DISCOVER
JAZZ

JOHN EDWARD HASSE

TAD LATHROP

PEARSON

Boston   Columbus   Indianapolis   New York   San Francisco   Upper Saddle River
Amsterdam   Cape Town   Dubai   London   Madrid   Milan   Munich   Paris   Montréal   Toronto
Delhi   Mexico City   São Paulo   Sydney   Hong Kong   Seoul   Singapore   Taipei   Tokyo

Editorial Director: Craig Campanella
Editor-in-Chief: Sarah Touborg
Executive Editor: Richard Carlin
Editorial Assistant: Lily Norton
Director of Marketing: Brandy Dawson
Executive Marketing Manager: Kate Mitchell
Marketing Assistant: Lisa Kirlick
Managing Editor: Melissa Feimer
Production Liaison: Joe Scordato
Pearson Imaging Center: Corin Skidds
Senior Operations Specialist: Brian Mackey
Manufacturing and Operations Manager
 for Arts & Sciences: Mary Fischer
Creative Director (Interior): Pat Smythe

Interior Design: Lisa Delgado/Delgado and Company
Cover Design: Laura Gardner
Cover Image: Dizzy Gillespie admiring the singing of Ella
 Fitzgerald at New York's Downbeat Club. Photographed ca.
 Sept. 1947 by William P. Gottlieb. Courtesy William Gottlieb
 Collection/Library of Congress
Senior Digital Media Editor: David Alick
Media Project Manager: Rich Barnes
Music Typesetting: Don Giller
Full-Service Management: GEX Publishing Services
Composition: GEX Publishing Services
Printer/Binder: The Courier Companies
Cover Printer: Lehigh-Phoenix Color

For Ann Moore and Alexandra Hasse
—John Edward Hasse

For Bert Dever, a true jazz spirit, and to Inga and Audrey
—Tad Lathrop

Credits and acknowledgments borrowed from other sources and reproduced, with permission, in this textbook appear on the appropriate page within text. Lyrics on the pages used with permission from Joni Mitchell, *Dry Cleaner from Des Moines* and *A Chair in the Sky*, Alfred Publishing Co., Inc.

10 9 8 7 6 5 4 3 2 1

Library of Congress Cataloging-in-Publication Data

Discover jazz / [edited by] John Edward Hasse, Tad Lathrop.
 p. cm.
 Includes bibliographical references and index.
 ISBN-13: 978-0-13-602637-2 (student ed. : pbk.)
 ISBN-10: 0-13-602637-0 (student ed. : pbk.)
 ISBN-13: 978-0-13-602645-7 (instructor's review copy)
 ISBN-10: 0-13-602645-1 (instructor's review copy) 1. Jazz—History and criticism—Textbooks. 2. Jazz—Analysis, appreciation—Textbooks. I. Hasse, John Edward. II. Lathrop, Tad.
 ML3506.D57 2012
 781.6509—dc23
                                                                              2011029111

Student Edition ISBN-10: 0-13-602637-0
Student Edition ISBN-13: 978-0-13-602637-2
Instructor's Review Copy ISBN-10: 0-13-602645-1
Instructor's Review Copy ISBN-13: 978-0-13-602645-7

DATE DUE

BRODART, CO.   Cat. No. 23-221

Contents

WITHDRAWN

Dear Readers:

A new form of musical expression emerged at the outset of the twentieth century, and more than a hundred years later it is still vital. It came from many corners of American life, from the poorest of the poor and from the well-to-do, from the musically educated and from many without musical training, but all with a vision of a new music that carried a message of freedom: freedom to improvise new forms of expression; freedom to cross cultural, economic, racial, and political boundaries. The new music was jazz, and *Discover Jazz* tells its whole story.

We were motivated to write this book by our lifelong interest in and love of jazz. For us, the music is a passion, without which our lives would be much less rich. While we can't guarantee that this book will make you fall in love with jazz, it's our highest hope that it inspires in you a lifelong curiosity about the music.

We hope that this book will not only open your ears to a beautiful style of music, but also open your eyes to an entire era of modern life that we rightfully could call the Jazz Era. Jazz is steeped in the history of our time, and our history has been inherently changed by its presence. *Discover Jazz* tells the whole story of how jazz changed our musical and cultural worlds.

John Hasse   Ted Lathrop

John Edward Hasse is a music historian, pianist, and award-winning author and record producer. Since 1984, he has served as Curator of American Music at the Smithsonian Institution's National Museum of American History, where he founded the Smithsonian Jazz Masterworks Orchestra and Jazz Appreciation Month. He is the author of *Beyond Category: The Life and Genius of Duke Ellington*, and co-producer/co-author of the book-and-six-disc set *Jazz: The Smithsonian Anthology*.

Tad Lathrop has authored, produced, or edited more than 50 books on music, including two lauded volumes on the business of music. Lathrop lectures on music and the recording industry at colleges and professional conferences, and is an accomplished guitarist who has performed at numerous venues, including New York's Blue Note.

Photo © Genevieve Shiffrar

Discover the Whole Story of Jazz!

DISCOVER JAZZ Is Inclusive

Discover Jazz recognizes that the story of jazz has many facets. It is an *inclusive* story, one that includes contributions from different ethnic groups, musical roots, men and women, and musicians from around the world. To tell this story, we have gathered a group of distinguished scholars to give their perspectives on different parts of the jazz story.

Jazz is a *global* music that appeals widely, bringing a unique message of freedom of expression across cultural boundaries. Since its earliest days, jazz musicians have engaged in an active dialogue with their contemporaries around the world. The influence of Latin American musicians on jazz has been well documented, but is not always honored in standard histories of the music. Similarly, jazz musicians in Europe, Asia, and Africa have taken the music in new and original directions.

Jazz & the Arts

Jazz and Tap

Who was responsible for the evolution of jazz, the musicians or the tap dancers? Ask tap dancers, and they'll tell you. Ask jazz musicians, and they just might admit it. The truth is, during the first half of the twentieth century, tap dance and jazz music were intricately intertwined and affected one another more than most realized.

In early twentieth-century American entertainment, musicians and tap dancers lived and worked in the same world—that of vaudeville, Broadway, and nightclubs. In these environments, the tap dancers were the stars and the musicians played the dancers' charts. The musicians watched and listened in wonder to the confoundingly complex syncopated rhythms tapped out by the dancers.

"Tap dancers had a big influence on drummers, no doubt about it," bandleader Jay McShann recalled. "They taught drummers when to play and when to stay out of the way. Reading music had little to do with it; it was a matter of developing your instincts."

Musicians listened day after day, night after night, year after year as tap dancers stretched the boundaries of early jazz to swing, from swing to bop, and from bop to modern jazz. According to the tap dancers, the musicians replicated their rhythmic ideas, and musical changes constantly followed.

By the mid-1930s, vaudeville was on its way out and a new form of entertainment called *presentation* was taking its place.

While vaudeville consisted of a lineup of variety artists, presentation focused on the music. The musicians were taken out of the orchestra pit and placed right up on the stage, and the bands were top-drawer swing orchestras. It was bandied about that every band had a tap-dance act and every tap dancer had a band. To name a few, Jimmy Slyde worked with Count Basie and Duke Ellington; Coles and Atkins with Cab Calloway and Basie; the Condos Brothers with both Jimmy and Tommy Dorsey, Benny Goodman, Ellington, Basie, and Sammy Kaye; Bunny Briggs with Ellington, Charlie Barnet, Earl Hines, and Basie; Bill Bailey with Ellington; Jeni LeGon with **Fats Waller** and Basie. Peg Leg Bates, perhaps the most ubiquitous of all, danced with Jimmy Dorsey, Barnet, Ellington, Erskine Hawkins, Calloway, Basie, Jimmie Lunceford, Claude Hopkins, Louis Armstrong, and Billy Eckstine.

So who changed jazz: musicians or tap dancers? Answers may differ depending on whom you ask. But without a doubt, jazz wouldn't have happened the way it did without music and dance interacting.

—Rusty Frank

Tap dancer Bill "Bojangles" Robinson.

DISCOVER JAZZ Is Contextual

The story of jazz is not one story but a series of different encounters between musicians, historical events, musical influences, and social forces. Jazz has had a huge impact on American social and cultural history. The birth of jazz occurred just as African Americans were beginning their century-long struggle for equality and freedom. Jazz played a crucial role in this struggle, helping to bridge the gap between the races through musical collaboration. Jazz influenced other musical forms, from classical to pop, and the other performing and visual arts. It's no exaggeration to say that the twentieth century was—at least culturally—the Jazz Era.

History & Culture

Parade and funeral regulars Henry Allen, Sr., and his brass band in Algiers, Louisiana (ca. 1905). Standing, left to right: Jack Carey, unknown musician, Jimmy Palao, August Rousseau, unknown musician, Joe Howard, Oscar "Pops" Celestin, Henry Allen, Sr.
PHOTO COURTESY FRANK DRIGGS COLLECTION.

Parading with a Brass Band

Boom! . . . Boom! . . . Boom! Those first thunderous blasts from the big bass drum signal the start of a musically led passage deep into the soul of New Orleans. Whatever the context of the drum call and improvised brass-band music that follow, be it a funeral march, a social club's annual

anchor everything with bass lines. Whether jazzing up a standard religious hymn, a traditional march, a popular song, a rag, or a blues, the band struts along and marks the time in easy, neither-too-fast-nor-too-slow dance tempos.

Each band is led by an elegantly dressed grand marshal, who waves his handkerchief and carries a

twisted, and stretched in favor of fresh creative expression that matches the wild passion of the dances and provides a taste of the freedom sought by its creators in everyday life. It's easy to become disoriented in this spirit world. As the dancing and the music reach

DISCOVER JAZZ Is Student-Friendly

We wanted *Discover Jazz* also to be accessible to you, because ultimately our goal is for you to discover your own relationship with jazz. Your love of jazz undoubtedly will begin with hearing a performance that moves you to listen to more. We want to help you learn how to listen to jazz by giving you the tools to become active listeners.

To make it easier for you to study, each chapter opens with a section titled "Take Note," which gives the key concepts explored in the chapter. These are repeated after the discussion of each concept occurs. At the end of the chapter, we return to these concepts to offer a summation of what we have studied.

To make the history come alive, we have created a lively design that we hope will help you become engaged with the music. Included in this design are links to our Web site, **MyMusicLab**, which was designed from the start to accompany the text. You'll find these icons throughout the text that guide you to the appropriate online material:

MYMUSICLAB ICONS:

((• **LISTEN:** Links to recordings and audio documentaries

👁 **WATCH:** Links to online videos and documentaries

✳ **EXPLORE:** Links to interactive demonstrations

✔• **STUDY AND REVIEW:** Links to chapter assessments

MyMusicLab

Educators know it. Students know it. It's that inspired moment when something that was difficult to understand suddenly makes perfect sense. Pearson's MyLab products have been designed and refined with a single purpose in mind—to help educators create that moment of understanding with their students.

The new **MyMusicLab** delivers **proven results** in helping individual students succeed. It provides **engaging experiences** that personalize, stimulate, and measure learning for each student. And, it comes from a **trusted partner** with educational expertise and an eye on the future.

MyMusicLab can be used by itself or linked to any learning management system. To learn more about how the new **MyMusicLab** combines proven learning applications with powerful assessment, visit www.pearsonhighered.com/newmylabs.

MyMusicLab—the moment you know.

Features

MyMusicLab provides **engaging experiences** that personalize, stimulate, and measure learning for each student.

- **Listening activities** help students identify key musical styles and composers. Instant feedback directs the student to resources to build listening skills.

- **Active listening and viewing guides** mirror those in the printed text and aid students as they analyze key pieces of music.
- **Streaming audio** for most of the key musical examples and **streaming video** of 18 historic performances from Bessie Smith to Weather Report enrich the learning experience.
- The **Pearson eText** lets students access their textbook anytime, anywhere, and any way they want—including listening online or downloading to an iPad.
- A **personalized study plan** for each student, based on Bloom's Taxonomy, arranges content from less complex thinking—like remembering and understanding—to more complex critical thinking—like applying and analyzing. This layered approach promotes better critical-thinking skills, and helps students succeed in the course and beyond.
- **Assessment** tied to every video, application, and chapter enables both instructors and students to track progress and get immediate feedback. With results feeding into a powerful gradebook, the assessment program helps instructors identify student challenges early—and find the best resources with which to help students.
- An **assignment calendar** allows instructors to assign graded activities, with specific deadlines, and measure student progress.
- **Class Prep** collects the very best class presentation resources in one convenient online destination, so instructors can keep students engaged throughout every class.

TIME	FORM	MELODY	INSTRUMENTATION	HARMONY (KEY)
0:00	CHORUS 1	The tune begins, without introduction or fanfare, with Miley and Nanton, tightly muted, moaning the haunting blues melody that echoes the traditional hymn *The Holy City*.	Muted trumpet and trombone.	B-flat minor.
0:24		Sonny Greer crashes his cymbals to announce the end of one section and the beginning of another.	Cymbal.	
0:25	VERSE	Otto Hardwick plays the contrasting second theme in a sweet style. After six bars, the band answers.	Alto saxophone.	B-flat major.
0:41		The second phrase (eight bars) of the verse begins. After six bars		

Listening Choices

Discover Jazz offers students quality recordings by major artists in the history of jazz. They are available as the following:

- **Streaming Audio:** Almost all of the recommended listening in the text is available in streaming audio as part of **MyMusicLab**.
- **Downloadable Set** (ISBN 0205259928): Students also have the option of purchasing a downloadable package to load all of the musical examples directly onto a portable music player or their own computers.
- **Two-CD Set** (ISBN 0136026427): The music is also available on a traditional two-CD set.

Pearson Choices

- **CourseSmart**
  ISBN: 0205210872

CourseSmart eTextbooks offer the same content as the printed text in a convenient online format—with highlighting, online search, and printing capabilities. *Approximate savings over a regular textbook: up to 60%.* www.coursesmart.com

- **Books a la carte**
  ISBN: 0205003524

Give your students flexibility and savings with the new Book a la carte edition of *Discover Jazz*. This edition features exactly the same content as the traditional textbook in a three-hole-punched, loose-leaf version—allowing students to take only what they need to class. The Books a la carte helps students save about 35% over the cost of a used book.

Create a Custom Text: Pearson Custom enables you to work with a dedicated Pearson Custom editor to create your ideal text—publishing your own original content or mixing and matching Pearson content. *Contact your Pearson Publisher's Representative to get started.*

Resources for Teachers

- Classprep: This feature within **MyMusicLab** collects the very best class presentation resources in one convenient online destination including PowerPoint slides, streaming audio and video, audio clips for class tests and quizzes, and all of the book's illustrations so you can create an interactive lecture.

- PowerPoints: Ready made PowerPoints® for your lectures with embedded audio and video, accessed through your **MyMusicLab** instructor account at www.mymusiclab.com.

- Instructor's Manual & Test Bank: This is an invaluable professional resource and reference for new and experienced faculty. Each chapter contains the following sections: Chapter Overview, Chapter Objectives, Key Terms, Lecture and Discussion Topics, Resources, and Writing Assignments and Projects. The test bank includes multiple choice, true/false, short answer, and essay questions. Available for download on www.mymusiclab.com.

- MyTest: This flexible, online test-generating software includes all questions found in the printed Test Item File. Instructors can quickly and easily create customized tests with MyTest at http://www.pearsonmytest.com.

Acknowledgments

From the time the editors first conceived of this book to its current presentation in multimedia form, an international team of top-flight educators, historians, editors, photographers, and designers lent their talents to the project. Richard Carlin, our editor at Pearson, deserves special praise. Without his enthusiasm, creativity, collegiality, and rare combination of music expertise and publishing savvy, the book would not have become a reality.

In its early stages, the book benefited from the support of editor Paul Bresnick and our agents Andrew Stuart and Frank Weimann. Designer Nancy Carroll brought a meticulous hand, visual acumen, and technical expertise to production of this book's forerunner, *Jazz: The First Century*.

David Baker of Indiana University and Bruce Talbot made a number of invaluable suggestions throughout the project. In Paris, Philippe Baudoin read several portions of the manuscript and generously and repeatedly supplied helpful pieces of information. In New Orleans, Bruce Boyd Raeburn of Tulane University and Jack Stewart reviewed sections of the manuscript and kindly helped track down images. José Bowen, of Southern Methodist University, provided extensive advice and recommendations for updating the text.

The undertaking was greatly aided by our production editor Kelly Morrison; project manager Joe Scordato; editorial assistants Lily Norton, Tricia Murphy, and Emma Gibbons; and early-stage copy editor Jacqueline Dever and production assistants Curtis Carroll, Fredrick Schermer, and Francis Gilbert. For their work on **MyMusicLab**, we wish to thank Leslie Cohen for authoring the chapter assessment questions, Jim Scully for authoring the learning objectives, and William Christy for authoring the quick review and formative assessment questions.

For their gracious help with photographs, thanks to the late Bill Claxton, Frank Driggs, Andy Freeberg, the late William Gottlieb, the late Milt Hinton, Michael Jackson, the late Herman Leonard, Jim Quinn, Chuck Stewart, Lee Tanner, Jack Vartoogian, and Michael Wilderman. Tom Alexios, *Down Beat* magazine's director of special projects, made an invaluable contribution by helping to acquire photos and, in particular, arranging the loan of images from the magazine's archive; *Down Beat* editorial director Frank Alkyer cheerfully and generously facilitated that loan in countless ways. Ted Hershorn at Rutgers University's Institute of Jazz Studies was also extremely helpful in researching and providing images for this text.

Thanks, of course, to the book's many knowledgeable contributors, as well as to Larry Appelbaum, Lida Belt Baker, Bob Blumenthal, Jerry Brock, Myles Faulkner, Krin Gabbard of SUNY Stony Brook, Deborah Gillaspie, Vince Giordano, Beverly Hennessy, Terri Hinte, Arnold Hirsch, Andy Jaffe, Ann K. Kuebler, Stacy Lewis, Isabelle Leymarie, Don Lucoff, Wynn Mathias, Stephen F. Pond of Cornell University, José Rizo, Lina Stephens, Steve Teeter, Michael Ullman, Kevin Whitehead of the University of Kansas, and Jim Wilke.

Finally, appreciation above all to the jazz men and women whose art has enriched the lives of hundreds of millions of people around the world.

JOHN EDWARD HASSE
TAD LATHROP

Reviewers and Class Testers

We have benefited from the feedback from many reviewers and class testers throughout the development of this book. We'd like to thank them all for their insights and suggestions, many of which were incorporated into the final version of the text and Web site.

Alabama
Andrew Dewar, University of Alabama
Christopher Kozak, University of Alabama

California
David Borgo, University of California, San Diego
Jeremy Brown, Mt. San Jacinto College
Leslie Drayton, Ventura College
Karlton Hester, University of California, Santa Cruz
Anne Kilstofte, Glendale Community College
Paul Rinzler, California Polytechnic State University
Jim Scully, California State University, Bakersfield

Colorado
Malcolm Baker, University of Denver
John Davis, University of Colorado, Boulder
Curtis Smith, University of Colorado, Colorado Springs

Connecticut
Brian Torff, Fairfield University
Nicholas Conway, Trinity College

Florida
Richard Rose, Miami Dade College
Tim Walters, Florida Atlantic University

Georgia
David Springfield, Valdosta State University

Idaho
Marcus Wolfe, Boise State University

Illinois
Richard Kelley, Southern Illinois University Carbondale
Gabriel Solis, University of Illinois

Indiana
Daniel Weiss, Purdue University

Iowa
William Carson, Coe College
Steve Shanley, Coe College

Kentucky
N. Michael Goecke, Northern Kentucky University
Jerry Tolson, University of Louisville
Gordon Towell, Morehead State University

Louisiana
Richard Schwartz, Southeastern Louisiana University

Massachusetts
Paul Beaudoin, Fitchburg State College
Theodore Brown, University of Massachusetts, Amherst
Timothy Crain, University of Massachusetts, Lowell

Thomas Everett, Harvard University
Andy Jaffe, Williams College
Sonya Lawson, Westfield State University
Allen Livermore, Berkshire Community
  College
Edward Orgill, Westfield State University
Duncan Vinson, Suffolk University

Michigan

Paul Anderson, University of Michigan

Minnesota

Jeffrey Hess, Normandale Community
  College

Missouri

Arthur White, University of
  Missouri-Columbia

Nebraska

Clarence Smith, Metropolitan Community
  College

New Jersey

Michael Conklin, Brookdale Community
  College
P.J. Cotroneo, Ramapo College
Timothy Newman, William Paterson
  University
Lewis Porter, Rutgers University, Newark
Ralph Anthony Russell, College of
  New Jersey

New Mexico

Chris Beaty, Eastern New Mexico
  University Main Campus

New York

David Lalama, Hofstra University
Howard Mandel, New York University
Steven F. Pond, Cornell University

North Carolina

Chad Eby, University of North Carolina at
  Greensboro
John Harding, Central Piedmont
  Community College
Judith Porter, Gaston College

Ohio

William Christy, Ohio University Zanesville
Timothy Dickey, Ohio Wesleyan University
Tammy Kernodle, Miami University
Zachary J. Kreuz, Owens Community
  College
Ted McDaniel, The Ohio State University

Oregon

Walter Carr, Portland Community
  College

Pennsylvania

Paul Fehrenbach, Pennsylvania State
  University
Joshua L. Kovach, Community College of
  Philadelphia
Barry Long, Bucknell University
Michael Stephans, Bloomsburg University
  of Pennsylvania

South Carolina

L. H. Dickert, Winthrop University

Texas

Philippe Baugh, Tarrant County
  College NE
Kim Corbet, Southern Methodist
  University
Graeme Francis, University of Texas,
  San Antonio
Ryan Gabbart, University of Houston
Jeff Hellmer, University of Texas
  at Austin
John Murphy, University of North Texas
Dr. Nico Schuler, Texas State University

Virginia

James Carroll, George Mason University
Richard Cole, Virginia Polytechnic
  Institute and State University

Washington

David Deacon-Joyner, Pacific Lutheran
  University
Paul de Barros, Seattle Pacific University

Washington, D.C.

Saïs Kamalidiin, Howard University
Kip Lornell, The George Washington
  University

West Virginia

Christopher Barrick, West Liberty
  University

Wisconsin

Robert Holt, University of Wisconsin
  Colleges Online
Thomas L. Patterson, University of
  Wisconsin - Waukesha

Canada

Andrew Homzy, Concordia University

CHAPTER 1

Introducing Jazz

by Tad Lathrop and John Edward Hasse

TAKE NOTE

- How do you listen to jazz for the first time?
- What are the defining elements of jazz?
- What is the relationship of jazz to our history and culture?

There's something about the experience of jazz that is unique. The combination of surprise, delight, insight, satisfaction, and appreciation that can come from listening to an improvised jazz performance is fundamentally different from the experiences that come from listening to other kinds of music. This critical difference accounts in part for why jazz has become an art form of importance and depth, the focus of study and research, and a rich set of ideas always ripe for continuing development.

Jazz has a reputation for being "difficult." Because of this, many people shy away from trying to appreciate it. But in some ways jazz is easy to understand. The most modest knowledge of how it works yields pleasure in listening. Many aspects of jazz require no special knowledge at all. A great singer, such as **Billie Holiday**, can give chills even to a non-expert. The power of a big band can inspire awe in anyone. A masterful jazz guitarist can be appreciated by the least jazz-aware listener.

Wayne Shorter, 2004.
PHOTO COURTESY MICHAEL WILDERMAN.

Yet part of the beauty of jazz is that the deeper the knowledge, the greater the rewards. This is why musicians and listeners alike are attracted to jazz for its challenges as well as its immediate payoffs. It is also why jazz is increasingly taught in colleges as an entry point to the study of music in all its aspects. Jazz exemplifies the many qualities that make music as rich an art as any that humans have developed.

Jazz also interacts with other aspects of modern life. By studying jazz and comparing it to related events and movements, you can gain insight into recent history and the contemporary world from a unique perspective. In the history of jazz you will find interplay with other art forms and social and political movements. You also will find reflections of technological developments and of changes in the pace of human life.

Because of its technical, social, and aesthetic aspects, jazz has relevance to the quantitative and social sciences as well as to the humanities and the arts. The relationships of pitches in a scale, the structures of rhythm and meter, and the musical qualities of loudness, texture, color, and tone have as much to do with mathematics and physics as they do with art. And the ability of a musician to absorb musical concepts and then draw from rich reserves of knowledge to create, instantaneously and on the spot, complex musical statements speaks to the psychology of memory and the neuroscience of brain function.

But if all this sounds a little too academic, remember that the understanding of jazz is primarily rooted in the sense of pleasure jazz elicits at its most basic level. We will start at that level, look at what is occurring there, and then explore further.

Jazz as an "American" Art Form

Is it accurate to describe jazz as "America's classical music"?

Jazz has special importance in the history of the United States. Many have referred to jazz as "an intrinsically American art form" and "America's classical music." This is because the origins of jazz can be traced to locales in the United States where cultures and traditions from all over the world merged, generating a hybrid art form that accurately reflects the diverse cultural identity of its birth country.

However, some object to calling jazz a "classical" music, because it assumes that European classical music is the standard against which all other musics are measured. Categorizing jazz as classical music suggests that it can be studied and appreciated in the same way as European music. But jazz has a unique history with its own styles, compositions, and performers. Is it fair to describe it as a "classical" art form?

And, given that much of today's jazz is created by musicians from around the world, can we still describe the music as "an intrinsically American art form"? Consider particularly Chapter 10, "Latin Jazz" and Chapter 11, "Jazz Worldwide."

—*Richard Carlin*

First Listening

For the first exposure to a jazz tune you don't need any special musical knowledge. You just need to listen with an open mind and simply pay attention as the music unfolds.

Watch and listen to **Count Basie's** *Boogie Woogie*. At the end of the clip, free associate: What are your impressions? What overall mood does the music convey? What kinds of events occur? What changes take place? What else do you observe? Make a note of your impressions.

Later, when you know more about the tune, its background, and its building blocks, you can listen more critically and can appreciate it on multiple levels. You will do that with *Boogie Woogie* after reading the tips for listening to jazz in Chapter 2.

Listening with Untrained Ears

You might know little about a recording when you first listen. It is possible you are coming into the experience without preconceptions, with fresh ears. Perhaps you have never heard of the artist and have little or no familiarity with the history of jazz. You may not be aware of the standard routines that musicians follow when they perform jazz. You might not know about the music foundations upon which jazz performances are built.

Still, you can respond to the music. You may be moved by its vitality or its calmness. As you pay attention to the flow of the music, the changes in the sound are noticeable. They may cause changes in your feelings. You become aware of speed and slowness, of loudness and softness. You can differentiate between the dense, thick texture of a full orchestra and the spare, intimate sound of a single performer. You might find the melody pleasing—perhaps for a reason no more complicated than, well, it just sounds good.

You derive meaning and, quite likely, pleasure from all these perceptions.

Yet a deeper appreciation is within reach. With guidance about what to listen for in jazz, the possibilities for a rewarding listening experience are multiplied many times over.

Being able to place a recording somewhere in the continuum of jazz history can add an important dimension to listening. It might help you to know why a musician plays the way he or she does and what historical influences are at work. Knowing this can add a layer of understanding about how the musician differs from those precursors and an appreciation of what the musician brings to the history that is new.

Aside from a recording's place in history, there are more immediate, as-you're-listening aspects to the sound that can be appreciated with guidance in how to separate them for individual attention. Focusing separately on rhythm, melody, form, and other elements can generate a multidimensional appreciation of a performance. But it won't, by any means, exhaust all the possibilities for exploring a well-crafted piece of jazz.

◉ **Watch** the video *Boogie Woogie* by Count Basie on
mymusiclab.com

Defining Jazz: A Beginning

A society matron reportedly once asked jazz pianist Fats Waller, "Mr. Waller, exactly *what is jazz?*" "Lady," he replied, "if you gotta ask, you're never gonna know." Though difficult to precisely define, we can point to many qualities and characteristics of jazz.

When you listen to jazz, what do you notice? And how do you know that the music you're hearing is jazz and not classical music, rock music, country music, hip-hop, or some other popular form?

Often, jazz is identifiable by sounds that have long been associated with it: for example, a saxophone blowing emotive melodies; a loose rhythm being tapped out on a drum or cymbal; a bass "walking" its notes underneath layers of other instruments; a piano's stabbing, punctuating chords behind a soloist's playing.

The term "jazz" is also associated with familiar ensemble configurations and styles of sound: a big band playing a brassy, swinging version of *One O'Clock Jump*; a vocalist scat-singing wordless melody variations on top of a propulsive rhythm; an electric guitar/organ/drums trio churning out pungent blues licks; a classic quartet of saxophone, piano, string bass, and drums working out on a favorite old tune.

Jazz has so many variations that it can be difficult to pin down those elements that make it jazz. Some of the variations that have been identified over the years—mostly by record companies and radio stations in need of labels for marketing purposes—include "trad" or traditional jazz, swing, bebop, cool jazz, hard bop, mainstream jazz, free jazz, Latin jazz, bossa nova, fusion, and smooth jazz.

Elements of jazz can be heard or used in other types of music: **Western swing** employed jazz-soloing guitars and saxophones; classical pieces—Gershwin's *Porgy and Bess*, for example—have made use of jazz phrasings; **hip-hop** records have used jazz samples.

So how can we define jazz's unique character? One way to start is by addressing improvisation.

✳ Explore Jazz Instruments on **mymusiclab.com**

Western swing a mixture of jazz and country music, popularized in the 1930s by Bob Wills and His Texas Playboys and, later, Asleep at the Wheel.

hip-hop a largely African American popular music characterized by talk-sung rhymes over funk-derived beats.

Improvisation in Jazz

Much music outside jazz (classical and concert music, for example) consists of compositions created for later performance, with listener appreciation focused on the musicians' precision, polish, and interpretive skill in bringing the music to life. Jazz, in contrast, emphasizes **improvisation**: on-the-spot composition. This provides much of jazz music's characteristic excitement, surprise, and sense of tension and resolution.

What makes great jazz begins with improvising: it's the core of the art. The great masters of jazz are capable of creating, on the spot, solos of such originality and brilliance that they are listened to and remembered for decades. The improvised solo is the criterion by which the jazz musician is judged above all.

While improvisation is the most obvious hallmark of jazz, it is not true that jazz *has* to be improvised. Some big-band jazz, for instance, doesn't leave much room for improvisation. And some jazz musicians—pianist **Art Tatum**, for example—worked out solos and played them largely the same way time after time.

Improvisers often begin their solos in an understated way. "You're going to start down," says pianist Kenny Barron, "so that you can have somewhere to go. It can build to different points in different parts of the solo. It's hills and valleys."

Then, through elaboration and dramatic effects, changes in rhythm and melody and tone colors, and variations in energy level, improvisers sustain interest and, often, build intensity. A solo is said to "tell a story." The story may not be reducible to words, but it's a story nonetheless, with a beginning, a climax, and an end.

While an improvised solo can be based on a lifetime of accumulated skills, it is also very much "in the moment": the improviser is highly sensitive to what the other musicians are playing, and interaction among the players shapes the results. The venue, audience, acoustics, and, if present, dancers can also greatly affect the course of an improvisation. As music scholar Paul Berliner has observed, "performers and listeners form a communication loop in which the actions of each continuously affect the other." That's one reason that performances or *live* jazz recordings are often exciting: the audience lends another unpredictable variable to the mix.

Jazz improvisation occurs on a number of levels simultaneously: technical (how to finger a passage), theoretical (what scales go with what chords), intellectual (consciousness of other musicians' versions of a tune), intuitive (anticipating what, say, the pianist will do in the next moment), and emotional (what feelings to express in

✳ Explore the Jazz Timeline on **mymusiclab.com**

---

improvisation spontaneous composition; one of the central elements in jazz.

the solo). Some also consider it spiritual (being in touch with a divine force). Thus playing—or listening closely to—jazz is immediate, deep, and powerful.

The jazz musician's art is full of risk: playing improvised solos before an audience is akin to a high-wire act. If architects or writers or composers make a mistake, they can simply use an eraser to correct it, but if a jazz player makes a mistake, it will be there for everyone to hear. In jazz improvisation, the dangers of playing wrong notes, stumbling during solos, or failing to play a coherent solo are offset by the opportunities to experiment, freshen an existing piece, and make a musical statement that, even if only eight bars in length, no one has made before. Jazz players, working night after night on the bandstand with no safety net, have raised risk taking to a great art.

Other Dimensions of Jazz

Apart from improvisation, jazz exhibits a defining characteristic in its searching, innovative spirit. Many jazz musicians share an inclination to explore and invent. Jazz also encompasses distinctive approaches to melody, harmony, rhythm, form and structure, color and texture, voice and feel, and musicians' individual and collective roles. These categories are all discussed in Chapter 2, along with tips for applying them to your listening.

TAKE NOTE

- What are the defining elements of jazz?

Jazz and Society

As is true of any art form, jazz intersects with other fields of activity and aspects of life. Because of its rapid growth in the twentieth century, the vibrancy and volatility of its changes, its multiracial constituency, and its overall popularity, jazz offers an especially penetrating lens through which to view and understand the world in which it thrived. Through other art forms, social and political movements, technological developments, national identity, and international relations, jazz affords a unique way to think about our world.

Jazz and the Arts

Movies, painting, writing, dancing—all of these forms of expression and more have, at one time or another, converged conceptually with jazz.

Cinema shared with jazz its relative youth as an art form. As the two matured in parallel, they came together from time to time. Jazz infused movies with a sense of the urban—and sometimes the urbane. In painting, 1950s abstract expressionists found commonalities with jazz in the breaking from convention—from literal representations of subjects—just as jazz broke from traditional conceptions of ear-pleasing harmony.

So, too, have poetry, literature, drama, dance, and other forms drawn from jazz for inspiration and raw expressive material. For many artists in the twentieth century, jazz represented the exotic, the new and innovative, the free, the urban, the unconventional, the taboo, the abstract, the personal, or the spiritual.

Social Life and Issues

Jazz has found itself on the fault lines of social divisions. Paradoxically, it has also provided a bridge across social divisions.

Class distinctions have at times been illuminated by jazz. In its earliest days, jazz was decried by some as the abrasive, untutored utterances of society's underclass. The origins of jazz in New Orleans dance halls, party scenes, and brothels set it up for dismissal by "polite society" as a "low" art form. In its early years, jazz was the subject of a vigorous cultural battle, pitting traditionalists and moralists against modernists and seekers of the new.

Jazz has sometimes been equated with social deviance. The stereotype of the junkie, the outcast, and the social misfit—fueled by real-life stories such as that of Charlie Parker's heroin addiction and stoked by images created in Hollywood—have long dogged the art form.

But over time those stereotypes have lost their edge, countered by growing evidence of the art form's cultural and social elevation: saxophonist Joshua Redman turning down an offer to attend Yale Law School to instead follow the path of jazz; trumpeter **Wynton Marsalis** ascending to the helm of Jazz at Lincoln Center; presidents Carter, Clinton, and Obama hosting jazz in the White House. In recent years, jazz has become synonymous with the upscale and refined, as evidenced by marketing that equates jazz with luxury brands: for example, Marsalis modeling an expensive Movado watch.

Yet throughout its history, whatever the social differences separating individuals, the love of jazz has tended to provide common ground. Jazz was ahead of the curve in helping to bridge racial differences. Long before American society was racially integrated, jazz musicians were recording in multiracial bands and becoming celebrities across the color line.

Jazz and Historic Trends

The extraordinary rate of change in jazz—in a little over a hundred years growing from a local dance accompaniment to an international art with an **avant-garde** edge—matched the speed of transformation throughout society. As just one example, compare the Original Dixieland Jazz Band's *Livery Stable Blues* (CD I, Track 7/Download Track 7), one of the first jazz recordings, with world jazz musician Nguyên Lê's *Ting Ning* (CD II, Track 13/ Download Track 37).

During that rapid evolution, the shapes jazz took made it a musical analog to broader events and trends. Nightclub jazz and dancehall swing of the 1920s and 1930s, for example, rose on a wave of postwar optimism and a surging youth culture. The music's multi-ethnic flavors—heard in the Afro-Cuban beat of Dizzy Gillespie's *Manteca* (CD II, Track 9/ Download Track 33), the Middle Eastern rhythms of Dave Brubeck's *Blue Rondo à la Turk* (CD I, Track 2/ Download Track 21), or the bossa nova of Stan Getz's *The Girl from Ipanema* (CD II, Track 10/Download Track 34)—emerged with both the growth of U.S. immigration and the increasing interconnectedness of world cultures due to advances in communications and transportation. Progressive bebop of the 1940s articulated the new assertiveness of African Americans, and the even more progressive free jazz of the 1960s echoed the calls for freedom and equality of the civil rights and counterculture movements. Post-sixties jazz synthesizers and electronics signaled alliance with the digital information revolution. The kaleidoscopic sonic arrays of some twenty-first-century jazz reflect the increasingly fractured and data-bombarded state of today's world.

National Identity

Jazz tends to embody many aspects of the United States' traditional national identity. America, a country built on immigration and forced migration, is a social tossed salad—various types are all mixed together; jazz is a tasty musical salad, drawing from America's many cultural traditions. In its political, social, and economic structures, the United States tends to blend the individual with the collective; jazz reflects the same balance, valuing the group sound while giving voice to individual soloists. In the United States, the entrepreneurial spirit powers all kinds of activities; in jazz, that same spirit guides the invention and innovation that are at jazz's core.

Racial Identity

The development and popularization of jazz, which was led to a significant degree by African Americans, has been closely linked with African American identity. As one of the United States' unique global exports, jazz has introduced the world to the African-ness of American culture. The pervasiveness of the African influence on American performing arts, perhaps represented in its highest and most original form by jazz, attests to the centrality of the African American story to that of the nation as a whole.

During the 1950s and 1960s civil rights movement, jazz and jazz musicians played a significant role in speaking out against the oppression of African Americans in the United States. As only one example, the violence surrounding school desegregation in Little Rock, Arkansas, inspired musician Charles Mingus to compose *Fables of Faubus*, a direct comment on then-governor Orval Faubus's resistance to racial integration. Many feel that jazz musicians' long-time stand against racial discrimination—among both black and white players—helped pave the way for the landmark civil rights and voting rights acts of the 1960s.

Watch the documentary *Jazz Clubs* on mymusiclab.com

---

avant garde experimental, unconventional, cutting edge

 Watch the documentary on civil rights on mymusiclab.com

Jazz as African American Music

Is jazz a purely African American musical style?

Jazz has some major roots in African music, and many of its formative artists were black. Does this mean that jazz is, essentially, a black music? Does it mean that jazz played by whites or Latinos is not authentic, but rather something appropriated?

This question has permeated the story of jazz since the early days and continues to do so, reflected, for example, in controversy over exclusively black concert programming in the early 1990s at Jazz at Lincoln Center (see "Jazz and Race Revisited," page 334).

Jazz's African-originated inflections and rhythmic qualities, some contend, cannot be adequately performed by non-black musicians.

The invention of the blues by African Americans—infused with feeling born of the black experience in America—and the foundational role of the blues in jazz, have been cited as indicators of jazz's exclusively black provenance.

On the other hand, European influences on jazz, the accomplishments of many non-black players, and the increasing stylistic inclusiveness of jazz are proof to some that jazz has no exclusive owner— that jazz can be "authentic" regardless of the player's race.

One narrative has it that jazz may have started out as black music but over the years it evolved into a multi-style music influenced by many racial and ethnic groups.

A countering thesis is that the multi-style "jazz" of later years is not jazz at all. The only real jazz is the black-originated material.

Think about these issues as you read this book. Who do you think deserves the credit for originating jazz? Are there limitations on the ability of one racial or ethnic group to play music originated by another? Can a Japanese singer do bluegrass music? Can a Kenyan sing Italian opera? Can an Italian sing Kenyan music?

—*Tad Lathrop*

Cultural Significance

Jazz in the twenty-first century remains a lively and enduring musical art. Among many other benefits, jazz offers the following:

- A shared, community-binding field of social activity
- A contribution to community economic growth, through attraction of audiences to venues and surrounding neighborhoods and businesses
- A touchstone to history
- A springboard to new creation and the emergence of new musical stars
- A field of study and practice rich with opportunity for exploration and development
- A set of expressive building blocks adaptable to infinite forms, styles, and structures
- A genre of music with an endless capacity for self-renewal and reinvention

TAKE NOTE

- What is the relationship of jazz to our history and culture?

TAKE NOTE

- How do you listen to jazz for the first time?

Jazz can be enjoyed by an untutored listener, but deeper appreciation is possible with knowledge of jazz history, performance practices, and structural elements. When first listening to jazz, try to approach each recording with open ears, letting yourself be moved by the music itself.

- What are the defining elements of jazz?

Jazz shares elements with other styles of music, yet it offers characteristics that are uniquely "jazz." It can be appreciated across a number of musical dimensions, which include melody, harmony, rhythm, form and structure, color and texture, voice and feel, and musicians' individual and collective roles. What makes great jazz begins with improvisation—on-the-spot composition.

- What is the relationship of jazz to our history and culture?

Jazz has intersected with other art forms, including film, painting, writing, drama, and dance.

It has found itself on the fault lines of social divisions—of class, race, and social mores. Paradoxically, jazz has also provided a bridge across social divisions, especially in race relations.

DISCUSSION QUESTIONS

1. Talk about your general impressions of jazz. Do you know a lot about it? Just a little? Share what you do know.
2. Discuss an important way in which jazz differs from other kinds of music.
3. What aspects of U.S. national identity are reflected in jazz?
4. Think of important issues and events in U.S. history in the twentieth century. What do any of them have to do with jazz?
5. Jazz and other arts have found common themes. Cite some of them.
6. Discuss the ways in which presenting jazz might benefit a community—economically, culturally, socially.
7. After watching Count Basie's *Boogie Woogie*, what are some of your first impressions? What can you say about it? What kinds of feelings does it evoke? Do you like it? Why or why not?

KEY TERMS & KEY PEOPLE

avant garde 6	Billie Holiday 2	Art Tatum 4
Count Basie 3	improvisation 4	Western swing 4
hip-hop 4	Wynton Marsalis 6	

CHAPTER 2

Listening to Jazz

by Tad Lathrop and John Edward Hasse

TAKE NOTE

- How should you listen to a jazz melody?
- What is distinctive about jazz harmony?
- What types of rhythms are commonly heard in jazz?
- What are typical jazz forms and structures?
- What roles do color and texture play in jazz?
- How do individual voice, feel, and expression affect a jazz performance?
- Why is improvisation a key element of jazz?
- In jazz, what does style mean?
- What are the tensions between individual and collective performance in jazz?
- What factors can help us determine the quality of a jazz performance?

A s pointed out in Chapter 1, listening to jazz can be gratifying without deep knowledge of its underlying structure. So, too, can the history of jazz be studied without musical expertise. But knowing about the music's history can enhance listening. And the most rewarding experience of jazz requires some attention to its structural elements and characteristics. The listening and viewing guides throughout this book will help you learn how to understand these elements. Before using these guides, we need to address some basic elements of jazz and how to identify them. Once we've done that, we will return to Count Basie's *Boogie Woogie*, which was introduced in Chapter 1, with a viewing guide that demonstrates how to focus on the music's elements and features.

Guitarist John Scofield, an alumnus of mid-1980s Miles Davis bands. PHOTO COURTESY DAVID REDFERN/REDFERNS/GETTY IMAGES.

Melody

The ever-searching, exploratory, inventive nature of jazz plays out in the realm of melody. Jazz musicians, over time, have listened to countless types of music from the United States and around the world, pored over the structure of music itself, and found vast banks of source material from which to imagine new kinds of melodies.

As in much other music, **melody** serves in jazz as the main musical statement: the tune of the song, if you will, the theme. For jazz musicians, it is often just the starting point. Rather than a fixed sequence of **notes** to be performed faithfully, as written, the melody may be a jazz player's point of reference for creating embellishments, variations, countermelodies, and entirely new melodies. It serves as a tool for personal expression beyond what the original composer may have had in mind.

What is a melody? Reduced to its basics, a melody is a series of notes. They may vary in pitch (highness and lowness) and in duration (longness and shortness). Strung together in groups, notes may form **phrases**. Phrases may be made up

---

melody   an organized succession of notes.

note   a single sound that has pitch and duration.

phrase   a short sequence of notes expressing an idea, analogous to a musical clause or sentence; sometimes constructed from shorter sequences called motifs; typically employed as units of longer melodies.

✳ **Explore** the *Elements of Jazz* on **mymusiclab.com**

👁 **Watch** the video of *Boogie Woogie* by Count Basie on **mymusiclab.com**

of shorter groups called **motifs**. A set of phrases may be arranged to form longer groupings—complete songs or sections of a song.

The melody of Count Basie's *Boogie Woogie*, for example, is built on a three-note motif (see diagram; each black bar represents a musical note, with the vertical position representing **pitch**—highness or lowness—and length of bars and spaces representing **duration**.)

The motif, similar in sound to *Three Blind Mice*, repeats to form a phrase—like a comment or statement one might make in speech. The three-note motif then repeats again, twice in varied form (quicker, lowering the first note and adding a fourth note) and once in original form, to make up a second phrase. A third phrase, not shown here, completes the melody.

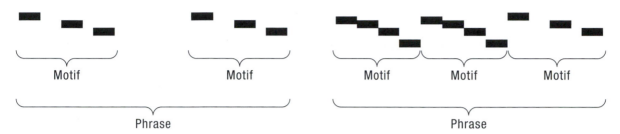

Melody from Boogie Woogie

In the introduction to Weather Report's *Birdland*, a synthesizer plays a phrase made up of a three-note motif that repeats in slightly varied form, abbreviating the third note and adding a higher fourth note. This added note lends a sense of completion to the phrase.

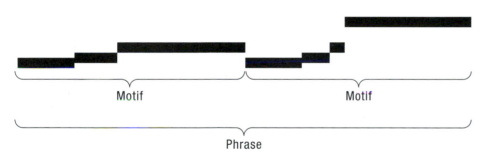

Introductory phrase from Birdland *(CD II/Track 5)*

A phrase from the melody of Nguyên Lê's *Ting Ning* is more complex, as the graphic representation shows. An up-and-down patterned motif repeats, changing slightly in the number and length of its notes, until resolving into a single sustained note.

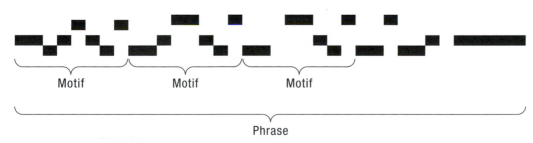

Bluesy phrase from Ting Ning *(CD II/Track 13, at 2:32)*

motif (or motive) a brief pattern of notes; typically the building blocks of longer phrases.

pitch the aspect of sound related to highness and lowness, determined by sound wave frequency; in music, pitches are given letter names from A to G; the pitch A above middle C has a frequency of 440 hertz (cycles per second).

duration length in time.

When jazz musicians study—both playing through songs and practicing **scale** and motivic exercises—they pay close attention to the logic of melody structures. They analyze the ways notes are strung together. They notice whether movement from one note to the next is **conjunct** (stepwise) or **disjunct** (a jump to a note several steps away). They feel the expressive effects of different sequences of notes. Movement among notes close to each other in pitch may sound soothing, comforting, but unsurprising. But movement among notes that are far apart—wide jumps and drops—may sound disjointed and surprising (a desirable effect in some cases). Musicians internalize these perceptions and memorize the note groupings that produced them. That's because these shards and scraps and bits of melody become the building blocks they can use to form their own **improvisations** later on.

Musicians attempt to master and mentally store every possible sequence of pitches. These become the internalized "phrases" and "**licks**" of their musical literacy and fluency. When improvising, musicians tap into this store of material and make split-second decisions—more like instinctive responses—about which ones to use in the immediate context of the solo.

This is not quite the same as the formulaic improvisation discussed later (page 18). The signature licks that many musicians develop consist not only of melody but also expressive devices, adding up to more personal constructions. Like saxophone virtuoso Charlie Parker, musicians may rely on many such licks.

The melodic motifs that jazz musicians use—the brief arrangements of notes that are the building blocks of longer phrases—number in the thousands.

Listening Tips for Jazz Melody

- Does the melody sound smooth or jagged?
- Does the melody consist of brief phrases or long lines?
- Are there few notes or many notes?
- Does the melody move in stepwise fashion or are the notes disjunct?
- Do you notice lots of repeated notes?
- Do the notes vary widely in pitch (high and low) or stay within a narrow pitch range?
- Is the melody easy to remember?

---

scale   a sequence of consecutive notes arranged in a particular order of steps.

conjunct   stepwise melodic motion.

disjunct   melodic movement to a note several steps away.

improvisation   spontaneous composition; one of the central elements in jazz.

lick   a brief melodic idea or phrase.

- How should you listen to a jazz melody?

Harmony

Harmony consists of more than one note occurring simultaneously, moving in time. In jazz this correlates with the terms **harmonic progression** or **chord changes**—the sequential arrangement of changing stacks of notes (**chords**) that accompany melodies.

Think of a choir, or a gospel group, or a glee club, or an instrumental ensemble accompanying a singer of a melody. They are providing *harmony* to the melody. When they change notes—move to a new *chord*—they change the feeling of the harmony and create movement. The direction and shape of this movement over the length of a tune—the *progression* of the movement—is an important element of the tune's architecture.

Jazz melds European harmonic traditions with "non-Western" traditions, yielding an amalgam unique to jazz. The West African tradition of vocal call-and-response, sometimes heard in field hollers in America's rural south during the nineteenth century, merged with the European-style harmonies of hymns and folk songs to yield a fundamental harmonic sequence called the blues. More than any other progression of chords, the three-chord, three-phrase structure of the blues has served as a central structure in jazz (as well as in many other styles, from rhythm and blues to rock).

The simplicity of **blues form**—starting with a "home" chord (called the **tonic**), moving away to a secondary chord (called the **subdominant** chord), and

---

harmony   the combination of two or more pitches, melodies, or melodies and chords; the aspect of music related to combinations of pitches changing in progression for expressive effect.

harmonic progression   a sequence of chords, also called a *chord progression*; also informally called *chord changes* or simply *changes*; serves as the harmonic architecture of a tune.

chord changes   a sequence of chords; also called a *chord progression*.

chord   a stack of notes played simultaneously.

blues form   typically, a twelve-bar musical structure comprising three lines of lyrics with the form AAB, consisting of a statement (A) sung over the home (tonic) chord, repetition of the statement (A) sung over the subdominant chord, and resolution of the statement (B) sung over the dominant chord resolving to the home chord.

tonic   the root of a key.

subdominant   the fourth degree of the scale.

Duke Ellington at the piano (ca. 1946).
PHOTO COURTESY WILLIAM P. GOTTLIEB/WILLIAM P. GOTTLIEB
COLLECTION/LIBRARY OF CONGRESS PRINTS & PHOTOGRAPHS
DIVISION.

Listening Tips for Jazz Harmony

Listen to sounds other than the main melody and the rhythm.

- What do you hear changing? Is there a lot of movement? Not much movement?
- Do you feel that the accompaniment has a significant effect on the overall sound? If so, how might you describe that effect?
- Does the sound strike you as consonant, "right," happy, pleasant? Or do you feel it is dissonant, unresolved, dark? Does it alternate between the two? Does the music take you to different kinds of feelings? Or does it keep you essentially in one type of feeling?
- If there are points of tension, do you feel that they resolve satisfyingly?

TAKE NOTE

- What is distinctive about jazz harmony?

moving further to a third chord (the **dominant** chord) that resolves back to the home chord—has offered ample room to jazz musicians for creating variations. Indeed, many famous jazz tunes, although they may sound complex, can with analysis be reduced back to this basic blues structure.

A particular focal point of variation in jazz has been the "third chord" of the blues: the dominant chord. Listeners hear in it the sound of irresolution, a sense of transience that would be resolved by a return to the tonic (the home chord). This transient, not yet resolved nature of the dominant chord in the blues has inspired jazz musicians to experiment with substitutions for it, creating unusual and sometimes discordant variations. The idea has been that you can go practically anywhere harmonically in place of the dominant chord as long you resolve satisfyingly back to the tonic.

Jazz has, of course, moved far beyond a focus on "complexifying" the blues. Musicians such as Cecil Taylor and Ornette Coleman have brought to jazz conceptions that in some instances do away with harmony altogether.

---

dominant   the fifth degree of the scale.

Rhythm

Rhythm is critical to defining jazz: a musician could play the exact same piece with one set of rhythms and it wouldn't be jazz, but the musician could then take another set of rhythms—a syncopated melody played in a swinging way—and it would be jazz. Rhythm has been important to jazz since the music's birth. The influence of West African percussion, propulsiveness, and **polyrhythm**—multiple rhythms of different **meter** occurring simultaneously—has informed jazz since its inception.

Jazz was originally a dance music—music intended to accompany dancing in dance halls, ballrooms, and other venues—and remained so for at least 50 years. The connection to physical human movement is hard-wired into jazz.

---

rhythm   the aspect of music related to the structuring of sound in patterns of unfolding time; the aspect of music that most people think of as "the beat."

polyrhythm   multiple rhythms played simultaneously.

meter   the pattern of beats underlying a tune's rhythm; the number of beats occurring in a measure and the kind of note—quarter note, eighth note, or whatever—that is counted as a beat.

Dancers in a Washington, DC, jazz club (1940s). PHOTO COURTESY WILLIAM P. GOTTLIEB/WILLIAM P. GOTTLIEB COLLECTION/LIBRARY OF CONGRESS PRINTS & PHOTOGRAPHS DIVISION.

A prominent rhythmic characteristic of jazz is **swing**. This quality resists precise definition, but you can consider it a forward momentum that makes you want to snap your fingers or move another part of your body. Duke Ellington called swing "that part of rhythm that causes a bouncing, buoyant, terpsichorean urge." Many listeners are familiar with the **walking bass** in jazz. Its precise time keeping, in combination with the surrounding accents and syncopations of drums and other instruments, holds much of the key to the feeling of swing: a palpable rhythmic sensation marked by a forward propulsion.

 Watch the video on walking bass on **mymusiclab.com**

---

swing a rhythmic characteristic of much jazz, swing is a forward momentum, an elasticity of the pulse, that defies precise definition.

(to) swing to play with a perceptible forward momentum, a propulsive rhythm, and a flowing beat; found in much African-rooted music.

walking bass the bass technique of producing a steady beat while playing and connecting notes of a chord progression.

But swing is far from the only rhythm used in jazz. In its embrace of music from all over the world and from other genres, jazz has assimilated a massive collection of rhythmic approaches. You may hear Afro-Cuban jazz, Brazilian bossa nova and samba, Indian asymmetric meters, marching music, funk, rock—the list goes on.

In jazz, revolutions in instrumental technique have extended to the drums. In marching bands—the early models of jazz bands—the bass drum kept the beat. Later drummers, among them Kenny Clarke in the 1940s, shifted the beat-keeping function to the cymbals, freeing the bass drum to provide accents, punctuation, and highlights. The drum set in jazz opened up dynamically, becoming as expressive and colorful an instrument as any other.

Listening Tips for Jazz Rhythm

Pay attention to the following:

- Tempo—whether the music is fast or slow
- Meter—what the "count" is (repetitive groups of four, or three, or two, or some other grouping)
- Feel—the effect it has on you physically, whether calming you, making you sway, making you want to tap your feet, or pulling you in different directions
- Level of complexity—whether the rhythm is simple and straightforward (basically just keeping the beat) or full of activity and changing emphasis

TAKE NOTE

- What types of rhythms are commonly heard in jazz?

Form

A piece of music's larger **form**—its order of events, its architecture—is a key focal point for listening to and understanding the piece. Jazz, like classical music, employs many different kinds of architecture, some of which are unique to jazz.

One common structure in jazz consists of the band playing the tune's theme—its **head**—and then proceeding through solos that are improvisations over the **chord progression** of the head. At the end of solos, the band restates the head. For example,

head—solo 1—solo 2—solo 3—head

---

form architecture or organization of a piece of music and its subdivisions.

head in jazz, the main melody of a tune.

chord progression a sequence of chords; also informally called *chord changes* or just *changes*; serves as the harmonic architecture of a tune.

(This is not related to a common jazz term **head arrangement**, which refers to a musical arrangement that is played from memory rather than from the page.)

The head portion of the head-solo-solo-solo-head structure is essentially a statement of a tune or theme, which itself has a defined form. There are three commonly used forms in jazz, which can be grouped into two overall types: chorus forms and compound forms.

Chorus Form

A **chorus form** consists of one set of melodic-harmonic material—whether 12 bars, 32, or another length—that repeats over and over. There are two main types of chorus forms: the blues and the popular-song form.

The simplest form in jazz is that of the blues. The simple and expressive but extraordinarily elastic blues chord progression or "blues progression" (typically 12 bars, but sometimes 8 or 16) runs throughout jazz—indeed, is its most basic musical structure. Within this simple form, however, jazz musicians have created dozens of variations and thousands upon thousands of blues tunes.

You may not know it, but you've probably heard dozens of pieces of music that use the blues form. If you know the songs *Baby, Please Don't Go*, which has been recorded by singers ranging from Muddy Waters to Van Morrison to BeauSoleil; Lieber and Stoller's *Kansas City*; or the well-known tunes *Got My Mojo Working, Dust My Broom, Mystery Train, Cross Roads Blues*, or *Statesboro Blues*, you've heard the 12-bar blues.

A structure that found favor in the nineteenth century and reached its peak of expression in the twentieth is the **popular-song form**. Most American popular songs, at least through the mid-twentieth century, were in two main parts: the verse (16 or 32 bars) and the refrain or chorus (most often 32 bars). But jazz musicians rarely play the verses of popular songs, usually just the refrains. So in jazz, the term "popular-song form" refers to a structure built typically of four 8-bar phrases.

In the most typical popular-song construction, the first 8-bar musical phrase (typically labeled letter A) is usually repeated, followed by a contrasting phrase (letter B), and a return to the first phrase,

yielding the schema AABA. The B section is typically called the "bridge" as it bridges the phrase heard most often in the song, the A phrase, and its return at the end of the refrain. Examples of pieces that use this format are George Gershwin's *The Man I Love* and *Oh! Lady Be Good*, *Honeysuckle Rose* recorded by Benny Goodman and His Orchestra (CD I, Track 13/Download Track 13), and *Body and Soul* recorded by Coleman Hawkins (CD I, Track 14/Download Track 14). Antonio Carlos Jobim's *The Girl from Ipanema* (CD II, Track 10/Download Track 34; see Example 2.1) adds 8 bars to its B section.

Within popular-song form, the second most commonly used construction is ABAC. Examples of this format are Hoagy Carmichael's *Stardust*, Vincent Youmans's *Tea for Two*, Rodgers and Hart's *My Romance*, Morgan Lewis's *How High the Moon*, Sonny Rollins's *Airegin* (performed by Tito Puente; CD II, Track 8/Download Track 32), and George Gershwin's *Love Is Here to Stay* and *Summertime* (*JTSA* Disc 3/ Track 18; see Example 2.2).

Compound Form

The other major type of form is **compound form**. This is a longer, more complex form. Sometimes, for instance, a blues form might be subsumed within a popular-song

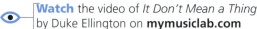

Watch the video of *It Don't Mean a Thing* by Duke Ellington on **mymusiclab.com**

---

head arrangement an arrangement worked out, usually collectively, on an impromptu basis and typically played from memory.

chorus form a formal structure, typical in jazz, consisting of one set of harmonic-melodic material—12 bars, 32 bars, or another length—that repeats over and over.

popular-song form a standard architecture in American popular song and jazz: 32 bars, consisting of four 8-bar phrases, AABA, with a contrasting bridge or B section.

compound form a structure with multiple discrete sections; also called *multisectional form*; came to jazz from marches and rags; an example is AABBACCDD (*Maple Leaf Rag*).

Example 2.1 *The Girl from Ipanema* (words by Norman Gimbel, music by Antonio Carlos Jobim, 1961)

PHRASE LENGTH	8 BARS	8 BARS	16 BARS	8 BARS
MUSIC	A	A	B	A
LYRICS	Tall and tan and young and lovely, the girl from Ipanema goes walking and when she passes, each one she passes goes "Ah!"	When she walks she's like a samba that swings so cool and sways so gentle, that when she passes, each one she passes goes "Ah!"	Oh, but I watch her so sadly. How can I tell her I love her? Yes, I would give my heart gladly, but each day when she walks to the sea, she looks straight ahead not at me.	Tall and tan and young and lovely, the girl from Ipanema goes walking, and when she passes I smile, but she doesn't see. She just doesn't see. No, she doesn't see.

SOURCE: WORDS BY NORMAN GIMBEL, MUSIC BY ANTONIO CARLOS JOBIM, 1961. LEONARD BERNSTEIN MUSIC PUBLISHING COMPANY, LLC, PUBLISHER.

Example 2.2 *Summertime* (words by DuBose Heyward, music by George Gershwin, 1938)

PHRASE LENGTH	4	4	4	4
MUSIC	A	B	A	C
LYRICS	Summertime, and the living is easy,	Fish are jumpin', and the cotton is high.	You're daddy's rich, and your mama's good-lookin',	So hush little baby, don't you cry.

SOURCE: WORDS BY DUBOSE HEYWARD, MUSIC BY GEORGE GERSHWIN, 1938. ALFRED PUBLISHING CO., INC.

Example 2.3 *Maple Leaf Rag* (Scott Joplin, 1899)

SECTION LENGTH	16	16	16	16	16	16	16	16	16
MUSIC	A	A	B	B	A	C	C	D	D
KEY	A-flat	A-flat	A-flat	A-flat	A-flat	D-flat	D-flat	D-flat	D-flat

form: for example, Richie Powell's *Jacqui*, recorded by Clifford Brown (1955). In the early years of jazz, composers often used the compound form, deriving from marches and instrumental rags. A famous example is Scott Joplin's *Maple Leaf Rag* (CD I, Track 6/Download Track 6; see Example 2.3), which incorporates a change of key partway through.

In the 1920s, composer, pianist, and bandleader Jelly Roll Morton employed elaborate multisectional or multithematic forms, such as that he used in his canonical recording *Black Bottom Stomp* (CD I, Track 9/Download Track 9; see Example 2.4).

A long multisectional or compound form may fill up an entire recording. However, when musicians play using chorus forms, it takes a number of renditions of the chorus form—three times through, six times through, etc.—to fill out a recording or performance.

Listening Tips for Jazz Form and Structure

- Pay attention to the overall structure. Try to identify sections that repeat, and determine how many sections make up a complete statement of the form. See if, by identifying sections with letters (A, B, and so forth), you can discern a structure, such as AABA.
- One way to identify the form in the cases of many mainstream jazz tunes is to focus on the music before the solos begin. This part usually consists of one or two iterations of the "head" or theme. Focus on its structure and subsidiary phrases. Notice how they carry through the solos. Listen to how the head recurs after all solos.

TAKE NOTE

- What are typical jazz forms and structures?

Example 2.4 *Black Bottom Stomp* (Jelly Roll Morton and His Red Hot Peppers, 1926)

TIME	MUSIC	LENGTH	INSTRUMENTATION
0:00	INTRO	8 bars	Ensemble
0:07	A1	16	Ensemble
0:22	A2	16	Trumpet alternates with ensemble
0:37	A3	16	Clarinet
0:52	INTERLUDE/MODULATION	4	Trumpet with ensemble
0:56	B	20	Ensemble
1:15	B	20	Clarinet
1:33	B	20	Piano
1:51	B	20	Trumpet
2:10	B	20	Banjo
2:29	B	20	Ensemble
2:48	B	20	Ensemble
3:08	CODA	2	Ensemble

Color and Texture

Some instruments produce warm, soothing sounds; others sound piercing and bright. These aspects of sound are referred to as **tone** color, also called **timbre**. The **color** of sound is a critical component of jazz, just as color is vital to painting, and it is a focus of musicians' attention when composing and playing.

Texture can be thought of as the density and quality of instrumentation. The texture of a jazz big band can be described as dense, thick, saturated. In contrast, a piece may have spare instrumentation—a voice accompanied only by string bass, for example.

 **Explore** Jazz Instruments on **mymusiclab.com**

Listening Tips for Jazz Color and Texture

Focus on the sound qualities of individual instruments.

- Is there variety of tone color? Is the sound mostly monochromatic?
- Can you identify brass instruments? reeds? strings? percussion? piano? guitar? anything else?
- How would you describe the individual sounds you hear?

Now focus on the overall sound—the ensemble as a whole.

- Is it thick, dense, rich? Is it thin, sparse?
- Are there different textures within the overall sound? Areas of roughness? Layers of smooth softness?
- How does the texture of sound change as the music progresses?

TAKE NOTE

- What roles do color and texture play in jazz?

---

tone the quality of sound as determined by properties other than pitch, primarily sound shape, or waveform; also sometimes used to mean a note or pitch.

timbre tone quality, or color, of musical sound.

color in music, the timbre or tone of a sound.

texture the quality of sound determined by the density of instrumentation.

Voice, Feel, and Expression

In jazz, every good musician strives to have his or her own "voice": a distinctive, personal musical identity. Because of jazz's emphasis on individual improvisation, the personality or style the player brings to the solo is especially important. Tenor saxophonist Dexter Gordon was known for a dense and grainy sound and a relaxed, slightly-behind-the-beat feel. Billie Holiday's vocals sounded almost talk-sung, and she draped them loosely around the beat. Pat Metheny's guitar work tends to be understated, precise, clean, and highly articulate.

Part of a musician's expressiveness has to do with the ideas expressed. As with speech, some musical expression may be complex and long-winded; others may be abbreviated, pointed, concise. The "message" itself expresses the personality.

But a musician can also apply a number of expressive devices to embellish and add nuance to messages, and these may become part of his or her signature

Bille Holiday performing at the Club Downbeat, New York City (ca. February 1947).
PHOTO COURTESY WILLIAM P. GOTTLIEB/ WILLIAM P. GOTTLIEB COLLECTION/LIBRARY OF CONGRESS PRINTS & PHOTOGRAPHS DIVISION.

style. One player might employ a lot of **vibrato** (a wavering embellishment of the note); another may play "dry"—without much vibrato. Many Brazilian singers, such as Astrud Gilberto, heard on *The Girl from Ipanema* (CD II, Track 10/Download Track 34) take the dry approach. One might apply a hard attack to the beginnings of notes; another might prefer a softer attack.

Listening Tips for Voice, Feel, and Expression

Veteran jazz fans are often able to quickly identify their favorite performers. (*Down Beat* magazine's famous "Blindfold Tests" challenge musician-listeners to do just that.) To focus on the qualities that make players identifiable, listen to the sound as you would to a speaking style. Is it any of the following:

- Strong and forceful?
- Understated and tentative?
- Broad and round?
- Thin and pinched?
- Loose and imprecise?
- Tight and articulate?
- Heavily ornamented?
- Devoid of ornamentation?
- A sound in which the musician uses certain devices habitually, such as slurs, slides, and swells?

TAKE NOTE

- How do individual voice, feel, and expression affect a jazz performance?

Improvisation

Improvisation—the spontaneous composition that provides much of the excitement in jazz—can be said to have three types: paraphrase improvisation, formulaic improvisation, and motivic improvisation.

Some jazz solos, such as the first eight bars of Coleman Hawkins's celebrated *Body and Soul* (1939, CD I, Track 14/Download Track 14), are based on the melody of a given tune: the improviser will paraphrase, comment upon, vary, and take off on flights from the original melody. Using the song's melody as the basis of further development is called **paraphrase improvisation**.

 **Explore** *Jazz Performance Techniques* on **mymusiclab.com**

Another approach, **formulaic improvisation**—the most common in jazz of all periods—involves what jazz musicians call their "licks": a kitbag of formulae that they have so internalized that they can insert them seamlessly in a fast-moving solo at will. In Hawkins's *Body and Soul*, after the first eight bars he largely abandons the melody to engage in formulaic improvisation. Charlie Parker brilliantly incorporated and creatively manipulated a vast number of **formulae** into his playing, for example, in *Embraceable You* (1947, CD I, Track 16/Download Track 16). The challenges of this approach are to insert the formulae and manipulate them on the fly, hide the fact that they are formulae, and avoid turning them into clichés.

Still another approach is that of **motivic improvisation**—using and repeating short motifs (or motives) that are in plain "sight"—for example Benny Carter's solo on the Chocolate Dandies' *I Can't Believe That You're in Love with Me* (JTSA Disc 2/Track 9), or John Coltrane's solo on Miles Davis's *So What* (CD I, Track 22/Download Track 22).

Although these three approaches are different, they can be intermixed within a single solo.

Listening Tips for Jazz Improvisation

- See if you can tell when the music is being improvised (rather than played as written). The original, written melody is usually played at the beginning of a performance, and sometimes at the end as well.
- Remember the tune's melody, and notice if the improvised solo is the same or different. Does the solo stay close to the melody? Does the solo bear only a distant relationship to the melody?
- Listen to the beginning and end of the solo, and notice the differences. Where has the soloist taken you?
- Listen to changes in the solo—in loudness and softness, in tempo, in **register** (highness and lowness). Is there a lot of variety in the solo? Or does it sound much the same from beginning to end?
- Is the soloist trading phrases or otherwise interacting noticeably with the other players?

---

formulaic improvisation   creating solos by manipulating, at the speed of thought, musical formulae or patterns that one has worked out and internalized.

formula   a memorized or routinized musical pattern that becomes a building block for improvising solos, especially at fast tempos; popularly called a *lick*.

motivic improvisation   improvisation that focuses on repeating a given motif by retaining its essential pattern but changing the pitches to match the changing chords of the compositional structure.

register   highness or lowness of pitch (melody).

---

vibrato   type of ornamentation or articulation in which a pitch is fluctuated slightly to enrich or intensify a tone.

paraphrase improvisation   paraphrasing, varying, and commenting upon—but not abandoning—the original melody.

- Why is improvisation a key element of jazz?

Style and Experimentation

Style refers to a distinctive way of mixing and presenting musical ingredients, and jazz offers a wide menu of styles, from boogie-woogie to bebop and beyond. Being able to recognize a style grows from hearing many examples and understanding the expressive devices that define the style. For example, compare Miles Davis's performance of *So What* to Count Basie's *Boogie Woogie*. Davis's improvisation is restrained, low-key, and full of space, in contrast to more energetic, full-bore performances such as Count Basie's.

While some jazz musicians enjoy specializing in a single style, many others are seekers, searchers, and adventurers, ever questing for original ideas, new ways to express themselves, and fresh sounds to absorb and work with. The search for the new has propelled jazz forward in an accelerated evolution, expanding from a relatively narrow array of styles in the beginning to today's more expansive palette. The spirit of exploration and discovery has made jazz a musical panorama of sounds. Jazz is an open system: It has embraced music from all over the world. It has peered into the inner workings of other kinds of music—classical and rock and hip-hop, for example—and taken what it has found intriguing.

Trumpeter Dizzy Gillespie, a bebop pioneer in the 1940s, was so enamored of Afro-Cuban rhythms that he built a big band with a Latin flavor. Trumpeter Miles Davis, years later, heard excitement in the sounds of rock guitarist Jimi Hendrix and funk band leader Sly Stone and began making rock-infused recordings. Today, players such as West African guitarist Lionel Loueke, Panamanian pianist Danilo Perez, Vietnamese-French guitarist Nguyên Lê, and Iraqi-American trumpeter Amir ElSaffar freely draw from a deep well

Louis Armstrong singing at New York's Carnegie Hall (ca. Feb. 1947). PHOTO COURTESY WILLIAM P. GOTTLIEB/WILLIAM P. GOTTLIEB COLLECTION/LIBRARY OF CONGRESS PRINTS & PHOTOGRAPHS DIVISION.

of international sounds. (Listen to Nguyên Lê's *Ting Ning*, CD II, Track 13/Download Track 17.)

Beyond styles, back in the realm of pure music, jazz has been a think tank for musical progress. The jazz tendency toward experimentation has made jazz one of the leading "research and development" sectors in musical art.

Jazz has consistently questioned the accepted wisdom, the status quo, and offered innovative alternatives. When Ornette Coleman appeared in 1959 with improvisations untethered from standard song structures and harmonies, he was introducing a whole new way of thinking about improvising, a clear break from the tradition of "running the chords" (soloing over chord progressions). There have been so many instances in jazz of musicians breaking from tradition that the phenomenon is itself a jazz tradition.

Listening Tips for Style and Experimentation

- Does the music remind you of anything you've heard before? Can you think of a specific musical approach that sounds similar? Is there a name for it?
- Are there multiple ingredients in the mix? Can you identify instruments representative of different styles? Of music from different countries?
- Does the music sound completely alien, unfamiliar, unrelated to what you know? Identifying the ways in which it is different can provide insights into the thinking of the musicians.

✳ **Explore** the basic elements of jazz composition on **mymusiclab.com**

👁 **Watch** the videos of Miles Davis's *So What* and Count Basie's *Boogie Woogie* on **mymusiclab.com**

- In jazz, what does style mean?

Musicians' Roles, Individual and Collective

The individual musician has a heightened role in jazz. A symphony musician may remain largely unknown to the public or audience because the focus of attention remains on the larger ensemble, but in jazz, every player in a group tends to hold the spotlight at some point in time.

It didn't start out that way. The original brass bands and dance ensembles of the early twentieth century made their names on the basis of group effort and sound. But when Louis Armstrong's cornet solos on his Hot Five and Hot Seven recordings (1925–28) showcased his musicianship and ability to personalize the tunes he played, he created a new focus: an emphasis on individual players. Since then jazz has offered, at its best, an optimum balance between the individual and the group, between the personal and the collective.

In support roles—as collaborators—musicians contribute to the collective whole. The results can be as distinctive as the Duke Ellington Orchestra's characteristic range of color, texture, and dynamics, or the Count Basie Orchestra's famous riff-based rhythmic drive.

As individuals, musicians stamp their solos and accompaniments with their own personalities. With the support of bandmates, the jazz musician "steps out" in ways not heard in some other types of music. The individual becomes a creator rather than, as in classical music, an interpreter.

Style & Technique

The Team Sport of Jazz

You can look at the performance of a jazz piece as an unusual kind of ball game. The closest analogy is basketball, where the ball is almost constantly in motion. As in basketball, where the ball is passed from player to player, in jazz the melody or solo is often passed among the soloists. In a jazz band, each player might "hold the ball," so to speak, for eight, twelve, sixteen, or more bars, but then he or she will typically pass it to another player. In basketball, part of the thrill of a good performance is watching what each player does when he or she has the ball and is in the spotlight of everyone's attention; in jazz, part of the thrill is *hearing* what each player does when it's his or her turn to take the forefront.

But in jazz, things get more complicated than in basketball. For one thing, every move is done to a rhythm—or even a series of overlapping rhythms—and the rhythms have to fit within a steady beat. (Can you imagine basketball players *having* to coordinate their every move to a steady beat?) For another, no matter who has the "ball" in a jazz performance, the other players are often interacting—the pianist is feeding chords to the band, the bassist is anchoring the beat off which everyone else plays, and the drummer is urging on and reacting to the soloists. You could even imagine these ongoing interactions as being like smaller basketballs. Viewed in this way, you have a game with a main basketball and a number of smaller balls all in play at the same time—creating multiple layers of interest, suspense, and excitement, not to mention complexity.

—*John Edward Hasse*

As in jazz, where individual players pass the melody back and forth, in basketball players have to keep passing the ball. Here, Kareem Abdul-Jabbar looks for a free teammate to take the ball. PHOTO COURTESY TONY TOMSIC/ WIREIMAGE/GETTY IMAGES.

In jazz, the interaction among players is important—it's part of the excitement and key to the notion of improvisation. The soloist listens to and is supported, prodded, sometimes even led, by the drummer or another accompanist. In some bands, the improvisation may occur among several musicians soloing simultaneously, thereby becoming a conversation in music.

In jazz, the audience also has a role to play. If you're witnessing a live performance, or listening to a recording made before an audience, pay attention to the interaction between the performers and audience. Can you detect any? Do you notice the audience—through applause or verbal interjections—urging on the players? Depending on the venue and audience, you might hear audience exclamations such as "Take your time!" "Play it!" "Talk to me!" "All right!" or "Yeah!" These are like the interjections one might hear in an African American sanctified or down-home church, and they testify to the traditional importance of the audience in jazz performance—a retention of African music, as we will learn in Chapter 3, where there is no rigid line separating performers and audience and one encourages the other.

In a jazz concert, it's perfectly okay to applaud after a solo—something that is against the unwritten rules of conduct at a classical music concert. The kind of interaction that you often find in a jazz performance is another indication of the African contributions to jazz.

Listening Tips for Musicians' Interaction

Choose two instruments from the ensemble—for example, a melody instrument and the drums, or the bass and the piano—and try to focus on them exclusively. Imagine them as a duo.

- Are the two responding to each other? Is a change in energy by one player followed by a corresponding change by the other player?
- Describe the relationship between the two. What do you think their jobs are in relation to each other? Do you think they are fulfilling those roles?
- Is one the soloist and the other the accompanist? Is one leading and the other following? Are they dueling, competing? Or are they dancing together, hand in hand?
- If they were talking to each other, what do you think they would be saying?

TAKE NOTE

- What are the tensions between individual and collective performance in jazz?

Jazz as an Art Form

All art forms have a basic set of criteria that is used to judge the quality of a specific work. In determining the quality of a jazz performance, musicians and critics alike tend to consider the following criteria (with not all applicable to every performance):

- **Technical mastery:** Adequate control of **intonation** (playing in tune), fingering, rhythm, and other mechanics of musicianship is the baseline criterion for performance quality. Poor technique is certain to break any "spell" the music might otherwise cast over a receptive audience.
- **Personality and originality:** Uniqueness of both concept and expression are highly valued in jazz. While competent replication of others' styles may warrant respect, it is the compellingly original voice that draws the most esteem. Thelonious Monk, for example, sounds like no other pianist—a factor that plays a significant role in his acclaim.
- **Innovation:** Like research scientists who push the bounds of knowledge, jazz musicians may introduce new techniques or concepts that change the way others think. Charlie Parker, in the 1940s, promulgated a complex new approach to improvising jazz melody. Cecil Taylor brought abstraction to jazz. Because true innovation is a rarity, its presence in a performance signals jazz of the highest order.
- **Power to engage:** In the best performances, the listener becomes transfixed, fully engaged emotionally and intellectually. The art, due to the power of its conception and presentation, creates a "world" in which the listener lives. It is the "spell" referred to earlier.
- **Balance:** This hard-to-define quality has to do with the "rightness" of structural and expressive elements. Is there internal consistency to the parts of the performance, adding up to a coherent, thoughtful whole? If an overall statement or mood can be discerned, do solos, dynamics, and all other factors support it?

TAKE NOTE

- What factors can help us determine the quality of a jazz performance?

Listening Tips Wrap-Up

When listening to tunes cited in this book, apply the first-listening approach described in Chapter 1 and then follow up with listening that focuses on the various jazz elements. In combination, these approaches can yield a rich, multilayered appreciation of the tune.

---

intonation   tuning, that is, playing or singing in tune.

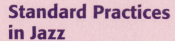
Standard Practices in Jazz

Jazz has been shaped by characteristic professional traditions among musicians. They have included woodshedding, jam sessions, cutting contests, and band battles.

Woodshedding—a metaphor for effort and time spent alone, as in a woodshed or other isolated place—refers to the focused private study and practice any musician needs to go through in order to develop chops. Famously, a young Charlie Parker proved himself inadequate for the demands of a Kansas City bandstand; after woodshedding for some time, he reemerged with mastery of his instrument, was hired by one of the city's top bands, and later helped pioneer modern-jazz improvisation.

Jam sessions are informal get-togethers in which musicians play for fun, as an opportunity to get practice in a band setting, to get to know other musicians, to demonstrate capabilities to other players, and to explore new ideas. Traditionally, they occurred on bandstands after regular paid gigs ended. Jam sessions at nightclubs in Harlem in the 1940s played a key role in the innovations that produced the style called bebop—a revolution at the time and a core methodology in jazz as time went on. In recent years opportunities for "jamming" have occurred primarily on college campuses, in community workshops, and in private homes.

Cutting contests are competitions between soloists—such as piano players—or even entire bands. They can take place during jam sessions. Musicians take turns soloing to see who has the best technique or develops the most interesting ideas. Many aspiring musicians have reconsidered their career plans after being "cut" on the bandstand by superior players. Others have emerged from these sessions with the aura of living legend.

Band battles attract audiences with the promise of drama: two or more bands vie for the title of winner. During the swing era of the 1930s—when big bands entertained larges audiences in dance halls and jazz peaked in popularity—battles of the bands raised the excitement level several notches above normal.

—*Tad Lathrop*

Band battles, like this 1938 face-off between the Chick Webb and Count Basie outfits, were hot attractions at Harlem's Savoy ballroom. COURTESY FRANK DRIGGS COLLECTION.

---

woodshedding   effort and time spent alone practicing.

chops   informal jazz term meaning technical skills on an instrument, as in "Wynton Marsalis has great chops."

jam session   informal playing session in which musicians play for each other.

cutting contest   in jazz, the practice of two or more pianists or bands competing with each other, each taking turns, to determine the winner; common in early New Orleans jazz and among Harlem pianists of the 1920s and 1930s.

band battle   a performance of two or more bands billed as a competition; especially prevalent in the swing era, and generally used to boost the appeal to audiences; also known as a battle of the bands.

Focused Listening

Watch and listen again to *Boogie Woogie*.

This time the listening can be more focused than before. Now, having explored characteristics of jazz, from improvisation to musicians' roles—along with the listening tips in each category—your new observations can target those characteristics. As you listen, make a note of your impressions.

The viewing guide demonstrates how to focus on the music's elements and features.

Watch the video of Count Basie's *Boogie Woogie* on **mymusiclab.com**

TAKE NOTE

- How should you listen to a jazz melody?

When we listen to a pop song, we usually focus first on its melody. We expect the melody to remain the same throughout the performance. On the other hand, jazz musicians often use a melody as the basis for embellishments, variations, countermelodies, and creating whole new melodies, rather than reproducing it exactly. Part of the enjoyment of jazz is hearing how each individual musician varies the "raw material" (the song or melody) that forms the basis for his or her improvisation.

- What is distinctive about jazz harmony?

Jazz harmony is sometimes built on the blues progression, based on the I, IV, and V7 chords. While the blues progression provides the basis for some jazz compositions, other harmonies are drawn from popular songs, classical music, and other genres.

- What types of rhythms are commonly heard in jazz?

A prominent rhythmic characteristic of jazz is swing, but swing is far from the only rhythm used in jazz. You may also hear Afro-Cuban jazz, Brazilian bossa nova and samba, marching music, funk, rock—the list is nearly endless.

- What are typical jazz forms and structures?

The simplest form in jazz is that of the 12-bar blues. The 32-bar popular song form AABA is perhaps the second most popular structure. Another commonly used 32-bar construction is ABAC.

- What roles do color and texture play in jazz?

The color of sound—also called tone color and timbre—is a critical component of jazz, just as color is vital to painting. Also important is texture, which can be thought of as the density and quality of instrumentation.

- How do individual voice, feel, and expression affect a jazz performance?

Every good jazz musician seeks to have his or her own "voice"—a distinctive, quite personal musical identity. A musician can also apply a number of expressive devices to embellish and add nuance to messages, and these may become part of his or her signature style. In this way, musicians can set themselves apart from the pack, and their dedicated fans will immediately recognize their performances.

- Why is improvisation a key element of jazz?

Improvisation is what sets apart jazz performance from many other types of music. In jazz, improvisers use three types of improvisation—paraphrase, formulaic, and motivic—to create new melodies.

- In jazz, what does style mean?

Style refers to a distinctive way of mixing and presenting musical ingredients, and it describes any jazz performance. Jazz offers a wide menu of styles, from boogie-woogie to bebop and beyond. While some musicians adhere to a single style throughout their careers, others like to experiment with different musical identities. Miles Davis, for one, became famous for reinventing himself stylistically and pioneering new sounds.

- What are the tensions between individual and collective performance in jazz?

Great jazz bands perfectly balance the individual talents of their players with true "team spirit." In jazz, we expect to hear the musicians interact with each other; the trumpeter's solo performance should influence how the saxophonist plays his or her part, for example. Balancing individual virtuosity with the need to create a unified band sound is the sign of a truly great jazz performance.

- What factors can help us determine the quality of a jazz performance?

The qualities that distinguish an outstanding jazz performance include technical mastery, personality and originality, innovation, the power to engage, and balance. While not all of these factors come into play for every performance, they are the general standards used by musicians and the jazz audience alike when judging a jazz work.

DISCUSSION QUESTIONS

1. What are the primary musical characteristics of jazz? Describe how each is important.

2. Think about musical innovators. Discuss any that you are aware of, either in jazz or in some other musical form such as rock or classical music. What did the innovators contribute?

3. Think of a song that you know well and recall its melody. Attempt to identify such subdivisions of the melody as motifs and phrases.

4. Think of a song that you know well. Attempt to describe its form in terms of sections such as A, B, and so forth. Then try to think of a popular song that uses AABA form.

5. Describe the distinctive "voice" of a musician whose work you know. What expressive characteristics come to mind?

6. Choose a favorite recording and listen to it. Discuss whether the piece succeeds in meeting the criteria for evaluating jazz as an art form presented on page 21.

KEY TERMS & KEY PEOPLE

blues form 12	jam session 22	scale 12
chord 12	melody 10	subdominant (note or chord) 13
chord changes 12	meter 13	swing 14
chord progression 15	motif (motive) 11	texture 17
color 17	note 10	timbre 17
dominant (note or chord) 13	phrase 10	tone 17
form 14	pitch 11	tonic (note or chord) 12
harmonic progression 12	polyrhythm 13	vibrato 18
harmony 12	popular-song form 15	walking bass 14
head 14	register 18	
improvisation 12	rhythm 13	

CHAPTER 3

The Birth of Jazz

by John Edward Hasse

TAKE NOTE

- What roles did African and European music play in the development of jazz?
- What were the special conditions in New Orleans that made it a fertile ground for jazz?
- What roles did blues and ragtime play in the development of jazz?
- How did jazz develop as an improvised music performed for dancing?
- Who were some of the early innovators of New Orleans jazz?
- What were some other early centers of jazz, and how did their music differ from that heard in New Orleans?

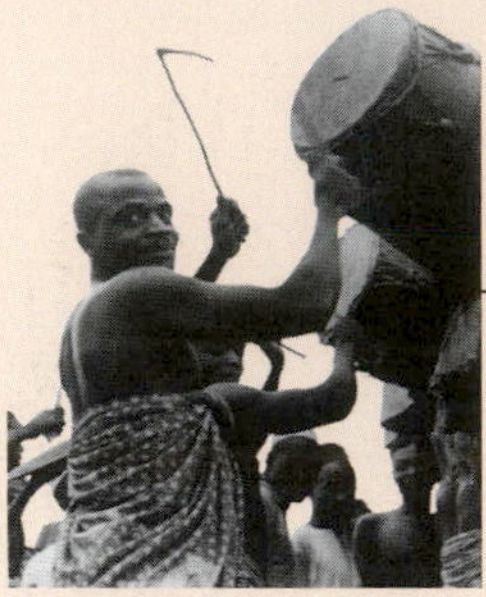

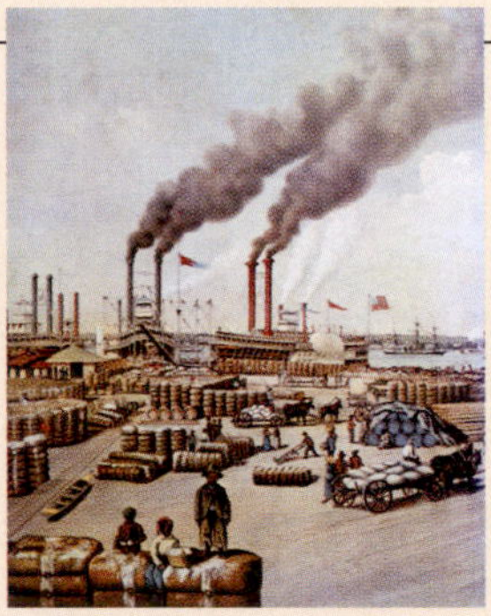

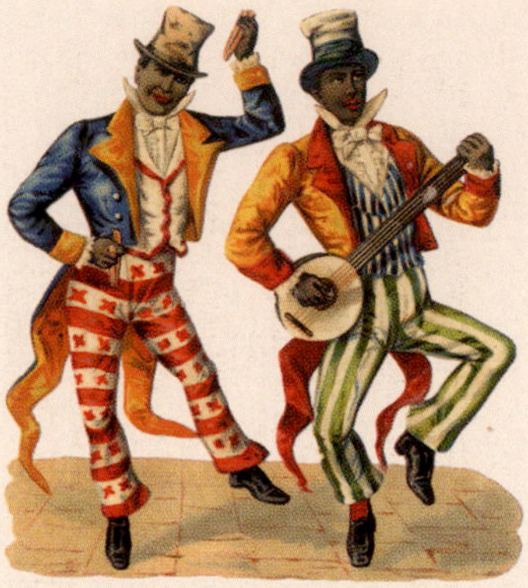

New Orleans established by the
French as La Nouvelle-Orléans ——————— ● **1718**

United States Declaration
of Independence ——————— ● **1776**

Approximately half of New
Orleans population is of
African descent ——————— ● **ca. 1800**

The Louisiana Purchase; New
Orleans and Louisiana become
part of the United States ——————— ● **1803**

New influx of French and
Creole peoples arrive in
New Orleans from Saint-
Domingue (now Haiti) ——————— ● **ca. 1810**

● **1840–80s** ——— Heyday of
minstrel shows

● **1850** ——— Stephen Foster's *Camptown Races*
becomes his first major hit; it is
popularized by Christy's Minstrels

The Civil War ——————— ● **1861–65**

Emancipation Proclamation frees slaves in the
rebellious Confederate states ——————— ● **1863**

Reconstruction Era; freed blacks win
some political power in the South ——————— ● **1865–77**

"Compromise of 1877" leads to
removal of federal troops from the
South and widespread enactment ——————— ● **1877** ——— Thomas Edison patents his cylinder
of "Jim Crow" laws reestablishing
segregation — recording machine

● **ca. 1880** ——— First major brass parade bands, the
Excelsior and the Onward, established
in New Orleans

Booker T. Washington ——————— ● **1881**
named first head of
Tuskegee Institute, an
all-black college; in
1895, he gives famous ● **1885** ——— Cornetist/bandleader Joe "King" Oliver
"Atlanta Address," born in Louisiana
establishing him as
national leader Made possible by the development of disc sound
recordings, the commercial phonograph and recording
● **1894** ——— industry gets underway

● **1895** ——— Cornetist
Buddy Bolden
forms his first
group in New
Orleans

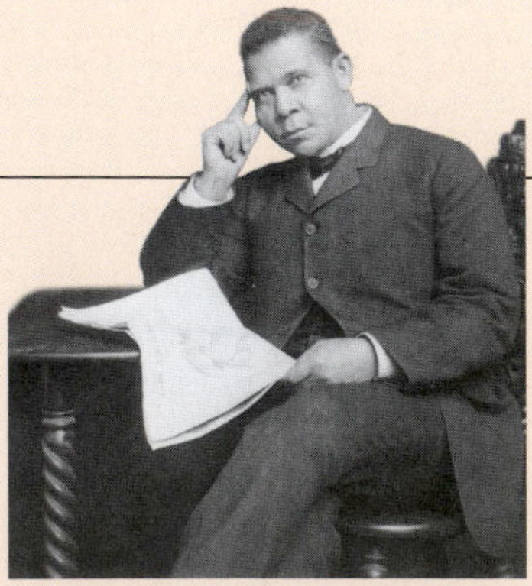

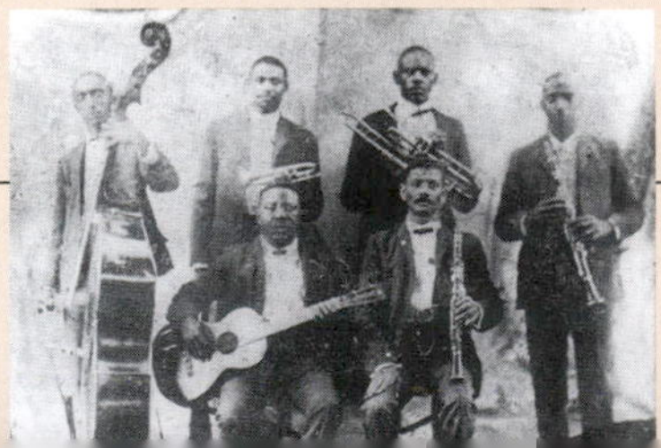

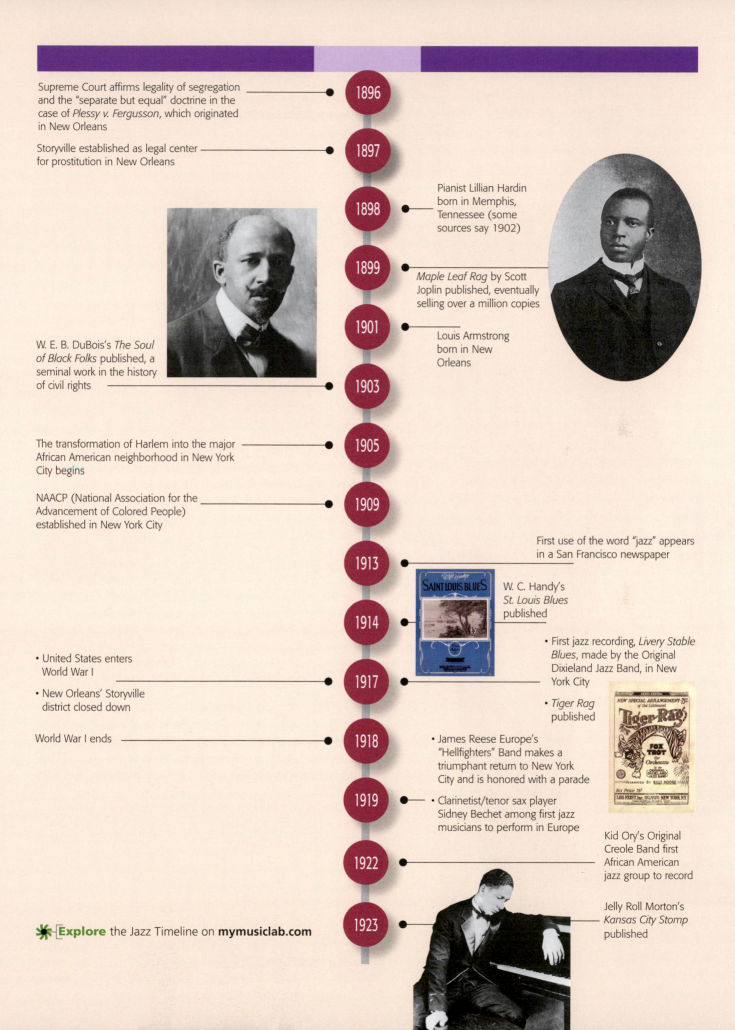

1896 — Supreme Court affirms legality of segregation and the "separate but equal" doctrine in the case of *Plessy v. Fergusson*, which originated in New Orleans

1897 — Storyville established as legal center for prostitution in New Orleans

1898 — Pianist Lillian Hardin born in Memphis, Tennessee (some sources say 1902)

1899 — *Maple Leaf Rag* by Scott Joplin published, eventually selling over a million copies

1901 — Louis Armstrong born in New Orleans

W. E. B. DuBois's *The Soul of Black Folks* published, a seminal work in the history of civil rights — **1903**

The transformation of Harlem into the major African American neighborhood in New York City begins — **1905**

NAACP (National Association for the Advancement of Colored People) established in New York City — **1909**

1913 — First use of the word "jazz" appears in a San Francisco newspaper

SAINT LOUIS BLUES

1914 — W. C. Handy's *St. Louis Blues* published

• United States enters World War I
• New Orleans' Storyville district closed down — **1917** — • First jazz recording, *Livery Stable Blues*, made by the Original Dixieland Jazz Band, in New York City

• *Tiger Rag* published

World War I ends — **1918** — • James Reese Europe's "Hellfighters" Band makes a triumphant return to New York City and is honored with a parade

NEW SPECIAL ARRANGEMENT
Tiger Rag
FOX TROT
for Orchestra
ARRANGED BY BILLY MOORE
Net Price 75¢
LEO. FEIST Inc. NEW YORK, N.Y.

1919 — • Clarinetist/tenor sax player Sidney Bechet among first jazz musicians to perform in Europe

1922 — Kid Ory's Original Creole Band first African American jazz group to record

1923 — Jelly Roll Morton's *Kansas City Stomp* published

✳ **Explore** the Jazz Timeline on **mymusiclab.com**

J azz, according to popular lore, was born and raised in Storyville, the New Orleans red-light district. When, to protect sailors, the U.S. Navy forced the area's closure in 1917, jazz musicians left the city and took the new music up the Mississippi River to Chicago. From there it spread across the nation.

Is that the way jazz actually came into being? Well, not really. This widely embraced notion is based on five misconceptions about the following:

1. Where the music started
2. Where it was played in New Orleans
3. When the exodus of jazz musicians began
4. Why the migration began
5. Where musicians went

Jazz did not originate in Storyville, and it was played not only in that district but all over New Orleans. Some musicians left New Orleans long before 1917, while others didn't leave for a number of years or never left. Those who did leave were motivated by the promise of greater economic opportunity elsewhere. None of the adventurers took the Mississippi River to Chicago (it doesn't go anywhere near Chicago). Some of the musicians who left went north, some went west to California, and others toured widely.

But historians are still far from unanimity about the origins and early development of jazz. In fact, the early years of jazz are shrouded in a kind of fog, which the passing decades have thickened rather than cleared. In the years leading up to the making of the first jazz records in 1917, the evidence—the prehistory of the music—is mostly silent. Lacking recordings of jazz musicians before 1917, the historian must rely on far less direct sources of information: contemporaneous recordings of other kinds of music, the reminiscences of musicians (which frequently are at odds with each other), newspaper notices, and photographs.

The very origin of the word *jazz* is in doubt—there are at least a half-dozen theories about its derivation. One holds that the word is an Afro-Caribbean term for "speed up." There are multiple indications that in early twentieth-century San Francisco, the word was in the air, meaning something like pep, enthusiasm, or "play with energy," while in New Orleans, the word was used to mean sexual intercourse. The first verified written use of it was in a San Francisco newspaper in 1913. In fact, the word was spelled variously "jas," "jass," "jaz," and "jazz" until at least 1918. In New Orleans, until the 1920s at the earliest, most musicians used the term "ragtime" for the music they played.

The early history of jazz may never be known precisely. Yet it's possible to identify a number of phenomena, conditions, and events that in combination seem to have given rise to the music and brought it before the public.

New Orleans cornet king Freddie Keppard left the city in 1914, taking his sound west to Los Angeles and north to Chicago. PHOTO COURTESY FRANK DRIGGS COLLECTION.

Old World Roots

The story of jazz begins with two of the most important population shifts in modern history: European emigrants seeking a better life in the New World and black Africans being brutally uprooted and transported to the Americas to be sold into slavery. In the Western Hemisphere, European- and African-derived cultural traditions—including musical traditions—intermingled gradually over a period of several hundred years, creating many different combinations that included jazz.

African Influences

Understanding jazz requires a look at a few facts about African music, and in particular the music of West Africa, where most of the slaves came from. A number of the characteristics of jazz are found in African music. They include group participation, a link with dancing, an emphasis on rhythm, a structure based on **call and response**, the use of improvisation, the application of vocal sounds to instruments, and the prevalence of short, repeated melodic phrases—called **riffs** in jazz. African music also tends to be passed on aurally, rather than in written form.

In Africa, music is such an integral and omnipresent part of the daily fabric that life without it is

---

riff a short, repeated melodic phrase.

syncopation accenting weak beats of a rhythm in a way that adds musical interest; a characteristic of jazz rhythm.

call and response a pattern, common in jazz and African American music, in which a singer or instrumentalist (or group of them) answers a phrase or short passage from another; also found in some church services when the congregation answers the "call" from the preacher.

Listening Focus

((• **Listen** to *Simpa (Fire)* by Hausa Drummers on **mymusiclab.com**
CD I, Track 1/Download Track 1

((• **Listen** to *On Mardi Gras Day* by "Hank" on **mymusiclab.com**
CD I, Track 1/Download Track 2

SIMPA (FIRE) • HAUSA DRUMMERS AND ON MARDI GRAS DAY • "HANK"

Simpa (Fire) by Hausa Drummers

Music: Traditional. Personnel: Hausa drummers (percussion ensemble and singers). Recorded by Ivan Annan, 1964, in Ghana. First issue: *Folk Music of Ghana*, Smithsonian Folkways FW08859. Timing: 2:04.

On Mardi Gras Day by "Hank"

Music: Traditional. Personnel: "Hank" (vocal, homemade percussion instrument). Recorded by Samuel Charters, 1957, in New Orleans. First issue: *Music of New Orleans, Vol. 1: Music of the Streets: Music of Mardi Gras*, Smithsonian Folkways FA 02461. Timing: 1:37.

Simpa is an example of traditional African drummers accompanying a group of vocalists. This recording, made in Ghana in 1964 by folklorist Ivan Annan, is performed by a group of Hausa-speaking recreational drummers. This recording is in many ways typical of the complexity of West African drum bands. In this performance, you can hear three different groups of percussion instruments: several high-pitched shakers; a group of mid-range drums performing **syncopated** patterns somewhat independent of the shakers; and deeper drums beating accents to the shaker lines. You can hear the first and third groups most clearly at the opening of the song, right after the crowd noise and applause drop down (at around 0:10). At 0:26 a thunderous clamor from the bass drums introduces the mid-range parts. While these may be difficult for you to hear, each is playing a different rhythm pattern; the patterns all together create the polyrhythmic sound. You should also listen for the interplay between the lead singer and the group; this is an example of the call-and-response style that is so prevalent in African and African American music.

Compare *Simpa* with a recording made by folklorist Samuel Charters of a street musician performing in 1957 on Mardi Gras day in New Orleans. This street entertainer is playing a homemade percussion instrument made out of a variety of sizes of tin cans mounted onto a wooden frame; he uses the rails from an old chair as his drumsticks. In this performance, you can hear the clear difference between the slow-moving, almost non-rhythmic vocal and the propulsive drum part (starting at approximately 0:06). Even within the drum part itself, the musician creates the illusion of several different lines by exploiting the different pitches and timbres of the cans. Listen (0:53 through 1:06) to how he plays a high-pitched line and then "responds" with a low-pitched part. The rhythmic complexity of the drum part builds through the entire performance, with the drummer cleverly creating the illusion of an instrumental "break" (at about 0:30) and, in the concluding part, imitating how a marching band would build to a dramatic conclusion.

—*Richard Carlin and John Edward Hasse*

An African drummer from the Gold Coast (now Ghana) plays the large "state drum" in honor of a visiting dignitary. PHOTO COURTESY BRITISH INFORMATION SERVICES.

of an interlocking, overlapping nature) between a leader and a chorus. Call and response also characterizes interplay between drummers in a drum ensemble and between a singer and accompaniment. In addition, it's reflected in African dance: sometimes a skilled dancer will step into a circle of dancers and take a solo that mirrors a call-and-response pattern in the music.

Call and response typically involves improvisation: the soloist will spontaneously invent musical statements and melodic variations and embellishments. The chorus responds to each improvised statement with a more stable melodic "answer" to the soloist. African American music, including jazz, is rich with improvisation and responsorial patterns. Examples can be heard in the music of 1930s big bands, in which a lead instrument improvises a melody over a background chorus of repeating riffs played by a horn section.

African music also makes use of the natural melodic quality of spoken language, applying it to both vocal and instrumental music. Most African languages are built on a melodic relationship between syllables (up-down, down-up, same-same), and thus speech patterns are easily transformed into song. African vocal music has such other speechlike characteristics as **glissandi**, dips and bends, a rising attack, and a falling release. Similar sounds can be produced with some instruments—the famous African "talking drums," for example, as well

inconceivable. Music involves group participation, and it is frequently performed to accompany dancing.

Drumming is a crucial mode of musical expression in West Africa. But it is just one aspect of the all-important twin hallmarks of African music: rhythm and percussiveness. West African music is marked by **"hot rhythm"**—rhythm that swings or has a strong forward-propelling motion. Musical ensembles often play **polyrhythms** and **polymeters**—several different rhythms and **meters** going on simultaneously.

A related dominant trait of West African music is a percussive approach to articulation. Musical instruments, whether struck or not, are given a crisp, precise attack, creating a kind of kick at the beginning of the note, a practice that would come to mark a great deal of jazz.

Much African music is structured in a two-part form called call and response—a kind of dialogue (often

---

hot rhythm   mid twentieth-century term for rhythm that swings or has a strong, forward-propelling motion.
polyrhythm   multiple rhythms played simultaneously.
polymeter   multiple meters played simultaneously.
meter   the pattern of beats underlying a tune's rhythm; the number of beats occurring in a measure and the kind of note—quarter note, eighth note, or whatever—that is counted as a beat.
glissandi   (Italian) plural of glissando, which means sliding upward or downward between two pitches.

as such melody-producing instruments as flutes, trumpets, and xylophones. Jazz trumpeters and trombonists would carry on this tradition by developing ways of using mutes and half-valving techniques to make their brass instruments "talk."

Long forms comparable to the European rondo or sonata are rare in traditional West African music, which prefers short, repeated forms—the kind that would show up in jazz as riffs and the repeating bass lines of boogie-woogie. While some African patterns are repeated exactly, often there is subtle variation.

European Influences

Other characteristics of jazz came from European music. First, even though there is a basic kind of harmony in some African music, and while the African scale is similar to the European, jazz took its harmonic system more from Europe. Second, jazz, when written down, is expressed using the European system of musical notation, slightly modified. Third, jazz derived most of its instruments—cornet, trumpet, trombone, the saxophone family, clarinet, piano, bass, and guitar—from European music. (Exceptions included the drum set, which was an American amalgamation of percussion instruments of various origin, and the banjo, an American commercial adaptation of an instrument, the *banza,* made by West African slaves in the New World.) Fourth, European music served as the source of several compositional forms common in jazz, notably the 32-bar popular-song form and the multi-strain form used in marches, rags, and such early jazz pieces as *Tiger Rag* (1917) and **Jelly Roll Morton**'s *Kansas City Stomp* (1923).

One example of Europe's impact on jazz is how European and especially Italian opera exerted a powerful influence on the New Orleans-born trumpeter **Louis Armstrong**. It can be heard in Armstrong's improvised quotations from various operas and, moreover, in his dramatic bursts of melody; florid embellishments; operatic, bravura musical gestures; and way of theatrically placing himself, as soloist, in the sonic foreground. Armstrong, through his clarion example, would make these characteristics common in jazz.

TAKE NOTE

- What roles did African and European music play in the development of jazz?

New Orleans

Many syntheses of African and European traditions took place in the Americas, and one of them was jazz. In the creation of that music, one American locale looms largest: New Orleans.

New Orleans was established in 1718 as an outpost in the French colony of Louisiana, and during its first century it had more in common geographically, economically, and culturally with the French and Spanish colonies in the Caribbean than it did with New York City or Boston. While the U.S. populace was largely Protestant (with some puritanical influence) and English-speaking, that of New Orleans was Roman Catholic and French-speaking. The French in the New World, through their cultural and religious worldview, were noted for tolerance of local cultures, which would help lay the groundwork for jazz in New Orleans.

At first, French culture predominated in New Orleans, reinforced by an influx of French and Creoles—New World natives of European, African, and mixed descent—from Saint-Domingue (now

Cargo being unloaded on the Levee in New Orleans, Louisiana, depicted in a Currier & Ives print from 1884. COURTESY LIBRARY OF CONGRESS.

Haiti) around 1810. At that time the city was awash in French-language opera (established in 1791, the first in North America), theater, and newspapers. Before the Civil War, New Orleans was often called "the Paris of America."

In 1800, more than half the population had African origins; the scent of African cooking, the sounds of African music, and the sight of Afro-Creole dancing flavored the cultural environment. The African influence was reinforced by the importation of slaves directly from Africa; although the federal government outlawed the practice in 1808, some slaves were brought in illegally up to the eve of the Civil War. The city boasts the oldest urban black community in the United States.

Following the Caribbean pattern, New Orleans developed something of a three-tiered racial structure: whites, blacks, and people of mixed descent.

Events in the city's history added to its ethnic pluralism. In 1783, France ceded Louisiana to Spain, which returned it to France in 1803. That year, the Louisiana Purchase transferred ownership to the United States. A flood of Anglo-American immigrants then challenged the Franco-African host culture of the city. Before the Civil War, the city took in many German and Irish immigrants and, after the war, an influx of Italians. Although Anglo-Americans were ascendant, New Orleans boasted an ethnic composition—including French, African, Caribbean, Italian, German, Mexican, and American Indian—of a diversity unprecedented in the South.

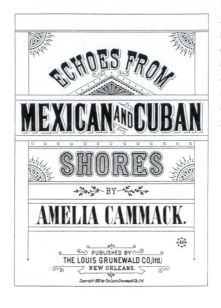

Music publishers responded to the demand for Latin-influenced music by issuing printed versions of songs and instrumentals. COURTESY JOHN EDWARD HASSE.

New Orleans's Six Jazz-Creating Conditions

New Orleans, with its multiethnic populace and pivotal location, claimed a unique set of six conditions that gave rise to jazz:

1. Loose cultural boundaries
2. Active Afro-Caribbean culture
3. Vital musical life
4. Strong dance tradition
5. Pervasive "good times" atmosphere
6. Numerous brass bands

Loose Cultural Boundaries. New Orleans possessed the loose boundaries needed for the exchange of culture. Until the Civil War, it was the second-largest port of immigration in the Western Hemisphere—both the Mississippi River and the Gulf of Mexico served as broad musical highways.

The city's residential patterns and musical activities promoted cultural intermingling. In most other U.S. cities, many ethnic groups typically lived in their own neighborhoods. New Orleans, however, had no such ghettos. People of one race lived cheek by jowl

👁 **Watch** the documentary on New Orleans on **mymusiclab.com**

with another: the black trumpeter **Buddy Bolden** lived two doors down from the white clarinetist Larry Shields and his musical family, and the black bassist Pops Foster lived next door to the Sicilian American clarinetist Leon Roppolo. Part of the city's fluid multiculturalism, this proximity provided many opportunities for musical interchange and helped jazz spread quickly beyond color lines.

Active Afro-Caribbean Culture. The city hosted a large contingent of free blacks—proud Afro-French Creoles—who established their own culture and small-market economy. By the late eighteenth century, on Sundays and religious holidays slaves and free people of color gathered in an open field that became known as the Place de Negres, later called Place Congo or Congo Square. It and a couple of other grassy commons in the city became probably the only places in North America where African dancing, drumming, and music making could occur openly. (Drumming also figured in ceremonies of an African-derived religion called **voodoo (or *vodun*)**, which some Africans and African descendants kept alive.)

New Orleans also absorbed elements of Caribbean cultures. Among them were the Cuban ***habanera*** and

---

voodoo (or *vodun*) religious beliefs and practices that combine African and Roman Catholic elements; practiced in parts of the Caribbean, especially Haiti, and in some parts of the Southern United States.

habanera (Spanish) a long-short-medium-medium rhythm from Cuba; a dance and music genre in $\frac{2}{4}$ time popular in Cuba in the late nineteenth century; adopted in Bizet's 1875 opera *Carmen* and widely exported to the Americas; named for Habana (Havana).

Parade and funeral regulars Henry Allen, Sr., and his brass band in Algiers, Louisiana (ca. 1905). Standing, left to right: Jack Carey, unknown musician, Jimmy Palao, August Rousseau, unknown musician, Joe Howard, Oscar "Pops" Celestin, Henry Allen, Sr.

PHOTO COURTESY FRANK DRIGGS COLLECTION.

Parading with a Brass Band

Boom! . . . Boom! . . . Boom! Those first thunderous blasts from the big bass drum signal the start of a musically led passage deep into the soul of New Orleans. Whatever the context of the drum call and improvised brass-band music that follow, be it a funeral march, a social club's annual parade, or a church anniversary, everyone is welcome to participate in the spirited—and often spiritual—occasion.

One, two, even three 10-piece brass bands—each member wearing a uniform and band cap—may line up for the procession. Each group might have three trumpets to improvise melodies, two trombones to slide and growl, a clarinet to sing and dance above the ensemble, and two saxophones to lay down powerful riffs. The foundation is a swinging rhythm section with a lightly rapping snare drum, a roaring bass drum to pour out endless syncopated rhythms, and a whopping tuba to anchor everything with bass lines. Whether jazzing up a standard religious hymn, a traditional march, a popular song, a rag, or a blues, the band struts along and marks the time in easy, neither-too-fast-nor-too-slow dance tempos.

Each band is led by an elegantly dressed grand marshal, who waves his handkerchief and carries a decorated umbrella as he gracefully dances along, establishing processional order amid the surrounding chaos. Then there are dozens of club members who spend thousands for the special day. Club divisions attempt to outdo each other in dance and dress. One group may wear boiled-shrimp-colored outfits from head to toe; another may wear cranberry red or avocado green.

As the parade proceeds, it collects an endless number of "second liners"—hundreds of anonymous onlookers who follow and dance alongside the parade. The music and dance interact in countless ways. Standard music rules are broken, twisted, and stretched in favor of fresh creative expression that matches the wild passion of the dances and provides a taste of the freedom sought by its creators in everyday life. It's easy to become disoriented in this spirit world. As the dancing and the music reach ever-higher levels of intensity, the participants may feel they're losing themselves in a swirling sea of people, motion, heat, scents, and sounds. For many, undoubtedly, the four-to-six-hour duration of the experience seems like mere minutes.

The parade ends with a rousing finale, and normalcy slowly sets in. Musicians and others begin to feel the ache of fatigue and the sting of blistered feet. But chances are that everyone has the same thought: it'll be a long wait until the next weekend, when they can do it all again.

—*Michael White*

Listening Guide

Listen to *In Gloryland* by Bunk's Brass Band on **mymusiclab.com**
CD I, Track 3/Download Track 3

IN GLORYLAND • BUNK'S BRASS BAND

Music: Emmett S. Dean, 1861. Personnel: Bunk Johnson (trumpet); Louis "Kid Shots" Madison (trumpet); Jim Robinson (trombone); George Lewis (E-flat clarinet); Isidore Barbarin (alto horn); Adolphe Alexander (baritone horn); Joe Clark (bass horn); Warren "Baby" Dodds (snare drum); Lawrence Marrero (bass drum). Recorded May 18, 1945, in New Orleans, Louisiana. First issue: American Music 101. Timing: 3:02.

Overview

Brass bands were among the early manifestations of New Orleans jazz. By the turn of the twentieth century, a tradition of brass bands playing for funerals, parades, and other social occasions was well established. When playing for funerals, the bands would play a slow dirge as they accompanied the casket to the cemetery, and then, to celebrate the deceased's life, strike up lively tunes, ragging and jazzing hymns such as *Down by the Riverside* and *When the Saints Go Marching In*, as a "**second line**" of mourners danced along the street.

"Bunk played funeral marches that made me cry!" said Louis Armstrong, recalling the 1910s in their native New Orleans, where trumpeter Bunk Johnson played in various bands and made a bit of a name for himself. Beginning in 1915, Johnson toured southern theaters, circuses, and clubs, but stopped playing in 1931, when he lost his teeth. Rediscovered in 1939 by historian William Russell, Johnson was swiftly hailed as history reborn and, along with clarinetist George Lewis, became an icon for the revival of New Orleans jazz that blossomed in the 1940s.

In 1945, Johnson assembled a brass band and recorded 11 tunes, including *In Gloryland*. *Just Over in the Gloryland*, its full title, is a white gospel song that was adopted by African American musicians. Johnson's was only the third jazz version on record and influenced the making of 150 recordings by bands as far-flung as Sweden and New Zealand.

Johnson's recordings are valuable as the earliest of a New Orleans brass band. Because they were recorded decades after the heyday of this style, how accurately they reflect original practices is open to some debate. There is a freshness, unpretentiousness, and even raggedness to the performance that strikes some listeners as primeval, others as authentic and charming.

Key Features

- Form: Johnson reverses the order in the published hymn, opening with the 16-bar refrain (chorus), then playing the 12-bar verse of the hymn. Then the band plays the refrain four times through.
- Instrumentation: This is a standard marching band of the time, with one or two trumpets playing the lead, a second trumpet sometimes ornamenting or embellishing, the trombone playing

other rhythms and dances. Dancers carried on African and Caribbean traditions in Congo Square until the mid-1850s, when increasing Americanization, with its more restrictive laws on matters of public amusement, drove those traditions out. But they lived on in cultural memory.

Vital Musical Life. In nineteenth-century New Orleans, music played an important role in community and civic life. "Of all the cities in North America," wrote cultural historian Berndt Ostendorf, "New Orleans had the oldest and most active musical public sphere." New Orleanians loved a good melody, and the city was awash with operatic airs such as the quartet from Verdi's *Rigoletto* (1851); French music-hall songs; such Creole tunes as *Eh la Bas*; *Old Dan Tucker* (1843) and other minstrel songs; spirituals such as *Down by the Riverside*; African American folk songs such as *Careless Love*; Italian, German, Mexican, and Cuban tunes; polkas and marches; and the latest popular songs from New York City. When an enormous Mexican military band played the city's Cotton Centennial Exposition in 1884–85, it created a sensation and sparked interest in Latin-influenced music. After the band broke up, some of its members remained in New Orleans, helping to extend the Latin musical influence in the city.

Strong Dance Tradition. Like its active musical sphere, the city's long-standing, insatiable demand for dancing transcended all boundaries of class and race. Dancing was the cheapest and most feasible form of entertainment in the frontier days; it jumped language barriers better than song. (Louisiana's first U.S.-appointed governor from 1803–09, William Claiborne, reportedly complained that the locals were ungovernable because they were preoccupied with dancing.) Early on, New Orleans hosted discrete dance traditions, but by the end of the nineteenth century it had developed a citywide dance culture. Out of this culture

---

second line   the procession of people marching and dancing behind a New Orleans jazz band parading down the street. A person who joins in is a "second liner."

countermelodies, and the clarinet playing high filigrees and fills. Two drummers keep time. (Later bands replaced the alto and baritone horn with alto and tenor sax.)

- Texture: This is ensemble music, not a showcase for soloists. In this style, the emphasis is on the sound of *all* the instruments, as multiple lines weave in, out, under, and over each other, creating **heterophony** and **polyphony**.
- Rhythm: The band plays in a jaunty, swinging $\frac{4}{4}$ meter, perfect for swaggering down the street. The musicians **rag** the melody of the original hymn, syncopating it in an early twentieth-century ragtime style.
- Function: Though this recording was made in a backyard setting, typically such brass bands were mobile as they played—marching in a parade or funeral, a custom that is still today a fundamental cultural tradition in New Orleans. (See "Parading with a Brass Band," page 33).

—John Edward Hasse

TIME	FORM/SECTION	MELODY	RHYTHM
0:00	Introduction		The snare drum, joined by three strokes on the bass drum, introduces the piece.
0:09	Refrain	Trumpeters Johnson and Madison carry the melody, with the trombone and clarinet providing counter-melodies and fills.	Jaunty $\frac{4}{4}$ march rhythm.
0:38	Verse		
0:56	Refrain 2	The melody having been stated is now embellished more freely without losing its essential quality.	The rhythm opens up as the melodic variation increases.
1:24	Refrain 3		The rhythmically freer playing continues.
1:53	Refrain 4		The trumpeters continue to play with the rhythms of the melody.
2:21	Refrain 5		Ragging the melody continues.
2:36	Ride-out Chorus	As the musicians reach the last eight-bar phrase of the refrain, they play more loudly.	The bass drum plays in **double time**, turning up the heat.
2:50	Coda		The snare drum fades out as if the band were marching down the street, out of earshot.

grew jazz, thanks to the bands that provided dance accompaniment.

Pervasive "Good Times" Atmosphere. The Big Easy loves to party, savors a holiday, relishes any festive occasion, and exercises a laid-back attitude toward sex and revelry. New Orleans is the only large U.S. city with a tradition of pre-Lent Carnival or Mardi Gras, and *Laissez les bon temps roulez* (Let the good times roll) is the city's unofficial motto.

Early on, New Orleans earned notoriety for its bohemian streak and for its elegance, extravagance, colorfulness, and, yes, wickedness. (During the 20-year period ending when Storyville was closed down in 1917, as many as 800 registered prostitutes worked 175 "houses," making Storyville the largest red-light district in the nation.) Whatever the setting for good times—whether dances, parties, parades, cabarets, sporting events, riverboat excursions, or even broth-els—jazz was on hand to provide the accompaniment.

Numerous Brass Bands. By the late nineteenth century, brass bands were popular across the United States, but especially in New Orleans; the city adored marching bands and parades, as observers going back at least as far as 1830 noted. During the Civil War and Reconstruction, brass bands proliferated in the city at large and among black musicians. By 1888, *Metronome* magazine was reporting that New Orleans had "twenty to twenty-five bands averaging twelve men apiece. The colored race monopolize the procession music." Such bands as the Excelsior and Onward, both established in the 1880s, were often hired by black fraternal organizations for parades and funeral marches—events that reflected African notions of responsorial group participation. These bands, which sometimes doubled as dance bands, provided musical training for many jazz musicians, contributed pieces

heterophony the simultaneous playing or singing of two or more versions of a melody.

polyphony multiple melodies occurring simultaneously.

rag (verb) to syncopate a melody in the style of ragtime.

double time twice as fast as the established tempo; used in jazz to create excitement.

The Original Superior Brass Band, New Orleans, in 1900, with acclaimed cornetist Bunk Johnson (standing, second from the left). Johnson later switched to the trumpet. PHOTO COURTESY FRANK DRIGGS COLLECTION.

to the jazz repertory, and influenced dance bands to change over from stringed instruments to the brass instruments that became central to jazz.

Particularly noteworthy—and colorful—were the funerals with brass bands, a tradition that continues to this day. Typically sponsored by local fraternal societies, the processions are subdued and reverent in the march toward the interment ceremony, but on the way out, the musicians, as pianist Jelly Roll Morton put it, "just tear loose," spiritedly celebrating the life of the departed.

TAKE NOTE

- What were the special conditions in New Orleans that made it a fertile ground for jazz?

Musical Antecedents

The Blues

While jazz drew on numerous cultural traditions, it also grew from, and built on, several earlier U.S.-originated musical forms. One of them was the blues, whose evolved three-chord structure ultimately served

as a popular framework for jazz compositions, and whose characteristic bent and slurred notes became common in jazz melodies.

The **blues**, like jazz, has roots in Africa. In his provocative book *Origins of the Popular Style*, scholar Peter van der Merwe argues that "the raw materials of the blues already existed in Africa, but mixed with an enormous wealth of other material. Gradually and unconsciously this other material was winnowed away, and what was left was the blues." At the same time, European influence—especially through settlers of Scots-Irish ancestry who found their way to Mississippi and other Deep South states—not only simplified complex African rhythms but added a few new rhythmic twists and exerted some sway over the structure and melodic contour of the blues.

---

blues a fundamental style of American music derived from the West African tradition of vocal call and response, reinvented as "field hollers" in America's rural south during the nineteenth century, combined with the European-style harmonies of hymns and simple folk songs; the three-chord, three-phrase structure of the blues has served as a central structure in jazz.

The blues may have begun when a nineteenth-century African American thought up the idea of accompanying a **field holler**—probably at first with a one-chord accompaniment. In this scenario, elaborations developed over time, and eventually the blues's familiar three-chord pattern coalesced. Tunes employed a "framework of melodically sensitive notes interspersed with less sensitive notes," as van der Merwe put it, emphasizing "**blue notes**" (bent or slightly raised minor third or seventh notes of the scale) in syncopated rhythm.

Blues lyrics typically comprise three lines, the second often repeating the first. While many people think the blues have to be woeful or complaining, in fact many blues songs are celebratory. But either way, they're packed with emotion and spirituality. When a jazz musician really plays the blues, he or she is dipping into a deep river of tradition that speaks of struggle, community, affirmation, and transcendence over adversity. The blues brings release to the performer as it uplifts the audience.

The blues no doubt arose in rural areas of the Deep South—songwriter **W. C. Handy** recalled hearing it around 1903—and then found its way into southern cities and eventually into the North. The music existed strictly in **aural tradition** (it was not written down, but rather spread by individual performers) until sheet music published in New Orleans and St. Louis began to reveal it in the first decade of the twentieth century. In the 1910s, songwriters began publishing bluesy pieces. Beginning in 1920, blues tunes were recorded on discs by Ma Rainey, Bessie Smith, and others. By then, the blues chord progression, blue notes, and even a blues sensibility had become firmly entrenched in jazz, and the blues would continue to evolve as a related but separate music.

What is the blues progression? For most jazz musicians, it's a 12-bar musical structure which, at its most basic, contains just three chords that always pull you back to the home, or tonic, chord. The following prototypical blues chorus, from W. C. Handy's *St. Louis Blues*

---

field holler   an extemporaneous, solo cry made by African Americans in Southern cotton-picking and other work settings; it's likely a forerunner of the blues.

blue note   a defining note in blues melodies and scales; a "bent" or slightly raised minor third or seventh.

aural tradition   the practice of passing along a story, song, or tune by ear, rather than by written means.

Listening Focus

((•   **Listen** to *Old John Henry Died on the Mountain* by Henry Grady "Big Boy" Terrill on **mymusiclab.com**
CD I, Track 4/Download Track 4

OLD JOHN HENRY DIED ON THE MOUNTAIN • HENRY GRADY "BIG BOY" TERRILL

Music: Traditional. Personnel: Henry Grady "Big Boy" Terrill (vocal and pickax). Recorded by Art Rosenbaum, 1984, in Athens, Georgia. First issue: *Folk Visions and Voices: Traditional Music and Song in Northern Georgia, Vol. 2*, Smithsonian Folkways 34164. Timing: 1:59.

This song reflects several related folk-music traditions: African American work songs and traditional railroad songs. One of the most popular of these songs is *John Henry*, which exists in many versions sung by black and white performers. In the song, John Henry works on the railroad driving spikes to secure the newly laid steel tracks. Management brings in a steam drill to replace the manual laborers, and Henry accepts a challenge to see if he can beat the drill. He does, but dies from his effort. For many years, it was believed that Henry was a fictional character based on the experience of real railroad workers. Recently, however, evidence has been found linking him to a steel driver who worked on the deep, challenging Big Bend Tunnel, built in the Blue Ridge Mountains of West Virginia by the C&O Railroad in 1870–72.

Folklorist Art Rosenbaum said singer Henry Terrill learned this song from an older man who had worked on a prison chain gang. Terrill said that a song like this would "make the day go faster," make the pickax swinging "go faster and get more willingness," and would "fool the man." He meant that the workers, by singing this song at a slow speed, could set their own rate, without the labor captain ("the man") insisting that they work more quickly. "Henry Terrill," wrote Rosenbaum, "could not sing this properly without a pick in hand, and recorded this in [a] back yard to the accompaniment of the pick and [an] excited dog."

The percussive *thud*s of the ax (at 0:02, 0:06, 0:10, etc.) serve not only as rhythmic accompaniment to the singing but act as a staccato response to the "call" of the vocal line. Call-and-response patterns are typical of much African and African American music—blues, gospel, jazz, soul, and other genres. Call and response can be heard on a number of well-known jazz recordings, ranging from Bessie Smith's *Back Water Blues* (1927) to Miles Davis's *So What* (1959) to *Neutralisme* by Martial Solal and Johnny Griffin (1999). There is even a 1960 Nat Adderley jazz standard called *The Work Song*—the lyrics include "Breaking rocks out here on the chain gang"—filled with responsorial patterns.

—*John Edward Hasse*

(1914), contains space (shown in purple) for a soloist to answer the singer.

Bar 1	Bar 2	Bar 3		Bar 4
I hate to see	the evenin' sun go	down		
C	F	C		C7
Bar 5	**Bar 6**	**Bar 7**		**Bar 8**
Hate to see	the evenin' sun go	down		
F	F	C		C
Bar 9	**Bar 10**	**Bar 11**		**Bar 12**
'Cause my baby	he done lef' this	town.		
G	G7	C		C

The simple and expressive but extraordinarily elastic blues progression (typically 12 bars, but sometimes 8 or 16) runs throughout jazz—indeed, its most basic musical structure. Within this simple form, however, jazz musicians have created dozens of variations and thousands upon thousands of blues tunes.

Sometimes blues tunes are easy to spot: obvious ones include the traditional *Careless Love* and *Frankie and Johnny*, the **Original Dixieland Jazz Band**'s *Livery Stable Blues* (1917), **King Oliver**'s *Chimes Blues* (1923), Count Basie's *One O'Clock Jump* (1937), Billie Holiday's *Fine and Mellow* (1939), Charlie Parker's *Now's the Time* (1945), and Miles Davis's *All Blues* (1959). In other cases, the composer camouflages the blues "changes": examples are Duke Ellington's *Creole Love Call* (1928) and *Ko-Ko* (1940), Thelonious Monk's *Misterioso* (1948) and *Straight, No Chaser* (1951), John Coltrane's *Chasin' the Trane* (1961), and Chick Corea's *Matrix* (1968).

---

pentatonic scale   scale consisting of five notes.

Listening Focus

((•— **Listen** to *Boll Weevil* by Pink Anderson on **mymusiclab.com** CD I, Track 5/Download Track 5

BOLL WEEVIL • PINK ANDERSON

Music: Traditional. Personnel: Pink Anderson (vocal, guitar). Recorded by Samuel Charters, 1961, in Spartanburg, South Carolina. First issue: *Carolina Medicine Show Hokum and Blues*, Smithsonian Folkways FS 3588. Timing: 3:07.

The lyrics of the country blues document everyday life, love, work, and conditions in the rural American South in the late nineteenth and twentieth centuries. By the 1920s, a small insect (less than .25" or 6 mm long) called the boll weevil had infested nearly all cotton fields in the South, becoming the scourge of cotton farmers and the manual laborers—often African Americans—they employed, typically as sharecroppers. The boll weevil became the subject of countless ballads and blues songs. Many of these songs approached their subject with irony, bemoaning the bug's devastating power to destroy one's livelihood yet admiring its tenacity and quiet power to subvert the agricultural ruling class. The boll weevil thus became a symbol of the sharecroppers' own resistance to the harsh conditions under which they worked.

The African American songster Pinkney "Pink" Anderson first learned to play the guitar at age 10, and as a teenager, danced in the street for tips. For decades he traveled around the rural South in a medicine show, providing entertainment to draw crowds so the show's sponsor could try to sell a medicine or tonic of dubious value. Anderson played guitar in the style of Southeast/Piedmont blues players. Unlike the more intense Mississippi Delta players, who preferred open tunings and heavy use of a glass or metal slide, Anderson and such other musicians as Rev. Gary Davis developed a ragtime-derived style in which the bass strings kept a regular beat and the treble strings played a syncopated melody.

While called "12-bar blues"—because the standard chorus runs 12 bars—many traditional blues singers would shorten or lengthen the chorus at will. When trained musicians such as W. C. Handy began playing blues, they tended to iron out these irregularities. Here, Anderson plays each chorus as 12 bars in length. You can clearly see the blues structure in the lyrics themselves; each line consists of four bars (lyrics and guitar response), with three lines equaling 12 bars:

> Woke up this mornin', woke up this mornin', heard somebody callin' me,
> Woke up this mornin', heard somebody callin' me,
> It must've been the mama weevil, that they call the stingeree.

Anderson's performance features a subtle kind of call and response: after singing each line of the blues, he brings the guitar from the background to the foreground (for example, at 0:08, 0:14, and 0:24), increasing the activity of the bass line as a kind of response to the "call" of his vocal. His vocal line follows almost completely a **pentatonic** or five-note scale common to many blues and blues-influenced songs.

—*John Edward Hasse*

St. Louis Blues

In 1909, Memphis bandleader W. C. Handy, inspired by the folk blues he had heard while traveling the South, composed a song called *Memphis Blues*. When published in 1912, it sparked a fad for blues songs and eventually became a jazz standard. Two years later, he published *St. Louis Blues*, which far surpassed *Memphis Blues* to become one of the most familiar, widely performed jazz standards and American songs of all time.

St. Louis Blues caught on slowly; it wasn't until the 1920s that it became a jazz staple. In that decade, more than 60 jazz recordings were made of it, and the number increased in the 1930s. Ultimately, *St. Louis Blues* became the second-most recorded American song (Hoagy Carmichael's *Stardust* is first), with versions by such artists as the Original Dixieland Jazz Band, Louis Armstrong, Duke Ellington, **Sidney Bechet**, Dave Brubeck, Herbie Hancock, and Sun Ra. The piece has been arranged for dozens of instrumental combinations and undergone numerous variations. Pianist Earl "Fatha" Hines recorded it as *Boogie-Woogie on Handy's St. Louis Blues* (1940), and Glenn Miller and His Orchestra issued a recorded version as *St. Louis Blues March* (1944).

Why was this the most successful blues of all time? The piece is much richer in musical form and contrast than typical blues tunes. It employs an AABC structure. Both the A and C sections comprise 12-bar blues progressions, while the contrasting B section is a 16-bar strain in *habanera*

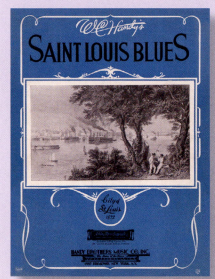

COURTESY JOHN EDWARD HASSE.

rhythm. (Handy's band had traveled to Cuba in 1900.) The A and C strains provide further interest by building in **breaks**, and those in the final C section contain some boogie-woogie bass figures. The three different melodies are singable and memorable. And the lyrics are striking; as scholar Philip Furia has pointed out, the words, particularly in the middle section, are "laced with more truncated slang, telegraphic syntax, and sharp imagery than would appear in popular lyrics until the 1920s."

The song was used in about 40 motion pictures, most notably the 1929 sixteen-minute short subject *St. Louis Blues*, in which Bessie Smith, in her only screen appearance, sings the song with great power and majestic sorrow.

---

break   a brief pause in a band's playing to feature a soloist or soloists; the beat continues, but is implied.

Watch the video *St. Louis Blues* by Bessie Smith on **mymusiclab.com**

The song also served as the title of a patronizing 1958 Hollywood biopic starring Nat "King" Cole as W. C. Handy. In the 1956 documentary *Satchmo the Great*, made two years before Handy's death, the cameras captured a touching moment in which Louis Armstrong performs *St. Louis Blues* while the aged, now-blind Handy, in the front row, listens transfixed to his masterpiece, dabbing tears from his eyes.

—*John Edward Hasse*

W. C. Handy, the leading popularizer of the blues, in 1932. PHOTO COURTESY FRANK DRIGGS COLLECTION.

Listening Guide

MAPLE LEAF RAG • DICK HYMAN

Music: Scott Joplin, 1899. Personnel: Dick Hyman (piano). Recorded 1975 in New York City. First issue: *The Complete Piano Rags of Scott Joplin*, RCA Victor ARL5-1106. Timing: 2:30.

Overview

For over a century, one ragtime piece has stood above all others: Scott Joplin's *Maple Leaf Rag*.

Born near Texarkana, Texas, to ex-slaves, probably in 1868, Scott Joplin settled in 1894 in the modest, maple-tree-lined railroad town of Sedalia, Missouri, where he wrote his most celebrated rag. *Maple Leaf Rag*, published in 1899, sold only 400 copies its first year. But it gradually picked up steam, selling 500,000 copies within 10 years and earning Joplin the rightful title of King of Ragtime Writers.

For a well-trained pianist, the notes on the pages don't look daunting. But perfecting the right-hand rhythms, establishing a groove with the bass part, and coordinating the two hands at a medium tempo or faster—that's a challenge. Embellishing the melody makes the task even tougher. And that's precisely what professional piano "perfessers" and "ticklers" were doing with *Maple Leaf Rag*—taking liberties, embellishing, and improvising. Although they also did it with other rags, *Maple Leaf* was a universally known "test piece" among them. In 1938, recording for Alan Lomax at the Library of Congress, Jelly Roll Morton made a now-famous demonstration of the "Missouri" or ragtime style of playing the *Maple Leaf*, followed by his own jazz version, showing how adaptable the piece is.

Although many improvised on its basic score, Joplin himself was a classicist and felt his pieces should be played as written. Joplin never made a record, but he did cut some piano rolls in 1916, the year before his untimely death. However, there is controversy surrounding his version of *The Maple Leaf Rag* because of additions to the roll that may have been made after the fact, plus the uneven rhythm at which the piece is played. This may have been due to advancing illness or a poor recording machine. Whatever the case, it is unfortunately impossible to hear Joplin play the piece as he originally envisioned it.

By the 1950s, there were about 70 versions on 78-rpm records, with dozens more to come on LPs and CDs. The tune has always been a favorite among pianists, but the range of artists who recorded it spans the century and an array of musical styles. They include the U.S. Marine Band; New Orleans musicians Sidney Bechet and Kid Ory; swing bandleaders Tommy Dorsey and Benny Goodman; the revivalist Lu Watters's Yerba Buena Jazz Band; the country-blues guitarist Reverend Gary Davis; the Brazilian guitarist Carlos Barbosa-Lima; the cutting-edge jazzmen Anthony Braxton (*JTSA* Disc 6/Track 1), Ran Blake, and Archie Shepp; the Australian folk-rock group the Seekers; and the rock band Emerson, Lake, and Palmer.

Why the appeal? First, there's the allure of ragtime's toe-tapping rhythms and the magical polarity between the rhythms of the right and left hands. Then there's the *Maple Leaf's* originality. Though it's not as highly developed as some of Joplin's late rags, none can match its exuberance, rhythmic drive, and triumphant note of optimism, especially as the last strain goes out with a burst of energy.

This recording of *Maple Leaf* is a straightforward version without embellishment or liberties, showcasing Joplin's composition rather than the pianist's improvisational abilities. Yet few pianists could match the combination of technique and interpretation that Dick Hyman brings to this piece: a light but definite touch; clean execution at a rather brisk tempo; a percussive attack; swinging, rock-steady rhythm; ability to negotiate the wide leaps of the *boom-chick* left hand; and excellent control of dynamics and phrasing. His performance is solidly within the tradition of playing ragtime-as-written yet it has the snap and swing of jazz.

Key Features

- Form: As with all piano rags, *Maple Leaf Rag* is multisectional or multithematic, specifically AABBACCDD—each section is 16 bars, a total of 96 bars. There is no introduction: the piece simply takes off with the opening syncopated figure.
- Modulation: After the statement of AABBA, there is a modulation up an interval of a fourth (from A-flat to D-flat). This was common in marches, whose form ragtime adopted. The contrasting section in the new key was often known as the "**trio**"—a marking Joplin used here. The modulation provided a harmonic and emotional lift partway through the piece, enhancing its excitement. *Maple Leaf's* D section returns to the home key of A-flat.
- Meter: Like most marches and rags, the piece is in $\frac{2}{4}$ meter. In the opening bars, however, Joplin appears to be "playing" with **ternary** time, with the left hand rendering, instead of the *boom-chick-boom-chick*, four *boom-chick-chick* patterns, which

are novel and subtly announce that *Maple Leaf* is no ordinary rag. *Boom-chick-chick* is also heard in the left-hand of the first measures of the D section (1:50).

- Rhythms: The major interest of the piece is its rhythms. The essence of ragtime was the tension between irregular (syncopated) rhythms of the right hand and regular ones of the left. Not every measure of *Maple Leaf* contains syncopation, but about 84 percent of them do.
- Melody: The melody opens with chordal notes, then alternates to banjo-like figurations. Mostly the top note in the right hand carries the melody, but at the beginning of the C section, the melody note is briefly in the thumb of the right hand in the middle of the texture.
- Tempo: Joplin marked this piece "Tempo di marcia"—march tempo—but Hyman, like most ragtime and jazz pianists, takes a brisker tempo. On some of his pieces, Joplin stipulated "Not fast" or "Do not play this piece fast. It is never right to play Ragtime fast. Composer." The fact that he had to insert such warnings indicates that many pianists were indeed playing the pieces at fast tempos. The "correct" tempo—if there is a correct tempo—at which to play ragtime has been a subject of controversy in ragtime circles for more than a century.
- Contrast: Joplin provides musical contrast in numerous ways: within two-measure phrases by interweaving single notes with octaves into his melodic lines; within sections (such as section C) by contrasting right-hand chords with single-note banjo-like lines; and within the piece by varying his dynamic markings from *p* (*piano* or soft) to *f* (*forte* or loud). In section A, after a mere four bars, he entirely halts the *boom-chick* left hand to insert four measures of **arpeggios**, followed by eight measures of steady chords (no *boom-chick*). To further create interest, Joplin also varies the register of both hands—for example, in the A section's eighth measure, going up high with both hands.

—John Edward Hasse

TIME	SECTION/FORM	MELODY	HARMONY	TEMPO
	A	The rag opens with a two-bar, 10-note syncopated figure, which is repeated once.	A-flat.	Brisk $\frac{2}{4}$.
0:16	A	Repeats.		
0:32	B	This section features an extension (now 12 notes) of the syncopation noted above; this 12-note figure is played five times.		
0:48	B	Repeats.		
1:04	A	The return to the A section provides an element of continuity.		
1:19	C or "trio"	New melodic theme.	Modulates to the subdominant (D-flat), brightening the feel.	
1:35	C or "trio"	Repeats.		
1:50	D	Final, triumphant theme.	Returns to the home key of A-flat.	
2:06	D	Repeats.		Tempo slows for finale, giving the piece a big send-off.

trio (1) a three-piece ensemble; (2) in a march or rag, a contrasting section that modulates to another key.
ternary composed of three parts.

arpeggio the notes of a chord played sequentially rather then simultaneously.

Ironically, such songs as *Birth of the Blues* (1926), *Basin Street Blues* (1928), and *Blues in the Night* (1941) are not considered blues by jazz musicians: none follow the blues chord progression. To recognize a real blues, you have to use your ears.

Ragging and Ragtime

Another musical precursor of jazz—**ragtime**—emerged in the late nineteenth century. It began, probably far back in U.S. history, as a practice of "ragging"—creatively altering and syncopating—an existing piece of music. In 1876, the Georgia-born

poet Sidney Lanier wrote, "Syncopations . . . are characteristic of Negro music. I have heard Negroes change a well-known melody by adroitly syncopating it . . . so as to give it a *bizarre* effect scarcely imaginable."

---

ragtime   a body of syncopated American popular music, especially popular from ca. 1897 to 1920; one of the roots of jazz. Ragtime included both instrumental or piano rags and ragtime songs.

ragging   the practice of creatively altering and syncopating an existing piece of music; a term from the early twentieth century, when *ragtime* music was popular.

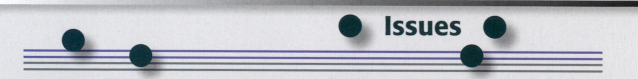

● Issues ●

The Ragtime War

Why did ragtime create such strong feelings—both pro and con—during its first period of popularity?

As the twentieth century dawned, across America a new music was creating both a sensation and unprecedented conflict. The struggle was so protracted and sometimes so vehement that it can be considered more than a battle—rather, it was a 20-year war of words.

On one side were the mostly young proponents of the new syncopated sounds called ragtime. On the other side were several types alarmed about this dangerous development: those vested in cultivated music who felt that ragtime cheapened and threatened their art, and people defending traditional values against perceived threats to acceptable morals and behavior.

The musical opponents of ragtime—which many thought of as any syncopated popular music—made several arguments. Ragtime would ruin the taste of the young. Karl Muck, conductor of the Boston Symphony Orchestra, charged, "I think that what you call . . . ragtime is poison. It poisons the very source of your musical growth, for

it poisons the taste of the young." Ragtime would ruin the technique of musicians, ran another argument. A piano teacher named Philip Gordon claimed in 1912 that "Ragtime will ruin your touch, disable your technic, misuse your knowledge of pedaling, and pervert whatever sense of poetry and feeling you have into superficial, improper channels. Shun it as you would the 'Black Death.'" Syncopation caused permanent

Ragtime pianists were often depicted as musical wildmen, much to the amusement of contemporary audiences.
COURTESY JOHN EDWARD HASSE.

brain damage, claimed some, and a *New York Times* editorial quoted a German musical professor asserting that ragtime would "eventually stagnate the brain cells and wreck the nervous system."

The moralist combatants attacked ragtime on other grounds. Ragtime was akin to drinking: "A person inoculated with the ragtime-fever is like one addicted to strong drink!" Warned writer Leo Oehmler in 1914 in the *Musical Observer*, "In Christian homes, where purity of morals are stressed, ragtime should find no resting place. Avaunt the ragtime rot! Let us purge America and the Divine Art of Music from this polluting nuisance."

A 1913 editorial in the *New York Times* declared that "'decent people in and out of the church are beginning to be alarmed' at the 'rude' and 'vulgar' music and 'loose conduct' accompanying it with 'dances defying all propriety.'" If ragtime music wasn't bad enough for "respectable" people, "undignified" ragtime dances—such steps as the Grizzly Bear, Turkey Trot, Bunny Hug, and Devil's Ball, which featured increased bodily contact—seemed licentious and shocking.

Over time, the technique was applied to new compositions. Songs and pieces for banjo and piano would be composed in a "ragged" or "raggy" style, with the syncopations an inherent, not an added-on, part of the music. Ragtime's characteristics, apart from syncopation, included polyrhythm, a strong rhythmic polarity between treble and bass, and multisectional forms.

COURTESY JOHN EDWARD HASSE.

((•— **Hear** composer/performer Eubie Blake discuss ragtime on **mymusiclab.com**

In the 1880s, ragtime could be heard in the Midwest, even as its reverberations radiated to surrounding parts of the country. By 1892, composer Charles Ives had come across ragtime in minstrel shows in his hometown of Danbury, Connecticut, and at the 1893 Chicago World's Fair, many people evidently heard the style for the first time. By 1896, the first pieces labeled "rag

To such traditionalists, ragtime generated not only cheap and tawdry lyrics and threatening sensuality, but also a diabolical, spreading contagion: "It is an evil music," one magazine cried, "that . . . must be wiped out as other bad and dangerous epidemics have been exterminated." Ragtime would lead to a disintegration of society's norms: "Its greatest destructive power lies in its power to lower the moral standards" was one claim. "Many ragtime songs as well as dances receive their inspiration in the brothel [and are] tossed upon the market to corrupt the minds of the young. . . ."

Though mostly couched indirectly in the ragtime war, white racism toward African Americans sometimes got expressed openly, as in a 1913 letter published in the *Musical Courier*: "Can it be said that America is falling pretty to the collective soul of the negro through the influence of what is popularly known as 'rag time' music?" The writer went on to link ragtime with the supposed sinful sexuality of African Americans.

While much of the ink spilled over ragtime was in the white press, ragtime sparked heated opposition with the middle-class black community as well. The African American pianist-composer Eubie Blake, born in 1883, recalled, "My mother was very religious and hated ragtime like all the high-class Negroes. . . . When

I played it at home my mother would yell, 'Take that ragtime out of my house.'" Even in the 1910s, the father of Fats Waller, who was born in 1904 and would become one of the great jazz pianists, considered ragtime "music from the Devil's workshop."

The struggle over ragtime can be viewed in religious terms; scholar Neil Leonard described "the highly spiritual and emotional tone of the argument and its core concerns of art, sex, race, class, and nationality, which lay not only at the center of the ragtime dispute but of other social and intellectual controversies of the day."

Prior to ragtime, mainstream America had never encountered music for which syncopation was so central, and many found those syncopations infectious. The contagious allure of its rhythms alarmed some of ragtime's opponents and attracted some of its proponents. Exclaiming "You simply can't resist it," in 1915, critic Hiram K. Moderwell told of his reactions: "I felt my blood thumping in tune, my muscles twitching to the rhythm."

Moderwell, the most redoubtable of the pro-ragtime spokesmen, argued that ragtime beautifully embodied the American character. "I like to think that ragtime is the perfect expression of the American city, with its restless bustle and motion . . . and its underlying rhythmic progress. . . . As you walk

up and down the streets of an American city you feel in its jerk and rattle a personality different from that of any European capital. This is American. Ragtime, I believe, expresses it. It is to-day the one true American music."

Moderwell urged that ragtime become the basis for a national American style of composition: "There will be no great American music so long as American musicians despise our ragtime." (Unbeknownst to Moderwell, the then little-known American composer Charles Ives had already incorporated ragtime into some of his classical compositions. And in a few years, composer George Gershwin, who got his musical start in ragtime, would, with his masterpiece *Rhapsody in Blue*, resoundingly answer Moderwell's call to develop a distinctively American art music by mining the rich mother lode of African American folk music and American popular song. [See Jeffrey Magee, "Jazz and Classical Music," page 74.])

By the late 1910s, ragtime was increasingly accepted by Americans, and the struggle over ragtime morphed into a clash over early jazz, which struck many as even more jarring than ragtime. The ragtime war heralded a series of conflicts and controversies throughout the history of jazz.

—*John Edward Hasse*

time" were being published. In 1897, twenty-some **piano rags** were published, and by 1899, the number had reached more than 120, including some issued in New Orleans. Ragtime became the "new thing" in music, appealing to young people across the nation (though their parents often hated it).

Ragtime was played largely on the piano, and two separate traditions developed: most amateurs played pieces from sheet music largely as written, while many professional pianists "faked"—that is, embellished and even improvised on the melodies, playing, in everything but name, an early form of jazz. So many pianists were showing off and taking liberties that by 1905, **Scott Joplin**, the "King of Ragtime Writers," felt compelled to mark his rags "Notice! Don't play this piece fast." And in 1913, ragtime composer Artie Matthews admonished, "Don't fake."

While the composition and publication of ragtime died out in the late 1910s, the music's characteristics were absorbed into the new jazz style.

> ### TAKE NOTE
>
> - What roles did blues and ragtime play in the development of jazz?

Jazz: An Improvisational Music for Dancing

The jazz style involved not only reading written music but also improvising—composing or making up melodies spontaneously, on the spot. The practice comes largely from the African side of the music's Afro-European heritage (although European music of the Baroque and Classical periods employed kinds of improvisation). "Jazz," observed Berndt Ostendorf, "is the result of a confluence of rural ear music and

---

piano rag a syncopated, multisectional composition for piano, such as Scott Joplin's *Maple Leaf Rag*.

---

urban eye music, of Western musical literacy and African musical memory"—in other words, jazz represents a merging of aural traditions (such as the blues) with notated forms of music.

Once jazz got under way in New Orleans, most of the city's jazz bands could both read notation and fake, or play by ear, which increasingly included improvising. The latter would eventually come to be regarded as a fundamental part of jazz. Players' ability to improvise satisfyingly would become at least as important as their technique, style, sound, choice of repertory and bandmates, and ability to communicate musically and connect with the audience.

Jazz started as a music primarily intended for dancing, and it would remain so for decades. European dance steps—the mazurka, polka, lancer, schottische, and variety—were prevalent in nineteenth-century New Orleans, accompanied by bands such as those under the leadership of John Robichaux and William Braun, whose members normally read music rather than improvised.

In the 1890s, New Orleans dancers began displacing the European steps with the American two-step and such erotic dances as the Grizzly Bear, Turkey Trot, Texas Tommy, and Todolo—some of which may have originated locally. As New Orleans experienced an influx of blacks migrating from other parts of Louisiana, as well as Mississippi and Alabama, these new residents danced to other vernacular steps, including the Black Bottom and the Funky Butt. As the racier dances became popular, the bands focused more on improvisational music, especially after midnight when the "nice people" went home and the remaining dancers got down and dirty. The dancers idolized such musicians as the African American cornetists Buddy Bolden and Bunk Johnson, who played a looser, hotter, bluesier style of dance music than did the Creoles.

There may have been a hundred or more bands in New Orleans at the time: besides Robichaux's long-lived orchestra, leading bands around 1910 were the Magnolia and Superior orchestras, Manuel Perez's Imperial Orchestra, Freddie Keppard's Olympia Orchestra, Frankie Dusen's Eagle Band, Frank Christian's Ragtime Band, and those led by

John Robichaux (seated, right) led one of New Orleans's most active dance bands from the 1890s into the new century. PHOTO COURTESY JOHN EDWARD HASSE.

Papa Celestin, Armand J. Piron, Kid Ory, Happy Schilling, Johnny Fischer, and **Jack Laine**. These bands kept the dozens of dance halls that were scattered throughout the city and in outlying communities—including Economy Hall, Masonic Hall, Globe Hall, Artesian Hall, Tuxedo Hall, Funky Butt Hall, Perseverance Hall, the Tin Roof Cafe, and the 101 Ranch—packed with dancers.

Some of these bands employed female pianists; from approximately 1921–37, Papa Celestin, for example, featured Emma Barrett, a New Orleans native who would return to prominence during the traditional jazz revival of the 1950s and 1960s. Young women were often taught the piano and many were exposed to the developing popular styles of marches, ragtime, and blues, so it's not surprising that they turned up in these early bands—despite the bias against women performing in dangerous bars and clubs. Another prominent early pianist on the New Orleans scene was Billie Pierce, who had accompanied blues singer Bessie Smith in her native Florida before relocating to the Crescent City in search of employment. Later, she would wed Creole

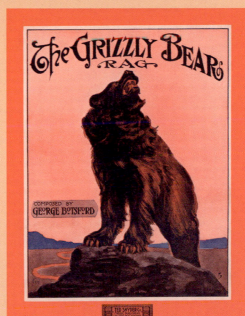

As the Grizzly Bear and other racy dances gained popularity, so did dance bands that improvised and played hotter, bluesier music than that of their more "polite" counterparts.

COURTESY JOHN EDWARD HASSE.

trumpeter Dede Pierce, and the two were "rediscovered" in the 1950s and subsequently recorded and toured over the following two decades.

TAKE NOTE

- How did jazz develop as an improvised music performed for dancing?

New Orleans Notables

Early on, nearly all New Orleans ragtime, jazz, and dance musicians had to have "day gigs"—jobs as barbers, carpenters, laborers, longshoremen, brick masons, cigar rollers—to support themselves. By the early 1910s, some were able to pursue music full-time, which must have looked enticing. At a time of growing racial discrimination, the profession of musician was one of only three (the others were teacher and minister) open to any great extent to African Americans, and music provided the hope of escape from poverty, anonymity, and powerlessness. For all, it provided a means of self-expression and opportunities to impress others; for many, it offered a chance to travel, to escape routine, and to earn good tips. But to pursue that profession, musicians found that they had to leave the city, which was in a gradual economic decline; in the 1910s most of the best—or at least the most ambitious—players migrated to pastures with more "green."

No one can say who was the first jazz musician in New Orleans. Cornetist and bandleader Charles "Buddy" Bolden was among the earliest. By 1895 Bolden was leading his own group, and by 1901, it comprised cornet, trombone, clarinet, guitar, bass, and drums, which became a prototypical lineup of instruments. He became famous playing in New Orleans dance halls, in outlying communities, and in the city's Johnson Park, where his band would "cut," or outplay and outdraw, the polite dance band of John Robichaux, who performed across the street in the more respectable Lincoln Park. Bolden is said to have been inspired by the music of a "holy roller" church, and he delivered sounds in many forms, from rough and loud to slow and low-down. A legend has it that he made a cylinder recording, but if so, it has never been found. He did leave indelible memories of the rhythmic and emotional power and the clarion example of his playing on such numbers as *Make Me a Pallet on the Floor*; *If You Don't Shake, You Don't Get No Cake*; and his signature tune, *Funky Butt* (recorded as *Buddy Bolden's Blues* by Jelly Roll Morton). In 1907, Bolden, suffering from apparent dementia, was institutionalized, and he remained so for the rest of his life. He assumed the status of a legendary father figure in jazz.

Drummer and bandleader George "Jack" (or "Papa") Laine was one of the oldest of the pioneers, born in 1873, four years earlier than Bolden. In the 1890s, he established his **Reliance Brass Band** and a series of offshoots that included both "readers" and "fakers." Through his bands passed many of the white players who would make their names in jazz of the 1910s and 1920s in such groups as Tom Brown's Band from Dixieland, the Original Dixieland Jazz Band, Jimmy Durante's Original New Orleans Jazz Band, and the **New Orleans Rhythm Kings**. Though the Reliance bands never recorded, Laine achieved lasting importance as a nurturer of jazz talent.

Cornetist **Freddie Keppard** began his professional career in 1906. At that time, Keppard led the Olympia Orchestra and worked in other bands. In 1914, he headed west to Los Angeles, where he joined the Original Creole Band. Though it never recorded, this important band of New Orleans musicians played the vaudeville circuit for mostly white audiences for four years, spreading the city's novel jazz sound across the nation. Other musicians found Keppard's youthful skills praiseworthy: "There was no end to his ideas," recalled Jelly Roll Morton. "He could play a chorus eight or ten different ways." Legend has it that Keppard—who was, like many vaudeville performers, leery of having others "steal their stuff"—turned down an offer from the prestigious Victor Talking Machine Company to become the

Perhaps the very first jazz band, led by cornetist Buddy Bolden (standing, second from left). This photograph, the only known image of Bolden, was probably taken between 1895 and 1900. PHOTO COURTESY FRANK DRIGGS COLLECTION.

Having built a reputation in New Orleans, cornetist Joe "King" Oliver (third from the left) moved to Chicago and made history with his Creole Jazz Band. In 1921, the band—shown here in San Francisco—included clarinetist Johnny Dodds (third from the right) and pianist Lil Hardin (forth from the left). Cornet prodigy Louis Armstrong would join later—and would marry Hardin. PHOTO COURTESY FRANK DRIGGS COLLECTION.

first New Orleans band to record; the honor of making the first jazz record then went to a white group, the Original Dixieland Jazz Band. By the time Keppard would record in the 1920s, he was past his influential period and would sound dated and archaic compared to the cutting-edge Louis Armstrong.

It was in approximately 1907 that Joe Oliver began playing in dance bands, brass bands, and small units across New Orleans. Another cornet "king," he developed an expressive vocabulary of blueslike pitches and rhythmic nuances. He also became an early master of mutes, creating "wah-wah" and other effects that would be copied by many a musician, the Ellington trumpeter Bubber Miley, for one (see Chapter 4). After moving to Chicago in 1919—part of a general migration, during and after World War I, of blacks seeking more opportunity and a better life in the North—Oliver formed his own band in 1920 and became a respected bandleader. He played in California before returning to Chicago in 1921 and establishing King Oliver's Creole Jazz Band, which, when joined by the younger Louis Armstrong on second cornet, would make history.

Also in Oliver's band was a talented young pianist named **Lillian Hardin**. She was born in Memphis, Tennessee, probably in 1898, and raised in a middle class black home. She was trained as a classical pianist and attended Nashville's famous Fisk University, and then moved with her mother to Chicago. Hired as a pianist by a music store to demonstrate music for customers, she met other jazz players and eventually landed a job as house pianist at the Dreamland Café, where she joined Oliver's band in 1921.

When Armstrong joined the band, Hardin was at first unimpressed by his country manners and wardrobe. Soon, however, she recognized Armstrong's enormous talents and that Oliver was holding him back by keeping him in the role as second trumpeter. The two married, and Hardin encouraged Armstrong to leave Oliver and go to New York to work with Fletcher Henderson, and she also pushed him to record on his own. Hardin also composed some of the pieces that Armstrong recorded with his Hot Five and Hot Seven groups in the mid-1920s, including *Struttin' With Some Barbecue* and *Hotter Than That*. She also

JELLY ROLL MORTON'S BRILLIANT ORCHESTRATIONS ARE EVIDENT IN *BLACK BOTTOM STOMP* AND *GRANDPA'S SPELLS*.

These two compositions exemplify call and response, improvisation, logical harmonies, and breaks. In a Library of Congress recorded interview, Morton discussed elements of jazz, including "breaks" (when the band stops and gives a soloist a brief chance to play alone). He cited "the Spanish tinge," referring to the Afro-Cuban influence present in New Orleans. His acknowledgment of this strain combined with swing

Explore on mymusiclab.com

foreshadowed what was to come in jazz over the next 50 years, and divulged some of the cultural exchanges going on at the turn of the century in New Orleans. Morton also delineated the difference between jazz, ragtime, and blues. He referred to the latter two as specific musical forms, and noted that ragtime was a specific repertoire. Morton said, "Jazz is a style that can be applied to any type of tune."

—*Jeff Rupert*

The Red Hot Peppers' Rhythm Section

Morton's Red Hot Peppers rhythm section included Andrew Hilaire on drums, John Lindsay on bass, and a superb banjo soloist, Johnny St. Cyr. This rhythm section was one of the liveliest of its time and its precision was evident in the breaks of Morton's compositions, as well as in its seamless transitions from each section.

Omer Simeon • Clarinet

Simeon performed not only with Morton, but also King Oliver, Louis Armstrong, and Kid Ory. Like many early jazz musicians, he was born in New Orleans, and migrated to Chicago. His superb clarinet playing was exemplary of the New Orleans style.

PHOTO COURTESY FRANK DRIGGS COLLECTION.

Kid Ory • Trombone

Ory was a key figure in early jazz as exemplified by recordings made with Morton and Louis Armstrong's Hot Five and Hot Seven. Originally from Louisiana, he worked with Armstrong and Morton in Chicago, which by 1917 was the center of jazz. Ory's "tailgate" or swooping style of playing the trombone was key to early jazz trombone playing. As a band leader himself, Ory made the first recordings by a black jazz band.

George Mitchell • Cornet

Mitchell's hard driving cornet playing was underrated in jazz history, perhaps being eclipsed by the genius of his contemporary, Louis Armstrong. His playing was articulate, imaginative, and representative of the style.

Jelly Roll Morton • Piano

Morton, a.k.a. Ferdinand Joseph Lamothe, was a pianist, self-proclaimed "inventor of jazz," and above all, jazz composer. Born in 1890, he was one of the first jazz musicians, and his *Jelly Roll Blues* (1915) was one of the first published jazz pieces. His fierce personality spilled through his band's timeless recordings of 1926. By 1907 Morton left his home town of New Orleans, never to return. Musicians recall having heard him from New York to the West Coast. His death in 1941 happened just as a revival of New Orleans music began. In 1992 his life was dramatized in the Broadway show *Jelly's Last Jam*.

Sidney Bechet (far right) played Paris with Benny Peyton's Jazz Kings in 1921. He had already been hailed as a genius in Europe. PHOTO COURTESY FRANK DRIGGS COLLECTION.

played on most of these classic sides. Although the couple broke up in the late 1920s, Hardin remained active, leading her own bands and composing for decades to come.

From 1912 to 1919, trombonist Edward "Kid" Ory led one of New Orleans's most respected bands. Settling in California, he formed a unit known as Kid Ory's Original Creole Band, which, in 1922, became the first African American New Orleans group to make a record. He was the best-known trombonist in the loud, smeary, "**tailgate**" style, and he composed the standard *Muskrat Ramble* (1926).

Pianist, entertainer, and composer Jelly Roll Morton (born Ferdinand Joseph Lamothe, 1890–1941) was descended from free Creoles of color who had roots in Saint-Domingue. Raised with the colored Creoles' social and ethnic sensibilities, Morton

---

tailgate trombone an uninhibited style of jazz trombone—with considerable slides, glides, and slurs—characteristic of early New Orleans players such as Kid Ory and New Orleans revival or Dixieland players.

preferred to work with other downtown mulattoes more than with the uptown African Americans.

In 1907, after playing the Storyville district, Morton began touring in vaudeville and working sometimes as a solo pianist, with a drummer, or as a bandleader. His travels took him through the Gulf Coast and on to Memphis, St. Louis, New York, Texas, and the Midwest. He settled in Chicago from 1914 to 1917 and then on the West Coast from 1917 to 1922. Like Oliver, Keppard, Bechet, and Louis Armstrong, Morton remained unrecorded until 1923. But in the 1910s he had already composed a number of works (by then probably including *New Orleans Blues, King Porter Stomp, Georgia Swing,* and *Winin' Boy Blues*), published an important early blues (*Jelly Roll Blues,* 1915), and registered a composition with the copyright office (*Frog-I-More Rag,* 1918).

A colorful personality who made money as a pool shark and wore a diamond in his tooth, Morton bragged that he "invented" jazz in the first decade of the century—an assertion that was met with derision by many. Yet by the 1910s he was already a piano wizard of the first rank who could evidently transform

The Original Dixieland Jazz Band (ODJB) in 1917. From left to right: Tony Sbarbaro, Eddie Edwards, Nick LaRocca, Larry Shields, and Henry Ragas. PHOTO COURTESY FRANK DRIGGS COLLECTION.

all sorts of music into jazz, embellishing, paraphrasing, and improvising, smoothing out the rhythms of ragtime, and making everything flow and swing.

Two years older than Morton was trombonist Tom Brown, who played in Jack Laine's Reliance bands before starting his own around 1910. After opening for a short but influential run at Chicago's Lamb's Cafe in May of 1915, his Brown's Band from Dixieland became one of the first New Orleans jazz acts to make a splash—for itself and the new music—in the North.

Among the second generation of pioneer jazzmen, clarinetist and soprano saxophonist Sidney Bechet stands the tallest. By 1910, when he was in his teens, he had found work as a clarinetist in New Orleans jazz bands; in 1916, he left to play in touring shows, and in 1917 he settled briefly in Chicago, where he picked up the soprano saxophone, which became his primary instrument. In 1919, he became one of the first Americans to spread jazz to Europe, prompting the Swiss conductor Ernest Ansermet to famously call him "an extraordinary clarinet virtuoso . . . an artist of genius" who played blues "equally admirable for their richness of invention, force of accent, and daring in novelty and the unexpected." Bechet played with great intensity, soaring passion, and, like Armstrong, operatic bravura that, heard on recordings, can still

raise goosebumps. At the end of his life, he wrote an autobiography, *Treat It Gentle* (1960)—as warm, lyrical, and eloquent as the best of his music.

TAKE NOTE

- Who were some of the early innovators of New Orleans jazz?

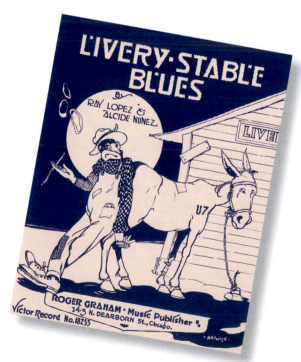

The ODJB's 1917 recording of Livery Stable Blues *sold a phenomenal 1.5 million copies. Ironically, given the denigrating caricature on the sheet-music cover, the music owed a great debt to African-American musicians.* COURTESY JOHN EDWARD HASSE.

Listening Focus

LIVERY STABLE BLUES • THE ORIGINAL DIXIELAND JAZZ BAND

Music: Ray Lopez and Alcide Nunez (authorship disputed by Dominic J. LaRocca, who copyrighted the piece as *Barnyard Blues*), 1917. Personnel: Dominic J. "Nick" LaRocca (cornet, director); Eddie Edwards (trombone); Larry Shields (clarinet); Henry Ragas (piano); Tony Sbarbaro (drums). Recorded February 26, 1917, in New York. Issued as Victor 18255. Timing: 3:11.

The Sicilian American cornetist Nick LaRocca was a mainstay of the Original Dixieland Jazz Band (ODJB), a dance outfit organized in Chicago in 1916, which included five New Orleans musicians. Clarinetist Larry Shields became known as its best player. In January of 1917, the ODJB opened at Reisenweber's Restaurant in New York City, where it played for 18 months. Its performance created a sensation, attracting record executives from the Victor label to invite the group to record. It became the first jazz band to make recordings, in February 1917. Although its recordings reveal a band short on improvisational ability, it was also full of drive and energy and was considered strikingly novel by the American public; the ODJB's 1917 recording of *Livery Stable Blues* sold, by some estimates, over a million copies.

Livery Stable Blues is widely considered one of the very first jazz recordings. That's because the ODJB was the first recorded band to use the word "jazz" (or "jass") in its name; a number of its compositions became jazz standards; it played a lively, syncopated music rooted in New Orleans (as well as in minstrel and vaudeville

traditions); and this tune takes the form of an African American blues, a major root of jazz.

Like *St. Louis Blues*, *Livery Stable Blues* comprises three sections, but in contrast to Handy's piece, all three sections are 12-bar blues. This performance takes the form Intro AA BB CC A B CC Coda.

The ODJB didn't improvise solos as we know the practice today, but rather it emphasized well-rehearsed breaks, where the band would drop out and the rhythm abruptly stop to highlight a specific sound or musical moment. What made this piece such a smashing success was the four breaks conveying barnyard effects (hence the alternate title *Barnyard Blues*). At 1:19, 1:37, 2:30, and 2:48, you can hear, in quick succession, the clarinet crowing like a rooster, the cornet whinnying like a horse, and the trombone braying like a donkey. Besides the novel animal effects, what created a sensation? This music was unprecedented in its lively tempo, noisy humor, brash energy, overall impertinence, and musical subversiveness challenging established conventions. The band reveled in outlandish stage antics (such as playing the trombone with the foot), it used the audacious slogan "Untuneful Harmonists Playing Peppery Melodies," and leader Nick LaRocca piqued the press with statements like "Jazz is the assassination of the melody, it's the slaying of syncopation." Like punk rockers 70 years later, its group members gleefully proclaimed their outsider status in the musical world.

Today's listeners may have some difficulty listening to this recording. Made before the days of electrical microphones, this recording suffers poor fidelity. There is variation in the performance, but no out-and-out soloing as we know it. The music is repetitive and doesn't seem to build to a climax. *Livery Stable Blues* will strike some as painfully old-fashioned, even humorous in unintended ways.

The ODJB's social and cultural importance surpassed its music: it introduced the word *jazz* to many people, popularized the music to audiences far from New Orleans, and deeply influenced a generation of young musicians, from Louis Armstrong (who liked the band's recordings) to young white mid-westerners such as cornetist Bix Beiderbecke and clarinetist Benny Goodman, who would go on to become renowned masters of the jazz idiom. This and other recordings of the ODJB helped pave the way for the 1920s to become "The Jazz Age."

The ODJB performed in England in 1919–20 and played a leading role in spreading jazz to a mass audience abroad as well as in the United States. Five of the band's numbers—two from 1917, *Tiger Rag* and *Dixieland Jass Band One-Step* (later called *Original Dixieland One-Step),* and three 1918 pieces, LaRocca's and Shields's *At the Jazz Band Ball* and *Fidgety Feet* along with *Clarinet Marmalade* (by Shields and the ODJB's H.W. Ragas)—became jazz standards.

—*John Edward Hasse*

New Orleans Style and "Jass" Variants

The style developed by New Orleans musicians weaved separate melody lines into a captivating counterpoint—a "hot" sound of group embellishment and improvisation. The melody was typically passed

from instrument to instrument, but by the 1920s, the cornet usually punched out the melody, the trombone smeared a countermelody or doubled the bass line, and the clarinet filled in with bursts of melody. "In the early days . . . [n]one of the guys took their horns down for a chorus to let another guy play a solo," recalled Pops Foster. "About 1920 or '21 guys started taking down their horns, after they'd blown a chorus." In the 1920s, especially through the influence and genius of trumpeter Louis Armstrong and saxophonist Sidney Bechet—and the indelibility of recordings—jazz would become a soloist's art. The growing diaspora of Crescent City players spread the sound, and it caught the fancy of many young people at a time when, across the nation, public dancing was becoming a craze and nightlife was increasing as a part of urban culture. However much the youngsters liked the new jazz sound, many oldsters resisted it on musical or moralistic grounds, joining a heated controversy that had raged over ragtime and now erupted into a war over jazz. "Does Jazz Put the

---

ride-out chorus   climactic final chorus, often with collective improvisation; term used especially in early jazz.

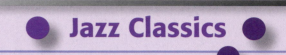

Jazz Classics

Tiger Rag

First recorded by the Original Dixieland Jazz Band on August 17, 1917, in New York City, *Tiger Rag* is the quintessential New Orleans jazz composition and one of the best known and most-recorded jazz pieces of all time.

A long-running controversy shrouds its origins. Although the song was published by the Leo Feist company in New York, with the Original Dixieland Jazz Band's cornetist Nick LaRocca listed as the composer, pianist-composer Jelly Roll Morton later claimed he developed the piece from an old French quadrille popular in New Orleans. Legendary New Orleans bandleader Jack Laine and his men said it was alternately known as *Meatball, Praline, Number One, Number Two,* and the *Reliance Rag* and that it was a "put-together" piece. LaRocca explained that the piece resulted from combining many elements. These include an extension of a popular two-bar phrase known as "Get Over Dirty," a simplified stop-time version of the children's song *London Bridge Is Falling Down,* a chorus melody built on the chord progressions of the standard march *National Emblem* (1906), and a downward "rip" after the lyric "Hold that

tiger" that imitates the alto horn part in German bands. *Tiger Rag* as recorded by the ODJB also incorporates an eight-bar excerpt from Schubert's *Sixteen German Dances, Opus 33.*

Tiger Rag's source material turned up in other songs as well. The *National Emblem* chord progressions appear in many popular pieces from the time—including *Zacatecas March* (1891), *Bill Bailey, Won't You Please Come Home* (1902), and *Washington and Lee Swing* (1910).

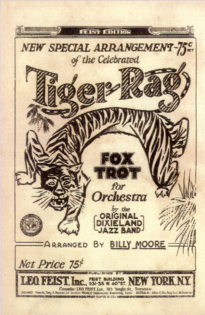

COURTESY JOHN EDWARD HASSE.

Watch the video of Louis Armstrong's *Tiger Rag* on **mymusiclab.com**

By 1942, jazz musicians had recorded *Tiger Rag* more than 130 times. It became a favorite of Louis Armstrong and every traditional-style New Orleans jazz band, as well as guitarist Django Reinhardt, pianist Art Tatum (*JTSA* Disc 2/Track 6), and bandleader Duke Ellington. Lyrics by Harry de Costa were added in 1932, and pop artists ranging from the Mills Brothers to Liberace to Bobby Short recorded the piece. *Tiger Rag* also became one of the fight songs of the Louisiana State University Tigers football team.

Tiger Rag achieved enduring popularity because it contains many simple yet effective devices that hold interest and build intensity. Through two 32-bar verses and a 128-bar chorus, it uses appealing chord progressions, two key changes, three different extended riffs, numerous breaks, and the signature tiger "rip" to build to a rousing finish in a **ride-out chorus**. It has often been noted that everyone played the *Maple Leaf Rag,* and it can also be said that everybody played, and still plays, *Tiger Rag.*

—*Jack Stewart*

Sin in Syncopation?" asked a 1921 article in *Ladies Home Journal*, answering its own question with an emphatic affirmative.

But opposition couldn't contain jazz. New Orleans wasn't the only source of the music in the 1910s. During the middle and late teens, early jazz was emerging in Los Angeles, San Francisco, Chicago, Kansas City, New York, and Washington, DC. There and elsewhere, musicians were experimenting. They were trying out looser rhythms, exploring syncopation, bending notes, embellishing melodies, varying familiar songs, devising their own "breaks," and creating their own tunes.

Some of the musicians leading the way worked in New York City, the hub of show business and the home of storied Tin Pan Alley. By 1913, pianist **James P. Johnson** was playing dance halls in the "Jungles" section of the rough Manhattan neighborhood Hell's Kitchen, working out a driving keyboard style that, beginning in 1917, was captured on player-piano rolls. He and fellow pianists Abba Labba, Luckeyth Roberts, and Eubie Blake were creating an eastern style of ragtime—flashy, tricky, with syncopation in the left hand as well as the right—that would develop into the Harlem "**stride**" style of jazz piano.

By the close of the 1910s, jazz had emerged outside the confines of New Orleans, lighting up nightspots on the South Side of Chicago, in Hell's Kitchen and Harlem, and on the West Coast. While expanding geographically, jazz had also moved from the tenderloins into dance halls and vaudeville houses. Through sheet music, piano rolls, and especially phonograph recordings, jazz had entered the parlors and living rooms of average Americans, undergoing a transformation from a localized style of music making to a budding and controversial national phenomenon. It had sailed the ocean and penetrated Europe. In the next decade, jazz would, along with its associated dance steps, bring an unprecedented number of Americans into dance halls and ballrooms, capture the imagination of painters and writers and composers, and produce the first momentous evidence of its foremost practitioners' depth and genius when Sidney Bechet, Jelly Roll Morton, Louis Armstrong, and Duke Ellington made records.

✳ **Explore** Key Recordings on **mymusiclab.com**

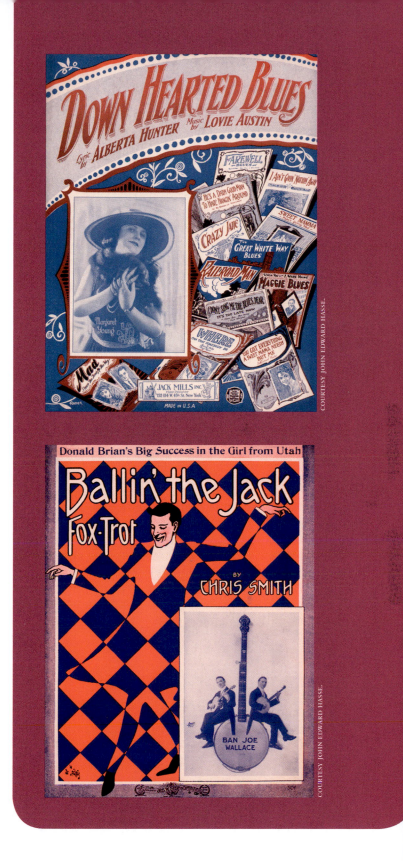

COURTESY JOHN EDWARD HASSE.

COURTESY JOHN EDWARD HASSE.

---

stride   a style of jazz piano developed in the 1910s and 1920s, derived from ragtime and featuring large, striding leaps in the left hand and syncopated figures in the right hand; pioneered by James P. Johnson; also called stride piano or Harlem stride piano.

TAKE NOTE

• What were some other early centers of jazz, and how did their music differ from that heard in New Orleans?

- **What roles did African and European music play in the development of jazz?**

African music contributed to jazz powerful propulsive rhythms, call-and-response form, an emphasis on the natural melodic quality of spoken language, a link with dancing, short repeated melodic phrases, and percussive attack. European music contributed harmony; musical notation; compositional forms such as the 32-bar song; and an array of instruments, including brass, woodwinds, piano, bass, and guitar.

- **What were the special conditions in New Orleans that made it a fertile ground for jazz?**

New Orleans, with its mixed population of African Americans, Creoles, Native Americans, and Europeans, had a unique set of six conditions that gave rise to jazz: loose cultural boundaries, active Afro-Caribbean culture, vital musical life, strong dance tradition, pervasive "good times" atmosphere, and numerous brass bands.

- **What roles did blues and ragtime play in the development of jazz?**

Jazz drew on many earlier African American musical forms in its development. The blues's three-chord structure has served as a popular framework for jazz compositions, and its characteristic bent and slurred notes became common in jazz melodies. Ragtime contributed the use of syncopation and polyrhythms, a strong rhythmic separation between treble and bass parts, and multisectional forms to jazz.

- **How did jazz develop as an improvised music performed for dancing?**

By the 1890s, African Americans had developed many unique dance styles, which demanded a new type of accompaniment. Their looser, more sexually suggestive dances were best accompanied by a hotter, bluesier style of music. Jazz developed as the ideal accompaniment for these modern dance styles.

- **Who were some of the early innovators of New Orleans's jazz?**

Cornet player Charles "Buddy" Bolden is generally considered among the first true jazz musicians and bandleaders; he was leading a group as early as the mid-1890s. Other innovators included cornetist/bandleader Joe "King" Oliver, saxophonist and trombonist/leader "Kid" Ory, pianist Jelly Roll Morton, and clarinet master Sidney Bechet. The Original Dixieland Jazz Band (ODJB) was the first to record and make a major impression outside of New Orleans, helping to spread the new music.

- **What were some other early centers of jazz, and how did their music differ from that heard in New Orleans?**

During the middle and late teens, early jazz was emerging in major cities across the country, notably New York, Los Angeles, and Chicago. While New Orleans jazz featured ensemble playing and group improvisation, talented soloists like Louis Armstrong and Sidney Bechet brought an emphasis on individual virtuosity and personality to the music.

DISCUSSION QUESTIONS

1. Before you read this chapter, what impressions did you have of early jazz? Did this chapter change your outlook, and if so, how?

2. Jazz was a music of young people—musicians and dancers—and many older people didn't like it. Draw comparisons with other forms of music in the twentieth century, such as early rock or rap and hip-hop.

3. Discuss the roles that dancing and parading played in the genesis of jazz.

4. What aspects of the origins of jazz may have contributed to the view of the music as disreputable, impolite, and immoral?

5. Could jazz have originated in a midwestern city as successfully as it did in New Orleans? Why or why not?

6. What elements of African culture and music are found in jazz? What elements of European music are in jazz?

7. Discuss two of jazz's musical roots (musical styles born in the United States) and what each contributed to jazz.

8. If you had to single out the two most important musicians or bands in early jazz, to whom would you point and why?

KEY TERMS & KEY PEOPLE

Louis Armstrong 31
arpeggio 41
Sidney Bechet 39
blues 36
Charles "Buddy" Bolden 32
break 39
call and response 29
field holler 37
glissandi 30
habanera 32
W. C. Handy 37

Lillian Hardin 47
James P. Johnson 53
Scott Joplin 44
Freddie Keppard 46
George "Jack" (or "Papa")
   Laine 45
meter 35
Jelly Roll Morton 31
New Orleans Rhythm Kings 46
Joe "King" Oliver 38
Original Dixieland Jazz Band 38

piano rag 44
pentatonic scale 38
ragtime 42
Reliance Brass Band 46
riff 29
second line 34
stride 53
syncopation 29
tailgate trombone 49
trio 40

CHAPTER 4

The Jazz Age

by Michael Brooks

TAKE NOTE

- How did jazz develop in Chicago in the 1920s, and who were some of its key players?
- What distinguished Kansas City jazz from other regional styles during the 1920s and early 1930s?
- Why was New York City an important jazz center in the 1920s, and who were some of its leading players?
- Who were some of the primary vocalists to emerge during the Jazz Age?
- What role did arrangers play in creating the sound of early jazz bands?
- Why were regional bands important during this period?

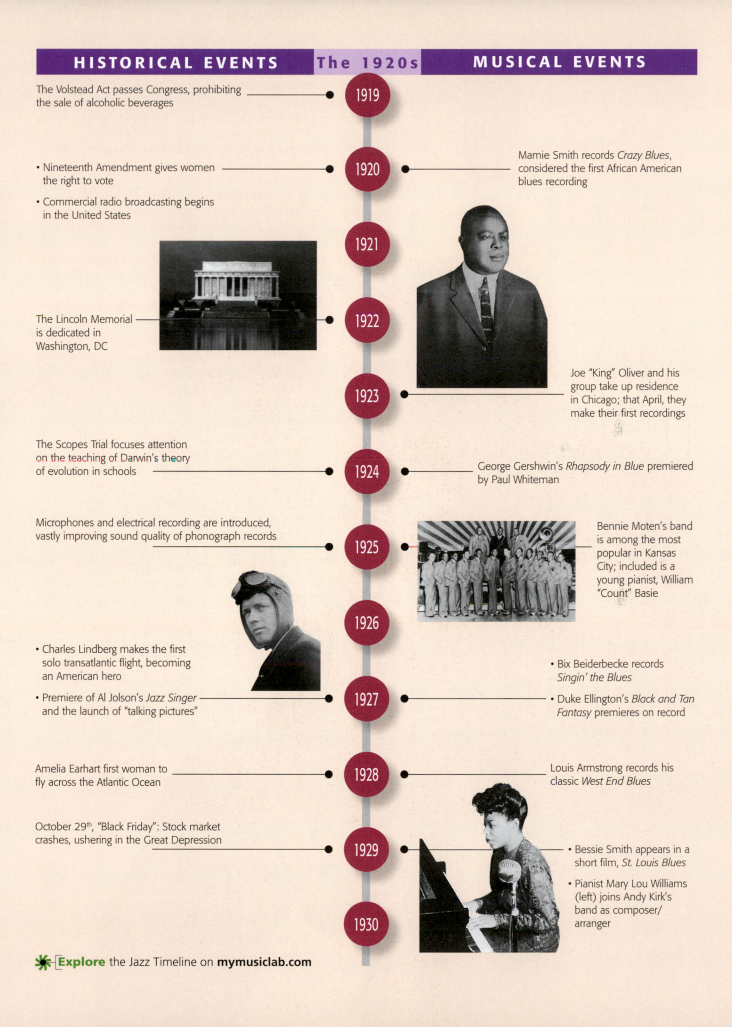

HISTORICAL EVENTS   The 1920s   MUSICAL EVENTS

1919

The Volstead Act passes Congress, prohibiting the sale of alcoholic beverages

1920

- Nineteenth Amendment gives women the right to vote

- Commercial radio broadcasting begins in the United States

Mamie Smith records *Crazy Blues*, considered the first African American blues recording

1921

1922

The Lincoln Memorial is dedicated in Washington, DC

1923

Joe "King" Oliver and his group take up residence in Chicago; that April, they make their first recordings

The Scopes Trial focuses attention on the teaching of Darwin's theory of evolution in schools

1924

George Gershwin's *Rhapsody in Blue* premiered by Paul Whiteman

Microphones and electrical recording are introduced, vastly improving sound quality of phonograph records

1925

Bennie Moten's band is among the most popular in Kansas City; included is a young pianist, William "Count" Basie

1926

- Charles Lindberg makes the first solo transatlantic flight, becoming an American hero

- Premiere of Al Jolson's *Jazz Singer* and the launch of "talking pictures"

1927

- Bix Beiderbecke records *Singin' the Blues*

- Duke Ellington's *Black and Tan Fantasy* premieres on record

Amelia Earhart first woman to fly across the Atlantic Ocean

1928

Louis Armstrong records his classic *West End Blues*

October 29th, "Black Friday": Stock market crashes, ushering in the Great Depression

1929

- Bessie Smith appears in a short film, *St. Louis Blues*

- Pianist Mary Lou Williams (left) joins Andy Kirk's band as composer/arranger

1930

✳ **Explore** the Jazz Timeline on **mymusiclab.com**

Jazz began as a music associated with dancing, and it remained that way as it moved into the 1920s with one overriding difference: in earlier years, live jazz, still in embryonic form, was hard to find outside of New Orleans and a few other cities. But in the 1920s it took shape as a distinct musical style known and embraced by young audiences the world over.

Its first creative geniuses—**Louis Armstrong**, **Duke Ellington**, **Sidney Bechet**, and Jelly Roll Morton—produced key work during the twenties, transforming what had once been a rough iteration of ragtime, the blues, and marching music into an art of sophistication and depth. Through vision and force of personality, they established new artistic benchmarks and conventions that would last through the remainder of the century: Where jazz had once been an ensemble sound, artists in the wake of Armstrong shifted the focus to soloists. Where jazz composition had formerly been narrowly conceived, new artists envisioned it as broader, more open-ended. Where band sounds had been limited, innovators expanded the sonic palette, introducing new timbres and combinations of instruments. And making their accomplishment all the more remarkable was the fact that they did it in the restrictive sphere of popular entertainment, where the first order of business was to keep the crowds coming.

Nightlife and the surrounding social whirl, whatever the creative limitations it placed on performers, had everything to do with jazz coming into public favor. New trends in the use of leisure time—trends that favored the public consumption of music—had emerged in the years surrounding and during World War I. Growing and diversifying populations in urban industrial centers, combined with changing social attitudes, had spiked demand for new kinds and places of entertainment. A dance craze swept U.S. cities from 1912 to 1916, fueled by a new permissiveness that made public dancing socially acceptable for both women and men. The opening of New York City's Roseland Ballroom in 1919 heralded a boom in dance halls in the 1920s, and dance bands played for young people who

Louis Armstrong (ca. 1932). PHOTO COURTESY DOMINIC WINTER/DK IMAGES.

The Charleston and other popular dances of the 1920s came out of musical revues such as those produced and choreographed in Harlem by Clarence Robinson (ca. 1925).

wanted to forget the war and instead look forward to a brighter future.

With the passage of the Volsted Act in 1919, Prohibition had come into force, outlawing the manufacture and sale of alcohol. But instead of eliminating consumption, Prohibition drove it underground, where nightclubs, cabarets, and speakeasies lured late-night crowds with the promise of illegal booze and unregulated revelry.

The Roaring Twenties, with its taste for the new, the exciting, and the exotic, found in jazz the perfect sonic accompaniment. So great a part of the cultural fabric was the new music that novelist F. Scott Fitzgerald dubbed the 1920s the Jazz Age.

Jazz also rode in on the coattails of a growing white fascination with African American culture. In August 1920, singer Mamie Smith made what is considered the first blues record, *Crazy Blues*, which opened the floodgates for "**race records**"—discs made expressly for blacks, but that whites also

race records a music industry term from the 1920s and 1930s to connote phonograph discs made expressly for blacks (whites could also purchase the discs); applied to blues, gospel, and some jazz recordings.

purchased. In New York City, the home of the largest concentration of African Americans in the United States, all-black revues and musicals were the rage on Broadway, fueling a market for other types of black entertainment and art. But even more pivotal was the explosion of interest in African American–derived dancing. One 1923 revue, *Runnin' Wild*, popularized the **Charleston**. **James P. Johnson**—the show's composer—says he first saw the dance in New York City, performed by transplants from Charleston, South Carolina, and adapted its snappy rhythm to his song. The step became a national fad for several years and created a vogue for other dances—and for the jazz that accompanied them.

Further laying the groundwork for the spread and development of jazz in the 1920s were advances in communications and recording technology. Radio became a mass medium in the middle part of the decade, exposing listeners all over the United States to the sound of the new music. At the same time, new innovations in phonograph recording vastly improved the quality of recorded sound and inspired such jazz composers as Duke Ellington to create more detailed and intricate musical arrangements.

In the 1920s, New York City remained the center of the entertainment industry, but thanks to a still-vital **vaudeville** circuit, musical acts spread across the country on lengthy tours, bringing up-to-date entertainment into any town large enough to have a theater. Jazz too, especially as black musicians moved north and east from the economically waning South, found its way into other cities. Chief among them were Chicago and Kansas City.

👁 **Watch** the documentary on jazz in Chicago on **mymusiclab.com**

Chicago

Because of its central location and access to waterways, Chicago has long been one of the great commercial hubs of North America, and at the dawn of the 1920s it was especially active. The city's population was booming, Prohibition had given rise to a thriving black market in vice, money was pouring in from illicit liquor stills, and booze was being smuggled in from Canada. Speakeasies, brothels, nightclubs, movie houses, and dance halls were proliferating—all of them craving musical entertainment. The musicians followed, coming into LaSalle Station from the South with cases containing not submachine guns but trumpets and saxophones.

It took a few years for white musicians from New Orleans—who made most of the first Chicago jazz records—to shake off their Crescent City roots, but by the mid-1920s a distinctive new style of jazz

---

Charleston a fast, rhythmic African American dance step of the 1920s characterized by knocking the knees together and kicking out the lower legs. At the heart of the Charleston dance was the rhythm:

vaudeville the popular theatrical entertainment style of the late nineteenth and early twentieth centuries in which different kinds of acts—singers, comedians, dancers, magicians, acrobats—would share billing; presaged later television variety shows and provided a career launching pad for many star musicians and performers.

When cornetist and bandleader Joe Oliver hired Louis Armstrong in 1922, the two turned Chicago on its ear. Their paths then diverged. Armstrong moved on to New York and international stardom. Oliver's career went into decline and his health began to fail; he eventually moved to Georgia, where his final job was that of a poolroom attendant. PHOTO COURTESY FRANK DRIGGS COLLECTION.

had emerged. It was quite different from the sound produced in New Orleans: here, the music had an edgy $\frac{4}{4}$ rhythm with angry staccato solo work that was not out of keeping with the trigger-happy philosophy of the surroundings.

There were few black jazz records until 1923, when **Joe "King" Oliver** returned from a stint in California to take up residence in Chicago's Lincoln Gardens—along with a new addition to the band, the young cornetist Louis Armstrong—and the Gennett Record Company invited Oliver's Creole Jazz Band to cut some sides in their Richmond, Indiana, studios. Gennett's outside-the-hub location and lack of a nationwide distribution system ordinarily meant it couldn't attract big-name artists. But a year earlier, it had recorded the New Orleans Rhythm Kings (NORK), a group of young white musicians in residence at Chicago's Friar's Inn, and the records were selling well. Inspired by both the Original Dixieland Jazz Band and cornetist King Oliver, the NORK, with solid ensemble playing and memorable solos by clarinetist Leon Roppolo, created a sound—on recordings such as *Weary Blues* and *Tin Roof Blues* (both 1923)—that would influence a coterie of white Chicago players. Roppolo's biting tone cut through the other instruments and made expressive solos with the NORK (*Panama*, 1922; *Wolverine Blues*, 1923), causing audiences to demand that he be featured.

In April 1923, King Oliver's Creole Jazz Band, one of the great jazz ensembles from New Orleans, made its first recordings for Gennett. Oliver's records followed the classic New Orleans pattern of ensemble playing, but with an important difference: the interplay between Oliver and Armstrong exhilarated the listeners, making them more aware of individual instrumentalists.

A momentous break from the New Orleans small-group sound came with the legendary Louis Armstrong Hot Five and Hot Seven sides, made for OKeh Records in Chicago from 1925 to 1928. The group never existed outside of the recording studios, but the music it made is as important as any jazz in the twentieth century. The group's first recording

---

polyphonic having a multi-melodic texture.

plunger mute a type of brass mute, such as an ordinary sink plunger without the stick, that is cupped and manipulated against the bell of the instrument with the left hand. It produces human-voice-like tone colors. Trombonist "Tricky Sam" Nanton and trumpeters Bubber Miley and Cootie Williams—all in Ellington's band—were brilliant exponents of the plunger mute.

wah-wah (1) a mute that, when manipulated over the bell of a trumpet or trombone, creates a vocal-like wah-wah sound. Popularized by King Oliver and a series of Ellington trumpeters. (2) The sound achieved by using such a mute. (3) From the 1960s on, an electronic pedal used by guitarists (popularized by Jimi Hendrix and Eric Clapton) and keyboard players.

coda (Italian for "tail") the ending of a musical piece.

tag a phrase tagged on or added to the end of a chorus or, more commonly, a piece; the latter is formally known as a *coda*.

Listening Focus

((•• **Listen** to *Dipper Mouth Blues* (1923) by King Oliver's Creole Jazz Band on **mymusiclab.com** CD I, Track 8/Download Track 8

DIPPER MOUTH BLUES • KING OLIVER'S CREOLE JAZZ BAND

Music: Louis Armstrong, 1923. Personnel: King Oliver, Louis Armstrong (cornet); Honore Dutrey (trombone); Johnny Dodds (clarinet); Lil Hardin (piano); Bill Johnson (banjo, vocal break); Baby Dodds (drums). Recorded: April 6, 1923, in Richmond, Indiana. First issue: Gennett 5132. Timing: 2:18.

In Oliver's most typical recordings, the densely **polyphonic** ensemble playing is the real "star." However, on his most celebrated recording, *Dipper Mouth Blues* (1923), it's the soloists—clarinetist Johnny Dodds and especially Oliver himself—who shine. (The piece was named for Armstrong, who as a youth was nicknamed "Dippermouth" for his big mouth, and who here plays second cornet.) Oliver leads his septet through nine 12-bar, smoothly swinging blues choruses. After two ensemble choruses of collective improvisation, Dodds (at 0:36) takes a two-chorus solo as the band plays in stop-time. In another ensemble chorus (1:06), Armstrong plays melody while Oliver rests. Then, (1:22) King Oliver blows a well-constructed three-chorus solo beginning on a bluesy, or flatted, third degree of the scale, demonstrating the profound influence blues had on early jazz. As Oliver opens and closes a **plunger mute** over the bell of his cornet, he achieves expressive **wah-wah** sounds. His earthy solo would become a familiar set piece, copied by countless trumpeters. In one of the most memorable vocal interjections in jazz, the banjoist calls out (2:05), "Oh, play that thing!" One final, rousing ensemble chorus (2:07) rounds out the performance, followed by a two-bar **coda**, or **tag**. On the basis of Oliver's recordings, *Dipper Mouth Blues* and a variant called *Sugar Foot Stomp* became staples of traditional jazz.

—*John Edward Hasse*

Listening Guide

Listen to *West End Blues* by Louis Armstrong and His Hot Five on **mymusiclab.com**
CD I, Track 11/Download Track 11

WEST END BLUES • LOUIS ARMSTRONG AND HIS HOT FIVE

Music: Clarence Williams and Joe Oliver, 1928. Personnel: Louis Armstrong (trumpet, vocal, leader); Fred Robinson (trombone); Jimmy Strong (clarinet); Earl Hines (piano); Mancy Carr (banjo); Zutty Singleton (drums). Recorded June 28, 1928, in Chicago. First issue: OKeh 8597. Timing: 3:17.

Overview

The most celebrated of the 89 Louis Armstrong recordings made from 1925 to 1928 with his Hot Five and Hot Seven recording groups, *West End Blues* helped usher in a new era in American music, emphasizing the brilliance of improvisation, the supremacy of the soloist, the unique "voice" of the individual, and the powerful example of a genius.

In these recordings, Armstrong abandoned the two- and four-bar breaks of New Orleans jazz in favor of entire choruses of improvisation. He helped transform jazz from a group practice into an art form for the individual soloist. In the 1920s, Armstrong emerged as the dominant musician in jazz and as the man who would take the role of the soloist to new heights in American music. He

set such a sky-high benchmark of originality and artistry that he came to influence—directly or indirectly—just about every instrumentalist and singer in jazz, and ultimately, many performers of other kinds of music too. He is the single most influential musician in American history.

Still musically fresh and emotionally compelling after 80-some years, *West End Blues* is an all-time American classic.

Key Features

- Blues: *West End Blues* takes the form of a standard 12-bar blues, repeated five times.
- Instrumentation: The typical New Orleans-style small group of the day, with three **front line** instruments (trumpet, trombone, and clarinet), and a **rhythm section** of piano, banjo, and drums.
- Melody: *West End Blues* is a rather mournful, somewhat stately slow blues.
- Rhythm and percussion: The tempo is a slow $\frac{4}{4}$. In much jazz, the drummer keeps time and provides rhythmic propulsion and

accents. Here, time is kept mostly by Hines's piano, and rhythms are produced primarily by the three soloists and Hines; percussionist Singleton is audible only in the second chorus.
- Improvisation: Armstrong's and Hines's solos provide most of the solo interest. In chorus 3, in a call-and-response with clarinetist Strong, Armstrong scats a solo that, in contrast, is more elaborated and is plaintive in tone. After the understated chorus by Strong and Armstrong, Hines bursts in with fast, flowery downward and upward runs, playing, at 2:00, a flourish of 26 notes in one measure. Hines alternates these rapid runs with less rapid right-hand octaves—critics have called this his "trumpet" style. His solo delivers the greatest amount of melodic and rhythmic activity in the recording. In his closing solo, Armstrong demonstrates his gifts as a musical dramatist, improvising a theatrical and well-shaped solo.

—*John Edward Hasse*

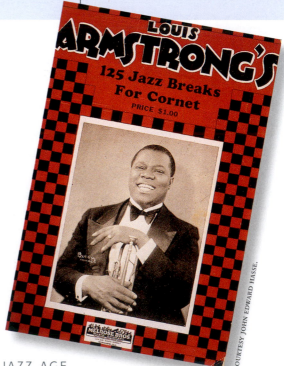

COURTESY JOHN EDWARD HASSE.

My Heart (1925), essentially follows the old formula, with a few short solo breaks and Armstrong playing a strong lead. But on the **flip side**, *Gut Bucket Blues*, Armstrong introduces each sideman, the first time this had occurred on record, and gives each one generous space. The floodgates for soloists had opened, and a new era was born.

---

front line in New Orleans marching and jazz bands, the melody instruments of trumpet, trombone, and clarinet; by extension, *front line* in later jazz means the instruments played by musicians standing in front of the rhythm section—typically trumpet, trombone, and sax.

rhythm section the core instrumentation of the jazz ensemble: piano, bass, drums, and sometimes banjo or guitar.

flip side the reverse side of a 78-rpm or 45-rpm phonograph record; unlike CDs, these records were played on both sides.

TIME	FORM	MELODY	INSTRUMENTATION	RHYTHM
0:00	INTRODUCTION	Armstrong offers a surprising introduction: a cadenza that showcases his technical virtuosity, daring, and musical imagination and announces that this is no ordinary or typical piece but rather something truly extraordinary.	Unaccompanied trumpet.	Out-of-tempo.
0:16	CHORUS 1	Armstrong plays the slow blues melody as the clarinet and trombone accompany and respond to him.	Trumpet lead with band accompaniment.	Slow tempo; regular rhythmic accompaniment with prominent strummed banjo.
0:50	CHORUS 2	Blues melody repeats.	Trombone lead, with piano and percussion accompaniment.	Rhythmic clip-clop accompaniment on pop cymbals by drummer Singleton.
1:25	CHORUS 3	Call-and-response duet between the clarinetist Strong and Armstrong's scat-singing. Strong plays a minimalist but effective series of mostly three-note phrases that Armstrong answers freely.	Clarinet and Armstrong's scat vocal, with banjo accompaniment.	Regular strummed chords on the banjo.
1:59	CHORUS 4	Pianist Earl Hines plays flowery downward and upward runs, playing, at 1:59, a flourish of 26 notes in one measure.	Unaccompanied piano solo by Earl Hines.	
2:11		Hines plays an improvised melody line in octaves (2:10–2:22), his famous "trumpet" style that helped distinguish him from pianists playing the earlier ragtime or stride styles.		
2:33	CHORUS 5	Armstrong's solo opens dramatically with a long soaring note held almost four bars (2:34–2:45).	Trumpet with band accompaniment.	
2:45		Solo reaches a dramatic climax.		Armstrong plays in double time (2:45–2:55).
2:57	CODA	A short coda concludes the piece, beginning with the piano playing descending chords linked by melodic runs.	Piano.	
3:05		Trumpet returns with mournful notes answered by chords played by the lead instruments.	Trumpet with lead instruments.	

On *Big Butter and Egg Man* (1926), Armstrong delivers one of his most celebrated, perfectly constructed solos, while *Potato Head Blues*, *Struttin' with Some Barbecue*, and *Hotter Than That* (all 1927) reveal his growing gifts as cornetist and improviser: technical mastery of his instrument; a big, beautiful tone; rhythmic daring; a fertile imagination as a soloist; and the ability to personalize his material. With these talents, Armstrong would assert more influence on the course of jazz than any other musician in the twentieth century.

By 1923 OKeh Records had hired black pianist Clarence Williams as its director of "race records"; the Columbia and Brunswick labels also recognized the commercial possibilities of signing black artists. Only the Victor Company stood aloof, but it finally capitulated in 1926, signing Jelly Roll Morton to an exclusive contract.

Morton is now recognized as the first great jazz composer and **arranger**—a pioneer in working variety and improvisation into the structure of his compositions—and as one of the most meticulous of early bandleaders, who would spend hours rehearsing for each record date. (See Chapter 3 for more on Morton's early career.) His piano solos reflect the ragtime style of his youth, and there are echoes of gavottes and mazurkas too (*Seattle Hunch* and *Pep*, both 1929). His early Red Hot Peppers sides are equally

Watch the video of *Tiger Rag* by Louis Armstrong on mymusiclab.com

arranger one who applies styling and instrumentation to a musical composition.

Listening Guide

BLACK BOTTOM STOMP • JELLY ROLL MORTON AND HIS RED HOT PEPPERS

Music: Jelly Roll Morton, 1926. Personnel: George Mitchell (cornet); Kid Ory (trombone); Omer Simeon (clarinet); Jelly Roll Morton (piano, leader); Johnny St. Cyr (banjo); John Lindsay (bass); Andrew Hilaire (drums). Recorded: September 15, 1926, in Chicago. First issue: Victor 20221. Timing: 3:12.

Overview

In the 1920s, Ferdinand "Jelly Roll" Morton composed, arranged, and recorded a series of brilliant small-group recordings—*Original Jelly Roll Blues*, *Grandpa's Spells*, *King Porter Stomp*, *The Pearls*, and others—that established him as the first great composer in jazz. His compositions typically employed the three- and four-strain march form that ragtime composers such as Scott Joplin utilized. Each change of section provided Morton the arranger with the opportunity to introduce changes in texture and dynamics.

Morton thought out his compositions, structured and arranged them carefully for his band, and mastered the element of contrast. His superior musicianship, meticulous preparation, and sense of form and drama set a high standard for all subsequent jazz composers. Morton achieved a remarkable integration of improvisation, contrast, and variety in his compositions. He was a careful and assiduous rehearser. His recordings with the Red Hot Peppers reached the peak of the New Orleans style of group embellishment and collective improvisation with its trademark **heterophony** and polyphony.

The Black Bottom was an African American dance step that originated in the Deep South in the early twentieth century. The step's five-note off-beat rhythm can be heard numerous times during this performance, for example, in the final two measures of the second clarinet solo (1:31) and at the end of the piano solo (1:49).

In *Black Bottom Stomp*, we hear a real composer at work, with a rich formal plan and all sorts of procedures to create and sustain interest: lively themes, a modulation, meticulous dynamics, breaks, stop-time phrases, and four different beats—all within a little more than three minutes.

Morton balances his composed parts with carefully planned spaces for improvisation, and all the soloists acquit themselves admirably. Unusual for the time is Johnny Lindsay's bass line, which sometimes goes into a walking bass pattern that became more common in the 1930s and later.

Black Bottom Stomp is Morton's masterpiece, above all because he brilliantly creates a study in formal, textural, and rhythmic contrast. In 1999, a transcription of this recording was published in the series Essential Jazz Editions. In 2006, *Black Bottom Stomp* was added to the Library of Congress's National Recording Registry.

Key Features

- Form: While most of Morton's compositions adhered to the three- or four-strain plan of marches and piano rags, here he offers essentially two strains. *Black Bottom Stomp* is a two-section work (labeled A and B in the listening chart) enriched with an introduction, a transition, and a coda. Morton creates structural, textural, and rhythmic contrast by the use of stop-time (1:51–2:09) and the **break** (1:01, 1:20, 2:16, 2:35, and 2:55).
- Tempo: Taken at approximately 126 beats per minute, this performance sets a lively tempo for dancing.
- Improvisation: The first three choruses are played as written by Morton in an edition published in 1925. (The piece was originally printed as *Queen of Spades*,

and republished in 1926 with a new title: *Black Bottom Stomp*.) After 0:56, all the choruses contain improvisation. Both the clarinet and banjo solos (at 1:15 and 2:11, respectively) are built around a tricky, repeating three-note pattern that harkens back to similar patterns in such piano rags as *Dill Pickles* (1906), *Black and White Rag* (1908), and *12th Street Rag* (1914). (This repeating three-note pattern, which shifts its rhythmic accent each time it's played, is sometimes given the name **secondary rag**.)
- Dynamics: Note how the thinner textures such as solo piano (1:13) and banjo with bass (2:11) naturally create less volume. In section B7, when the full band re-enters (2:49), the volume rises. Then, in the last chorus (2:49), Morton ratchets up the overall volume to end the piece with intensity. Such driving, final, or **out choruses** became popular in jazz of the 1920s.
- Instrumentation: The septet contains three "melody" instruments (cornet, trombone, and clarinet), and four "rhythm section" instruments (piano, banjo, bass, and drums). The cornet often carries the melody, while the clarinet plays filigrees and countermelodies in a higher register and the trombone comments in a lower register. All three front-line players—cornet, clarinet, trombone—play masterfully, demonstrating their leader's motto: "Always give 'em melody with plenty rhythm." During the 1920s, some bands employed the tuba to play the bass line, and **Fletcher Henderson's** band included the tuba as late as 1932, but the tuba was on its way out in favor of the fleeter string bass, heard here.

—*John Edward Hasse*

TIME	SECTION	LENGTH	MELODY/INSTRUMENTATION	RHYTHM
0:00	INTRO	8 bars	Opens in B-flat. Full ensemble plays four-bar intro, and repeats it.	Two-beat.
0:07	A1	16	The first four bars feature a slow-moving melody (one note per measure), followed by four bars of faster-moving melody; this pattern repeats, creating something of a call-and-response effect.	Four-beat; the bass plays mostly two beats per measure, but from 0:15 to 0:18 it plays one note per measure. At 0:12 and 0:19, bass plays a measure of **walking bass** (four beats per measure).
0:22	A2	16	Cornet takes the lead, engaging, every four measures, in call-and-response with entire ensemble.	
0:37	A3	16	Clarinet takes the lead as banjo accompanies; full ensemble in background, except trombone drops out until end of chorus.	
0:52	TRANSITION	4	Ensemble modulates from the key of B-flat to E-flat.	
0:56	B1	20	Cornet improvises a solo. Two-bar trombone break at 1:02.	
1:15	B2	20	Clarinet solo built around a repeating secondary rag three-note pattern. Clarinet break at 1:20.	At 1:32, the chorus ends with the band playing the five-note, off-beat rhythm of the Black Bottom dance.
1:33	B3	20	Morton plays a piano solo in two-handed stride style, while the other six instruments completely drop out until the last two bars (1:50). Note how Morton builds intensity throughout his solo by playing more actively.	Four-beat rhythm until 1:50 when band plays Black Bottom rhythm.
1:52	B4	20	Cornet solo	Stop-time, Black Bottom rhythm played by band.
2:11	B5	20	Banjo with bass. From 2:11 to 2:18, the banjo plays repeating three-note patterns (secondary rag). Bass plays percussive "slap" bass and, from 2:19 to 2:29, plays on every beat (walking bass). Banjo break at 2:16.	Four-beat.
2:29	B6	20	Full ensemble, now reverting to two-beat rhythm. Cymbal break at 2:35.	Two-beat rhythm; chorus ends (2:47) with the Black Bottom rhythm.
2:48	B7	20	Final, "hot" chorus: full ensemble plays more loudly, with more strongly accented rhythms. Clarinet and trombone play in a higher register than previous chorus. Colorful trombone break at 2:55.	Drums play a heavy **backbeat** (playing on beats 2 and 4). Bass does more mixing of two-to-the-bar and four-to-the-bar.
3:06	CODA	2		

heterophony   the simultaneous playing or singing of two or more versions of a melody.

break   a brief pause in a band's playing to feature a soloist or soloists; the beat continues, but is implied.

secondary rag   a melodic-rhythmic pattern that repeats three eighth or sixteenth notes, each repetition placing the accent on a different beat of the measure. Used to create a catchy effect in such piano rags as *Dill Pickles*, *Black and White Rag*, and *12th Street Rag*.

out chorus   the final chorus of a performance (see *chorus*, definition 1); the out chorus ends the piece, unless there is a coda or tag.

walking bass   the bass technique of producing a steady beat while playing and connecting notes of a chord progression.

backbeat   emphasis on the 2 and 4 of a four-beat measure; a fundamental example of syncopation, characteristic of African American music, and in contrast to the European march rhythm emphasizing the 1 and 3.

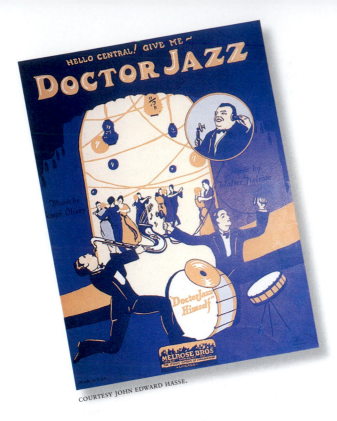

COURTESY JOHN EDWARD HASSE.

impressive. *Grandpa's Spells*, recorded with a seven-piece band in 1926, is a wondrously complex piece of arranging, replete with breaks and a variety of contrasting textures and dynamic levels. His masterpiece *Black Bottom Stomp*, from the same year, is rich in structure, contrast, and musicality using **stop-time** (an intermittent statement of the beat), breaks, varying rhythms, exchanges of four-bar phrases, and outstanding improvised solos. *Doctor Jazz*, also from 1926, offers trumpeter George Mitchell's tight, economical lead and clarinetist Omer Simeon's long, sustained notes and liquid phrasing.

The Lincoln Gardens—the site of King Oliver's 1923 post-California stint—was situated on Chicago's South Side. Until the crash of 1929, the zone had three times as many theaters and nightclubs as New York City. Along the "Stroll," a nine-block stretch of South State Street, jazz lovers had a choice of the Panama, Dreamland, and Elite cafés, or they could take in two silent movies and a musical program at the Monogram or Vendome theaters. At the latter, Erskine Tate led a big band with Louis Armstrong and pianist Earl "Fatha" Hines among its sidemen. The one record that they made, *Static Strut* backed with *Stomp Off, Let's Go* (1926), is a

heavy-footed yet immensely exciting pairing, with Armstrong spraying out notes with the ferocity of a double-crossed gangster. The black music scene later shifted to 35th and Calumet (honored by a 1934 Mezz Mezzrow recording), where you could hear Armstrong at the Sunset Cafe, drummer Sonny Clay or King Oliver at the Plantation, or clarinetist Jimmie Noone and Earl Hines at the Apex Club.

Although the "Stroll" was in a black neighborhood, there was no segregation in force, and it quickly became the haunt of some white students who attended the Austin High School. The nucleus of jazz-seeking teenagers included cornetist **Jimmy McPartland**, tenorman Bud Freeman, drummer Dave Tough, and reedman Frank Teschemacher. They were joined in their obsession by such future stars as guitarist **Eddie Condon**, cornetists Muggsy Spanier and **Leon "Bix" Beiderbecke**, and pianist Joe Sullivan. (Listen to Eddie Condon's *That's a Serious Thing*, JTSA Disc 1/ Track 13.) The youngsters bought records by King Oliver and the New Orleans Rhythm Kings, played them till the grooves wore flat, and dreamed of making their own mark on recorded jazz. This dream became reality in 1926 when they met up with a St. Louis **disc jockey** named William "Red" McKenzie, whose lack of musical ability was counterbalanced by his genius for promotion. In quick succession he persuaded the Chicago **A&R** man of the prestigious OKeh Record Company to record four sides in December 1927, including *Nobody's Sweetheart* and *Liza*. Two months later he wangled a date with Paramount Records; the date included *Sister Kate* and *Bullfrog Blues*. On the strength of the OKeh session, most of the musicians left for New York, where the local talent frowned on their use of $\frac{4}{4}$ rhythm and the standard of competition was much tougher.

One of the most romantic of the early jazz figures was Bix Beiderbecke, out of Davenport, Iowa. When he hit Chicago with the Wolverines, a midwestern group of limited talent, his drive and tone on such records as *Jazz Me Blues* and *Copenhagen* (both 1924) set the other musicians on their collective ear. Eddie Condon and the Austin High Gang claimed him as one of their own, but he never recorded with them, and judging by his later work among the more sophisticated New York

((•—**Hear** a profile of Beiderbecke on **mymusiclab.com**

---

stop-time   a technique to draw attention to a soloist; a stop-time passage typically suspends the beat except for one beat every one or two bars; for example, in King Oliver's *Dipper Mouth Blues* (CD I, Track 8/Download Track 8) and Jelly Roll Morton's *Black Bottom Stomp* (CD I, Track 9/Download Track 9).

disc jockey   in radio, the on-air host who plays records; also called a "deejay."

A&R   artists and repertoire, a term used in the recording industry; an "A&R man" was a staff record producer, but now most recording sessions are supervised by independent producers.

Another major figure on the Chicago jazz scene, **Earl Hines**, went little noticed by later generations of jazz musicians. This is particularly surprising because—in the 1920s—he revolutionized jazz piano, releasing it from the exciting but musically limiting constraints of ragtime and stride and paving the way for such higher-profile figures as Bud Powell and Thelonious Monk. Before he made a remarkable series of piano solos in 1928—including *Caution Blues*, *57 Varieties*, and *Off Time Blues*—most jazz pianists relied heavily on the unfaltering rhythm of the left hand to propel the music along. Hines departed from the regular left-hand patterns of alternating chords and single notes, instead introducing countermelodies or his own inventive harmonies while still retaining a strong beat. For the right hand he created his celebrated **trumpet style**, interjecting single notes or octave doublings to cut through the

---

trumpet style   a descriptor applied to Earl Hines's right-hand piano style, in which he played more like trumpeter Louis Armstrong—improvising single-note melody lines—than like other pianists.

Earl "Fatha" Hines, one of the leading pianists in all of jazz, ruled the Chicago scene with Louis Armstrong in the 1920s. His career stretched into the 1980s.
PHOTO COURTESY FRANK DRIGGS COLLECTION.

musicians, it is difficult to imagine him in their rough-edged company.

Beiderbecke became known for his lyrical, well-constructed solos and distinctive tone. (His notes, said his friend Hoagy Carmichael, "weren't blown—they were hit, like a mallet strikes a chime.") And he made a series of influential recordings—perhaps none more revered by musicians than *Riverboat Shuffle*; *I'm Coming, Virginia*; and especially *Singin' the Blues* (*JTSA* Disc 1/Track 7), all with Frank Trumbauer's band in 1927. But his recording career was brief. Though Beiderbecke was both talented and sweet-natured, he had little capacity for dealing with day-to-day living. Saxophonist Trumbauer, who met Beiderbecke while they were with the **Jean Goldkette** band, tried to be a father figure to him, but it was a losing battle. Time ran out for Beiderbecke and he died, alone, of acute alcoholism in 1931 at the age of 28.

sound of the orchestra. He also developed a devastating **tremolo** on the keyboard to imitate the vibrato of a wind instrument.

From 1926 to 1928 Hines and Louis Armstrong were musically joined at the hip, recording a series of small-group masterpieces under the banner of the resuscitated Hot Five. Their output included one of the greatest jazz records of all time, *West End Blues*, with Armstrong's breathtaking opening cadenza, and culminated in their brilliant and assured duet *Weather Bird* (both 1928; listen to *West End Blues* by Louis Armstrong, CD I, Track 11/Download Track 11, and *Weather Bird* by Earl Hines and Louis Armstrong, *JTSA* Disc 1/Track 12).

As the Great Depression unfolded, Chicago underwent a transformation. Money dried up, gangster Al Capone's stranglehold on Chicago was broken by federal tax laws, Prohibition was repealed, and a new type of club rose from the ashes, while the surviving ballrooms were taken over by legitimate businessmen who favored the **sweet bands** of such leaders as Hal Kemp, Don Bestor, or Guy Lombardo. Jazz continued to thrive, but a new set of players arrived on the scene, and most of the older ones either retired or moved on to other cities.

((•—[Hear] a profile of Earl Hines on **mymusiclab.com**

TAKE NOTE

• How did jazz develop in Chicago in the 1920s, and who were some of its key players?

Kansas City

Like a seedling planted in fertile soil, jazz burst into opulence in the fecund atmosphere of Kansas City, Missouri. Because of the city's economic importance, bands from all over the South and Southwest, the Great Plains, and the Midwest passed through, some to play local dates, others to use the city as a stopover where they indulged in fierce **cutting contests** with local

---

tremolo dynamic effect achieved by rapid alternation of a note's loudness levels.

sweet bands a term, often used derogatorily in jazz, from the 1920s and 1930s to denote commercial dance bands that featured minimal improvisation—the opposite of *hot bands*.

cutting contest in jazz, the practice of two or more pianists or bands competing with each other, each taking turns, to determine the winner; common in early New Orleans jazz and among Harlem pianists of the 1920s and 1930s; also called a "carving contest."

Bennie Moten (in black) led the most successful band in Kansas City in the 1920s. In 1931, it included Bill (later "Count") Basie (second from the left), "Hot Lips" Page (third from the left), Eddie Durham (front, sixth from the left), and Jimmy Rushing (top right). PHOTO COURTESY AMERICAN JAZZ MUSEUM/18TH & VINE.

Pianist Bill Basie followed his tenure in the Moten band by forming his own outfit and taking the nickname "Count." PHOTO COURTESY WILLIAM P. GOTTLIEB/ WILLIAM P. GOTTLIEB COLLECTION/LIBRARY OF CONGRESS PRINTS & PHOTOGRAPHS DIVISION.

musicians. Kansas City became known for a style of big-band jazz steeped in the blues of the South and old Southwest and rich with riffs and rhythmic drive.

Kansas City jazz thrived in a setting not unlike that of Prohibition-era Chicago. The city's nightlife— its unbridled vitality assured by the fact that it lined the pockets of political boss Tom Pendergast—spilled forth in such storied clubs as the Reno, Hey-Hay, Cherry Blossom, Harlem Club, Lucille's Band Box, and Sunset Crystal Palace. "Most of the [Kansas City] nightspots were run by politicians and hoodlums, and the town was wide open for drinking, gambling, and pretty much every form of vice," recalled pianist **Mary Lou Williams**. "Naturally, work was plentiful for musicians."

The biggest name in Kansas City in the 1920s was that of pianist **Bennie Moten.** Born in 1894, he studied with former pupils of composer Scott Joplin and began playing in the city as early as 1916. By the mid-1920s he had the most successful band in town, with whom he made many recordings for the Victor Company. His records from the 1926–28 period, such as *Kansas City Shuffle* (1926) and *South* (1928), employ a heavy, rolling rhythm, prominent banjo and tuba, and novelty effects. Although the Moten band was immensely popular in Kansas City and attracted

big crowds on the road, its music was old-fashioned even for its time. In 1928, Moten staged a battle of the bands with **Walter Page's Blue Devils** and was so impressed by the latter group that he hired away trumpeter Oran "Hot Lips" Page and vocalist **Jimmy Rushing**. Later, a young pianist from Red Bank, New Jersey, by the name of **William (later "Count") Basie** took over the piano chair, leaving Moten to concentrate on leading. These and other personnel changes, including the additions of trombonist Eddie Durham, bassist Walter Page, and tenorman Ben Webster, transformed Moten's band into a powerhouse. The band's final session came in 1932 when, broke and hungry, it crashed Victor Records' studios in Camden, New Jersey, and recorded 10 tunes, including *Toby, Lafayette,* and *Moten Swing* (*JTSA* Disc 1/Track 16). These recordings—which capture the band's swinging rhythm section (featuring Basie), "horizontal" flow of rhythm, exciting breakneck tempos, and impressive virtuosity—exploded off the records in much the same way as the first Parker-Gillespie sides would in the next decade. Although these last Moten discs sold abysmally on their first release, their ultimate influence brought the 1930s into the swing era. Basie would prove a dominant figure in that era with his own band, composed in part of former Moten sidemen.

The George Lee Orchestra, one of the top Kansas City bands of the 1920s, with Lee (fourth from the left) on saxophone and his sister Julia on piano (shown here in 1926). PHOTO COURTESY FRANK DRIGGS COLLECTION.

Another prominent group in Kansas City was that of George E. Lee, a singer who had learned to play saxophone after military service. His band, with his sister Julia on piano and vocals, can be heard on *Paseo Street* and *Won't You Come Over to My House?* (both 1929). Julia possessed an earthy, full-throated delivery and a mean left hand, but she wasn't to achieve full recognition until the 1940s, when she made the West Coast her home.

Kansas City also served as the base for the band of **Andy Kirk**. In 1929 he hired the beautiful, willowy Mary Lou Williams, whose fragile appearance belied hands that could leave other pianists in the dust. She also possessed a keen musical intelligence; such Williams arrangements as *Mess-a-Stomp* (1929), *Walkin' and Swingin'* (1936), and *A Mellow Bit of Rhythm* (1937)—with their combination of drive and subtlety—would make the Kirk outfit one of the top bands of the mid-1930s. Her vital contribution to the Kirk ensemble would be aptly celebrated in their 1936 recording *The Lady Who Swings the Band*.

TAKE NOTE

• What distinguished Kansas City jazz from other regional styles during the 1920s and early 1930s?

New York City

If Chicago and Kansas City were the nation's cultural mixing bowls, New York City was the full store of ingredients. Immigrants from almost every country on earth streamed through Ellis Island until its closure in 1954, bringing their music with them as a reminder of the Old Country and incorporating it into the strains of other nationalities.

At the same time, New York hosted a growing black population, fueled, during World War I, by a massive migration from the southern states. By the 1920s, African American cultural life had found its center in the Harlem section of uptown Manhattan, and in that decade—during what is now called the

Harlem Renaissance—music, entertainment, literature, and art were thriving.

But early New York jazz owed as much to Italians and Jews as it did to blacks. Manhattan's Jewish ghetto on the Lower East Side was one of the most densely populated areas on earth, while on the southernmost tip of the island Irish and Italians lived cheek by jowl in far from harmonious conditions. Yet harmony emerged. One of the earliest New York jazz bands, the Original Memphis Five, was composed of three Italians, a Jew, and a white Protestant. All New Yorkers, they took the name from W.C. Handy's 1912 standard *Memphis Blues*. This frequently recorded group, under the leadership of trumpeter Phil Napoleon, favored contemporary pop tunes that would appeal to the general public, with carefully tailored solo passages. Their later recordings, including *Fireworks* (1928) and *Kansas City Kitty*

👁 **Watch** a documentary on Harlem on **mymusiclab.com**

Pianist, arranger, and bandleader Fletcher Henderson. PHOTO COURTESY DOWN BEAT ARCHIVES.

(1929), both of which featured Napoleon's strong trumpet and Tommy Dorsey's trombone, are particularly appealing.

Henderson, Hawkins, Armstrong, and Bechet

The first important big band was led by Fletcher Henderson, a classically trained pianist from Georgia. Henderson eventually became known as one of the fathers of the swing big-band sound, but his earliest recordings, such as *Dicty Blues* (1923) and *Teapot Dome Blues* (1924), are remembered primarily for the contributions of such outstanding musicians as alto saxophonist Don Redman and tenorman **Coleman Hawkins**.

Hawkins was a pioneer of his instrument; prior to his arrival on the scene, the saxophone (usually the alto or C-melody sax) was employed as a novelty instrument in dance orchestras. Hawkins kept some of the flashiness but combined it with ferocious, stop-time

The Lafayette, at 131ˢᵗ Street in Harlem, hosted 1927's Jazzmania *revue featuring Duke Ellington.*
PHOTO COURTESY FRANK DRIGGS COLLECTION.

bombs; a lyrical, romantic approach on slow tempos; and, above all, a sense of swing hitherto unheard on the instrument. His solos with Henderson (*The Stampede*, 1926 [*JTSA* Disc 1/Track 4]; *Wherever There's a Will, Baby*, 1929; and *It's the Talk of the Town*, 1933) influenced an entire generation of tenor reedmen, and his fat tone remained the ideal until Lester Young, in the late 1930s, pioneered a light, airy sound.

Late in 1924, Henderson—who had just begun what would become a long-running association with New York's Roseland Ballroom—hired Louis Armstrong away from King Oliver. Armstrong was the alchemist who turned a collection of first-rate but disparate ingredients into gold. His clarion sound, swinging rhythm, and natural genius, evident in his solos on *Shanghai Shuffle* (1924), *When You Do What You Do* (1925), and *Sugar Foot Stomp* (1925), cloaked the Henderson band in a sheen of brilliance that lasted even after Armstrong returned to Chicago in 1925. Right into the early 1930s, on such recordings as *D Natural Blues* (1928), *Comin' and Going* (1931), and *Queer Notions* (1933). Henderson's was the premier black band, often challenged but never vanquished, despite numerous personnel changes. Its ultimate demise was due to its lack of a top-notch manager and its leader's

decreasing ambition, probably caused by the aftereffects of a serious car accident in 1928.

Louis Armstrong's and Coleman Hawkins's chief rival in the mid-1920s was the brash soprano saxophonist Sidney Bechet. He was away from the U.S. music scene for long periods and during the Depression retired temporarily, opening a tailor's shop in Harlem with Henderson alumnus Tommy Ladnier. That hiatus, and Bechet's adherence to the notoriously difficult soprano saxophone, have led him to be overlooked by some jazz historians. Few jazz musicians even attempted to make the soprano sax their instrument of choice in the 1920s. Johnny Hodges (with Ellington) and Charlie Holmes (with Luis Russell) occasionally employed it in solo work, but both preferred the more stable alto sax. Bechet, perhaps mindful of the soprano's tendency to go out of tune, used it like a blowtorch. So strong was his attack that on most small-group recordings he dominated even the brass instruments.

Armstrong was one of the few who could take him on head to head. Some of Bechet's best work (and some of the most exciting jazz ever recorded) are his records with Armstrong under the leadership of pianist-composer Clarence Williams, including *Texas Moaner Blues* (1924) and *Santa Claus Blues* (1925). Armstrong and Bechet did not like one another; their work together resembles a shootout rather than a cutting contest. Probably their finest effort is Williams's OKeh version of *Cake Walking Babies from Home* (1925), in which, still keeping the traditional New Orleans format, they weave and intertwine; it's like a death battle between a cobra and a mongoose, set to music. Some find Bechet more acceptable in a big-band setting, where his aggression fuels the excitement rather than upsets the balance, as some feel it did in a small group. He is arguably at his best with the Noble Sissle Orchestra on such tracks as *The Basement Blues* and *Roll On, Mississippi, Roll On* (both 1931).

Prominent White Bandleaders and Players

In the first five years of the 1920s, the two most prominent white bands were **Paul Whiteman's** orchestra and Ed Kirkeby's California Ramblers. Whiteman was a Denver-born violinist who laid aside his instrument for a baton. He matched an imposing presence on the bandstand—he was tall and heavily built—with a mastery of self-promotion. He soon became known as the "King of Jazz": he didn't believe the hype, but the public did.

Whiteman did recognize talent in others. He helped advance the career of composer **George Gershwin**, staging the first public performance of his *Rhapsody in Blue* at

Saxophonist Johnny Hodges, a mainstay of the Ellington band.
PHOTO COURTESY FRANK DRIGGS COLLECTION.

---

bomb a pronounced or unexpected accent, most typically on a bass drum.

a famous 1924 concert at New York's Aeolian Hall and recording many of his early compositions. But his band was stilted and fussy and its arrangements pretentious. It wasn't until 1927, when he hired a number of musicians from the defunct Jean Goldkette Orchestra and added arrangers Tom Satterfield, Bill Challis, and William Grant Still, that jazz could be applied to the name of Whiteman. His biggest coup was acquiring from the Goldkette band those disparate but inseparable musical twins, cornetist Bix Beiderbecke and saxman Frank Trumbauer. The former was pure blazing heat with an unearthly tone; the latter cool and languid, with a vibratoless tone and phrasing that oddly predated the bebop players of the 1940s. Whiteman's augmented personnel produced his greatest recordings of this, or any other era, including *Changes* (1927), *From Monday On* (1928; *JTSA* Disc 1/Track 10), and *Louisiana* (1928).

The California Ramblers, led by former recording executive Wallace T. "Ed" Kirkeby and anchored by the massive bass saxophone of Adrian Rollini, packed its repertoire with ephemeral pop tunes and novelty items—including *She Knows Her Onions* (1926) and *Crazy Words, Crazy Tune* (1927)—and became immensely popular with the fast college crowd. Despite the superficiality of the Ramblers's output, Kirkeby filled the band with top white jazz players of the period. In 1930 trumpeter Jack Purvis joined the band. A blazing talent who spent much of his life in prison, he electrified such otherwise mundane dance records as *Charming* and *The Stein Song* (both 1930). Heard today, the sides hint at what the Jay Gatsby crowd might have danced to in West Egg.

In the middle and late 1920s, the finest white musicians held lucrative jobs playing dance music in hotel bands or radio house orchestras. Trombonist Tommy Dorsey and his reedman brother, Jimmy, worked with Fred Rich's Astor Hotel band; **Joe Venuti**, **Eddie Lang**, Miff Mole, and Fud Livingston were with Roger Wolfe Kahn; and **Red Nichols** was with CBS's Don Voorhees.

Violinist Guiseppe "Joe" Venuti had a short fuse and a penchant for practical jokes that made him a liability in the eyes of some orchestra leaders. He collaborated with guitarist Eddie Lang on a series of remarkable duet and small-group recordings—including *Stringin' the Blues* (1926) and *My Honey's Loving Arms* (1928)—that amply displayed his rich tone and facile technique and made him the first to gain the violin acceptance as a jazz instrument. Lang was known for his single-string solos and his consummate accompanying, favored by such top vocalists as Bing Crosby. He also recorded guitar duets with bluesman **Lonnie Johnson**, including *Handful of Riffs* (1928; *JTSA* Disc 1/Track 14) and *Bullfrog Moan* (1929).

Many of these musicians supplemented their regular incomes with freelance jazz record dates under various names—some real, some fictitious. Most of the lucrative

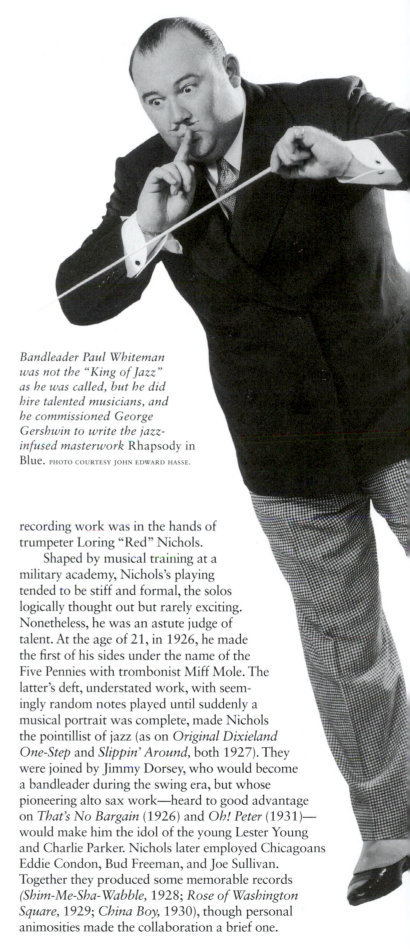

Bandleader Paul Whiteman was not the "King of Jazz" as he was called, but he did hire talented musicians, and he commissioned George Gershwin to write the jazz-infused masterwork Rhapsody in Blue. PHOTO COURTESY JOHN EDWARD HASSE.

recording work was in the hands of trumpeter Loring "Red" Nichols.

Shaped by musical training at a military academy, Nichols's playing tended to be stiff and formal, the solos logically thought out but rarely exciting. Nonetheless, he was an astute judge of talent. At the age of 21, in 1926, he made the first of his sides under the name of the Five Pennies with trombonist Miff Mole. The latter's deft, understated work, with seemingly random notes played until suddenly a musical portrait was complete, made Nichols the pointillist of jazz (as on *Original Dixieland One-Step* and *Slippin' Around*, both 1927). They were joined by Jimmy Dorsey, who would become a bandleader during the swing era, but whose pioneering alto sax work—heard to good advantage on *That's No Bargain* (1926) and *Oh! Peter* (1931)—would make him the idol of the young Lester Young and Charlie Parker. Nichols later employed Chicagoans Eddie Condon, Bud Freeman, and Joe Sullivan. Together they produced some memorable records *(Shim-Me-Sha-Wabble*, 1928; *Rose of Washington Square*, 1929; *China Boy*, 1930), though personal animosities made the collaboration a brief one.

Jazz and Classical Music: The First Half of the Twentieth Century

In 1895, when Antonin Dvořák heard the future of American music in "negro melodies and Indian chants," the "negro melodies" he had in mind were spirituals, not ragtime or jazz. Yet Dvořák proved remarkably prescient. Much of the vitality and many of the "American" qualities of twentieth-century classical music have links to "negro melodies" (and rhythms), and the reason for this link is jazz.

The seeds were sown in the ragtime era. Among the composers taking Dvořák's charge to heart, Henry Gilbert stands out as the most committed, with a series of works spanning two decades, including *The Dance in Place Congo* (1908). Charles Ives alludes to ragtime in a few works, most notably *Central Park in the Dark* (1906), featuring a "ragtime war" leading to a cacophonous climax. Meanwhile, Scott Joplin, the "King of Ragtime Writers" after the publication of his *Maple Leaf Rag* (1899), strove to compose in larger European forms and realized his dream in the operas *The Guest of Honor* (1903) and *Treemonisha* (1911).

When jazz and blues began to reach larger audiences in the late 1910s and early 1920s, composers for the concert hall were quick to respond. In fact, jazz was soon enlisted in the effort to define a modern American classical music. Jazz was nothing less than "the voice of the American soul," as George Gershwin put it. The Chicago composer John Alden Carpenter made an early impact with his "jazz pantomime," *Krazy Kat* (1921), based on a popular comic strip, and with his ballet *Skyscrapers* (1924).

But the key figure was Gershwin. Despite success and wealth as a composer of popular songs and Broadway shows, this Brooklyn-born son of Russian-Jewish immigrants wanted to be taken seriously. With *Rhapsody in Blue* (1924), commissioned by Paul Whiteman, Gershwin put the classical music world on notice that he had arrived. From the opening, siren-like yawp of the solo clarinet, to the blues-drenched melodies and infectious rhythms—all embedded in a conception heavily indebted to nineteenth-century European Romantics such as Franz Liszt—Gershwin threw down the gauntlet for American composers seeking a distinctively modernist American idiom.

As if taking up Gershwin's challenge, Aaron Copland (another native Brooklynite of Russian-Jewish parentage) answered with his own *Piano Concerto* (1926), whose two movements illustrated what Copland believed to be the two moods of jazz, "the blues and the snappy number." Copland had already engaged jazz in such works as *Music for the Theater* (1925), but *Piano Concerto* raised the stakes, as it was premiered by the prestigious Boston Symphony Orchestra under the direction of the great conductor Serge Koussevitsky.

Gershwin and Copland thrived in an era that espoused the notion that Jewish musicians were the leading "jazz composers," assuming the "primitive" noise of black improvisers served chiefly as raw material for the refined product heard in the concert hall. The tables have turned, of course. The narratives of jazz history now tend to relegate the composers to a sidebar,

George Gershwin composed such jazz-inflected concert works as Rhapsody in Blue *(1924) and* Porgy and Bess *(1935).*
PHOTO COURTESY FRANK DRIGGS COLLECTION.

at best, among the appropriators of "authentic" jazz.

Meanwhile, several European composers found in jazz a bracing medium through which to escape the burdensome weight of Teutonic Romanticism. The impulse was especially strong in France. Erik Satie ignited interest with his unique ballet *Parade* (1917). Darius Milhaud soon followed with his own ballet score, *La Creation du Monde* (1923), featuring a jazzy blues theme as a fugue subject. And Maurice Ravel embraced jazz in the "Blues" movement of his *Sonata for Violin and Piano* (1927) and a piano concerto. Igor Stravinsky also captured the new spirit in such works as *Ragtime* (1919) and, after he emigrated to America, the *Ebony Concerto* (1945), composed for Woody Herman's big band.

—*Jeffrey Magee*

Duke Ellington was an extremely influential and prolific composer and arranger, as well as a gifted soloist and pianist, whose career spanned six decades. Even though the main traits of swing-era dance music are present in his work, there is great variety and depth in his music. He went beyond the confines of swing style by exploring innovative orchestration and extended compositional

✳ Explore on **mymusiclab.com**

forms. This photo shows Ellington's band in about 1940. Many of his musicians worked with him for two or three decades, and he made a point of showcasing their unique talents in his compositions.

—*Jeff Rupert*

Juan Tizol, Joe Nanton, Lawrence Brown (l. to r.) • Trombones

The trombone section of swing-era big bands contained usually two to three musicians. Trombone and trumpet players formed the brass section. Typical big band arrangements used the sax and brass sections as the two main melodic voices. These two groups were used prominently in call-and-response sections, but Ellington was unconventional and liked to voice instruments *across* sections.

Sonny Greer • Drums

Drums in swing-era big bands were mostly timekeepers so that the beat could be better communicated to dancers. The use of hi-hat cymbals was introduced during this period. Drummer Sonny Greer worked with Duke Ellington for 31 years.

Johnny Hodges, Ben Webster, Otto Hardwick, Harry Carney (l. to r.) • Alto, Baritone, Tenor Saxes

The sax section contained three to five reed players, some often doubling on clarinet. Individual players would also be featured soloists.

Wallace Jones, Cootie Williams • Trumpets

The trumpet section of swing-era big bands contained two to five musicians, usually three.

PHOTO COURTESY MICHAEL OCHS ARCHIVES/GETTY IMAGES.

Barney Bigard • Clarinet

One of Ellington's best-known longtime collaborators, Barney Bigard also doubled on sax, the instrument he's holding here. However, his best solo work was as a clarinetist.

Duke Ellington • Piano

Pianists in swing-era big bands were not limited to playing chords and embellishments, but could also play melody. The rhythmic style of accompaniment included stride and occasionally "comping," a way of playing chords in improvised, flexible syncopated rhythms that complement and interact with the soloist. Ellington used stride style in his early years, but thereafter developed his own, sometimes percussive, original style.

Fred Guy, Jimmie Blanton • Guitar, Bass

Guitarists and bassists in this era were primarily timekeepers. They mostly played a "two-feel" (playing on the first and third beat of a bar) or a "walking" bassline (playing on all four beats).

Rex Stewart • Cornet

The cornet, an instrument that was losing its popularity during the swing era, is sonically almost indistinguishable from the trumpet.

In 1928 a new star hit town. Trombonist **Jack Teagarden** came roaring in from Texas like an uncapped oil well and set the town on its ear. If Miff Mole was the Seurat of jazz, Teagarden was Gauguin, all exotic colorings and broad sensual tones, as on *Knockin' a Jug* with Louis Armstrong (1929) and *Makin' Friends* under the name of the Whoopee Makers (1930). He became a fixture at the Park Central Hotel with Ben Pollack's Orchestra, alongside clarinetist Benny Goodman, trumpeter Jimmy McPartland, and trombonist Glenn Miller. Drummer Pollack was another impeccable judge of talent, and his 1933 orchestra formed the nucleus of the outstanding Bob Crosby big band.

Harlem and the Cotton Club

New York during the period 1926–30 hosted what may have been the richest cultural life in North America. Theater, literature, art, and music flourished as never before or since. Broadway theater alone served as the stomping ground for playwright Eugene O'Neill; actors Alfred Lunt, Lynne Fontanne, and the Barrymores; and songwriters Jerome Kern, George and Ira Gershwin, Richard Rodgers and Lorenz Hart, Cole Porter, Harold Arlen, and Dorothy Fields and Jimmy McHugh.

Much of New York City's cultural glow emanated from Harlem, and Broadway's leading lights had a way of sneaking uptown incognito, uninvited but not unwelcome. The Harlem clubs may not have been as sumptuous as those downtown, but the music more than compensated for the lack of silk brocade. The Savoy Ballroom opened in 1926, and blacks and whites happily mingled there, much to the chagrin of the authorities. The equally famous Cotton Club had a white-patrons-only policy, and the socialites flocked there.

Before his Cotton Club tenure, Duke Ellington led a smaller group at the Kentucky Club in midtown Manhattan. His first recordings (*Trombone Blues*, 1925; *Li'l Farina*, 1926) show little indication of what was to come. But once he signed with Columbia and Victor he quickly embraced the new electrical recording techniques that permitted clearer, more detailed sound. The results included such beautifully realized tracks as *East St. Louis Toodle-Oo* (1926) and *Black and Tan Fantasy* (1927).

Ellington's move to the Cotton Club in December 1927 was the break of a lifetime for the young Washingtonian. Taking advantage of the sophisticated clientele, the first-class floor shows, and the media coverage, he shrewdly combined Fields-McHugh tunes written for the club revues (*Freeze and Melt*, 1928; *Hot Feet* and *Arabian Lover*, both 1929) with his own three-minute masterpieces (*Black Beauty*, *Creole Love Call*, both 1927, and *The Mooche*, 1928) and further broadened his fan base by recording for every major record label, under a barrage of pseudonyms. Ellington has been rightly acclaimed as one of this century's greatest composers—for his distinctive harmonic language and tonal palette, among many other attributes—but not enough tribute has been paid to his genius for shaping an orchestra as a showcase for his work, penning arrangements to highlight his soloists' strengths, and hiring musicians from other bands only to totally retool their styles to suit his needs.

A case in point is his transformation of conventional soloists Bubber Miley and Cootie Williams (trumpets) and Joe "Tricky Sam" Nanton (trombone) into masters of the mute. Other beneficiaries of the Ellington touch include Lawrence Brown, an unheralded musician with the Los Angeles-based Paul Howard Orchestra, whom Ellington helped transform into the most lyrical of trombone soloists (*The Sheik of Araby*, 1932), and Albany "Barney" Bigard, whose work with the 1926–27 King Oliver band barely merits a second listen yet whose liquid, New Orleans clarinet Ellington used to perfection in such classics as *Mood Indigo* (1930) and *Slippery Horn* (1932). Few of Ellington's soloists who moved on ever duplicated the successes of their time with him.

Ellington, under the management of Irving Mills, stayed at the Cotton Club for three years, until February 1931, when he and his band began non-stop touring. During an absence in 1930 when he and his orchestra went to Hollywood to be featured in RKO's Amos and Andy film *Check and Double Check*, they were replaced by the singer-showman **Cab Calloway**.

Beyond the Cotton Club

Another Irving Mills-managed group, the Blue Rhythm Band, was assigned the role of benchwarmer at the Cotton Club, standing in for Ellington, Calloway, Henderson, and other Harlem big bands when they were playing on the road. While the Blue Rhythm Band lacked great soloists (except for the pianist, Edgar Hayes), it had a gritty brass section that snarled its way through such tunes as *Blue Rhythm* and *Levee Low Down* (both 1931).

Watch the documentary on Duke Ellington on **mymusiclab.com**

The Ellington orchestra accompanies Ethel Waters at the Cotton Club, 1933. PHOTO COURTESY FRANK DRIGGS COLLECTION.

The Cotton Club

Harlem's nightlife became a magnet in the 1920s, and one of its greatest attractions was the Cotton Club.

Of New York City's illegal drinking establishments, numbering an estimated 32,000 to 100,000, the Cotton Club was a standout. Its owners were gangsters. The employees were black. The customers were white. And the entertainment included a heady mix of dancing, vaudeville, and such musicians-on-the-rise as Duke Ellington and Cab Calloway.

Located on 142nd Street near Lenox Avenue, the Cotton Club opened in the fall of 1923. It had a log-cabin exterior and interior and featured jungle décor, a proscenium stage, and a dance floor.

Cab Calloway, who first performed there in 1930, vividly recalled the venue as "a huge room. The bandstand was a replica of a southern mansion with large white columns and a backdrop painted with weeping willows and slave quarters. . . . The waiters were dressed in red tuxedos, the butlers in a southern mansion, and . . . there were huge cut-crystal chandeliers."

During Ellington's tenure, which began in 1927, the club typically opened at 10 p.m. and closed at 3 a.m. Showtimes were specifically designed to attract a high-spending, after-theater crowd.

"There were brutes at the door," observed writer and cultural critic Carl Van Vechten, "to enforce the Cotton Club's policy which was opposed to [racially] mixed parties." Occasionally, a star black performer such as singer Ethel Waters or dancer Bill "Bojangles" Robinson could get a table for friends.

Beginning in 1926, the shows were staged and produced by singer, dancer, and comic Dan Healy. Jimmy McHugh wrote the songs, usually with lyricist Dorothy Fields, through 1928.

The performers' costumes were sensational, as Calloway observed: "The soloists, dancers, and singers were always dressed to the hilt—the women in long flowing gowns, if that was appropriate, or in the briefest of brief dance costumes. . . . Low cut and very, very risqué." The cast could be large. The spring 1929 revue had 30 in the company, plus Ellington's orchestra.

The Cotton Club's shows were sensational. And the club also exposed whites to African American culture—a rarity at a time when such opportunities were circumscribed in many ways. What's more, the club provided Ellington with an opportunity to work out many important musical ideas, and, via its radio broadcasts, to reach a national audience.

The original club closed in 1936. Late that year, the owners opened a new Cotton Club in the heart of the downtown theater district at 48th Street, but the club closed in 1940.

—*John Edward Hasse*

Listening Guide

Listen to *Black and Tan Fantasy* by The Washingtonians (Duke Ellington and His Orchestra) on **mymusiclab.com**
CD I, Track 10/Download Track 10

BLACK AND TAN FANTASY • THE WASHINGTONIANS (DUKE ELLINGTON AND HIS ORCHESTRA)

Music: Duke Ellington and Bubber Miley, 1927. Personnel: Bubber Miley, Louis Metcalf (trumpet); Joe "Tricky Sam" Nanton (trombone); Otto Hardwick (alto saxophone); Rudy Jackson (tenor saxophone); Harry Carney (baritone saxophone); Duke Ellington (piano, leader); Fred Guy (banjo); Wellman Braud (bass); Sonny Greer (drums). Recorded October 26, 1927, in Camden, New Jersey. First issue: Victor 21137. Timing: 3:06.

Overview

In the 1920s, many nightclubs, even in the north, permitted only whites to attend. "Black and tan" was the name given to speakeasies—in such places as Harlem and Chicago's Bronzeville—which blacks and whites could both frequent, though their interaction was socially stylized. *Black and Tan Fantasy*, composed by Duke Ellington and his star trumpeter, Bubber Miley, can be interpreted as a mournful prayer, a biting commentary, or an unusual satire about the state of black–white relations during the Jazz Age.

At the time of this recording, Ellington was in the early years of his career, on his way to becoming arguably America's greatest *all-around* musician—composer, orchestrator–arranger, bandleader–conductor, accompanist, and pianist.

His growing genius lay partly in his relationships with his musicians. Deeply appreciating the value of individuality and stylistic diversity, Ellington sought out musicians with distinctive, personal sounds on their instruments. He learned their strengths and weaknesses, and composed for them in ways that avoided their shortcomings and brought out the best that each had to offer. He composed not for the instrument, but for the specific person playing the instrument in his band. He inspired his players to perform at, or beyond, their best.

Ellington created and led a classic example of what business writer Warren Bennis calls a "great group," in which "the leader finds greatness in the group, and he or she helps the members find it in themselves." In Ellington's case, the inspiration worked both ways—he inspired his players, and they inspired him.

Ellington led one of the great collaborative organizations, and *Black and Tan Fantasy* is a prime example. Bubber Miley—Ellington's greatest soloist of his early years—created the main melody, based on the nineteenth-century hymn *The Holy City*, and Ellington contributed the second theme. The solos of trombonist Joe "Tricky Sam" Nanton and especially Miley help make the recording outstanding, but it took Ellington to put all the pieces together.

A 1929 short film titled *Black and Tan* shows Ellington purportedly working out the theme of *Black and Tan Fantasy* and then the Ellington band performing the work, this time with trumpeter Arthur Whetsol. This remarkable piece helped make Ellington's reputation, and it remained in his repertoire throughout his life.

Recalling the Great Depression years, novelist Ralph Ellison wrote, "And when the *Black and Tan Fantasy* was played we were reminded not only of how fleeting *all* human life must be, but with its blues-based tension between content and manner, it warned us not only to look at the darker side of life but also to remember the enduring necessity for humor, technical mastery, and creative excellence. It was immensely danceable and listenable music and ever so evocative of other troubled times and other triumphs over disaster. It was also most Negro American in its mocking interpolations from Chopin's B-flat minor piano sonata. . . ."

Key Features

- Form: A 12-bar blues form with a 16-bar verse. After the single statement of the verse, the rest of the piece consists of choruses of 12-bar blues.
- Tempo: A slow-to-moderate dance tempo, at 120 beats per minute.
- Personnel: Ellington's band at this time included 10 players. In the 1920s and 1930s, Ellington kept enlarging his band: each time he added personnel, it gave him more tone colors with which to compose and arrange.
- Tone colors: The solos by Miley and Nanton are rife with vocal inflections—bent notes, slurs, wah-wahs, growls—thus humanizing their brass instruments.
- Contrast: Ellington was a master at integrating opposites into an aesthetically satisfying whole. In this classic recording, he integrates the familiar (*The Holy City* and a bit of Chopin's *Funeral March*) with the unfamiliar (the brand-new second theme and the solos). He juxtaposes and integrates the two divergent themes—a minor-key (somber, moaning, sacred-rooted) theme and a major-key (jaunty, urbane, secular) theme. It's not only the very different melodic lines that create contrast, it's also the orchestration: Ellington assigns the dark main theme to Miley and Nanton, playing muted horns, and gives the second, much lighter theme to the silken-toned saxophonist Otto Hardwick. Juxtaposed between the vocal-inflected solos of Miley and Nanton is Ellington's buoyant piano solo.
- Signifying: Because of the way Ellington reuses the preexisting themes of *The Holy City* (as filtered by Miley) and Chopin's *Funeral March*, *Black and Tan*

Fantasy can be interpreted as an example of the African American practice of **signifying**—what Henry Louis Gates called "repetition with a signal difference."

- Solos: Nanton and Ellington each deliver satisfying solos. Miley's three solo choruses are, however, the highlights of the piece. His first solo (0:57) opens dramatically with a soft, high B-flat held for four bars—presaging a similar solo-opening gesture with the same note made by Louis Armstrong in his famous *West End Blues* eight months later. In his majestically constructed first solo, Miley—a master of tone colors and showmanship—demonstrates his gifts as Ellington's best soloist of this period. Who else would open with a four-measure-long high B-flat and then break loose into a bluesy and dirty—yet measured and beautiful—creation? Miley's solo ranks as one of the greatest plunger-mute trumpet solos ever recorded.

—*John Edward Hasse*

TIME	FORM	MELODY	INSTRUMENTATION	HARMONY (KEY)
0:00	CHORUS 1	The tune begins, without introduction or fanfare, with Miley and Nanton, tightly muted, moaning the haunting blues melody that echoes the traditional hymn *The Holy City*.	Muted trumpet and trombone.	B-flat minor.
0:24		Sonny Greer crashes his cymbals to announce the end of one section and the beginning of another.	Cymbal.	
0:25	VERSE	Otto Hardwick plays the contrasting second theme in a sweet style. After six bars, the band answers.	Alto saxophone.	B-flat major.
0:41		The second phrase (eight bars) of the verse begins. After six bars, the band answers differently.		
0:55		Greer's three cymbal crashes punctuate the end of this section.	Cymbal.	
0:57	CHORUS 2	Miley's trumpet solo begins dramatically with a B-flat held for four measures.	Trumpet.	
1:05		Miley contrasts the relative calm of his long held note with an active, blues-drenched, vocalized line.		
1:21	CHORUS 3	Miley continues his beautifully constructed solo.		
1:25		Miley adds a growling effect to enhance the texture and tone color.		
1:46	CHORUS 4	Duke Ellington plays an amiable solo in stride piano style.	Unaccompanied piano.	
2:05		Ellington plays a passage of "trick" or offbeat left hand.		
2:09	CHORUS 5	Tricky Sam Nanton begins his solo with his trombone muted tightly.	Trombone, tightly muted.	
2:13		Nanton eases his mute to increase the volume and intensity of his sound. Nanton peppers his entire solo with vocal-like wah-wah effects.	Trombone, less muted.	
2:24		Nanton interjects a horse whinny.		
2:33	CHORUS 6	Bubber Miley opens his second solo with a rapid-fire succession of B-flat notes, an octave lower than the long B-flat he held in chorus 2.	Plunger-muted trumpet.	
2:37		In a call-and-response, the rhythm section answers Miley with an exclamation point.	Rhythm section.	
2:41		Another exclamation point from the rhythm section. The chorus is abbreviated to 10 bars.		
2:54	CODA	In a four-bar coda, Miley and the band play a quotation from Chopin's *Funeral March*, ending the piece, as they began, in a minor key.	Trumpet and orchestra.	B-flat minor.

signify an African American rhetorical device featuring indirect communication or persuasion and the creating of new meanings for old words and signs; or in the words of Henry Louis Gates, "repetition with a signal difference."

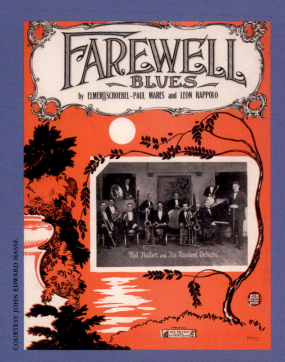

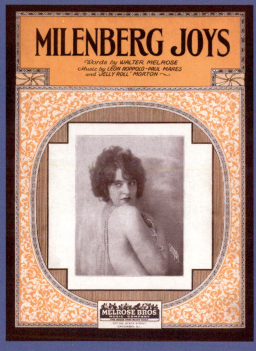

for musicians to cluster around a large acoustic horn used to capture sound, opened up new possibilities. On records, reed sections evolved from mud to clearly delineated instruments, strings became crystal-clear, and the grunting tuba and cutting banjo were replaced by the more flexible string bass and guitar.

By the second half of the decade, jazz arranging was beginning to emerge, in the scoring for Fletcher Henderson's band by Don Redman (*Copenhagen*, 1924); by Henderson himself (*King Porter Stomp*, 1928); by Benny Carter (*Keep a Song in Your Soul*, 1930); and in John Nesbitt's work for McKinney's Cotton Pickers (*Put It There*, 1928). Redman is widely credited for pioneering the clarinet trio scoring in jazz. When questioned years later, Redman laughed and said, "Oh, I stole that—from the polka bands."

Other arrangers included Bill Challis (who scored for Whiteman, as on *Changes*, 1927) and reedman Walter "Fud" Livingston, noted for angularity (Frank Trumbauer's *Humpty Dumpty*, 1927) and a preference for stop chords, in which staccato phrasing and sudden changes of key were employed to build excitement (*Oh! Baby*, 1928). His technique was also favored by Don Redman and adopted in the early work of Livingston's prodigy, Glenn Miller. The flowering of the big bands in the 1930s saw jazz arranging come into its own as a vital addition to the big-band sound.

TAKE NOTE

- What role did arrangers play in creating the sound of early jazz bands?

Regional Bands

Every major city in the country had one or more jazz bands, but aural documentation is sparse. The major record companies had offices and recording studios in New York, Chicago, and Los Angeles, but there was a lot of country in between. All that survives of regional or "territory" bands under the names of Speed Webb, Thamon Hayes, Peck Kelly, Doc Ross, Ligon Smith, Leslie Sheffield, and countless others are fading memories, since they never recorded. The few that did survive were usually confined to one session on a record label's field trip. Examples include Hal Kemp's *Peg-Leg Stomp* (Atlanta, 1926); Jesse Stone's *Boot to Boot* (St. Louis, 1927); and Celestin's Original Tuxedo Jazz Orchestra's *Black Rag* (New Orleans, 1927).

Two **regional bands** that did record prolifically and thus achieved a national following, were the Detroit-based Jean Goldkette Orchestra and McKinney's Cotton Pickers. Both groups used Detroit's gigantic Graystone

the instrumentation of jazz orchestras into choirs of brass, reeds, and a rhythm section. Mostly, orchestra leaders were content to get their **stock arrangements**, while small jazz groups mainly improvised or relied on informal, unwritten "head" arrangements. The introduction of electrical recording in 1925, which employed microphones and thus abolished the need

---

stock arrangement   standard, published orchestration of a tune, used by musicians in lieu of an original interpretation.

regional band   similar to a *territory band*.

Jazz: Musical Virtue or Vice?

Why did some people feel that the new jazz style was "corrupting" music and social morals?

Controversy swirled around jazz almost from its birth. When media commentators weren't decrying it as a "musical vice" *(New Orleans Times-Picayune, 1918)*, others were blaming it for a range of social ills.

"Ellington Refutes Cry That Swing Started Sex Crimes!" blared one *Down Beat* headline in 1937. At issue was a prominent educator's charge that a wave of sexual assaults stemmed from the "hot" jazz that was in vogue at the time.

The debate over jazz was actually a continuation of a long-running war of words about ragtime (see pp. 42–43, Chapter 3). The opponents of ragtime—conservative members of the older generation, people with vested interests in classical music, and defenders of public morality—attacked the music on multiple grounds: its words, its racial (that is, African American) origins, and its supposed perils. "In Christian homes," wrote the *Musical Observer* in 1914, "where purity and morals are stressed, ragtime should find no resting place. . . . Let us purge America and the Divine Art of Music from this polluting nuisance."

When jazz became the focus of controversy, traditionalists linked it with sinful sexuality and with public dancing, which in the early 1920s was still controversial. "Moralists," wrote John Edward Hasse, "drew a close link between dancing, loose language, immodest dress, sex, and jazz."

Opposition to the music occurred not just among whites.

In many middle-class black homes, parents opposed jazz and blues as disreputable and even as "the devil's music." Clarinetist Garvin Bushell recalled of the 1920s, "You usually weren't allowed to play blues and boogie-woogie in the average Negro middle-class home. That music supposedly suggested a low element."

But if some saw jazz as "appealing only to the lover of sensuous and debasing emotions" (Lucien White, in *New York Age*, ca. 1921), others saw the music as posing life-threatening danger: in 1936 a series of suicides were attributed to the Billie Holiday song *Gloomy Sunday*, resulting in its being banned from the radio airwaves. Many, apparently, shared a view of jazz as "an atrocity in polite society . . . [with great] possibilities of harm" *(New Orleans Times-Picayune, 1918)* or as "a return to the humming, hand-clapping, or tomtom beating of savages" *(New York Times, 1924)*.

When a U.S. Senate committee conducted an investigation of the American Federation of Musicians' 1942–44 ban on recording, they concluded that "if the ban on recording wipes out jitterbug music, jive, and boogie-woogie, it might be a good thing all around."

But some of the most heated controversy occurred within the jazz community itself. An ongoing point of dissension was any new form of jazz. Musicians often voiced the loudest opposition to the latest styles—or any styles that differed from their own. "Of all the cruelties in the world, bebop is the most phenomenal," Fletcher Henderson said, while Louis Armstrong charged that "bop is

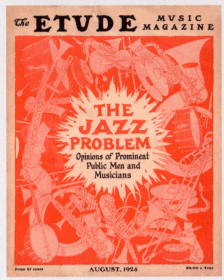

COURTESY JOHN EDWARD HASSE.

ruining music . . . and the kids that play bop are ruining themselves."

Writers did their parts to raise the critical decibel level: in 1961, critic John Tynan decried a free-jazz performance by John Coltrane and Eric Dolphy as "a horrifying demonstration of what appears to be a growing anti-jazz trend . . . Coltrane and Dolphy seem intent on deliberately destroying [swing]. They seem bent on pursuing an anarchistic course in music."

None of the controversy should have been surprising. Jazz was born with a rebellious streak; Alain Locke wrote that jazz represented "a reaction from Puritan repressions . . . an escape from the tensions and monotonies of a machine-ridden . . . form of civilization." If Hoagy Carmichael was right in calling jazz a rejection of "the accepted, the proper, the old," jazz was bound to stir up antipathy among those with a stake in the accepted, the proper, and the old.

—Tad Lathrop

Ballroom as their base and both were under the management of the French-born Goldkette. McKinney's was led by alto saxophonist and arranger Don Redman, who had left Henderson. Although much of the Cotton Pickers' output was dance music and novelty material with commercial vocals (*There's a Rainbow 'Round My Shoulder*, 1928; *Never Swat a Fly*, 1930), the group could play with rhythmic complexity (*Peggy*, 1929); with ensemble precision (*Stop Kidding*, 1928); or with abandon (*Milenberg Joys*, 1928), justifying the claims that on "coloreds-only night" 3,000 people packed the place.

The Goldkette band boasted an array of star jazz soloists—including Beiderbecke, Trumbauer, Venuti, Lang, Tommy and Jimmy Dorsey, and arranger Bill Challis—and on one famous occasion in 1926 even bested Fletcher Henderson's band on its home turf at the Roseland Ballroom in Manhattan. Victor's A&R man confined the Goldkette band's studio dates to commercial fare, leaving only a few recordings—*My Pretty Girl* and *Clementine* (both 1927)—for the annals of jazz.

Goldkette's band broke up in 1927, but 18 months later he took out of Toronto a band called the Orange Blossom Orchestra. The name was changed to the Casa Loma Orchestra, and in the fall of 1929 it went down to play at the Roseland. A recording date was set at OKeh's Union Square studios, and early in the morning of October 29, 1929, a weary band cut its first record date, including *Happy Days Are Here Again*. Meanwhile down on Wall Street the world was ending: it was Black Thursday. The tune became the anthem of the Great Depression and the band one of the harbingers of the swing era.

During the Jazz Age of the 1920s, Louis Armstrong had transformed jazz from a group art into a soloist's art; Morton and Ellington had set the standard for jazz composition; Redman and Henderson had worked out the fundamental format for big-band arrangements; and a varied group of voices—from Bessie Smith to James P. Johnson to Bix Beiderbecke—had established clarion, individual styles that would resonate for decades to come. Jazz, now a widely known style of music, was poised to enter its period of greatest commercial success.

TAKE NOTE

- Why were regional bands important during this period?

 Explore Jazz Classics and Key Recordings on **mymusiclab.com**

TAKE NOTE

- How did jazz develop in Chicago in the 1920s, and who were some of its key players?

In Chicago, jazz moved away from the small-group ensemble sound popular in New Orleans to an emphasis on exciting soloists, such as Louis Armstrong. During the 1920s, jazz developed from a largely improvised music to an emphasis on carefully planned compositions that featured contrasting instrumental sounds and distinctive melodies. Musicians Louis Armstrong, Duke Ellington, Sidney Bechet, and Jelly Roll Morton produced dominant work during the period, lifting jazz to an art form of sophistication and depth.

- What distinguished Kansas City jazz from other regional styles during the 1920s and early 1930s?

Kansas City became known for a style of big-band jazz steeped in blues and rich with riffs and rhythmic drive. Bennie Moten was a pianist/bandleader who helped establish the Kansas City style, mentoring key musicians including future bandleader William "Count" Basie and trumpeter "Hot Lips" Page. Andy Kirk's band was also influential, thanks to the work of pianist/arranger Mary Lou Williams.

- Why was New York City an important jazz center in the 1920s, and who were some of its leading players?

By the 1920s African American cultural life had found its center in the Harlem section of uptown Manhattan. In that decade—during what is now called the Harlem Renaissance—music, entertainment, literature, and art were thriving. A large audience supported many nightclubs, including Harlem's Cotton Club, which became famous for its floorshows. Fletcher Henderson, Coleman Hawkins, Louis Armstrong, and Sidney Bechet were some of New York's key jazz innovators in the 1920s. Paul Whiteman and Duke Ellington were important bandleaders. Whiteman nurtured talented musicians and commissioned George Gershwin's *Rhapsody in Blue*. Ellington's career took off after he and his ensemble were hired to become the house band at the Cotton Club. He began composing more ambitious compositions to take advantage of the skills and personalities of principal performers in his group.

- Who were some of the primary vocalists to emerge during the Jazz Age?

The Jazz Age was the era of the great blues singers, most notably Bessie Smith, who performed and recorded prolifically. Bandleader Cab Calloway became famous for his vocals on novelty numbers like *Minnie the Moocher*, which he sang to great comic effect at Harlem's Cotton Club. And Paul Whiteman innovated in 1927 when he was the first bandleader to hire full-time vocalists the Rhythm Boys, including a young Bing Crosby.

- What role did arrangers play in creating the sound of early jazz bands?

During the 1920s, bands moved from using "stock" arrangements to hiring their own arrangers to create pieces that would help them build a distinctive sound. Arrangers such as Don Redman and Fletcher Henderson helped create the main elements that would become the basis for big-band swing (see Chapter 5).

- Why were regional bands important during this period?

Regional bands—groups that played in specific cities or small areas around the country—popularized jazz music among local audiences. Although many never rose above local fame, a few were important as innovators and became known nationally, notably two Detroit-based bands, the Jean Goldkette Orchestra and McKinney's Cotton Pickers.

DISCUSSION QUESTIONS

1. An important aspect of jazz through most of its history has been the elevation of individual musicians to stars and heroes—to jazz "giants." Discuss the origins of this phenomenon.

2. Discuss the social, cultural, demographic, geographic, economic, and technological forces that contributed to the spread and growing popularity of jazz in the 1920s.

3. What event in 1920 opened the floodgates for African American musicians to make records, and why was this important?

4. Explain why, after New Orleans, the next jazz center was Chicago.

5. What characteristics were shared by Chicago, Kansas City, and New York that made them centers of jazz? What were some of the differences?

6. Important milestones in the career of Louis Armstrong occurred in the 1920s. What do you think they were, and why were they important?

7. Compare and contrast Louis Armstrong and Bix Beiderbecke.

8. Talk about race relations in jazz of the 1920s. Did musicians of all colors have equal opportunities? What about audiences—could they enter any dance hall or club?

KEY TERMS & KEY PEOPLE

Louis Armstrong 58
arranger 63
backbeat 64
Bill "Count" Basie 69
Sidney Bechet 58
Leon "Bix" Beiderbecke 66
break 64
Cab Calloway 76
Charleston (dance) 60
Eddie Condon 66
Duke Ellington 58
George Gershwin 72
Jean Goldkette 67
Coleman Hawkins 71

Fletcher Henderson 64
Earl "Fatha" Hines 67
James P. Johnson 60
Lonnie Johnson 73
Andy Kirk 70
Eddie Lang 73
Jimmy McPartland 66
Bennie Moten 69
Red Nichols 73
Joe "King" Oliver 61
polyphonic 61
race records 59
Ma Rainey 83
regional band 84

rhythm section 62
Jimmy Rushing 69
Bessie Smith 82
Jack Teagarden 76
tremolo 67
trumpet style 67
vaudeville 60
Joe Venuti 73
wah-wah 61
walking bass 65
Thomas "Fats" Waller 80
Walter Page's Blue Devils 69
Paul Whiteman 72
Mary Lou Williams 69

CHAPTER 5

The Swing Era

by John Edward Hasse

TAKE NOTE

- How did jazz become a "mass attraction" during the swing era?
- What were the key African American bands of the swing era and why were they important?
- What were the main white bands of the swing era and why were they important?
- What were the challenges in keeping a band together and financially successful?
- Why did all-female bands arise during this period, and how did they help advance women's role in jazz?
- How did arrangers help create the successful big band sound?
- What roles did smaller ensembles, instrumental soloists, and singers play during this era?
- Why did the big bands decline at the end of World War II?

HISTORICAL EVENTS	The 1930s	MUSICAL EVENTS

1926 — Savoy Ballroom opens in New York City, later becomes a center for swing dancing

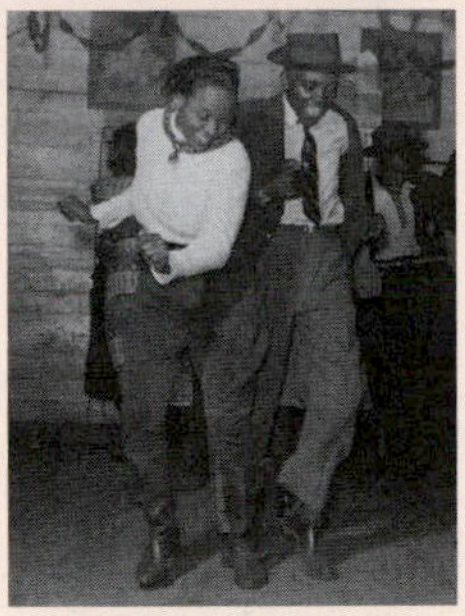

1927 — Casa Loma Orchestra forms in Detroit, first major white swing band

1928

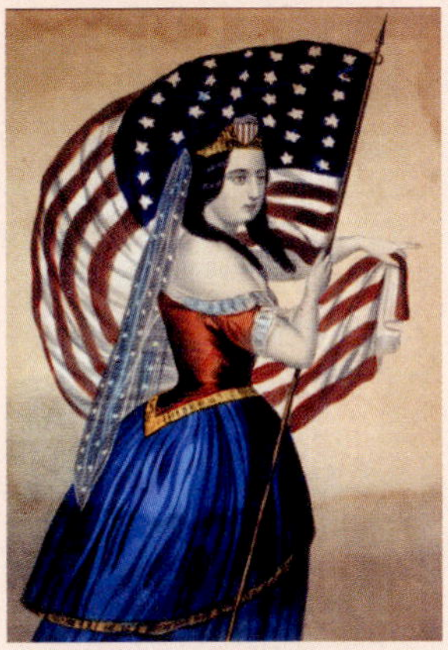

1929

1930

1931 — *The Star-Spangled Banner* is officially made the National Anthem of the United States

1932 — Franklin Delano Roosevelt elected president, and launches the New Deal in 1933 to fight the Depression

1932 — Duke Ellington records *It Don't Mean a Thing (If It Ain't Got That Swing)*, whose title predicts the national mania for swing several years later

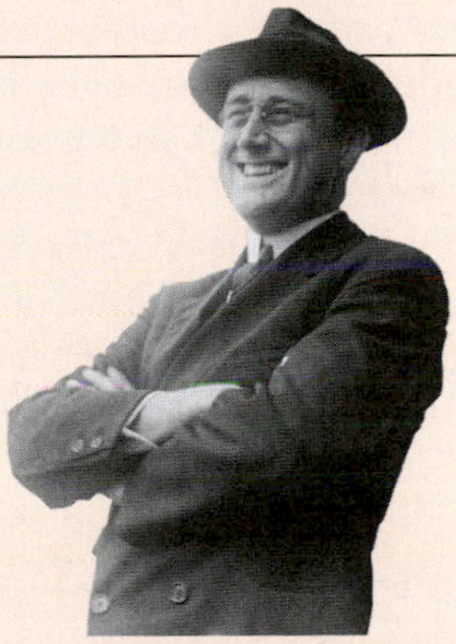

1933

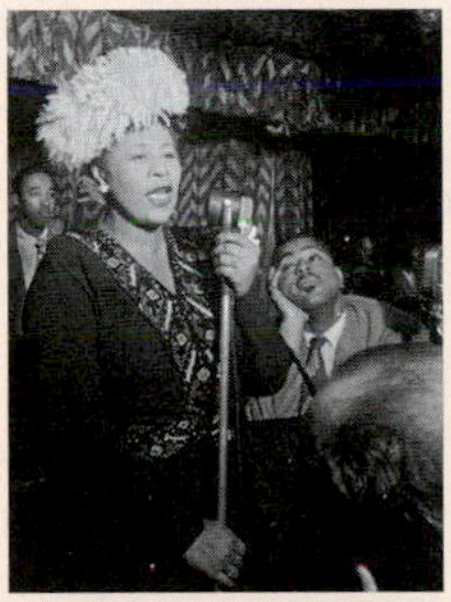

- Tommy Dorsey forms his big band
- Bandleader/drummer Chick Webb hires a young Ella Fitzgerald to be his group's vocalist

1934

- Benny Goodman band opens at Los Angeles's Palomar Ballroom

1935 — Social Security is passed by Congress, giving benefits to elderly Americans

- *Porgy and Bess* by George and Ira Gershwin debuts on Broadway

1936

Count Basie band makes its New York City debut

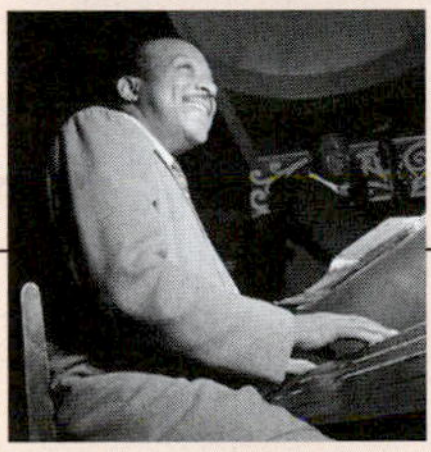

1937 — Golden Gate Bridge opens in San Francisco, California

1937 — Artie Shaw forms his first big band

1938

NATIONAL ARCHIVES AND RECORDS ADMINISTRATION.

1939 — Prompted by the actions of Nazi Germany's leader Adolph Hitler, World War II begins in Europe, although the United States remains officially neutral

- Glenn Miller leaps to fame thanks to his band's national radio broadcast
- All-female band International Sweethearts of Rhythm forms

Explore the Jazz Timeline on **mymusiclab.com**

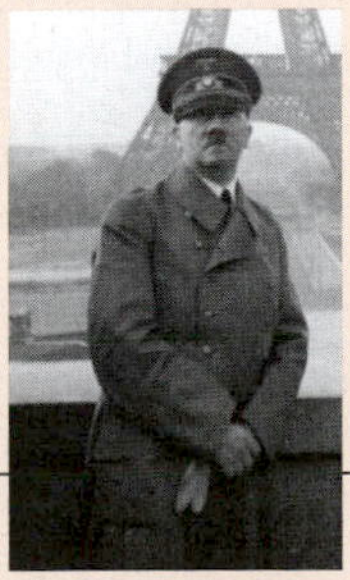

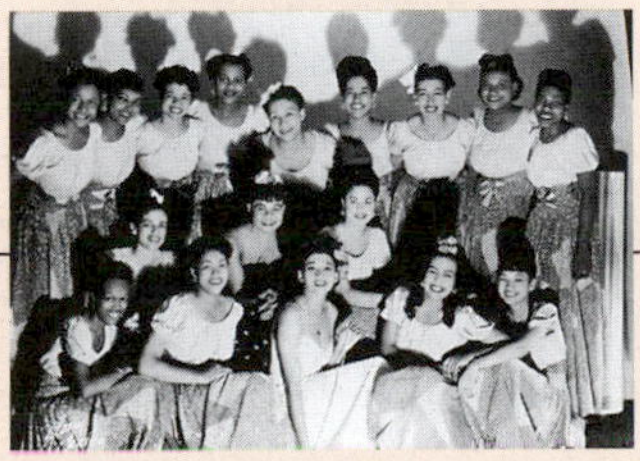

I f novelist F. Scott Fitzgerald had it right when he called the 1920s the Jazz Age, then the 1930s through the mid-1940s could even more aptly be termed the swing era. That's because during that time, the swing pulse and impulse transformed jazz—and through it, much of American vernacular music.

Swing music and dancing became a huge phenomenon, almost a national obsession, taking jazz to heights of popularity never achieved before or since. More jazz musicians gained favor with the general public—more audiences turned to jazz as a backdrop for dancing and entertainment—than at any other time in history. Never before had jazz so dominated the field of popular music. At no other time was jazz such a catalyst for thousands of fans queuing up for a performance, for turn-away crowds so large and enthusiastic that the police had to be called in to keep order, for so many live radio broadcasts carrying the music to waiting listeners coast-to-coast, and for heated band battles that became the stuff of legends.

Many people helped create swing, but two musicians, **Fletcher Henderson** and **Louis Armstrong**, were especially influential.

In the 1920s, Fletcher Henderson's orchestra had popularized a fundamental format for, and style of, big band arranging. Henderson and his principal arranger, Don Redman, fully developed a basic framework that featured **sections** of reeds and brass pitted against each other, sometimes in call-and-response patterns, and sometimes with one section playing supporting motifs or riffs (short, repeated phrases).

What separated **swing** from jazz that preceded? Most of all, its rhythm. Louis Armstrong's rhythmic innovations loosened up the beat of jazz, provided a greater variety of rhythms, and made its momentum more flowing. Between 1930 and 1935, Armstrong influenced other musicians to play slightly ahead of the beat and, in so doing, transformed the rhythmic feel of jazz.

In its most original and most fundamental sense, swing is a verb meaning to play with the feeling of forward momentum, the propulsive rhythmic quality that is found in much African-rooted music. It's a looseness, almost an elasticity of the pulse. "Swing is not a kind of music," **Duke Ellington** told an interviewer in 1939. "It is that part of rhythm that causes a bouncing, buoyant, terpsichorean urge."

---

section subdivision of an ensemble defined by instrument group (as in reed section) or function (as in rhythm section).

swing a rhythmic characteristic of much jazz, *swing* is a forward momentum, an elasticity of the pulse, that defies precise definition.

(to) swing to play with a perceptible forward momentum, a propulsive rhythm, and a flowing beat; found in much African-rooted music.

Harry James paid dues in territory bands before becoming one of the most popular swing era bandleaders. PHOTO COURTESY DOWN BEAT ARCHIVES.

Frank Sinatra's popularity echoed the success of big bands in the 1930s. The singer first rose to fame with the Harry James and Tommy Dorsey orchestras. This portrait was taken in early 1947.

The change in the rhythms of jazz became more pronounced as bands, over time, began replacing traditional instruments and introducing new instrumental techniques. The plodding tuba, originally used to keep a two-to-the-bar beat, gave way to the fleeter string bass, which promoted an even, flowing feel of four-to-the-bar. The banjo was abandoned in favor of the more versatile guitar. Drummers shifted the fundamental pulse from the drum itself to the hi-hat cymbal. These changes made the music feel less staccato and jerky, and more long-lined, forward-moving, and, well, swinging.

Singers also became an important part of the swing era. Paul Whiteman was among the first bandleaders to feature a vocalist (Bing Crosby), and in 1931 Duke Ellington hired Ivie Anderson. Other bandleaders began to follow their lead: in the 1930s, **Benny Goodman** offered singer Helen Ward, **Count Basie** had Jimmy Rushing, **Chick Webb** featured **Ella Fitzgerald**, **Earl Hines** engaged Billy Eckstine, **Harry James** employed **Frank Sinatra**, and **Artie Shaw** presented Helen Forrest and **Billie Holiday**. At its essence, however, swing was an instrumental music. "In the middle and late thirties," wrote Barry Ulanov, "swing lost its standing as a verb and was elevated to the stature of a noun and a category. Jazz was dead, long live swing."

To most people, swing meant big band jazz.

Watch the documentary on the swing era on **mymusiclab.com**

Jazz: A Mass Attraction

The 1920s and 1930s were, as Russell Nye has observed, the time when "public dancing in America reached its highest point of popularity and profit, and the dance hall became one of the nation's most influential social institutions."

The kind of dance hall that drew the largest attendance was the dance palace: "Huge, brilliantly lighted, elaborately decorated with columns, gilt, drapes, mirrors, and ornate chandeliers, often with two bands, these became synonymous with glamour and romance," wrote Nye. The most celebrated dance palaces were the Roseland and Savoy in New York City, the Trianon and Aragon in Chicago, the Graystone in Detroit, the Indiana Roof Garden in Indianapolis, and the Avalon Casino on Santa Catalina Island, California. A step down in space and luxury were the Marigold in Minneapolis, the Pla Mor in Kansas City, and the Madrid in Louisville, Kentucky. Several nightclubs with big ballrooms became famous, including Glen Island Casino in New Rochelle, New York; Castle Farm in Cincinnati; and Shadowland in San Antonio, Texas.

Public dancing became, by the 1930s, one of the key American courtship rituals. For many young people, swing music and dancing served as important emotional outlets; for others, they offered a much-needed escape from the economic difficulties of the lingering Depression. With partner in hand, caught up in shared euphoria and momentary forgetfulness, dancers could stomp and swing themselves into states of transcendence. While the music's time surged forward, real-world time, paradoxically, seemed to stop. Ears flooded with irresistible melodies and intoxicating rhythms, skin flushed with excitement (and perhaps desire), and pulses

---

Lindy Hop   a fast swing dance step that burst forth in 1928, and became widely popular in the 1930s; it featured improvised "breakaways" and athletic aerial movements; named for aviator Charles Lindberg.

Jitterbug   another name for the *Lindy Hop*, a fast swing dance step that emerged in 1928.

Jazz & the Arts

The Swing Dances

From the beginning, ragtime, jazz, and often blues had been music to dance to, spawning a progression of famous steps—the Slow Drag, the Grizzly Bear, Ballin' the Jack, the Mooche, the Shimmy, the Black Bottom, the Charleston, and others. Most of the steps originated among southern African Americans in down-home juke joints and, in expurgated versions, eventually reached the stages of northern nightclubs, vaudeville theaters, and Broadway.

During the swing era, jazz dancing reached its apex of public participation, attention, and virtuosity. "The beat," asserted dancer Norma Miller, "is what swing dancing is all about. . . . Swing music. There's never been any music so perfectly attuned to what the body can do."

As always, hip dancers were open to new steps, and the 1930s saw a parade of them, including the Shim-Sham (also known as the Shim-Sham-Shimmy) and the Big Apple, which featured a "caller" shouting out the steps. Some dances originated in Harlem ballrooms or as Cotton Club production numbers—Truckin' (1933), the Suzy-Q (1936), Peckin' (1937), and the Scronch (1937)—and then, as fads, spread widely to dance halls and ballrooms.

The most spectacular and exciting dance step of the swing era, the fast, furious **Lindy Hop**, had burst forth in 1928—probably from the Savoy Ballroom. It was developed there in the 1930s and taken to exceptional heights, literally and figuratively. The dance, encompassing a tension between partnering and individual expression, featured improvised "breakaways" and athletic aerial movements or "air" steps—pioneered by the Harlem dancer Frankie Manning—in which women were tossed into the air like rag dolls. As the Lindy Hop caught on, energetic young dancers expanded its routine of floor and aerial steps at ballrooms and competitions. Known in white communities as the **Jitterbug**, the step drew young enthusiasts across America. Twirling dancers, swirling skirts, exuberant smiles, youthful energy, virtuosic displays, the night charged with excitement—this was the Lindy Hop. A dancing audience gave musicians a charge, too. "Outstanding musicians inspire

quickened as dancers Lindy-Hopped, Suzy-Q'ed, Shim-Shammed, and Shagged the nights, and their cares, away. If ballrooms had won public acceptance in the 1920s and offered a diversion from the Depression of the early 1930s, in the late 1930s they reached their all-time height of popularity. Most of the dancers were young people, and swing took center stage in American youth culture, just as rock and roll would two decades later.

Swing may have been a national phenomenon, but Manhattan was the music's capital and Harlem its absolute epicenter. There, "uptown," one could catch swing at ballrooms such as the Savoy and Renaissance; such theaters as the Apollo and the Harlem Opera House; such nightclubs as Monroe's Uptown House, Small's Paradise, and the Rhythm Club; and all sorts of lesser spots. Outside of Harlem, swing venues dotted the map of New York City, but they were concentrated in three areas of Manhattan: one ran along a stretch of West 52nd Street (also known as Swing Street or simply the Street), where the basements of brownstones crammed in dozens of nightspots, among them the Onyx Club, the Famous Door, the Three Deuces, and the Hickory House. The prominent midtown hotels—among them the Waldorf, the Edison, the New Yorker, and the Pennsylvania—provided another locus for swing dancing and listening, albeit for affluent white people. And finally, Greenwich Village offered such swinging clubs as the Village Vanguard, Black Cat, and Café Society.

Throughout the nation, swelling masses of listeners and dancers created an explosion in the popularity of jukeboxes, on which swing recordings were increasingly heard. The number of jukeboxes in the United States jumped dramatically from 25,000 in 1933 to 300,000 in 1939, by then consuming 13 million discs a year. Spurred on by the swing music craze, the recovering economy, the popularity of the phonograph, the jukebox boom, and the new low-priced (35-cent) discs issued by music-industry upstart Decca Records and others, the record industry climbed back to recovery. From a low of 10 million units sold in 1933, sales surged to 33 million in 1938 and 127 million in 1941.

great dancers and vice versa," observed saxophonist **Lester Young**. "The rhythm of the dancers," he added, "comes back to you when you're playing." Duke Ellington, when performing in stage shows became routine for his musicians, liked to take his band out for a string of dance gigs, because "when they see people moving around the floor, they've got to put snap and ginger into their work."

And so the musicians and the dancers would form a swinging union, the band's music interplaying with the dancers' limbs and feet, creating what novelist Ralph Ellison called "that feeling of communion which was the true meaning of the public jazz dance. The blues, the singer, the band, and the dancers formed the vital whole of jazz as an institutional form, and even today neither part is quite complete without the rest."

—*John Edward Hasse*

Big Band, Big Sound

Much of the appeal of big bands had to do with the sheer depth, breadth, textural variety, and volume of their sound. Where combos of two to five or six musicians tended to thrive in small, intimate surroundings, big bands were geared to fill vast spaces and envelop large audiences.

To create that sound, they employed **instrumentation** that filled the entire sonic spectrum, from the string bass anchoring the low end to clarinets, trumpets, and piano defining the highest limits of the music's range.

In between, musical events varied depending on the band but generally unfolded along the following lines.

The rhythm section (drums, string bass, piano, and guitar) served as the foundation of the sound. The drums would keep time, generally on the **hi-hat cymbal** and bass drum, and provide rhythmic kicks, accents, and fills on the **snare drum**, **tom-tom** drum, and other cymbals. The string bass would serve a double function, reinforcing a steady beat by "walking" in sync with the drums and simultaneously outlining the harmony by playing the lowest notes of the changing chords or providing **counterpoint**— complementary melodies—to the main melody. The guitar would also keep time and establish harmony with chords generally played four-to-the-bar, with occasional rhythmic accents. The piano served a somewhat freer role, keeping time and providing chordal accompaniment while sometimes playing melody and inserting melodic **fills** in musical spaces. In some bands, the vibraphone was used in much the same way as a piano, adding an airy yet percussive timbre to the overall sound.

Melody and solos would be played by any of a number of instruments, including clarinet, saxophone, trumpet, or trombone.

The distinctive big band quality came from the use of brass (trumpets and trombones) and woodwind, or "reed," instruments (primarily clarinet, alto saxophone, tenor sax, baritone sax) to fill out the sound. They were used in sections to create chordal blocks of sound that could be used to punch out rhythmic accents or provide smooth harmonic textures under and around the melody. They could also play repeating melodic figures (riffs) or serve as a kind of chorus answering the main melody.

The different tonal qualities of the instruments—crisp, bright, and metallic brass (sometimes greatly altered with the use of mutes) and warm, reedy woodwinds—allowed for contrast, with the brass and the winds often interacting as separate sections. In Duke Ellington's band, however, instruments were frequently combined in unusual ways to create entirely new tone colors and moods.

—*Tad Lathrop*

In 1937, swing bands and Hollywood films had comparable clout in the marketplace. Theater operators doubled their drawing power by pairing the two types of entertainment.

PHOTO COURTESY DOWN BEAT ARCHIVES.

Bands had always competed for popularity, but in the swing era competition between dance bands came to the fore, taking on the characteristics of rivalry between great athletic teams. Bands attracted ardent followers, orchestras engaged in sometimes epic band battles, and jazz magazines and black newspapers ran readers' polls to select the top groups. Fans kept track of changes in bands' personnel and argued the merits of one band over another.

One cause of swing's ability to draw so many passionate adherents was the depth of its meaning: it affirmed the joys of dance, music, and youthful court-ship; of risk-taking improvisation; and of a dynamic African American–inspired force challenging and chang-ing mainstream America. Like rock and roll would a generation later, swing drew young people powerfully, giving rise to a musical subculture. And swing affirmed the human spirit at a time when the country was still struggling to come out of the Great Depression.

Swing also provided a context for forward strides in race relations, contributing to the development of a more inclusive concept of American identity. Before the swing era, jazz reflected the nationwide racial divide between blacks and whites. When, in 1935, Benny Goodman established a racially mixed band, he made it safe for other bands to do so. Some swing bands became interracial institutions a decade before baseball and the armed forces were integrated.

Prior to the swing era, most white Americans had been only vaguely aware of black jazz musicians, whom the record companies relegated to the "race" catalogs marketed mainly to black buyers. In the 1930s, however, swing led jazz of all colors into the American mainstream.

---

instrumentation   the array of instruments called for in a piece of music or provided by a band.

hi-hat cymbal   a percussion instrument consisting of two fac-ing cymbals on a stand operated with a foot pedal; pressing on the pedal brings the two cymbals together; functions as a time-keeping component of a drum set; can be played with a drumstick or brush in open and closed position.

snare drum   narrow drum with a band of metal wires called "snares" stretched across the underside, which provide a distinctive rasp when the drum is struck on top with a drum stick; a central component of the rock, funk, and blues drum kit, where it typically supplies the backbeat; in bebop jazz it became used more for accenting.

tom-tom   midrange drum used in the drum kit for sounds higher than a bass drum but lower than a snare drum; there are several sizes of tom-toms.

counterpoint   interaction of two or more melodies. Music with counterpoint is characterized as having polyphony or being polyphonic.

fill   an improvised phrase inserted between phrases of a main melody.

Jazz began as a local music, deeply rooted in African American musical traditions. Prior to the 1930s, most jazz and dance bands—whether head-quartered in Atlanta, Kansas City, or Chicago—played in a limited region or territory (and thus were called "**territory bands**") and found limited access to radio and recording—the means of reaching greater numbers of listeners (see Chapter 4). But by the height of the swing era, jazz was dominated by national bands managed by white businessmen and marketed to a mass, predominantly white, nationwide audience.

Twelve national swing bands—some black and some white—stand out for their excellence, influence, and historical importance. None of these bands played jazz exclusively; surviving in the entertainment market-place meant their **band books** had to include pop vocals and commercially oriented fare. But at their best, these groups produced jazz of enduring quality.

TAKE NOTE

- How did jazz become a "mass attraction" during the swing era?

The Great African American Bands

In the 1920s, Fletcher Henderson and his orchestra had served as a model for Duke Ellington and other bandleaders (see Chapter 4). Henderson was esteemed for his talented musicians—such as Louis Armstrong, cornetist Rex Stewart, and tenor saxophonist **Ben Webster**—and his pioneering arrangements, but he possessed neither business acumen nor a shrewd manager. In 1934, not long after recording two of his best compositions, *Down South Camp Meeting* and *Wrappin' It Up*, Henderson's band broke up. He went to work as an arranger for Benny Goodman, and when Goodman and swing became hugely popular, it

---

territory band   in the 1920s and early 1930s, a jazz or dance band that played in a limited region or territory and found limited access to radio and recordings; some talented musicians, such as Harry James, rose from the ranks of territory bands to gain renown in national bands of the swing era.

band book   a band's repertoire of tunes.

Fletcher Henderson's last push as a bandleader came in the mid-1930s when his outfit boasted Chu Berry (far left) and Roy Eldridge (foreground, leaning on piano). PHOTO COURTESY FRANK DRIGGS COLLECTION.

was, ironically, Henderson's arranging that provided the framework.

The short, hunchbacked Chick Webb may have lacked physical stature, but he made up for it in the respect he earned as a bandleader and drummer. His excellent control of dynamics, imaginative drum breaks and fills (abundantly displayed in *Stompin' at the Savoy* and *Blue Lou*, both from 1934, and *Harlem Congo* [JTSA Disc 1/Track 25] and *Liza* from 1938), and plucky personality won him many avid fans. Webb's band played at the Savoy Ballroom from 1927 on, and from 1931 to 1939 it served more or less as the house band; he routinely defeated other groups in band battles. In 1935, Webb hired Ella Fitzgerald as vocalist. Upon Webb's untimely death from tuberculosis in 1939 at the age of 30, Fitzgerald became the nominal leader of his group until it disbanded in 1942 and she went on as a solo singer.

Soon after attracting acclaim with his 1928 recordings with Louis Armstrong, pianist Earl "Fatha" Hines established a band at Chicago's posh Grand Terrace, where he would hold many residencies until 1940. Unlike Ellington or Basie, Hines never built a consistent sonic personality for his band, which nonetheless made a number

Ella Fitzgerald singing at New York's Downbeat club in September 1947, while Dizzy Gillespie looks on in admiration. PHOTO COURTESY WILLIAM P. GOTTLIEB/WILLIAM P. GOTTLIEB COLLECTION/ LIBRARY OF CONGRESS PRINTS & PHOTOGRAPHS DIVISION.

of solid, impressive recordings, such as *Cavernism* (1933) and *Grand Terrace Shuffle* (1939). A great talent scout, in the 1940s Hines employed Dizzy Gillespie and Charlie Parker, who were on their way to developing an advanced style that would be dubbed bebop.

Though Hines's orchestra lacked a consistent arranging style, the leader's forceful gifts as a pianist firmly marked the band's sound and propelled Hines into the jazz pantheon. Indeed, some jazz critics consider him the greatest of all jazz keyboard artists. With his linear lines, unpredictable phrasing, use of silence, razor-sharp inventiveness, and technical skills (for example, extending a tremolo for two minutes), he deeply influenced other pianists, notably **Teddy Wilson**. Hines's piano recordings spanned a half century; his swing era masterworks included the showpieces *Pianology* (1937), *Rosetta* (1939), and, taken at the dizzying tempo of 276 beats per minute, *Piano Man* (1939).

Watch the documentary on Ella Fitzgerald on **mymusiclab.com**

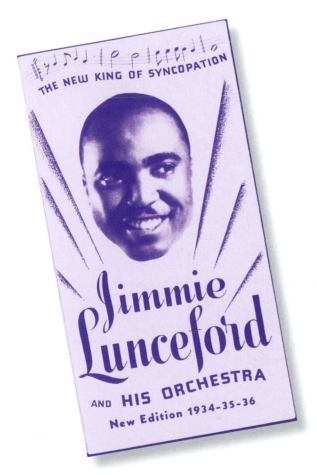

Jimmie Lunceford's orchestra was unmatched for its showmanship, which kept the band at the top of the swing scene for a decade starting in 1934. COURTESY FRANK DRIGGS COLLECTION.

Stompin' at the Savoy

"Three nights a week, we were at the Savoy Ballroom," recalled the painter Romare Bearden. "The best dancing in the world was there, and the best music." Opened on March 12, 1926, in Harlem, the Savoy became famous for its hot jazz music, torrid dancing, and special events. Adroit showmanship and promotion helped make the Savoy the most talked-about ballroom in America, "the home of happy feet," as new dances originated there, songs were written about it (*Stompin' at the Savoy*, *Savoy*, and *House of Joy*), and **radio remotes** (live broadcasts made from the ballroom) sent the music coast to coast. Normally two bands were featured at a time, alternating sets between two bandstands, so the dance music never stopped.

Situated at 596 Lenox Avenue, it ran the length of the block between 140th and 141st streets. The Savoy boasted a spacious lobby, a marble staircase leading to the ballroom on the second floor, and a 50-by-200-foot polished-maple dance floor. Management billed it as "the world's most beautiful ballroom." The Savoy employed 120 people, including 15 bouncers to keep order, and its dress code required male customers to wear coats at all times.

Most of the important bands of the swing era played there, including those of Duke Ellington, Cab Calloway, Andy Kirk, Count Basie, Roy Eldridge, and **Benny Carter**. A shrine of public dancing and a center of popular style, the Savoy was not only a highly influential venue but also a demanding one for the bands. "If you didn't swing, you weren't there long," recalled trombonist Dicky Wells.

The Savoy hosted legendary band contests, positioning the contesting groups on adjoining bandstands. On May 15, 1927, the Savoy hired four bands and promoted a battle of New York versus Chicago, which brought out the riot squad. Another contest featured six bands in a battle of the North versus the South. Legendary battle royals pitted Chick Webb's band (the house favorite) against Count Basie's and Webb's against Duke Ellington's. Most sensationally, on May 11, 1937, in "The Music Battle of the Century," Webb's black band battled the white band of Benny Goodman, who had gotten several of his biggest hits from Webb's arranger Edgar Sampson. As the two bands competed heatedly, reported the *New York Age*, thousands "battled mounted cops and patrolmen for places near enough to the Savoy to hear the music of the two great orchestras." The verdict: Webb beat Goodman.

The Savoy welcomed black and white patrons alike. "At one stage, about half the people at the Savoy were white and half were colored," Savoy manager Charles Buchanan recalled. "The cops used to hate it."

By the time the Savoy closed its doors in 1958 and was demolished to make way for a housing project, 250 bands had performed there for an estimated 30 million stomping feet.

—*John Edward Hasse*

radio remote a radio broadcast not from the station's studio but rather from a remote location such as a nightclub, ballroom, or theater.

Like Paul Whiteman and Cab Calloway, **Jimmie Lunceford** stood in front of his band to conduct it. His band emphasized ensemble playing over solos, offered a joyous swing, and projected infectious enthusiasm in such numbers as *Organ Grinder's Swing* (1936), *For Dancers Only* (1937; JTSA Disc 1/Track 23), and *Margie* (1938); many were arranged by Sy Oliver, whose apparently simple arrangements often masked deep sophistication and offered imaginative contrasts in dynamics and **tone colors**.

Lunceford's band established a strong reputation for its "three p's": precision, polish, and presentation. While other bands matched its musicianship, none matched its showmanship. His players always wore sharp outfits; the trombonists would point their slides skyward; the trumpeters would, in unison, toss their instruments into the air and catch them; and the audience could watch everyone in the band sharing a contagiously good time.

While swing bands typically followed the lead of Fletcher Henderson and voiced their instruments in discrete sections (sax section, trumpet section, trombone section), Duke Ellington often mixed instruments together in unusual ways, creating distinctive and unique tone colors—for example, pairing a tightly muted trumpet with a low-playing clarinet and a high-playing trombone in *Mood Indigo* (1930). In contrast to bandleaders Goodman, Basie, Lunceford, Webb, and Tommy and Jimmy Dorsey, Ellington was not merely a gifted instrumentalist and leader; he personally created most of the music played by his orchestra. Unlike many other bandleaders, Ellington wasn't interested primarily in establishing a good beat for dancing; he wanted to explore his musical imagination. Memories, sound colors, moods, emotions—these were his focal points, as you can hear in the astonishing train ride conveyed in *Daybreak Express* (1933), the quiet daydream of *Azure* (1937), the intense drama of *Ko-Ko* (1940), and the sexuality and sensuality of *Warm Valley* (1940).

👁 **Watch** the video of *It Don't Mean A Thing* by Duke Ellington on **mymusiclab.com**

---

tone color same as *timbre*.

Earl "Fatha" Hines, pianist and bandleader (ca. 1947). PHOTO COURTESY WILLIAM P. GOTTLIEB/WILLIAM P. GOTTLIEB COLLECTION/LIBRARY OF CONGRESS PRINTS & PHOTOGRAPHS DIVISION.

With musical insight and sensitivity, Ellington composed pieces with his players in mind—for example, *Concerto for Cootie*, *Cotton Tail*, and *Jack the Bear* (all 1940) were each written for a specific musician in his band (respectively, trumpeter Cootie Williams, tenor saxophonist Ben Webster, and bassist Jimmie Blanton)—and in so doing, lifted individuality within his band to an artistic zenith.

The scope of his musical interests—and his success in pursuing them—set Ellington apart from other leaders of big bands: historically, he ranks as the supreme composer and orchestrator for the medium of the jazz orchestra or big band.

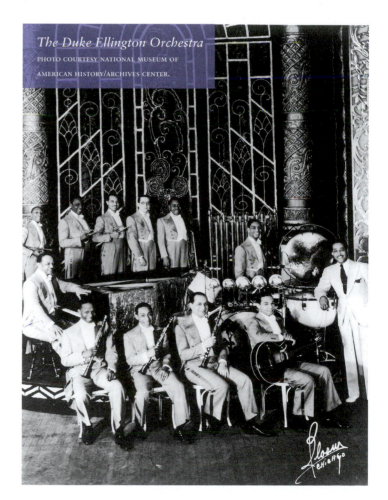

The Duke Ellington Orchestra PHOTO COURTESY NATIONAL MUSEUM OF AMERICAN HISTORY/ARCHIVES CENTER.

Listening Guide

KO-KO • DUKE ELLINGTON AND HIS ORCHESTRA

Music: Duke Ellington, 1940. Personnel: Rex Stewart (cornet); Cootie Williams, Wallace Jones (trumpet); Joe "Tricky Sam" Nanton, Juan Tizol, Lawrence Brown (trombone); Barney Bigard (clarinet, tenor sax); Johnny Hodges (alto sax); Otto Hardwick (alto sax, clarinet); Ben Webster (tenor sax); Harry Carney (baritone sax); Duke Ellington (piano, leader); Fred Guy (guitar); Jimmie Blanton (bass); Sonny Greer (drums). Recorded March 6, 1940, in Chicago. First issue: Victor 26577. Timing: 2:43.

Overview

From its opening tom-toms to its final crescendo, *Ko-Ko* fascinates with its drama, reportedly depicting slaves' frenetic dancing in New Orleans's legendary Congo Square. *Ko-Ko* includes memorable solos but it's the orchestral writing, especially, that makes it unique. Musically and harmonically sophisticated, emotional and intellectually stimulating, *Ko-Ko* ranks as one of Ellington's most esteemed recordings.

Key Features

- Blues: *Ko-Ko* is a sterling example of Ellington's use of the blues. Though it might not be obvious at first, the piece is a 12-bar blues.
- Form: An 8-bar introduction, seven blues choruses, and a 12-bar coda that begins with the repeat of the introduction.
- Instrumentation: Standard big band arrangement, with sections of trumpets, trombones, and saxophones, and a rhythm section of piano, bass, guitar, and drums.
- Melody: The melody (0:12) is in a minor key and is rendered in a call-and-response fashion: trombonist Juan Tizol states a four-note motif and the saxes play a seven-note answer.
- Harmony: The minor key and Ellington's orchestral writing imbue *Ko-Ko* with an exotic, almost unearthly, quality—somewhat dark and menacing. The piece is dramatic, eerie, and compelling.
- Stylistic variety: Ellington directed a jazz orchestra comprising highly individualistic voices, and you can hear four of them in *Ko-Ko*: valve trombonist Juan Tizol plays the melody in the first chorus (0:12), then slide trombonist Nanton comes in (0:31) with an entirely different trombone sound. Ellington's distinctive piano style is heard in the fourth chorus (1:07) and bassist Jimmie Blanton, with his outsized sound, in the sixth (1:43).
- Dynamics: Ellington was known for his sensitivity to dynamics, and you can hear how he builds each chorus in intensity and volume, as in a ***bolero***. The first chorus (0:12) is soft, and the last chorus (2:01) reaches a peak of volume.

—*John Edward Hasse*

TIME	FORM	MELODY	ACCOMPANIMENT
0:00	INTRODUCTION	Trombones play the eight-bar melody.	Baritone sax plays a **pedal point** (a single bass note).
0:12	CHORUS 1	Trombonist Juan Tizol states the four-note melody; saxes respond with a seven-note answer.	Call-and-response.
0:31	CHORUS 2	Trombonist Tricky Sam Nanton plays a solo. Listen for his unique *ya-ya* sound in contrast to Tizol's style, also on trombone.	
0:49	CHORUS 3	Nanton continues his solo, gaining volume and presence.	
1:07	CHORUS 4	Ellington plays a dissonant piano solo.	Sax riffs in background.
1:25	CHORUS 5	The muted trumpets play riffs and the saxes respond.	Call-and-response.
1:43	CHORUS 6	Bassist Jimmie Blanton and the band trade two-bar exchanges.	Call-and-response.
2:01	CHORUS 7	The entire band wails at full volume.	
2:20	CODA	Trombones play the 12-bar coda.	Baritone sax pedal points, then full orchestra.

bolero   (Spanish) originally, a Spanish dance in $\frac{3}{4}$. In Cuba, it became a slow, romantic $\frac{4}{4}$ genre akin to jazz ballads.

pedal point   held or repeated note of one pitch, typically in the bass; sometimes used to create contrast with simultaneous melodic motion in other instruments.

✳ Explore on mymusiclab.com

COUNT BASIE AS A LEADER

William "Count" Basie formed his orchestra in Kansas City from former members of the Blue Devils and the Bennie Moten Orchestra, following Moten's passing. The bluesy and swinging feeling in the Blue Devils band became the model for Basie's sound. An empathetic relationship within Basie's rhythm section (nicknamed the "All American Rhythm Section") developed and their tightly knit interplay propelled the orchestra and its soloists in a new way.

THE BAND

The Basie band is pictured here at the Apollo Theater in 1940. Virtually all of its members became key figures in jazz.

—*Jeff Rupert*

Walter Page • Bass

Walter Page redefined bass playing in the jazz band. Basie had originally heard him with his own band, the Blue Devils. That occasion changed Basie's musical conception. The bluesy and swinging feeling in the Blue Devils became the model for Basie's sound. Page's concept of a walking bass line (playing on all four beats of the measure) was perhaps the main driving force behind the Basie band's swing feel, and ultimately the Kansas City sound of the late 1930s.

Freddie Green • Guitar

Freddie Green strummed his guitar on all four beats of the bar. (Strumming chords to keep time is known as rhythm guitar playing.) His unobtrusive yet deceptively important role within the rhythm section allowed for a crucial change; it freed up Basie from having to be a timekeeper. Because of Green's driving rhythm guitar, Basie was able to play light fills and seemingly float over the rest of the rhythm section. In short, Green enables Basie's light, refined style.

Trumpet Soloists

Buck Clayton and Harry "Sweets" Edison were two important soloists in the Basie band. Both had a tremendous impact on the band, and they ultimately had solo careers of their own.

PHOTO COURTESY FRANK DRIGGS COLLECTION.

Count Basie • Piano

Basie's piano style emanated from the stride piano tradition, with strong influence from Fats Waller and James P. Johnson. But by the mid-1930s, Basie developed his own style—spare, drenched in riffs and blues—that embodied the Kansas City sound. For several years, Basie performed in Kansas City, whose style of jazz was built around the rhythm section.

Jo Jones • Drums

Jo Jones was an integral part of the Basie sound and jazz drumming. Jones was known for elegant solo fills and for his use of the hi-hat cymbal (pictured here to Jones's left) in a new way—utilizing it for syncopation and for keeping the swing feel, even on ballads or slow tempos. Prior to Jones, the jazz beat was kept on the bass drum, rather than cymbals. Jones played the bass drum at times softly on all four beats, but he began using it just for accents. Jo Jones's overall feel created a feeling of light, but driving, forward motion.

Other Soloists

High-note trumpet player Al Killian; trombonist Vic Dickenson. Tenor saxophonist Buddy Tate (third from left), while influenced by Lester Young, came into his own as a soloist.

Lester Young

Lester Young—nicknamed Pres (short for president) by vocalist Billie Holiday—was the premier soloist in the Basie band during the late 1930s and early 1940s. His light, floating style was the antithesis of his contemporaries, Coleman Hawkins and Ben Webster, who both had deeper, huskier tones than Young. Young's approach contrasted with the driving aspect of the rhythm section; his round tone, swing feel, and melodic improvisations were light and unaffected. Together, Lester Young and the Basie rhythm section created a new sound in jazz. Note the characteristic way in which Pres holds his horn and twists his head.

Listening Guide

ONE O'CLOCK JUMP • COUNT BASIE AND HIS ORCHESTRA

Music: Count Basie. Personnel: Buck Clayton, Ed Lewis, Bobby Moore (trumpet); George Hunt, Dan Minor (trombone); Earle Warren (alto sax); Herschel Evans, Lester Young (tenor sax); Count Basie (piano); Freddie Green (guitar); Walter Page (bass); Jo Jones (drums). Recorded July 7, 1937, in New York. First issue: Decca 1363. Timing: 3:05.

Overview

This recording demonstrates why composer-author Gunther Schuller called the Basie band "the quintessence of swing." Basie's conception and execution of swing was exceptional, largely because of his stellar rhythm section, which maintained steady personnel from 1937 to 1947. Drummer Jones modernized jazz rhythm by moving the beat from the bass drum to the **ride cymbal** and hi-hat cymbals. Guitarist Green made his rhythmically precise downstroke slightly ahead of bass player Page's line. Jones, Green, and Page played four-beats-to-the-bar, accenting all four almost equally. The result was swing with a feeling of lightness, openness, and suppleness.

Basie's rhythm section combined the lightness of a balloon, the precise time-keeping of a Swiss watch, the forward propulsion of an express train, and the infectiousness of great big grin. Dancers found his beat irresistible.

This recording highlights the band's extraordinary swing, spirit, and ensemble style, not to mention a deceptively simple arrangement and several fine solos.

The Basie band originated this piece when it was playing at Kansas City's Reno Club, a small, gangster-run nightspot with a whites-only clientele, where the band performed in 1935–36 and where the band would stretch out this piece for as long as 30 minutes. There is conflicting evidence on who contributed what to the piece; saxophonist Buster Smith said in 1962 that he, Hot Lips Page, and Jack Washington each contributed elements before they left the Basie band in 1936, and that Basie and trombonist Dan Minor supplied others. Eddie Durham is also usually credited as an arranger. The piece was not written down originally, but was rather a head arrangement. Basie took formal credit as composer, but

the piece is really a superb example of creative collaboration in music.

Originally titled *Blue Balls*, the off-color name was changed to the more polite *One O'Clock Jump* during a radio broadcast that took place at about 1 a.m.

His first hit, *One O'Clock Jump* became Basie's **theme song** and one of the most iconic anthems of the swing era. Best-selling recordings were made by Harry James and Benny Goodman. In 1957, the singing group Lambert, Hendricks, and Ross made a memorable **vocalese** (sung) version.

Key Features

- Form: This is a classic 12-bar blues. Within the form, there is also call-and-response, for example, between the trombone figure and trumpet answer in choruses 8 through 10.
- Tempo: Basie takes the piece at medium tempo—a very danceable 171 beats per measure.
- Riffs: This piece is a showcase for riffs—the arrangement employs eight different ones. From chorus 4 until the end, sections of the band play a succession of two-bar riffs. In the last three choruses, two riffs

But Ellington's work transcended jazz. Many consider him beyond category—a musician whose body of recordings ranks, as Gary Giddins has written, as "surely the finest representation of a composer's work since Edison invented the phonograph." More than just a snapshot of a particular musical style at a particular time, Ellington's music reflects, in the most sensuous terms, much of life in twentieth-century America—making him not only

a quintessential jazz musician but one of the greatest composers, from any stylistic background, that America has produced.

In some obvious ways Ellington was part of swing: he shared with the swing bands a similar instrumentation, employed a singer, played pop songs and original instrumentals, and performed

---

ride cymbal one of several cymbals used in a drum set, providing a splashy metallic accompaniment that contrasts with the tight time-keeping of the hi-hat cymbal, the dramatic statements of the crash cymbal, and the more exotic effects of the sizzle cymbal.

theme song the song or tune with which a musician or band is most associated; also called a signature tune.

vocalese the application of lyrics to an existing instrumental solo; notable practitioners have included Eddie Jefferson; Lambert, Hendricks, and Ross; and the Manhattan Transfer.

are heard concurrently: the sax section's riff over the brass section's riff. The latter is actually a two-part call-and-response: the trombones play a held note and the trumpets play a three-note syncopated figure. The brass's rhythm remains constant throughout these three choruses, establishing a feeling of control against which the saxes roll out a variety of riffs. In subsequent recordings of the piece, the Basie band played some of the same riffs as heard here and introduced others—one could do a fascinating comparison of the riffs played in this piece over time.

- Melody: Encountering this recording, the listener may be wondering, "Where's the melody?" Like **Coleman Hawkins**'s *Body and Soul* (CD I, Track 14/ Download Track 14), *One O'Clock Jump* does not open with a recognizable melody or "head." If this piece has a melody, it is the sax riffs in chorus 9 and perhaps 10.
- Arrangement: In the choruses 3 through 6, the soloists alternate between saxes and brass instruments, and the accompanying riffs alternate as well: the brass riffs behind the sax soloists, and the saxes riff behind the brass soloists.
- Solos: Three solos stand out particularly: Herschel Evans's big-toned solo (0:45); Lester Young's (1:19), which begins by hitting a B-flat 24 times, and which was memorized by legions of tenor sax players; and Buck Clayton's estimable, well-shaped trumpet solo (1:36), replete with expressive bent notes.

—*John Edward Hasse*

TIME	SECTION	MELODY
0:00	INTRO	Basie and the rhythm section open with an eight-bar boogie-woogie piano introduction.
0:11	CHORUS 1	Basie improvises a single-note melody line, interspersed with spaces (rests).
0:28	CHORUS 2	Basie continues his solo, including some **octave tremolos**. He abruptly modulates from the key of F (his favorite) to that of D-flat.
0:45	CHORUS 3	Big-toned Herschel Evans (tenor sax) solos over muted five-note brass riffs.
1:02	CHORUS 4	George Hunt (trombone) solos over nine-note sax riffs.
1:19	CHORUS 5	Lester Young (tenor sax) solos over biting nine-note brass riffs.
1:36	CHORUS 6	Buck Clayton (trumpet) solos over six-note descending sax riffs.
1:53	CHORUS 7	Page prominently plays a walking bass line, punctuated by very spare right-hand jabs by Basie.
2:10	CHORUS 8	Saxes play a two-bar riff six times over the brass's call-and-response counter-riff.
2:27	CHORUS 9	Saxes play a different, longer (13-note, four-bar) riff three times. Most people consider this riff the piece's melody. Brass counter-riff continues.
2:43	CHORUS 10	Saxes play a descending four-note riff 10 times; brass counter-riff continues. Jones whacks the snare drum every two measures.

rhythmic music typically for dancing. But overall, Ellington operated in an artistic sphere different from swing's. His music expressed a greater range of emotions than did the swing bands, employed more sensitive dynamics and more of a sense of theater than most, featured the most distinctive players and most varied sounds, experimented and innovated more than any others, was less prone to fads, and presented more original (and challenging) pieces, particularly on records.

In a swing band, the drummer kept the time and drove the band—examples include the great Jo Jones in the Count Basie band, Chick Webb in his own orchestra, and **Gene Krupa** with Benny Goodman.

Ellington's drummer Sonny Greer took a different course: he was less a driver of the band than a master colorist, with his subtle brush playing, tasteful stick work, and novel use of percussive effects (for example, on the evocative *Caravan*, 1937). Producer-entrepreneur **John Hammond** called Greer "the most intricate of all percussionists."

Even the best of the other big bands suffer a certain sameness if their recordings are listened to one after the other, but Ellington's recordings, taken together, offer variety, contrast, and even surprise. The Duke Ellington Orchestra predated the swing craze by a decade, helped in fact to foster it, popularized its catchphrase "It don't

◉ **Watch** the documentary on Count Basie on mymusiclab.com

octave tremolo a rapidly repeating oscillation between two notes that are one octave apart.

mean a thing if it ain't got that swing," and provided its highest benchmarks of originality.

Other than the Ellington aggregation, the greatest swing era ensemble was led by pianist and bandleader William "Count" Basie. His band, which he organized in Kansas City, was steeped in the blues and its traditions, from blues chord progressions and blue notes (certain "bent" notes) to bluesy riffs (short, repeated phrases often rendered behind soloists).

Soon after the band arrived in New York in 1936, it became champion of the hotly competitive Harlem ballrooms, edging out the orchestras of Ellington, Webb, and Lunceford. Basie's band became famous for its outstanding soloists and its peerless "rhythm section"—Basie on piano, Freddie Green on guitar, Walter Page on string bass, and Jo Jones on drums—whose light but relentlessly forward-moving propulsion, or swing, was the envy of many other bands. The Basie rhythm section influenced others to play more flexibly and more responsively to the horn players. In such recordings as *Taxi War Dance* (1939), Basie's rocking Kansas City rhythm proved irresistible to dancers. His use of freewheeling **"head"** (unwritten) **arrangements**, in which a player might blow for several choruses, made his performances even more exciting.

By 1939, the band comprised 15 instrumentalists and 2 singers, Helen Humes (who replaced Billie Holiday in 1938) and Jimmy Rushing. Basie's band was dominated by great soloists: tenor saxophonists Lester Young (*Lester Leaps In*, 1939) and Herschel Evans (*Doggin' Around*, 1938); trumpeters Buck Clayton (*One O'Clock Jump*, 1937) and Harry "Sweets" Edison (*Shorty George*, 1938); trombonist Dicky Wells (*Texas Shuffle*, 1938); and Basie himself (*Doggin' Around*). His own early playing followed the two-handed ragtime approach, but in the mid-1930s he switched to a relaxed, spare style—imbued with subtlety and wit—that led beautifully into his instrumentalists' solos. From the piano keyboard, Basie cued, directed, and "swung" the band.

From the 1950s on he chose a style rather different from his classic 1930s sound, but Basie's band remained an enduring musical institution.

TAKE NOTE

- What were the key African American bands of the swing era and why were they important?

Watch the video of *Basie's Boogie* by Count Basie on **mymusiclab.com**

head arrangement an arrangement worked out, usually collectively, on an impromptu basis and typically played from memory.

The Great White Bands

Established in Detroit in 1927 as the Orange Blossoms, the **Casa Loma Orchestra** became the first notable white swing band and a model for later bands. With such arrangements as *Casa Loma Stomp* and *San Sue Strut* (both 1930), arranger Gene Gifford transformed the Casa Loma Orchestra from a semi-hot dance band into a jazz outfit known for its precise ensemble playing, fast tempos, and rhythmic energy that could bring dancers to the floor and raise the temperature of any ballroom.

Their flashy uptempo numbers (up to 250 beats per minute) such as *White Jazz* (1931) required great teamwork. When asked later how the Casa Lomans managed to play such demanding charts, clarinetist Clarence Hutchenrider—the band's leading soloist—quipped, "We practiced hard between drinks." But the Casa Loma Orchestra balanced its repertory, mixing fast numbers with such slow-dance ballads as *Smoke Rings* (1932).

The band enjoyed its greatest popularity from 1930 to 1935. Its youthfulness and exuberance attracted followers on the college circuit, while it also performed for older dancers at plush hotels, including New York's Essex House, where it held a residency for nearly two years, in 1933–34.

When compared with music by the best black bands of the 1930s, the Casa Loma Orchestra's recordings reveal more technical virtuosity (some would say mechanical exactness) than soulfulness or creativity, and they lack the looseness evident in the best of swing. Nonetheless, the ensemble exerted a strong influence, even on black bands. (Eddie Barefield, who played and arranged for the Bennie Moten band in the early 1930s, recalled that "we all admired the Casa Loma band, and tried to ape them.") Its precise ensemble playing, well-crafted arrangements, and appeal to college students provided a model for Benny Goodman and other bandleaders.

Clarinetist and bandleader Benny Goodman played a key role in moving jazz from the margins of American culture to the mainstream. He boasted superb technique on his instrument, excellent control, and a clear, light tone. He led the most influential, for a time the most popular, and perhaps the most polished of the big bands of the period. They sent a ripple of excitement through the nation after wowing an audience at the Palomar Ballroom in Los Angeles on August 21, 1935, and, for many who hadn't been paying close attention, seemed to launch the swing era. In 1937 his band attracted screaming bobby-soxers at the Paramount Theatre in New York City, and their performances often ignited audience passions to the point that fans rushed the stage to jitterbug to Goodman's music.

Watch the documentary on Benny Goodman on **mymusiclab.com**

Clarinetist Benny Goodman (front) came to prominence as a leader of a big band. Later, he established a trio, a quartet, and a sextet. His orchestra is shown here at Chicago's Congress Hotel shortly after a 1935 breakthrough engagement at the Palomar in Los Angeles. With him at the time were vocalist Helen Ward and drummer Gene Krupa. PHOTO COURTESY FRANK DRIGGS COLLECTION.

A perfectionist and strict taskmaster, Goodman demanded a high level of musicianship from his players and became famous for his glare, dubbed "the ray." His band suffered legendary turnover; singer Helen Forrest said she left the band "to avoid having a nervous breakdown."

Like Louis Armstrong, but unlike Duke Ellington, Goodman took most of the band's solos himself. But it wasn't for lack of talent among his employees.

Goodman's band boasted possibly the most esteemed trumpet section—Ziggy Elman and Harry James were key players—of any big band of the swing era. Trumpeter Bunny Berigan sparkled on Goodman's recordings of *King Porter Stomp* and *Sometimes I'm*

sweet bands a term, often used derogatorily in jazz, from the 1920s and 1930s to denote commercial dance bands that featured minimal improvisation—the opposite of hot bands.

Issues

The Commercial Success of White Swing Bands

Did white bands profit from swing music at the expense of the black musicians who created the style?

When Benny Goodman's band launched the swing era after appearing at Los Angeles's Palomar Ballroom, some black bandleaders groused that Goodman was profiting from a style that they had been performing—less successfully—for years. This was compounded by the fact that Goodman purchased arrangements from Fletcher Henderson, a leading black

bandleader (see Chapter 4) whom many credit with creating big band swing style. Although Goodman led a racially integrated small group, many felt that the reason he was successful was because he and most of his band members were white, making them more acceptable to book at better hotels and clubs (and thus being able to command higher pay), for radio broadcast, and to appear in movies.

Some argued that while Goodman and some others truly captured the spirit of swing, other white bands just took some simple elements—such as the call-and-response between sections—and

incorporated them into their more conservative style of playing. Many of the popular white bands were labeled "**sweet**" because they focused on pop tunes for dancing and weren't considered to be bona fide swing outfits.

The problem of untangling musical inspiration and separating that from mere imitation runs throughout the history of jazz—and popular music as a whole. Were blacks exploited? Did whites add something beyond mere imitation in popularizing swing music and thus deserve some credit for its success?

—*Richard Carlin*

Listening Guide

Listen to *Honeysuckle Rose* by Benny Goodman and His Orchestra on **mymusiclab.com**
CD I, Track 13/Download Track 13

HONEYSUCKLE ROSE • BENNY GOODMAN AND HIS ORCHESTRA

Music: Fats Waller. Lyrics (not heard here): Andy Razaf, 1928. Personnel: Ziggy Elman, Jimmy Maxwell, Johnny Martel (trumpet); Red Ballard, Vernon Brown, Ted Vesely (trombone); Benny Goodman (clarinet); Toots Mondello, Buff Estes (alto saxophone); Jerry Jerome, Bus Bassey (tenor saxophone); Fletcher Henderson (piano, arranger); Charlie Christian (electric guitar); Artie Bernstein (bass); Nick Fatool (drums). Recorded November 22, 1939, in New York. First issue: Columbia 35319. Timing: 2:59.

Overview

Pianist Fats Waller composed *Honeysuckle Rose* in 1929 and it soon became a jazz perennial. At the time Goodman recorded it, there were 80 jazz recordings; by the 2010s, it had become one of the most-recorded jazz standards, with more than 1,200 versions. Waller's original song caught on with the public partly because his melody featured much repetition—which always makes tunes easier to remember. Waller's A section offers a phrase played three times, followed by second phrase played twice. The B section presents a slow-moving, ascending **scalar** melody, followed by a more active answering phrase; then this pattern is repeated a whole-step higher (an example of a musical **sequence**).

By the late 1930s, Benny Goodman had become the best-known and most popular jazz bandleader in America.

In the period preceding this recording, Goodman's band had suffered high turnover in personnel, yet the band still boasted tight ensemble playing, superb solos, and swing perhaps unmatched by any band except Count Basie's.

The arrangement by Fletcher Henderson, one of more than 200 that he made for Goodman, showcases the former's well-vetted approach. Eschewing the verse of the popular song, Henderson's charts typically concentrate on the better-known chorus section, typically using the form AABA. After a brief introduction, the statement of the melody consumes the first chorus, with solos over riff ensemble passages, and a final chorus setting forth a riff-based variation on the original melody.

The 23-year-old guitarist Charlie Christian joined the Goodman band just a few months before this recording, and he quickly became the most prominent guitarist in jazz. While Goodman had previously assembled a racially integrated trio and quartet, this was among his first recordings boldly fielding an integrated big band: both Henderson and Christian were African American, while the rest of the band was white.

Key Features

- Melody: In the first chorus of this performance, Henderson's arrangement presents Waller's melody in a recognizable fashion while at the same time dressing it up with numerous embellishments and small variations. After the first chorus, the original melody is not repeated.
- Form and structure: As was typical by the 1930s, this jazz arrangement of a popular song omits the verse section, leaving the 32-bar AABA chorus as the architecture. The straightforward formal plan entails a four-bar introduction followed by five readings of the chorus.
- Improvisation: The arrangements that Goodman commissioned for his band always allowed room for improvisation. Goodman featured his own soloing on virtually every performance, typically giving some solo space to one or two of his musicians. Here guitarist Charlie Christian, trumpeter Ziggy Elman, and Goodman himself are each featured—Goodman twice.
- Tempo: As was typical for the time, this performance is taken at a brisk clip—220 beats per minute. "People used to dance fast in those days," recalled saxophonist Russell Procope, "in ballrooms, they were used to playing fast."
- Riffs: In the 1920s, Fletcher Henderson had done much to develop a widely adopted approach to big band arranging, pitting one section (saxes, trumpets, trombones) of the band against another, and using frequent riffs. Here he employs riffs in two different ways: as background under soloists (Goodman's first solo, as well as

Happy (both 1935). Drummer Gene Krupa swung *Sing, Sing, Sing* (1937). Goodman himself shone on *Riding High* (1937), *Blue Room* (1938), and *Mission to Moscow* (1942).

Prior to Goodman, there had been occasional interracial bands, but primarily at after-hours jam sessions or in recording studios. For example, the Creole pianist Jelly Roll Morton recorded with the white New Orleans Rhythm Kings (1923); black guitarist Lonnie Johnson recorded with white

guitarist Eddie Lang (listen to *Handful of Riffs*, 1928, *JTSA* Disc 1/Track 14); and Louis Armstrong recorded with a range of white artists in the late 1920s, including trombonist Jack Teagarden, singer Hoagy Carmichael (1929), and country singer Jimmie

---

scalar related to a scale.

sequence a short melodic phrase repeated at different pitch levels.

Christian's and Elman's solo turns), and as replacements for the original melody, creating, in effect, two alternative melodies (one from 2:14 to 2:22, the other from 2:23 to 2:40 and 2:49 to 2:57). Introducing new melodies, instead of returning to the **head**, works in part because by 1939 *Honeysuckle Rose* was familiar to every jazz fan. Creating a new, riff-based melody set up, in the listener's head, an implied contrast between the original tune and Henderson's new melodic line.

- Voice, feel, and expression: Soloists Benny Goodman, Charlie Christian, and to a lesser extent Ziggy Elman all display their trademark playing styles, and Fletcher Henderson's arranging "voice" is very recognizable. This recording exudes a bright, cheerful kind of energy that motivated dancers to get out there and swing, swing, swing. And because of its high standard of virtuosity, artistry, variation, and contrast, it also works extremely well for listening and re-listening.

—*John Edward Hasse*

TIME	SECTION	FORM	MELODY
0:00	INTRODUCTION		The band plays a catchy four-bar introduction.
0:04	CHORUS 1	A	The band plays the song's melody. For the first four bars (0:04–0:08), the saxes render the melody as the brass comment with **staccato** punctuations. Then for the next four bars (0:08–0:13), the brass section plays the melody.
0:13		A	The preceding pattern is repeated: saxes take the melody for four bars (0:13 to 0:17), and then the brass play the melody for four bars (0:17–0:22).
0:22		B	Saxes continue the melody with brass punctuation.
0:32		A	Saxes continue playing the melody until the brass take over from 0:35 to 0:39.
0:40	CHORUS 2	AABA	Goodman plays a solo chorus, with artful mixing of fast passages, held notes, and rests. In the B section (starting at 0:58), Goodman interweaves his solo so tightly with the band it sounds like part of the arrangement, but it was improvised.
1:16	CHORUS 3	AABA	Charlie Christian takes an exceptional electric guitar solo in his influential style that used single-note lines rather than chords. Because his sound isn't as penetrating as either Goodman's clarinet or, in the next chorus, Elman's trumpet, arranger Henderson tones down the ensemble background so the guitar can be heard.
1:51	CHORUS 4	AA	Trumpeter Ziggy Elman improvises a well-crafted 16-bar solo, beginning with 10 D-flat notes. Note his effective use of a plunger mute at 1:54 and again at 2:03.
2:08		B	Goodman improvises a very active solo on the bridge, as the ensemble provides contrast by playing minimally: in succession, four notes, each held for two bars.
2:16		A	The saxes plays an eight-note riff, completely different from the original melody.
2:25	CHORUS 5	AA	The ensemble plays a different, rolling eight-note riff. To provide contrast, the band plays the first two statements of the riff (2:25–2:29) at lowered volume and the next two statements (2:29–2:33) at a higher volume. This happens in both statements of the A section here.
2:43		B	In the B section, the ensemble plays a stripped-down variation—two ascending scalar patterns—of the original B-section melody.
2:52		A	In the final A section, the ensemble returns to the second eight-note riff.

Rodgers (1930). But Goodman pioneered interracial bands playing *in public*: in 1935 Goodman formed a trio, with Gene Krupa on drums and Teddy Wilson on piano; the following year he added vibraphonist Lionel Hampton. His combos—later including the guitar virtuoso **Charlie Christian**—produced some of the most classic of small-group swing, exemplified by such performances as *After You've Gone* (the Benny Goodman Trio, 1935), *Avalon* (the Quartet, 1937), and *Breakfast Feud* (the Sextet, 1941).

Offering a cool contrast to the hot playing style of Goodman was fellow clarinetist Artie Shaw. From the first bars of his dark theme song, *Nightmare* (1938), one could tell that Shaw was a bandleader of a different order. After failing to win public

head   in jazz, the main melody of a tune.

staccato   played with shortened duration, detached from other notes in a phrase; not legato.

acceptance for a group based around a string quartet, he formed a conventional big band in 1937; in 1938 he enjoyed an enormous hit with the challenging 108-bar Cole Porter tune, *Begin the Beguine*. Propelled by this success, Shaw became a rival to Goodman, and even a matinee idol. But the introspective Shaw, conflicted about his huge celebrity and unhappy about playing the same hits over and over again, broke up his band in 1939. Thereafter his disbandings became almost as frequent as his marriages (eight, including those to glamorous actresses Lana Turner and Ava Gardner).

Between its hiatuses, however, the Shaw band produced some of the finest jazz of the era, such as *Traffic Jam* (1939) and *Lucky Number* (1945). With celebrated choruses by trumpeter Billy Butterfield, trombonist Jack Jenney and Shaw himself, the band's *Stardust* (1940; *JTSA* Disc 2/Track 10) ranks as a masterpiece of jazz, the quintessential big band recording of Hoagy Carmichael's perennial. Shaw assembled a small group called the Gramercy Five in 1940, 1945, and 1954 to make such memorable recordings as *Summit Ridge Drive* (1940), *Special Delivery Stomp* (1940), and *Yesterdays* (1954).

In 1939, the Shaw band made a short film called *Free Wheelin'*, which featured a medley of their well-known numbers, including their theme song *Nightmare* followed by *Table D'Hote*, composed by

Shaw, and the pop song *I Have Eyes*. In the film's opening sequence, the makeup of a typical big band is illustrated, with the roles of each instrumental section demonstrated. Despite the somewhat dated dialogue, the film gives a good snapshot of the Shaw band at the height of its powers.

Trombonist **Tommy Dorsey** and his younger brother clarinetist Jimmy Dorsey formed the Dorsey Brothers Orchestra in 1934, but in 1935 Tommy Dorsey walked off the stage in a pique, his famous hot temper showing, and formed his own band. He turned heads with his silky-smooth, lyrical playing, especially on such ballads as *I'm Getting Sentimental over You* (1935). Many of the band's recordings were of novelty tunes and pop songs in uninspired arrangements, though his soloists (trumpeters Bunny Berigan and Yank Lawson, and drummer Buddy Rich) could sometimes transform this kind of mediocre material into an artistic creation: for example, Berigan's solo on Dorsey's *Marie* (1937) became one of his most polished, enduring statements.

Still, prior to 1939, Dorsey's dance band had little to do with jazz. Then when Dorsey hired Sy Oliver (who had been with the Jimmie Lunceford band) as his chief arranger in 1939, the bandleader finally

👁 **Watch** the video *Free Wheelin'* by Artie Shaw on **mymusiclab.com**

Tommy Dorsey (standing, with trombone) led a band that in 1941 included vocalist Jo Stafford (back row, second from left), Frank Sinatra (back row, right), and drummer Buddy Rich. PHOTO COURTESY FRANK DRIGGS COLLECTION.

Moonlight Serenade *(1939)* *and many other hits helped earn the Glenn Miller Orchestra a vast following of swing fans.*
PHOTO COURTESY DOWN BEAT ARCHIVES.

achieved something he had lacked: a swinging jazz sound and style, as Oliver's masterful *Well, Git It!* (1942) and *Opus One* (1943) so amply demonstrate. After Oliver's arrival, the band's repertory proceeded on two lines: the jazz-swing material and the romantic pop vocals sung by Jo Stafford, Frank Sinatra, and the Pied Pipers; the band reached its peak of popularity from 1940 to 1942.

Like Dorsey, his friend **Glenn Miller** was a bespectacled trombone player who emerged as a bandleader during the late 1930s, becoming a driving taskmaster and a successful musician-businessman. During the late 1930s and early 1940s, Miller led the most popular swing band of its day. Never a remarkable trombone soloist, he left his mark as a band arranger, organizer, and especially leader. Miller's band was known not so much for its rhythmic drive or great improvisatory ability—it boasted only one important jazz soloist, Bobby Hackett—as for its precision and musicianship. The band's most characteristic sound featured a clarinet playing the melody an octave above four saxophones.

Miller organized his first band in 1937. He leaped to national fame in 1939 through live radio broadcasts from the Glen Island Casino and the Meadowbrook

Ballroom and through his own *Moonlight Serenade* radio series.

In its brief four-year life, the Miller orchestra enjoyed many hit recordings, including pop ballads and novelties, but it's best remembered for riff-based instrumental pieces such as *In the Mood* (1939), *Tuxedo Junction* (1940), and *A String of Pearls* (1941). He disbanded his group in 1942 to join the U.S. Army Air Force and in the service organized a first-rate band, which entertained extensively in Britain. In December 1944, Miller's airplane disappeared over the English Channel; widely mourned, he was hailed as a war hero.

Woody Herman's band formed in 1936 when Isham Jones retired and six of his players decided to form a new group, electing clarinetist Herman as the front man. The new group became known as "the band that plays the blues," and with the million-selling head arrangement *Woodchopper's Ball* (1939), it attracted national attention.

By 1944, his band, now dubbed **Woody Herman's Herd**, featured such outsized personalities as tenorman Flip Phillips, trombonist Bill Harris, drummer Dave Tough, and bassist Chubby Jackson, as well as arrangers Neal Hefti and Ralph Burns. The Herd

Woody Herman's bands—which were numerous over his long career—became known as incubators of talented young players. Shown here is Herman's Second Herd. L to r: Fred Otis, piano; Mary Ann McCall, vocalist; Woody Herman; Harry Babasin, bass; Stan Getz, tenor sax; Serge Chaloff, baritone sax; Shorty Rogers, trumpet; Ernie Royal, trumpet; Ollie Wilson, trombone; Zoot Sims, tenor sax; Bernie Glow, trumpet; Earl Swope, trombone; Irving Markowitz, trumpet. COURTESY INSTITUTE OF JAZZ STUDIES, RUTGERS UNIVERSITY.

built a reputation for its modern, progressive swing, as on such 1945 recordings as *Caldonia*, *Bijou*, and *Northwest Passage*, and the driving, stand-up-and-cheer exuberance of *Apple Honey* (based on *I Got Rhythm* chord changes). The band won numerous polls, a sign of the respect Herman commanded for the originality, force, and influence of his music. Two works from 1946 pushed the limits of the jazz-band repertoire: Ralph Burns's twelve-minute *Summer Sequence* and *Ebony Concerto*, which Igor Stravinsky wrote for Herman's band (augmented by harp and French horn) and which they premiered at Carnegie Hall.

Herman disbanded the Herd in 1946. A year later he formed his Second Herd, rooted in bebop, with a front line of saxophonists—Stan Getz, Serge Chaloff, Zoot Sims, and Herbie Steward—that became famous as the Four Brothers after being featured on a recording by that name (*JTSA* Disc 2/ Track 19). The Second Herd disbanded in 1949, but Herman continued to lead bands for the rest of his career. His greatest talent was for organizing and sustaining ensembles boasting exceptional arrangements and bright young musicians, and for balancing changing musical tastes with his fundamental musical integrity.

TAKE NOTE

- What were the main white bands of the swing era and why were they important?

Big Band Care and Maintenance

As swing became the rage, hundreds of bands were formed to satisfy young Americans' craving for the music. By 1939, there would be an estimated 200 "name" bands, employing some 3,000 musicians, playing swing across the United States.

The leaders of the big bands—from Charlie Barnet and Count Basie to Claude Thornhill and Chick Webb—received the most publicity and, generally, the greatest adulation. But they also endured the headaches of keeping a bunch of mostly single young men in line on the road, meeting a payroll, and dealing with booking agents and dance hall operators. Maintaining order and discipline was demanding, in part because most of the swing bandleaders of the 1930s were themselves relatively young men; most were in their 30s, and Goodman and Shaw were only in their 20s. Some leaders—Goodman and Lunceford, for example—were strict disciplinarians, while others, notably Ellington, took a laissez-faire attitude toward band-member behavior.

If leading a swing band presented many challenges, playing in the bands wasn't an easy job either. Apart from the demands of the leaders and audiences, the constant travel, and the late hours (no wonder the swing bands were composed mostly of young people), the musicians had to perform under great pressure, most of all in the recording studio. Whereas in later styles of jazz, musicians often soloed for a chorus or more, during the swing era the tight arrangements typically allowed soloists only six or eight bars in which to make a musical statement. You had to be concise,

Charlie Barnet (on sax) and his band going for a "keeper" with the tape rolling, 1949. The dark-shirted trumpet player (center), Doc Severinsen, would go on to lead the Tonight Show Band during Johnny Carson's tenure as host of that long-running television program. PHOTO COURTESY ZINN ARTHUR/DOWN BEAT ARCHIVES.

coherent, and consistently good; if you frequently flubbed your solo spot, you were out.

The constant travel was hard on both the leaders and the players; while many of the white bands had the luxury of playing in theaters, hotels, or ballrooms for extended stays, many of the black bands had to tour non-stop. For example, in 1942 Lunceford estimated that "we do a couple of hundred one-nighters a year, fifteen to twenty weeks of theaters, maybe one four-week location, and two weeks of vacation. All in all, we cover about forty thousand miles a year!" For the black bands, travel invariably meant bad hotel rooms (or splitting up to sleep in homes in black neighborhoods), spotty access to food, racial insults, and sometimes threats.

TAKE NOTE

- What were the challenges in keeping a band together and financially successful?

Conservatory trained Tommy Douglas (standing), one of Charlie Parker's musical influences, fit a large band into a small tour bus in 1938. PHOTO COURTESY FRANK DRIGGS COLLECTION.

All-Women Bands

If black bands faced challenges, so did the "all-girl bands," whether black or white. Women musicians faced greater demands regarding their appearance. Sexism was open and rampant and took many forms: some men belittled women as not being able to swing or play jazz; jazz magazines objectified women, making musical expression always secondary to looks; and men in positions of power often demanded sexual favors from women in exchange for places in bands or on radio programs. A Connecticut law forbad women from working after 10 p.m., making it illegal for female musicians to perform typical nighttime engagements. Despite these and other obstacles, a number of all-female bands managed to survive and even, for a few years, thrive.

In addition to pianist Lil Hardin Armstrong's several female ensembles, African American "all-girl" big bands of the 1930s included the Dixie Rhythm Girls, the Harlem Playgirls, and the Dixie Sweethearts. The most popular white female band was Ina Rae Hutton and Her Melodears (1934–39).

Hutton, a singer, was dubbed "The Blonde Bombshell of Rhythm," and in the words of *Variety* magazine, she "spelled box office forward and backward."

Foremost of the all-female bands was the International Sweethearts of Rhythm, which was formed at Piney Woods Country Life School in Mississippi, in 1939. The "International" in its name referred to the diversity of its members—women of black, white, Latina, and Chinese descent. Their ranks included such fine instrumentalists as drummer Pauline Braddy, tenor saxophonist Vi Burnside, and bassist Carline Ray. By 1941, they severed their ties with the Piney Woods School and toured to enthusiastic reception: at Washington, DC's Howard Theater, they set a new weekly record when 35,000 fans turned out for the show. They played the Apollo Theater through 1953, and, according to the Apollo's owner/manager Jack Schiffman, "Only the prevailing prejudices prevented the Sweethearts from becoming a major attraction."

During the 1940s, the black all-female Prairie View Co-Eds, college students at Texas's historically

The International Sweethearts of Rhythm.
PHOTO COURTESY FRANK DRIGGS COLLECTION.

black Prairie View A&M College, toured during summers and also performed at Harlem's famed Apollo Theater. Eddie Durham's All-Stars was an all-girl band, which Durham provided arrangements for. They, too, played the Apollo in the 1940s, even backing Ella Fitzgerald.

Because of their visual appeal, women bands were captured more often on film than on recordings. Ina Rae Hutton and Her Melodears performed in *The Big Broadcast of 1936* (1935) and the film shorts *Accent on Girls* (1936) and *Swing, Hutton, Swing* (1937), while the International Sweethearts of Rhythm played in three short Soundie films from 1946: *Jump Children*, *She's Crazy with the Heat*, and *That Man of Mine*.

Some women became leaders of all-male bands: In the 1930s, singer Blanche Calloway, sister of bandleader-singer Cab Calloway, led a group that was popular at the Apollo Theater. After the death of bandleader-drummer Chick Webb in 1939, singer Ella Fitzgerald took over and "fronted" the band for three years. Pianist Mary Lou Williams led a number of small ensembles, and in the 1940s, Ina Rae Hutton led an all-male band.

TAKE NOTE

- Why did all-female bands arise during this period, and how did they help advance women's role in jazz?

Shapers of the Sound

To sonically fill the cavernous dance halls and theaters, and to create additional musical interest, the bands had been expanding their personnel. As larger bands became the norm in the late 1920s and the 1930s, they required more-skilled **orchestrations**. After all, even an aggregation of the best musicians will be severely limited without good material to play. Most of the famous bandleaders—Goodman, Dorsey, and Webb—possessed neither the skills, inclination, nor time to do their own arranging. Rather, they relied on the talents of behind-the-scenes orchestrator-arrangers who actually determined the characteristic style of a band more than did the soloists, singers, or bandleaders. In the hotly competitive environment of the swing era, with each band seeking its own sound, the arrangers—however invisible to the public—were crucial.

---

orchestration the assignment of instruments to the raw melodies and harmonies of a composition, affecting the color and texture of a performance.

Benny Carter, saxophonist, multi-instrumentalist, bandleader, sideman, and arranger, in 1944. PHOTO COURTESY GILLES PETARD/REDFERNS/GETTY IMAGES.

For his band's arrangements, Fletcher Henderson supplied his own while also turning to his brother Horace Henderson as well as to Don Redman and Benny Carter. Benny Goodman used arranger Fletcher Henderson, Edgar Sampson, Mel Powell, and Eddie Sauter. Glenn Miller was a good arranger, but he also employed Bill Finnegan, Jerry Gray, and Billy May to write his arrangements.

Some of the Count Basie band's pieces were head arrangements—made up collectively during rehearsals or recording dates, not credited to any one individual, and often not written down. Basie also secured written-out arrangements from Herschel Evans.

TAKE NOTE

- How did arrangers help create the successful big band sound?

What Does a Jazz Arranger Do?

Bandleaders hired arrangers to prepare **charts** of given pieces of music, specifying the parts to be played by each instrument in the band—in essence, turning a skeletal melody-and-chords composition into a fully orchestrated score customized to the band's sound and style.

In jazz, an arranger usually begins with certain specifications. Knowing which ensemble has commissioned the work, he or she will know the instrumentation and perhaps the players and the context (a dance piece? concert piece? record date? telecast?) and will have a general idea of the desired length.

During the big band era, some parameters were givens—especially duration and instrumentation. Until the advent of long-playing recordings in the 1950s, most arrangements were tailored to fit on a 10-inch 78-rpm record, which could hold three or four minutes of material. And big bands had a fairly standard instrumental lineup. In 1940, for example, Duke Ellington, Benny Goodman, and Artie Shaw each fielded a band of 15 instrumentalists, including themselves (all told, three trumpets, three trombones, five reeds, and a rhythm section of four).

But within these bounds, the arranger would have considerable leeway, deciding on the key; the general tempo (a ballad? a medium bounce? a "killer"?); the degree of reference to, or departure from, the original song or an earlier arrangement; the spirit and feel (sweet or sharp? droll or solemn? nostalgic or contemporary?); the overall architecture (include an altered verse or chorus? a new introduction and ending? a transitional passage?); the number of instruments that play at any given moment (should the trumpets drop out here?); which instruments state the melody and which take solos and at what points; changes in the original piece's harmony, melody, and rhythm; and specific instrumental voicings and tone colors.

Anatomy of an Arrangement

Much as different painters would render different still-life interpretations of the same assemblage of household objects, each arranger who tackled, say, *Mood Indigo* perceived its artistic possibilities in an individual way. When Ellington first arranged the composition (which he and his clarinetist Barney Bigard composed) for his band, the maestro voiced the main theme for tightly muted trumpet, trombone, and low-register clarinet, producing a brand-new tone color. By the early 1950s, he had rearranged the theme for two trombones and bass clarinet, and in 1966, for trumpet, flute, and bass clarinet.

Indeed, the Ellington musical archives at the Smithsonian Institution's National Museum of American History include no fewer than 10 different arrangements of *Mood Indigo*, which he reworked every few years to feature different players or to try a new sonic approach. His saxophonist, Russell Procope, commented that "a new arrangement would freshen [*Mood Indigo*] up, like you pour water on a flower, to keep it blooming. They'd all bloom—fresh, fresh arrangements."

Most of these were instrumental versions; however, four featured vocalists: Ivie Anderson (1940), Kay Davis in a wordless vocal (1945), Yvonne Lanauze (1950), and Rosemary Clooney (1956). The 1945 version, recorded for RCA Victor (reissued on the album *Black, Brown, and Beige*), features an outrageous series of key changes and dissonant chords. Billy Strayhorn's 1950 arrangement for the album *Masterpieces by Ellington* extends

Bandleader Artie Shaw (right) conferring with arranger Johnny Mandel.

the piece to 17 choruses and 15 minutes, through three keys and many contrasting sonorities, densities, and timbres.

Although Ellington "owned" the piece, a few other big bands recorded their own versions, among them Jimmie Lunceford (arrangement below by Willie Smith, 1934)

and Hal McIntyre (arranged by Syd Schwartz, 1944).

These diagrams show that Ellington made varying decisions regarding instruments stating the melody, inclusion of the piece's second theme, the length of the arrangement, and other elements. While Ellington's arrangements

maintained the dreamy mood of the original, Lunceford's version—with its punchy countermelodies—created an entirely different feeling.

—*John Edward Hasse*

---

chart informal term for the notation of a tune; written music read by musicians.

Duke Ellington and His Orchestra (12 players total), recorded on December 10, 1930, for RCA Victor

16 bars	4 bars	16 bars	16 bars	16 bars
Theme A	Passage	Solo	Solo/Theme B	Theme A
trumpet, trombone, clarinet	piano	muted trumpet	clarinet with band	trumpet, trombone, clarinet

Duke Ellington and His Orchestra (15 players total), filmed on March 14, 1952, for Snader Telescriptions (for TV stations)

4 bars	16 bars	16 bars	16 bars	16 bars	16 bars	2 bars
Intro	Theme A	Solo	Solo	Solo	Theme A	Coda
piano	2 trombones + bass clarinet	clarinet	trumpet	piano	2 trombones + bass clarinet	band

Duke Ellington and His Orchestra (15 players total), recorded on May 11, 1966, for RCA Victor (*The Popular Duke Ellington*)

16 bars	16 bars	16 bars	16 bars	16 bars	4 bars	4 bars
Introduction (a rubato variation on Theme A)	Theme A	Solo (variation on Theme B)	Theme A	Solo (variation on Theme B)	Passage	Coda (Theme A)
piano	8 bars trumpet, flute, bass clarinet; 8 bars add tenor sax obbligato	piano	12 bars band + 4 bars band w/clarinet obbligato	clarinet	piano	band

Jimmie Lunceford and His Orchestra (13 players total), recorded on September 11, 1934, for Decca

4 bars	16 bars	4 bars	16 bars	16 bars	16 bars	2 bars
Intro	Theme A	Passage	Solo	Theme A (embellished)	8 bars Theme A, 4 bars new material, 4 bars Theme A	Coda
band	muted brass (reeds play a punchy countermelody)	2 bars trumpet, 2 bars trombone	trumpet (band plays smooth background riffs, mostly based on Theme A)	muted trumpet (band plays staccato chords; piano, guitar, drums lay out)	8 bars trumpet, 4 bars sax tutti, 4 bars trumpet	band

Small Groups and Solo Artists

If the swing era remains for many people the time of the big bands, it should also be remembered for its classic small groups, engaging singers, and remarkable soloists.

Between 1935 and 1941, Ellington made 140 recordings with small groups, comprising 6 to 10 musicians drawn from his big band. These sessions yielded such enduring recordings as the mournful *Mobile Bay* (1940), released under the nominal leadership of cornetist Rex Stewart, and the exquisite *Passion Flower* (1941), under the name of Ellington's alto saxophone star Johnny Hodges. There were small groups within other big bands, too: the Count Basie Ensemble, the Benny Goodman Trio, Tommy Dorsey's Clambake Seven, Bob Crosby's Bob Cats, Chick Webb and His Little Chicks, Artie Shaw and His Gramercy Five, and Woody Herman's Woodchoppers.

In the 1920s, Louis Armstrong had emerged as the dominant soloist in jazz and as the individual who would, more than anyone else, take the role of soloist to new heights in American music. Now, in the 1930s, following in Armstrong's footsteps, soloists and singers emerged who boasted individual styles that clearly differentiated them from others and would project their voices well into the future.

Coleman Hawkins and Miles Davis, at the Three Deuces, New York, New York (ca. July 1947). PHOTO COURTESY WILLIAM P. GOTTLIEB/WILLIAM P. GOTTLIEB COLLECTION/LIBRARY OF CONGRESS PRINTS & PHOTOGRAPHS DIVISION.

Solo Instrumentalists

Among the most radiant soloists was tenor saxophonist Coleman Hawkins, who, during his tenure with Fletcher Henderson (1923–34), helped transform the saxophone from a novelty instrument into an expressive, recognized vehicle for jazz. After returning to the United States in 1939 from a five-year residency in Europe, he recorded the stunning *Body and Soul* (CD I, Track 14/Download Track 14). This recording—one of the most celebrated saxophone solos in history—instantly established Hawkins as a star soloist. With his emphatic attack, rhythmic flexibility, full-bodied vibrato, rich tone, and emotional conviction, he founded a whole school of tenor saxophone playing that would include Don Byas, Chu Berry, Herschel Evans, and Ben Webster.

If Hawkins's style was hot, with a pronounced vibrato and rhythmic emphasis, then tenorman Lester Young's style was cool, with a lighter swing and virtually no vibrato. As a member of the Count Basie band in 1936–40 and 1943–44, the soft-spoken Young gradually established his tenor style—more delicate and detached—as a counter to Hawkins's. One of Young's earliest recordings, *Oh! Lady Be Good* (1936, with a quintet from the Basie band), displays such hallmarks of his style as a relaxed sense of swing; a compression of the wide, arpeggio-inspired lines characteristic of Hawkins into more compact melodic shapes; and a freeing of improvisation from the underlying

The soft-spoken Lester "Pres" Young spoke volumes on the tenor sax, and the message registered with a generation of later musicians. PHOTO COURTESY MYRON EHREN BERG/DOWN BEAT ARCHIVES.

Roy Eldridge dominated the jazz trumpet field post–Louis Armstrong and pre–Dizzy Gillespie.

harmonic sequence. This latter innovation would have far-reaching consequences for jazz in the bebop era and beyond. Young's star vehicle, *Lester Leaps In* (1939, with a septet from the Basie band), showcases his superior choice of notes and interlinking melodic ideas. Young's new aesthetic, along with his long, flowing lines, made him the most influential musician in jazz between the rise of Louis Armstrong in the 1920s and that of Charlie Parker, beginning in the mid-1940s.

A focused pitch wasn't a priority for tenor saxophonist Ben Webster, who reveled in sheer sound and tone. With his breathy timbre and sensuality, Webster was a romantic of the highest order, spinning out eloquent solos on such ballads as *Stardust* and *All Too Soon* (both 1940 with the Ellington band). The fast and flashy *Cotton Tail* (also 1940) became a Webster trademark during his 1940–43 years with Ellington, but in fact Webster had a wide tonal and emotional range that encompassed the powerful, driving, and raspy as well as the warm, eloquent, and lyrical. These opposites led to the apt title for the biographical film *The Brute and the Beautiful* (1991).

After Armstrong, Roy Eldridge became the most original trumpeter in jazz until Dizzy Gillespie came to the fore in the 1940s. Taking his deep tone and

arpeggio-laden style from Coleman Hawkins, Eldridge became a powerful, virtuosic player, boasting dexterity over a three-octave range, as on the dazzling *After You've Gone* (1937). With its ease, authority, shape, and skill, his *Rockin' Chair* (1941, with Gene Krupa's orchestra) ranks among the greatest recorded jazz solos. The exuberant, good-humored, and keenly competitive Eldridge loved jam sessions and cutting contests. He helped to dismantle the color barrier in jazz during his stints with the bands of Gene Krupa (1941–43) and Artie Shaw (1944–45). For an example of Eldridge's playing, listen to Gene Krupa's *Let Me Off Uptown* (*JTSA* Disc 2/Track 11).

Trumpeter Bunny Berigan combined influences of Louis Armstrong and Bix Beiderbecke into a personal voice noted for its tone, lyricism, technical assurance, power and projection, exploitation of the trumpet's low register, and clarity of structure. These trademarks can all be heard on his masterpiece (and hit recording), *I Can't Get Started* (1937). Like Beiderbecke, Berigan suffered from alcoholism; he died at the age of 33.

Following in the footsteps of his fellow New Orleans trumpeter Louis Armstrong, Henry "Red" Allen brandished a style brimming with energy and authority. Known for his daring, rhythmic freedom, and large arsenal of timbral devices (slurs, growls, **rips**, **trills**, and half-valve effects), Allen was an outstanding interpreter of the blues. Three of his best solos were made in 1933 with Fletcher Henderson's orchestra: *King Porter Stomp*, *Queer Notions*, and *Nagasaki*.

Trumpet star Bunny Berigan.

---

rip a loud tonal slide (glissando) up to a note, often ending with a sharp accent; can be heard in the playing of trumpeters Bix Beiderbecke and Louis Armstrong, among many others.

trill for ornamentation, a rapidly repeating alternation of a note with its adjoining note.

Body and Soul by Coleman Hawkins

Johnny Green, the composer of *Body and Soul*, reported "that the question he most frequently heard was, 'When you were writing *Body and Soul*, did you realize that this was to be the most recorded **torch song** of all time?'" According to critic Will Friedwald, "Early on, he formulated a set response: 'No, all I knew was that it had to be finished by Wednesday.'" *Body and Soul* (CD I, Track 14/Download Track 14) is the best-known song written by Green, who, when he composed it in 1930, was a recent Harvard University economics graduate.

Body and Soul utilizes standard 32-bar AABA form. William Zinsser observed that the B section or **bridge** of *Body and Soul* is a gem of "unexpectedness. . . . a bridge unlike any other. The first four bars . . . are one-half-step above the home key of the song, while the next four bars . . . are one-half-step *below* the home key." This can make playing or singing the bridge tricky for veteran musicians, and perilous for beginners.

With its catchy melody and challenging harmonies, the song entered jazz tradition when Louis Armstrong recorded it in 1930, though his solo stuck fairly close to the melody. During that decade, Benny Goodman, Red Allen, **Art Tatum**, Django Reinhardt, and Roy Eldridge recorded it, but it was the 1939 version by tenor saxophonist Coleman Hawkins that immortalized *Body and Soul* among jazz lovers.

By the time of this recording, Hawkins had honed a style built on command of a wide range on his instrument and deep emotional conviction. *Body and Soul* demonstrates these qualities and showcases his biggest contribution to the development of jazz: exploring the outlines of chords for his solos rather than the then-standard practice of embellishing the melody.

The accompaniment throughout Hawkins's recording is bare-bones: even during the second chorus when the horns come in, the show belongs entirely to Hawkins. After a four-bar introduction by pianist Gene Rodgers, Hawkins begins (at 0:08) to both state and paraphrase the melody of *Body and Soul*. In the second A section (0:30), he departs more from the original melody, just hinting at Green's line. In the B section (0:50), which modulates from the key of D-flat major to the remote key of D major, Hawkins begins exploring a wider range on his instrument, incorporating notes that are higher and lower than previous ones. By the second chorus (1:30), Hawkins has completely abandoned Green's

The pianist Art Tatum, who was 85 percent blind, typically performed in small clubs and was at his best as a solo pianist, for he played a full, orchestral style that needed latitude so he could shape dramatic contrasts. His arpeggios and **runs** (fast-paced streams of notes) in the right (and even the left) hands astonished fellow musicians and the public; beneath his speed and dazzling, classically trained technique lay Tatum's daring and inventive reharmonizations—one could even say recompositions—of pop songs and show tunes. He favored formulas (many recordings followed a format of free/strict/free tempo) and worked out most solos

Art Tatum set new technical standards for jazz piano playing. PHOTO COURTESY FRANK DRIGGS COLLECTION.

torch song in popular music, a sad or sentimental song describing an unrequited love; from the expression "to carry a torch" for someone. Examples are *My Man, Stormy Weather, Lover Man, Body and Soul,* and *One for My Baby (and One More for the Road).*

bridge a segment of a tune, usually 8 or 16 bars, that departs from the main melody in order to provide contrast and development; the B in AABA form, for example.

run a rapid sequence of notes, ascending or descending.

melody and is playing on the chord changes. At 1:47, he renders several sequences. He continues to heighten the intensity, artfully saving his highest note of the solo (an F at 2:37) for the final A section. Throughout the 64 bars (two choruses), Hawkins builds to the climax, playing higher notes with louder volume, a more strident tone, and greater rhythmic intensity. He even nudges the tempo from an opening 95 beats per minute to 99 by song's end. Hawkins shapes his solo brilliantly; later, he would compare the arc of his solo to a lovemaking session.

Hawkins's approach on *Body and Soul*—making new melodies from the chords of an old piece—would become, in a few years, the new *modus operandi* of the beboppers. The recording represented the apotheosis of Hawkins's career and one of the most celebrated jazz improvisations ever recorded. Said pianist Randy Weston, "For me it's one of the greatest works of music of any kind from any era. When I first heard it I played it note for note on the piano . . . it was something that blew my mind."

In the 1940s and 1950s, *Body and Soul* became a test piece among tenor saxophonists from Lester Young to David Murray and a must-play piece for pianists—Nat "King" Cole, Art Tatum, Earl Hines, Thelonious Monk, Oscar Peterson, and Kenny Barron all recorded it.

Singers, too, took up *Body and Soul*. The somewhat awkward lyrics ("My life a wreck you're making") tell darkly of self-doubt, abandonment, weariness, and desperation ("It looks like the ending"). The sensual, sexual stance of offering both soul *and* body to the singer's ungrateful lover caused a sensation in the 1930s; some radio stations banned it from airplay.

For vocalists, the song posed not only challenging harmonic changes but the additional problem of a wide range: like *Stardust*, *Body and Soul* spans an octave and a fourth (only one whole step less than the devilishly difficult-to-sing *Star-Spangled Banner*).

Sarah Vaughan won an Amateur Night contest in 1942 at Harlem's famed Apollo Theater singing *Body and Soul*, thereby launching her

career. Billie Holiday recorded it memorably, always changing the lyrics from "a wreck you're making" to the franker "a hell you're making." Several remakes of *Body and Soul* offered new sets of vocalese lyrics to Coleman Hawkins's improvised solo line: singer Eddie Jefferson's version and one by the vocal group Manhattan Transfer.

In 1973 the National Academy of Recording Arts and Sciences inducted Hawkins's 1939 recording into the Grammy Hall of Fame. In 2004, the Library of Congress added it to the National Recording Registry of significant sound recordings. *Body and Soul* is such a memorable song and romantic phrase that it's been used as the title for six movies, scores of CDs, and more than 50 books, including, in 1993, Frank Conroy's hauntingly musical novel. As of 2011, jazz musicians alone had made nearly 2,000 recordings of this classic American song, making it easily the most-recorded piece in the history of jazz.

—*John Edward Hasse*

in advance. One of his most famous solos was on the standard *Tiger Rag* (*JTSA* Disc 2/Track 6).

Though he came to prominence during the swing era, Tatum's playing was never really of that era, nor of bebop or modern jazz—rather it stood apart, like Ellington's, in a class of its own. Tatum's style continued to mature, as demonstrated by such later masterpiece recordings as *Willow Weep for Me* (1949) and *Sweet Lorraine* (1955), recorded the year before he died.

In contrast to Tatum, Teddy Wilson was very much of the swing era; he was, in fact, its most important pianist. His style combined elements of Earl Hines's and Tatum's piano styles into one tailored for playing in ensembles.

In comparison to Tatum's splash and unrelenting energy, Wilson—with his clean lines and light textures—sounded more legato, subtle, reserved. As his left hand rendered a series of tenths and his right executed brief melodic figures in octaves, Wilson would sit boardupright at the keyboard, the very model of poise and control. He was the perfect pianist to play the Benny Goodman Trio's kind of chamber jazz—notably on

After You've Gone and *Body and Soul* (both 1935)—and to accompany Billie Holiday on *Mean To Me*, with Wilson's septet, (1937; *JTSA* Disc 1/Track 22).

What Coleman Hawkins did for the tenor saxophone, Red Norvo did for the xylophone: he took it out of vaudeville and put it firmly in the realm of jazz. Difficult to categorize, Norvo played with pre-swing, swing, and bebop musicians, first on the xylophone and later on the vibraphone as well. With his light sound, Norvo created a gentle sonic world of subtle surprises, swing, and imaginative solos, as on *In a Mist* (1933), *Dance of the Octopus* (1933), and *Remember* (1937).

The guitarist Charlie Christian was one of the first to amplify his instrument so that it could be heard among the winds and brass. His recording career lasted only from 1939 to 1941, his life cut short at age 25 by tuberculosis, but in those two years he set musicians and the public on their ears with his fluid and inventive single-line soloing, which for the first time gave the guitar the same kind of expressive power as the trumpet or saxophone. As a member of Benny Goodman's Sextet (*Breakfast Feud*, 1940 and 1941;

I Found a New Baby, 1941) and big band (*Honeysuckle Rose*, 1939 [*JTSA* Disc 2/ Track 5], and *Solo Flight*, 1941), Christian lifted his instrument to prominence in jazz and exerted an enormous influence on later guitarists from a wide range of musical styles.

Exposed as a Texas youth to African American spirituals at tent revival meetings, Jack Teagarden developed a deceptive ease of technique and forged a singing, lyrical, bluesy sound on the trombone (*Dinah*, with Red Nichols, 1929, and Jack *Hits the Road*, with Bud Freeman, 1940) and an equally personal, blues-drenched vocal style. Indeed, Gunther Schuller has called him "the finest white blues singer." Nowhere is his brilliance better demonstrated than on *St. James Infirmary* (with Louis Armstrong, 1947), which Teagarden transforms into a haunting masterpiece.

Louis Armstrong's reputation as a singer and entertainer grew in the 1930s and began eclipsing his renown as a trumpeter. COURTESY JOHN EDWARD HASSE.

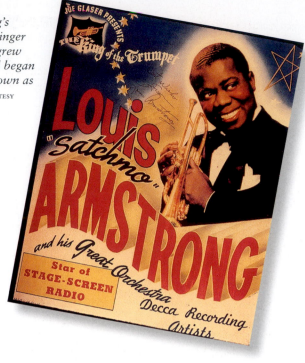

Singers

One of the greatest jazz singers of them all, Louis Armstrong, flowered in the 1930s, becoming a cultural hero of epic proportions, above all to musicians. He developed a vocal style—marked by his unique gravelly tone, passionate delivery, and superb vowel coloration—as distinctive as his seminal style on trumpet. On such recordings as *Stardust* and *Lazy River* (both 1931), he projected a sense of exultation somewhere between singing and shouting, as Henry Pleasants has noted, and this required singing at both a high volume and pitch.

Just as Armstrong lived his life, so he sang with feeling, energy, infectious *joie de vivre,* and good humor—listen

Trumpeter Louis Armstrong pretends to play the flute while trombonist Jack Teagarden mugs with a trumpet.
PHOTO COURTESY DOWN BEAT ARCHIVES.

John Hammond: Talent Scout, Jazz Catalyst

As a discoverer of talent, John Hammond had few if any peers. That's because many of the performers he helped lift from obscurity to the international spotlight went on to validate his sponsorship to a spectacular degree. Singer Billie Holiday, bandleader Count Basie, pianist Teddy Wilson, and guitarists Charlie Christian and George Benson—not to mention soul singer Aretha Franklin and the rock world's Bob Dylan and Bruce Springsteen—are just a few whom Hammond championed before they rose to the highest ranks of the twentieth century's popular artists.

Born in 1910 to a wealthy family (his grandfather was the railroad magnate Cornelius Vanderbilt), Hammond became enamored of jazz as a teenager. He began his career as a disc jockey and producer of jazz stage shows, worked as a music critic for *Down Beat* and *Melody Maker* magazines, went on to serve as a talent scout and tour manager for Benny Goodman (his future brother-in-law), and spent a number of years as a record producer and executive, most notably at Columbia.

Using his inherited wealth, he financed jazz recording sessions at a time when record sales were in the Depression-era basement. During one week in November 1933, he supervised the last recordings of Bessie Smith and the first sessions of Billie Holiday. "She was 17," he later said of Holiday. "I never heard anyone sing like this—as if she was the most inspired improviser in the world." The music business types gave him a hard time, he recalled: "Scratchy, unmusical voice. Where was the tune?"

When Hammond heard the little-known Basie band over a car radio in 1936, the excited producer traveled to Kansas City to hear them in person. As he'd done with Holiday, Hammond brought the Basie band to the attention of his contacts in the music business and helped set the wheels in motion for the group's entry onto the national stage.

Others who benefited from Hammond's support included arranger Fletcher Henderson; trumpeter Bunny Berigan; xylophonist Red Norvo; and saxophonists Benny Carter, Chu Berry, and Lester Young.

But Hammond's impact went well beyond the careers of individual musicians. In 1938 and 1939 he organized two landmark Carnegie Hall concerts of African American music, "From Spirituals to Swing," that helped legitimize jazz. Through his association with Goodman he helped spearhead the swing era. He sparked public interest in boogie-woogie by promoting the careers of pianists Meade "Lux" Lewis, Albert Ammons, and Pete Johnson. And Hammond, who called himself "a social activist," served as an important catalyst for racial integration in jazz.

—*Tad Lathrop*

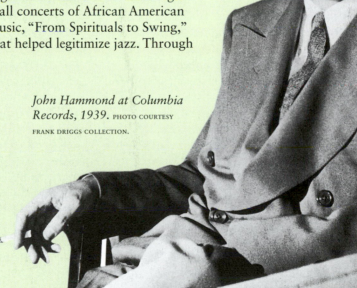

John Hammond at Columbia Records, 1939. PHOTO COURTESY FRANK DRIGGS COLLECTION.

The New Orleans Revival

Swing music, whether played by big bands or small groups, was not all that was happening in jazz during the swing era.

At universities such as Yale and Princeton, young men were collecting "hot" records of the 1920s, encouraged by articles in the men's magazine *Esquire*. In 1935, from within his big band, Tommy Dorsey organized the Clambake Seven, an octet to play Dixieland jazz, an offshoot of New Orleans jazz, and was followed within two years by Bob Crosby and his Bob Cats.

In the 1930s, partly as a reaction against what some saw as the overly arranged and overly commercialized character of swing, some musicians began consciously reviving the older, uncluttered, small-group jazz styles from New Orleans and Chicago. Attention to these styles took a big step forward in 1938: the year saw the first "From Spirituals to Swing" concert at Carnegie Hall, which stimulated interest in the history of jazz; the establishment of two independent record labels—Commodore and H.R.S.—that issued pre-swing jazz; and renewed recording activity for the New Orleans pioneers Sidney Bechet, Johnny Dodds, and Jelly Roll Morton (whose recordings that year, made by Alan Lomax for the Library of Congress, rank among the great sound documents in American culture).

Nineteen thirty-nine was a milestone year, with cornetist Muggsy Spanier forming his so-called Ragtime Band and making a series of influential recordings that included *At the Jazz Band Ball* and *Riverboat Shuffle*. That same year, the landmark book *Jazzmen* was

to *I'll Be Glad When You're Dead, You Rascal You* (1931), *Laughin' Louie* (1933), or *Swing That Music* (1936; *JTSA* Disc 1/Track 20) and you can't help smiling. He boasted an extraordinary ability to overcome commonplace material, often—with the force of his musical personality—transforming lackluster pop songs into enduring art (*Sweethearts on Parade*, 1930). And he set the standard for scat singing (*Basin Street Blues*, 1933), his example clarion and timeless. The title of Leslie Gourse's book on jazz singers—*Louis' Children*—is an apt reflection of Armstrong's profound influence on generations of jazz vocalists.

The novelist Ralph Ellison, who grew up in Oklahoma City listening to another local son, the big-voiced tenor Jimmy Rushing, wrote of that singer's "imposition of a romantic lyricism upon the blues . . . a romanticism which is not of the Deep South but the Southwest." The featured singer with Count Basie's band from 1935 to 1948, Rushing combined the sensitivity and precision of a ballad singer with the authority, earthiness, and robustness of a blues shouter, as on *Sent for You Yesterday* (1938), *Goin' to Chicago* (1941), *I'm Gonna Move to the Outskirts of Town* (1942), and especially the mournful *I Left My Baby* (1939), all with Basie.

The **Boswell Sisters**, from New Orleans, achieved their peak of popularity and influence from 1931–35, becoming, in the estimation of Will Friedwald, "the greatest of all jazz vocal groups." The trio sang in beautifully blended three-part harmony, with a remarkable sense of rhythm. Connee Boswell did most of the group's imaginative arrangements, replete with reharmonizations, scat singing, the instrument-like use of their voices, frequent tempo changes, and other creative elements that typically recomposed the original material (*Roll On, Mississippi, Roll On,* 1931; *Charlie Two-Step*, 1932; and *Everybody Loves My Baby*, 1932 [*JTSA* Disc 1/Track 17]). Ella Fitzgerald cited Connee Boswell as among her main musical influences.

The Boswells and the plaintive-voiced Mildred Bailey were the first white singers to absorb and master the African American jazz idiom of the 1920s. Bailey boasted fine diction; a pure, warm, and beautiful natural tone; and an ability to project a song's lyrics and convey sweetness, sincerity, and conviction. She performed Hoagy Carmichael's *Rockin' Chair* (notably a classic version recorded in 1937) so definitively that she became known as "the Rockin' Chair Lady." Her art also sings on in such memorable sides as *A Porter's Love Song to a Chambermaid* (with husband Red Norvo's band, 1936) and *Darn That Dream* (with Benny Goodman's orchestra, 1939).

Billie Holiday ranks close to Louis Armstrong among the greatest jazz singers. Acknowledging great inspiration from him, she practiced an instrumental

issued, drawing attention to New Orleans jazz and notably to Morton and the forgotten trumpeter Bunk Johnson. Within months of the book's publication, Morton was rediscovered by RCA Victor, which began recording him again (it had dropped him in 1930). Morton's rejuvenation was short-lived, however; he died in 1941 following an illness, his dream of a major comeback unfulfilled. Another independent, Blue Note Records, emerged in 1939 and immediately recorded Sidney Bechet.

Also in 1939, trumpeter Lu Watters organized the Yerba Buena Jazz Band in the San Francisco Bay Area to revive small-group New Orleans music in the style of King Oliver. In 1941, his band began recording old rags (*Maple Leaf Rag* and *Black and White Rag*) and early jazz pieces (*Tiger Rag*, *Fidgety Feet*, and *Muskrat Ramble*) with the polyphony of interweaving clarinet, trumpet, and trombone lines harking back to the music's early years. The band helped spark an international revival of New Orleans and Chicago jazz.

In the early 1940s, a number of African American jazz musicians, some of them, like Kid Ory and Bunk Johnson, in retirement from jazz, were recorded by younger white enthusiasts, as small but influential jazz-specialist magazines—notably *The Record Changer* and *The Jazz Record*—published articles on early figures. In 1944 actor-director Orson Welles's CBS radio program put Kid Ory's band—with clarinetist Jimmie Noone and trumpeter Mutt Carey—on the national map. The traditional jazz revival built up steam after World War II, and in 1947, Louis Armstrong dropped his big band in favor of a small-group format, the All Stars, with a traditional New Orleans lineup.

The old styles and the new bebop appealed largely to different groups of listeners, and a war of words broke out between the modernists and the traditionalists, whom the former derisively labeled "moldy figs." Each camp carried a vision of one true jazz; the combatants failed to recognize that by the 1930s, jazz had become a music of multiple styles that could exist side by side. Increasingly jazz would become a music synonymous with variety and, like the American population, pluralism.

—*John Edward Hasse*

approach to singing as she ranged freely over the beat, flattened out the melodic contours of tunes, and, in effect, recomposed songs to suit her range, style, and artistic sensibilities. Her voice was physically limited, but she achieved shadings, nuances, color, and variety by sliding along the thin line separating speech and song. Her collaborations with Lester Young (*I Must Have That Man* and *Mean To Me*, *JTSA* Disc 1/ Track 22, both recorded with Teddy Wilson's group, 1937) are justifiably celebrated, as is her courageous recording of the harrowing anti-lynching song *Strange Fruit* (1939) and her haunting studio recording, with strings, of *Lover Man* (1944).

In 1957, jazz critic Nat Hentoff arranged for Holiday to be part of a television program on contemporary jazz. Although her powers were in decline, she sang a fine version of *Fine and Mellow* which featured Coleman Hawkins, Ben Webster, and Lester Young (her old compatriot) on alto saxes. Holiday's voice is huskier than in her youth, but she displays strongly her talent for elevating a contemporary popular song into majestic and tragic grandeur.

After recording the memorable *All or Nothing at All* in 1939 with Harry James's band, Frank Sinatra joined the Tommy Dorsey Orchestra and, with his new kind of natural phrasing, rich baritone, jazzy inflections, and depth of feeling, helped lead the band to its greatest acclaim with such recordings as *Everything Happens to Me* (1941). Not one to improvise, his singing nonetheless was influenced by—and in turn

Billie Holiday— Lady Day—the most hauntingly distinctive of jazz vocalists.
PHOTO COURTESY JAMES J KRIEGSMANN/DOWN BEAT ARCHIVES.

👁 **Watch** the video of *Fine and Mellow* by Billie Holiday on **mymusiclab.com** much admired by—jazz musicians. By the 1950s, he had become the quintessential American pop singer through his gift for conveying lyrics and ability to take a three-minute song and transform it into a virtual three-act play (*One for My Baby*, 1958).

TAKE NOTE

- What roles did smaller ensembles, instrumental soloists, and singers play during this era?

The End of the Swing Era

A major rupture in the swing era came on August 1, 1942, when the American Federation of Musicians, ruled by union boss James Petrillo, ordered its musicians to cease recording for record companies. At issue was the companies' refusal to contribute a payment per recording to the union's pension fund. In response, musicians were forced to stop making records for sale to the public indefinitely, with the exception of a few **transcription recordings** intended exclusively for radio stations. It took Victor and Columbia, the two largest companies, until November 1944 to finally cave in to the musicians' union.

During the recording ban of 1942–44, a group of young players had been experimenting in Harlem, and in 1945 they made their first important recordings. Employing heightened melodic and rhythmic complexity, they introduced a music that was intended far less for dancing than for listening in small clubs. Initially known onomatopoeically as "rebop" or "bebop," it finally took the shortened label "bop."

The bebop musicians worked outside previously standard career paths that required being entertainers or dance musicians; they relied for their livelihoods on an intense circle of jazz fans to an extent that a musician of the swing era generation would have found uncomfortable. Now, led by African American musicians searching for their own music not co-opted by the white-controlled music industry, many younger jazz players found swing too highly arranged, too formulaic, and too commercial and took up the new, startlingly different bop.

The musical developments occurred partly as a result of historical events. World War II brought more than a million blacks into uniform, and fighting abroad for freedom raised the expectations of returning servicemen. Hundreds of thousands of blacks moved north and west to work in war plants, and they helped support a style of black popular music that would in 1949 be dubbed "**rhythm and blues**" **(R&B)**. What became known as R&B was really a diverse group of styles. Sung by the likes of singer-saxophonist **Louis Jordan** and

Louis Jordan's jump blues helped usher in the post-swing era. PHOTO COURTESY JAMES J KRIEGSMANN/DOWN BEAT ARCHIVES.

his Tympany Five, Wynonie Harris, Big Joe Turner, and Ruth Brown and accompanied by guitar, piano, bass, drums, and saxophone, R&B offered accessible songs, a strong dance beat, and a fresh sound.

The pop music world was changing markedly. Exempt from the 1942–44 recording ban, many singers, despite the wartime shortage of shellac used on records, were continuing to make them and were gaining in popularity. This development, combined with an increase in the number of singers leaving their big band employers and striking out on their own (Frank Sinatra and Perry Como in 1942, Dick Haymes in 1943, and Jo Stafford and Peggy Lee in 1944) helped create an era of the "big singer."

The increasing popularity of singers and such emerging styles as R&B and bebop combined with other factors to push the big bands into a sharp decline, effectively ending the big band era. In November and December 1946, eight of the bands disbanded either

transcription recordings disc recordings made, especially in the 1930s and 1940s, exclusively for broadcast on radio stations; from the phrase "broadcast transcription."

rhythm and blues (R&B) style of popular music forged in the 1940s as an offshoot of urban blues; a precursor of rock and roll, soul music, funk, and hip-hop.

Boogie-Woogie

Swinging, eight-to-the-bar figures rumbling way down in the piano bass, meshing with bluesy, complex patterns higher up; a pianist, close to the audience, working the keyboard so powerfully that the piano and the floor could literally rock—this was **boogie-woogie**.

Jelly Roll Morton and W.C. Handy recalled hearing boogie-woogie in the South during the first decade of the twentieth century, and ragtime sheet music of that time began to hint at it. Taking its name from a dance step developed in the South by African Americans, boogie-woogie piano playing went north with the great black migration after World War I; St. Louis and Chicago became hotbeds. Pianists played boogie-woogie in barrelhouses, saloons, juke joints, honky-tonks, and rent parties, where its loud, rolling sound cut through the din, dominating the atmosphere and providing an all-but-irresistible call to the dance floor.

By the mid-1920s, boogie began to appear on "race records"—for example, Clay Custer's *The Rocks* (1923), Jimmy Blythe's *Chicago Stomp* (1924), and Pine Top Smith's *Pine Top's Boogie Woogie* (1928, with Smith shouting out dance instructions).

The general public "discovered" the style in 1938, after John Hammond presented three masters—Albert Ammons, Pete Johnson, and Meade "Lux" Lewis—in the landmark From "From Spirituals to Swing" concert at Carnegie Hall. A vogue for boogie then ensued during the late 1930s and the World War II years: the authentic boogie pianists such as Jimmy Yancey were widely recorded, and publishers put out method books for the masses of amateur pianists. There were big band versions (Count Basie's *Boogie Woogie [I May Be Wrong]*, 1936, and Benny Goodman's *Roll 'Em*, 1937) and pop songs hopping on the boogie bandwagon (*Boogie Woogie Bugle Boy [of Company B]*, 1941); but the music was quintessentially a piano style.

As with ragtime, the tension between the right and left hands' opposing roles made boogie-woogie at once discordant and appealing. Its expressive range was limited and its format highly stylized (almost entirely 8- and 12-bar blues progressions with a repetitive bass, typically fast and percussive). But within these limitations, the music's complex figures and powerful cross-rhythms could be insistent,

COURTESY JOHN EDWARD HASSE

hypnotic, and exciting. The style was virtuosic in its way and took great endurance.

Lewis ranks as the most stylistically advanced of the boogie artists. His masterpiece was *Honky-Tonk Train Blues* (JTSA Disc 1, Track 21), a colorful evocation of a train in motion, which he recorded 11 times between 1927 and 1961. Observers recall that he could improvise on this tune for 30 minutes, his fingers cascading over the keys, relentlessly rolling out the rhythms, dazzling everyone within earshot.

—*John Edward Hasse*

permanently or temporarily, including those of Benny Goodman, Harry James, Woody Herman, Tommy Dorsey, Benny Carter, and Les Brown. Additional reasons were higher costs, a short-lived postwar boom in movie-going, and preoccupation among returning servicemen with settling down and starting families. A new, suburban lifestyle, along with the imminent advent of network television, would create serious adjustments in social habits. Most younger listeners, some of whom in previous years would have become big band

fans, were attracted to more accessible vocal sounds or fresher and newer styles of music. "After the war," bandleader Les Brown recalled, "families settled down and the ballrooms went to hell. Before the war every town with 20,000 people had a ballroom, and my band could spend a month just doing one-nighters in Texas."

boogie-woogie   a form of blues, often for the piano, with a repeating or ostinato left hand or bass pattern.

But if the era when big bands predominated came to an end in the mid-1940s, the bands themselves never completely disappeared. Indeed, Duke Ellington kept his band together—and made many important recordings—up until his death in 1974. And in the decades after Ellington's death, big bands enjoyed something of a renaissance: jazz programs at American high schools and colleges and growing numbers of historically-oriented bands (for example, the Smithsonian Jazz Masterworks Orchestra and the Lincoln Center Jazz Orchestra) kept the canonical repertory alive, while others (the Muhal Richards Abrams Orchestra, for example) focused on newly written works for large jazz ensembles.

Swing rhythm became such an accepted and expected element of jazz that it came to be taken for granted. Swing rhythm also spread into R&B, the western swing music of Bob Wills, the propulsive beat of bluegrass, and into kinds of pop music. Beginning in the late twentieth century and continuing to today, North America has seen a revival of swing dancing among young people, and new retro pop bands—the Squirrel Nut Zippers, the Brian Setzer Orchestra, and the Royal Crown Revue—attracted younger fans by playing a revved up, edgy kind of swing. Reinventing itself in the grand tradition of American music, and adapting itself to changing musical times, swing continues to capture the ears of new generations.

TAKE NOTE

- Why did the big bands decline at the end of World War II?

Explore Jazz Classics and Key Recordings on mymusiclab.com

TAKE NOTE

- How did jazz become a "mass attraction" during the swing era?

Key to the popularity of swing music was the rise of public dancing and dance halls. Popular dances included the spectacular Lindy Hop, the Big Apple, and the Shim-Sham-Shimmy. The demand for music to accompany these dances formed a strong base for the big bands that traveled the country playing for dancers.

- What were the key African American bands of the swing era and why were they important?

The key African American bands of the period included the orchestras of Duke Ellington and Count Basie. In his work, Ellington brought a new level of instrumental sophistication and composition. He had the luxury of composing for the specific talents of his band members, many of whom remained with the band over several years (if not decades). Basie was responsible for popularizing Kansas City style jazz. His band was steeped in the blues and its traditions, from blues chord progressions and blue notes (certain "bent" notes) to bluesy riffs—short, repeated phrases often played by the band behind soloists.

- What were the main white bands of the swing era and why were they important?

The leading white bands of the period included those led by Benny Goodman, Artie Shaw, the Dorsey Brothers, and Glenn Miller. Goodman led the most influential, for a time the most popular, and perhaps the most polished of the big bands of the period. The Goodman and Shaw bands featured more jazz soloists than the Dorsey and Miller bands, which were more commercial.

- What were the challenges in keeping a band together and financially successful?

The physical strain of moving large groups of people—mostly young, single men—and their instruments around the country was one of the most daunting of all the challenges a big band faced. Personnel problems, discipline, and general management issues beset all the bands. Traveling constantly to play a series of one-night stands across the country took its toll on musicians and the bands' finances.

- Why did all-female bands arise during this period, and how did they help advance women's role in jazz?

Sexism in the music business was rampant, and it was hard for women to find acceptance as performing musicians. Nonetheless, several all-female bands were able to achieve commercial and popular success during the swing era, if only for their novelty value. Among the best-known were the International Sweethearts of Rhythm. Bands like this lay the groundwork for the gradual increasing acceptance of women as jazz performers.

- How did arrangers help create the successful big band sound?

Big bands required talented arrangers to create the complex scores for their musicians. While Count Basie relied on "head arrangements"—arrangements worked out on the fly by the band in rehearsal—most bands employed professional arrangers to create unique scores for them to perform. The arranger could be more important than the bandleader himself in creating an identity for a band.

- What roles did smaller ensembles, instrumental soloists, and singers play during this era?

Small ensembles—often made up of subgroups within the popular big bands—were popular during this era, as were talented solo instrumentalists and vocalists. Instrumental virtuosos, like saxophonist Coleman Hawkins, were able to establish themselves as major stars through their solo work.

Singing groups, like the popular Boswell Sisters, and individual vocalists—often employed by big bands as an "added attraction"—were also very popular during the swing era.

- Why did the big bands decline at the end of World War II?

The recording ban during the war years and the loss of personnel to the war effort weakened the bands, and many had folded at least temporarily. After World War II, big bands declined in popularity, due to the increasing popularity of smaller ensembles (including R&B and bop groups) and the cost of keeping a big band afloat.

DISCUSSION QUESTIONS

1. What was the impact of the Great Depression on popular entertainment of the 1930s?
2. Describe some of the key elements that contributed to the popularity of swing music and the big bands that played it.
3. How would you describe the sound of swing and big bands to someone who has never heard it?
4. What is a "section" in a big band? What instruments constitute a "rhythm section"?
5. Name the two figures most responsible for swing and briefly identify the role that each played in the development of swing.
6. Discuss several soloists who came to the fore during this period and what their contributions were to swing music.
7. What happened to American race relations during the swing era?
8. Describe what an arranger does. Identify three of the factors that an arranger considers when making an arrangement of a piece.
9. What were some of the factors that led to big bands losing popularity?

KEY TERMS & KEY PEOPLE

Louis Armstrong 90
boogie-woogie 125
Boswell Sisters 122
bridge 118
Benny Carter 98
Casa Loma Orchestra 101
Charlie Christian 108
chart 114
Count Basie 91
counterpoint 94
Tommy Dorsey 108
Duke Ellington 90
fill 94
Ella Fitzgerald 91
Benny Goodman 91
Coleman Hawkins 103

head 107
head arrangement 102
Fletcher Henderson 90
hi-hat cymbal 94
Billie Holiday 91
Jitterbug 92
Gene Krupa 101
Lindy Hop 92
Jimmie Lunceford 99
Glenn Miller 109
orchestration 113
rhythm and blues (R&B) 124
ride cymbal 102
run 118
section 90
sequence 106

Artie Shaw 91
snare drum 94
staccato 107
swing 90
Art Tatum 118
territory band 96
theme song 102
tom-tom 94
tone color 99
torch song 118
vocalese 102
Chick Webb 91
Ben Webster 96
Teddy Wilson 97
Woody Herman's Herd 110
Lester Young 93

CHAPTER 6

Bebop and Modern Jazz

by Bob Blumenthal

TAKE NOTE

- What musical movements began to replace big band jazz during the years following World War II?
- What is bebop and what roles did Charlie Parker and Dizzy Gillespie play in creating and popularizing it?
- Who were the early bebop pianists and how did they affect the growth of the musical style?
- What was cool jazz, who were its key proponents, and where did it develop?

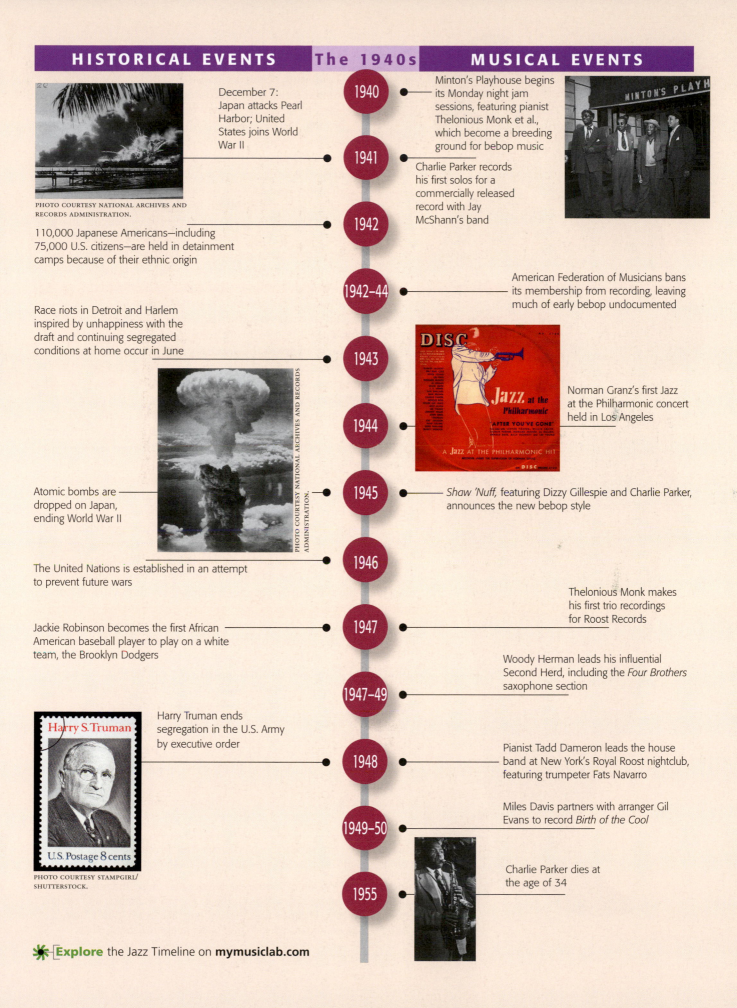

HISTORICAL EVENTS   The 1940s   MUSICAL EVENTS

PHOTO COURTESY NATIONAL ARCHIVES AND RECORDS ADMINISTRATION.

1940

Minton's Playhouse begins its Monday night jam sessions, featuring pianist Thelonious Monk et al., which become a breeding ground for bebop music

MINTON'S PLAYH

1941

December 7: Japan attacks Pearl Harbor; United States joins World War II

Charlie Parker records his first solos for a commercially released record with Jay McShann's band

1942

110,000 Japanese Americans—including 75,000 U.S. citizens—are held in detainment camps because of their ethnic origin

1942–44

American Federation of Musicians bans its membership from recording, leaving much of early bebop undocumented

1943

Race riots in Detroit and Harlem inspired by unhappiness with the draft and continuing segregated conditions at home occur in June

PHOTO COURTESY NATIONAL ARCHIVES AND RECORDS ADMINISTRATION.

1944

DISC
Jazz at the Philharmonic
"AFTER YOU'VE GONE"
A JAZZ AT THE PHILHARMONIC HIT

Norman Granz's first Jazz at the Philharmonic concert held in Los Angeles

1945

Atomic bombs are dropped on Japan, ending World War II

Shaw 'Nuff, featuring Dizzy Gillespie and Charlie Parker, announces the new bebop style

1946

The United Nations is established in an attempt to prevent future wars

Thelonious Monk makes his first trio recordings for Roost Records

1947

Jackie Robinson becomes the first African American baseball player to play on a white team, the Brooklyn Dodgers

1947–49

Woody Herman leads his influential Second Herd, including the *Four Brothers* saxophone section

Harry S. Truman
U.S. Postage 8 cents

PHOTO COURTESY STAMPGIRL/ SHUTTERSTOCK.

Harry Truman ends segregation in the U.S. Army by executive order

1948

Pianist Tadd Dameron leads the house band at New York's Royal Roost nightclub, featuring trumpeter Fats Navarro

1949–50

Miles Davis partners with arranger Gil Evans to record *Birth of the Cool*

1955

Charlie Parker dies at the age of 34

✳ Explore the Jazz Timeline on **mymusiclab.com**

Trumpeter and bebop innovator Dizzy Gillespie. PHOTO COURTESY WILLIAM P. GOTTLIEB/WILLIAM P. GOTTLIEB COLLECTION/ LIBRARY OF CONGRESS PRINTS & PHOTOGRAPHS DIVISION.

The Postwar Jazz Scene

The decline of the big bands and of jazz's status as popular music was precipitous during the World War II years. In 1940, the creative and commercial success attained by the bands of Duke Ellington, Count Basie, Benny Goodman, Artie Shaw, and others appeared beyond challenge. A mere five years later the big band era was waning and swing was passé. In its place, complex new sounds were entering the jazz lexicon.

The war years took their toll on big bands in many ways. Key musicians were drafted into the armed services, leaving many bands short-handed. Gasoline rationing increased the difficulty and expense of touring (most bands traveled by bus). The recording ban by the musicians' union from 1942–44 deprived the bands an opportunity to reach their fans, as well as taking from them a key source of income.

Several musical movements emerged to supplant the big bands as the leading forms of popular music. Singers, already critical components in the success of the bands, became even greater commercial forces. The phenomenal popularity of Frank Sinatra, who rose to fame with Tommy Dorsey's band but soon went off on his own, helped shift public taste from a swing beat to romantic ballads. Sinatra had been touched by jazz, and African American singing stars such as Nat Cole, Billy Eckstine, and Ella Fitzgerald reflected an even stronger jazz foundation in their work; yet public taste had turned to lushly arranged pop fare. Soon, even singers with unimpeachable jazz credentials, including Sarah Vaughan and Dinah Washington, were pulled into these more placid pop waters.

There was also the strong tidal pull of a more blues-based, dance-oriented development that can be traced back to the big bands through alto saxophonist Louis Jordan (a Chick Webb alumnus) and various editions of Lionel Hampton's orchestra. Originally referred to as **jump blues** or rhythm and blues and ultimately evolving into **rock and roll**, this extroverted style sustained the dynamic power of the big bands in a context that accommodated a more pronounced backbeat and the new sound of the electric guitar.

While pop balladeers and jump bands became music's new commercial champions, young, mostly African American improvisers were adding new elements to jazz and moving it far from the realm of pop entertainment. These players tended to be virtuoso instrumentalists who were schooled in the discipline of the big bands but were unwilling to settle for the limited solo opportunities available to orchestral sidemen. For black musicians particularly the big band era was a mixed blessing: Most of the bands that enjoyed commercial success where white, while the musical form itself had been developed by blacks. Further, black

jump blues a form of upbeat, jazz-tinged blues made popular in the 1940s and fifties by bandleader Louis Jordan and others.

rock and roll genre of youth-oriented popular music that emerged in the 1950s as an amalgam of jump blues, rhythm and blues, and country music; early stars included Elvis Presley, Jerry Lee Lewis, Chuck Berry, Buddy Holly; as it matured, its name became abbreviated to rock.

musicians who had served in World War II experienced new opportunities (despite the segregation of the armed forces) and hoped that their service would inspire a recognition of the need for equal rights by society at large. Many were disappointed when they returned from the war to find that little had changed.

These forces helped push the younger generation of jazz players toward a more assertive mode of expression. The blues and popular song structures still served as the base of their creations, but these artists favored more complex and irregularly accented melodies, more sophisticated harmonic modulations, and faster tempos than those favored by the big bands. In effect, the young jazz players were establishing a new inner circle, an exclusive countercultural "club" that required virtuosity of musicians and an open-eared

History & Culture

From left to right: Thelonious Monk, Howard McGhee, Roy Eldridge, and Teddy Hill at Minton's Playhouse, New York, 1948. PHOTO COURTESY WILLIAM P. GOTTLIEB/WILLIAM P. GOTTLIEB COLLECTION/LIBRARY OF CONGRESS PRINTS & PHOTOGRAPHS DIVISION.

After Hours at Minton's

Jazz's modern era was nurtured in the clubs of Harlem, where musicians would go to try out new ideas—or simply to seek playing opportunities that the big bands did not provide—after completing club, theater, and ballroom gigs. The jam sessions that resulted, with musicians testing their limits and challenging others to keep up with the latest discoveries, have become legendary; the center of the legend was at 210 West 118th Street, where the former dining room of the Hotel Cecil was converted by M. Henry Minton into the Playhouse, a club we now know simply as Minton's.

The Playhouse opened in 1938 but attracted little attention until two years later, when saxophonist and bandleader Teddy Hill signed on to manage the room. Hill decided to institute more musician-friendly policies, including a Monday-night jam session that set the tone for the innovations that followed. The key to Minton's success was its house band, a quartet co-led by Hill's former drummer **Kenny Clarke** and trumpeter Joe Guy and including an iconoclastic young unknown, **Thelonious Monk**, on piano. As word spread about Monk's adventurous harmonies and the daring rhythmic notions Clarke was adding from his drum kit, other musicians began frequenting Minton's to test their own new ideas. **Dizzy Gillespie**, another Teddy Hill alumnus, was a regular, and electric-guitar fountainhead Charlie Christian left an amplifier in the room so he could drop in as soon as his boss, Benny Goodman, was through for the night. Established stars, including Don Byas, Ben Webster, and Lester Young, often visited. Billie Holiday and **Charlie Parker** preferred Clark Monroe's Uptown House at 198 West 134th Street, which, as Barren Wilkins's Exclusive Club, had been the site of Duke Ellington's first steady New York job, in 1923; but they passed through Minton's as well. Some of the earliest evidence of the modern movement was captured at Minton's on a portable disc recorder by Columbia University student Jerry Newman, who documented Christian, Clarke, Gillespie, and Monk in full after-hours flight.

—*Bob Blumenthal*

attentiveness on the part of listeners. These performers would be the vanguard of a new musical style, which would come to be known as **bebop**.

Several heroes from the previous generation had paved the way for this new style. Tenor saxophonist Coleman Hawkins had exemplified the stream-of-consciousness creativity of the improvising soloist with his classic 1939 recording of *Body and Soul* and was among the first to demonstrate the feasibility of an instrumental soloist's playing for listeners rather than dancers—without singers or large orchestral accompaniment (see Chapter 5). As musicologist Scott DeVeaux has pointed out, Hawkins was *the* proto-bebopper: he was too proud to sing or otherwise try to please a mass audience and not inclined to lead a big band. Pianist Art Tatum, with his stupendous technique and harmonic knowledge, had revealed in such solo recordings as *Moonglow* (1934) and *Tea for Two* (1933) the complex potential of simple-seeming pop songs. The Count Basie

((•— **Listen** to CD I, Track 14/Download Track 14, *Body and Soul* by Coleman Hawkins

---

bebop   a style of jazz that emerged in the 1940s and established jazz as a music for listening rather than just dancing to; characterized by fast tempos, complex chord progressions, and virtuoso improvisation using multiple scales and altered tones; notable pioneers included Charlie Parker, Dizzy Gillespie, and Thelonious Monk.

---

band practiced a flowing, liberating sense of tempo, while Basie's star soloist, Lester Young, introduced an oblique, floating approach that pointed soloists toward musical abstraction. Charlie Christian, the electric guitar innovator, reflected a similar attitude in his solos with Goodman, and Ellington's new star, Jimmie Blanton, was revealing the untapped potential of the string bass.

TAKE NOTE

- What musical movements began to replace big band jazz during the years following World War II?

Parker, Gillespie, and the Birth of Bebop

Even before the United States entered World War II, new ideas were developing among young players inspired by their innovative predecessors. The disciples fueled the evolutionary process by refining and sharing discoveries after hours in Harlem spots such as Minton's Playhouse and Monroe's Uptown House. Several players were central to this effort, but none more so than alto saxophonist Charlie Parker,

◉— **Watch** the documentary on Bebop on **mymusiclab.com**

Charlie Parker, Miles Davis, Allen Eager, and Kai Winding in New York, 1949. PHOTO COURTESY © HERMAN LEONARD PHOTOGRAPHY LLC.

◉ **Watch** the documentary on Charlie Parker on **mymusiclab.com**

ultimately known via his legend to even the non-jazz world as "Yardbird" or "Bird."

Parker was born in 1920 and grew up in the fertile musical environment of Kansas City. By 1941 and his initial recorded solos with Jay McShann's band, on such tracks as *Swingmatism* and *The Jumpin' Blues*, he was displaying a heady approach that merged the virtuosity of Tatum and the melodic daring of Young—topped off with a blues-rooted intensity uniquely his own. When Parker finally recorded as a solo artist, in 1945, he could draw upon additional big band experience with Earl "Fatha" Hines and Billy Eckstine and the ideas he had shared with such contemporaries as trumpeter John Birks "Dizzy" Gillespie, who had apprenticed in the big bands of Teddy Hill and Cab Calloway; drummer Kenny Clarke, another Teddy Hill alumnus who had been among the first to introduce complex polyrhythms behind soloists; and pianist-composer Thelonious Monk, whose work was filled with startling dissonance and rhythmic displacements. You can watch the dynamic interplay of Charlie Parker and Dizzy Gillespie performing *Hot House* in a rare 1952 TV appearance, on mymusiclab.com. Parker's solo demonstrates his complete mastery of the instrument and the bebop idiom. In the final chorus, Parker, Gillespie, and the drummer trade four-bar phrases.

This core group of innovators—particularly the charismatic Parker—first demonstrated their discoveries in jam sessions, then landed nightclub engagements on New York's 52nd Street, before the new music was disseminated widely through recordings. As a result, a slightly younger group of talented musicians had already rallied around Parker and Gillespie before the larger audience learned of their existence. Pianists Earl "Bud" Powell and Al Haig, trumpeter **Miles Davis**, trombonist J. J. Johnson, saxophonist Edward "Sonny" Stitt, and drummer **Max Roach** were among the most prominent of these disciples, and together they represented a loose yet identifiable modernist school.

The lack of recorded evidence of the experimenters' early efforts resulted from the 1942–44 ban on recording ordered by the American Federation of Musicians. When the musicians' union's ban ended in late 1944, the new music was poised to emerge from its period of incubation, and it spread quickly in the following year on a series of historic records issued under Gillespie's and Parker's names. Gillespie began 1945 by recording composer **Tadd Dameron**'s *Good Bait* and his own composition *Bebop*, which quickly

◉ **Watch** the video *Hot House* by Charlie Parker and Dizzy Gillespie on **mymusiclab.com**

Fashions popularized by such boppers as Dizzy Gillespie and Thelonious Monk proved more than a rapidly passing fad; they spawned the berets-and-shades look associated with the beatnik counterculture of the 1950s. COURTESY JOHN EDWARD HASSE.

LADIES' GLITTER BE-BOP
For that slim figure. Beautiful lightweight Black, Brown, Blue Pearl or Pink Pearl frames. Gold decorated front and sides.
Style No. 131.......................**$3**⁹⁵

lent its name to the new style. Then Gillespie held two recording sessions—with Parker as a sideman—that introduced his pieces *Salt Peanuts* and *Groovin' High* as well as Gillespie and Parker's *Shaw 'Nuff*. Each of these recordings became modern classics. Parker's first session as a leader, which featured Miles Davis, Max Roach, and (on piano as well as trumpet) Gillespie, yielded its own classics: the blues themes *Now's the Time* and *Billie's Bounce* and the virtuosic variation on *Cherokee* called *Ko-Ko*.

Few recordings in jazz history proved as influential—and controversial—as these titles. Unsympathetic listeners disparaged the allegedly "thin" tones of the horn players, who had dispensed with the expressive vibrato of traditional soloists; lamented the irregular accents and dissonant harmonies such as the interval of the flatted fifth; and predicted that any music presenting such challenges to dancers had no future. Gillespie's former boss Cab Calloway had once called the trumpeter's more confounding experiments "Chinese music," and veterans as respected as Louis Armstrong attacked the new sounds in similar terms.

These reactions were further indicators of the uphill battle faced by the emerging modernists. Swing, as DeVeaux put it, had been "an integral part of the burgeoning entertainment industry. . . . All of the bebop musicians began their careers within this system. Their decision to break, or at least radically revise, their relationship to it was no casual act. Nor, given the realities of power in American society, could it hope to be entirely successful."

Not all of the older players rejected bebop. Ellington sax star Ben Webster loved to join the jam sessions at Minton's, pianist Mary Lou Williams became a mentor to the likes of Gillespie and Monk, and the harmonically audacious Coleman Hawkins

Listening Guide

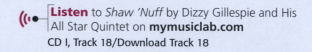
Listen to *Shaw 'Nuff* by Dizzy Gillespie and His All Star Quintet on **mymusiclab.com**
CD I, Track 18/Download Track 18

SHAW 'NUFF • DIZZY GILLESPIE AND HIS ALL STAR QUINTET

Music: Dizzy Gillespie and Charlie Parker, 1945. Personnel: Dizzy Gillespie (trumpet); Charlie Parker (alto sax); Al Haig (piano); Curly Russell (bass); Sid Catlett (drums). Recorded May 11, 1945, in New York. First issue: Guild 1002. Timing: 3:03.

Overview

Shaw 'Nuff is one of the first definitive modern jazz/bebop recordings. It contains several features that would become indicative of the style: unison melody lines by trumpet and alto saxophone, irregular rhythmic accents by both soloists and members of the rhythm section, trumpet and saxophone tones that place reduced emphasis on vibrato, and virtuosic improvisations—all at an accelerated tempo. The thematic choruses and solos are based on the harmonic progressions of Gershwin's *I Got Rhythm*, second only to the blues chorus as a preferred structure for improvisers, but these choruses are framed by an introduction/coda that adds a more uncommon structural element.

Key Features

- Improvisation: *Shaw 'Nuff* features rapid, technically dazzling improvising from its three soloists. Each plays a single chorus that displays great dexterity and variety.
- Rhythm: Both the written melodic material and the improvisations are filled with rapidly shifting accents that attack the symmetries of the form (see below) from a variety of angles, creating a headlong momentum that is sustained throughout the performance.
- Melody: Rather than building its theme exclusively in concise, symmetrical phrases, both the introduction/coda and the main melody of *Shaw 'Nuff* rely on complex melodic units of irregular length. Even the repetitive, riff-like sections of the theme employ these more jagged phrases.
- Harmony: While the underlying harmonic structure is taken from a popular standard, the soloists often expand upon this base by superimposing more complex **harmonic substitutions**.
- Sonority: By eliminating the vibrato that characterized earlier brass and reed soloists, Gillespie and Parker are able to execute their newly complex ideas with greater accuracy. This is particularly critical to the success of their unison passages.
- Musicians' roles: Among its other innovations, modern jazz marked a further liberation of the rhythm section, which is most evident in the support offered by the piano and drums. Both instruments place greater emphasis on spontaneous commentary: the piano through the replacement of sustained patterns with more spontaneous chords, and the drums by moving the primary time-keeping function to the ride cymbal and using tom-tom and bass drum for more diverse accents.
- Form and structure: The primary theme and solo choruses of *Shaw 'Nuff* employ the 32-bar, AABA chorus structure that is among the most common in popular music. This central form is surrounded, however, by a more harmonically static 16-bar section in AA'BC form that ends in a two-bar break that is omitted at the conclusion. Both Gillespie and Parker are credited as composers, and it is likely that one wrote the main theme while the other contributed the introduction/coda.

—*Bob Blumenthal*

TIME	SECTION	FORM	INSTRUMENTATION	MELODY	RHYTHM	HARMONY
0:00	INTRODUCTION		Piano, bass, drum, dominated by drum rolls on tom-toms		Static rhythm pattern.	
0:06	INTRODUCTION	AA'BC, 16 bars	Ensemble	Fanfare-like melody stated in unison by horns; ends with two-bar piano break.	$\frac{4}{4}$, sparsely stated with ride cymbal keeping the underlying beat.	Static harmony stated by rhythm section; bass plays repeated two-note figure.
0:20	MAIN MELODY	AABA, 32 bars	Ensemble	Rapid paced melody stated in unison by horns; phrases of irregular length throughout cut across the AABA structure.	$\frac{4}{4}$, ride cymbal states primary beat; rapidly shifting accents by pianist and drummer cut across the regular beat.	Based on *I Got Rhythm* chord changes.

TIME	SECTION	FORM	INSTRUMENTATION	MELODY	RHYTHM	HARMONY
0:33	MAIN MELODY	Bridge or B section	Ensemble	Stated in unison by horns; shorter contrasting phrases.		
0:40	MAIN MELODY	Return of A section	Ensemble	Stated in unison by horns.		
0:47	SOLO	AABA	Charlie Parker, alto saxophone	Parker begins with a relatively simple phrase, then quickly moves into more complex ideas.	Piano comping behind solo cuts across beat and symmetrical form.	At the bridge (1:01) Parker imposes substitute chord progression for four measures.
1:14	SOLO	AABA	Dizzy Gillespie, trumpet	Trumpet enters with a piercing glissando. Gillespie's solo is technically complex but with greater use of space and repeated phrasing than Parker's. The final eight bars (1:34) begin with repeated rapid triplets.		
1:41	SOLO	AABA	Al Haig, piano	Employs intricate phrases similar to those of Gillespie and Parker; however, Haig's bridge (1:55) hews more closely to the harmony, and his final eight bars (2:02) resolve into simpler ideas.	Walking bass emphasizes beat.	
2:09	MAIN MELODY	AABA, 32 bars	Ensemble	The opening ensemble passage is now played in reverse, beginning with a restatement of the theme.		
2:36	CODA		Piano, bass, drums with piano playing a repeated rhythmic pattern.		Return of initial static rhythm section.	
2:43	CODA	AA'BC, 16 bars	Ensemble	The unison introduction returns, but now the final two bars of solo piano have been omitted and replaced by a quiet piano **glissando**.		Static harmony stated by rhythm section; bass plays repeated two-note figure.

harmonic substitution   replacement of an established chord in a progression with an alternative to counter expectation and add interest.

glissando   a gliding slur or slide from one pitch to another.

Charlie "Bird" Parker playing at Birdland in 1949. The club's name was a nod to the alto saxophonist—and to his impact on the jazz world. PHOTO COURTESY © HERMAN LEONARD PHOTOGRAPHY LLC.

hired Monk and other young innovators as sidemen. Williams was particularly generous and supportive, opening her apartment as a spot for after-hours jam sessions, and encouraging Monk to continue to compose despite the fact that others in the young movement felt his playing was too eccentric. A new generation of musicians and non-dancing listeners—smaller than the audience that sustained the swing bands yet equally passionate—rallied to the modern sounds. The new fans responded to the music's restless energy and sophisticated virtuosity, and they identified with the countercultural trappings that already set the style's leading players apart. Jazz had been born outside the mainstream, and after the mass acceptance of the swing bands, bebop was returning the music to its niche of unconventionality. The new wave of players seemed intent on breaking rules both musical and nonmusical.

The most committed of the modern fans lived for each new Parker and Gillespie record, just as earlier

  Issues

Boppers versus Moldy Figs

Why did some older jazz fans resist the new bebop style?

Some people have a high need for the new and novel, others prefer the familiar, often leading to initial resistance to new artistic advances. The twentieth century alone is rife with conflicts over new styles, such as the famous 1913 Paris riot at the premiere of Stravinsky's modernist *Rite of Spring*, when the police had to be called in.

Bebop shared many commonalities with earlier jazz, but its dissimilarities attracted most of the attention and sparked a heated war of words. In 1946, the *Washington Post* described the strife as "an all-consuming holocaust." If that is an exaggeration, it was at least a fiery civil war— and sometimes not very civil.

On one side were the modernists —those who welcomed the innovations of Charlie Parker, Dizzy

Gillespie, and the other bop musicians. On the other side were proponents of either New Orleans-style traditional jazz, or swing music, or both—people who didn't understand, didn't like, or were threatened by the new style and much preferred the older, familiar music. The boppers derisively labeled them "moldy figs." Generational change was a big part of the clash: most of those attacking bebop were born in the 1890s or first decade of the twentieth century; those who promulgated it—musicians and critics—were mostly from the next generation, born in the 1910s and 1920s. Generational differences in—and struggles over—musical taste are, in fact, a recurring theme in American music.

The two jazz camps had their own adherents, detractors, sympathetic journalists, and nightclubs. Under the headline "Police Avert Clash of Dixieland and Re-bop," *Down Beat* reported in 1946 that New Orleans–style trombonist

George Brunis, performing on 52nd Street, decided to march across the street to where Dizzy Gillespie's bebop group was playing and have a battle of the bands, but the police intervened to break up what could have gotten out of hand. The *Washington Post* reported that New York City's famed 52nd Street tolerated "none of the Fundamentalists' Dixieland music and Greenwich Village, 'that little bit o' Basin Street in New York,' has squeezed out almost completely modern swing units."

On the traditionalist side, decrying the loss of the beat so prevalent in earlier jazz, concert violinist Sol Babitz wrote, "Such, alas, is the decay of jazz which started out by making everyone tap his foot because of the music and ends by asking you to tap your foot in spite of the music. . . . [Jazz is] coming to an onanistic end in the blind alley of New York where it has struck its head against a brick wall with an ominous 'bebop.'"

listeners had devoured the Armstrong Hot Fives and Hot Sevens and the Count Basie sides with Lester Young. Where the older disciples had copied the slang and mannerisms of Armstrong and Young, the new acolytes became similarly absorbed with their bop role models. Sporting Gillespie-inspired goatees, berets, and glasses was benign, but when Parker's heroin addiction became widely known and his followers mistakenly assumed that emulating this aspect of his lifestyle would allow them to produce music of similar brilliance, the hero worship had a far more destructive effect.

During his brief and often sensationalized lifetime, and to an even greater extent after his death in 1955 at the age of 34, Parker's music and life story evoked more passion—pro and con—than that of any of his contemporaries. Parker stood more clearly apart from previous jazz generations than did Gillespie, who was more of an accomplished entertainer—with his scat singing and onstage dancing—than the typical bopper. On the other hand, Parker was more approachable than the sometimes eccentric behaving pianist Thelonious Monk. Parker's music had a searing emotional quality that provided a fitting soundtrack to the drug and alcohol abuse, erratic behavior, and occasional hospitalizations that fueled his legend. Yet while Parker complained that many who came to hear him were only seeking a glimpse of "the world's greatest junkie, the supreme hipster," even his most casual fans were responding to a visceral intensity that gave jazz—and most particularly the blues sensibility so central to jazz—a contemporary immediacy. Together with the more commercial rhythm and blues players (including saxophone player Paul Williams who turned Parker's *Now's the Time* into the pop hit *The Hucklebuck* in 1948) and such raw urban-music innovators as Muddy Waters, Parker was taking the blues into the postwar era.

A writer named D. Leon Wolff castigated bebop:

> Bop violates one of the major characteristics of good art— ease. The best that is done, written, said, or played ordinarily gives the effect of grace and fluidity. . . . But bop has carried frantic jazz to the ultimate.

Some of the harshest criticism came from jazz musicians playing earlier styles. Swing arranger-bandleader Fletcher Henderson charged that bebop was the most "phenomenal cruelty in all the world." "Mistakes—that's all re-bop is," Louis Armstrong told *Time* magazine. Armstrong did however, praise Gillespie: "I'd never play this bebop because I don't like it. Don't get me wrong; I think some of them cats who play it play real good, like Dizzy, especially."

Among those who welcomed and defended the new style was Barry Ulanov, the editor of *Metronome* magazine, who in his article "Feud for Thought," responded to the banning of bop by Los Angeles radio station KMPC:

> Musically, men like Dizzy Gillespie are helping jazz to progress, are giving America's art greater harmonic depth, increasing its rhythmic and tonal resources. But as long as serious channels of information, such as a radio station and a leading newsmagazine [*Time*— quoted previously], misinform, mislead, distort and destroy, there will be no progress outside of the backrooms where the Dizzys make their rhythmic and harmonic explorations.

From the perspective of the twenty-first century, the word war may seem quaint, but while it lasted, it created a great deal of bad feeling. In retrospect, like many wars, it seems pointless. While bebop reigned as the progressive new music for some years, it did not vanquish the earlier styles to oblivion. Today, in major American cities, determined seekers can find all three styles being played—a victory not for one style or another, but rather for musical pluralism. SOURCE: BARRY ULANOV, "FEUD FOR THOUGHT," *METRONOME*.

—John Edward Hasse

Dizzy Gillespie wearing his trademark beret and horn-rimmed glasses.
PHOTO COURTESY WILLIAM P. GOTTLIEB/WILLIAM P. GOTTLIEB COLLECTION/LIBRARY OF CONGRESS PRINTS & PHOTOGRAPHS DIVISION.

Listening Guide

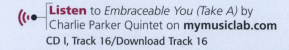 **Listen** to *Embraceable You (Take A)* by Charlie Parker Quintet on **mymusiclab.com**
CD I, Track 16/Download Track 16

EMBRACEABLE YOU (TAKE A) • CHARLIE PARKER QUINTET

Music: George Gershwin, 1930. Personnel: Charlie Parker (alto saxophone); Miles Davis (trumpet); Duke Jordan (piano); Tommy Potter (bass); Max Roach (drums). Recorded October 28, 1947, in New York. First issue: Dial 1024. Timing: 3:48.

Overview

The nickname "Bird" proves apropos as Charlie Parker pilots his alto saxophone on astoundingly rapid, darting flights of melodic exploration in this recording that captures the bebop pioneer at peak form. Working with his most famous quintet, which included the young trumpeter Miles Davis and the innovative drummer Max Roach, Parker recorded a number of tracks between October and December of 1947, *Embraceable You* being one of the earliest. Recently released from Camarillo State Hospital, where he had undergone treatment for drug addiction, Parker brought to the recording a renewed vitality.

While most bravura bebop performances rely on fast tempos, *Embraceable You* is a ballad. Yet Parker defied convention—which would typically dictate a slower, smoldering, ruminative approach to soloing—and instead used the slow pace as a wide-open platform for highly varied, sometimes hummingbird-fast melodic forays. The detail, precision, structural rigor, and sheer innovation of Parker's improvisations are testimony to the genius (there's no other word) that enabled such virtuosity at so young an age and without formal training. (But not without serious woodshedding: "I put quite a bit of study into the horn, that's true," Parker said in a 1954 interview. "I used to put in at least 11 to 15 hours a day. . . . I did that for over a period of three to four years.")

Miles Davis, on the other hand, had absorbed some formal training—at the Juilliard School of Music—and (though not necessarily as a consequence) his solo on the track is in stark contrast to Parker's. Davis is the reserved, cool foil to Parker's acrobatic, extroverted front man. Already, with his dry tone, vibrato-free delivery, and pensive stance, Davis is foreshadowing the cool jazz that he would help introduce in 1949 with his *Birth of the Cool* recordings and all but define in 1959 with his *Kind of Blue*. Although Parker dominates this recording, it's clear in retrospect that he is marking the pinnacle of a period style while Davis, less visible in the shadows, already holds a key to the future.

At the same recording session, a second take (Take B) of this performance was made that gives insights into how Parker shaped his solos in different renditions of the same piece. You can hear that second take on the download set of music that accompanies this book and follow an online listening guide on mymusiclab.com.

Key Features

- Improvisation: With melody entirely improvised, the tune encompasses Parker's 64 bars of soloing and Davis's 40. Parker builds his solo, in part, on a six-note figure that he echoes periodically.
- Accompaniment and rhythm: The rhythm section—pianist Duke Jordan, bassist Tommy Potter, and drummer Max Roach—provide solid, straightforward, and unobtrusive support as they leave the spotlight to the soloists. The meter is in **cut time**, moving in relaxed half notes.
- Melody and style: Parker chooses to not play Gershwin's melody at all, departing from tradition even more markedly than Coleman Hawkins did on *Body and Soul*

(see page 118), when Hawkins played only the first few bars of the original melody. Here, Parker's solo is a compact lexicon of bebop conventions, both melodic and rhythmic. Parker continually displaces his phrasing, starting and ending at unexpected points, which maximizes the listener's sense of uncertainty and surprise. He alters the velocity of his melodies. He offers endless variation of shape and contour, interweaving scalar melodies linked via **chromatic**, **passing**, and **neighbor tones** with harmony-outlining (or altering) **arpeggios**. He makes substantial melodic use of notes outside the base scale, including the flatted and sharped fifth and ninth. Accents are frequently on offbeats.

- Harmony: Based on George Gershwin's composition, the harmony hews to a major-key progression in the key of F, which Parker and company freely alter and embellish with substitute harmonies.

—Tad Lathrop

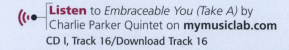 **Listen** to *Embraceable You* Take B on **mymusiclab.com**

---

cut time a meter emphasizing two beats per measure.

chromatic related to half steps, as opposed to diatonic and modal, which refer to arrangements of whole and half steps.

passing tone a note that connects two stable tones.

neighbor tone a note a step above or a step below another note.

arpeggio the notes of a chord played sequentially rather then simultaneously.

TIME	FORM	INSTRUMENTATION	MELODY
0:00	INTRODUCTION	Piano	Pianist Duke Jordan sets the mood with a four-bar intro previewing the first chords of the tune in F. The feeling is warm and intimate.
0:13	CHORUS 1	Alto sax	Charlie Parker ignores the written melody and begins improvising immediately with a six-note figure similar to the opening of the standard tune *As Time Goes By* (and possibly a direct quote of a 1939 song titled *A Table in a Corner*). He reworks the figure three times before (0:27) using it as the springboard for an extended phrase ending on a segment of the figure. (He's using the figure as a structural device for melodic development.) His next phrase (0:31) picks up where the last left off, but lower, and spills forward in a continuing, snaking path that closes the chorus characteristically on an arpeggio using altered (non-scale) notes resolving to the unexpected note D.
0:42	CHORUS 2		Entering before the **downbeat**, and now in double time, Parker hurtles forward, ascending and descending, before halving the time in bars two and three and ending (0:45) with a three-note figure of A, low A, B-natural. He repeats this start-fast-then-relax approach on the next four-bar phrase (0:48), punctuating it (0:55) with a complex chromatic flourish. A third phrase (0:57) revisits the opening figure at 1:00, then extends a bar past the expected fourth-bar (bar 12 of the chorus) ending. For the last two bars (1:07) he begins the next chorus unexpectedly ahead of schedule . . .
1:11	CHORUS 3		. . . playing through the downbeat and pausing in the first bar, then resuming (1:13) with an ornamented passage ending on a paraphrase of the opening figure (1:15), which he echoes, first higher (1:19), then lower (1:22). From the flitting gesture of a bird alighting on a branch (1:24–1:27), Parker slows down for an ascending phrase over a G minor chord climaxing with a high descending eighth-note figure (1:30) outlining a D-flat chord rather then the underlying C7 of the accompaniment.* He resolves to the home chord with three ascending iterations of a four-, then five-note arpeggiated motif. A final-bar descending cascade of sixteenth notes leads to . . .
1:41	CHORUS 4		. . . a pause on the note B-flat, then (1:43) lifting off to more flights of convoluted, corkscrewing, up-and-down melody, broken by brief stop-offs on a D-flat note (1:45) and an A (1:49). A slowed-down phrase rises to yet another iteration of the original figure (1:52), repeated with a lowered first note (1:54), then lowered further to—surprise!—a new motif, repeated a half-step lower (1:58); then it's raised back to—another surprise!—an extended resolving phrase that lands "home" on the third of the F scale (2:04). Parker transitions out with several more "afterthought" flourishes.
2:11	CHORUS 5	Trumpet	Taking a much different approach, Miles Davis stays mostly with the beat and plays less-busy melodies that could be sung. He emphasizes economy, playing fewer notes but choosing those that define (and maximize the feeling of) the tune's harmonic motion (2:18, 2:23, 2:32), which he connects via passing strings of melody. Davis sounds downright minimalist compared to Parker's gregarious, ostentatious, note-packed displays.
2:42	CHORUS 6		Davis continues in the same vein, while Parker makes occasional background musical comments. (At 3:02 Davis plays, and fluffs, a three-note figure that implies D-flat major—reminiscent of Parker's idea at 1:30.) This chorus extends for an additional eight bars (3:12–3:28) as Davis closes out his solo, ending with octave jumps from F' to F.
3:29	CODA	Band	Parker joins Davis in a harmonized coda lasting four bars, with a melody that suggests—but doesn't exactly replicate—the closing phrase of the original song.

*This characteristic Bird (and bop) practice involves making melodies out of altered (flatted or sharped) notes of the underlying scale or chord (the C7 chord in this example). At times these melodies may match the regular (unaltered) scale tones of a separate key (D-flat major in this example), making for two keys being implied simultaneously—the technical term for which is **polytonality**.

downbeat   the first beat of a measure; can also refer to the first beat of a tune.

polytonality   two or more keys played simultaneously.

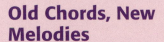
Old Chords, New Melodies

Many of the compositions created by bop-era musicians were **contrafacts**: new melodies written to the harmonic structures—what musicians call the chord changes (or simply "the **changes**")—of preexisting songs.

The practice is as old as jazz itself. It could be argued that every 12-bar blues is this type of "contrafact"; but the technique was applied to popular song forms as well, by some of the greatest jazz composers. Duke Ellington made use of the final harmonic sequence of the classic composition *Tiger Rag* (the "hold that tiger" strain) often in the early days of his orchestra, in such pieces as *The Creeper* (1928) and *High Life* (1929), and built *In a Mellotone* (1940) on the chords of *Rose Room*, while his collaborator Billy Strayhorn's immortal *Take the "A" Train* (1941) borrows harmonies from *Exactly Like You*. Such appropriations were hardly confined to Ellington's circle; witness the Kansas City staple *Moten Swing*, written in 1932 on the changes of the pop song *You're Driving Me Crazy*.

With the arrival of the modern-jazz era, the creation of such contrafacts grew exponentially. In a sense, using a familiar harmonic sequence simply verified the continuity between the new jazz and earlier styles, while also underscoring the melodic, rhythmic, and (through the addition or **substitution** of more complex **passing chords**) harmonic distinctions that the modernists had introduced. It was also an economic strategy to reap financial benefits from these new creations. While an improvised solo could not serve as the basis for generating earnings, at least the crafting of a new melody over chords that (like solos) enjoyed no copyright protection provided a source of royalties. Some record companies, determined to solidify their own profits and avoid payments to established composers, even insisted that musicians record original material with the label acting as publisher—a practice that generated even more contrafacts.

It did not take long for *I Got Rhythm* (1930) to become the jazz world's favorite harmonic sequence

For most of the decade (1945–55) during which he reigned as the acknowledged leader of the boppers, Parker's working life involved leading a combo—usually a quintet in which his alto saxophone was joined by trumpet, piano, bass, and drums—on recording sessions or in club and concert performances. Parker had played for dancers during his years of big band apprenticeship, yet his new ideas were better suited for listeners. This shift to jazz as listening music not only helped the nightclubs that were now the centers of instrumental music performance but also sustained a growing number of independent jazz labels that could not marshall the production budgets required for recording larger ensembles. (Coleman Hawkins and Lester Young had anticipated the shift to combos, club work, and independent jazz labels before and during the war years.)

The lineup of Parker's best-known group—with Miles Davis on trumpet, Duke Jordan on piano, Tommy Potter on bass, and Max Roach on drums—was ideal for expressing the premium the new music placed on speed of thought and execution. Parker recorded with these musicians for both the Dial and Savoy companies in 1947 and 1948, and the resulting performances, including *Scrapple from the Apple*, *Bird Gets the Worm*, and *Dexterity*, redefined the sound and textures of small-group playing. The shift in Parker's performing venues during these years—from the after-hours Harlem spots to the nightclubs on and around 52nd Street (which ultimately included a room named Birdland in Parker's honor) and finally to the bohemian haunts of Greenwich Village—also reflected the broader route this new style of jazz was traveling,

---

contrafact a composition that superimposes a new melody on a preexisting chord progression; employed extensively in the bebop era, notably in the writing of new melodies to the chords of *I Got Rhythm* and *Indiana*.

changes the arrangement of chords—the chord progression—that defines a tune; "*Rhythm* changes," for example, is jazz shorthand for "the chords of *I Got Rhythm*."

[chord] substitution replacement of a chord that is standard or written with another to create musical interest; most often applied to transitory chords such as the dominant seventh.

passing chord transitional chord that connects stable chords; chord that conveys a sense of irresolution and tension, resolved by movement to another chord.

after the blues, and for Charlie Parker to become the king of the *Rhythm* remakers. The harmonic motion of the Gershwin classic was ideal for jazz improvisation, and Parker mined it constantly with such new-melody reworkings as *Red Cross* (1944), *Anthropology* (1946), *Cheers* (1947), *Dexterity* (1947), *Chasin' the Bird* (1947), *Ah-Leu-Cha* (1948), *Steeplechase* (1948), and *Kim* (1952). Sometimes he worked variations into the practice, as on *Constellation* (1948) and *Merry Go Round* (1948), in which the primary themes are built on the main chordal scheme of *Honeysuckle Rose* and the second theme (or bridge) is based on the bridge of *I Got Rhythm*. Parker liked to play compositions based on other songs as well: Tadd Dameron's *Hot House* (1945), Miles Davis's *Donna Lee* (1947), and Benny Harris's *Ornithology* (1946), based on *What Is This*

Thing Called Love?*, *Indiana*, and *How High the Moon*, respectively.

When it came to such contrafacts, virtually everybody was doing it in the 1940s and 1950s. That is why such classic compositions of the period as Thelonious Monk's *Rhythm-a-ning* (1941), **Bud Powell**'s *Wail* (1946), and Sonny Rollins's *Oleo* (1954)—not to mention Duke Ellington's *Cotton Tail* (1940) and Lester Young's *Lester Leaps In* (1939)—can claim *I Got Rhythm* as a common point of origin.

—*Bob Blumenthal*

out of the black community to the precincts of the educated (primarily white) audience.

Parker was not confined exclusively to combos and clubs, however; a significant portion of his recorded legacy reveals that the new music was already functioning elsewhere. In addition to the triumphant recordings of *Ornithology*, *Yardbird Suite*, and the Gillespie composition *A Night in Tunisia*, all from 1946, some of the key products of Parker's stay in California between 1945 and 1947 include recorded performances with Jazz at the Philharmonic, a forum in which he and Gillespie demonstrated, to listeners who had open ears and minds, that their approach was perfectly compatible with that of predecessors Roy Eldridge, Coleman Hawkins, and Lester Young. When **Norman Granz**, the producer of Jazz at the Philharmonic (JATP), expanded upon the success of recordings from the concerts to create his own jazz label Clef in 1946, Parker was included on one of the first releases, *Slow Drag*, a JATP jam. Several of the saxophonist's studio projects under Granz's supervision announced even more far-reaching aspects of the new music.

Granz began by recording Parker with Machito's Afro-Cubans, the orchestra fronted by vocalist

Frank Raul "Machito" Grillo. Under the musical direction of Machito's brother-in-law, multi-instrumentalist Mario Bauzá, the Afro-Cubans had successfully merged Latin American rhythms and forms with big band concepts. Dizzy Gillespie, who had been introduced to Latin rhythms by Bauzá while both were members of the Cab Calloway trumpet section, had established himself as the prime champion of this Latin-jazz fusion by featuring Cuban conga drummer Chano Pozo on *Manteca* (*JTSA* Disc 2/Track 13) and *Cubana Be/Cubana Bop* in 1947. This stylistic conjunction continued to develop in the years before Parker's death: **Stan Kenton** paid tribute in a piece entitled *Machito* (1947); Latin bandleaders including Tito Puente and Tito Rodriguez followed Machito's lead and made frequent room for guest jazz soloists; and popular jazz combos of the early 1950s—led by pianist George Shearing and vibraphonist Cal Tjader—returned the compliment by incorporating Latin percussionists (see Chapter 10 for more on Latin Jazz).

Swing Street

It was called "Swing Street" and "the street that never slept." In its nightclub heyday—which lasted roughly from 1933 to the late 1940s—the stretch of Manhattan's 52nd Street that ran between 5th and 7th avenues served as a vibrant center of jazz activity.

Clubs such as the Onyx, the Famous Door, and the Three Deuces lit the street in neon. Over time, they also cast light on the changing face of jazz. In the late 1930s, a walk past a club marquee and downstairs into a basement would plunge a visitor into a crowded, smoke-filled setting alive with the sound of swing. Ten years later, that same descent would immerse the clubgoer in the hyperkinetic energy of bebop.

The Street offered a grab bag of options for fan and player alike. On any given night, a jazz seeker could snake from one brownstone to another and catch sets by Art Tatum, Coleman Hawkins, and Billie Holiday. The musicians themselves would hop from club to club, finishing up their regular shows and then rushing across the street or a couple of doors away to sit in with other bands. With new ideas and players circulating freely, tested for durability in late-night "**cutting sessions**," 52nd Street became a hothouse of innovation and evolving styles.

It was on the Street that many musicians heard sax innovator Charlie Parker for the first time, when he would drop in unannounced to jam. "Everybody just flipped," clarinetist Tony Scott recalled. Parker's influence would course through the Street's echoing basements and on into future jazz.

The clubs were numerous, and each had its own mini-history. There was the Onyx, one of the Street's earliest jazz venues, where in 1933 one could hear Tatum and the swing quintet Spirits of Rhythm; two years later, audiences could catch the sextet of violinist-singer Stuff Smith, who had a novelty hit in 1936 with *I'se a Muggin'*. By the mid-1940s Dizzy Gillespie was there, playing virtuosic bop trumpet with a group that included bassist Oscar Pettiford and drummer Max Roach. Across the street was the Famous Door, which played host, over the years, to the likes of Count Basie's big band, Gillespie, Lester Young, Ben Webster, and Jack Teagarden.

Another club, the Hickory House, opened its doors in 1934. By 1936 it was showcasing one of 52nd Street's first racially mixed groups, led by clarinetist Joe Marsala and featuring Red Allen on trumpet. Marsala seemingly couldn't leave: he played at the Hickory House off and on through 1945.

At the Club Downbeat, featured acts included Holiday, guitarist Tiny Grimes and his group, and Hawkins, who worked there with Thelonious Monk in 1944, at around the same time Gillespie was bringing bop to the Onyx.

Gillespie also played the Three Deuces. And in 1947 young trumpeter Miles Davis could be heard there, earning his stripes in a quintet led by saxophone sensation Parker and propelled by Max Roach.

Kelly's Stable was the site, in 1939, of Hawkins's debut engagement after an extended stay in Europe. Hawkins's classic Bluebird recording of *Body and Soul* was a product of his Stable stint. Nat Cole, Holiday, and Hot Lips Page were others heard there.

Two doors down from the Onyx was Jimmy Ryan's, a site that specialized in traditional jazz: Page, Allen, Earl Hines, Sidney Bechet, and Bob Wilber played there. The club outlasted the Street itself, closing in 1962.

After World War II, the Street's jazz began to slip away, drawn to clubs in other parts of town—clubs such as Bop City, the Royal Roost, Birdland, and Greenwich Village's Cafe Society and the Village Vanguard. Strip joints and pockets of vice replaced it. Several decades later, following its transformation into a gray stretch of nondescript office buildings, the "street that never slept" finally turned out the lights for good.

—*Tad Lathrop*

---

cutting session a jam session featuring informal competition among soloists.

52nd Street, New York City, 1948. PHOTO COURTESY WILLIAM P. GOTTLIEB/WILLIAM P. GOTTLIEB COLLECTION/LIBRARY OF CONGRESS PRINTS & PHOTOGRAPHS DIVISION.

Big Bands in the Modern Era

A combination of changing economics and changing tastes may have brought a close to the big band era, but it hardly extinguished all big bands. In addition to the ongoing enterprises of jazz's orchestral Olympians, Duke Ellington and Count Basie, a number of newer large ensembles emerged as jazz entered the modern era.

Unfortunately, the two big bands that became known as the incubators of the modern era were victims of the 1942–44 recording ban. These were the Earl Hines Orchestra of 1943, which included Dizzy Gillespie, Charlie Parker, and Sarah Vaughan, and the first edition of the band formed by Hines vocalist Billy Eckstine, which featured Gillespie, Parker, and Vaughan as well as such other leading modernists as trumpeter Fats Navarro, tenor saxophonists Gene Ammons and Dexter Gordon, and drummer Art Blakey. By the time Eckstine's band recorded, Gillespie and Parker had moved on.

The big band was a natural setting for Gillespie's virtuosic trumpet and extroverted showmanship, however; and in the latter half of the 1940s he led an orchestra of his own. The compositions *Things to Come* (1946), *Cool Breeze* (1947), and others demonstrated that the innovations heard most frequently in combos could also be applied to larger ensembles, while *Algo Bueno* (1947) and the two-part *Cubana Be/Cubana Bop* (1947) revealed the potential in merging jazz with Afro-Cuban music (see Chapter 10).

Modern ideas also drove what came to be known as the First and Second Herds of veteran bandleader Woody Herman—especially the 1947–49 Second Herd, which bore

COURTESY JOHN EDWARD HASSE.

the strong influence of both Parker and (in the sound of its *Four Brothers* sax section) Lester Young.

Another variety of modernism was purveyed by the bands of Stan Kenton, who used Jimmie Lunceford as the initial model for his band, yet by the end of the 1940s was the exemplar of all things "progressive." There was much pretense in Kenton's music (particularly in his constant recasting of 1943's *Artistry in Rhythm*), but much innovation as well, beginning with his use of bassist Eddie Safranski and the Kai Winding–led trombone section on such performances as *Collaboration* and *Minor Riff* (both 1947). Early-1950s editions featured the challenging scores of Bob Graettinger (*City of Class*, 1951) and Bill Russo (*23 Degrees North, 82 Degrees West*, 1952; *JTSA* Disc 3/Track 5). By that time, trumpeter

Billy Eckstine. PHOTO
COURTESY DOWN BEAT ARCHIVES.

Shorty Rogers, saxophonist **Gerry Mulligan** (who wrote the influential *Young Blood* [1952] but did not play in the band), and others had introduced ideas into Kenton's orbit that would also prove to be forerunners of "cool" jazz. Ultimately, however, the economics of bandleading proved prohibitive. By 1950, Gillespie had disbanded, Herman and Kenton only toured for parts of each year, and even Count Basie was temporarily reduced to leading a combo. Only Duke Ellington, in a class of his own as always, remained on the road, the exception that proved the rule that big bands had become an unaffordable luxury.

—*Bob Blumenthal*

Jazz at the Philharmonic was the first "live" jazz album ever released.
COURTESY BENCAR ARCHIVES.

Norman Granz, 1947. PHOTO COURTESY WILLIAM P. GOTTLIEB/ WILLIAM P. GOTTLIEB COLLECTION/LIBRARY OF CONGRESS PRINTS & PHOTOGRAPHS DIVISION.

Norman Granz and Jazz at the Philharmonic

Along with the annual Carnegie Hall concerts that Duke Ellington embarked on in 1943, producer Norman Granz's Jazz at the Philharmonic concert series was among the gathering indications that jazz could find a new home in formal settings that typically hosted symphony orchestras and classical soloists. Not that JATP, as it quickly became known, confined itself to the esoteric aspects of the music. The concerts were organized jam sessions, loose and extroverted and frequently derided for the solo displays of such regulars as tenor saxophonists Illinois Jacquet and Flip Phillips that approached the exhibitionism of rhythm and blues. In honoring Granz's preference for the spontaneous, JATP drove home the point that all "serious" music was not necessarily committed to manuscript paper; and at its best, as in the 1946 concert that produced Charlie Parker's solo on *Lady Be Good*, JATP presented

informal cross-generational summit meetings in which such young innovators as Parker and Dizzy Gillespie could stand shoulder-to-shoulder with such influential elders as Lester Young and Roy Eldridge.

JATP's 1944 debut concert at Hollywood's Philharmonic Auditorium had been organized by Granz to raise funds for Mexican American defendants in a murder case, and the producer's commitment to civil rights was further demonstrated by his insistence that integration take place both onstage and in the audience at all JATP concerts. The 1944 debut was also recorded, later appearing on 12-inch, 78-rpm records. These became the first commercially issued live jazz recordings, and their popularity made JATP an international concert phenomenon and Granz the first acknowledged jazz impresario. He continued to present JATP through

1957, generally with vocalist Ella Fitzgerald and the trio of pianist Oscar Peterson as the centerpieces of the star-heavy packages.

Granz also excelled as a recording executive and personal manager. He owned the labels successively known as Clef, Norgran, and Verve, which dominated independent jazz production throughout the 1950s by presenting Fitzgerald, **Stan Getz**, Gillespie, Billie Holiday, Parker, Peterson, Art Tatum, Young, and other stars. After selling Verve in 1960, Granz returned to recording with his Pablo label in 1973, where Basie, Fitzgerald, Peterson, and guitarist Joe Pass all found a home. Granz also personally oversaw the careers of Fitzgerald and Peterson and enjoyed a productive if less exclusive business relationship with Duke Ellington.

—Bob Blumenthal

The Jazz Musician as Outsider

Why are jazz musicians often perceived as being "outsiders" who shun the values of mainstream American life?

Part of the reason jazz music was controversial from the beginning was that the occupation of jazz musician challenged notions of middle-class respectability and normative behavior. Late hours, uncertain employment, and an often-itinerant work life—not to mention jazz's early associations with New Orleans sporting houses, scandalous dancing, drinking, and nightlife—led some parents to ask, "Would you want your daughter to marry a jazz musician?"

Sociologist Howard S. Becker has argued that jazz musicians, at least at mid-century, constituted a deviant subculture—deemed unorthodox by more conventional members of society—but nonetheless one that was stable and long lasting. Jazz musicians segregated themselves musically and felt a conflict with the non-musicians who hired them, and with people (musicians or not) outside of jazz, who were often thought to be "square"—the opposite of hip. Signs of the isolation of the jazz community, wrote Alan P. Merriam in *The Anthropology of Music*, included "special language, greeting rituals, titles, and dress; folk plots in stories which are traded among members; a lack of race prejudice. . . ."

Until the latter part of the twentieth century, few jazz musicians learned their craft in school; the image of the jazz musician as outsider was stoked by the fact that jazz existed largely outside of respectable institutions such as schools, colleges, and churches. The temptations and abuse of alcohol were ever-present for players whose main living was in nightclubs and dancehalls, where booze was easily consumed, as symbolized by the 1931 death from alcoholism of the brilliant cornetist Bix Beiderbecke, at the age of 28.

Drug use became part of jazz's public image—sometimes in good humor, as in Cab Calloway's signature song, *Minnie the Moocher* (1931), a light-hearted story of an opium smoker. Marijuana, popular among some jazz musicians, was memorialized in Don Redman's *Chant of the Weed* (1931) and the song *Reefer Man* (1932). Though hidden from the public, Louis Armstrong smoked weed, he said, every day of his adult life. Drummer Gene Krupa's 1943 arrest for possession of two marijuana cigarettes—he was given a three-month jail sentence—helped further a connection in the public's mind between jazz and drugs.

In the 1940s, the image of the jazz musician as abnormal ratcheted up considerably when Charlie Parker and Billie Holiday underwent well-publicized arrests and prison terms for heroin addiction. "Dope, heroin abuse, really got to be a major problem during the bebop era, especially in the late forties, and a lotta guys died from it," recalled trumpeter Dizzy Gillespie in his autobiography, *To Be or Not to Bop*. In the 1950s, a range of other musicians—Miles Davis, John Coltrane, Stan Getz, Ray Nance, Art Pepper, Bill Evans, and many others—would struggle with drug addiction, strengthening the image of jazz musicians as deviant outsiders.

Jazz musicians often actively cultivated the image of outsider, as it was their artistic prerogative to stand apart from, or outside, the main culture. Often jazz players looked down on other kinds of music, creating the word "corny" to refer to non-jazz sweet pop music. Their stance as outsiders helped them to develop unconventional, highly personal ways of playing and improvising, even speaking and dressing. Indeed, innovation and creativity are often linked with "outsider" behavior; in the creative arts generally, high creativity and deviant behavior have often gone together, from Vincent van Gogh to Jack Kerouac, William Burroughs, and Andy Warhol. During the 1950s, as part of a countercultural literary movement dubbed "the Beat generation," writers such as Kerouac and Lawrence Ferlinghetti embraced jazz and held poetry readings with live jazz, reinforcing the image of the jazz musicians as oddball "beatniks" or outsiders.

The stereotyping of the jazz musician as outsider would ultimately be challenged, if not shattered, by the rise of Wynton Marsalis, in the 1990s and the 2000s, as an immaculately attired, eloquent, powerful cultural figure who was equally at home teaching in an inner-city school, hosting his own show on PBS television, lobbying on Capitol Hill, or performing at the White House. But the image of the outsider jazz artist would last a very long time.

—*John Edward Hasse*

Granz also recorded Parker with a string section, fulfilling one of the saxophonist's lifelong ambitions and inspiring a small but steady stream of similar performances from soloists with the artistic or commercial clout to merit such lavish treatment. Parker was extremely proud of his work with strings, especially his stunning interpretation of the standard *Just Friends* (1949), and the *Charlie Parker with Strings* recordings (1949) were easily his most popular.

Parker's diehard fans were able to preserve many of his more typical quintet performances, because his music was broadcast frequently from nightclubs on radio "remotes" and could be saved through the new home-recording technology. Fans made their own copies of these "**airchecks**" as well as in-person dubs of concerts, club sets, and even informal rehearsals and jam sessions. This activity generated an astounding number of unauthorized Parker recordings, which began surfacing before his death and continued to emerge over the decades. These multiple versions of the same stable of bebop compositions, together with many alternate studio **takes** saved by the labels for which Parker recorded, testify to his inexhaustible creativity. Several location recordings are masterpieces, such as the 1953 Massey Hall concert in Toronto in which Parker, Gillespie, Powell, Roach, and bassist Charles Mingus held something of a bebop summit. Even the rough and unpolished snippets of Parker's alto preserved elsewhere, with ensembles and solos by other band members omitted to save precious tape or discs, include brilliant improvisations and reinforce Parker's status as a cult figure.

Parker's image as a self-destructive outsider established an unfortunate stereotype for his musical generation. This romantic notion of the doomed jazz genius done in by his or her addictions actually predates Parker and can be traced back at least as far as the 1920s cornetist Bix Beiderbecke. Still, the identification of jazz with drug abuse grew stronger in the 1940s, boosted by Gene Krupa's and Lester Young's marijuana-related run-ins with the authorities, Parker's erratic behavior leading to his commitment in California's Camarillo State Hospital, and Billie Holiday's imprisonment for heroin possession. Frank Sinatra's portrait of fictional drummer Frankie Machine in *The Man with the Golden Arm* (1955) plus later movie biographies of Holiday and Parker contributed to an environment in which extramusical notoriety often

overshadowed artistic achievement. Notwithstanding the distortions and racial double standards that fed such sensational depictions of many great musicians, there is no denying that substance abuse was a particularly devastating scourge in the jazz world during this period and interrupted the careers of many prominent musicians. For such innovators as baritone saxophonist Serge Chaloff, tenor saxophonist Wardell Gray, and trumpeter Theodore "Fats" Navarro, as well as Parker and Holiday, these addictions would prove fatal before the 1950s ended.

TAKE NOTE

- What is bebop and what roles did Charlie Parker and Dizzy Gillespie play in creating and popularizing it?

Piano Modernists

Even in the face of such problems, players in the 1940s and early 1950s generated a vast quantity of great music, beginning with the work of those who formed Parker's immediate circle as his style took hold. Much of the most interesting music came from the era's pianists. Bud Powell—the musician who best transferred

Pianist, composer, and bandleader Tadd Dameron.
PHOTO COURTESY WILLIAM P. GOTTLIEB/
WILLIAM P. GOTTLIEB COLLECTION/
LIBRARY OF CONGRESS PRINTS &
PHOTOGRAPHS DIVISION.

---

aircheck a recording made from a radio broadcast by the station for its own purposes; sometimes, years later, they were issued.

take in a recording session, one run-through; several takes may be required in order to achieve an acceptable rendition.

the speed and complexity of Parker's alto playing to the piano—worked with Parker only infrequently, yet he defined the standard for modern piano in several early trio, solo, and quintet recordings and became, arguably, the most influential modernist after Parker. Powell was at best an erratic presence. Psychiatric problems that had apparently been caused or exacerbated by a police beating in 1945 led to lengthy incarcerations, during which Powell underwent shock treatments that left the pianist even more disoriented and withdrawn. The toll taken on Powell's technique became increasingly audible in his playing; yet the pianist's initial recordings between 1947 and 1951, including *Dance of the Infidels*, *Tempus Fugit*, *Parisian Thoroughfare*, *Indiana* (*JTSA* Disc 2/Track 17), and *Un Poco Loco*, capture some of the era's most brilliant and completely realized music.

Tadd Dameron also played piano but is primarily remembered as one of the era's most gifted

Piano modernist Bud Powell. PHOTO COURTESY © HERMAN LEONARD PHOTOGRAPHY LLC.

bandleaders and composers (*Good Bait*, 1944; *Hot House*, 1945; *Our Delight*, 1946; *If You Could See Me Now*, 1946). During his period of greatest activity, 1947–49, Dameron led a significant band at the Royal Roost on 52nd Street. His featured trumpeter was Fats Navarro, whose melodic gifts and balanced technique were easier for other trumpeters to emulate than those of the more virtuosic Gillespie. Prior to his death in 1950, Navarro made several important studio recordings with Dameron (*The Squirrel*, 1947, and *Lady Bird* [*JTSA* Disc 2/Track 21], 1948) and Powell (*Bouncing with Bud* and *52nd Street Theme*, 1949), as well as aircheck recordings with Dameron and Parker, that continue to enhance his legend.

The late 1940s marked the first recordings by a third important pianist-composer, one who had

The melodic trumpet style of Fats Navarro (left, shown with Illinois Jacquet) was easier to emulate than that of the more virtuosic Dizzy Gillespie. PHOTO COURTESY DOWN BEAT ARCHIVES.

Listening Guide

Listen to *Misterioso* by Thelonious Monk Quartet on **mymusiclab.com**
CD I, Track 19/Download Track 19

MISTERIOSO • THELONIOUS MONK QUARTET

Music: Thelonious Monk, 1948. Personnel: Thelonious Monk (piano); Milt Jackson (vibraphone); John Simmons (bass); Shadow Wilson (drums). Recorded July 2, 1948, in New York. First issue: Blue Note 560. Timing: 2:47.

Overview

Misterioso employs the most common of jazz structures, the 12-bar blues, to new and audacious ends. Unlike much of the new music of its period, it sets aside the more obvious signs of virtuosity for equally refined uses of sonority, rhythmic displacement, and melodic development, together with a more consistent emphasis on harmonic dissonance. The angular nature of the theme, the more brazen ensemble sound, and the tensions of the rhythms (which sometimes seem to lurch yet always swing) define the personality of composer/pianist Thelonious Monk, as distinctive a musical presence as jazz has known.

Key Features

- Melody: *Misterioso* employs simple melodic ideas to complex effect. For most of its length, the melody uses the interval of a sixth in a see-saw pattern that has sometimes been described as "walking sixths." The sixths are taken through the standard harmonic structure of the blues, leading at the end of the chorus to a single minor seventh (the "blue" seventh), creating an unresolved feeling that carries dramatic tension.
- Harmony: Monk makes extensive use of dissonance, both in his own solo lines and the chords with which he accompanies Milt Jackson's vibraphone solo.
- Rhythm: Monk is masterful in the way he employs slight adjustments of his phrases, anticipating or delaying his attack to constantly surprising effect.

- Tempo: While a medium-slow tempo is employed for most of the performance, it is doubled excitingly in the final theme chorus.
- Color and texture: Both Monk and Jackson use the sustaining qualities of their instruments in a manner that extends the drama and harmonic resonance of the performance.
- Stylistic variety: There is great contrast in the approach of the two soloists, with Jackson more technically fluent while Monk is deliberate. At the same time, both display an unquestioned affinity for the emotional terrain of the blues.
- Form and structure: With the exception of the four-bar introduction, the entire performance consists of standard blues choruses; yet Monk has taken great pains to ensure variety through changes in texture and rhythmic emphasis, creating a complex totality rivaling

Thelonious Monk at Minton's, 1949. PHOTO COURTESY WILLIAM P. GOTTLIEB/ WILLIAM P. GOTTLIEB COLLECTION/ LIBRARY OF CONGRESS PRINTS & PHOTOGRAPHS DIVISION.

mentored Powell at Minton's and collaborated actively with Parker and Gillespie in defining the modern jazz vocabulary. It took far longer, though, for the public and even many musicians to see beyond Thelonious Monk's personal idiosyncrasies and hear beyond the passing dissonances of his bold, unpredictable creations. Wearing dark glasses and a variety of distinctive hats and given to occasional cryptic pronouncements, Monk was an ideal candidate for the role of jazz's leading eccentric, earning him the nickname of "the high priest of bebop." From his first recordings as a leader in 1947 until he began his influential series of albums for the Riverside label eight years later, Monk was a man ahead of his time, valued, if at all, for his quirky yet undeniably fascinating compositions (*Misterioso*, *Evidence*, *'Round [About] Midnight*, *Little Rootie Tootie*) but frequently challenged regarding his percussive, jarring keyboard attack. It did not help that Monk

such earlier blues classics as Duke Ellington's *Ko-Ko*.

An alternate take of *Misterioso* exists, and was first issued on Blue Note 1509. It reduces the length of the piano solo to one chorus and retains the original unison for the final theme statement, while featuring different improvisations by Jackson and Monk.

—*Bob Blumenthal*

TIME	FORM	INSTRUMENTATION	MELODY
0:00	INTRODUCTION	Piano solo	Monk states the two-bar phrase that is the final resolution of the melody twice as an introduction. The phrase ends on a minor seventh, creating an unresolved feeling after the walking sixths. This introductory section announces the two melodic/harmonic ideas—the major sixth and minor seventh—that provide the substance of the composition.
0:11	THEME	Full quartet	The full quartet, in unison, plays the melody, which is a four-note see-saw pattern played in sixths, thus creating an echo effect. The phrase, one measure in length, is modulated through the form and harmonic progressions of the 12-bar blues, with a melodic adjustment at the end of bar eight (0:34) and the climactic minor seventh at bar 12 (0:43).
0:46	CHORUS 1	Vibraphone with piano, bass, drums	Milt Jackson begins his vibraphone solo by anticipating the beginning of the next chorus. Jackson's solo lasts one chorus, with Monk's support limited to the minor seventh phrase at the end of the melody while the drummer and bassist play in the medium-slow $\frac{4}{4}$ tempo of the performance.
1:22	CHORUS 2-3	Piano with bass and drums	Monk plays two solo choruses on piano, which include such techniques as descending **whole tone scales**, parallel octaves (2:02), and a frequent return to the minor seventh that has taken on a defining character for the composition. His unexpected accents and use of space gain added impact against the steady support of bassist Simmons and drummer Wilson.
2:39	THEME	Full Quartet	The theme returns, but now Wilson is playing in double time and, while Jackson states the melody, Monk is creating further tension by playing only one or two notes in each bar, while varying the placement of those notes from bar to bar. In the eighth bar of the restatement (3:02), Monk rejoins Jackson in **unison**, the tempo slows, and as the final note is sounded (3:14), Monk adds a concluding whole tone scale.

had taken a drug rap for one of his musician friends, losing, in the process, the "cabaret card" license that was required for performers seeking work in New York establishments where alcohol was served. For years, Monk did much of his playing in his West Side apartment, where young musicians, including tenor saxophonist Sonny Rollins and pianist Randy Weston, would come for intensive tutorials. Monk's day would arrive in the late 1950s. But during the period he helped inaugurate, Monk's brilliant recordings were widely ignored, and he remained a prophet without honor. (For Monk's work in the 1950s and beyond, see Chapter 7.)

Another pianist and bandleader often considered as "far out" as Monk had a more immediate impact. While still in his native Chicago, **Lennie Tristano** developed a personal philosophy of improvisation and began attracting students. He spent hours learning classic recorded performances of Armstrong, Eldridge, Young, and others by ear. His work showed off his strong melodic imagination, while he downplayed more traditional piano techniques, such as the use of tone color and a rhythmically active accompaniment. The style was best captured in a series of 1949 recordings—including *Wow* (JTSA Disc 2/Track 24)—in which Tristano was joined by his two leading disciples, alto saxophonist Lee Konitz and tenor saxophonist Warne Marsh. Two of these performances—*Digression* and *Intuition*—were totally improvised and are now viewed as harbingers of the free-jazz movement that emerged a decade later. While Tristano's influence was significant,

whole tone   a whole step.

whole tone scale   scale consisting only of whole steps; in jazz improvisation, especially applicable to the augmented chord.

unison   simultaneous playing of the same pitch or melody by different voices.

Watch the video of *Blue Monk* by Thelonious Monk on **mymusiclab.com**

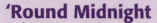

'Round Midnight

'Round Midnight (also known as 'Round About Midnight), with music by Thelonious Monk and Cootie Williams and lyrics by Bernie Hanighen, is one of the most enduring compositions to come out of the modern-jazz era. In the decades since its birth, there have been more than 1,400 recordings of this remarkable piece by such diverse artists as Miles Davis, Wes Montgomery, Ella Fitzgerald, Bobby McFerrin and Chick Corea, Cecil Taylor, the Art Ensemble of Chicago, Sun Ra, June Christy, Laurindo Almeida, Linda Ronstadt, Eydie Gorme, Eileen Farrell, the Kronos Quartet, and virtually every major modern-jazz instrumentalist and singer.

'Round Midnight dates from 1944, when it was first recorded by trumpeter Williams. Like so many other works by Monk, it stands successfully as a composition with or without improvisational embellishment; unlike the great majority of jazz pieces, it is almost always presented with the written introduction and coda intact.

The piece was the focal point of collegial reciprocity between Monk and Dizzy Gillespie, whom Monk introduced to the harmonic and compositional potential of the half-diminished chord (also known as the minor sixth chord) with the sixth in the bass. In turn, the introduction of 'Round Midnight drew from Gillespie's use of the chord in the ending of his own I Can't Get Started (recorded in 1945). The coda of 'Round Midnight is, again, Gillespie's invention, based loosely on the chord changes to the bridge of Gillespie's Con Alma (1954). The half-diminished chord, which Gillespie also used in Woody 'n' You (1944) and other tunes, and which composer Tadd Dameron used so prominently in Hot House (1945), seems to hold a special fascination for both jazz and art-music composers and performers. Few classically trained musicians escape a discussion of this so-called Tristan chord, so named because of its prominence in the Tristan theme of Richard Wagner's opera Tristan und Isolde.

The body of 'Round Midnight is beautifully structured, with a perfect balance between chordal and scalar lines, rising and falling phrases, constantly unfolding sequences, and the illusion of inevitability of resolution without a hint of predictability. Its two main themes are among the most alluring, haunting, and memorable in jazz literature—romantic without being sentimental or maudlin, tender but with muscularity and sinew, and capable of capturing both heart and mind.

The piece is one of a very few works by jazz composers (Ellington excepted) that have become popular successes as well as jazz standards. It's one of two works of Monk's that have become titles of successful movies: Straight, No Chaser (a biographical documentary) and 'Round Midnight (a fictional story of a jazz musician who is a loose composite of Lester Young and Bud Powell). In the minds of many, 'Round Midnight is Monk's magnum opus.

—David Baker

---

particularly in Europe thanks to Konitz's recordings and appearances, it might have been more keenly felt had the pianist not made teaching his priority from 1951 until his death in 1978.

Tristano's systematic methods and dispassionate approach—perhaps reinforced by the fact that he and his circle were white rather than African American—made his work appear to be a more cerebral or "progressive" alternative to bebop. In fact, Tristano was one of Parker's most individualistic disciples, the creator of a music that could not have existed without bebop and the harmonic discoveries of Art Tatum as primary sources. Then again, with rare exceptions (such as Erroll Garner, a pianist who rose to popularity with a merger of swing and modern elements, or young classicists such as cornetist Ruby Braff and clarinetist Bob Wilber, who played in more traditional styles with older players), it is hard to identify any young musicians from the period who were not working from a bebop foundation.

TAKE NOTE

- Who were the early bebop pianists and how did they affect the growth of the musical style?

Metronome All-Stars Billy Bauer (guitar), Eddie Safranski (bass), Charlie Parker, and Lennie Tristano, 1949. PHOTO COURTESY © HERMAN LEONARD PHOTOGRAPHY LLC.

Cool Jazz and the West Coast Scene

Also based on bop, although often viewed as independent of it, was the music that came to be known as "**cool**" or "**West Coast**" **jazz**. As it gained popularity and turned briefly into a marketable commodity, cool jazz became identified with lighter, vibrato-free lines (similar in this respect to Tristano's music); the use of flute, French horn, tuba, and other instruments that were uncommon in earlier jazz styles; and a greater emphasis on counterpoint and other supposedly classical techniques. The style was identified with California, even if such leading cool lights as Stan Getz, Gerry Mulligan, and Shorty Rogers had grown up on the East Coast. One of the most popular figures, **Dave Brubeck**, would cross over into popular, mainstream success with his work of the late 1950s and early 1960s (see Chapter 7). Cool was also taken by many to be the exclusive domain of white musicians, even though the leader of the recordings that mark the style's emergence was Miles Davis, and the ensemble most deeply immersed in European influences was the **Modern Jazz Quartet**. Once again, nomenclature disguised evolutionary continuity, because cool jazz was as rooted in the Kansas City continuum of Count Basie, Lester Young, and Charlie Parker as it was in any alternative geographical or cultural soil.

A primary source for the light, floating sounds of cool jazz was the dance orchestra led in the 1940s by pianist **Claude Thornhill**, which employed symphonic

cool jazz a style of jazz developed in the late 1940s and 1950s, in part a reaction to bebop; notable for its understatement, restraint, lighter vibrato-free lines, use of counterpoint, and use of atypical jazz instruments such as the French horn, tuba, and flute.

West Coast jazz the collective name for jazz that emerged from Los Angeles and San Francisco in the 1950s and 1960s, generating much of what became known as cool jazz, but also offering experiments in instrumentation, composition, and counterpoint by such musicians as Dave Brubeck, Gerry Mulligan, and Jimmy Giuffre.

Stan Getz (ca. 1955). PHOTO COURTESY BOB WILLOUGHBY/REDFERNS/GETTY IMAGES.

The rich, understated sound of pianist Claude Thornhill's orchestra (here with Lee Konitz, back row, third from the left, on alto sax), shaped in part by arranger Gil Evans, offered a moody alternative to the high energy of bop and helped pave the way for the cool jazz movement.

brass and woodwinds in addition to the more standard big band instruments. **Gil Evans**, Thornhill's primary arranger beginning in 1941, was fascinated by the colors these additional instruments placed at his disposal and began employing them to obtain a range of impressionistic tonal effects. Evans was influenced by a movement that some called **third stream**, an attempt to wed classical technique and instrumentation with a jazz sensibility. While admiring classical tonalities, he embraced the new sounds of the modern-jazz combo.

In 1947, Evans orchestrated the Parker recordings *Yardbird Suite* and *Donna Lee* and the Parker-Gillespie collaboration *Anthropology* for Thornhill as features for the band's distinctive new alto sax soloist, Tristano student Lee Konitz. Evans also began sharing ideas around this time with younger musicians from the Parker quintet such as Miles Davis and future Modern Jazz Quartet leader John Lewis, as well as composers Gerry Mulligan, John Carisi, and George Russell. Their interaction produced the

---

third stream compositions blending jazz elements with classical forms and techniques; term coined in 1957 by composer Gunther Schuller.

short-lived but seminal Miles Davis Nonet, a compact version of the Thornhill band featuring the solos of Davis, Konitz, and Mulligan and the writing of Evans (*Boplicity*), Mulligan (*Jeru*), Lewis (*Move*), and Carisi (*Israel*).

The Davis Nonet obtained only one booking, in the fall of 1948, but it managed to record on three later occasions, and the dozen titles it produced—which were later collectively named *Birth of the Cool*—had a powerful impact. Their influence extended most directly to the work of Milton "Shorty" Rogers, a young trumpet player and arranger who made similar use of a midsize ensemble in recordings by his Giants group (*Popo* [*JTSA* Disc 3/Track 3] and *Didi*) that began to appear in 1951. Rogers also drew heavily on the riff-based example of the Count Basie band and the surface restraint of Lester Young, whose influence on young soloists predated Parker's and was still widely felt. The "cool" that Rogers represented echoed jazz's most emphatically swinging sources, as did the playing of a favorite Rogers collaborator, alto saxophonist Art Pepper.

Like many other former big band sidemen adjusting to shifts in the music industry, Rogers found a new outlet for his playing and writing in

Miles Davis's 1949–1950 recordings later released as *Birth of the Cool* employed a nine-piece group whose approach marked a distinct shift, in color and texture as well as in performance style, from the bebop style that preceded it. French horn and tuba, unusual instruments in jazz, were included in the nonet. The musicians and the arranger (Gil Evans) brought in "classical" orchestral techniques. The result was an understated "cool" mix of jazz expressiveness delivered with an orchestral sheen.

✳ **Explore** on **mymusiclab.com**

Kai Winding • Trombone

Trombonist Kai Winding played on this recording session, but J. J. Johnson played trombone on some of the other sessions for this album. Both were considered to be great trombonists in jazz, and recorded together (*The Great Kai and J. J.*, 1960). The *Birth of the Cool* is a testament to racial integration reaching greater acceptance by the late 1940s and early 1950s.

Miles Davis • Organizer and Trumpet

Davis spearheaded the innovation of a new style. His association with the Charlie Parker Quintet (1945–1948) revealed a trumpet style completely different from that of Dizzy Gillespie, the main force in bebop trumpet playing. Early on, Davis's style embodied an understated and introspective approach within the bebop idiom.

The Rhythm Section

This rhythm section comprised piano (Al Haig), bass (Joe Shulman), and drums (Max Roach). The drummer Max Roach is not pictured here, but the drums can be seen behind the baffle (a moveable wall used in recording studios). This rhythm section's approach was very similar to the bebop style but with less volume and fewer accents. The drive and forward momentum of the rhythm section was deceptively concealed by the serene nature of the performance.

PHOTO COURTESY FRANK DRIGGS COLLECTION.

Bill Barber • Tuba
Junior Collins • French Horn

Unlike its role in early jazz, the tuba was used here for color instead of playing a bass line. Behind the tuba in this photograph is a French horn (an unusual choice for the jazz band), which was also used experimentally in jazz. The arranger Gil Evans had experience with these instruments from his earlier work with Claude Thornhill's band. The wind instruments for the *Birth of the Cool* band were arranged in pairs, high and low: trumpet and trombone, alto and baritone sax, and French horn and tuba.

Gerry Mulligan • Baritone Sax

In addition to performing as a soloist and playing section parts on this record date, Gerry Mulligan arranged five of the twelve pieces on the *Birth of the Cool* sessions. Aside from being less intense than bebop, the "cool" movement revisited counterpoint, which was an element of New Orleans jazz. As a compositional practice, counterpoint reached its zenith in the works of Bach. Counterpoint is a property of polyphony, whose antithesis is homophony (a single melody over chords), which characterizes a lot of the swing era big band music.

Lee Konitz • Alto Sax

Miles Davis's original consideration for this chair was Charlie Parker's contemporary and perhaps disciple, Sonny Stitt. However, Gerry Mulligan believed that Stitt's allegiance to the style of Charlie Parker would overshadow the originality and focus of the recording session. Mulligan instead recommended Lee Konitz as a fresh alternative, whose light alto saxophone sound (unlike Charlie Parker's) harkened back to that of Lester Young. Most saxophonists (including Gerry Mulligan) of the cool era were profoundly influenced by Young's saxophone tone.

the Hollywood studios, where music for films and television began to take on a jazz flavor. (As time went on, studio work for the film, television, and advertising industries—as well as for popular-music recordings—would become a key source of income for some jazz musicians.)

The movie industry's growing infatuation with jazz scores was only the latest of Hollywood's inter-actions with jazz, which had long included the use of jazz as subject matter for dramatic, musical, and comedic films. But racial discrimination had prevailed in Hollywood, helping to explain the predominance of white jazz musicians in California (although

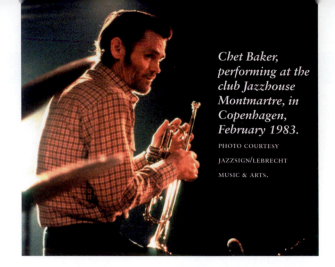

Chet Baker, performing at the club Jazzhouse Montmartre, in Copenhagen, February 1983.
PHOTO COURTESY JAZZSIGN/LEBRECHT MUSIC & ARTS.

Listening Guide

((•)) **Listen** to *Boplicity* by Miles Davis Nonet on **mymusiclab.com**
CD I, Track 20/Download Track 20

BOPLICITY • MILES DAVIS NONET

Music: Miles Davis, 1949. Personnel: Miles Davis (trumpet); J. J. Johnson (trombone); Sandy Siegelstein (French horn); Bill Barber (tuba); Lee Konitz (alto saxophone); Gerry Mulligan (bari-tone saxophone); John Lewis (piano); Nelson Boyd (bass); Kenny Clarke (drums); Gil Evans (arranger). Recorded: April 22, 1949, in New York. First issue: Capitol 57-60011. Timing: 3:03.

Overview

Boplicity, one of the dozen tracks recorded in 1949–50 by the Miles Davis Nonet and compiled several years later into the influential album *Birth of the Cool*, melded divergent ideas as well as interesting person-alities. In its tightly knit ensemble passages interwoven with brief solos, the Nonet joined improvisatory jazz with a more arranged, orchestral approach. Davis's ensemble fused the cool, airy, but understated sound of the earlier Claude Thornhill orchestra (employing some of its players) with the more active, syncopated melo-dies of bebop. It brought together musicians who themselves combined disparate inclinations—toward "classical" compositional techniques on the one hand and jazz expressive qualities on the other. Most notably, on the people side, it partnered Miles

Davis with Thornhill's former arranger Gil Evans, a collaboration that some years later yielded such orchestral jazz masterworks as *Porgy and Bess* and *Sketches of Spain*. In *Boplicity*, the Davis-penned melody is colored and thickened by Evans's orchestration.

Key Features

- Style: Bebop's angularity, synco-pation, and swing combine with impressionistic orchestral color to yield an early example of cool jazz.
- Form and structure: An AABA melody stated at the outset becomes obscured as composed passages and solo statements unfold, returning to a final full-band recapitulation of A at 2:40.
- Improvisation: Rather than domi-nating, the ad-libbed segments are nestled within constructs of fixed composition. Soloists must have their "say" within strictly limited durations.
- Melody and harmony: The angular melody is less a singable "tune" than a string of characteristic bebop devices: eighth-note lines varied with rests, triplets (0:02), syncopation (0:04), and double-time embellishments (0:08), following the underlying chord

progression but including altered notes (0:04, 0:07, 0:13). The harmonic progression proceeds simply, in the key of F major, through the two A sections, and in the B section it departs into a progression in descending half steps from C minor, leading back to the A section. The progression is conventional, yet the ensemble writing adds color and complexity.
- Color and texture: Instrumentation is a pared-down version of Claude Thornhill's orchestra, including the French horn and tuba that were common in European chamber music but were rare in mid-century jazz ensembles. The texture is thick and rich, with tight ensemble harmony on the melody line, yet smooth and fluid. At points, space opens up for individual soloists.
- Voice, feel, and expression: Note the horns' chordal swells (0:13, 0:27), the melodic accents on offbeats (0:34–35), and the tight rendering of sixteenth-note embellishments (0:06, 0:29), all of which contribute to expressiveness and a feeling of swing.
- Pulse: The $\frac{4}{4}$ pulse is subdued.

—Tad Lathrop

African American veterans such as Benny Carter and Harry "Sweets" Edison were quietly cracking barriers in the segregated system).

Not all the white musicians who ventured west sought studio work. Gerry Mulligan wrote the influential *Young Blood* for the Stan Kenton band when he relocated to Los Angeles in 1952, but the move also led him to form a quartet for appearances at a nightclub called the Haig. The group featured an inspired blend of Mulligan's virtuosic playing of the baritone saxophone and the fragile, lyrical trumpet of **Chet Baker**, a self-taught newcomer who had impressed no less a figure than Parker himself.

Mulligan and Baker would frequently improvise simultaneously, a practice that harkened back to early New Orleans music yet took on a modern feeling that was enhanced by the absence of a piano in the quartet's rhythm section. The lean, witty Mulligan sound proved as definitive of West Coast cool as that of any band's, and it turned both Mulligan and Baker into international stars.

 Watch the video of *Indiana* by Gerry Mulligan on **mymusiclab.com**

---

comping playing chordal accompaniment for a soloist.

TIME	SECTION	FORM	INSTRUMENTATION	MELODY
0:00	HEAD (CHORUS 1)	32 bars: A (0:00) A (0:14) B (0:28) A (0:42)	Trumpet leads full ensemble	Without an intro, the swinging melody begins, fully harmonized. Listen to the final chord of each A section: it sounds unresolved, intentionally, due to the addition of a note (B-natural) from outside the tune's key signature (F major). Notice the bass line, which occasionally departs from walking (keeping time) to join the melody (0:54).
0:57	CHORUS 2	AA	Baritone sax solo with piano accompaniment	Gerry Mulligan solos over two A sections as the horns drop out and John Lewis provides punchy chordal backing on piano. Mulligan's melodies follow the bop conventions of linear "swing" eighth notes broken up by occasional rests (1:08, 1:11) and dressed up with sixteenth-note figures (1:09, 1:21).
1:25		Extended B	Ensemble minus trumpet; trumpet returns at 1:36 for solo	The texture changes as the ensemble re-enters (minus trumpet) with a six-bar flowing unison melody that soon sprouts a spinoff line (1:36) led by Davis on trumpet. For the next four bars (1:36 to 1:43), Davis solos in the foreground backed by the ensemble in a composed passage.
1:43		A	Ensemble	The passage seems to spill over into the next section—a new, robust-sounding melody variation by the ensemble, loosely referencing the harmony of the A section.
1:57	CHORUS 3	AA	Ensemble; trumpet solo begins on the second bar	The ensemble continues into the first bar of chorus 3, which plays out over variations on the A-section chord progression. Davis begins his solo in bar two, soloing with bebop eighth-note phrases and a showy sixteenth note-passage (2:08), as he's accompanied by horn-ensemble countermelodies and then (2:12) by **comping** on the piano. After a pause, Davis continues (2:18) with a Charlie Parkerish anticipation of the downbeat, proceeding through four bars of swinging arpeggiated and scalar lines connected by chromatic passing tones and embellishments.
2:26		B	Piano with ensemble	In the B section, John Lewis's piano emerges from the background with a spare two-note syncopation that develops into a long phrase. He pauses, then (2:35) plays a second phrase in the bop style of the preceding soloists. Drummer Kenny Clarke switches to brushes to achieve a softer sound under the pianist.
2:40		A (extended from eight to nine bars)	Ensemble	As the drummer returns to playing his instrument with drumsticks, the ensemble returns for a final statement of A. They hold the last note (2:54 to 2:57) for an extra measure, making this section nine, instead of eight, bars.

Jazz and Film

They grew up together. At the same time in the late nineteenth century that audiences were first paying to see images projected on a screen, musicians in New Orleans were beginning to stir up a musical gumbo we now call jazz. Both movies and jazz started out as scandalous, "low" entertainment but quickly won huge popular followings; today they are regularly hailed as art. From the outset, however, jazz and the movies have both been typically American, typically romantic means of expression in which artists and audiences alike have explored their dreams and aspirations.

The two art forms interacted from the beginning. Musicians improvised in theaters while customers watched such "silent films" as *The Jazz Bandits* (1920) and *Children of Jazz* (1923). By 1927, key jazzmen like Duke Ellington and Bix Beiderbecke were creating groundbreaking work. In that same year the movies first began to talk, appropriately in a film called *The Jazz Singer*. Two years later, Ellington was playing a serious composer and bandleader in Dudley Murphy's 19-minute short, *Black and Tan*.

The dignity afforded Ellington in *Black and Tan* was not typical of the film industry's treatment of jazz musicians, however. Also in 1929, director Murphy cast Bessie Smith in *St. Louis Blues* as an abused, gin-swilling woman who sings not because she is an artist like Ellington but simply because her man has left her. Jazz musicians fared much better if they happened to be white, like Paul Whiteman, who regally presided over the bizarre revue *The King of Jazz* (1930).

In the 1930s jazz artists of color were more likely to appear in short subjects or even cartoons than in full-length features. Eubie Blake played the piano, Nina Mae McKinney sang, and the Nicholas Brothers danced their hearts out in the nine-minute *Pie, Pie, Blackbird* (1932). Louis Armstrong played a cannibal in a 1932 Betty Boop cartoon, and Cab Calloway was cast as an animated dancing walrus in another short feature with Ms. Boop. In the full-length films *Check and Double Check* (1932), *The Big Broadcast* (1932), and *King of Burlesque* (1935), artists such as Ellington, Calloway, and Fats Waller were carefully segregated in brief segments that could easily be edited out for people who were unnerved by the sight of black men.

Jazz in the movies probably came of age in the 1940s. Films with all-black casts—among them *Cabin in the Sky* (1943) and *Stormy Weather* (1943)—offered great performances by Ellington, Armstrong, Calloway, Waller, and singer Lena Horne. Interracial casts appeared in *Birth of the Blues* (1941), inspired by the Original Dixieland Jazz Band, and *Syncopation* (1942), which cast the great cornetist and jazz writer Rex Stewart as a character based on cornetist King Oliver. Audiences were given behind-the-scenes dramas about the immensely popular swing bands in *Orchestra Wives* (1942) and *The Fabulous Dorseys* (1947). *Jivin' in Be-Bop* (1947) served as a vehicle for Dizzy Gillespie and his orchestra, and *Rhythm in a Riff* (1946) featured the early bebop

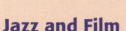

Explore the Viewing Guide for *St. Louis Blues* on **mymusiclab.com**

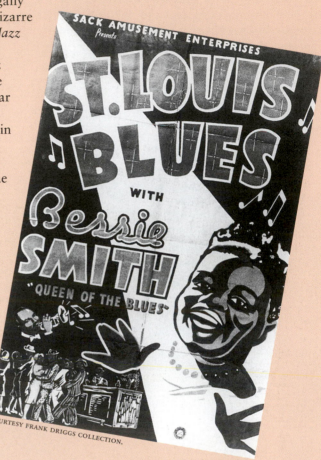

COURTESY FRANK DRIGGS COLLECTION.

band of Billy Eckstine. In 1948's *A Song Is Born*, jazz was portrayed as an art form with a history (albeit a history so willfully misconceived that it emphasized Spanish explorers and ignored the slave trade).

Some filmmakers found jazz to be useful as a sign of corruption and criminality. In Frank Capra's *It's a Wonderful Life* (1946) the jazz that plays in bars and nightclubs signifies the decadence of "Pottersville," the nightmare alternative to the small-town paradise of Bedford Falls. In *The Wild One* (1953) a gang of motorcyclists in

black leather listen not to rock and roll but to big band music that suggests Stan Kenton. And in *The Rat Race* (1960) a group of talented jazz musicians steal Tony Curtis's saxophones and flutes at a fake audition.

After jazz ceased to be a popular music in the 1950s, it was most likely to be heard in nostalgic biopics about bandleaders from the swing era (among them, *The Benny Goodman Story*, *The Glenn Miller Story*, and *The Five Pennies*); in grainy, "independent films" like *Shadows* (1960) and *The Connection* (1961); or in such documentaries as *Jazz on a Summer's Day* (1960) and *The Last of the Blue Devils* (1974). Jazz also became a musical flavor of choice in movie

soundtracks, most memorably in *A Streetcar Named Desire* (1951), *Man with the Golden Arm* (1955), and *The Pawnbroker* (1964), not to mention *Anatomy of a Murder* (1959), with its great score by Duke Ellington and Billy Strayhorn. In the 1970s, Hollywood tried valiantly to make hit movies focusing on jazz with *Lady Sings the Blues* (1972) and *New York, New York* (1977). A decade later, the ambitious biographical jazz films *'Round Midnight* (1986) and *Bird* (1988) drew even smaller audiences.

At the end of the twentieth century, the most revealing treatment of jazz could be found in such documentaries as *Thelonious Monk: Straight, No Chaser* (1988), *Let's Get Lost* (the 1988 film about the life of Chet Baker), and *A Great Day in Harlem* (1995). But filmgoers could hear bits and pieces of jazz in many Hollywood films, especially in scenes establishing emotional intimacy. Although jazz had become an art music, in the movies it was still very much the music of romance.

—*Krin Gabbard*

COURTESY FRANK DRIGGS COLLECTION.

Some of the new West Coast sounds emerging from California actually *were* created by musicians with roots west of the Mississippi. Saxophonist and clarinetist Jimmy Giuffre, a Texan, had gained early fame as the composer of *Four Brothers* (1947; *JTSA* Disc 2/Track 19) for Woody Herman's Second Herd (a bebop-oriented follow-up to the swing-heavy band Woody Herman's Herd; see Chapter 5). After studying advanced compositional techniques, Giuffre began to explore more compact, folkish themes in his intimate *Jimmy Giuffre 3*, a band that eliminated drums and even, in one unusual clarinet-trombone-guitar configuration, bass. The Giuffre 3 featured the gentle abstractions of guitarist Jim Hall, who had made his debut in the quintet of former Mulligan drummer Chico Hamilton. With its emphasis on flute, cello, and atmospheric percussion, the Hamilton quintet established two Los Angeles natives, Hamilton and woodwind master Buddy Collette, among the leading figures in the cool style.

Beyond the Cool

The Modern Jazz Quartet, which was based in New York, made many of the same inroads with college and concert-hall listeners. The MJQ had originated as the rhythm section in Dizzy Gillespie's 1946 big band, where it comprised pianist John Lewis, vibraphonist Milt Jackson, bassist Ray Brown, and drummer Kenny Clarke. Shortly after it began performing as a unit in 1952, with Percy Heath in place of Brown and (beginning in 1955) Connie Kay in place of Clarke, the MJQ cultivated a veneer of chamber-music propriety in such recordings as *Vendome* (1952), *Django* (1954; *JTSA* Disc 3/Track 7), and *Milano* (1954). The members often appeared in tuxedos and played compositions that recalled Baroque fugues. Yet the jazz bona fides of Jackson, one of the music's most exceptional blues and ballad players, and the rest of the MJQ could not be denied. They were cool jazz modernists forthright enough in their playing to also connect with the hard bop style that emerged around the time of Charlie Parker's death.

This cool/hard dichotomy was increasingly the rule as jazz continued to evolve. In this regard, no musician exemplifies the frustrations of drawing

Watch the video of *The Golden Striker* by the Modern Jazz Quartet on **mymusiclab.com**

Hear a profile of John Lewis on **mymusiclab.com**

stylistic boundaries more vividly than Miles Davis. First an important member of the Parker quintet, then the harbinger of cool with his nine-piece band, Davis also laid the groundwork for the bluesy, percussion-driven hard bop style in *Dig*, *Walkin'*, and other of his early 1950s recordings. These investigations of a more assertive and emotional style would hardly exhaust the trumpeter's curiosity or temper the innovations he introduced subsequently. More than any of his peers, more than even his mentors Parker and Gillespie, Davis demonstrated that, as modern jazz came of age, it remained a miraculous engine for change.

TAKE NOTE

- What was cool jazz, who were its key proponents, and where did it develop?

Explore Jazz Classics and Key Recordings on **mymusiclab.com**

The Modern Jazz Quartet (clockwise from upper left): drummer Connie Kay, pianist John Lewis, vibraphonist Milt Jackson, and bassist Percy Heath. PHOTO COURTESY JAMES J KRIEGSMANN/DOWN BEAT ARCHIVES.

Jazz Poetry

For more than three quarters of the twentieth century, poets responded both to jazz and to jazz musicians. While the term "jazz poetry" tends to conjure stereotypical images from the 1950s (coffee houses, black berets, and the like), the complex history of jazz-related poetry offers a far more diverse collection of poetic styles and sensibilities.

The earliest published jazz poems were written by white writers, such as Carl Sandburg, whose *Jazz Fantasia* (1920) was one of the first to appear in print. Many of his contemporaries, including e.e. cummings and Vachel Lindsay, associated racial and sexual anxieties with jazz; much of the poetry from the 1920s displayed an ignorance of the jazz aesthetic. In 1926, however, Langston Hughes published *The Weary Blues*, a collection of poems that, for the first time, embraced jazz as an art form integral to American and African American culture. Hughes published prolifically, including two exceptional jazz-related poetry collections, *Montage of a Dream Deferred* (1951) and *Ask Your Mama: 12 Moods for Jazz* (1961). Although several writers from the 1930s and 1940s made substantial contributions to jazz poetry—chiefly Sterling Brown and Melvin Tolson—Hughes's achievements outweigh the efforts of any other writer from the first half of the century.

The popularity of bebop generated a stunning number of jazz poems, particularly among Beat poets. In 1957 Lawrence Ferlinghetti and Kenneth Rexroth performed their work with a jazz band in San Francisco, spurring a series of live poetry-read-to-jazz

Poet Langston Hughes created The Story of Jazz for Folkways Records as an introduction to the musical style for young listeners.
COURTESY BENCAR ARCHIVES.

performances and recordings by such writers as Kenneth Patchen and Jack Kerouac. Ultimately, most of the writers and musicians had great reservations about these performances, and the fad virtually died out by the end of that decade. Since then a number of poets—most notably Amiri Baraka (LeRoi Jones) and Jayne Cortez—have more successfully integrated their work with jazz musicians. The 1970s group the Last Poets fused poetry with black pop—and laid the groundwork for 1990s rap music and hip-hop.

Although poets have celebrated hundreds of jazz musicians, two saxophonists dominate the list: Charlie Parker and John Coltrane. Poets in the late 1950s—mainly white writers from the West Coast—repeatedly found inspiration in Parker's artistic innovations as well as his self-destructive lifestyle. Many of these homages conferred a godlike status on Parker and, in doing so, lost the humanity of the man; against the barrage of bad verse, Bob Kaufman

worked diligently to make words sound like jazz and best captured some of Parker's magnetism. In the late 1960s, African American poets began to identify Coltrane's music with the black civil rights movement. Major voices from that time—including Don L. Lee (Haki Madhubuti), Baraka, Sonia Sanchez, and Larry Neal—invoked Coltrane's sound as a direct political commentary on race.

Compared to the work from the 1950s and 1960s, jazz poems after 1970 were rather quiet in tone and strongly narrative, but the number of jazz poems rose exponentially. Some of the major voices included Al Young, Hayden Carruth, Sherley Anne Williams, Akua Lezli Hope, Yusef Komunyakaa, and William Matthews. The growing volume of activity—combined with increasing critical interest in jazz-related literature after 1990—suggests that poets will continue to explore the unlimited associations between poetry and jazz as long as the music survives.

—*Sascha Feinstein*

- What musical movements began to replace big band jazz during the years following World War II?

Several musical movements emerged to supplant the big bands as the leading forms of popular music. Vocalists broke away from the big bands to enjoy success on their own, singing popular ballads and songs. A more blues-based, dance-oriented music was developing, originally called jump blues. Exemplified by the small group led by saxophonist/vocalist Louis Jordan, this dynamic style wed the power of the big bands with a pronounced backbeat and the new sound of the electric guitar. Finally, a new style of jazz was on the horizon that would change all of the rules: bebop.

- What is bebop and what roles did Charlie Parker and Dizzy Gillespie play in creating and popularizing it?

Bebop was developed, following the decline of big band swing music, mostly by younger, African American improvisers. They favored complex and irregularly accented melodies, more sophisticated harmonies, and faster tempos than those of the big bands. A standard practice of bebop was to write and improvise new melodies to preexisting songs, and devise interesting-sounding substitutions for some of the underlying chords. Saxophonist Charlie Parker was known for his lightning-fast playing and rich musical imagination; he became the model for dozens of future boppers. Dizzy Gillespie, with his outstanding compositional skills and sense of showmanship, was a prime spokesperson for the movement and helped spread its popularity.

- Who were the early bebop pianists and how did they affect the growth of the musical style?

Thelonious Monk was among the best-known of the original bebop pianists. His angular compositions and percussive piano playing helped define the bebop style. Bud Powell was another important pianist, although personal problems shortened his playing career. Lennie Tristano was a more melodic, cerebral pianist than Monk, and had a strong impact on the growth of West Coast cool.

- What was cool jazz, who were its key proponents, and where did it develop?

A school of jazz arose on the West Coast and came to be known as "cool jazz." Arranger Gil Evans shared ideas with Parker associate Miles Davis and others, yielding the important cool jazz recording *Birth of the Cool*. Saxophonist Gerry Mulligan participated in that recording, and his baritone sax work, often in association with trumpeter Chet Baker, helped popularize the new style. The Modern Jazz Quartet took cool in a classical direction, using sophisticated compositions to create chamber jazz.

DISCUSSION QUESTIONS

1. Had you heard bebop before reading this chapter and listening to the selections? If so, in what contexts had you heard it? What were your impressions of it? What did it remind you of? Do you feel differently about it now? How?

2. What factors led musicians of the early 1940s away from commercial popular music and toward more individualized and experimental music?

3. Do you think the names "bop" and "bebop" served the music well? Why or why not?

4. Describe some of the important differences between bebop and swing music.

5. Why do you think that bebop created such vehement negative reactions among some jazz musicians and listeners?

6. How would you compare and contrast Dizzy Gillespie and Charlie Parker?

7. The image of the jazz musician as a doomed genius was fed by Charlie Parker. What other instances of this image have you seen? Have there been some in later musical eras? How has the image been promoted in movies? In literature?

KEY TERMS & KEY PEOPLE

arpeggio 138
Chet Baker 155
bebop 132
Dave Brubeck 151
changes 140
[chord] substitution 140
chromatic 138
Kenny Clarke 131
comping 155
contrafact 140
cool jazz 151
cut time 138
Tadd Dameron 133
Miles Davis 133
downbeat 139
Gil Evans 132
Stan Getz 144
Dizzy Gillespie 131
glissando 135
Norman Granz 141
jump blues 130
Stan Kenton 141
Modern Jazz Quartet 151
Thelonious Monk 131
Gerry Mulligan 143
neighbor tone 138
Charlie Parker 131
passing tone 138
polytonality 139
Bud Powell 141
Max Roach 133
rock and roll 130
Shorty Rogers 143
third stream 132
Claude Thornhill 151
Lennie Tristano 149
unison 149
West Coast jazz 151
whole tone 149

CHAPTER 7

Mainstream Jazz

by Neil Tesser

TAKE NOTE

- What currents in American society influenced the development of jazz in the 1950s?
- Why was Miles Davis among the most important musicians of this period?
- How did hard bop develop in response to bebop and other styles?
- What distinguishes West Coast bop from other variants, and who were the key players in this style?
- What are the different saxophone styles of Dexter Gordon, Sonny Rollins, and John Coltrane?
- How were the musical approaches of composer-pianists Thelonious Monk and Dave Brubeck similar and how were they different?
- What is soul jazz and how does it differ from hard bop?
- How did earlier jazz traditions and groups grow and thrive during this period?
- What vocalists were important during the mainstream era?
- What other jazz styles were prominent during this time and how did they differ from the more dominant styles?

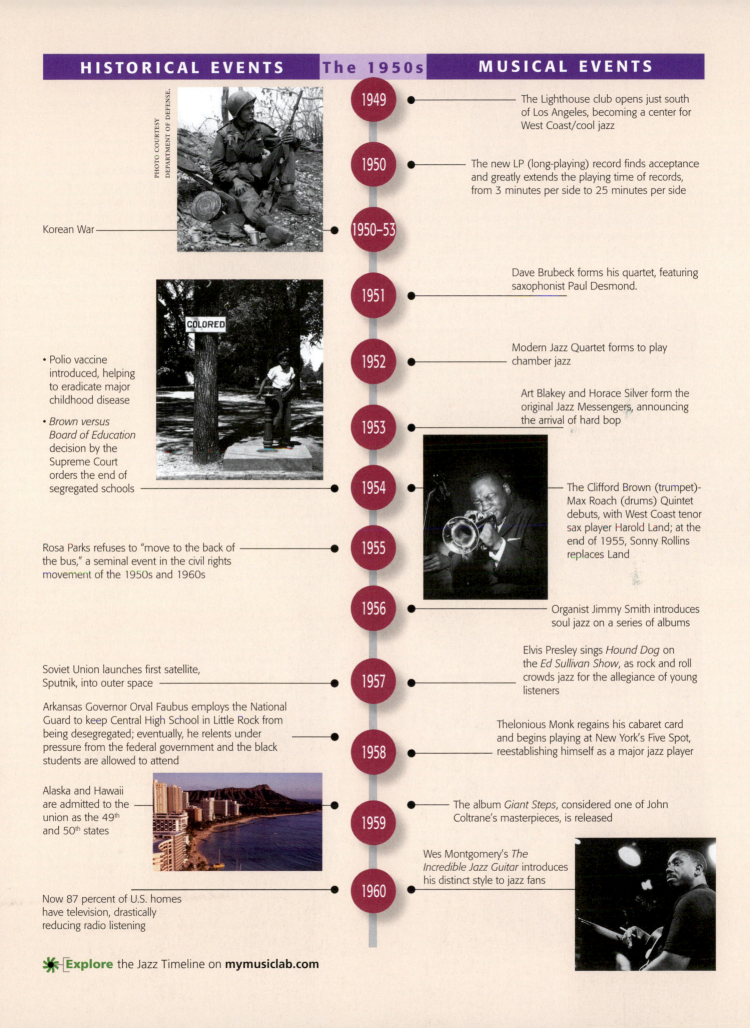

HISTORICAL EVENTS · The 1950s · MUSICAL EVENTS

PHOTO COURTESY DEPARTMENT OF DEFENSE.

1949 — The Lighthouse club opens just south of Los Angeles, becoming a center for West Coast/cool jazz

1950 — The new LP (long-playing) record finds acceptance and greatly extends the playing time of records, from 3 minutes per side to 25 minutes per side

Korean War — **1950–53**

1951 — Dave Brubeck forms his quartet, featuring saxophonist Paul Desmond.

• Polio vaccine introduced, helping to eradicate major childhood disease

1952 — Modern Jazz Quartet forms to play chamber jazz

1953 — Art Blakey and Horace Silver form the original Jazz Messengers, announcing the arrival of hard bop

• *Brown versus Board of Education* decision by the Supreme Court orders the end of segregated schools

1954 — The Clifford Brown (trumpet)-Max Roach (drums) Quintet debuts, with West Coast tenor sax player Harold Land; at the end of 1955, Sonny Rollins replaces Land

Rosa Parks refuses to "move to the back of the bus," a seminal event in the civil rights movement of the 1950s and 1960s — **1955**

1956 — Organist Jimmy Smith introduces soul jazz on a series of albums

Soviet Union launches first satellite, Sputnik, into outer space — **1957** — Elvis Presley sings *Hound Dog* on the *Ed Sullivan Show*, as rock and roll crowds jazz for the allegiance of young listeners

Arkansas Governor Orval Faubus employs the National Guard to keep Central High School in Little Rock from being desegregated; eventually, he relents under pressure from the federal government and the black students are allowed to attend — **1958** — Thelonious Monk regains his cabaret card and begins playing at New York's Five Spot, reestablishing himself as a major jazz player

Alaska and Hawaii are admitted to the union as the 49th and 50th states — **1959** — The album *Giant Steps*, considered one of John Coltrane's masterpieces, is released

Wes Montgomery's *The Incredible Jazz Guitar* introduces his distinct style to jazz fans

1960

Now 87 percent of U.S. homes have television, drastically reducing radio listening

✳ **Explore** the Jazz Timeline on **mymusiclab.com**

The innovations of bebop—at first considered radical—eventually became jazz conventions. And as a growing number of up-and-coming players built on and reacted to those conventions, jazz entered what is perhaps its best-known phase. It was a time of maturation, a period in which jazz became firmly established and widely embraced as a distinct, deeply developed musical idiom. And it was a time dominated by jazz "giants"—musicians whose names even a casual observer of jazz history can't fail to recognize. **Art Blakey**, **John Coltrane**, **Bill Evans**, Herbie Hancock, **Charles Mingus**, the Modern Jazz Quartet, **Thelonious Monk**, **Wes Montgomery**, and **Horace Silver** are just a few of the players who either emerged or reached the peak of their artistry during the 1950s and 1960s and whose influence—and some of whose careers—stretched into the twenty-first century.

It's as difficult to imagine one stylistic description applying to all these musicians as it is to imagine a jazz world without any of them. Nonetheless, much of the music recorded during these years is now identified as **mainstream jazz**. The term emerged in the mid-1950s, and it came to embody the lyrical, cleanly structured music that predominated during that decade and remained central to the jazz experience through the remainder of the century. Within the mainstream, however, surged a number of musical currents—from cool jazz to hard bop and including such offshoots as chamber jazz and modal jazz—that were set in motion by the galvanic impact of bebop.

Miles Davis, whose influence dominated jazz in the second half of the twentieth century.
PHOTO COURTESY VERN SMITH/DOWN BEAT ARCHIVES.

Setting the Stage

American society in the 1950s is often described as a bridge between the rigors of World War II and the turbulent social changes of the 1960s. The decade witnessed widespread societal conformity but also technological advances in many areas, including aviation (jet aircraft), chemistry (plastics, Velcro), electronics (transistors, computers), aeronautics (the "space race"), and recording—when the **long-playing (LP) record** album replaced the 78 rpm records of previous decades. For the first time, musicians could record performances longer than about three minutes, which had been the limitation of the

mainstream jazz   acoustic jazz as practiced in the 1950s and 1960s and preserved in the present day; some define mainstream jazz as including earlier classic jazz.

long-playing (LP) record   a disc recording that plays back on a turntable moving at 33⅓ revolutions per minute (rpm); the principal music delivery medium from about 1950 through the 1980s, until it was replaced by the digital compact disc (CD).

older format. For jazz musicians, this new freedom provided the opportunity to record music that more closely reflected the live-concert setting, whereby lengthier improvisations helped define and advance the art.

Even as the fledgling idiom of rock and roll was taking flight, jazz maintained a strong and steady audience, largely because of the increasing importance of college life in America. Peacetime affluence allowed more people to send their children to college, where students sought out the cool and intellectual jazz sounds that had supplanted their parents' swing era dance bands. In addition, the GI Bill provided servicemen returning from World War II the opportunity to complete their education; many of these older students had developed a taste for jazz as popular music during the war. As the 1960s dawned, jazz musicians began to incorporate the earthy, bluesy sounds of the gospel church into what would eventually be known as "soul jazz," anticipating (perhaps subconsciously) the epochal struggle for civil rights that would peak during that decade.

TAKE NOTE

- What currents in American society influenced the development of jazz in the 1950s?

Miles Ahead

Miles Davis, more than any other musician, dominated the mainstream era. Although Davis had made his initial reputation working with Charlie Parker, not until the 1950s did he emerge as an innovator of enormous impact. During this period, he first showed the ability to synthesize emerging jazz sounds into coherent styles that others would embrace as new movements—an ability that would ultimately make Davis the most important jazz figure in the second half of the twentieth century in the minds of many.

Davis sometimes seemed to be doing it all with mirrors. On such tunes as *All of You* and *My Funny Valentine* (both first recorded in 1956, then burnished in repeated performances through the mid-1960s), Davis played introspective solos in a vulnerable, diffident trumpet voice, which boasted virtually none of bebop's trademark fireworks and clever one-upsmanship. Old-school trumpeters derided his technique, but Davis's style became the template for jazz expression among musicians and audiences for the next 20 years. The bands he assembled were small miracles: many of his musicians would brilliantly execute his concepts, exceeding what anyone expected of them, before going off on their own. Many never made music of the same

Watch the documentary on Miles Davis on mymusiclab.com

quality again. Davis himself wrote relatively few songs, but time after time his recording of an old standard or a modern jazz tune became the definitive one, emulated by his contemporaries and successors. (Good examples include the Davis Quintet's 1956 versions of *Bye Bye Blackbird* and *'Round Midnight*.) And no jazz sound could have better mirrored the existentialist philosophy coloring Western society in the 1950s than Davis's lonely, emotionally naked sorties.

Davis often turned his back on his audience or left the bandstand entirely when not soloing (a practice immortalized in singer Eddie Jefferson's lyrics to one of Davis's best-known recordings, the 1959 track *So What*). And he turned his back on jazz entirely as the 1950s began, dropping out of sight and sound for the better part of two years to overcome the heroin habit he'd learned from Parker. But even in absentia, Davis wielded influence: the "cool school" inspired by his Nonet recordings became the "new sound of jazz." By the time Davis returned to the scene in 1953, "cool" had begun seeping up from the jazz underground to become the primary concern of American art, from film to fashion to literature to theater. From 1954 on, Davis's bands would brilliantly capture the hard bop style, but his own trumpet work never abandoned the hooded stance that characterized cool jazz.

TAKE NOTE

- Why was Miles Davis among the most important musicians of this period?

The Birth of Hard Bop

In the words of author Joe Goldberg, the cool breezes from the Pacific "went largely unnoticed by musicians in the East, except as an irritant." The cool school had offered its reaction to bebop, but in New York, Chicago, Philadelphia, and Detroit, the jazz of the 1950s derived primarily from bebop to become the style dubbed **hard bop**.

While such Miles Davis recordings as *Four* (1954) and *Walkin'* (1954) suggest the arrival of hard bop, the real parents were drummer Art Blakey and pianist Horace Silver. In the autumn of 1954, the two formed a cooperative quintet, the Jazz Messengers, and in 1955 they recorded a jubilee shout in the form of the 16-bar blues *The Preacher*, (*JTSA* Disc 3/Track 8) composed by Silver: as Goldberg put it, "The reaction to the reaction had taken place." To be sure, the hard boppers were responding to cool's constraints with

---

hard bop a post-bebop style marked by simpler chord progressions and earthy soulfulness, in contrast to the cool restraint of another post–bop style, cool jazz.

their explosive emotionalism. But they were also reacting to the calcifications of bebop.

The hard bop musicians used much the same vocabulary and grammar as bebop, but they turned the language to somewhat different ends to suit the demands of a new decade. They relaxed the tempos that had often made bebop a breathtaking steeplechase, and they simplified the knotty melodies that had delighted Parker and Dizzy Gillespie. In so doing, the hard bop players brought back an earthy soulfulness that had receded during the boppers' quest for more "serious" recognition.

This soulfulness had its roots in the ecstasy of church and gospel music, which provided the first listening experience for many black musicians, and which permeates such hard bop classics as pianist Bobby Timmons's *Moanin'*, recorded by the Jazz Messengers in 1958, and keyboardist Joe Zawinul's *Mercy, Mercy, Mercy*, recorded by **Cannonball Adderley** in 1966. The hard bop players dug even deeper into the blues than had their bebop predecessors, and minor-key melodies—such as Silver's *Señor Blues* (1956) and cornetist Nat Adderley's *Work Song* (1960; *JTSA* Disc 4/Track 8)—became increasingly popular. The hard boppers also made use of the new

Horace Silver in 1956; he was one of the fathers of hard bop, writing many jazz standards. PHOTO COURTESY SONY BMG MUSIC ENTERTAINMENT/GETTY IMAGES.

long-playing (LP) record format to stretch out on extended solos, and the most important players went further still: they saw in the LP a chance to reconceive the jazz solo as a vehicle for large-scale thematic development.

The most important hard bop bands all developed under the guidance of bebop veterans: Davis, Blakey, drummer **Max Roach**, and Silver. In 1956, Silver left the Jazz Messengers to form a quintet concentrating on his own remarkable compositions. Many of these, such as *Doodin'* (1955), *Nica's Dream* (1956), *Sister Sadie* (1959), and *Song for My Father* (1964), have entrenched themselves in the mainstream repertoire. Meanwhile, Blakey assumed full command of the Jazz Messengers after Silver's departure and proved himself a brilliant leader. The band epitomized hard bop until Blakey's death in 1990; the Messengers became jazz's answer to the Naval Academy, training a steady parade of new recruits to navigate the mainstream as leaders in their own right (see Chapter 12).

Horace Silver's post-Messengers career as a leader extended through the 1990s, during which he issued dozens of recordings. Like the Jazz Messengers, Silver's groups helped launch the careers of many important musicians, including saxophonists Joe Henderson and Junior Cook and trumpeters Art Farmer and

Art Blakey, 1955. Blakey nurtured upcoming talent in his long-running band the Jazz Messengers. PHOTO COURTESY BILL SPILKA/GETTY IMAGES.

Watch the video of *Build A New World* by Art Blakey on **mymusiclab.com**

Listening Guide

🔊 **Listen** to *The Preacher* by Horace Silver and the Jazz Messengers on **mymusiclab.com**
CD II, Track 1/Download Track 25

THE PREACHER • HORACE SILVER AND THE JAZZ MESSENGERS

Music: Horace Silver, 1955. Personnel: Kenny Dorham (trumpet); Hank Mobley (tenor saxophone); Horace Silver (piano); Doug Watkins (bass); Art Blakey (drums). Recorded: February 6, 1955, in Hackensack, NJ. First issue: *Horace Silver Quintet Vol. 2*, Blue Note 5062 (10" LP). Timing: 4:20.

Overview

The Preacher embodies key qualities that Silver brought to post-bop jazz: a turn to soulfulness and earthiness, and a welcoming sense of music whose every note feels heartfelt and engaging. In it we hear gospel, blues, swing, and the seeds of rock and roll. Silver's accessibility and down-home emotionalism brought a joy and populism to jazz that contrasted with bebop's intellectualism and exclusiveness.

Key Features

- Form and structure: The chorus consists of four 4-bar phrases, reminiscent of gospel tunes. The first three phrases, A, A1, and A2 vary slightly, followed by a resolving phrase, B. Soloists improvise over the full 16-bar chorus.
- Rhythm: For the first two choruses, the beat saunters in half time ($\frac{2}{2}$). During the solos the time doubles to $\frac{4}{4}$, with the bass and drums leading the way, setting a more uptempo-feeling groove to support solos.
- Melody and harmony: The melody is simple compared to the convoluted lines used in bebop. The melody is accessible and singable. The harmony stays within the confines of standard gospel and blues tunes—nothing groundbreaking here.
- Improvisation: Three soloists, Kenny Dorham, Hank Mobley, and Horace Silver draw from bebop concepts but play them engagingly, making them accessible to non-jazz listeners.
- Color and texture: A prominent texture is provide by the trumpet and tenor sax playing in harmony on the melody.

—*Tad Lathrop*

TIME	FORM	INSTRUMENTATION	MELODY
0:00	CHORUS 1 HEAD	Band	The jubilant 16-bar melody launches straightaway, with trumpet and tenor saxophone in harmony backed by the three-piece rhythm section. (The tune slightly resembles the old-time standard *Bill Bailey, Won't You Come Home*, 1902.) The beat is ebullient, sauntering in counts of two. The melody unfolds in four phrases—in the form of A, A1, A2, B—posing a statement, varying it, and resolving conclusively.
0:23	CHORUS 2		The melody repeats.
0:44	CHORUS 3	Trumpet solo	Trumpeter Kenny Dorham ascends to a soaring F, holds it, and spills forward with jazz-blues phrasings mainly in eighth notes. The bass shifts from half notes to walking quarter notes, picking up the energy.
1:06	CHORUS 4		Trumpeter Dorham continues, repeating the opening figure of the first chorus and shooting up to an even higher F—heightening the excitement. He stays within the blues (rather than getting too "outside") and keeps the energy high.
1:27	CHORUS 5	Tenor sax solo	Hank Mobley's fat-sounding sax picks up Dorham's opening figure and launches into a solo that mixes blues ideas with irregular phrasings that draw from bebop.
1:48	CHORUS 6		Sax continues, now emphasizing straight-ahead bop lines until (2:04) ascending in half steps to a melodic curlicue of an ending.
2:09	CHORUS 7	Piano solo	Horace Silver enters with bluesy, rhythmic chording, shifting to single notes at 2:21.
2:30	CHORUS 8		Silver continues, establishing a downward-tumbling phrase (two-bars long) that he repeats at 2:33, 2:35, and 2:40, followed by a five-note figure (2:43) that he repeats lower and then truncates as he closes out the chorus.
2:50	CHORUS 9	Piano solo with backing	Silver continues with syncopated chordal statements that sax and trumpet "answer" with unison (an octave apart) blues riffs.
3:11	CHORUS 10		Silver keeps up his rhythmic chordal improvising as sax and trumpet continue their unison riffing.
3:31	CHORUS 11	Band	Head.
3:52	CHORUS 12		Head repeats.

New York Nights

"It was the same every night when we were closing at 4 a.m.," recalled Max Gordon, owner of the venerable Village Vanguard club in New York City. "There were always a few insomniacs and night prowlers left in the place who never wanted to go home."

Quite possibly, those night owls were still buzzing from the energy of a set by John Coltrane or Miles Davis or **Sonny Rollins**: the Vanguard, from the 1950s on, was the leading small venue for jazz, launching many an illustrious career and sustaining others that were already aloft. Jazz front-liners from Charles Mingus to Thelonious Monk regularly played there, and some immortalized the stints on LPs (notably Bill Evans's *Sunday at the Village Vanguard,* 1961, and several by Coltrane). Even Monday nights—typically off-nights in the club world—drew crowds, thanks to weekly sets by the Thad Jones-Mel Lewis Orchestra.

The Vanguard was smack in the middle of Greenwich Village, itself a focal point of live jazz following the demise of the 52nd Street nightclub strip in the late 1940s. The emergence of jazz in the Village reflected the growing interest in and identification with the music among college students, artists, and other cultured denizens of that neo-bohemian neighborhood.

Other downtown clubs that nurtured the latest jazz styles included the Five Spot, which booked such forward-looking players as Cecil Taylor and Ornette Coleman for lengthy residencies that helped their music develop; the Half Note, for

nearly 20 years a host to the likes of Charles Mingus, Lennie Tristano, and Coltrane; Slug's Saloon on East 3rd Street, where hard bop thrived in the hands of such proponents as Art Blakey, **Lee Morgan**, and Freddie Hubbard (and where Morgan was shot dead by his mistress on the night of February 19, 1972); and the Village Gate on Bleecker Street, another home of hard bop—and, like the Vanguard, a favored location for live recording sessions. Further uptown, at 1678 Broadway, the post-boppers could get a hearing at Birdland—a club named after their patron saint, Charlie "Bird" Parker.

But more traditional sounds also had their New York show spots, in both the Village and other parts of

Pee Wee Russell, Muggsy Spanier, Miff Mole, and Joe Grauso, at Nick's Tavern, New York, New York (ca. June 1946). PHOTO COURTESY WILLIAM P. GOTTLIEB/WILLIAM P. GOTTLIEB COLLECTION/LIBRARY OF CONGRESS PRINTS & PHOTOGRAPHS DIVISION.

town. In the mid-1960s, such established stars as **Sarah Vaughan**, Louis Armstrong, Count Basie, and Lionel Hampton would occasionally take their acts to Basin Street East on 48th Street, and swing veterans Red Allen, Coleman Hawkins, and Roy Eldridge could sometimes be heard at the Metropole, on the western end of that same street. Meanwhile, Dixieland jazz enjoyed an extended life at Nick's, located on 7th Avenue in the heart of the Village.

Jazz may have livened up Boston, Chicago, Los Angeles, San Francisco, and other locales in the 1950s and 1960s. But the surging energy of New York made that town—and still makes the town—the jazz capital of the world.

—*Tad Lathrop*

Donald Byrd. Silver's music proved durable: it modeled a funky soul-and-jazz hybrid whose influence can be traced through the popular 1960s recordings of pianist Ramsey Lewis to the 1970s disco and jazz-funk tracks of Donald Byrd and jazz fusion of Weather Report and the Crusaders to the 1980s R&B-jazz fusion of David Sanborn and many others.

It was during his early development that Silver encountered the root sounds that he later brought to jazz. Silver's father had migrated to the United States from the Portuguese island colony of Cape Verde, off the coast of West Africa, where Portuguese, Caribbean, African, and Brazilian musical influences coalesced. The latter influence, and echoes of his father's jam sessions during Silver's youth, eventually inspired Silver's most popular tune, *Song for My Father*. But he also grew up on boogie-woogie, the blues, and **gospel music**, and he got an early start in mixing them into his own highly accessible brand of jazz. By the time he joined Blakey in the Jazz Messengers, Silver had toured and recorded at age 22 with Stan Getz, backed up Coleman Hawkins and Lester Young, and recorded his own tunes as a sideman and a leader. With 1955's *The Preacher*, recorded under the name Horace Silver and the Jazz Messengers, his funky, gospel-inflected signature sound was firmly in place.

The most brilliant of the hard bop bands was the one that bore the closest resemblance to bebop's fire. In 1954, Roach enlisted the startling young trumpeter **Clifford Brown**, creating one of the most respected partnerships in jazz history. (It was also one of the shortest lived: 30 months later, Brown died in a car crash that also killed the band's pianist, Bud Powell's younger brother Richie.) "Brownie" played with a honeyed tone, a sunny and exquisite lyricism, and a precision that challenged and at times eclipsed even the virtuosity of his idols, Dizzy Gillespie and Fats Navarro. Roach thought enough of Brown to grant him co-star status, and the Clifford Brown-Max Roach Quintet, with West Coast tenorman Harold Land, achieved overnight success with a sound typified by their take-no-prisoners romp on the bop favorite *Cherokee* (1955). The precocious genius Sonny Rollins replaced Land at the end of 1955, and for the next six months—until Brown's death—this

Drummer Max Roach, co-leader of the Brown-Roach Quintet. PHOTO COURTESY © HERMAN LEONARD PHOTOGRAPHY LLC.

band was fueled by the highest-octane front line in jazz.

Before joining the Brown-Roach Quintet, Rollins had participated in several memorable sessions led by Miles Davis, which produced the first recordings of the classic Rollins tunes *Airegin*, *Oleo*, and *Doxy* (all 1954). When Davis prepared to form his own hard bop band in 1955, he thought immediately of the tall, contemplative tenorist, whose playing had already begun to turn heads. But Rollins was unavailable, off in Chicago on the first of three celebrated hiatuses, so Davis turned instead to a relatively obscure saxophonist from Philadelphia, John Coltrane.

Their yin-yang collaboration—with Davis's progressively simpler solos set in bas-relief against Trane's increasingly complicated chromaticism—made this the most influential group of its time. With an unimpeachable rhythm section anchored by bassist Paul Chambers and drummer "Philly" Joe Jones, Davis turned out a series of album masterpieces

Trumpeter Clifford Brown co-led the Brown-Roach Quintet, one of the most influential hard-bop bands. PHOTO COURTESY © HERMAN LEONARD PHOTOGRAPHY LLC.

---

gospel music demonstrative African American religious music originating in the early twentieth-century United States, associated with Protestant denominations.

(*Workin'*, 1956; *'Round About Midnight*, 1955–56; and *Milestones*, 1958) that exemplified the hard bop style—and transcended it. For in the midst of this decidedly hard bop landscape stood the distinctly cool figure of Davis himself, turning the band into a bridge between the decade's two prevalent jazz idioms.

TAKE NOTE

• How did hard bop develop in response to bebop and other styles?

West Coast Bop

Although California was a hotbed of cool jazz, it also supported important musicians who had little to do with the style. But many of these musicians didn't fit the East Coast hard bop mold, either. Some of them—such as pianist Sonny Clark, trumpeter and flugelhornist Art Farmer, bassist Charles Mingus, tenor saxophonist Teddy Edwards, and drummer Shelly Manne—managed to consolidate key virtues of both schools: Clark, for instance, recorded with the cool-oriented Lighthouse All-Stars before moving to New York, where he worked with Sonny Rollins and led some of the era's most representative hard bop dates (such as *Cool Strutting*, 1958).

Other West Coasters—most notably pianist Hampton Hawes and the alto saxophonists **Art Pepper** and Sonny Criss—concocted a potent version of bebop. This music contrasted sharply with that of their cool compatriots, but it also differed from hard bop, which offered a somewhat relaxed adaptation of bop's frenzy; listening to the aptly named Pepper on such tracks as *Surf Ride* (featuring Hawes, from 1952) and the supersonic *Straight Life* (1954), most people have trouble believing the sessions took place anywhere near the Pacific Ocean. On the other hand, Pepper utilized certain "West Coast" devices to great effect, most notably the studied counterpoint that distinguished the quartet of baritone saxophonist Gerry Mulligan. But Pepper played it hot instead of cool: that same recording of *Straight Life* boasts a fast and furious bit of two-part invention for Pepper and tenor saxophonist Jack Montrose.

Pepper blurred the line further with *Art Pepper Meets the Rhythm Section*, the widely respected 1957 album on which he partnered with the rhythm section from the Miles Davis Quintet (pianist Red Garland, bassist Paul Chambers, and drummer "Philly" Joe Jones). By this time Pepper had arrived at one of the most compelling styles of the decade, a personal and deeply felt compendium of bebop, cool, California, and New York. A similar description would apply to pianist Hawes,

who—on the albums *Hampton Hawes Trio* (1955) and *Four* (1958)—proved himself one of the few pianists able to capture not only the virtuosity but also "the scorching intensity of Bud Powell's pianism," as music historian Ted Gioia put it. "He was, in his own words, the man with the 105-degree fever." Both Hawes (who died in 1977) and Pepper (who died in 1982) fought substance-abuse problems their entire adult lives.

Other than the members of Brubeck's and Mulligan's bands, the best-known West Coast jazzmen belonged at one time or another to the Lighthouse All-Stars, a loose-knit amalgam of players associated with the club called the Lighthouse. Just south of Los Angeles in Hermosa Beach, the Lighthouse was a restaurant down on its luck in 1949, when bassist Howard Rumsey convinced the owner to institute Sunday jam sessions. These sessions often displayed the bristling

Art Pepper, 1948. Pepper would emerge as an important purveyor of West Coast bop in the 1950s. PHOTO COURTESY WILLIAM P. GOTTLIEB/
WILLIAM P. GOTTLIEB COLLECTION/LIBRARY OF CONGRESS PRINTS & PHOTOGRAPHS DIVISION.

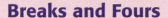
Breaks and Fours

Jazz musicians have developed a number of common practices; two of the best known are breaks and fours. Both provide contrast and drama and allow the soloists to show off.

A break is a short solo passage by a single instrument or group of instruments—or, less commonly, a short period of complete silence. During a break the rhythm section lays out, but the meter, tempo, and beat remain intact and are ongoing. Breaks usually occur at the ends of sections, especially in the final phrase of a blues or a multi-strain composition.

The break serves a number of purposes: providing the soloist with a springboard into a solo; briefly changing the texture, which is typically otherwise constant; serving as a structural device to herald the next solo; and creating tension and excitement leading to the beginning of a new section. Breaks were found frequently in early jazz, and Jelly Roll Morton used them brilliantly in such recordings as *Black Bottom Stomp* and *Grandpa's Spells* (both 1926). By the 1940s, breaks had become less common, but Charlie Parker took a memorable one to set up his solo on his Dial recording of *Night in Tunisia* (1946). Other modern instances of breaks include John Coltrane's *Locomotion* (1957) and Stan Getz's *Night and Day* (1964).

Another venerable tradition in jazz performance is that of soloists' trading improvised phrases. Exchanging phrases of four measures is called playing fours, trading fours, or simply **fours**, while alternating phrases of eight bars is called **eights**, and so on. The length of these phrases is usually some equal subdivision of the tune's form. In playing a 12-bar blues, musicians could exchange complete *twelves*, two *sixes*, three *fours*, or four *threes*. In a 32-bar form, the phrases might be two, four, eight, or sixteen measures in length.

These exchanges most often follow a round of extended solos, affording the soloists space to build on what the previous soloists have played, revisit their own improvisational ideas, engage in friendly musical combat, and collect their thoughts between cyclical occurrences. The exchanges occur in a number of different settings, often between a solo instrumentalist and a drummer. They also frequently take place in a "round robin" of two or three instrumentalists in a small group setting, whereby a competition of improvisation ensues: for example, **Dexter Gordon** and Wardell Gray on *The Chase* (1947), Johnny Griffin and Eddie "Lockjaw" Davis on *Blues Up and Down* (1961), and trombonists J. J. Johnson and Kai Winding on *It's All Right with Me* (1976). Sometimes a number of like instruments trade phrases, as the saxophones do on Woody Herman's *Four Brothers* (1947). Trading phrases—quite common in jam sessions—gives participants opportunities to express their personalities through concise statements.

—David Baker

Big band drummer **Buddy Rich** *(shown here in 1954), demonstrated dazzling technique when trading fours or taking long solos.* PHOTO COURTESY © HERMAN LEONARD PHOTOGRAPHY LLC.

---

fours trading fours: the jazz practice of showcasing a different soloist every four measures.

eights the jazz practice of showcasing a different soloist every eight measures, as in "trading eights."

energy associated with hard bop on the opposite coast; nonetheless, as the schedule expanded to every night of the week, the Lighthouse emerged as headquarters for such important cool jazz musicians as Shelly Manne and saxophonist Bud Shank, who led innovative groups that balanced composition with improvisation. Soon the club and its "house band," the Lighthouse All-Stars—which at various times included Shank, Manne, pianist Claude Williamson, tenor saxophonists Bob Cooper and Bill Perkins, and brass men Conte Candoli, Shorty Rogers, Frank Rosolino, and Jack Sheldon—came to embody West Coast jazz to most listeners.

Meanwhile, the cool trumpet voice of **Chet Baker**, one of the original West Coast stars, began a fadeout into the jazz background. Drugs took their toll on him, as they had on Pepper and Hawes.

TAKE NOTE

- What distinguishes West Coast bop from other variants, and who were the key players in this style?

Three Tenor Torchbearers: Gordon, Rollins, and Coltrane

The 1950s produced a number of important alto saxophonists—among them Cannonball Adderley, **Jackie McLean**, and Phil Woods. But the virtuosic genius of Charlie Parker remained an unmatchable benchmark for most alto players, so the spotlight shifted to the

tenor sax. The sound of bebop had belonged to trumpet and alto; the sound of hard bop was the tougher, more full-bodied sound of trumpet and tenor. In retrospect, the Sonny Rollins title *Tenor Madness* (1956), which paired Rollins with John Coltrane, could well describe the entire decade.

Both Rollins and Coltrane owed a huge debt to Dexter Gordon, the first important bebop tenorist, whose adaptability made him a vital voice in hard bop as well. Gordon fused the two streams of earlier jazz tenor playing, combining the huge sound and harmonic ingenuity of Coleman Hawkins with the light vibrato and quixotic grace of Lester Young; he also expanded upon Young's narrative abilities, playing solos that almost unfailingly told a story. (Excellent examples include *Dexter Rides Again* by Dexter Gordon and Wardell Gray (*JTSA* Disc 2/Track 15), *It's You or No One* from the Blue Note album *Doin' Allright* (1961), and his solo on Herbie Hancock's famous *Watermelon Man* (1962). Gordon's style fed two new streams, represented by Rollins and Coltrane, which then provided the primary inspiration for the next generation or three of jazz saxophonists.

Although he was four years younger than Coltrane, it was Rollins who first grabbed the attention of jazz cognoscenti, including Davis: in the section of Harlem in which he'd grown up, his neighbors included such towering figures as Hawkins, Monk, and Bud Powell, all of whom encouraged his interest in jazz. (As a teen, Rollins would wait on Hawkins's doorstep for the chance to see his first idol.) Rollins's first recordings with Powell in 1949—especially *Wail* and *Dance of the Infidels*—showed a youngster still mastering bebop's complexities but already possessing a distinct sound and innovative ideas. Before long, the intense young saxophonist had arrived at a style of unusually cogent thematic development, heard on such tunes as *I'll Remember April* (1956) with the Brown-Roach Quintet. Rollins's best improvisations—heard throughout the albums *Saxophone Colossus* (1956), *Sonny Rollins* (1957), *A Night at the Village Vanguard* (1956), and *The Bridge* (1962)—gracefully unfolded across multiple **choruses**. His solos sounded like spontaneous compositions rather than a series of fragments strung between harmonic signposts, and they set a new standard for jazz improvisation.

Sonny Rollins (right) playing with his early mentor Coleman Hawkins, 1963. PHOTO COURTESY LEE TANNER.

Watch the documentary on John Coltrane on **mymusiclab.com**

***

chorus (1) in jazz, an iteration of a main theme; each time a jazz performer plays through, for example, a 12-bar blues or a 32-bar popular song, he or she is playing a chorus of that tune; (2) an improvised solo, as in "take a chorus"; (3) in a popular song, the main part of the song, which typically repeats, often preceded by its verse.

COLTRANE FORMS HIS GROUP

✳ Explore on **mymusiclab.com**

John Coltrane's "classic" quartet came to fruition when Coltrane left the Miles Davis band in 1960 and struck out on his own as a leader. Coltrane's experiences in jazz up to that point were rich, and they included associations with Dizzy Gillespie, Charlie Parker, bluesman Earl Bostic, and famous groups led by Miles Davis. This background, combined with his fervor for practicing and his spiritual exploration through music, spurred his and the quartet's innovative performances and recordings.

—*Jeff Rupert*

Jimmy Garrison • Bass

Jimmy Garrison had a depth of sound that anchored Coltrane's quartet. Coltrane had experimented with numerous bass players and settled on Garrison, whose rhythmic feel was in sync with the group. While he did not have the technique of some other bass players, his addition to the Coltrane group exemplified the importance of tone and feel in music.

McCoy Tyner • Piano

McCoy Tyner's "voice" in the quartet was crucial; his rhythmic approach was fierce, buoyant, and relentless, qualities embodied by the entire quartet. Tyner was an original soloist in jazz, relying somewhat on pentatonic techniques (five-note scales, as compared to eight-note scales), and quartal harmony; that is, harmony based on musical intervals of fourths, rather than thirds, which had been the basis for European harmony.

PHOTO COURTESY MICHAEL OCHS ARCHIVES/GETTY IMAGES.

Elvin Jones • Drums

Elvin Jones was the rhythmic center, or the heartbeat, of Coltrane's quartet. Jones's feel on the drums had an unrivaled buoyancy and propulsion. His conceptualization tended toward horizontal motion with vertical inflections, and he epitomized polyrhythmic (more than one rhythm at once) drumming, a West African carryover to jazz. Jones's physical strength enabled him to accompany Coltrane, who at this point would perform for hours without rest. Performances often consisted of one tune, with drum and sax duets in the middle.

John Coltrane • Saxophone

Although primarily a tenor saxophonist, Coltrane also played soprano. His approach was unique; at times his tone resembled an Eastern reed instrument (as exemplified on *India* from his album *Impressions*). Coltrane has been referred to as a "cosmopolitan" of religion. He studied Western and Eastern religious beliefs, all of which are embodied in his music. His jazz improvisation had an entirely different rhythmic approach than that of those who preceded him; at times he played so many notes that one critic referred to him as playing "sheets of sound." Equally, he could play a tender ballad or a driving blues. In all cases he had a unique and identifiable swing feel that created an uplifting air.

Listening Guide

CD I, Track 23/Download Track 23

GIANT STEPS • JOHN COLTRANE QUARTET

Music: John Coltrane, 1959. Personnel: John Coltrane (tenor sax, leader); Tommy Flanagan (piano); Paul Chambers (bass); Art Taylor (drums). Recorded May 5, 1959, in New York. First issue: Atlantic 1311. Timing: 4:47.

Overview

The title tune from Coltrane's breakthrough album, *Giant Steps* became a proving ground for the next two generations of jazz musicians. It consists of a rather simple melody, with only two notes per measure. But almost every note has a different chord attached to it; and these chords move through three keys, changing key as often as twice per measure. Taken at a blistering tempo, it remains one of the most challenging sets of chord changes ever designed for improvisation—an advanced study of harmonic interrelationships—requiring significant preparation in advance. (Coltrane had reportedly been working with these chords for nearly two years prior to the recording.) As an aside, consider the following: The 1930s Rodgers and Hart tune *Have You Met Miss Jones?* has a bridge with nearly the same changes, though a half step lower and at half the pace—making it a great warm-up for playing *Giant Steps*—and perhaps an inspiration for Coltrane's chord changes.

Key Features

- Form: The theme consists of a 16-bar melody that is then repeated, with a slight alteration in the last four measures.
- Rhythm: Much of the recording's propulsion comes from the pronounced use of evenly spaced eighth notes, as opposed to the "swinging" style of dotted eighths alternating with sixteenths.
- Improvisation: Coltrane takes one long solo (12 choruses) and then, after piano and bass, a shorter solo (two choruses) before restating the theme—a relatively unusual structure, previously used to strong effect by Sonny Rollins.
- For such a busy and forceful solo—and one that would become synonymous with Coltrane's early style—this improvisation features relatively little melodic novelty. Instead, it relies on Coltrane's ability to mix and match a handful of motifs to relentlessly explore the harmonic framework. Virtually all of these motifs are introduced within the first choruses of the solo.
- The song's difficulty is illustrated by the fact that seeing the sheet music for the first time at the recording studio, Tommy Flanagan—among the most accomplished post-bop pianists—could manage only a sparse, simple solo that all but ignores the rigorous harmony.
- Dynamics and texture: Variations in dynamics play no role in this performance. It succeeds entirely on speed and urgency, as opposed to gradations in volume or texture.

A nattily dressed Dexter Gordon.

PHOTO COURTESY MICHAEL OCHS ARCHIVES/GETTY IMAGES.

Coltrane's solos, on the other hand, seemed to burst directly from the horn rather than the head, even though they grew from his deep study of modern harmony; his first professional experience came in rhythm and blues bands, and the soulful passion of that music remained with him during his short life (he died in 1967, at the age of 40). Playing with Davis, Coltrane garnered a huge audience for his hell-for-leather style, which featured cyclonic, note-filled solos informed by a relentless appetite for harmonic permutations. Coltrane's albums with Davis, as well as his own *Blue Train* (1957) and *Soultrane* (1958), document the progression of his style, which became increasingly controversial: one reviewer criticized him as "anti-jazz," and Davis supposedly once told him, "Coltrane, you can't play everything at once!" The climax of these investigations came on his 1959 masterpiece, *Giant Steps*, the title track a tricky slalom of careening

- Usually, such concepts as "voice" and "expression" depend entirely on the musician's actual timbre. But here, the song and tempo also contribute to the instrumental voice: the yearning nature of Coltrane's sound gains extra power from the energy required to navigate the rapidly changing chords at fast tempo.
- The rhythm section is given little responsibility other than maintaining the speed of the performance and providing chordal mileposts for the tenor solo.

—*Neil Tesser*

TIME	SECTION	MELODY/INSTRUMENTATION
0:00	THEME STATEMENT	Standard quartet arrangement, except that rather than offering traditional "comp" rhythms, pianist Flanagan doubles the saxophone melody (using chords). Theme is restated in Chorus 2.
0:26	CHORUS 3	Coltrane begins his 12-chorus solo, introducing one of the dominant recurring motifs—call it figure A—an ascending four-note figure (at 0:30–0:32).
0:40	CHORUS 4	Coltrane begins this chorus with a single note held for almost five beats: a virtual eternity within the context of this swiftly moving solo. This contrasting trope—figure B—will also reoccur frequently.
0:43	CHORUS 4	Reappearance of figure A.
0:53	CHORUS 5	Intermittent use of figure A, from 0:53–0:59.
1:06	CHORUS 6	Variations on figure A reoccur at 1:06 and 1:10, and of figure B at 1:16–1:17 and 1:20.
1:46	CHORUS 9	Brief use of an ascending scalar figure introduces a new element and builds momentum.
2:26	CHORUS 12	Coltrane begins this chorus with a restatement of figure A.
2:52	CHORUS 14	As Coltrane concludes, drummer Art Taylor—most likely signaled by a visual cue from Coltrane—marks the solo's end with a series of rimshots that lead into Tommy Flanagan's piano solo.
2:55	CHORUS 14–16	Piano solo.
3:31	CHORUS 17	Pianist Flanagan plays chords, allowing bass line to be heard more clearly.
3:44	CHORUS 18–19	Second tenor sax solo (recapping elements of the first).
4:10	CHORUS 20–21	Restatement of theme.
4:35	CODA	Final flurry of notes against sustained final chord.

chords. Afterward, Coltrane set about assembling his own band, which by the end of 1961 had coalesced into his galvanic "classic quartet": McCoy Tyner (one of the period's most influential pianists), bassist Jimmy Garrison, and drummer Elvin Jones. The empathic interplay of the four reached a peak on *A Love Supreme* (1964; *JTSA* Disc 5/Track 3).

The track *Tenor Madness* (also from *Saxophone Colossus*) is the only on-disc meeting of Rollins and Coltrane, and it remains the perfect starting place to compare and contrast their styles. Both men benefited from Monk's tutelage, and their work under his name—on *Brilliant Corners* (1956) and *Monk with Coltrane* (1957), respectively—further illuminates their different approaches. Coltrane's music altered in the 1960s, and he became an iconic figure of the jazz avant-garde. Rollins also made significant changes, but not until the 1970s, when he unveiled a technique that was bluesier and far less refined than his music of the 1950s. (For more on Coltrane's free jazz recordings, see Chapter 8.)

As for Dexter Gordon, his battle with narcotics addiction made him something of a shadow figure in the 1950s: he spent almost six years in jail and recorded only one album between 1951 and 1959. When he re-emerged in the 1960s, he showed that he had big enough ears to appreciate Coltrane and Rollins—and a small enough ego to adapt some of their innovations to his own style, as on *Both Sides of Midnight* (1967). This adaptability allowed Gordon to flourish throughout the 1960s and 1970s, and as an "elder statesman" in the 1980s, when he made his film debut in *Round Midnight* (and received an Academy Award nomination for best supporting actor).

TAKE NOTE

- What are the different saxophone styles of Dexter Gordon, Sonny Rollins, and John Coltrane?

Two Takes on the Piano

In the 1950s, most jazz fans would have considered Thelonious Monk and **Dave Brubeck** polar opposites. However, Monk and Brubeck played similar roles in their respective musical camps—that of the stubborn iconoclast, the exception that proves the rule. In his book *West Coast Jazz*, Ted Gioia offers an analysis of their unexpected similarities, pointing out that instead of the dominant 1950s piano style, characterized by hornlike single-note lines and sparse chords, "Brubeck and Monk brought out the intrinsically pianistic and orchestral qualities of the instrument. . . . Both began adopting more complex harmonic structures than their peers. . . . Both emphasized (almost to an extreme) the percussive nature of the piano . . . and focused as much on composing as on playing." And although both men were active in the 1940s, Brubeck and Monk—the second and fourth jazz musicians to appear on the cover of *Time* magazine—really wrote their legacies during the 1950s.

By far the most popular musician to emerge from California was pianist Dave Brubeck, a product of studies with classical composer Darius Milhaud and experiments in counterpoint and **atonality** in late-1940s San Francisco. Brubeck's first band was an octet that proved too esoteric for popular tastes, but subsequent trio recordings planted the seeds of a mass following that blossomed after the addition of alto saxophonist Paul Desmond made the Brubeck group a quartet. The contrast between Desmond's limpid elegance and Brubeck's weightier complexities, and the conversational improvisations that the pair generated on such recordings as *Over the Rainbow* (1952) and *You Go to My Head* (1952) carried particular appeal for the growing audience that approached jazz as a challenging intellectual experience. With an uncanny sense of where both technology and the public were headed, Brubeck began recording nightclub performances on 33⅓-rpm long-playing (LP) records, then

Hear Dave Brubeck describe how he composed *Blue Rondo à la Turk* on **mymusiclab.com**

---

atonal composed without being based in traditional rules of harmonic relationships; for example, not in a key.

The Dave Brubeck Quartet. From left to right: Paul Desmond (alto saxophone), Joe Dodge (drums), Dave Brubeck (piano), and Ron Crotty (bass). PHOTO COURTESY JOHN BROOK/DOWN BEAT ARCHIVES.

obtained bookings on college campuses and recorded those concerts as well—one of them, the album *Jazz Goes to College*, achieved commercial success in 1954.

Brubeck's popularity grew at a steady clip, but he refused to coast on his success, or on the West Coast phenomenon he nominally represented. He continued to develop his classically influenced compositions and to challenge himself and his listeners with unusual meters. This process culminated in his landmark 1959 album *Time Out*, featuring the famous *Take Five* (written by his saxophonist, Paul Desmond). *Time Out* was the first jazz album to sell a million copies—even though it was almost shelved by its label, Columbia, which thought it too "radical" for the record-buying public.

On the other hand, Monk's success in the 1950s represented a return to grace, as the jazz public began to rediscover his quirky compositions and one-of-a-kind piano style. This resulted from a combination of factors. In 1955 a fledgling jazz label, Riverside, decided to "rehabilitate" Monk's image with two albums designed to show him as less "far out" than generally believed: *Thelonious Monk Plays Duke Ellington* and a standards date, *The Unique Thelonious Monk* (a redundant title if ever there was one). Subsequent albums such as *Monk's Music* (1957) proved his stature, with Monk leading groups that mingled respected veterans with fiery newcomers; meanwhile, a few other musicians (most notably soprano saxophonist Steve Lacy) began to revisit his deceptively simple, elegantly constructed compositions and proselytize for them. In 1957 Monk regained his New York City cabaret card and took up residence at the Five Spot club, leading a quartet that featured the skyrocketing Coltrane and propelling himself into the jazz limelight; in 1959, his compositions were arranged for nonet for a famous concert at Town Hall (released on disc as *The Thelonious Monk Orchestra at Town Hall*). By the early 1960s, when Monk established his long-running quartet starring saxophonist Charlie Rouse, he was hailed as one of jazz's true geniuses. Monk tunes were still favorites decades later, having proved adaptable to a wide range of musical settings.

TAKE NOTE

- How were the musical approaches of composer-pianists Thelonious Monk and Dave Brubeck similar and how were they different?

Soul Jazz

As the 1950s drew to a close, one hard bop strain dominated all others. To be sure, the gospel-tinged but down-and-dirty sounds of "**soul jazz**"—simple, funky melodies, danceable rhythms, and plenty of the blues—had exerted a strong influence since the idiom took shape. But now, inspired by the successes of Horace Silver's group and the remarkable keyboardist **Jimmy Smith**, jazz players began turning out one album after another on which they sought to parlay "the funk" into commercial success.

No one had a more important hand in this process than Smith, the Philadelphia pianist who started to play the electric organ in 1951. By 1956 he had mastered his driving, slashing, sophisticated combination of bebop and rhythm and blues. On his Blue Note Records debut, *A New Sound . . . A New Star* (volumes 1 and 2) and the follow-up *The Incredible Jimmy Smith*, all recorded in 1956, he established the model for the ultra-streamlined "**organ trio**" in jazz; it featured only a drummer, either a guitarist or saxophonist, and Smith himself, both hands and feet in constant motion on the organ's keyboards and pedals as he handled the chores of bassist, keyboard accompanist, and dynamic lead soloist. On subsequent albums, Smith was joined by a number of Blue Note hornmen in jam-session performances that fully exploited the new long-playing record format, with tracks that ran 15 minutes or more.

A similar format became a favorite of guitarist **Kenny Burrell** on such late-1950s "jam" albums as *All Day Long* (1957) and *Blue Lights* (1958). He had already worked on albums by Dizzy Gillespie, John Coltrane, and many of his colleagues from Detroit, which throughout the decade funneled jazz stars from its fertile, vibrant scene into New York. Burrell's mellow tone and easygoing style made him a leading guitarist of the time; in 1959, and then again decades later, he hooked up with Smith on such exceptional Blue Note dates as *Home Cookin'* (1958–59) and *The Master* (1993).

Smith's organ trio showcased the electric guitar to a degree not often heard in earlier jazz, paving the way for the success enjoyed by two other guitarists, Wes Montgomery and Grant Green. In his hometown of Indianapolis, Montgomery formed a trio with his brothers Buddy and Monk, but before long his virtuosity resulted in an extraordinarily successful solo career, best represented by his Riverside album *The Incredible Jazz Guitar* (1960). Montgomery played with a deep, soulful swing that gave his melodies unusual propulsion, and he was the first guitarist to improvise in octaves, a startling technique that at first

---

soul jazz a funky, bluesy style of jazz made popular in the 1950s and 1960s by such musicians as organist Jimmy Smith; guitarists Wes Montgomery, Kenny Burrell, and Grant Green; and saxophonist Cannonball Adderley.

organ trio a distinctive ensemble configuration consisting of electronic organ (usually a Hammond B-3), electric guitar or saxophone, and drums; introduced as part of the soul jazz and hard bop movements in the 1950s and 1960s primarily by organist Jimmy Smith.

Listening Guide

))) Listen to *Blue Rondo à la Turk* by The Dave Brubeck Quartet on **mymusiclab.com**
CD I, Track 21/Download Track 21

BLUE RONDO À LA TURK • THE DAVE BRUBECK QUARTET

Music: Dave Brubeck, 1959. Personnel: Paul Desmond (alto saxophone); Dave Brubeck (piano); Eugene Wright (bass); Joe Morello (drums). Recorded August 18, 1959, in New York. First issue: *Time Out*, Columbia CL 1397. Timing: 6:46.

Overview

Blue Rondo à la Turk is memorable for four reasons: its use of a meter ($\frac{9}{8}$) then virtually unknown in jazz; its incorporation of European rondo form; its unusual approach to the blues; and the contrasting playing styles of its two soloists.

Dave Brubeck considered himself as much a composer as a pianist, had long been incorporating classical-music forms in his compositions, and in the 1940s—under the influence of composer Darius Milhaud—Brubeck composed a piece he called *Rondo*. (In classical music, a **rondo** is a multisectional form—such as ABACA—with a repeating theme in the tonic or "home" key.) One of the most famous rondos in classical music was Mozart's "Rondo Alla Turca," the third movement of his Sonata no. 11 for piano, which had been inspired by a vogue for Turkish music, and Brubeck based *Blue Rondo à la Turk* loosely on Mozart's "Rondo Alla Turca." The incorporation of the European rondo form (and its use in the title) imbue this recording with aspects of third stream music (see page 152)—a blending of classical music and jazz.

In 1958, Brubeck's quartet traveled to the Middle East and India, and in Istanbul, Turkey, he heard street musicians playing in the unfamiliar meter of $\frac{9}{8}$—a rhythm from a folk dance called a *karşılama*. "I was on my way to a radio station to be interviewed in Turkey," said Brubeck in a Smithsonian oral history interview. "I was walking through the streets. There were street musicians playing in $\frac{9}{8}$." He repeated the rhythm over and over, and was inspired to build *Blue Rondo à la Turk* around the rhythm.

Blue Rondo was included in Brubeck's 1959 album *Time Out*, consisting entirely of pieces with unusual time signatures or meters. Defying the recording company's reluctance ("undanceable," an executive sniffed), *Time Out* became one of the best-selling jazz recordings ever. Two tunes from that album—*Blue Rondo à la Turk* and *Take Five* (in $\frac{5}{4}$ meter)—were issued in 1960, on opposite sides of a 45-rpm disc, selling an extraordinary million copies—highly unusual for a jazz recording.

Key Features

- Instrumentation: This recording exemplifies one of the most popular small ensembles in jazz: a quartet of piano, bass, drums, and saxophone (another common quartet consists of piano, bass, drums, and trumpet).
- Rhythm: The tempo is 140 beats per minute—what jazz musicians called "medium-up." What was highly unusual, even innovative, about the rhythm was its use of $\frac{9}{8}$ meter and the way the measures of $\frac{9}{8}$ were subdivided into rhythmic groupings. Whereas in classical music, works in $\frac{9}{8}$ rhythm were divided regularly into beats of 3+3+3, here the main theme features three measures subdivided 2+2+2+3—an irregular rhythm—followed by a measure subdivided 3+3+3. In the middle of the recording, the band alternates between $\frac{9}{8}$ and $\frac{4}{4}$, and then goes into eight choruses of straight $\frac{4}{4}$ rhythm. These large and small rhythmic shifts took considerable skill to perform and took audiences some getting used to.
- Style: The two soloists—Brubeck and Desmond—play in contrasting styles. Brubeck's firm piano playing—sometimes in block chords—tends to ground the performance, while Desmond's ethereal lines lift it skyward.
- Musicians' roles: The piano and bass take the lead not only in keeping the time but in switching time signatures from $\frac{4}{4}$ to $\frac{9}{8}$ and back and forth. Pianist Brubeck switches among four different roles: as sole presenter of the melody (for example, from 0:00 to 0:11 and 0:22 to 0:32); as co-presenter, with saxophonist Desmond, of the melody; as improvising soloist (3:52 to 5:32); and, from 2:13 to 3:51, as silent partner: during Desmond's solo, Brubeck stops playing completely.
- Form and structure: This recording features perhaps the most complex structure of any discussed in this book. Composer Brubeck has created a unique form that accentuates considerable contrast, juxtaposing the following: major- and minor-key melodies; exacting rapid-fire melodies with space for easy playing; a weighty piano lead with the airy alto sax sound of Paul Desmond; the non-danceable $\frac{9}{8}$ with a swinging $\frac{4}{4}$.
- Voice, feel, expression: A cool ambience is conveyed by Paul Desmond's airy, light Lester Young–like sound on alto saxophone. Although part of the piece is in blues form, there is very little blues tonality—blue notes, vocal-like slides and slurs—and the performance seems somewhat restrained emotionally in comparison with much jazz.

—*John Edward Hasse*

TIME	FORM	BARS	METER	MELODY/INSTRUMENTATION
0:00	A	8	$\frac{9}{8}$	Piano states main theme, built around a descending two-note figure in F major. At 0:05, bass joins piano: each measure, the bass plays four notes on the same pitch. Drummer plays few notes on cymbal.
0:11	A'	8		Sax enters to play a variation on the first four measures in A minor. Drums more active.
0:22	A	8		Sax drops out; piano plays main theme in F major. Drums now play continuously.
0:33	B	8		B theme (in A minor) is a variation of the A theme: built around repeating two-note figures, first ascending, then descending.
0:44	A	8		Sax and piano play main theme in F major in two-part harmony.
0:55	C	8		Piano, bass, drums alone.
1:07	A	8		Sax plays main theme in F major.
1:18	D	14		Percussive theme in A minor—played alternately by piano and sax—with longer notes than themes A or B.
1:38	E	8		From 1:38, no sax: piano plays thunderous chords. In key of A minor.
1:52	F	12	$\frac{4}{4}$ alternates with $\frac{9}{8}$	Now in F major. An ingenious transition from the preceding material to blues choruses that follow. Sax improvises two bars in $\frac{4}{4}$; sax drops out for two measures as piano plays A-section melody in $\frac{9}{8}$ meter. Bass walks during the $\frac{4}{4}$ measures; reverts to four unison notes per measure in $\frac{9}{8}$ passages.
2:13	G: IMPROVISED SOLOS	12	$\frac{4}{4}$	Piano drops out; sax plays solo over 12-bar blues progression. Walking bass defines the harmonic movement through the blues progression.
2:37		12		Second blues chorus: Desmond leaves space (rests) so that his solo line can breathe.
3:01		12		Third blues chorus.
3:26		12		Fourth blues chorus. Sax has built solo to climax, playing higher notes and blues inflections (3:25 and 3:36).
3:52	H: IMPROVISED SOLOS	12	$\frac{4}{4}$	Sax drops out; piano solo (12-bar blues): Brubeck transitions smoothly from the piano-less solo of Desmond by initially avoiding left-hand chords, instead playing single-note lines in his right hand. Walking bass continues.
4:16		12		Second blues chorus: By bar five (4:25), Brubeck has built to full chords.
4:43		12		Third blues chorus: He maintains the intensity of the previous chorus.
5:08		12		Fourth blues chorus: Brubeck returns to a single-note line to prepare for the transitional section with sax. He incorporates rests, which both serve to outline his phrases and draw attention to the playing of the bassist and drummer.
5:33	F	12	$\frac{4}{4}$ alternates with $\frac{9}{8}$	Band repeats material from 1:52 to 2:12, again ingeniously transitioning out of the blues into the main theme in $\frac{9}{8}$ meter.
5:54	A	8	$\frac{9}{8}$	The band restates the theme in F major. Sax is silent until 5:57.
6:03	D	14		In A minor, sax plays two bars with piano doubling the melody. Then piano plays two bars with no sax. This pattern repeats several times.
6:23	E	9		Sax drops out. Piece ends in A minor.

---

rondo a multisectional musical form, dating from the Baroque period, in which the principal theme alternates with other themes; for example ABACADA.

Jazz and Religion

Does jazz have a spiritual dimension?

At first glance, jazz and religion may seem as incompatible as gambling and God. Indeed, early on, jazz and the blues were often denounced as "the devil's music," regarded as disreputable by middle-class blacks and whites alike. Such attitudes took many years to soften. But jazz and religion have been connected in a number of ways—even beyond the obvious link between certain musicians' tastes and their formative experiences hearing church singing.

Early New Orleans jazz musicians performed such religious songs as *Glory, Sing On, In Gloryland* (*JTSA* Disc 1/Track 2), and *Down by the Riverside*. Still, in 1938, Louis Armstrong raised some eyebrows when he made swinging recordings of *Bye and Bye, When the Saints Go Marching In*, and other Negro spirituals.

Some jazz composers went to the spiritual well for inspiration. Duke Ellington composed the ravishing *Come Sunday* for his epic *Black, Brown, and Beige* (1943) and, commissioned by San Francisco's Grace Cathedral, wrote the controversial *Concert of Sacred Music* (1965). Two other sacred concerts followed (1968, 1973).

Bassist-composer Charles Mingus, inspired in part by his mother's visits to Methodist and Holiness churches, wrote *Wednesday Night Prayer Meeting* (1958) and *Better Git It in Your Soul* (1959; *JTSA* Disc 4/Track 5) —raucous, wailing pieces with hand-clapping, shouting, spontaneous bursts of emotion, and simultaneous improvisation. Gospel-influenced pieces such as Horace Silver's *The Preacher* (1955) and Cannonball Adderley's *Sermonette* (1956) echoed call-and-response patterns of down-home African American churches. Pianist Mary Lou Williams composed a

cantata, *Black Christ of the Andes* (1963), and three masses, and Django Reinhardt and Lalo Schifrin each wrote a jazz mass.

John Coltrane, after experiencing a religious awakening in 1957, composed and recorded a number of spiritual works that included *Amen* and *Dear Lord* (both 1965) and the mighty *A Love Supreme* (1964). "God," he wrote, "is gracious and merciful. His way is in love. . . . truly—a love supreme."

Beyond specific religiously inspired pieces, many people found jazz meaningful on a deep, spiritual basis. Perhaps echoing the ancient African integration of music, dance, ritual, religion, and daily life, jazz's "mysterious power to evoke ecstasy" and transcendence, as scholar Neil Leonard observed, made it magical or sacred to countless participants. No wonder many jazz adherents maintain such deep allegiance to the music.

—*John Edward Hasse*

---

made listeners think he'd gone back to overdub his solos. In the mid-1960s, he became one of the most popular jazz performers due to a series of albums with orchestra that emphasized his flowing sound (but not his brilliant solo constructions). Montgomery also formed a partnership with Jimmy Smith heard on *Jimmy & Wes: The Dynamic Duo* (1966) and *The Further Adventures of Jimmy and Wes* (1966), the latter including the track *King of the Road* (*JTSA* Disc 5/ Track 6).

Green, meanwhile, came out of St. Louis with a ringing, shouting tone—tailor-made for soul jazz—and a powerfully direct style of soloing that placed him in great demand as a member of the Blue Note Records "stable": in 1961 alone, he served as either leader or sideman on 19 different record sessions, most notably on *Green Street* (1961). These three guitarists did much to make the instrument an increasingly strong

Wes Montgomery, one of the most significant and influential jazz guitarists, infused bop-blues phrasing with swinging energy. PHOTO COURTESY LEE TANNER.

Down Beat and the Jazz Magazines

Jazz magazines have come and gone with dizzying frequency. More than 800 jazz periodicals have been published in the United States and abroad, but most long ago ceased publication. At the end of jazz's first century, the best known included *Down Beat*, *Jazz Times*, and *Jazziz* (all in the United States); *Coda* (Canada); *Jazz Journal International* (United Kingdom); *Jazz magazine* and *Jazz hot* (France); *Orkester Journalen* (Sweden); *Musica Jazz* (Italy); and *Swing Journal* (Japan). In the early twenty-first century, several of them were no longer publishing. But others expanded with robust Internet sites, and newer entrants such as allaboutjazz.com redefined the notion of jazz coverage, combining journalism with multimedia programming and services for the jazz community. The Internet enabled a proliferation of other special-interest jazz information sites.

One of the jazz magazines, *Down Beat*, boasts a special place in jazz history. Of the English-language jazz magazines, it has survived the longest: since 1934. And along the way—through jazz's roller-coaster ride through changing sonic landscapes and jumps and dips in popularity—it stayed on track as the magazine that U.S. fans and musicians thought of first when seeking jazz information.

With its record and concert reviews, interviews, readers' polls, and educational features, *Down Beat* not only supported the efforts of working musicians but also inspired new generations to follow in the footsteps of their musical heroes.

The magazine helped launch the careers of some leading jazz writers, among them Dan Morgenstern, Nat Hentoff, and Gary Giddins. It also invited musicians to submit commentary, and many—including Jelly Roll Morton, Duke Ellington, Marian McPartland, Kenny Dorham, and Ornette Coleman—took them up on it, with sometimes controversial results. *Down Beat* ultimately codified musician participation in a feature called the Blindfold Test, in which musicians would listen to unidentified recordings and offer their critiques.

The magazine rose to popularity during the swing era, linking its fortunes with those of the big bands and players it advocated—including Duke Ellington, Benny Goodman, Woody Herman, and Jimmy Dorsey. When those fortunes began to sag, *Down Beat* was left seeking ways to maintain financial viability at a time when jazz—in its new bebop, cool, and experimental incarnations—was becoming a music of the devoted few rather than the general public.

Its answer, in part, was to focus on jazz education; by providing instructional articles, drawing attention to young talent in a "First Chorus" column, co-sponsoring instrumental clinics and music festivals, and conferring scholarships through its Student Music Awards, it would build its future readership. That approach took *Down Beat* into the 1960s and what some observers consider the magazine's heyday, as it was, to an extent, a heyday of mainstream jazz.

The arrival of the rock era and of magazines that chronicled its culture—*Rolling Stone*, for one—brought another turning point. With jazz eclipsed by the popularity of the Beatles, Jimi Hendrix, and other rock stars, the magazine faced the quandary of maintaining its strictly jazz focus or branching out and covering the many other new popular styles. It chose the latter route, and its decision to do so reflected what many jazz musicians were doing: drawing from increasingly varied musical sources for creative fuel and inspiration.

Down Beat later adapted to evolving technology, too, launching a Web site. The magazine's broadened content and expanded media reach were further indicators of the growing pluralism—and resilience—of jazz itself.

—*Tad Lathrop and John Edward Hasse*

COURTESY JOHN EDWARD HASSE.

Kenny Burrell's precision, taste, and warm tone embodied mainstream jazz guitar. PHOTO COURTESY MICHAEL WILDERMAN.

in Ghana (1960), and Morgan's *The Sidewinder* (1964).

Morgan and Freddie Hubbard (his successor on trumpet in the Jazz Messengers) both came naturally to this idiom, having played a fair amount of "the funk" with Blakey. And both were able to transcend the rapidly accumulating soul-jazz clichés to create rich and lasting albums, including Morgan's *Search for the New Land* (1964), Hubbard's *Ready for Freddie* (1961) and *Breaking Point* (1964), and their 1965 face-off, the aptly titled *Night of the Cookers*.

Many of these albums starred pianist Herbie Hancock, for whom soul jazz held the greatest value. A child prodigy who performed with the Chicago Symphony at the age of 12, Hancock was a vital member of Miles Davis's progressive 1960s quintet. But on his own, Hancock showed a penchant for soul jazz, beginning with his Blue Note debut, *Takin' Off* (1962), an album that included *Watermelon Man*, which became a funk standard. A prolific and important composer, Hancock hit his stride on the 1965 album *Maiden Voyage*, a jazz exploration of the ocean's mysteries that remains a mainstream milestone.

presence in jazz during the 1960s, paralleling the rise of guitar-driven rock.

Around 1960, soul jazz became the preferred description for this branch of hard bop, after the term was applied to the recordings of alto saxophonist Cannonball Adderley. A technically brilliant and emotionally dynamic player, Adderley sported a brimming, almost fulsome tone and an impressive bag of expressive tricks. He and his younger brother, cornetist Nat, had moved in 1955 from their native Florida to New York, where jazz aficionados quickly discovered the white-hot talent beneath Cannonball's heavy drawl and country manner. After leaving Miles Davis's band in 1960, Cannonball founded a quintet with his brother; it also starred a noted Jazz Messengers alumnus in pianist and composer Bobby Timmons, and it quickly emerged as the most popular band on the hard bop scene. Prime examples of Adderley's soul jazz are present on the retrospective album *Phenix* (1975).

Even musicians whose main interests lay elsewhere—the progressive Charles Mingus, the darkly emotional alto saxophonist Jackie McLean, and Lee Morgan (a tough and even menacing presence on trumpet)—recorded famous examples of soul jazz. These include Mingus's *Better Git It in Your Soul* (1959; *JTSA* Disc 4/ Track 5), McLean's *Appointment*

Cannonball and Nat Adderley performing in Denmark, 1961. PHOTO COURTESY JP JAZZ ARCHIVE/ REDFERNS/GETTY IMAGES.

Jazz Festivals

The proliferation of jazz festivals—events showcasing multiple artists, sometimes over several days—occurred in tandem with the increasing perception of jazz as music to listen to rather than simply to dance, imbibe, or converse to.

Festivals offered audiences and musicians alike an alternative to cramped, noisy, smoky clubs. In often idyllic settings, listeners could enjoy a broad spectrum of artists playing a range of jazz styles—or different approaches to one style if the festival happened to focus on a particular theme.

For musicians, jazz festivals provided an important outlet. With hundreds of such gatherings presented around the globe every year, they added up to an international "circuit" that could keep bands on the road when nightclub gigs were hard to come by.

An International Jazz Congress was held in Chicago in 1926, but the festival idea didn't catch on until the presentation of the Festival Internationale du Jazz, held in Paris in 1949, which offered a wide range of U.S. and European performers. In years that followed, the Newport Jazz Festival (launched in 1954 and captured on film in the 1960 documentary *Jazz on a Summer's Day*) emerged as a leading stateside showcase, as did the Monterey Jazz Festival, founded in 1958 by disc jockey Jimmy Lyons and jazz critic Ralph Gleason. A half century later, continuing U.S. festivals included George Wein's Jazz Festival in New York, the Concord Jazz Festival in California, the still-active Monterey fest, the Chicago Jazz Festival, and the New Orleans Jazz and Heritage Festival.

COURTESY JOHN EDWARD HASSE.

Events also cropped up in other parts of the world, including nearly every European country.

Switzerland hosted one of the world's highest-profile yearly jazz events, the Montreux Jazz Festival (over time, mixing jazz with varied kinds of pop music); France drew visitors yearly to its Paris Jazz Festival; Germany staged festivals in Berlin, Köln, and Frankfurt; the Netherlands' North Sea Jazz Festival enjoyed a long run and gained a reputation as the world's largest jazz festival; the UK's offerings included an Edinburgh-based event; and Canada staged jazz fests all across the country, from Halifax and Montreal in the East to Victoria and Vancouver in the West.

Theme-based events included the Imatra Big Band Festival in Finland, the Festival of New Orleans Music in Switzerland, and the free-jazz Total Music Meeting in Germany.

Eventually, jazz festivals were being held in such far-flung places as St. Petersburg, Istanbul, Melbourne, Tokyo, Beijing, and even the islands of St. Lucia and Jamaica—proving that jazz had truly become a global art form.

—*Tad Lathrop*

In his early, pre-synthesizer years, Herbie Hancock penned such mainstream classics as Maiden Voyage and Dolphin Dance. He is shown here in performance in 2004.
PHOTO COURTESY MICHAEL WILDERMAN.

Continuing Traditions

During this period, earlier jazz styles didn't just fold up and die. In fact, every previous idiom not only coexisted but also still thrived—and usually in the work of the musicians who had invented it. In 1955, such legends as Louis Armstrong and Earl Hines were still in early middle age, many of the swing giants maintained rigorous performing schedules, and the bebop rebels had just approached their prime. Jazz had yet to place Duke Ellington, Billie Holiday, Parker, and Gillespie on pedestals; fans were too busy checking out their latest records.

In fact, during the 1950s Ellington entered the second great arc of his storied career, during which his fame eclipsed even his previous success. This "comeback" began at the Newport Jazz Festival in 1956, where Paul Gonsalves's intense, 27-chorus tenor saxophone solo on Ellington's *Diminuendo in Blue* set the crowd (and then those who bought the *Ellington at Newport* album) on fire. From then until the end of his life (1974), Ellington and Billy Strayhorn spent increasing amounts of time on larger works, many of which are considered their greatest accomplishments: *Such Sweet Thunder* (1956–57), based on characters and themes from Shakespeare; Ellington's score for the film *Anatomy of a Murder* (1959); their *Far East Suite* (1966); and the *Second Sacred Concert* (1968).

In the work of other artists, the various eras of jazz flowed together, combining aspects of swing, bop, and

Listen to *Isfahan* from Duke Ellington's *Far East Suite* (*JTSA* Disc 5/Track 7)

Hear the Thad Jones-Mel Lewis Orchestra live at the Village Vanguard on **mymusiclab.com**

Soul jazz made dozens of converts, moving mainstream jazz further toward funk (and recapturing some of the audience that had turned to rock and roll). Pioneers and newcomers alike rubbed shoulders in the recording studios of Blue Note, Prestige, and Atlantic Records. Soul jazz even found its way into the relatively few big bands that established themselves during the 1960s as descendants of engines that powered the swing era.

In this sector, two important figures rose above the rest. Trumpeter and composer-arranger Thad Jones built upon his experience in the Count Basie Orchestra to add soul jazz to the big-band repertoire; the **Thad Jones-Mel Lewis Orchestra**, which began as a Monday night "**rehearsal band**" at New York's Village Vanguard, eventually set the standard for modern big band power. And saxophonist Oliver Nelson, who had worked for jump–band leader Louis Jordan in the early 1950s, offered imaginatively soulful renditions of his own tunes, notably on the album *The Blues and the Abstract Truth* (1961)—a perennial favorite led by its centerpiece, *Stolen Moments*.

TAKE NOTE

- What is soul jazz and how does it differ from hard bop?

Cool jazz man Stan Getz got hotter as the 1950s unfolded.
PHOTO COURTESY DOWN BEAT ARCHIVES.

---

rehearsal band   group of musicians who meet to rehearse and play for each other rather than for the public.

((•— **Listen** to *I'll Remember April* by Errol Garner
(*JTSA* Disc 3/Track 9)

cool into styles both unique and popular. Pianist **Erroll Garner**, for example, used an insistent left-hand pulse (à la the 1930s), angular bop syncopations, and richly chorded harmonies in creating perhaps the most popular jazz sound of the 1950s, heard on best-selling records (*Concert by the Sea*, 1955) and network-television variety shows. The song *Misty* (1954), for which Garner wrote the music, is one of the most performed 1950s-era compositions. The brilliant tenor saxophonist Stan Getz, previously associated with bebop and cool, reflected both schools in his spectacularly communicative style, at home in both the intimate setting of a quintet, as on *Stan Getz Plays* (1952–54), and the grand stage of orchestral strings, as on his 1961 collaboration with arranger Eddie Sauter, *Focus*.

TAKE NOTE

- How did earlier jazz traditions and groups grow and thrive during this period?

Vocalists of the Mainstream Era

The 1950s didn't launch many new vocalists, largely because so many of the "old" ones were still around—and in many cases sounding better than ever. The swing

Billie Holiday, though past her prime, continued to work during the 1950s. Time had diminished her vocal range but seasoned her interpretative abilities. PHOTO COURTESY DOWN BEAT ARCHIVES.

Frank Sinatra and Ella Fitzgerald, both master song stylists. PHOTO COURTESY DOWN BEAT ARCHIVES.

era star Ella Fitzgerald reinvented herself not once but twice: in the 1940s she had become a terrific bop singer, and now she recorded a series of "songbook" albums celebrating the great American composers of popular music—including George and Ira Gershwin, Irving Berlin, Harold Arlen, Rodgers and Hart, and Cole Porter—that made her a national treasure. Sarah Vaughan, meanwhile, had to refashion herself only once: from the bebop rebel who scatted with Bird and Diz to a voluptuously swinging pop star who never lost her jazz roots. Yet when she placed her voice before a symphony orchestra—as on *Sarah Vaughan Sings George Gershwin* (1954–57)—she became the closest thing to an operatic diva jazz has ever known. (Listen to her version of *Wrap Your Troubles in Dreams*, *JTSA* Disc 4/Track 9). The work of Mel Tormé, the gifted wunderkind who had achieved fame in the 1940s, gained depth and chiseled his credentials as a great improviser on a par with Fitzgerald (as on *Mel Tormé Swings Shubert Alley*, 1960); the same could be said of **Anita O'Day,** who had created the mold for cool jazz singers as a member of Stan Kenton's band in the 1940s and, on such albums as *Pick Yourself Up* (1956), proved herself among the most intelligently swinging vocalists of the 1950s and 1960s. (Listen to early O'Day on *Let Me Off Uptown*, *JTSA* Disc 2/Track 11.)

Nat "King" Cole, best known as a pop singing star, was also an influential pre-bebop pianist and one of the great jazz singers. His rich baritone, liquid phrasing, excellent diction, warmth of tone, and superb musicianship won him a huge following among audiences, black and white, starting with his hip hit from 1943, *Straighten Up and Fly*

Jazz & the Arts

Jazz on Television

Television may have become a vast wasteland, as critics liked to point out, but jazz fans could occasionally find their music on the "box"—though it wasn't always easy. In television's early years, traditional jazz styles could be found on *Eddie Condon's Floor Show* (NBC and CBS, 1949–50), with such regulars as Wild Bill Davison and Pee Wee Russell; *Chicago Jazz*, featuring Art Van Damme and the Tailgate 7 (NBC, 1949); and *Adventures in Jazz* (CBS, 1949). The music was upbeat and accessible, and it usually stayed within the bounds of mainstream tastes—and racial preferences.

But at a time when segregation was still legal in much of the United States, television's increasing use of African American musicians in the 1950s helped chip away at the color line. Black jazz musicians not only performed on television but often did so in racially integrated groups. Well before the civil rights movement reached its peak, pianist Hazel Scott had her own network series (Dumont, 1950). What's more, television presented black musicians as artists, not just entertainers. On "The Sound of Miles Davis" (*The Robert Herridge Theater*, CBS, 1958), there was no shucking or jiving, no corny comedy bits; it was filmed with all the dignity and respect given to symphonic broadcasts. In the button-down Eisenhower era, *The Sound of Jazz* (CBS, 1959) enabled Americans to experience the work of such iconoclasts and nonconformists as Thelonious Monk and Lester Young.

Still, there was resistance to jazz on the part of some program sponsors. *The Nat "King" Cole Show* (NBC, 1956–57) featured **Ella Fitzgerald**, Billy Eckstine, and stars from Jazz at the Philharmonic, including Coleman Hawkins, Roy Eldridge, and **Oscar Peterson**, but the show was canceled due to sponsors' fears of alienating white southern viewers. Some shows got around such fears by appealing to a more highbrow, presumably more tolerant, audience. *Omnibus* (CBS and ABC, 1953–57), with host Alistair Cooke, is remembered for its sophisticated approach to classical and jazz music; on one broadcast it offered a reunion of the groundbreaking, racially integrated Benny Goodman Trio with Teddy Wilson and Gene Krupa.

Musicians Duke Ellington, Steve Allen, and Billy Taylor were instrumental in bringing jazz to a wider TV audience. Ellington was charming, articulate, and telegenic, as evidenced by his appearances on the *Bell Telephone Hour* (NBC, 1959 and 1967); *The U.S. Steel Hour* (CBS, 1957); and *Duke Ellington: Love You Madly* (National Educational Television [NET], 1967). On such shows, he achieved the rare balance of art and entertainment.

Pianist, composer, and comedian Steve Allen also managed to straddle the highbrow-middlebrow divide. *The Steve Allen Show* (NBC, 1956–58) featured jazz artists on a regular basis, including a memorable remote broadcast from Birdland by Count Basie's orchestra.

Pianist Billy Taylor became a mainstay jazz figure on TV, from

his musical-directorship of NET's first jazz series, *The Subject Is Jazz*, in 1958 to his ongoing role as arts correspondent for CBS's *Sunday Morning*.

When jazz wasn't the focal point its sound was used to evocative ends. Crime and detective shows used jazz music to suggest gritty realism or to convey a character's inner thoughts, notably on *Naked City* (ABC, 1958–63), with its theme by Billy May; *M Squad* (NBC, 1957–60) with music by Count Basie; *Asphalt Jungle* (ABC, 1961), for which Ellington wrote the opening music; and the highly successful jazz score by Henry Mancini for *Peter Gunn* (NBC and ABC, 1958–61).

In the late 1950s and early 1960s, network television largely ignored jazz, but things were different over at public television. NET—the precursor to the Public Broadcasting System (PBS)—didn't rely on ratings or sponsors, so it occasionally ventured into more modern, even avant-garde territory. Ralph J. Gleason's *Jazz Casual* series, for example, bravely devoted entire programs to performances by the quartets of John Coltrane (1964) and Charles Lloyd (1968). Another NET series, *Music U.S.A.*, presented a program titled "The Experimenters" with groups led by Charles Mingus and Cecil Taylor, including analysis and commentary by critic Martin Williams and novelist Ralph Ellison (1967). In tandem with America's rightward turn in the Reagan era of the 1980s, PBS programming became more conservative. But jazz continued to find airtime, notably in

Woody Herman on Cavalcade of Bands, *which ran from January 1950 to September 1951.* PHOTO COURTESY WILLIAM KAHN/ DOWN BEAT ARCHIVES.

alternative hip hop. In 2009, jazz was dropped and BET J was rebranded as Centric, a general-interest channel aimed at African American adults.

In 2001, PBS broadcast an ambitious 19-hour documentary miniseries titled *Jazz: A Film By Ken Burns*, featuring a narrative script written by Geoffrey C. Ward, historic film clips, and extensive interviews with prominent musicians, critics, and academics. The series stirred considerable controversy and criticism in jazz circles due to what some perceived as conservative bias and short shrift given to jazz after 1960. Five years later, PBS broadcast 12 episodes of a new series, *The Legends of Jazz*, hosted by Ramsey Lewis and featuring live studio performances and interviews.

As broadcast and cable outlets struggled with dwindling audiences, new and historic jazz television performances found a home on video-sharing Web sites such as YouTube, allowing collectors to post clips from off the air and from older video and film formats, many of which are commercially unavailable. YouTube and other such sites have been criticized and sued for failing to ensure that their online content adheres to copyright laws.

—*Larry Appelbaum*

the series *American Masters* and *Great Performances*.

Meanwhile, jazz found an increasingly hospitable place on commercial cable television. BET on Jazz, backed by Robert Johnson's Black Entertainment Television, became the United States' most ambitious attempt to create a channel devoted solely to jazz music and its offshoots. However, at the close of the century it was still struggling to find an audience and sponsor. In an attempt to increase audience and market share, BET re-branded by changing the name of the channel to BET Jazz in 2002, then in 2006 to BET J as it shifted from jazz to R&B, neo soul, and

Listening Guide

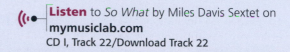**Listen** to *So What* by Miles Davis Sextet on
mymusiclab.com
CD I, Track 22/Download Track 22

SO WHAT • MILES DAVIS SEXTET

Music: Miles Davis, 1959. Personnel: Miles Davis (trumpet, leader); Cannonball Adderley (alto saxophone); John Coltrane (tenor saxophone); Bill Evans (piano); Paul Chambers (bass); Jimmy Cobb (drums). Recorded March 2, 1959, in New York. First issue: Columbia CL2126. Timing: 9:26.

Overview

Like the other four pieces on Miles Davis's 1959 album *Kind of Blue, So What* remains a cultural touchstone as well as a splendid and memorable musical experience. The entire album introduced the general public to a new organizing principle for jazz: modal improvisation. *So What*, the leadoff track and arguably the catchiest piece on the album, became a jazz standard, thanks to the original recording's evocation of "cool"; to the galvanic sax solos; and in part to the lyrics written and recorded later by vocalist Eddie Jefferson, which captured Davis's ambivalent public persona ("Miles Davis walked off the stage / *So what!*").

Key Features

- Melody: The melody of *So What* is almost comically simple. The entire melody consists of the same two-measure phrase, repeated 16 times (although it is transposed in measures 17–24). The melody updates the call-and-response technique found in field hollers, blues, and gospel, with Paul Chambers's bass stating the main line, answered every two measures by a two-note response.
- Form: A **rubato** (non-rhythmic) introduction by piano and bass precedes the 32-bar theme. This theme conforms to the traditional AABA structure, but is also novel in its simplicity. The first 16 measures essentially rest on one chord, followed by the bridge—which is nothing more than eight measures of the exact same melody, transposed up a half-step to a new harmonic center—and then a return to the initial chord.
- Blues feeling: Because the only harmonic movement is to the key one-half step up from the **tonic**—which here serves a function similar to that of the **subdominant** in the blues—the tune has a different form than the blues. But it still retains the emotional feel of a mid-tempo jazz blues.

Watch the video of Miles Davis's *So What* on **mymusiclab.com** for a comparison with this recorded performance.

Compare the video version of *So What* on **mymusiclab.com**

- Improvisation: The three main soloists present a striking variety of post-bop jazz solo styles: Davis, the spare, cool architect rebelling against bop's flurrying complexity; Coltrane, the fiery explorer, seeking new avenues for that complexity; and Adderley, the lyrical exponent of the soul jazz style that would grow especially popular in the 1960s.
- Davis's solo uses notes outlining chords as a unifying principle; he begins his solo outlining a D minor seventh chord, shifts to scalar melodies, and then returns to chord tones. Coltrane starts simply, but quickly launches into his famous "sheets of sound"; the tune's modal framework is quite congruent with his scalar approach. Adderley's solo incorporates both Davis's interest in chord tones and Coltrane's interest in

A much more blatant attack on convention than that of Bill Evans marks the work of Charles Mingus. Although his fluid and inventive technique raised the bar for jazz bassists, history remembers him mainly as a brilliant (if mercurial) bandleader—and the most important jazz composer after Duke Ellington. A self-professed descendent of Ellington and Monk, Mingus wrote the tenderest of ballads—among them his elegant threnody for Lester Young, *Goodbye Pork Pie Hat*, from the 1959 masterpiece *Mingus Ah Um*—as well as the most boisterous hard bop anthems (*Haitian Fight Song*, 1955, and *Hora Decubitis*, 1963). Some pieces, such as *The Clown* (from the 1957 album of the same name) combine jazz and poetry; on such tunes as *Wednesday Night Prayer Meeting* (1959) and *Hog Callin' Blues* (1961), Mingus combined soul jazz and satire. Like Ellington, he envisioned jazz on a wider scale than did most of his contemporaries, then used the musical materials of the time—in this case, the sharply angled melodies and vibrant rhythms of hard bop—to realize his vision.

The blind visionary and multi-instrumentalist Roland Kirk created a quite different blend of jazz tradition with the freedom cry. In the mid-1960s, Kirk adopted the name Rahsaan, which he said had come

Watch *Up With the Lark* by Bill Evans on **mymusiclab.com**

---

rubato   freely; played expressively without adhering to a strict beat.

tonic   the root of a key.

subdominant   the fourth degree of the scale.

scales, but also includes examples of his irrepressible tunefulness.
- Stylistic variety: This piece, like the rest of *Kind of Blue*, belongs to both the past and its own future. It mostly contains familiar, mainstream elements, yet offers a path to improvisatory freedom, which would influence the avant-garde and progressive-jazz styles that supplanted bop in the 1960s.
- Dynamics: This track ranges from the pianissimo introduction to the full-throated cries of Adderley's alto. The theme statement itself, with the main melody carried by the bass, offers a radically different sound and texture than those found in most music of the day.

—*Neil Tesser*

TIME	SECTION	INSTRUMENTATION	MELODY
0:00	INTRO	Piano and bass	Piano and bass set a mysterious, out-of-tempo mood.
0:33	CHORUS 1 (THEME)	Bass lead, piano, horns	Bassist Paul Chambers presents the melody, with call-and-response replies from piano and then horns (0:50).
1:31	CHORUS 2	Trumpet	Davis begins two-chorus trumpet solo with notes from the D minor seventh chord. (2:01) He shifts to scalar movement, then, at the final A, returns to chord tones.
2:28	CHORUS 3		Davis starts the next chorus with notes outlining an A minor seventh chord—even though the key is D minor. This juxtaposition highlights the unique character of the underlying modal scale.
3:26	CHORUS 4	Tenor saxophone	Coltrane picks up on the last phrase of Davis's solo to start his own, then (3:40) returns to scalar movement. (4:08–4:19) Repeating a phrase hinted at earlier in the solo, Coltrane finds a motif that propels his solo into its second chorus.
4:19	CHORUS 5		This "propeller" motif bridges and unifies the two choruses of Coltrane's solo.
5:16	CHORUS 6*	Alto saxophone	After extensive use of scalar movement *and* larger intervals, Adderley "turns the time around" with a phrase that intersects the bridge and the last A section of his first chorus.
6:23	CHORUS 7*		Adderley lands on an idea—five notes on the beat—and repeats it.
7:06	CHORUS 8*	Piano	In the piano solo, the call-and-response pattern is reversed: the "response" (horn figure) moves to the front of each phrase, with Evans's piano "call" coming in response.
8:03			This unusual eight-bar insertion marks time until the theme returns.
8:15	THEME**	Bass lead, piano, horns	Bass plays main melody; piano and horns answer.
9:12	SLOW FADE**		

*In order to fit the accompanying CD I, choruses 6–8 are omitted. The full recording is on the mymusiclab.com download and also on *JTSA*.
**On the CD version the Theme begins at 5:16 and the Slow Fade starts at 6:13.

to him in a dream; another dream inspired him to resurrect two archaic reed instruments, the manzello and stritch. These he played simultaneously with his main instrument, the tenor saxophone—three horns at once, with Kirk using countermelodies to accompany himself and **circular-breathing** techniques to play for minutes at a time without stopping for a breath. His critics saw only a freak show, but Kirk's extraordinary musicianship (as on *The Inflated Tear*, 1968) allowed him to bridge genres and impart a great deal of Mingus-like humor and satire.

But as the 1950s closed, it was Miles Davis who once again shifted the mainstream in a new direction.

Davis had already combined jazz and classical techniques on a series of Columbia albums, starting with *Miles Ahead* (1957), that reunited him with his *Birth of the Cool* (1949–50) colleague, arranger Gil Evans. These were really jazz concertos, as Evans's limpid, textured writing supported and engaged Davis's trumpet; on the famous *Sketches of Spain* (1959–60), Evans adapted a classical piece, *Concierto de Aranjuez*, penned by Joaquin Rodrigo in 1939.

With the 1959 landmark *Kind of Blue*, however, Davis instigated the most significant development in jazz since his creation of *The Cool*. On this album, he fully explored modal improvisation—which had shown up a year earlier on *Milestones* (1958)—instructing his band members to use preselected modes as the basis for their solos. These modes were specific scales named by the ancient Greeks, including but not

---

circular breathing   technique used in playing wind instruments that permits continuous, unbroken phrasing.

limited to the standard major and minor; they replaced the chord progressions that had controlled jazz improvisation since bebop, liberating the soloists from bop's "tyranny of chords" and forcing them to look in new directions. (To further spark innovation, Davis presented this new musical puzzle to his players just a few hours before the recording session.) This new style was called **modal jazz**.

The aesthetic and commercial success of *Kind of Blue* pointed to new possibilities, specifically for musicians such as Jackie McLean—a fiery alto saxist who had never quite fit in as a hard bopper but who embraced the new freedom with such albums as *One Step Beyond* (1963). McLean's work—and that of his Blue Note Records colleagues vibraphonist Bobby Hutcherson, trombonist Grachan Moncur III, pianist Andrew Hill, and keyboardist Larry Young—widened the jazz mainstream considerably, incorporating the revolutionary spirit that would soon rock every aspect of the 1960s.

Davis himself found it impossible to stand pat. By 1964 he had completely rebuilt his quintet into a band that artfully dodged easy characterization—except for "Miles Davis's greatest band." Its brilliant balance of talents reached an acme on *Miles Smiles* (1966), in

---

modal jazz   a style of jazz developed in the late 1950s in which modal scales serve as the basis of improvisation.

performances that remained "mainstream" but reveled in looser song structures descended from Davis's modal music. The music pivoted on the elastic interplay between drummer Tony Williams (who joined Davis in 1963, at the age of 17) and pianist Herbie Hancock (only six years older than Williams). Ron Carter's malleable bass glued the rhythm section. And Wayne Shorter's elliptical solos presented a new model for modern tenor saxophonists, while his concise and memorable compositions—among them *Witch Hunt* and *Infant Eyes* (both 1965), *Footprints* and *Dolores* (1966), and *Pinocchio* (1967)—marked him as the most important writer since Monk and Mingus.

With this band, Davis sailed swiftly through the 1960s and 1970s, helping to pilot jazz through its most turbulent period in three decades. Others who made their marks in the 1950s and 1960s would be there as well, continuing to hone their skills and exploring new ways to apply them.

✳ **Explore** Jazz Classics and Key Recordings on mymusiclab.com

TAKE NOTE

- What other jazz styles were prominent during this time and how did they differ from the more dominant styles?

TAKE NOTE

- What currents in American society influenced the development of jazz in the 1950s?

Although the 1950s are remembered as a decade when conformity and mainstream values flourished, there were also innovations in technology and race relations during the period. New, longer recording formats allowed jazz musicians to express themselves more fully. The building movement for civil rights was leading to a greater respect for African Americans and their art forms.

- Why was Miles Davis among the most important musicians of this period?

Miles Davis, more than any other musician, dominated the mainstream era. During this period, he first showed the ability to synthesize emerging jazz sounds into coherent styles that others would embrace as new movements—notably cool jazz and then modal jazz. He was also an expert bandleader and talent spotter, bringing to the fore such musicians as John Coltrane, Cannonball Adderley, and Bill Evans.

- How did hard bop develop in response to bebop and other styles?

Hard bop emerged in the mid-1950s. It featured more relaxed tempos, simpler melodies, and a more soulful emotionalism, with roots in the blues and gospel music, than did bebop. Some of the key proponents of hard bop were pianist Horace Silver and drummer/bandleader Art Blakey.

- What distinguishes West Coast bop from other variants, and who were the key players in this style?

In California, an offshoot of bebop developed that ran hotter than cool jazz but still carried forward some of its characteristics such as counterpoint. Saxophonist Art Pepper and pianist Hampton Hawes were innovators in this style.

- What are the different saxophone styles of Dexter Gordon, Sonny Rollins, and John Coltrane?

Where alto saxophone had typified the sound of bebop, the tougher, more full-bodied sound of tenor saxophone embodied hard bop, including Sonny Rollins and John Coltrane. Dexter Gordon, the first important bebop tenorist, combined the huge sound and harmonic ingenuity of Coleman Hawkins with the light vibrato and quixotic grace of Lester Young. Gordon's style fed two new streams, represented by Rollins and Coltrane. Rollins was the more intellectual, while Coltrane the more purely emotive player. Both extended the vocabulary of jazz performance.

- How were the musical approaches of composer-pianists Thelonious Monk and Dave Brubeck similar and how were they different?

Both were stubborn iconoclasts who emphasized the percussive and pianistic aspects of their instrument and focused as much on composing as performing. Monk continued to follow his own muse in the 1950s, but his music found a new audience that was more open to his quirky compositions and personality. Dave Brubeck, whose *Time Out* was the first jazz album to sell a million copies, brought jazz to a hip new audience of college students. His classically influenced compositions and experiments with unusual meters were typical of "third stream" experiments of the era.

- What is soul jazz and how does it differ from hard bop?

Soul jazz features both simple and funky melodies, danceable rhythms, and blues-gospel underpinnings. It grew out of hard bop's more aggressive style, but was more rooted in African American vernacular traditions, seeking a broader audience. Jimmy Smith brought elements of gospel organ into jazz and established the organ-trio format as a highly popular one for the music.

- How did earlier jazz traditions and groups grow and thrive during this period?

Almost all earlier forms of jazz continued to be performed during the 1950s, many by the styles' originators. Duke Ellington's career enjoyed a second renaissance, thanks to a successful appearance at the 1956 Newport Jazz Festival and Ellington's evolution as a composer. Such mainstream performers as pianist Erroll Garner created a listenable blend of jazz and pop styles to score major hits.

- What vocalists were important during the mainstream era?

Such mainstream singers as Frank Sinatra and Ella Fitzgerald set new standards for jazz vocalists. Fitzgerald was particularly influential through her series of *Songbook* albums, which featured the output of America's greatest popular song composers. The vocal trio Lambert, Hendricks, and Ross were among the few vocalists capable of matching the high-energy bebop style. Carmen McRae and Betty Carter emulated hard bop's phrasing and power in their singing.

- What other jazz styles were prominent during this time and how did they differ from the more dominant styles?

A search for artistic freedom and self-expression can be found in many of the alternate styles that emerged in the 1950s. Experiments ranged from Bill Evans's attempt to free the piano, bass, and drums from their traditional roles in his trio performances to bassist/bandleader Charles Mingus's blend of humor, social criticism, and soulful jazz in his compositions.

DISCUSSION QUESTIONS

1. What are the key differences between bebop, hard bop, cool jazz, and soul jazz?
2. Before you read this chapter, had you heard of any of the major mainstream musicians? Name some of the musicians associated with hard bop and soul jazz.
3. In the world of business, it is believed that concentrations of an industry in specific geographic regions can lead to high innovation and growth. Describe how that effect might apply to jazz and offer an example.
4. Describe some of the effects of evolving recording technology, such as the development of long-playing records, on the composition and performance of jazz.
5. Trace the line of influence in jazz trumpet playing, starting with New Orleans brass bands and Louis Armstrong and proceeding through swing, bop, cool jazz, hard bop, and modal jazz.
6. Discuss key players of the saxophone and how they influenced each other, starting from Coleman Hawkins and Lester Young and proceeding through bebop, cool jazz, hard bop, and modal jazz.

7. Trace the line of influence in jazz piano playing, starting with Jelly Roll Morton proceeding through swing, bop, cool jazz, hard bop, and modal jazz.

8. Bebop was a breakthrough style when it first emerged. What aspects of it were restrictive in ways that compelled musicians to seek alternative styles?

KEY TERMS & KEY PEOPLE

Cannonball Adderley 166
atonal 176
avant-garde 191
Chet Baker 172
Art Blakey 164
Clifford Brown 169
Dave Brubeck 176
Kenny Burrell 177
chamber jazz 190
chorus 172
John Coltrane 164
Miles Davis 165
Bill Evans 164

Ella Fitzgerald 186
fours 171
Erroll Garner 185
Dexter Gordon 174
gospel music 169
hard bop 165
mainstream jazz 164
Carmen McRae 188
Charles Mingus 164
modal jazz 194
Thelonious Monk 164
Wes Montgomery 164
Lee Morgan 168

Anita O'Day 185
Art Pepper 170
Oscar Peterson 186
Buddy Rich 171
Max Roach 166
Sonny Rollins 168
Horace Silver 164
Jimmy Smith 177
soul jazz 177
Thad Jones-Mel Lewis
   Orchestra 184
Sarah Vaughan 168

CHAPTER ⑧

Free and Exploratory Jazz

by John Litweiler

TAKE NOTE

- Why was 1959 such a pivotal year in jazz history?
- What were the roots of free jazz?
- What were the innovations introduced by free jazz in melody, rhythm, harmony, and performance style?
- Who were the leading innovators in the free jazz movement?
- What role did cooperatives and independent performance spaces play in free jazz?

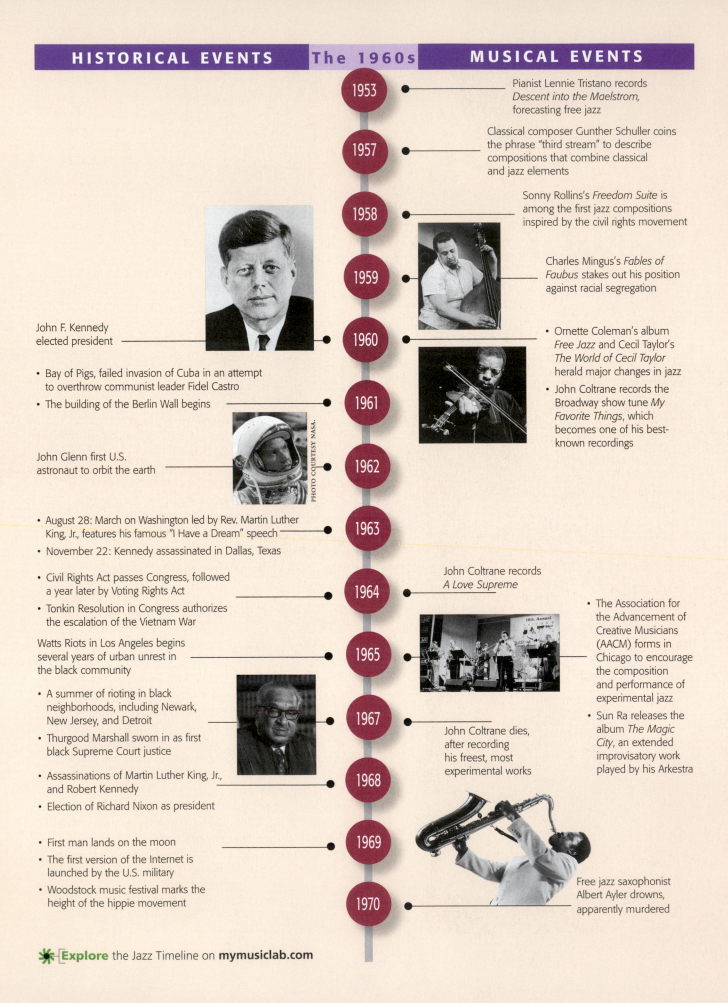

HISTORICAL EVENTS   The 1960s   MUSICAL EVENTS

1953
Pianist Lennie Tristano records *Descent into the Maelstrom*, forecasting free jazz

1957
Classical composer Gunther Schuller coins the phrase "third stream" to describe compositions that combine classical and jazz elements

1958
Sonny Rollins's *Freedom Suite* is among the first jazz compositions inspired by the civil rights movement

1959
Charles Mingus's *Fables of Faubus* stakes out his position against racial segregation

John F. Kennedy elected president

1960
• Ornette Coleman's album *Free Jazz* and Cecil Taylor's *The World of Cecil Taylor* herald major changes in jazz

• Bay of Pigs, failed invasion of Cuba in an attempt to overthrow communist leader Fidel Castro
• The building of the Berlin Wall begins

1961
• John Coltrane records the Broadway show tune *My Favorite Things*, which becomes one of his best-known recordings

PHOTO COURTESY NASA.

John Glenn first U.S. astronaut to orbit the earth

1962

• August 28: March on Washington led by Rev. Martin Luther King, Jr., features his famous "I Have a Dream" speech
• November 22: Kennedy assassinated in Dallas, Texas

1963

• Civil Rights Act passes Congress, followed a year later by Voting Rights Act
• Tonkin Resolution in Congress authorizes the escalation of the Vietnam War

1964
John Coltrane records *A Love Supreme*

Watts Riots in Los Angeles begins several years of urban unrest in the black community

1965
• The Association for the Advancement of Creative Musicians (AACM) forms in Chicago to encourage the composition and performance of experimental jazz

• A summer of rioting in black neighborhoods, including Newark, New Jersey, and Detroit
• Thurgood Marshall sworn in as first black Supreme Court justice

1967
John Coltrane dies, after recording his freest, most experimental works

• Sun Ra releases the album *The Magic City*, an extended improvisatory work played by his Arkestra

• Assassinations of Martin Luther King, Jr., and Robert Kennedy
• Election of Richard Nixon as president

1968

• First man lands on the moon
• The first version of the Internet is launched by the U.S. military
• Woodstock music festival marks the height of the hippie movement

1969

1970
Free jazz saxophonist Albert Ayler drowns, apparently murdered

✳ **Explore** the Jazz Timeline on **mymusiclab.com**

1 959: A Turning Point in Jazz History

Nineteen fifty-nine brought a turning point in jazz. The spring marked the deaths of three great swing era figures: saxophonist Lester Young, singer Billie Holiday, and soprano saxophonist-clarinetist Sidney Bechet. In that same season, the immensely popular Miles Davis Sextet disbanded, leaving two breakthrough albums in its wake: Davis's modal masterwork *Kind of Blue* and the supremely lyrical *Giant Steps* by Davis's departing tenor saxophonist, **John Coltrane**.

At the time, **Ornette Coleman** was still an obscure alto sax player, yet the three albums he recorded in California that year were as significant as those other key events. Two of the albums were by his own, carefully trained, pianoless quartet—*The Shape of Jazz to Come* and *Change of the Century*—and they announced a new era in jazz as surely as did Louis Armstrong's Hot Fives and Hot Sevens in 1926–27 or the first Charlie Parker-Dizzy Gillespie groups in 1945. And when the Coleman quartet played its first nightclub gig in New York City, in November 1959, it was the most combustible of all jazz debuts, igniting an explosion of exploratory creative activity by jazz musicians.

Of course, jazz musicians, those notorious nonconformists, have been explorers ever since New Orleans cornetist Buddy Bolden first played ragtime variations. But traditional jazz, swing, and bop improvisations were all based on the harmonic structures—the chord changes—of the songs the players played. Ornette Coleman's greatest innovation, on the other hand, was playing without fixed harmonic structures.

What Coleman did wasn't exactly unprecedented. A handful of musicians—among them, woodwind improviser Joe Maneri in Boston in the 1940s and alto saxophonist Joe Harriott in London in the 1950s—reportedly preceded Coleman in abandoning chord changes, though their early adventures weren't documented. Pianist Lennie Tristano's sextet created two notable recordings without preset chord changes in 1949, though the players instinctively imply conventional song form in the more successful piece, *Intuition*; more radical is Tristano's intense, atonal, overdubbed, aptly titled piano solo *Descent into the Maelstrom* (1953). As early as 1933 there were the strange, tumbling key changes of xylophonist-vibraphonist Red Norvo's *Dance of*

Ornette Coleman used the term harmolodic *for his approach to improvisation, which broke away from the chord-based soloing of bebop and mainstream jazz.* PHOTO COURTESY LEE TANNER.

Trombonist Tyree Glenn and tenor saxophonist Chu Berry photographed by bassist Milt Hinton while on the road (ca. 1940). PHOTO COURTESY © MILTON J. HINTON PHOTOGRAPHIC COLLECTION.

Jazz: The Sound of Freedom

At the time jazz musicians began freeing themselves from traditional harmony, sound, and form, many turned the same impulse toward social issues, especially the burgeoning civil rights movement. The music and activism that resulted were only the latest manifestations of a desire for individual freedom—and with it, racial equality—that had long been present in jazz. "Jazz was not just a music," Sonny Rollins said. "It was a social force in this country, and it was talking about freedom and people . . . not having to worry about whether they were supposed to be white, black, and all this stuff."

Not that the racial discrimination coursing through the United States during the twentieth century wasn't also reflected in the world of jazz—and experienced firsthand by its musicians. From the start, the

the *Octopus*, and during the bebop era there were plenty of works pointing to a world beyond bop. *Dalvatore Sally*, by George Handy for the Boyd Raeburn band (1946); Ellington's atonal theme of *The Clothed Woman* (1948); *A Bird in Igor's Yard*, George Russell's bright fusion of classical composer Igor Stravinsky and bop saxophonist Charlie Parker, played by the Buddy DeFranco band (1949); early experiments by drummer Shelly Manne and reedman Jimmy Giuffre—these are especially noteworthy examples of musicians' stretching the boundaries of jazz. But these works were isolated experiments, even though most of the artists were repeat experimenters throughout their lives.

"The new music," "the new thing," "'outside' jazz," "free jazz"—there was never a universally accepted name, such as swing or bop, for the idiom that grew out of Coleman's innovations. Early journalists took to the term **free jazz**, partly because Coleman recorded an album titled *Free Jazz* (1960) and also because this music's freedom of expression came at a time of great social change.

The changes, in fact, were some of the most far-reaching of the twentieth century: freedom was in the air. The civil rights movement—a crystallization of African Americans' growing insistence on equal opportunity and the public's increasing awareness of the value and vitality of African American culture—was at its height, marked by the passing of the Civil Rights and Voting acts (1964–65). Among jazz musicians, the civil rights movement had a powerful

---

free jazz a style of jazz introduced in 1959 and developed in the 1960s and 1970s that relies on neither key nor chord progressions for improvisational structure.

👁 **Watch** the documentary on free jazz on **mymusiclab.com**

prevailing social order guaranteed inequality of opportunity for black and white players: although black musicians may have played the first "jass" in New Orleans, it was a white group, the Original Dixieland Jazz Band, that first became famous.

For many years into the evolution of jazz, working conditions remained far from equal for white and black bands. In many parts of the United States, hotels and restaurants that served black customers were hard to find. And in some areas, particularly the South, black bands faced very real dangers. Cab Calloway recalled a 1931 gig in Virginia Beach, Virginia, in which the mostly white audience grew angry and "somebody shouted, 'Let's take this nigger out and lynch him.' And all this while I was trying to sing."

Integration onstage—pioneered in part by Benny Goodman's employment of a few major black musicians in his small combos—remained a rarity until the bebop era, when the increasing assertiveness of bop musicians began dovetailing with a free-thinking youth counterculture.

It was in the jazz realm that some of the earliest cracks in the wall of discrimination appeared. From the beginning, the music attracted both black and white musicians and audiences; for many white listeners, racial prejudice began to crumble when they found themselves admiring black jazz players. And exchanges of ideas among musicians of both races were at the core of jazz evolution—in the 1920s, for example, virtually all of the white, Chicago-style musicians were powerfully influenced by Louis Armstrong, while in the 1930s the white Casa Loma Orchestra had a strong impact on black bands of the time.

The jazz world's advocacy of freedom and racial equality ultimately became more overt and direct. In 1950, Duke Ellington vowed that proceeds from his composition *Harlem* would be used to "stamp out segregation, discrimination, bigotry, and a variety of other intolerances." In the 1960s, calls for social liberation—whether in the form of songs such as Eddie Harris's *Freedom Jazz Dance* (1965) or even band names (**Charlie Haden**'s Liberation Music Orchestra)—became plentiful. Bassist Charles Mingus's 1960 tune *Original Faubus Fables* overtly called for "no more Ku Klux Klan" and entreated, "Oh, Lord, don't let 'em shoot us . . . stab us . . . tar and feather us!" Saxophonist John Coltrane responded to the 1963 killing of four young girls in Birmingham, Alabama, by composing *Alabama*, its sound inspired by the cadences of the speech Martin Luther King, Jr., delivered at the memorial service. Drummer Max Roach issued the passionate 1960 album *We Insist! Freedom Now Suite*, and he remained a highly active vocal (as well as musical) advocate of civil rights.

Martin Luther King, Jr., himself recognized the connection between jazz and civil rights. "Much of the power of our Freedom Movement in the United States has come from this music," he remarked in his opening address at the 1964 Berlin Jazz Festival.

To many, the very idea of jazz became synonymous with freedom. "If jazz means anything," Ellington once wrote, "it is freedom of expression."

"Jazz," said Rollins, "has always been the music that had this kind of spirit."

—*Tad Lathrop and John Litweiler*

resonance. Louis Armstrong made headlines with his scalding criticism of President Eisenhower during the Little Rock, Arkansas, school integration crisis in 1957. There were civil rights inspired albums, including tenor saxophonist Sonny Rollins's *Freedom Suite* (1958), drummer Max Roach's *Freedom Now Suite* (1960), and drummer Art Blakey's *The Freedom Rider* (1961). And the free jazz musicians, mostly young and most black, were unanimous, often vocal, in their support of the struggle for social freedom.

 Watch the documentary on civil rights on **mymusiclab.com**

TAKE NOTE

• Why was 1959 such a pivotal year in jazz history?

Free Jazz Ancestors

Of the ancestors of free jazz, two offered especially powerful advances in technique and sensibility: composer-bassist Charles Mingus and composer Bob Graettinger.

Mingus based his music on chord changes and modes, but his passion was certainly a precedent for free jazz. Such Mingus works as *Pithecanthropus Erectus* (1956) and his *Tijuana Moods* album (1957) are volatile and full of complex activity and raw-edged playing, foreshadowing the sound of early 1960s groups with woodwind virtuoso **Eric Dolphy**; this is music that raises blisters. Along with beautiful melodies, he also composed the socially conscious pieces *Fables of Faubus* (1959), his musical assault on segregationist Arkansas governor Orval Faubus, and *Cry for Freedom (Prayer for Passive Resistance)* (1960). Of Mingus's big band works, quite the most important

As uncompromising in business as he was in music composition, bassist Charles Mingus made numerous career moves to counteract what he saw as restrictive commercialism in jazz. With drummer Max Roach, he ran a record label, Debut, in the early 1950s. In 1960 he and Roach organized Newport Rebels, an alternative to the mainstream Newport Jazz Festival. Such enterprises served as models for later musician-controlled record labels and organizations.

is his grand *Epitaph* suite (1962–89), encompassing decades of composition (including reconstruction by composer **Gunther Schuller**) and not performed until 1989, a decade after his death.

As for Graettinger, the works he composed for Stan Kenton's jazz orchestras bear only passing resemblance to any other jazz or twentieth-century classical music. His large-scale compositions sound like immense dreams. Graettinger's *City of Glass* (1950 version) and *This Modern World* (1951–53) are

atonal—without a harmonic foundation—and dense with polyphonic and polyrhythmic movement, lovely instrumental blendings, cold and bleak passages, blazing ensemble climaxes, and fugitive solo moments. These works are almost overwhelming in their complex, ever-changing activity; it's notable that every vivid, beautiful image evaporates.

TAKE NOTE

- What were the roots of free jazz?

Free Jazz Innovations

With all this diverse activity as a precedent, what was it about Coleman that made him such a powerful stimulus? And what is free jazz? To answer the second question first, there were four main areas of innovation in free jazz: sound, harmony, form, and rhythm. New conceptions of these four elements grew out of Coleman's early music.

Sonic Freedom

While early jazz and swing were rich with the personal sounds of expressive individuals, bebop's quest for virtuoso lyricism yielded a narrower range of sonorities. You hear this especially in brass instrumentalists. For instance, the smooth sound introduced by J. J. Johnson was pervasive among bop trombonists. In free jazz, on the other hand, the sonic range was unlimited. The emotive trombonist Roswell Rudd, a former Dixieland musician, brought back the rich intonation and slippery slides and blasts of swing, while such successors as George Lewis and Craig Harris went on to further exploit the trombone's power, range, and capacity for expression. Meanwhile, such trumpeters as the vividly dramatic **Lester Bowie** and the lyrical Leo Smith added new dimensions of humor and sweetness, fire and abstraction, and loud-soft contrasts. It's no accident that Leo Smith was once inspired by Joe Smith's (no relation) lyric trumpet accompaniments to Bessie Smith, or that Bowie was originally inspired by Louis Armstrong's epic solos; both Bowie and Leo Smith, like other free players, were returning to the quest for personal expression that was at the very root of jazz.

Coleman himself, for a time, played a white plastic alto saxophone, which had a rather dry sound

((•—[**Hear** a profile of Ornette Coleman on **mymusiclab.com**

---

atonal composed without being based in traditional rules of harmonic relationships; for example, not in a key.

Trumpeter Lester Bowie explored free improvisation and "freak" sounds as a member of both the Association for the Advancement of Creative Musicians and the Art Ensemble of Chicago. PHOTO COURTESY MICHAEL WILDERMAN.

Harmonic Freedom

What startled listeners most when they first heard Ornette Coleman was the harmonic structure of his soloing. In swing and bebop solos, chord changes provided emotional shape and tension, and the harmonic tensions were almost inevitably resolved, creating a familiar pleasure for listeners. The singular quality of modal jazz was its reduced structural tension, for modal jazz had slower and subtler harmonic movement, especially in its early years.

Coleman had a third solution. "Before I met Ornette," said his bassist Charlie Haden, "I would sometimes feel to play not on the changes of the song; sometimes I would feel to play on the inspiration and the feeling of the song, and create a new chord structure to it in my solo. . . . And the first time I played with Ornette, he was doing that." Coleman recalled that when he taught his new music to his first quartet partners, Haden, trumpeter **Don Cherry**, and drummer Billy Higgins, "the most interesting part is: what do you play after you play the melody [theme]? That's where I won them over . . . finally I got them to where they could see how to express themselves without linking up to a definite maze."

that emphasized the crying quality in his melodies. His sound sometimes changed from phrase to phrase as he soloed ("I realized that you can play sharp or flat in tune," Coleman said). **Multiphonics**, or split tones (two or more notes at once), and **overtones** (notes higher than a horn's normal range) became commonplace in the music of Coltrane and **Albert Ayler** and later among the multitude of saxophonists whom they inspired. Instruments almost wholly new to jazz improvisation appeared from Africa, Asia, and the realm of classical music. The **Art Ensemble of Chicago** made a deliberate search for new sounds, adding hundreds of gongs, bells, whistles, and toys to the usual instrumentation. Oddly enough, although free jazz coincided with the development of the synthesizer, only bandleader **Sun Ra** and a handful of others created important work on the instrument. One of those others was trombonist George Lewis, who played duets with a computer he programmed to improvise music.

Years later, when world music and heavy metal rock were popular, the sounds the free jazz musicians made didn't seem quite as astonishing as they once had. On the other hand, Lester Bowie, later in his career, proposed forming a literally heavy-metal band—with sousaphones, bass saxophones, and steel drums.

Don Cherry played pocket trumpet in Ornette Coleman's quartet before recording as a leader. In later years Cherry attained renown as a pioneer in world music. PHOTO COURTESY FRANK DRIGGS COLLECTION.

---

multiphonics   two or more notes played at the same time by a single instrument.

overtones   harmonic overtones; in acoustics, secondary tones that are subdivisions of a fundamental tone or frequency; generated in stringed instruments by touching, rather than plucking, the string at points marking shorter segments of the string length that generates the main tone; also called harmonics.

An alumnus of Ornette Coleman's Shape of Jazz to Come *quartet (1959), bassist Charlie Haden pursued a range of interests that included work with Gato Barbieri, Carla Bley, Keith Jarrett, and the groups Old and New Dreams and his own Liberation Music Orchestra.* PHOTO COURTESY MICHAEL WILDERMAN.

(1959) only the drummer of the Ornette Coleman Quartet kept time, while the trumpeter and saxophonist played the haunting melody in freely changing tempos and the bassist strummed spaced, arhythmic accents. And after the balladlike theme of *Beauty Is a Rare Thing* (1960) the Coleman quartet improvised together in freely moving lines with no fixed tempo or meter at all. Like free harmonic structure, free rhythmic structure was here.

Trumpeter Don Ellis's early combos played free-time pieces, and Jimmy Giuffre's trio created the daring *Free Fall* (1962), an album of free-time, "outside" improvisations. Ellis went on to compose big band scores using complex Indian rhythmic patterns, while four drummers—Sunny Murray, Andrew Cyrille, Milford Graves, and **Rashied Ali**—took the more radical step of abandoning fixed rhythm entirely, instead playing pure accent and momentum. What those drummers did was certainly revolutionary. And why not? Coleman's example was leading musicians to question the foundations of the entire jazz tradition.

Giuffre's and the drummers' explorations led to unaccompanied horn solos and free improvisation, which evolved largely in Chicago and England in the late 1960s. In free improvisation, soloists or groups (almost always small groups) of musicians improvised without themes, harmonic or rhythmic structures, or fixed forms.

Formal Freedom

Without chord changes, did Coleman's solos turn into chaos, as detractors once claimed? Quite the contrary: his music's formal unity was an important source of its power. He structured his solos by using fragments of melody, which he would alter and incorporate into virtually every phrase. This theme-based method was widely influential, though a good many alternatives followed. There were the free-association forms of Eric Dolphy; the cyclic forms of Coltrane; the grand architecture of pianist **Cecil Taylor**'s solos; the meticulously mounted lines of saxophonist Steve Lacy; the dramatic shapes of **Roscoe Mitchell** and Lester Bowie; the freely moving lyricism of saxophonist Fred Anderson—there were even vestiges of the classic building climax-anticlimax swing and bop form in the sonic adventures of tenor sax player Albert Ayler. Free jazz implied not freedom from form but freedom to choose form.

Rhythmic Freedom

Jazz had typically been played in $\frac{2}{4}$ and $\frac{4}{4}$ time, or occasionally in $\frac{3}{4}$ and $\frac{6}{4}$ meters, and the bassist and drummer marked the time. But in *Lonely Woman*

TAKE NOTE

- What were the innovations introduced by free jazz in melody, rhythm, harmony, and performance style?

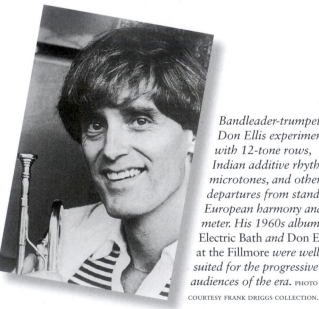

Bandleader-trumpeter Don Ellis experimented with 12-tone rows, Indian additive rhythm, microtones, and other departures from standard European harmony and meter. His 1960s albums Electric Bath *and* Don Ellis at the Fillmore *were well suited for the progressive audiences of the era.* PHOTO COURTESY FRANK DRIGGS COLLECTION.

How to Listen to Free Jazz

With many of the signposts for understanding standard jazz not applicable to free jazz, finding meaning in free jazz requires a shift of attention to different kinds of qualities.

You might apply a three-point approach to listening:

1. Open listening. At first, don't try to analyze or "make sense" of what you hear. Instead, focus on yourself: What are you feeling as you listen? What thoughts spring to your mind as you listen? How are you reacting to the music? Articulate answers to yourself (or in discussion) as precisely as you can. Then focus back on the music: how would you identify and describe some of the specific events and sounds that made you react as you did? This exercise should prompt an initial sense of engagement with the music.

2. Listening for familiar characteristics. Many of the tips for listening presented in Chapter 2 apply to free jazz.

Melody: Listen for shapes, contours, and durations. Are small melodic building blocks (motifs) being used to create longer phrases? Notice whether phrases repeat. If there is minimal or no repetition, decide whether another kind of logic is driving melodic development.

Color and texture: Listen to the spectrum of tone colors you hear. Is there much variety? Inventory the tone colors used in the piece. Are they bright? dark? woody? metallic? And listen for texture. Are there many instruments, creating a dense texture? Or are there only a few, leaving a sparse sound?

Voice, feel, and expression: You may hear more varied and unusual inflections and expressive devices in free jazz than in more traditional styles. Sounds may include those outside of an instrument's typical range or role. Blasts, squeals, squawks, whispers, murmurs are all part of the free jazz lexicon. You may even hear sound-producing devices—such as a car siren or bicycle horn—that are not normally considered musical instruments. Think about the expressiveness of what you hear and how you might describe it.

Musicians' roles, individual and collective: Pay attention to the relationships among players. Note whether there seems to be a leader and accompanist(s), a succession of different leaders, a "conversation" among equals, or some other arrangement of roles.

3. Making sense of the unfamiliar. In the areas of free jazz's greatest departures—form and harmony, for example—you need to reach beyond standard criteria for understanding.

Form: Chord progressions may not be present, so looking for an architecture based on them, with repetitions and variations, may not be relevant. You need to look for other elements on which form may be based. You might listen to changes in dynamics—soft sections and loud sections. Or you might listen to changes in texture, or musicians' roles. There may be fragments of melody that repeat and transmute, or change in contour. The key is to recognize a larger architecture that emerges from the development of any of these elements over the length of the piece. It's conceivable, of course, that no overarching form may be discernible.

Harmony: The sense of movement in a free piece may not rely on resolution to a "home" chord (the tonic) the way traditional jazz or European tonal harmony does. But harmony may exist in the sense of chords forming, changing, sounding **consonant** (agreeably "in tune") or **dissonant** (discordant), and voiced closely (notes of the chord clustered close together) or openly (notes wide apart). Listen for tension and resolution, stasis versus motion, consonance versus dissonance, and change of mood.

Rhythm: In the absence of a repetitive, steady beat, or of any discernible rhythmic unity among musicians, look for patterns where you can find them and focus on how they may be repeating or developing. Focus your attention on one player, and notice not only the rhythm of the playing but also how it interlocks with (or ignores) surrounding rhythms. Attempt to discern rhythmic structure—unless there is none.

—*Tad Lathrop*

---

consonant   notes or harmonies sounding agreeably "in tune"; the opposite of dissonant.

dissonant   sounding discordant; the opposite of consonant.

Free Jazz Innovators

Coleman, Taylor, and Coltrane

The force behind Ornette Coleman's spearheading of free jazz came from the emotion in his music. He played without chord changes because it was in his nature to do so. "I think jazz should express more kinds of feelings than it has up to now," he said, and among his classic early pieces, *Peace* (1959), *Compassion* (1959), and *Sadness* (1962) convey the emotions of his song titles with a subtlety new to jazz. There is also the optimistic swagger of *Ramblin'* (1959), the electricity of *Free* (1959) and *Forerunner* (1959), the stark blues of *Lonely Woman* (1959), the sorrow of *Lorraine* (1959), the anger of *Kaleidoscope* (1960) and *Blues Connotation* (1960)—all shown in sharp relief. In his early solos he achieved rhythmic tension as acute as Charlie Parker's, though his own broken phrases are rhythmically simpler than Parker's. Like Parker's, Coleman's melodies are rich with blues; his angular

Ornette Coleman played violin and trumpet as well as saxophone.
PHOTO COURTESY MICHAEL WILDERMAN.

Listening Guide

CD II, Track 2/Download Track 26

RAMBLIN' • ORNETTE COLEMAN

Music: Ornette Coleman, 1959. Personnel: Don Cherry (cornet); Ornette Coleman (alto sax); Charlie Haden (bass); Billy Higgins (drums). Recorded October 8, 1959, in Hollywood. First issue: *Change of the Century*, Atlantic LP1327. Matrix no. 3874. Timing: 6:38.

Overview

It's only right that this masterpiece, with its blues and folk-music elements, is a loving reflection of America's frontier myth, for Coleman's discoveries opened the jazz frontier to possibilities that have been the main area of jazz development ever since 1959.

Key Features

- Improvisation: The first two phrases of Coleman's wonderfully flowing solo capture the jaunty feeling of the theme. They provide a motif that recurs in many subsequent lines, varied, embodied, or (as at 1:28) repeated.

In the fifth chorus a very blue sax phrase is mocked by a light, dancing phrase (1:58). This provides Coleman with new motif that leads to swaggering phrases. At 2:19 he moves into darker, bluer phrases that, by 2:30, morph back into the original optimistic mood. A long growl (2:27) foreshadows the end of this eight-chorus solo. Hear, especially, the beauty of Coleman's melodies.

Don Cherry's pocket trumpet solo offers four choruses of fine bop melodies. His form is almost classic, including (3:30) a climactic chorus centered on repeated notes.

Charlie Haden's simple, strummed bass solo (4:00) is derived from his vamp accompaniments to the horns. It sounds like variations on a nineteenth-century cowboy song of lonely, wide-open spaces. At 4:40 Haden strums a new melody that suggests a country fiddle song (*Old Joe Clark?*).

- Rhythm: A $\frac{4}{4}$ meter and an ideal medium-up tempo for inspiring improvisation with exhilarating swing.
- Harmony: Coleman's harmonic structure only irregularly matches the bass's blues changes, for it is essentially implied by his melodic lines. Cherry's solo follows Haden's chord changes more closely.
- Dynamics: The final contrast between fading bass and stabbing horns is a delightful surprise.
- Voice, feel, and expression: Coleman's sax sound ranges from light to full-bodied to (beginning at 0:58) mock-angry growls. The sound of Cherry's small trumpet is light, with a one-octave treble range. Haden's bass attack is especially aggressive.
- Musicians' roles: Traditional horn and rhythm-section roles, though without the customary support of a piano.

—John Litweiler

note choices and shifting keys added further tension, as did the accompanying interplay of harmonically ambiguous bass and drums. Coleman also explored **collective improvisation**—where every musician is free to improvise his part during a performance—most notably in the 40-minute *Free Jazz*, with eight musicians bandying lines back and forth over a fixed tempo—a kind of far-out Dixieland.

By the mid-1960s Coleman was also playing violin and trumpet, both with wild, spontaneous phrasing and unorthodox, self-taught technique. Over the years he retired from public performing several times, usually to compose. Few of his orchestral or chamber-music compositions have been performed; the best known is his *Skies of America* (1972) for symphony orchestra and improvisers. Following the mid-1970s, he played most often with his band Prime Time—which employed electric guitars and drums—in a hybrid jazz-rock idiom that he invented. These unique fusion-music adventures were rhythmically stimulating, but little of his latter-day music had anything like the power and excitement of his early recordings on the Atlantic and Contemporary labels.

The commotion over Coleman at the start of the 1960s drew attention to two other highly advanced jazzmen: Eric Dolphy and Cecil Taylor. The almost human sounds—squawks, grunts, cries, blurts, mutters—of Dolphy's **bass clarinet** and Charles Mingus's bass in improvised mock arguments (*What Love*, 1960) were a fabulous spectacle, as was Dolphy's soaring, biting alto sax soloing (*Original Faubus Fables*, 1960): here at last was a passionate interpreter to match Mingus's own passion. Dolphy played with a full,

---

collective improvisation   spontaneous composition performed simultaneously by members of an ensemble.

bass clarinet   the lowest-pitched instrument in the clarinet family.

hambone   practice of using the human body as a rhythm instrument by using one's hands slapping against thighs, arms, chest, and other parts of the body.

TIME	SECTION	MELODY/INSTRUMENTATION
0:00	FIRST THEME, OPENING PHRASE	Four bars of horns, four bars of strummed bass vamp. This jaunty melody sets the feeling of *Ramblin'*. While the three-phrase theme resembles blues form, Coleman actually expands upon blues. So the initiating four-bar melody is answered by Haden's strummed bass chord, in a dancing "**hambone**" pattern derived from folk music.
0:09	SECOND THEME PHRASE	Two bars of horns, four bars of bass vamp. The down-turned phrases and abrupt, comic distortion of the melody suggest a realistic corrective to the optimism of the opening phrase.
0:15	THIRD THEME PHRASE	Two bars horns, four bars bass vamp. After this five-note return to optimism, the trumpet rides over the bass.
0:25	FIRST CHORUS	Follows the three-phrase form of the first, except that over the last bass vamp . . .
0:46	ALTO SAX SOLO	. . . Ornette Coleman begins his alto sax solo.
1:02		Alto solo continues over the bass's straight-ahead $\frac{4}{4}$ meter. For the rest of Coleman's solo, Haden alternates between 12-bar straightahead choruses on blues changes, and 16-bar choruses of strummed folk-dance variations.
2:56	TRUMPET SOLO	Drummer Billy Higgins switches to higher cymbals.
4:00	BASS SOLO	Higgins taps accompaniment on cymbal stand.
4:58	FIRST THEME, REPEATED ONCE	The band returns with the initial theme for two choruses.
5:43		Ending of the last theme phrase. Now both alto sax and trumpet ride in melodic counterpoint over the bass's cowboy-song strums. The bouncy horn melodies over the bass suggest a wagon train riding the prairie into the sunset. As the horns fade at 6:23, the strummed western song continues until . . .
6:28	CODA	. . . the final phrase. Horns and drums snap out the second (reality) phrase of the theme, for an irresolute conclusion. Perfect!

clear sound on all his horns—and on the flute—and employed wide harmonic leaps and dissonances that often sounded atonal, even though he maintained that "every note I play has some reference to the chords of the piece." In later years, he made many recordings with George Russell, Booker Little, Coltrane, Coleman, and others before his untimely death from diabetes at the age of 36.

Even before Coleman, Cecil Taylor was playing piano solos so dissonant and free they sounded atonal. Such classical composers as Béla Bartók and Igor Stravinsky influenced his music, as did Ellington and modern jazz pianists; a good introduction is his album *The World of Cecil Taylor* (1960). After that, turmoil grew in his highly complex solo forms, which often used fragmentary phrases to generate grand designs; he also composed knotty pieces with many mood changes and stops and starts. By the late 1960s, he was playing violently, as fast as humanly possible (and Taylor may be the most virtuosic of all jazz pianists), with dissonances crashing like thunder through the high ("astral" he called it), middle ("surface of the earth"), and low ("abyss") registers of the keyboard. He usually overpowered the horn soloists who played with him. He also improvised long, intense, unaccompanied pieces, full of detail, almost as demanding for the listener as for the performer; "To feel is the most terrifying thing in this society," he said. For an example of his playing of this era, listen to *Jitney No. 2* (*JTSA* Disc 5/Track 14). A lyrical side of his music subsequently grew in importance, especially in the 1980s. The most remarkable recording project built around a free jazz artist was Cecil Taylor in *Berlin '88*, a collection of 11 solo, duet,

Eric Dolphy's playing exuded warmth, humanity, and intelligence, notably in his innovative work on the bass clarinet. PHOTO COURTESY INSTITUTE OF JAZZ STUDIES, RUTGERS UNIVERSITY.

trio, and big band albums in which he was joined by a succession of excellent, mostly European players.

In subsequent decades, Taylor remained active while assuming a role—through teaching and performing—as a figurehead of experimental jazz. In 1990, he was recognized as a Jazz Master by the National Endowment for the Arts. Over the years, alumni of his college ensembles, at Antioch College and elsewhere, fanned out into the professional jazz community, promulgating his ideas.

John Coltrane was by far the most popular "outside" jazz artist, in large part because he had, according to Taylor, "great insight, a feeling for the hysteria of the times, and a conception that goes beyond that of his own horn." (For Coltrane's early career, see Chapter 7.) After 1960, Coltrane's solos became long, passionate conflicts in which he alternated lyrical playing with longer cycles that became progressively more

Cecil Taylor's stormy atonality drew on twentieth-century European music as well as jazz. PHOTO COURTESY MICHAEL WILDERMAN.

((•⦁ **Hear** a profile of Cecil Taylor on mymusiclab.com

The Loft Scene

Each jazz era brought its characteristic venues. During the swing era, dancers flocked to ballrooms to hear big bands; after World War II, nightclubs, concert auditoriums, and outdoor festivals became the centers of jazz. The jazz recession of the early 1960s, coinciding with the emergence of a generation of free jazz musicians, pointed to a need for different kinds of performance settings—ones where adventurous musicians could ply their trade without the pressures imposed by more commercial nightclubs.

At the south end of Manhattan, where many of the most renowned "outside" musicians lived, the most daring music of the 1960s could be heard at coffee houses, little theaters, and especially in the large lofts where musicians maintained rehearsal spaces. Among the leading artists who conducted their early careers in these settings were pianist Cecil Taylor; saxophonists Albert Ayler, **Archie Shepp**, and Marion Brown; trumpeter Don Cherry; drummer Sunny Murray; and trombonist Roswell Rudd.

Lofts and other alternative venues offered informal surroundings, tended not to serve alcohol, and charged low admission prices. Attendees were typically young and liberal. Writer-poet LeRoi Jones noted in 1963 that "many serious young jazz listeners now seem more willing to go sit on the floor in a loft and hear good music than go to the formal clubs downtown and hear well-known chumps." Due in part to the close connection between artists and listeners fostered by the loft scene, the new music became the center of an underground community.

In the early 1970s, Ornette Coleman led his band in occasional concerts at his rehearsal space, Artists House, below his living quarters at 131 Prince Street. The veteran tenor saxophonist Sam Rivers and his wife, Bea, opened Studio Rivbea, 24 Bond Street, in 1971. Other jazz lofts followed, including several operated by musicians—Ladies' Fort (singer Joe Lee Wilson), Ali's Alley (drummer Rashied Ali), and the Brook (saxophonist Charles Tyler) were among them. The lofts provided key support for noncommercial musicians. When Edward Blackwell needed money for a kidney operation in 1973, fellow drummers Billy Higgins and Roger Blank organized benefit concerts, featuring a parade of top jazz artists, at Artists House. Several lofts joined forces to present festivals that competed with the annual Newport Jazz Festival in New York; the festivals showcased important musicians who had been excluded from the Newport bash.

Loft jazz wasn't confined to New York City; other centers included Philadelphia, Detroit, Chicago, Vancouver, and the San Francisco Bay Area. The roots of free improvisation, in fact, are traceable to the activities of drummer John Stevens and his cohorts in the 1960s at the aptly named Little Theatre in London.

What kind of music was played in the lofts? It wasn't always free jazz. Also heard were jazz veterans, now out of fashion at a time when nightclubs were few and their fare was limited. Ex-Basie arranger-tenorist Frank Foster led his Loud Minority big band in lofts, and a number of boppers such as Clifford Jordan, Sheila Jordan, Lee Konitz, and Hank Mobley alternated with a colorful variety of free players. Coleman and Konitz recorded albums at Artists House, saxophonists Tyler and Arthur Blythe recorded albums at

Saxophonist Sam Rivers and his wife, Bea, founded the Studio Rivbea loft. PHOTO COURTESY LEE TANNER.

the Brook, and five noted recordings from Studio Rivbea documented the 1977 Wildflowers festival that Rivers produced, which featured leading "liberated" musicians from California, Chicago, Philadelphia, and New York.

Most lofts disappeared after a few years. The longest lasting, Studio Rivbea, survived and even thrived until 1978, when a dispute with the landlord brought the music to an end. New York theaters and nightclubs were regularly presenting "outside" jazz by 1981, when Sam Rivers said, "Now there's not much need for loft spaces anymore except for rehearsals and for students." Since then, lofts have served as occasional concert spaces in New York and other principal cities, even as the audience for free jazz grew and small nightclubs, theaters, universities, and other venues emerged to accommodate musicians and listeners.

—*John Litweiler*

removed from the central harmony, leading to further cycles of multiphonics and overtone screams. These were terrifically intense solos, and much of Coltrane's tension derived from his harmonic straining against his pieces' modal non-structures. His tone was tender in his occasional ballad solos (as on the album *Ballads*, 1961–62) and iron-hard in his longer virtuoso pieces (*Traneing In*, 1957, and *Good Bait*, 1958). Sometimes he soloed on soprano saxophone for variety, as in his famous interpretation of the Rodgers and Hammerstein song *My Favorite Things* (1960; *JTSA* Disc 4/Track 10) from their musical *The Sound of Music*. Typical Coltrane quartet pieces featured extensive duets in which the powerful Elvin Jones played dense, multiple rhythms on a resonant drums-and-cymbals kit, creating huge waves of sound around the tenor saxophone.

After the spiritual turmoil of his album *A Love Supreme* (1964), Coltrane progressed to his greatest extremes of violent sound and harmony. The track *Acknowledgement* from that album is one of the best-known examples of his later style (*JTSA* Disc 5/Track 3). *Interstellar Space*, recorded shortly before his death in 1967, consists wholly of duets with drummer Rashied Ali. Coltrane recorded often, and he liked to encourage younger free jazz players; his quartets and quintets rivaled Miles Davis's quintet as the most popular jazz groups of the mid-1960s.

After Coltrane's death in 1967 his wife and final piano accompanist, Alice Coltrane, perceptively adapted his saxophone phrasing and forms to piano, harp, and organ. Her style resulted in highly ornate impressionism and her repertoire included blues-infused versions of traditional Hindu chants.

Born Alice McLeod in 1937, Alice had studied classical piano before becoming drawn to jazz. She backed mainstream guitarist Kenny Burrell and saxophonist Lucky Thompson in the early 1960s and, in 1966, replaced pianist McCoy Tyner in John Coltrane's group, offering up empathetic, harmonically ambiguous chordal accompaniments for his increasingly avant-garde soloing. From 1968 through the 1970s she issued a number of solo albums, including *Journey in Satchidananda*, echoing the spiritualism of her husband's

late work and paralleling the related efforts of such other John Coltrane protégés as **Pharoah Sanders** (whose 1969 *The Creator Has a Master Plan* is a fine, mesmerizing example of sensuous modal jazz). She retired from music in the late 1970s to commit herself to religious pursuits—while managing the John Coltrane estate—and founded the Vedantic Center, an ashram for the study of religions, in Los Angeles. She resurfaced in 2004 with the album *Translinear Light*, on which she was joined by her tenor and soprano saxophonist son Ravi Coltrane, sounding at times eerily like his father, and her altoist son Oran. Alice died in 2007, leaving a legacy of musical spirituality, along with her musical offspring to carry the family torch.

Jazz Underground

Controversy followed this music, far more and far longer than it did bop in the 1940s. Miles Davis's comment on first hearing Ornette Coleman is famous—"Hell, just listen to what he writes and how he plays. If you're talking psychologically, the man is all screwed up inside." A *Down Beat* reviewer called a Coltrane-Dolphy performance "a horrifying demonstration of what appears to be a growing anti-jazz

Saxophonist Archie Shepp (shown here in 1967) studied drums and played in R&B bands before emerging as a key free-jazz player via work with John Coltrane, Cecil Taylor, and others. His later work reflected his view of jazz as an expression of black culture and freedom. PHOTO COURTESY JAZZSIGN/LEBRECHT MUSIC & ARTS.

Pharoah Sanders's fat, raspy tenor saxophone sound brought him a modest degree of commercial success. His 1969 album Karma, *recorded with yodeling singer Leon Thomas, reached the pop charts. He is shown here at the New Orleans Jazz and Heritage Festival in 2007.*
PHOTO COURTESY EBET ROBERTS/REDFERNS/GETTY IMAGES.

All of this meant that Taylor and the younger free players found work only irregularly, and the music became an underground art in the 1960s. Coleman; his liberated, lyrical trumpeter Don Cherry; and especially Coltrane became father figures to a lively underground New York scene that included the dramatic tenor saxophonist-poet-playwright Archie Shepp, alto saxman Charles Tyler, tenor player Pharoah Sanders, trumpeter Bill Dixon, and pianist Paul Bley among others.

The new underground musicians, by and large, shared the social concerns and liberal attitudes of their jazz predecessors, and some—reflecting the era's social and political unrest—carried these attitudes further. "Outside" jazz musicians offered works that reflected uniquely African American experiences, while Coltrane's *Alabama* (1963) and Shepp's *The Funeral* (1963) and *Rufus* (1965) mourned victims of racist murders. Some young free musicians and audiences went on to favor black nationalism, violent revolution, and even Marxism, for which poet, author, and critic LeRoi Jones (later known as Amiri Baraka) was the most militant spokesperson on the jazz scene: "We want poems that kill!" he wrote.

Other Free Instrumentalists

Some players normally oriented toward chord changes, including tenor saxophonist Sonny Rollins, experimented with free playing. Even Miles Davis moved to Coleman-like freedom in his mid-1960s quintet, which had a remarkable rhythm section centered around the impulsive young drummer Tony Williams (see Chapter 9). Younger modal players, notably vibraphonist Bobby Hutcherson and pianist Andrew Hill, conducted several daring free jazz adventures. The change from "inside" to "outside" playing was permanent for some, including soprano saxman Steve Lacy. "It happened in gradual stages," he said. "There would be a moment here, a fifteen minutes there, a half hour there, an afternoon, an

trend," and jazz magazines were filled with columns about how "outside" jazz would destroy or save Western civilization.

At the same time that controversy was stalling the careers of free musicians, the 1960s rock-music industry was having a devastating effect on jazz. Motown Records artists, the Beatles, Bob Dylan, and other pop stars were winning over the young generation that had accounted for a large portion of the jazz audience. On a downswing from the height of modern jazz's popularity at the beginning of the 1960s, jazz clubs closed in cities all over the United States.

The remaining club and festival producers struggled with the new jazz economics by booking bop and swing acts that had already been dependable attractions. All of the leading jazz record companies, each with hundreds of titles in its catalog—Riverside, Savoy, Contemporary, Pacific Jazz, Blue Note, Prestige, Verve—scaled down operations drastically, went out of business, or were sold, usually to rock record tycoons. Significantly, the new Impulse! label, unlike its competitors, embraced new jazz wholeheartedly; it issued Coltrane albums about every three months and thrived.

evening, and then all the time." A highly influential artist, the prolific Lacy ranged from sweet melody to high overtone abstraction on his instrument, in contrast to the narrower soprano sax sounds employed by latter-day jazz traditionalists and newly emerging "fusion" players. Lacy and pianist Mal Waldron were unusual for their alternately free and bop-era repertoires.

Critics mocked free jazz as "outer-space music." But composer, bandleader, and poet Sun Ra might have considered that a compliment. "I've chosen intergalactic music, or it has chosen me," he said. "Intergalactic music concerns the music of the galaxies. . . . I'm actually painting pictures of infinity with my music. . . . The real aim of this music is to coordinate the minds of people into an intelligent reach for a better world, and an intelligent approach to the living future." Sun Ra's shows were always spectacles, with his Arkestra, as he called it, in vivid, glittering robes and space helmets, parading and

dancing through nightclubs and concert halls chanting "Next stop, Jupiter! Next stop, Jupiter!"

Sun Ra was among the first composers to work extensively with modal structures in the 1950s. His Arkestras employed exotic sounds, at least for jazz: oboe, piccolos, timpani, throbbing percussion, paired baritone saxes. By 1965 and *The Magic City*—a long, completely improvised piece—he was conducting spontaneous compositions by signaling his musicians to play in changing groupings. The climaxes of his shows were often his own extended solos on the synthesizer: dissonant, crashing, virtuosic; they were sustained explosions of sound. *A Call for All Demons* recorded in 1956 but not issued until its appearance on the album *Angels and Demons at Play* in 1965 is a good example of the Arkestra's sound (*JTSA* Disc 3/Track 13).

"It's late now for the world. And if I can help raise people to new plateaus of peace and understanding, I'll feel my life has been worth living as a spiritual artist," said Albert Ayler. The most radical free jazzman of the 1960s, he tried to reinvent the

((•●─[**Hear** a profile of Sun Ra on **mymusiclab.com**

Listening Guide

((•●─ **Listen** to *Ghosts: First Variation* by Albert Ayler on **mymusiclab.com**
CD II, Track 4/Download Track 28

GHOSTS: FIRST VARIATION • ALBERT AYLER

Music: Albert Ayler, 1964. Personnel: Albert Ayler (tenor saxophone); Gary Peacock (bass); Sunny Murray (drums). Recorded: July 10, 1964, New York. First issue: ESP-Disk 1002. Timing: 5:12.

Overview

The pure force and extremeness of Ayler's sound, with his high, overtone cries and split tones (multiphonics, or several notes at once), hits the unwary listener like a thunderbolt. *Ghosts*, the most popular of his songs, sounds at first like a children's nursery ditty—until it shifts to extraordinarily challenging free improvisation. "From simple melodies to complex textures to simplicity again" was how Ayler described his forms; this solo fits that description. Ayler's radical improvising style made him the most influential jazz saxophonist after Ornette Coleman and John Coltrane.

Key Features

- Improvisation: Ayler begins improvising in cyclic form in which each strain of theme

variations is further and further removed from the *Ghosts* melody. As he progresses, all references to the theme vanish altogether and his solo becomes a flow of pure sound in his horn's extreme ranges—overblown, honking, crying sounds that saxophone teachers traditionally teach students to avoid. Like Ayler's other mid-1960s solos, this is an adventure in pure sound.

- Rhythm: The 16-bar tenor sax theme is in the conventional meter of $\frac{4}{4}$; the rest of the performance is arhythmic. Before his variations progress very far, Ayler abandons the meter, and simply plays many notes very fast. Meanwhile the bass line has a much slower momentum while the drum line is a cymbal shimmer, with snare-drum raps that imply an intermediate momentum. The bassist and drummer are responding to the tenor sax lead rather than accompanying it in any standard sense.

- Harmony: After the theme statement Ayler quickly abandons all suggestion of harmonic structure. In fact, his imprecise pitch, the speed of his tenor sax lines, his overtone cries, and his split-multiphonics passages make the very idea of tonality irrelevant. The bassist, by contrast, is more conventionally atonal.

- Dynamics: Next to the extreme *fortissimos* of Ayler's tenor sax, the other instruments sound *piano* (soft) at the very most.

- Voice, feel, and expression: The work is an almost dizzying flight into the tenor saxophone's extreme ranges and techniques. Ayler's dominating presence yields excitement, energy, and exhilaration.

- Musicians' roles: The comparative simplicity of the bass and drum lines are the opposite of Ayler's complexity.

—*John Litweiler*

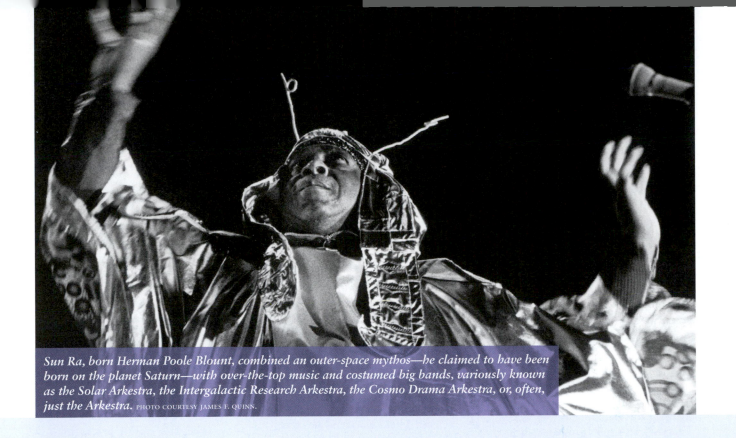

Sun Ra, born Herman Poole Blount, combined an outer-space mythos—he claimed to have been born on the planet Saturn—with over-the-top music and costumed big bands, variously known as the Solar Arkestra, the Intergalactic Research Arkestra, the Cosmo Drama Arkestra, or, often, just the Arkestra. PHOTO COURTESY JAMES F. QUINN.

TIME	SECTION/INSTRUMENTATION	MELODY
0:00	THEME, FIRST PHRASE	Ayler plays the first strain of the simple, diatonic theme unaccompanied, distorting some of the notes.
0:11	THEME, SECOND PHRASE	As Ayler plays the second strain, bassist Gary Peacock enters with a few out-of-tempo notes, quite unrelated to the melody. Sunny Murray, playing only on a cymbal and a snare drum, joins them.
0:21	BRIDGE	Instrumentation as in preceding phrases.
0:33	THEME, FINAL PHRASE	Ayler completes the thematic idea.
0:43	TENOR SAX SOLO	Ayler begins playing variations on the theme, adding rough, dissonant distortions and embellishments. He plays approximate notes rather than precise ones.
0:55		A second strain of theme variations, further from the melody.
1:06		Further strains of the theme variation . . .
1:17		. . . each of which is more distant, twisted.
1:23		Now the theme is scarcely a memory and the solo is pure sound. While Ayler does not play in a fixed tempo or meter, his momentum is fast and becomes faster as he progresses into atonality. His lines seems to career uncontrollably into multiphonics passages and high, wobbly overtones, but . . .
2:11		. . . with a fierce low honk for contrast, Ayler emphasizes his control of the solo. Approximate phrase lengths recurringly imply faint references to the theme until the end.
2:48	BASS SOLO	Gary Peacock's bass solo begins at a slower momentum, starting with spaced phrases, while the patter of Sunny Murray's snare drums and his ongoing cymbal sound provide background in a slightly faster momentum. As this solo progresses, the bass phrases become longer and busier (more notes), and the momentum become faster.
4:12	THEME	After all these adventures in atonality, Ayler returns playing a brief improvisatory melody in the bass register and then returns to the simple, diatonic theme (at 4:21), almost without variation or embellishment, over the atonal bass and arhythmic drums.

Listening Guide

BUSH MAGIC • ART ENSEMBLE OF CHICAGO

Music: Malachi Favors and Famoudou Don Moye, 1980. Personnel: Lester Bowie (trumpet); Roscoe Mitchell and Joseph Jarman (flute, wooden flute, piccolo, small percussion); Malachi Favors (first balafon, bass); Famoudou Don Moye (second balafon). Recorded May 5-6, 1980, live at the Amerika Haus, Munich, Germany. First issue: *Urban Bushmen* (ECM (G)1211/12). Timing: 5:06.

Overview

The most innovative and musically important free jazz group is the Art Ensemble of Chicago, formed in 1966. Its original members were together with few interruptions until Lester Bowie's death in 1999. For most of the AEC's history it was a quintet. Bowie was the most influential trumpeter since the mid-1950s, with a wide, mercurial emotional range and uniquely human expressive resources. Roscoe Mitchell created intense music on woodwinds and percussion, sometimes in very quiet sounds amid silence, sometimes in furiously violent alto or soprano sax solos. Joseph Jarman was capable of dizzying lyrical heights on woodwinds; the great Malachi Favors (a.k.a. Maghostut) created forceful bass lines; and Famoudou Don Moye added drama and rhythmic energy with his many percussion instruments. In the twenty-first century

Mitchell and Moye continued the Art Ensemble of Chicago.

Bush Magic is not a self-contained work but rather a quiet lull in an otherwise often dramatic, even exciting concert. It follows the concert's irresistibly catchy drum introduction by Moye. In its free jazz idiom, *Bush Magic* seems to move from emotional abstraction (the balafons) to subtle, complex feelings (the bass solo).

Key Features

- Improvisation: *Bush Magic* is wholly improvised, with no composed elements. It is almost wholly a **balafon** solo and a bass solo. Occasional percussion sounds accent, a held wooden-flute tone (1:11) and a piccolo (1:54) provide passing colors, then quiet trumpet tones appear (2:42).

  A lower balafon improvisation by Favors opens, and does not fade until 0:29. Meanwhile, Moye's high-register balafon solo becomes the foreground. Favors's bass solo begins in chords and becomes the group's foreground line.

- Rhythm: *Bush Magic* has no meter or fixed tempo. Nevertheless, very fast momentum arises from Moye's unbroken, many-noted balafon

solo. Favors's bass solo begins without tempo; after 4:11, momentum emerges and grows forceful.

- Melody: All improvised. The tiny notes of Moye's balafon solo only seem static, for close listening reveals a highly active line. The greater range and rhythmic variety of the bass solo yields a rich melodic line, mostly in long phrases.
- Harmony: Atonal or pan-tonal.
- Dynamics: A narrow range in the solos, with some quiet interjections by whistles, bells, horn sounds, percussion whacks, and a bicycle horn (3:26).
- Color and texture: *Bush Magic* is a relatively monochromatic lull in an otherwise mostly bright, multi-colored concert.
- Voice, feel, and expression: The balafon's treble range is small. By contrast, Favors's bass solo ranges high and low, in a true, unamplified sound, revealing fervent feeling.
- Musicians' roles: Moye and Favors solo, others comment quietly on their unusual instruments. This is worlds away from the standard horns-and-rhythm jazz combos.

—*John Litweiler*

TIME	INSTRUMENTATION	MUSICAL EVENT
0:00	LOWER-REGISTER BALAFON, PERCUSSION	A musical line begins on a fast rhythmic pattern.
0:16	HIGHER-REGISTER BALAFON; FLUTE (ENTERS AT APPROX 0:17); LIGHT PERCUSSION CONTINUES	A stream of tiny, very fast notes, with no rests; this stream of notes continues to 2:46.
2:33	BASS, ENTERS FOR THE FIRST TIME	The bassist (Favors) plays double-stops (chords) that now begin a foreground melodic line. Saxophone briefly comments at approx. 2:53.
3:05	BASS SOLO, WITH PERCUSSION ACCOMPANIMENT	The bassist solos alone.
3:52		Added tension enters the bass solo. A crucial phrase of up-bent tones, separated by space, appears. It leads to steady momentum after 4:11. By 4:30 the insistence of Favors's fast, undecorated line suggests emotional harshness, even anger, including demanding, repeated tones.
4:55	HORNS	Horns enter, announcing the end of the *Bush Magic* interlude. The concert's next episode (not heard here) begins with a comic march and soon moves into animated improvisations by the ensemble. Later in the concert Favors himself creates especially stark, forceful bass commentary to Bowie's ballad *New York Is Full of Lonely People*.

entire jazz tradition. The themes he composed—as in *Bells* and *Spirits Rejoice* (both 1965)—were like nineteenth-century pop songs, hymns, and bugle calls that sounded to writer Dan Morgenstern "like a Salvation Army band on LSD." Ayler played with a big tenor saxophone sound ("the biggest human sound I ever heard," critic Larry Kart said) and a wide, quavery vibrato. At fast tempos—and Ayler was another who played in the fastest tempos humanly possible—he did not play notes at all; rather, he approximated notes with distorted sounds, multiphonics, overtone screams, and wild, long, careening phrases. "It's a matter of following the sound . . . " said his brother and trumpeter Donald Ayler, "the pitches, the colors, you have to watch them move." Albert drowned, apparently murdered, in 1970; his own style became almost as influential as Coltrane's and Coleman's.

Terrifically fast tempos; dissonances and extreme sounds; and long, furious, exhilarating collective improvisations all characterized late-1960s New York free jazz—"energy music"—inspired by Coltrane, Ayler, Shepp, and Taylor. But energy music was emotionally narrow, even obsessive, compared to the music that was emerging in Chicago, where free jazz could be lyrical, soft as well as intense, simple as well as complex, composed as well as improvised, even swinging or humorous. The Chicagoans—members of the cooperative AACM (Association for the Advancement of Creative Musicians)—played in big bands led by veteran pianist-composer **Muhal Richard Abrams** as well as in small groups. One of them, the trio of altoist Roscoe Mitchell, trumpeter Lester Bowie, and bassist **Malachi Favors** (a.k.a. Maghostut) created musical lines that included "freak" sounds (bells, whistles, and

toys) and silences. In time they were joined by **Joseph Jarman**—who had achieved an unparalleled virtuosity in his alto saxophone's extreme ranges—and drummer Famoudou Don Moye, and they took the name the Art Ensemble of Chicago.

Like them, altoist **Anthony Braxton** explored free improvisation and unaccompanied soloing (his 1968 *For Alto Saxophone* album inspired a generation of horn players to play a cappella solos); like them, Braxton went on to master a number of different horns and became a prolific composer. More than the rest, he returned often to the bebop-era repertoire, with bop accompanists. To the early concept of free jazz—freedom from traditional harmonic, rhythmic, and formal restraints—the Chicagoans added a crucial element: freedom of choice. On his 1976 recording of Scott Joplin's *Maple Leaf Rag* (*JTSA* Disc 6/Track 1), Braxton along with fellow AACM member Muhal Richard Abrams on piano preserve the piece's essential spirit while playfully extending its melodic and harmonic roots.

Free Spaces

Where could the new musicians play? With night-clubs vanishing in Chicago, the AACM was formed to produce concerts by its member musicians. Churches, art galleries, high schools and colleges,

---

balafon   West African tuned percussion instrument, played by hitting tone bars with mallets.

The Association for the Advancement of Creative Musicians (AACM).
PHOTO COURTESY MICHAEL WILDERMAN.

Jazz Cooperatives and Performance Spaces

The notion of musicians cooperating in business was a long-held one in jazz; members of early jazz bands often pooled income and shared responsibilities and decision making. But as jazz developed along less commercial lines, some musicians found it desirable to take more active steps to ensure their creative and economic survival. This inclination gave rise to jazz cooperatives—organizations formed for their members' mutual benefit.

In 1960, bassist Charles Mingus and drummers Max Roach and Jo Jones formed the **Jazz Artists Guild** to produce their own musical events. Though the Guild didn't last long, it planted an important seed: the idea that musician-run enterprises could work.

The Jazz Composers Guild, formed by trumpeter Bill Dixon in 1964, included a number of New York free jazz artists, among them Archie Shepp, Cecil Taylor, Sun Ra, and Paul and **Carla Bley**. The Guild produced weekly concerts in a New York City loft and sought to negotiate members' contracts with clubs

and record companies. Its efforts led to the formation of the **Jazz Composers Orchestra Association (JCOA)**, which lasted through much of the 1970s. The JCOA performed and recorded large-scale, big band compositions by its directors, composers Mike Mantler and Carla Bley, and other "outside" composers; its New Music Distribution Service distributed albums of free jazz produced by small labels, some of which were musician-owned.

There were other musicians' cooperatives, based outside New York. In 1961, pianist-composer Horace Tapscott formed the Union of God's Musicians and Artists Ascension (UGMAA) to produce concerts by his big band in Los Angeles. The **Association for the Advancement of Creative Musicians (AACM)**, the most successful cooperative, was founded in May 1956 and had its base in Chicago. Its longevity rested in part on its school, which produced the organization's later generations of musicians and teachers.

Inspired by the AACM, Oliver Lake, Julius Hemphill, and other St. Louis musicians formed the **Black Artists Group (BAG)**, which

was active at the turn of the 1970s; like the AACM, it emphasized the sharing of creative discoveries as a vital by-product of cooperation. In the 1980s, in Chicago, came a music lovers' cooperative, the all-volunteer Southend Musicworks, which produced a variety of jazz and even contemporary classical concerts.

Grants from the National Endowment for the Arts (founded in 1965), state arts councils, and private philanthropies helped support the teaching and performance programs of the AACM and its successors. In time, as free jazz found its way into a growing number of venues, and as the music gained favor with a younger generation of listeners, the need for cooperative efforts declined. And as individual musicians arrived at different levels of musical and popular success, the cooperative, all-for-one feeling often dissipated. Nevertheless, for a number of important modern jazz artists, participation in cooperatives marked a crucial stage of their careers.

—John Litweiler

The Art Ensemble of Chicago launched in 1966 and purveyed sonic explorations using the basic vehicle of trumpet, saxophones, drums, and bass. They also became known for embracing unusual instruments (including African instruments, bells, whistles, and musical toys). The Ensemble continued to perform together through trumpeter Lester Bowie's death in 1999.

✳ Explore on mymusiclab.com

Famoudou Don Moye •
Drums and Percussion

Moye preceded his tenure in the Art Ensemble with experiences that supported an adventurous approach to rhythm. Work with such forward-thinking musicians as guitarist Sonny Sharrock and saxophonist Pharoah Sanders, as well as involvement in African and Caribbean percussion, help extend his interests far beyond standard beat keeping—which fit ideally with the "free" aesthetic.

Roscoe Mitchell • Alto and Soprano Saxophone, Woodwinds, and Percussion

Mitchell emerged in mid-1960s Chicago as an especially imaginative improviser, as apt to use silence as sound in his solos. In the Art Ensemble of Chicago he brought variety, humor, and an unconventional, multi-instrumental voice to the group "discussions."

Lester Bowie • Trumpet

Bowie made "freak" sounds—blurts, smears, chuckles, squeals—an intrinsic part of the Art Ensemble sensibility. In so doing, Bowie played as strong a role as any of the other band members in casting the group's ensemble work as near "conversations"—at times a seeming convocation of voices from Maurice Sendak's *Where the Wild Things Are*.

PHOTO COURTESY FIN COSTELLO/REDFERNS/GETTY IMAGES.

Malachi Favors • Bass

Favors brought an earthy, swinging solidity to the Art Ensemble's free-ranging explorations. Like the other band members, he played more than one instrument: among them were the zither, banjo, and harmonica. But it was his rigorously honed bass technique—he had played bop with Dizzy Gillespie, Freddie Hubbard, and Andrew Hill before joining the AEC—that most distinguished his Art Ensemble role.

Joseph Jarman (not shown) • Flute, Saxophone, Wind Instruments, and Percussion

Jarman was an early member of the Association for the Advancement of Creative Musicians, the cooperative that spawned the Art Ensemble. Jarman's mastery of saxophone enabled him to play outside the instrument's standard register and timbre, and make audible his vast range of imagined unearthly sounds. He left the Art Ensemble in 1993, delved into Zen Buddhism, and later joined pianist Myra Melford and violinist Leroy Jenkins in the trio Equal Interest.

neighborhood taverns, a lodge hall, and a historic settlement house became concert sites for the AACM players, who booked, advertised, and sold tickets for concerts, then swept the floors and turned out the lights once the music was over. The AACM was not the first self-producing effort by musicians, but it lasted arguably the longest. For over three decades, beginning in the late 1960s, it ran a music school for inner-city youth; some excellent musicians, including saxophonists Douglas Ewart and Edward Wilkerson and trombonist George Lewis, were graduates.

In New York, jazz musicians and music lovers converted lofts in old factory buildings into concert sites; the best known of these were Artists House, owned by Ornette Coleman, and Studio Rivbea, operated by saxophonist Sam Rivers. In this respect, too, free jazz was revolutionary. Just as swing thrived primarily in ballrooms and bop in nightclubs, free jazz became a music of concert venues and performance spaces. And if free jazz began as underground experiments, in time it was featured at jazz festivals and major concert halls. Without a dominating figure such as Armstrong, Ellington, or Parker, free jazz took off in many different directions. Unlike leading postwar combos (the Modern Jazz Quartet, Horace Silver, Art Blakey, Miles Davis, Dave Brubeck, and Thelonious Monk), the most popular free jazz groups were only intermittently active—their members had too many other musical interests. So, for example, the members of the Art Ensemble of Chicago and the multisaxophone virtuosos of the **World Saxophone Quartet** (originally David Murray, Julius Hemphill, Hamiet Bluiett, and the brilliant, Dolphy-inspired Oliver Lake) also maintained individual careers as composers, sidemen, and leaders of small and large groups. (For an example of the World Saxophone Quartet's sound, listen to *Steppin'* [1981, *JTSA* Disc 6/Track 6].)

Similarly, the free jazz scene was geographically dispersed. New England and upstate New York (notably the Creative Music Studio, a school in Woodstock) were new-music centers, and handfuls of musicians sparked activity in Houston, Toronto, New Orleans, Detroit, and a number of other cities throughout North America. In San Francisco were the far-ranging ROVA Saxophone Quartet, which played works by its members and commissioned music by others. In Los Angeles

two of Ornette Coleman's former associates—Bobby Bradford, a wonderful lyric trumpeter, and John Carter, who brought the clarinet back to jazz—formed a longtime team. Carter also composed a series of five **suites**—including *Castles of Ghana* (1985) and *Fields* (1988)—interpreting the historic black experience in the United States. Fred Anderson and Hal Russell, two pioneering free players, were catalysts in reviving the Chicago scene, beginning in the late 1970s: Anderson led bands and played endlessly creative, lyrical, blues-rich tenor sax, and the late multi-instrumentalist, composer, and teacher Russell led the freewheeling, often hilarious N-R-G Ensemble. None of the later AACM generations were much influenced by the innovations of the first generation, except for Anderson's protégés, especially saxophonist Douglas Ewart.

TAKE NOTE

- Who were the leading innovators in the free jazz movement?

Experimental Composers

One of the most radical departures of the era was undertaken in the traditional-jazz idiom by the Australian jazz and ragtime composer David Dallwitz. The subject of his *Ern Malley Suite* (1975) is a notorious down-under literary hoax. Imagine a singer like the young Billie Holiday warbling surreal lyrics ("Come, we will dance sedate quadrilles/A pallid polka or a yelping shimmy/ Over these sunken sodden breeding-grounds! . . . / Culture, forsooth! Albert, get my gun") while a fine Dixieland band plays strange ragtime melodies.

"Outside" experiments came from the realm of

Anthony Braxton's compositions, titled with diagrams instead of words, reflected his interest in the mathematical aspects of music. PHOTO COURTESY VAL WILMER/DOWN BEAT ARCHIVES.

---

suite a musical work with multiple movements or major sections; examples are Tchaikovsky's *Nutcracker Suite*, Ellington and Strayhorn's *Far East Suite*, and Mary Lou Williams's *Zodiac Suite*.

classical composition as well. In the 1950s, composer Gunther Schuller had conceived of "third stream" music, a fusion of the classical and jazz traditions. Two of his 1959–60 works are considered modern landmarks: *Abstraction* offers a string quartet playing an atonal piece in pyramid form with, at the apex, an unaccompanied Ornette Coleman alto solo; in the four *Variants on a Theme by Thelonious Monk (Criss Cross)*, improvisers including Coleman, Dolphy, and bassist Scott LaFaro enjoy interplay with each other and with a string quartet.

Performances by composer Carla Bley's big bands were often as entertaining and humorous as they were challenging. PHOTO COURTESY PHILIP RYALLS/REDFERNS/GETTY IMAGES.

Other classical composers, some encouraged by Schuller, contributed new works. They included Milton Babbitt's *All Set* (1958) and Krystof Penderecki's *Actions* (1971). The score of the 1997 opera *Amistad* by Anthony Davis included free jazz improvisers with the orchestra's symphonic musicians. Pianist-teacher Ran Blake advanced the third-stream idea to include the fusion of any ethnic and art-music traditions, whether improvised or composed.

Variations of the third-stream concept pop up in most extended pieces by free jazz artists, including Coleman. Carla Bley composed her "chronotransduction" *Escalator over the Hill* (1968–71) for a crowd of improvisers, singers, and reciters. For Charlie Haden's Liberation Music Orchestra, Bley's suites, such as *Dream Keeper* (1990), link Spanish and Latin American folk music with original pieces; her best scores for her own big bands, including *Spangled Banner Minor and Other Patriotic Songs* (1977), are notable for balancing distinctive elements and for a recurring whimsical humor. Cecil Taylor's large works for big band fuse composition and improvisation in grand polyphonic designs, as in *Alms/Tiergarten (Spree)* (1988). AACM artists, including Abrams, Jarman, Leroy Jenkins, Douglas Ewart, and **Henry Threadgill**, all composed large works. The largest is Anthony Braxton's *For Four Orchestras* (1978); among the most musically successful are Braxton's jazz-band scores and Leo Smith's *Return to My Native Land II* (1981).

Some other composers worked specifically within jazz traditions. The big band, octet, and saxophone ensemble scores of Julius Hemphill,

David Murray, and Edward Wilkerson (especially for his group Eight Bold Souls) gained vigor from Ellington sonorities and swing and bop phrasing. The potent trio Air (Henry Threadgill, woodwinds; Fred Hopkins, bass; Steve McCall, drums) created free interpretations of Scott Joplin rags as well as of Threadgill themes. In the 1980s Threadgill composed works—such as *Subject to Change* (1984) and *Theme from Thomas Cole* (1986)—with memorable melodies and countermelodies; rich harmonies; expressive soloing; and constant, ongoing, nervous activity for his sextet. As a composer, Roscoe Mitchell made some of the most far-reaching innovations of jazz form, including *Nonaah* (1976), originally a saxophone solo that he recomposed several times for wind and string ensembles. He created *L-R-G* (1978) for himself (woodwinds) and two brass instrumentalists (Leo Smith and George Lewis), in ever-mobile disparities; *The Maze* (1978), by contrast, contains the interactions of eight percussionists. In these works—Mitchell called them "sound collages"—form and musical line evolve from the unique sounds created by the performers.

Despite the artistic success of these big band and orchestra compositions, most were seldom performed because of the expense of paying so many musicians. Self-contained orchestras, including Sun Ra's Arkestra, whose members lived together in Philadelphia, or local phenomena like the AACM big band (Chicago) and Either/Orchestra (Boston) were rare. Needed were repertory ensembles dedicated to playing new music, just as the Lincoln

Jazz and Classical Music: The Second Half of the Twentieth Century

In the first half of the century, most composers who adopted jazz—whether in America, France, or elsewhere—did so as outsiders seeking modernist energy in a musical idiom beyond their own cultural heritage. And none of their works invited improvisation. In the second half of the century, however, the most notable developments in concert-hall hybrids came from jazz musicians writing in extended musical forms that provided space for improvisation. Duke Ellington paved the way with his landmark *Black, Brown, and Beige* (1943), a multimovement "tone parallel to the history of the Negro in America," that premiered at Carnegie Hall. Ellington composed several other large-scale works, mixing notated and improvised music, such as *Harlem* (1950), commissioned by Arturo Toscanini and the NBC Symphony (though never played by them), and his and Billy Strayhorn's witty, swinging versions of Grieg's *Peer Gynt Suite* and Tchaikovsky's *Nutcracker Suite* (1960).

Inspired, in part, by Ellington's model, other jazz composers followed suit. Charles Mingus's masterpiece *The Black Saint and the Sinner Lady* (1963) lasts nearly 40 minutes, and combines written composition, extensive improvisation, and considerable editing and overdubbing overseen by the composer. At a time when Ellington was conceiving and performing a series of sacred concerts, Mary Lou Williams composed several jazz masses, most notably *Mary Lou's Mass* (1971). The renowned jazz musician, composer, and educator David Baker contributed such works as *Le Chat qui Peche*, for soprano, orchestra, and jazz quartet (1974); *Three Ethnic Dances*, a clarinet concerto (1992); and *Roots II* for piano trio (1992).

Gunther Schuller, the omnivorous composer, conductor, crossover French-horn player, and one time president of the New England Conservatory, acted as a figurehead among jazz musicians pursuing serious composition. In 1957, Schuller coined the term "third stream" to acknowledge and encourage compositions that blended genuine jazz elements and classical forms and techniques. Schuller's own works, such as *Transformation* (1957), *Seven Studies on Themes By Paul* Klee (1959), and *Abstraction* (also 1959), put his ideas into practice. Other important third stream composers included Ran Blake, Jimmy Guiffre, John Lewis, and George Russell.

In the 1980s and 1990s, jazz itself enjoyed a newly elevated status as a kind of classic music, and as a result, efforts to blend jazz and "classical" elements seemed less urgent. Yet such efforts continue in surprising, artistic, and ambitious ways. Perhaps the most prominent transformation of the impulse at the beginning of the twenty-first century could be found in the work of Wynton Marsalis, who wrote a series of works for Jazz at Lincoln Center. His *In This House, On This Morning* (1992) and his jazz oratorio *Blood on the Fields* (1997), which won a Pulitzer Prize, demonstrated the ongoing possibilities of extended, jazz-based concert music and its capacity to earn prestigious prizes and institutional support. So too does a series of pieces by the composer-reed player Paquito D'Rivera, a Guggenheim award winner, who has earned commissions from such groups as the National Symphony and the Turtle Island String Quartet and reinvigorated the Latin jazz tradition with fresh musical hybrids. Together, works by Marsalis and D'Rivera answer Dvořák's call (discussed in "Jazz and Classical Music: The First Half of the Twentieth Century," page 74) beyond his wildest imaginings.

—*Jeffrey Magee*

Center and Smithsonian orchestras would focus on playing earlier jazz. In fact, for a time in the 1970s, trumpeter Mike Mantler maintained the Jazz Composers Orchestra as a workshop for New York composers. But most orchestral performances of jazz works were ad hoc, often resulting from grants by arts philanthropies. The largest arts funder, the National Endowment for the Arts, provided significant support for jazz composition in the 1970s and 1980s.

European jazz composers fared better than their U.S. counterparts. For over two decades, beginning in 1966, the Globe Unity Orchestra, comprising the best European free players, gathered almost annually to tour and debut new works by leader Alex Schlippenbach and other members. Bassist Barry Guy

The experimental big bands led by composer Muhal Richard Abrams yielded future members of the AACM and the Art Ensemble of Chicago. PHOTO COURTESY BILL ABERNATHY/DOWN BEAT ARCHIVES.

Staying Free

In the twenty-first century a few major figures such as Ornette Coleman and Cecil Taylor remained attractions at jazz concerts. Pharoah Sanders, Henry Threadgill, and David Murray were among the prominent free jazz performers in mainstream nightclubs, concerts, and festivals. Communities of free jazz artists kept busy presenting concerts and nightclub gigs in Boston, the San Francisco Bay Area, Chicago, New York, London, and Berlin, among other hot spots. The leading U.S. festival devoted entirely to free jazz and free improvisation was the annual Vision Festival, in New York City, which offered veteran explorers from around the world and introduced bold young creators.

While the U.S. government encumbered visiting European artists with red tape, Canada had few such restrictions, so festivals such as those in Vancouver, British Columbia; Edmonton, Alberta; and Victoriaville, Quebec, annually presented international free jazz performers. Several European festivals, including the Total Music Meeting and Moers annual affairs (both in Germany), also showcased artists who played the new music.

U.S. radio coverage of experimental jazz, which had always been limited, became more so in the 1990s and 2000s. In keeping with that period's fashion for conservative playlists, a good many public radio stations eliminated innovative jazz entirely, leaving college and university stations to pick up the slack.

Buyers of jazz compact discs needed to be alert, because jazz albums tended to be yanked from the market a few months after release. The rock-music conglomerates that controlled most of the recording industry in the twenty-first century eliminated most jazz recording activity. On the other hand, some musicians made downloads of their work available on the Internet, while independent labels in the United States and Europe—such as Delmark, Intakt, Hat ART, and Emanem—released many albums, and many of their CDs remained available.

All of which served to underscore what had always been the case: the determined explorers at the frontiers of jazz are willing to do whatever it takes to expand the music's boundaries.

TAKE NOTE

- What role did cooperatives and independent performance spaces play in free jazz?

formed and re-formed the London Jazz Composers Orchestra often, from 1970, to play his massive settings (including *Harmos*, 1989) for band and top British improvisers; the Italian Instabile Orchestra served as a similar showcase for Italian players.

Guy, who maintained dual careers as a jazz and classical musician, was one of a number of Europeans advancing the third-stream concept. Other successes included the fiery Brotherhood of Breath, 1970s South African exiles and English musicians who merged free jazz with black South African folk-pop; Pierre Dørge's New Jungle Orchestra (Denmark), fusing Ellington, free jazz, and West African music; and Willem Breuker's Kollektief (Holland), playing the leader's mad, satiric mélanges of jazz, classical, folk, and dance musics.

- Why was 1959 such a pivotal year in jazz history?

In 1959, saxophonist Ornette Coleman ignited an explosion of exploratory creative activity by jazz musicians. The musical idiom that emerged was given names such as "the new thing," "outside jazz," and "free jazz." Free jazz sought to remove all conventional ideas of melody, rhythm, harmony, and performance to allow for total individual expression.

- What were the roots of free jazz?

Free jazz emerged at a time of great social change. The passing of the Civil Rights and Voting Rights acts in the mid-1960s codified African Americans' insistence on racial equality, in itself manifesting a broader desire for personal freedom. Two important ancestors of free jazz were bassist Charles Mingus, who composed complex and challenging music, and composer Bob Graettinger, whose works for the Stan Kenton Orchestra incorporated atonality, polyrhythmic movement, and ever-changing activity.

- What were the innovations introduced by free jazz in melody, rhythm, harmony, and performance style?

In free jazz, melodies, rhythm, and harmony were freely improvised by each player. Musicians were encouraged to abandon preexisting or familiar riffs, harmonies, or rhythmic patterns. Performance style was assertive and uncompromising, taking bebop's anti-commercial stance to its logical conclusion. Free jazz was the most defiant attempt of jazz musicians to challenge their audience, rather than to aim for widespread success.

- Who were the leading innovators in the free jazz movement?

Although Ornette Coleman is considered the spiritual father of free jazz, the style was carried forward by a wide range of performers, including mainstreamers who embraced the new style (such as John Coltrane) and young innovators (pianist Cecil Taylor). Among the more adventurous were bandleader/keyboard player Sun Ra and saxophone players Albert Ayler and Anthony Braxton. The Art Ensemble of Chicago was an important ensemble that wed free jazz with an Afro-centric composition and performing style.

- What role did cooperatives and independent performance spaces play in free jazz?

The Chicago-based Association for the Advancement of Creative Musicians (AACM) and New York's Black Artist Group (BAG), among others, helped nurture the careers of young musicians, composers, and music promoters. Cooperatives enabled musicians to have a space in which to explore new musical formats. Alternative performance spaces similarly allowed for the new music to be heard, without having to be commercially successful.

DISCUSSION QUESTIONS

1. Identify several ways that 1959 was a turning point in the history of jazz.

2. Free jazz emerged in the 1960s. What else was going on in the 1960s that paralleled the revolution against jazz traditions?

3. Identify some of the major differences between free jazz and the jazz styles that preceded it.

4. Identify at least one way in which free jazz, as revolutionary as it was, can be said to be carrying on a jazz tradition.

5. Compare the roles of Louis Armstrong, Charlie Parker, and Ornette Coleman in their respective time periods and jazz movements.

6. Discuss the relationships between emerging popular music such as Motown and rock and the dwindling commercial prospects of free jazz.

7. Do you think free jazz musicians should have expected acceptance by a wide audience? Why or why not?

8. Why do you think there have been relatively few women instrumentalists in jazz? Discuss which instruments have had more female players and which instruments have had fewer. What are the differences?

KEY TERMS & KEY PEOPLE

CHAPTER 9

Fusion Jazz

by Stephen F. Pond

TAKE NOTE

- What is fusion jazz and how does it compare to other jazz styles?
- What were some of the early forms of fusion jazz?
- What were some of the key fusion bands of the early 1970s, and how did their styles differ?
- How did fusion jazz become more commercial by fusing with R&B music?
- How has fusion continued to develop and who are some current performers?

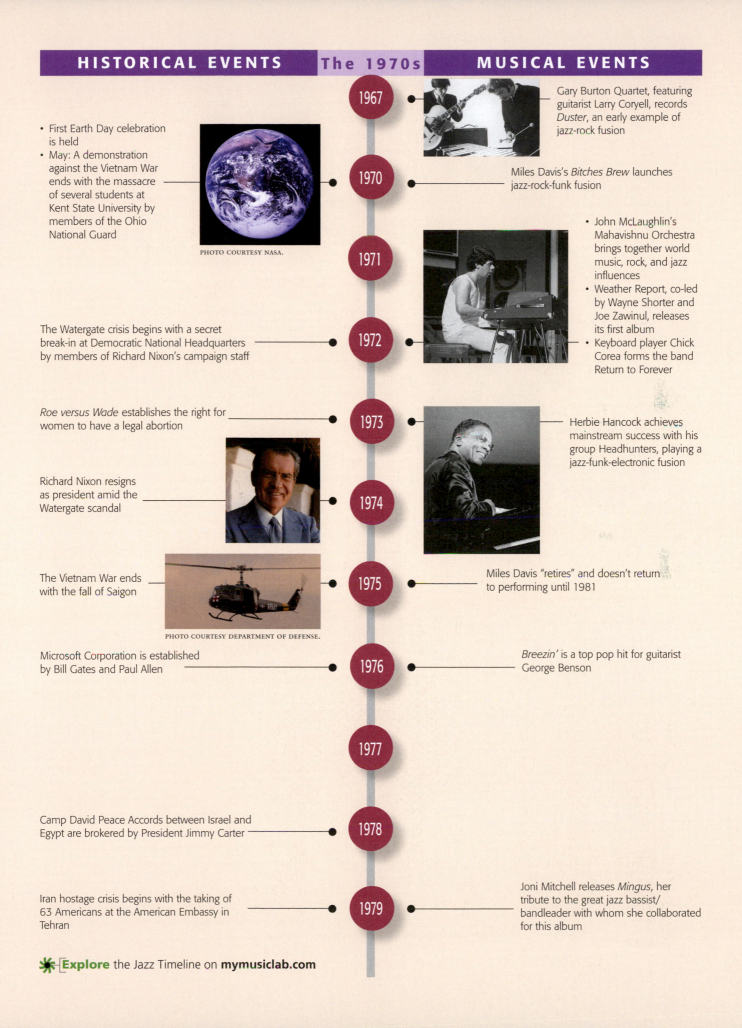

1967

Gary Burton Quartet, featuring guitarist Larry Coryell, records *Duster*, an early example of jazz-rock fusion

- First Earth Day celebration is held
- May: A demonstration against the Vietnam War ends with the massacre of several students at Kent State University by members of the Ohio National Guard

PHOTO COURTESY NASA.

1970

Miles Davis's *Bitches Brew* launches jazz-rock-funk fusion

1971

- John McLaughlin's Mahavishnu Orchestra brings together world music, rock, and jazz influences

The Watergate crisis begins with a secret break-in at Democratic National Headquarters by members of Richard Nixon's campaign staff

1972

- Weather Report, co-led by Wayne Shorter and Joe Zawinul, releases its first album
- Keyboard player Chick Corea forms the band Return to Forever

Roe versus Wade establishes the right for women to have a legal abortion

1973

Herbie Hancock achieves mainstream success with his group Headhunters, playing a jazz-funk-electronic fusion

Richard Nixon resigns as president amid the Watergate scandal

1974

The Vietnam War ends with the fall of Saigon

1975

Miles Davis "retires" and doesn't return to performing until 1981

PHOTO COURTESY DEPARTMENT OF DEFENSE.

Microsoft Corporation is established by Bill Gates and Paul Allen

1976

Breezin' is a top pop hit for guitarist George Benson

1977

Camp David Peace Accords between Israel and Egypt are brokered by President Jimmy Carter

1978

Iran hostage crisis begins with the taking of 63 Americans at the American Embassy in Tehran

1979

Joni Mitchell releases *Mingus*, her tribute to the great jazz bassist/bandleader with whom she collaborated for this album

Explore the Jazz Timeline on **mymusiclab.com**

Jazz musicians in the 1960s explored breaking down the boundaries of meter, structure, and harmony, but a significant number also branched out to experiment with expressive elements associated with other musical styles. They used these elements to expand their expressive palettes, while leaving their core jazz identities intact. Another set of players sought to graft their jazz styles to other popular styles in more fundamental ways. By the 1970s, many jazz musicians were turning to rock, soul, funk, avant-garde, classical music, and a variety of non-Western musics in search of new approaches to harmony and rhythm, new production methods, and new audiences. These fusions of jazz with other musical styles also brought jazz back to the popular music audience in a way that had not been seen since the swing era.

Guitarist John McLaughlin with his twin-neck electric guitar (ca. 1974).
PHOTO COURTESY SONY BMG MUSIC ENTERTAINMENT/ GETTY IMAGES.

Fusion jazz expanded the diversity of musical styles that could be considered jazz. In fact, although we can talk about fusion as a musical movement, trying to pin it down stylistically can be difficult. Rather than a *style*, fusion jazz emerged (and continues today) as an *approach* to music making, one in which jazz musicians both embraced jazz's recent past and distanced themselves from it.

Defining Fusion Jazz

Since the mid-1970s, the term fusion jazz has encompassed a variety of approaches and styles. Some of the more well-known fusion styles are as follows:

- Music played in rock's straight dance groove rather than jazz's swing rhythm (**Mahavishnu Orchestra**, **Return to Forever**)
- Funk/dance-pop inspired players that make heavy use of synthesizers (**Herbie Hancock**, **Weather Report**, George Benson)
- Groups like Blood, Sweat and Tears that feature a jazz horn section with a rock lead singer and rhythm section
- Hybrids of instrumental jazz and pop, like the very popular music played by Kenny G
- New age/impressionistic players like **Pat Metheny**
- World music fusions that might incorporate South Indian elements (**John McLaughlin** with Shakti), Afro-Brazilian ones (Oregon, Weather Report), or Spanish flamenco (**Al Di Meola** with Paco de Lucia)

It's difficult, and maybe impossible, to locate a set of stylistic principles that weaves these diverse strands together into a single fabric. Yet all of them thread through music that has been labeled fusion.

Another way to think about fusion jazz (or any kind of music) is to consider how the music is marketed to its consumers. Who listens to it and ultimately buys it? Prior to the late 1960s, the jazz press rarely mentioned rock performers, and popular music magazines rarely mentioned jazz

---

fusion jazz   a mixture of different musical styles; introduced in the 1960s as a term for the blend of jazz with rock and funk pioneered by Miles Davis, Weather Report, and others.

musicians. By 1970, that segregation was breaking down. Around the same time, a similar eclecticism showed up in the rise of free format (free-form) FM radio, a precursor to today's independent college radio, in which fiercely independent deejays routinely served up what they deemed best from widely diverse fare. Record labels also began cross-marketing the same music to several audiences at once—and to all these audiences as newly integrated. Together, free-form radio and cross-marketing confronted the fiction that people listen to only one type of music. (Students in surveys rarely claim to like only one type of music, although they sometimes do claim to *hate* one or two styles.)

The same can be said for the musicians themselves. As **Miles Davis**'s mid-1980s bassist and collaborator Marcus Miller commented, "It's just music, and the lines dividing these things aren't as thick as people think. . . . Musicians coming from urban situations are exposed to all these kinds of music at one time, in equal amounts." The multiplicity of tastes Miller described in the 1980s was equally true in the 1960s. For many musicians of that era, it seemed a natural outcome to incorporate elements from any and all of these musical exposures.

A working definition of fusion jazz, then, is two-pronged: the music resulting from musicians' attempts to extend jazz's traditional aesthetics of adventure and improvisation, borrowing from a range of other music styles; and the drawing together of jazz audiences with others formerly beyond jazz's reach.

TAKE NOTE

- What is fusion jazz and how does it compare to other jazz styles?

Foreshadowing Fusion

Early Mixes

Many of the jazz styles explored in this book can be linked to certain historical eras. Bebop, for example, emerged in the 1940s, and it makes sense to examine bebop in the context of the era's musical, social, and economic forces, and as a continuing presence in jazz since then. Fusion jazz can also be discussed in this way as a response to these same trends in the 1960s and 1970s. But fusing in jazz—jazz musicians incorporating elements from outside jazz—has a long history, and though it proved a highlight of jazz activity in the 1960s and 1970s, it continues to this day.

Jazz has always drawn on other popular musical styles as a basis for its own repertory. From its earliest days, to "jazz" a blues or military march meant

to play a popular tune in the vocabulary of jazz, and bebop players of the 1940s routinely used popular music as fodder for creative reworking. At various times, as in the case of the **western swing** played by Bob Wills and the Texas Playboys, musicians outside of jazz returned the favor. Wills played country and western songs in a modified big band format, blending the lilt and sway of the "territory" big band to his core "country" instruments of fiddle and steel guitar and a homespun vocal delivery. Beginning in the mid-1940s, **jump blues** was a hard-driving, small-group swing style, one of the styles that collectively came to be coined "rhythm and blues" (R&B), exemplified by tenor saxophonist Louis Jordan (*Choo Choo Ch-Boogie*, 1946) and by vocalist Big Joe Turner. Other jazz hybrids abound. Afro-Caribbean and Afro-Brazilian musics, for example, have never been far from jazz's core, a fact explored and highlighted in the **mambo**, **Cubop**, and **bossa nova** styles of the twentieth century's middle decades (see Chapter 10). In fact, hybridizing—fusing—is a long-standing practice in jazz.

Rock, Funk, and the Climate for Fusion

As the 1960s unfolded, rhythm and blues and rock and roll took on new identities. Soul (especially the polished, pop soul of Motown Records) incorporated more sophisticated lyrics and a wider range of orchestration and recording techniques than its jump blues and **doo-wop** predecessors. Rock recordings paralleled and, as in the case of the Beatles' mid-decade LPs, intensified these changes (*Revolver*, 1966, and *Sgt. Pepper's Lonely Hearts Club Band*, 1967). Rock guitarists embraced the practice of distorting their

---

western swing a mixture of jazz and country music, popularized in the 1930s by Bob Wills and His Texas Playboys and, later, Asleep at the Wheel.

jump blues a form of upbeat, jazz-tinged blues made popular in the 1940s and 1950s by bandleader Louis Jordan and others.

mambo (Bantu) a highly syncopated instrumental genre created by Cuban bandleader Pérez Prado and first performed by him in Mexico; a dance style highly popular in the 1950s that was a precursor to salsa.

Cubop from "Cuban" plus "bebop"; Afro-Latin-flavored bebop, pioneered in the 1940s by Cuban trumpeter-arranger Mario Bauzá; later known simply as "Latin jazz."

bossa nova Portuguese for "new tendency"; a syncopated, sensuous musical style refined from the samba and introduced in the late 1950s in Rio de Janeiro, Brazil.

doo-wop popular vocal music of the 1950s and 1960s, in which a lead singer was backed by harmony vocalists. A style of rhythm and blues, doo-wop was often sung a cappella (without instrumental accompaniment).

instruments' sounds, using fuzz-tones, amplifier feedback, wah-wah effects, and other add-ons to extend the timbres that had been so important to their blues forebears' style.

Guitarist **Jimi Hendrix**, whose virtuosity seemed to announce a new expressive universe, became a towering influence for rock musicians as much through his stunningly creative use of controlled noise as through his inventive note choices or his high-velocity melodic runs. Live rock performances by such late 1960s/early 1970s groups as Cream featured extended guitar solos. Borrowing licks, songs, and—perhaps most importantly—sounds from T-Bone Walker, Muddy Waters, Albert King, and other urban blues guitarists of the 1940s and 1950s, Cream often played whole sets consisting of a single, extended song—even over a single, cycling riff.

At about the same time, soul artist James Brown introduced a new style that featured stripped-down, raw-edged vocals, punctuating a tight matrix of sounds from his big band in a driving funky rhythm (*Papa's Got a Brand New Bag*, 1965). Grounding the groove on the bass guitar and the bass's pronounced arrival on the **downbeat** (the "one" of the bar), Brown spread the rest of the groove throughout the band, the musicians—even horn players—playing as percussively as possible, making each sound an essential part of a groove matrix. Other groups, notably Sly and the

Family Stone, would soon pick up the groove-matrix technique, the foundation of an increasingly pervasive style that became known as **funk**.

Playing extended solos over riffs or over short, repeating song forms has a long history in jazz, too. Territory bands during the swing era famously mastered the riff tune (as in Count Basie's *One O'Clock Jump*, 1937; Disc I, Track 12/Download Track 12). Paul Gonsalves's 27-chorus blues solo on Ellington's *Diminuendo and Crescendo in Blue* at the 1956 Newport Jazz Festival brought the normally staid audience to its feet, demonstrating the ability of a mere 12 bars, repeated many times, to build creative tension to the frenzy point. John Coltrane used modal vamps in such pieces as *My Favorite Things* (1960, issued 1961) and *Acknowledgement* from *A Love Supreme* (1964, issued 1965; JTSA Disc 5/Track 3) to provide surprisingly flexible frameworks for his extended solos.

With modal playing and with the free jazz movement, jazz musicians were finding routes outside of the normal approaches to harmony that had driven Western music for four centuries and that also had provided the chord progressions for bebop. Given rock's and soul's attentiveness to timbre and groove, described previously, and given jazz's readiness to wander from harmonies that were beginning to seem predictable and confining, a closer encounter between rock, soul, and jazz seemed to beckon. Each style offered creative openings to the others.

The way rock musicians were packaged offered an additional area for jazz adaptation: fusion jazz musicians largely adopted the rock model of a self-contained band with a stable set of musicians. To be sure, some prominent jazz group personnel had remained steady—the Modern Jazz Quartet, the Dave Brubeck Quartet, the second "great" Miles Davis Quintet, and the John Coltrane Quintet of the mid-1960s are examples of this—but the most common organization for jazz musicians entailed a shifting constellation of players (**sidemen**) orbiting a lead musician. In this environment, a three-month tour would seem an oasis of stability. Fusion jazz groups, in contrast, tended to assume a group identity (thus, "Weather Report," not the "Wayne Shorter-Joe Zawinul Quintet." This relative stability added

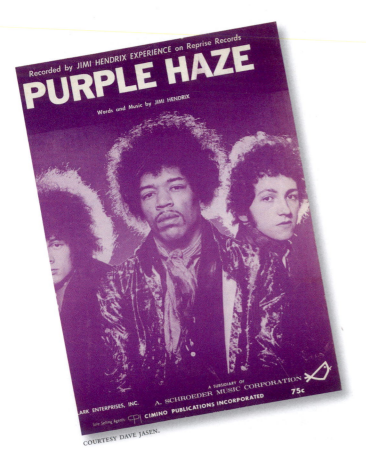

downbeat   (1) the first beat of a tune; (2) the first beat of a measure.

funk   a style of late–twentieth century African American popular dance music, evolved from rhythm and blues and soul music, with a strongly accented first beat in each bar and highly refined syncopated rhythm—or groove—expressed throughout the ensemble.

sideman   an accompanying or supporting musician, in contrast to the leader; a member of a backup band.

impetus, as we will see, to a later trend within the fusion movement that favored intricate compositions over the bebop-derived structure of playing a sequence of solo choruses over a popular song's chord progression, the approach that had held sway for some 30 years.

Early Fusions

Fusion began to emerge in the mid- to late 1960s, although its labeling as such didn't occur right away. Fusion was first hinted at in the experiments of a number of groups on both the rock and jazz sides. In the **progressive rock (prog rock)** movement, for example, there were echoes of hard bop and avant-garde jazz, and of avant-gardism in Western art music. The Soft Machine, formed in England in 1966; the Los Angeles-based Mothers of Invention (especially in 1967–71), led by Frank Zappa; and the Beatles were among the rock-based groups that made use of word play, *musique concrète* techniques ("found" sounds edited to express musical ideas), electronic instruments (including the theremin and other early synthesizers), and atonality and extreme dissonance as expressive tools. All of these also were part of the avant-garde's stock in trade.

Rock also drew on jazz traditions to extend its range. A number of groups grafted big band horn sections onto their basic rock-combo instrumentation. These included Blood, Sweat & Tears (formed in 1967), Chicago Transit Authority (1967, later shortened to Chicago), and Tower of Power (formed in 1967). Still others flirted with jazz by inserting hard bop elements into their rock-based sound. Van Morrison's 1968 album *Astral Weeks*, for example, sported top-notch jazz players, and his 1970 track *Moondance*, from the album of the same name, would become a jazz staple.

The Jimi Hendrix Experience took influence from jazz, in the interplay between Hendrix's and drummer Mitch Mitchell's improvisations, in Mitchell's drumming style generally, and in songs that overtly addressed jazz, wrapped in Hendrix's signature guitar style (*Third Stone from the Sun* and *Up from the Skies*, both 1967).

Larry Coryell (left) pioneered a mixture of jazz and rock, starting with the Free Spirits and then the Count's Rock Band, in 1966–67. The Gary Burton (right) album Duster *featured Coryell's brittle guitar work.* PHOTO COURTESY DOWN BEAT ARCHIVES.

At about the same time, young jazz musicians, who had grown up listening also to rock and soul, saw exciting potential in melding all the parts of their musical personalities. Flutist Jeremy Steig, for example, played with jazz avant-gardist Paul Bley and folk-blues-rock singer Richie Havens before forming Jeremy and the Satyrs in 1967, a group whose first album was heavily marketed to the rock audience. Fusion jazz guitarist **Larry Coryell** later recalled loving the Rolling Stones as well as Wes Montgomery: "We wanted people to know we [were] very much part of the contemporary scene, but at the same time we had worked our butts off [to master jazz]." Arriving in New York in 1965, Coryell met other like-minded young musicians, forming the Free Spirits (1966) with a line-up that included drummer Bob Moses. The Free Spirits' promising blend of jazz improvisation and the emerging **psychedelic rock** sound was undercut by amateurish lyrics, and the group did not survive. By the next year, Coryell had hooked up with vibraphonist **Gary Burton**.

Burton, arriving on the jazz scene as a teenage prodigy, quickly established a formidable reputation, working with pianist George Shearing, who had blended a cool jazz style with Afro-Cuban rhythms; the Stan Getz Quartet; and his own projects. In 1967, Burton formed a quartet, recording *Duster* with Coryell, bassist Steve Swallow, and drummer Roy

---

progressive rock (prog rock)   rock music characterized by structural complexity and instrumental virtuosity.

musique concrète   (French) musical composition created by recording and manipulating natural sounds; pioneered in 1948 by the French composer Pierre Schaeffer.

---

psychedelic rock   a style forged in the late 1960s with an aesthetic influenced by the hallucinogenic experience induced by mind-altering drugs such as LSD; notable practitioners included the Grateful Dead and Jefferson Airplane.

Listening Guide

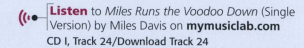

Listen to *Miles Runs the Voodoo Down* (Single Version) by Miles Davis on **mymusiclab.com**
CD I, Track 24/Download Track 24

MILES RUNS THE VOODOO DOWN (SINGLE VERSION) • MILES DAVIS

Music: Miles Davis, 1969. Personnel: Miles Davis (trumpet); Wayne Shorter (soprano saxophone); Bennie Maupin (bass clarinet); Chick Corea (electric piano, right channel); Josef Zawinul (electric piano, left channel); John McLaughlin (electric guitar); Dave Holland (electric bass); Harvey Brooks (electric bass); Don Alias (Charles Donald Alias, drums, left channel), Jack DeJohnette (drums, right channel), Jumma Santos (credited as "Jim Riley," shaker). Recorded: August 20, 1969, in New York. First issue: Original 14:04 version issued on the album *Bitches Brew*, Columbia P 26 CBS 66236. First issue of this radio promotion version: *Bitches Brew: The Singles*, Columbia CSK 41598, 1998. Timing: 2:49.

Overview

Harmonically, this song is constructed of a vamp on a single modal scale; there are no chord changes at all. The laid-back tempo and static harmony would seem to be a recipe for a boring performance, yet *Miles Runs the Voodoo Down* conveys a sense of mounting tension. Three elements, all building gradually, contribute to the excitement: volume, register, and texture. The texture—the density of notes at a particular moment—begins sparely and gradually becomes a bubbling cauldron of activity. This slow but sure shift is mirrored in an equally protracted crescendo overall. An instrument's "high-ness" or "low-ness" within the instrument's range of possible pitches is its **register**. Here, Davis's trumpet solo uses a gradual shift from his trumpet's low to high registers and back again, creating the sense of an "arch." But at key moments, Davis breaks the continuity with a startlingly high note, using the element of surprise to add tension overall.

This recording is one of several single-length tracks that Columbia Records sent to radio deejays as a promotion. Although shorn of four-fifths of the original length, this version captures Davis's approach to improvisation as well as his emphasis of groove over the harmony as a compositional foundation.

Key Features

- Drums and bass: Don Alias (drums, left channel) and Harvey Brooks (bass) take primary responsibility for establishing the basic groove, allowing drummer Jack DeJohnette (right channel), Dave Holland (bass, beginning at 0:42), and guitarist John McLaughlin to add interesting flourishes and fills along the way.
- Electric pianos (**Chick Corea**, right channel; **Josef Zawinul**, left channel) play mostly jabbing tightly clustered chords to add texture.
- Wayne Shorter, who plays on the original version of the recording, is not heard on this shortened one.
- Shadings on the chart indicate growing loudness and density of instrumental texture.

—*Steven F. Pond*

Haynes. The album is frequently cited as one of the first important jazz-rock recordings, although the acoustic bass, clean guitar sound, and relative absence of bass drum in the mix undermine the rock side of the equation. By the second album, *Lofty Fake Anagram* (1967, now with Bob Moses on drums), the two styles were more evenly balanced.

By the 1968, the fusion circuitry was there. Someone had to connect it; that someone was trumpeter Miles Davis, who always seemed to be restlessly seeking a new sound.

Miles Davis: Fusion Pioneer

Miles Davis incorporated rock and funk elements into his music over a period of years. For decades, the classic harmonic progressions of blues and popular songs had formed the backbone of jazz. While bebop players extended the harmonic vocabulary, they continued to base their music on pop standards. In the late 1950s, Davis had challenged bebop-era harmonic progressions, with his turn to modal playing in the soundtrack for the Louis Malle film *Ascenseur pour l'Échafaud* (*Elevator to the Gallows*, recorded 1957 and released 1958), *Milestones* (1958), and his landmark 1959 album, *Kind of Blue*. Having re-formed his group with stunning young players—saxophonist Wayne Shorter, pianist Herbie Hancock, bassist Ron Carter, and drummer **Tony Williams**—he pushed further away from jazz's harmonic past in 1965. This second "classic" quintet, with Davis at the helm, seemed to brush aside the very notion of chord progressions, relying instead on the ability to sense and react to

 Watch the video of *Children's Songs* by Gary Burton and Chick Corea on **mymusiclab.com**

---

register the range of the pitch spectrum, from low to high, available to an instrument or voice.

TIME	INSTRUMENTATION	MUSICAL EVENT
0:00	DRUMS, BASS, CONGA	Quiet, sparse groove; the "moan" sound is supplied by the conga player, rubbing its head with his thumb. The combination is vaguely portentous.
0:14	PLUS GUITAR	Guitar joins in, with jarring dissonance.
0:20		Dramatic cymbal flourish. Second drummer continues basic groove.
0:24	PLUS BASS CLARINET	Bass clarinet trills in lowest register (these will continue intermittently).
0:27		Guitar chords simulate a **vamp** borrowed from soul music, but of a kind more variable than in soul.
0:34	TRUMPET SOLO	Davis's solo begins on a long, low, wavering pitch, drenched in echo.
0:44-0:52		Davis hovers near the bottom of the trumpet's range, his echo-y notes allowed to die off in the distance.
0:54		Sudden interjection in the horn's high register; two drummers and second bassist become subtly but perceptibly "busier."
0:55-1:26		Davis's sudden high note elongates into a descending gesture, coming to rest again near the bottom of the trumpet's range, amid the bass clarinet's trilling.
1:26		Davis renews his solo, now in the middle register, perceptibly louder. Electric pianos jump in more aggressively with cluster-style chords.
1:41		Davis's notes, already higher, are now more clipped and percussive. Drums are more active, more cymbal-drenched.
1:46-1:53		Another sudden, high, and loud trumpet interjection that winds down in a short descent. Guitar "soul vamp" chords are high on the neck of the guitar, drums are more active with fills.
2:02-2:16		Davis plays a long, stuttering **glissando** that uses echo to build force and tension to a climax point (2:07) before descending to a resting point.
2:22-2:50	Ensemble	With the rhythm section boiling underneath, the guitar and electric pianos are playing high and loud; Davis hits a glass-shattering high note and ends in a dense stream of notes as the recording fades out.

each others' changes in tempo, melody, and timbre. These changes were all set against a regular beat stated by Ron Carter's insistent walking bass line.

A further innovation in Davis's playing occurred in 1968, when he emphasized the groove as an organizing core. Expressive tension could be created by establishing a groove and stacking others on it (related in principle to stacking riffs in the swing days) or by allowing one groove to morph into a new one, or by moving out of a regular-time feel altogether. By this time, Davis's music and stage persona were taking on some of the dance orientation, colorful tone, and flamboyant style of rock and funk. For Davis, the musical attractions of rock had to do with its timbres and rhythms; rock's cultural attractions had to do with its embrace of youth-oriented, countercultural expressivity.

Watch the video of *Directions* by Miles Davis on **mymusiclab.com**

Simultaneously, Davis mined rock's amplified, distorted, and electronic sounds for new creative pathways. *Stuff* on *Miles in the Sky* (1968) features Herbie Hancock, now on electric piano, and Ron Carter on electric bass, with Tony Williams providing a groove that hovers between rock and soul. This extended jam on a single chord challenged jazz fans used to their heroes "running the changes." Noted rock critic Lester Bangs greeted Davis's 1969 album *In a Silent Way*, with this effusive endorsement: "There is a new music in the air, a total art which knows no boundaries or categories." Bangs recognized that Davis's music was not exactly rock but it was "nothing stereotyped as jazz either." Davis's other albums of this period—*Bitches Brew* (1969, issued 1970), and *A Tribute to*

vamp a brief chord pattern, repeated an indeterminate number of times, used as filler and most commonly to introduce a piece.

glissando sliding upwards or downwards between two pitches.

"Miles wants you." When musicians got that call, they answered. It was like being anointed. PHOTO COURTESY ANDY FREEBERG.

Jack Johnson (1970, issued 1971)—made it clear that he was seriously committed to the jazz-rock hybrid. Taken together, they trace Davis's growing fascination with electric instruments and the possibilities of groove.

Bitches Brew stands as the moment when rock, jazz, and funk collided and fused, as a *fait accompli*. The double album sold more than 300,000 copies during its first year, an astounding success for jazz—jazz albums routinely sold in the 3,000 to 5,000 range at the time, and sales of 15,000 copies were considered a hit. With an expanded group featuring heavily amplified and distorted electric guitar, electric bass, up to three electric keyboards, bass clarinet and soprano saxophone alternating with the more conventional tenor saxophone, Afro-Caribbean percussion, and drums, *Bitches Brew* created a molten environment over which Davis's trumpet soared—now altered with echo and wah-wah effects. Beyond this reframing of the sound, Davis and his long-time producer, Teo Macero, embraced the pop industry's use of post-production recording techniques, particularly splice editing and multitrack recording. Moments that had been recorded for one take might be found in an entirely different one, or a guitar solo might be shortened and grafted elsewhere. This material was then presented as a series of extended jams, rather than as individual "songs" as had appeared on jazz albums in the past.

Receiving the endorsement of so towering a jazz figure as Miles Davis meant that jazz and rock musicians could pursue each others' idioms at will. For others more nostalgic for the "old" Miles, his new turn was confusing and off-putting. Despite (or perhaps partly because of) his rising sales numbers, the jazz mainstreamers cried foul, accusing Davis of pandering to the youthful audience that had come so completely to dominate the music scene.

In today's world it may be impossible to appreciate the unprecedented impact of youth on American society in the 1960s and early 1970s. Using 1972 music industry data, Steve Chapple and Reebee Garofalo reported that "[a]bout 80 percent of recorded music is rock music." During the Kennedy years, marketers began to stress youthfulness ("Now it's Pepsi, for those who think young," 1961), and the youth demographic drove the advertising mill in the mid-1960s (the "Pepsi generation" in 1963). By the early 1970s, youth dominated the advertising landscape. Coca Cola's television advertising suggested a love-in ("I'd like to teach the world to sing in perfect harmony," 1971); youth seemed to offer a tired world a transformative future.

Jazz, though, was the soundtrack for an earlier time. A generation of jazz musicians had seen their youth appeal erode as they and their audiences aged. Now, in the generation-gap atmosphere embodied in the slogan "Don't trust anyone over thirty," Davis was performing at the Fillmore East, Fillmore West, and other major rock venues. His shift away from the standard songbook and his renunciation of traditional harmony, along with his embrace of loud and distorted sound, and of the popular music industry's production and marketing techniques, prompted astonishment and anger in some corners. For some critics, these moves amounted to a renunciation of jazz, which could only be explained as Davis's chasing the big sales and notoriety that the rock world could confer. This argument was strengthened by Davis's obvious relishment of his enhanced wealth and fame.

Jazz magazines found that they now had to find a way to accommodate popular music. *Down Beat*, the leading jazz magazine since 1934, added "jazz-blues-rock" to its masthead, beginning with the July 22, 1971, issue, bringing in young music writers Gary Giddins to review jazz and Alan Heineman to review rock, with fusion up for grabs.

TAKE NOTE

- What were some of the early forms of fusion jazz?

Fusion in the Early 1970s

Several key groups, notably **Lifetime**, the Mahavishnu Orchestra, Weather Report, Return to Forever, and the **Headhunters**, spun off from Davis's *Bitches Brew* ensemble. While they by no means account for the majority of fusion activity in the 1970s, they do illustrate several streams of development as the decade progressed.

Lifetime

As a teenager in Boston, drummer Tony Williams had played in avant-garde jazz settings. He had also played in several hard-bop organ trios, and had later been a fan of the Beatles. In the mid-1960s, a time when resentment ran high among jazz musicians over what they saw as a connection between rock's ascendance and their own shrinking audiences, Williams's attraction to popular music seemed odd to some. After all, he sat in the drum chair in one of the preeminent jazz combos of the age. Undaunted, Williams pestered Miles Davis to listen to rock throughout his tenure in Davis's quintet, and Williams encouraged Davis's gradual move to electronic and amplified instruments. In 1969, just prior to *Bitches Brew*, Williams left Davis to form his own band, Lifetime, with Larry Young (a.k.a. Khalid Yasin; organ) and John McLaughlin (electric guitar), later joined on bass and vocals by Jack Bruce, formerly of the blues-rock supergroup Cream. Young,

History & Culture

Offspring of *Bitches Brew*

The recording sessions that yielded *Bitches Brew* (issued 1970) and all but one track of *Big Fun* (issued 1974) spanned nearly half a year: August 19, 1969, to March 3, 1970. Almost all of the musicians who played on those sessions went on to perform in important fusion jazz ensembles or to back key fusion headliners. This family tree shows the major players and the groups that they went on to form or join.

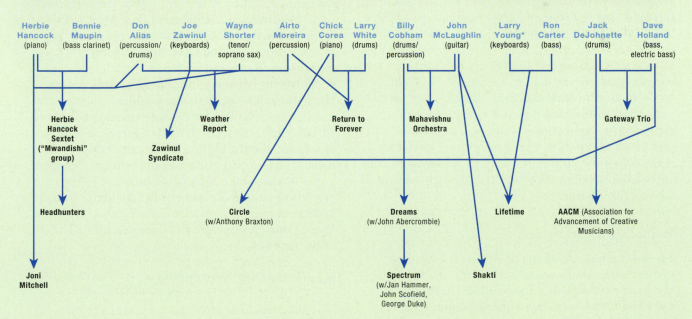

*aka Khalid Yasid

Tony Williams, founder of Lifetime, on stage at the Newport Jazz Festival in 1970.
PHOTO COURTESY DAVID REDFERN/REDFERNS/ GETTY IMAGES.

style of the French guitarist Django Reinhardt (see Chapter 11) at an early age, and as a young man became enamored of the harmonic approaches of both Thelonious Monk and John Coltrane. His early career included stints in hard bop organ trios and in the hard-edged blues revival band the Graham Bond Organization, where he first encountered future Cream bassist Jack Bruce. It was Tony Williams who brought McLaughlin to the attention of Miles Davis. Davis invited McLaughlin into the recording sessions that produced *Bitches Brew* and invited McLaughlin to join his band permanently. McLaughlin, however, had already committed himself to Tony Williams and Lifetime. Far from acting jilted, Davis encouraged McLaughlin to form his own band when it became clear that Lifetime was destined to fold.

The band that McLaughlin formed, the Mahavishnu Orchestra, helped establish fusion's image as stunningly virtuosic (among its fans) and slightly pretentious (among its detractors). McLaughlin, using a guitar with two necks (allowing him to alternate between a traditional six-string and a twelve-string instrument), brought all of his interests into play. He unleashed rock's creative use of distortion combined with Coltrane-esque melodies of dense, complex note groupings; his harmonies included Coltrane's **modalism** and extreme dissonance, coupled with a penchant for lightning fast, **flamenco**-styled runs. His bandmates matched McLaughlin's abilities and intensity, especially Czech synthesizer keyboardist Jan Hammer, electric violinist Jerry Goodman, and Panama-born Billy Cobham, an ambidextrous speed-wizard on the drums. Audiences gaped at the Mahavishnu Orchestra's impossibly fast, crystalline runs and penchant for challenging, odd meters. *Celestial Terrestrial Commuters* (JTSA Disc 5/Track 11), in $\frac{19}{8}$ time, demonstrates all of these qualities.

((•● **Hear** John McLaughlin discuss the influence of John Coltrane on his music on **mymusiclab.com**

modal jazz a style of jazz developed in the late 1950s and 1960s in which modal scales serve as the basis of improvisation.

flamenco (Spanish) a body of dance and music—guitar playing, singing, and percussion—from Andalusia in southern Spain.

supported by McLaughlin's agile, forceful, and imaginative approach to improvisation, had found a way to graft John Coltrane's advancements in harmony, dense clusters of melodic notes, and fearless give-and-take among brilliant equals (reminiscent of the John Coltrane-Elvin Jones relationship). The result pushed beyond anything resembling the blues organ grooves of a decade before. The group's potential for fame floundered, through a combination of lackluster promotion, substandard recording quality, and a tendency toward bombastic lyrics. Nevertheless, Lifetime brought together Williams's attraction to rock and avant-gardist experimentation, his decade at the top of the jazz world, and his background with organ trios. Lifetime also adapted the rock concept of the supergroup to fusion jazz.

Mahavishnu Orchestra

John McLaughlin split his time between Lifetime and the Miles Davis ensemble before forming the Mahavishnu Orchestra, the band he became most known for. McLaughlin had been part of the coterie of young English blues fanatics whose ranks eventually swelled the leading British Invasion bands of the 1960s, such as the Rolling Stones, the Yardbirds, Cream, and Led Zeppelin. But he also drank deep from the wells of jazz and flamenco music. McLaughlin dedicated himself to learning the

Fans also paid attention to McLaughlin's spiritual attraction to Eastern religious philosophies and Hindustani music. Eventually the group splintered, riven by fractious personality conflicts and musical disagreements. McLaughlin configured a short-lived second Mahavishnu Orchestra, and then pursued a more overt amalgamation of jazz with Indian music with a new group, Shakti.

Beginning in 1971, McLaughlin had studied South Indian music at the University of Connecticut, and had commissioned an acoustic guitar fitted with drone strings to simulate the similar strings on a North Indian **sitar** or south Indian **veena**. While at Connecticut, McLaughlin jammed with leading North Indian (Hindustani) and South Indian (Carnatic) musicians, eventually forming Shakti, a fusion of jazz with both Indian traditions. (The aesthetic gulf that Hindustani **tabla** drummer Zakir Hussain and Carnatic mridangam drummer Ramnad Raghavan traversed was as broad as the gulf either faced with McLaughlin.) Through both the Mahavishnu Orchestra and Shakti, John McLaughlin provided visionary leadership in the harmonic, metric, and stylistic expansion of jazz.

Weather Report

By 1970, saxophonist Wayne Shorter had moved on from the Miles Davis Quintet. Shorter had been a driving force in the quintet for the better part of a decade, providing a signature saxophone role while also contributing compositions for some of Davis's most significant albums (*E.S.P.*, *Footprints*, *Nefertiti*). Keyboardist Joe Zawinul had recorded with Davis on *In a Silent Way*, *Bitches Brew*, and *Big Fun*, although, as a member of Cannonball Adderley's group for a decade, he had not toured with Davis. When Ron Carter left the Miles Davis Quintet in 1968, Davis hired Czech bassist Miroslav Vitous to fill in. Zawinul recalled, "As it happened, Miles and Miroslav couldn't get it together. . . . [Vitous] called Wayne and Wayne called me. We had a meeting." They formed Weather Report, which, after an initial bit of personnel

((•—**Hear** a profile of Joe Zawinul on **mymusiclab.com**

shuffling, included Zawinul, Shorter, Vitous, and a succession of drummers and Afro-Brazilian percussionists (some of whom went on to other key fusion groups or became sought-after **session players**). Throughout Weather Report's decade-and-a-half run, Zawinul's embrace of the **synthesizer** keyboard, coupled with changes in the bass chair, fueled a remarkable evolution in Weather Report's sound. The bass role begun by Vitous, primarily an acoustic bass player, shifted to a far funkier direction with Alphonso Johnson on electric bass (1974–76).

Then the group took a major leap into new expressive territory, sparked by Johnson's replacement, **Jaco Pastorius** (1976–81), the self-proclaimed "greatest bass player in the world." Pastorius's bold inventiveness on the fretless electric bass proved as influential as Jimi Hendrix had been on guitar. Beyond his startling technique, a penchant for playing countermelodies, and a virtuosic use of a variety of **harmonic overtones** lay his mastery of distortion effects (all Hendrix trademarks). For his part, Zawinul, ambidextrous and able to play intricate lines on two instruments simultaneously, began to add multiple synthesizer keyboards to his arsenal. Weather Report's music emphasized an architecture of successive **grooves**, energized with layers of timbre: Afro-Brazilian percussion interlocking with virtuosic improvisational drumming, Pastorius's everywhere-at-once bass playing, and multi-voiced synthesizers providing a landscape over which Shorter could dip and soar.

Return to Forever

Like Weather Report and Herbie Hancock's group Headhunters, Chick Corea's band Return to Forever (RTF) explored the new frontier of the synthesizer and Africa-diasporic percussion. By the time RTF was formed in 1971, 30-year-old Corea had spent a decade playing hard bop, Latin jazz, and avant-garde jazz at the top professional level (*Matrix*; *JTSA* Disc 5/Track 9).

 Watch the video of *Boogie Woogie Waltz* by Weather Report on **mymusiclab.com**

---

session player   a musician who plays in recording studios.

synthesizer   a sound production device that blends waveforms to create new sounds; the device stores the sounds, which are playable via a keyboard or other controller.

harmonic overtones   in acoustics, secondary tones that are subdivisions of a fundamental tone or frequency; generated in stringed instruments by touching, rather than plucking, the string at points marking shorter segments of the string length that generates the main tone.

groove   the rhythmic architecture, or *feel*, of a tune, especially in late twentieth-century popular dance music and *funk*.

---

sitar   Indian stringed instrument consisting of a resonating gourd and a long neck supporting seven principal strings, plus 12 to 20 sympathetic strings.

veena   (also *vina*) Indian stringed instrument with a resonating gourd and a long neck supporting four melody strings and three drone strings.

tabla   a pair of drums of North India, played with the fingers, palms, and hands.

Listening Guide

Listen to *Birdland* by Weather Report on
mymusiclab.com
CD II, Track 5/Download Track 29

BIRDLAND • WEATHER REPORT

Music: Josef Zawinul, 1976. Personnel: Joe Zawinul (synthesizer, piano, voice); Wayne Shorter (soprano and tenor saxophones); Jaco Pastorius (electric bass, voice); Alex Acuña (drums); Manolo Badrena (percussion). Recorded October 1976, in Hollywood. First issue: *Heavy Weather*, Columbia CK 34418. Timing: 5:59.

Overview

Birdland is one of the best-known examples of mid-1970s jazz-rock-pop-funk fusion. The band behind it, Weather Report, started out as a jazz supergroup fronted by Josef Zawinul (keyboards, composer) and Wayne Shorter (saxophones). Personnel changed over several albums until young electric bassist Jaco Pastorius and percussionists Alex Acuña and Manolo Badrena were brought in for the album *Heavy Weather*, generating what many consider to be the band's defining sound. The introduction of the virtuosic Pastorius was a key to the success of both the album and its first track, *Birdland*.

The tune represents an evolution of Zawinul's R&B-jazz sensibility, first established with his 1967 hit song *Mercy, Mercy, Mercy*, now electrified, polished, and liberated from strict song form.

Birdland is a musical tribute to the famous New York nightclub named after 1940s saxophonist Charlie "Bird" Parker—and to jazz itself. Zawinul once said, "Birdland was the most important place in my entire life. . . . I had a concept for this album to go back to those good old days when stuff was happening in New York. I wanted to show some of the feeling happening in those days, man . . . Exactly like when I used to come down the stairs at 2 o'clock and Count Basie or Duke used to be working there."

Key Features

- Improvisation: Less soloing is featured than is typical in jazz. The piece is primarily a fixed composition, with space provided for several understated solos by keyboardist Zawinul (2:36) and saxophonist Shorter (3:07). Improvisations use **paraphrase** (keyboard, 5:12), **formulaic** (keyboard, 5:44), and motivic (saxophone, 3:38) approaches.
- Stylistic variety: The tune blends sounds from the blues (0:18), funk (1:47), gospel (2:02), and swing era big bands (2:02).
- Harmony: Unlike the complex harmonies of many older jazz pieces, the framework of *Birdland* rests on one tonal center, or chord. It's a blues chord: a major chord with a minor seventh. But the movement of "voices" and rhythms in the orbit of that central tonality is varied and complex.
- Rhythm: The overall feeling is upbeat, energetic, and exciting, propelled by powerful rock-style rhythm and drumming as aggressive as that found in 1970s rock and funk. The meter (beat) is in fours.
- Form and structure: An overarching ABA' form lays out a series of smaller themes (see Listening Guide grid). Section A presents four different themes, surrounded by periods of rest and transition. Section B encompasses a two-part interlude with synthesizer and saxophone solos. Section A' reiterates the first part in more condensed form, and includes a synthesizer solo over the final theme.
- Color and texture: Electric instrumentation—synthesizer, electric bass—matches the colors and textures of 1970s pop and rock. Thin sounds (acoustic piano) contrast with fat, rich tones (electric bass). Electronic sounds contrast with acoustic ones. Textures change throughout: sections of spare instrumentation (1:01) contrast with the full band (3:59). The changes appropriately match the tune's rich variety of themes.
- Voice, feel, and expression: One of the most distinctive voices is that of the bassist, Jaco Pastorius.

---

by member Patrick Gleeson. Despite critical enthusiasm, audiences dwindled. Adding to the problem, for Hancock, was the loss of young, hip, black faces in the audience; Hancock despaired over jazz's loss of relevance to its original black constituency. The group lasted only three years.

By 1973, Hancock was growing increasingly attracted to the funk of James Brown and Sly and the Family Stone. He was intrigued by black popular music on two counts. Playing a concert with the Pointer Sisters, a popular vocal quartet, Hancock was floored by the frenzied rapport between the singers and their audience; a recent convert to Nichiren Buddhism, Hancock saw their music as inclusive and populist. Musically, he was slightly mystified by Sly's and Brown's funk: he knew he could play

Hear a feature on Headhunters by Herbie Hancock on **mymusiclab.com**

---

paraphrase improvisation   quoting another tune in an improvisation.

formulaic improvisation   creating solos by manipulating, at the speed of thought, musical formulae or patterns that one has worked out and internalized.

He alternates popping, smartly articulated phrases with slurring, almost weeping-sounding statements in a style he pioneered. Wayne Shorter, too, is easily identifiable due both to his sound on soprano saxophone and the seeming ease with which he can dispense complicated flurries of melodic material.

- Musicians' roles: The tune combines a tight group sound with plenty of opportunity for individuals to shine. The electric bass plays a prominent role, providing melodies that at times are in the foreground (0:18) and at other times blend and interact with other melodies (0:42).

—*Tad Lathrop*

TIME	FORM	MELODY/INSTRUMENTATION
0:00	INTRODUCTION	Introductory phrases, each with seven notes consisting of two similar stepwise **motifs**.
0:18	SECTION A, THEME A	Bass and percussion enter, providing a brisk syncopated beat. The melody played on electric bass over the intro phrase, moves quickly and mostly stepwise, with a bluesy sound (repeated at 3:35).
0:42	SECTION A, THEME B	The full band enters powerfully. The melody moves mostly stepwise in motifs of three notes (long-short-short); it is supported by a contrasting countermelody on bass. Saxophone and synthesizer simulate the sound of a big band horn section.
1:02	SECTION A, THEME C	A new melody is introduced on piano, with two phrases of seven notes each, played with a stabbing rhythmic quality. In contrast, long, slurring notes are played on the bass (1:19).
1:32	INTERLUDE	Saxophone re-enters, playing the opening melodic phrases (see 0:00), "answered" by the piano. Saxophone sustains a high note.
1:47		The bass trades sharp, punctuated sounds with the piano, ending on a sustained low note.
1:59	SECTION A, THEME D	All instruments join in an upbeat, joyful chorus, with two brief three-note motifs, followed by a long note leading to a bouncy four-note phrase.
2:36	SECTION B: SYNTHESIZER SOLO	A long, low note on synthesizer note introduces a synthesizer solo, played on low-sounding notes (the lower register).
3:07	SECTION B: SAXOPHONE	Descending chords support a solo by the saxophonist, who seems to dart around the cascading chords with flurries of phrases.
3:35	SECTION A': THEME A	The bass repeats the first theme (see 0:18), and is joined by the saxophone.
3:59	SECTION A': THEME B	Repetition of the first full-band entrance (at 0:42).
4:12	SECTION A': THEME C	Repetition of punchy melodies on piano.
4:23	SECTION A': THEME D	Restatement of the earlier upbeat chorus (with a wordless vocal added at 4:35) supports a final synthesizer solo.

the notes but wanted to understand funk more deeply. For his next album, *Head Hunters* (1973), Hancock retained reed player **Bennie Maupin** from his Mwandishi and *Bitches Brew* days as part of a new band, the Headhunters. The balance of the new lineup focused on young, hip players versed in both jazz and funk. *Head Hunters* relentlessly explored funk's dance groove while providing room for extended improvisation on reeds (Maupin, on soprano and tenor saxophones and bass clarinet) and keyboards (Hancock, on piano, electric piano, and a variety of synthesizers). The album drew fire from critics who challenged whether it was jazz at all, but it became the first platinum-certified (million-selling) album on *Billboard* magazine's newly created Jazz Album chart category. (Previously, jazz recordings had been charted as popular music or rhythm and blues.) A follow-up, *Thrust*, continued both the sales success and critical consternation.

Hancock would continue to draw critical fire and praise. He helped to kick-start a "neo-bop" movement with V.S.O.P., a reunion band of the mid-1960s

---

motif (motive)   a brief pattern of notes; typically the building blocks of longer phrases.

Listening Guide

Listen to *Watermelon Man* by Herbie Hancock and the Headhunters on **mymusiclab.com**
CD II, Track 6/Download Track 30

WATERMELON MAN • HERBIE HANCOCK AND THE HEADHUNTERS

Music: Herbie Hancock, 1962. Personnel: Herbie Hancock (Fender Rhodes electric piano, Hohner D6 clavinet, ARP Odyssey synthesizer, ARP Soloist synthesizer); Bennie Maupin (soprano saxophone); Paul Jackson (electric bass); Harvey Mason (drums); Bill Summers (beer bottle *hindewhu*, tambourine, congas, *shekere*). Recorded September, 1973, in San Francisco. First issue: *Head Hunters*, Columbia KC32731. Timing: 6:29.

Overview

Hancock combines four elements, all distinct, to create a recording that invites contemplation of something lost but remembered. These elements are a musical reference to Africa, a funky bass line, jazz harmonies, and an echo effect. The interlocking whistle-and-voice segment that opens and closes the piece are recreations of a central African tradition (*hindewhu*), performed by percussionist Bill Summers. As the *hindewhu* fades out, it becomes more and more drenched in echo: the African reference is a memory, a dream. Ebbing away, the sound of Africa remembered is soon replaced by the echo-less, funky bass groove; we are jolted back to the present. The spare, plucking accompaniment and almost nonexistent tenor sax melody lead to a sharply punctuated set of descending chords on the electric piano, re-setting the form (1:44). These chords recall Hancock's post-bebop jazz history, and serve to remind us of jazz's central place in the mix. African *hindewhu*, an echo-drenched fade-out, jazz harmonies, and funky bass—each of these conveys something specific (African cultural memory, loss, jazz, and black youth) in ways that suggest possible interpretations but leave Hancock's intention slightly indistinct and vaporous.

Key Features

- The overall dynamics of the piece are restrained, even quiet. The percussive-sounding **clavinet** sounds like barely plucked, muted guitar strings. The overall texture is sparse.
- The tempo is slow and relaxed, but slightly faster than a typical ballad.
- Improvisation is kept to a minimum in this recording.

—*Steven F. Pond*

TIME	SECTION	MELODY/INSTRUMENTATION
0:00	INTRODUCTION: "AFRICA REMEMBERED"	*Hindewhu* entrance.
0:14		Second *hindewhu* track.
0:26		Third *hindewhu* track.
0:33		Fourth *hindewhu* track, including handclaps. Echo begins to elongate as *hindewhu* fades out.
0:45		Bass entrance establishes the groove.
0:58		Drums join the groove as *hindewhu* continues to fade out.
1:18	FIRST CHORUS	Clavinet seems to add another layer to the groove, but it's also outlining the song melody.
1:44		With punches by the Fender Rhodes electric piano, the tenor sax discretely plays the close to the blues melody.
2:04		The section ends. Melody fragment by "guitar" is doubled by the saxophone (2:09).
2:30	SECOND CHORUS	Saxophone now plays melody more clearly, but still quietly, almost tentatively.
2:40		The drums' "dry" sound—with resonating heads removed—add to the overall sense of dynamic restraint. Without the resonant echo, the drum's "bigness" becomes ambiguous.
3:25	THIRD CHORUS	Saxophone plays clearest statement of the melody yet, slightly louder and more assertively. The piano chords return, but this time opening a new section, based on a new bass vamp.
4:08	FUNK INTERLUDE	The group plays louder and punchier.
4:17		Ramping up the energy, the sax offers improvisational commentary on the repeated "electric guitar" melody fragment.
4:37	CODA	The climax being reached, the bass-drums-clavinet groove returns.
5:00		As the groove continues, it is joined by the *hindewhu* layers, the full complement now heard as an interactive complex.
5:26	ECHO-DRENCHED FADE OUT	As the *hindewhu* tracks build, the echo becomes more pronounced. The sound gradually becomes indistinct and fades out.

The Soul-Funk Connection

In addition to the jazz figures who explored R&B, soul, and funk, several key artists whose careers are more closely associated with R&B have incorporated jazz into their work, further demonstrating the permeable borders between jazz and black popular music. Here are a few prominent examples:

- James Brown remains the single most important figure in the development of funk, and he holds a seminal position in rhythm and blues of the 1950s and soul of the 1960s. In his memoir, Brown relates that he fundamentally saw his roots as being in jazz, not the urban blues of B. B. King and others.
- Maurice White gained journeyman experience as a session drummer behind jazz saxophonist Sonny Stitt and jazz pianist Ramsey Lewis prior to forming the funk-pop supergroup Earth, Wind & Fire.
- Robert "Kool" Bell and his brother Ronald (later known as Khalis Bayyan) grew up in a jazz-loving household and formed the Jazziacs. In the 1970s, they emerged as the R&B/funk/disco powerhouse Kool and the Gang.
- Producer-songwriter Quincy Jones's career has crossed many genres. He has produced some of the most significant recordings in black popular music (including Michael Jackson's landmark *Thriller*, 1982, the best-selling album of all time) and has collected an astounding 27 Grammy awards as of this writing. His early career included stints with Lionel Hampton and Dizzy Gillespie, and he has frequently returned to his jazz roots.

As funk and R&B records gained extensive play in dance clubs in the 1970s, spawning the disco phenomenon, certain fusion recordings found their way onto deejays' turntables. Brazilian keyboardist Eumir Deodato's 1972 adaptation of *Also Sprach Zarathustra* (the Richard Strauss orchestral prelude included in the soundtrack for the Stanley Kubrick film *2001: A Space Odyssey*),

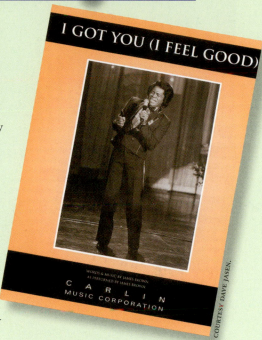

I GOT YOU (I FEEL GOOD)

WORDS & MUSIC BY JAMES BROWN.
AS PERFORMED BY JAMES BROWN.

CARLIN MUSIC CORPORATION

COURTESY DAVE JASEN.

Herbie Hancock's *Chameleon* (1973), guitarist George Benson's *Breezin'* (1976), and flugelhorn player Chuck Mangione's *Feels So Good* (1977) became widespread disco favorites. So popular did these recordings become on the disco circuit that, to critics, the artists' jazz credibility suffered.

—Steven F. Pond

Miles Davis Quintet substituting Freddie Hubbard (and later Wynton Marsalis) on trumpet, a move that gained critical approval. His forays into funk and **hip hop** had jazz traditionalists gnashing their teeth, but Hancock went on to silence this criticism with masterful acoustic jazz recordings such as *Gershwin's World* (1998) and *River* (2007), a collection of **Joni Mitchell**'s songs.

---

clavinet an electronic keyboard with a distinctive staccato, guitar-like sound; used notably for the main riff in Stevie Wonder's 1972 hit *Superstition*.

hip hop a largely African American popular music characterized by talk-sung rhymes over funk-derived beats.

TAKE NOTE

- What were some of the key fusion bands of the early 1970s, and how did their styles differ?

R&B Fusion

By now it should be clear that fusion artists looked beyond rock music for influence. Another important, if underreported, strain stemmed from rhythm and blues and its derivatives: soul, Motown, and funk. Just as important, this fusion style owed much to the "soul jazz" and other hard bop jazz styles of a decade or so before. The Jazz Crusaders (dropping the "Jazz" from their name in 1971) are an example of this trend. The

Walter Becker and Donald Fagen of Steely Dan, 1977.
PHOTO COURTESY CHRIS WALTER/WIREIMAGE/GETTY IMAGES.

group's members were originally from Houston, Texas, but then settled in Los Angeles, where they played in a mainstream hard bop style. However, the addition of electric bass and electric guitar marked a shift in a funkier direction. Their signature sound stemmed from a simple variation on the standard bebop procedure of trumpet and alto saxophone playing the "head" melody in unison: now the unison melody was carried by the tenor saxophone and trombone, with the funky rhythm section boiling underneath. Along with a group of other local musicians—including saxophonist Tom Scott, post-bebop alto saxophonist Phil Woods, and drummers Harvey Mason (based in Los Angeles) and Steve Gadd (based in New York)—they formed a critical mass of "first call" recording session players who turned up on each others' albums as well as on rock and R&B recordings. For example, they formed the musical core for the rock band Steely Dan's mid-1970s albums *Katy Lied* (1975, featuring Woods, and members of **the Crusaders**), and *Aja* (1977, with Woods, the Crusaders, and Wayne Shorter). Jazz musicians have long been favored as sidemen for pop music recording sessions, and now this coterie of fusion jazz players found themselves in high demand.

The R&B and funk flavors of fusion maintained an audience, and the musicians to entertain them, on into the next decades. Bassists proved especially able frontmen in this realm—due in part to their technical proficiency inspired by the likes of Jaco Pastorius and their use of the overtly rhythmic **slap-bass** technique pioneered by Larry Graham of Sly and the Family Stone, Marcus Miller (sideman to many, including Miles Davis), and other bassists. Miller, Stanley Clarke

(of Return to Forever), Alphonso Johnson (of Weather Report), and Gordon Edwards (myriad pop, funk, soul, and Latin sessions) all spearheaded either solo careers or notable group efforts. Guitarists, too, gravitated toward funk-laden fusion. Blues-based 1960s guitar "hero" Jeff Beck embraced the kind of popping, stop-on-a-dime rhythmic precision heard on Stevie Wonder's hit *Superstition*—among other sounds—for his own electric, and electrifying, brand of fusion. Los Angeles session guitarist Larry Carlton fronted his own albums of astoundingly fluid and melodically inventive soloing over tightly rendered pop-funk rhythm, for decade after decade. The northern California blues player Robben Ford, who replaced him in the Crusaders and in singer Joni Mitchell's backup band, also expanded into fusion (backed by Los Angeles session players the Yellowjackets) before delving back into his trademark state-of-the-art electric blues (with a jazz edge).

Of the bands that purveyed R&B-jazz into the 1980s, 1990s, and 2000s, Pieces of a Dream—essentially a rhythm section (drums, bass, and keyboard) supplemented by assorted instrumentalists and sometimes vocalists—proved prolific. Also popular were saxophone-led Spyro Gyra, the keyboard-based Jeff Lorber Fusion, and, through the 1980s, the Brecker Brothers.

Polishing and Popularizing Fusion

The idea of building a "stable" of key session musicians held appeal for record labels. Producer Creed Taylor, a key figure in the important 1960s jazz labels Impulse! and Verve (with credits including the classic *The Girl from Ipanema*, 1963 [CD II, Track 10/Download Track 34]) founded his own CTI label (Creed Taylor International). With CTI, Taylor built a label identity showcasing top jazz performers with accessible "easy-listening" arrangements, high-quality sound production, glossy album art, and a core group of "first call" session players, who frequently appeared on each other's albums. Prominent among these were tenor saxophonist Grover Washington, Jr., alto saxophonist David Sanborn, keyboardist-arranger-composer Bob James, and guitarist-singer George Benson. Likewise, GRP Records—the brainchild of composer-keyboardist Dave Grusin and producer Larry Rosen—built its own sound, frequently using studio professionals to back up featured artists.

At the same time, the Crusaders and others maintained their independence, preferring to work as independent contractors. Nevertheless, they and their

---

slap bass   an acoustic bass technique made by pulling and releasing the strings sharply against the fingerboard, producing loud snapping, popping sounds; on the electric bass produced by slapping the thumb down on a lower string and plucking a higher string with the fore- and middle fingers.

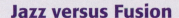

Jazz versus Fusion

Was fusion music the "path of the sell-out" or an invigorating new direction for jazz?

From the start, critics, historians, and musicians have fiercely debated in print over fusion's place in jazz, indeed whether it can be considered jazz at all. Assessing the state of jazz on the first day of the 1980s, journalist-producer Leonard Feather wondered publicly if "slickly packaged fusion sounds" topping the charts could be considered jazz. "Virtually every jazz critic the world over would answer all three questions in a resounding negative." Historian Grover Sales exemplified the contempt that an outspoken purist faction held for fusion. In his 1984 book *Jazz: America's Classical Music*, Sales sniffed, "Some bored rock artists had been gravitating toward jazz, while some jazz players dallied with rock to recapture their dwindling audience."

In the 1990s, the critique turned venomous. Peter Watrous, assessing Wayne Shorter's career, commented in 1995, "Like his peers who inhabit jazz's loftier realms—Herbie Hancock, Ornette Coleman, Sonny Rollins—[Shorter] has spent the last quarter century flashing bits of his grand talent, then finding the nearest drain down which to dump the rest." Watrous laid the blame at the feet of Miles Davis, calling Shorter's artistic slide evidence of the "Miles Davis Curse." To Watrous, Davis's former sidemen pursued fame at the expense of their art. Critic Stanley Crouch, in an assessment titled "Play the Right Thing," amplified the venomous characterization of Miles Davis's turn to fusion as "rapaciously commercial."

Davis never tried to justify his artistic decisions to his audience or his critics. Nonetheless, he did argue that his 1980s and 1990s recordings—which showed funk, R&B, and hip hop influences—were his attempt to reach a contemporary audience for artistic as well as commercial reasons. Davis noted that this was the music of the young, urban audience, and he wanted his music to be equally relevant to them as these popular forms. Through his entire career, he had repudiated the idea of "jazz" representing a static style that had to be preserved for future generations, but rather was a style to be explored and expanded as musical times changed.

Another response to such a toxic critical atmosphere has been to play up fusion's connections to jazz's history of high-art aspirations. Stuart Nicholson, whose *Jazz-Rock: A History*, is one of the few large-scale studies of this music, proposed *two* separate jazz subgenres. After complaining that "people doing the defining wanted jazz to be what it used to be, not what it is," he went on to distinguish jazz-rock from fusion "and its latter-day equivalents, variously marketed as smooth jazz, quiet storm, lite-jazz, hot tub jazz, or yuppie jazz." Guitarist Pat Metheny famously raged, on a blog post, over smooth-jazz saxophonist Kenny G's temerity in deciding to overdub himself onto Louis Armstrong's vocal recording of *What a Wonderful World*. Metheny wrote, "Kenny G has created a new low point in modern culture—something that we all should be totally embarrassed about—and afraid of."

Despite these controversies, fusion musicians have continued to follow their tastes. Herbie Hancock, Chick Corea, Pat Metheny, John McLaughlin, and many others have played a variety of musics—from bebop to fusion, to avant-garde, to funk, to flamenco—as the spirit moves them and as opportunities present themselves. Herbie Hancock, when asked if his 1976 reunion concert with V.S.O.P. (the Miles Davis Quintet with Freddie Hubbard substituting for Davis), was a repudiation of fusion jazz, commented, "Not at all. I mean, neither was doing the *Head Hunters* thing a move away from doing acoustic stuff." He continued, "I think that our society kind of supports the idea that you can only do one thing, and the fact of the matter is human beings can do many things. But in most cases we never get to find that out. Because if we find one thing that we can do, we have a tendency to rest on our laurels and enter a holding pattern there, because it's safe."

—Steven F. Pond

label-bound counterparts established such powerfully consistent "sounds" that the labels eventually suffered from a certain generic quality, ultimately to their artistic cost. By the late 1970s and early 1980s their aggregate sound was fostering a new, smooth, "quiet storm" or "smooth jazz" style that critics lamented as no longer jazz even as it proved the most commercially successful "jazz" style.

So successful was smooth jazz that 30 years later it still thrived. From its first minting through its worldwide circulation in the twenty-first century, smooth jazz soothed audiences—and sometimes infuriated jazz purists who deemed it safe and simplistic—in a range of flavors. Some of them included the R&B tinge of the group Pieces of a Dream and their stylistic kin. Saxophonist David Sanborn plied a distinctive and highly polished update of the early rough-hewn R&B sax style of King Curtis (also audible in the sound of Bruce Springsteen's sax player Clarence Clemons) to great success. Soprano saxophonist Kenny G (born Kenneth Gorelick), while playing a decidedly smoother sax style in mellower musical settings than Sanborn, nevertheless shared some stylistic traits, including a distinctive "cry" gesture, often at the ends of phrases. Kenny G's pop-oriented style yielded album sales in the millions, dwarfing the yield of the typical jazz recording and prompting heated criticism from jazz purists. One of G's highest-profile critics, guitarist Pat Metheny, has himself issued sounds described by some as smooth jazz, while Los Angeles session guitarist Lee Ritenour (sometimes with his group Fourplay) comfortably rode the smooth jazz airwaves through most of his career. Not jazz per se, the vocalist Sade and her group nonetheless demonstrated the kind of commercial success attainable by jazz-influenced players when focused on simplicity, groove, color, and mood.

dyad   two notes.

Listening Guide

CD II, Track 7/Download Track 31

BRIGHT SIZE LIFE • PAT METHENY

Music: Pat Metheny, 1975. Personnel: Pat Metheny (electric guitar); Jaco Pastorius (fretless electric bass); Bob Moses (drums). Recorded December, 1975, in Ludwigsburg, Federal Republic of Germany. First issue: *Bright Size Life*, ECM 1073. Timing: 4:43.

Overview

This recording captures ascending talents, and points the way toward later stellar developments. At the time of this recording, Metheny was making a name for himself as a guitar prodigy. Enrolling and then teaching at Boston's Berklee School of Music, he had found himself in the Gary Burton Quartet—all before his 20th birthday. Metheny was already developing his signature sound—a dark, midrange-heavy tone, with a pronounced delay effect (he now uses two digital delay devices), and very little distortion. The resulting sound was somewhat like guitarist Wes Montgomery's, but slightly smoothed over and glossy. The trio of Metheny, Pastorius, and Moses had been gigging around Boston when they made this recording in the German studio of Manfred Eicher. Eicher, whose ECM label was already setting a standard for high recording quality because of his fanaticism for clean, clear sound, was intensely selective about the artists he would record. Eicher's endorsement added luster to Metheny's fledgling reputation; this recording helped propel Metheny (and Pastorius) into jazz's top ranks.

Pastorius reveals the stunning skills that would soon cause electric bass players everywhere to re-learn their art, much the same effect Jimi Hendrix had had on electric guitar players nearly a decade before. Pastorius displays the penchant for countermelody, lightning runs, and bold use of chords—especially **dyads**, two-note chords that he plays in a bending gesture (called "bent dyad" in the chart). Added to these, he favors harmonic overtones (lightly touching the string to produce a higher, ringing note; for example, Pastorius's second note is a dyad of overtones), and other techniques that caused jaws to drop.

Moses's prodding drum style feeds rhythmic ideas throughout, in this three-way conversation. Even so, Moses has lamented that this recording does not capture the group's live sound.

Key Features

- The form is AABA, and it follows the bebop tradition of head melody/ solo choruses/out-chorus. The rising, sawtooth-shaped melody is used as an organizing element.
- The rhythm, especially the drum pattern, suggests either a funk or an Afro-Caribbean angularity (a "Latin feel") without referencing a specific tradition. Moses consistently heads for a funky feel in each bridge (the B section of the AABA form). However, the high, resonant tuning of his drums and his cymbal-laden playing style underscore the trio's jazz sound. (Compare Moses's sound to Harvey Mason's tuning and playing style on Herbie Hancock's *Watermelon Man*.) Metheny would later live for a while in Brazil, soaking up Afro-Brazilian traditional and popular music idioms.
- Metheny's soloing style foregrounds clean, clear groups of notes, sometimes with subtle bends. This sometimes lends a "folk" sensibility, although he does not reference any folk song material directly. At the same time, his solo gestures derive from the single-note lines of earlier jazz guitarists Charlie Christian, Wes Montgomery, and Tal Farlow, whom he cites as influences.
- Pastorius, in the perceptive words of Stuart Nicholson, "regarded the electric bass as an electronic instrument rather than an amplified acoustic one, in the way Jimi Hendrix revolutionized the electric guitar."

—*Steven F. Pond*

- How did fusion jazz become more commercial by fusing with R&B music?

Later Fusions

Guitarist Pat Metheny is one artist who garnered both acclaim and raised eyebrows in the 1970s and 1980s. A onetime teenaged prodigy, Metheny, with his principal collaborator, keyboardist Lyle Mays, combined formidable technique and harmonic sophistication with a smoothed-out, gentle guitar sound and a penchant for nostalgic images of Americana in his playing and album art (for example, *American Garage*, 1979, issued 1980). Metheny was influenced by a variety of sources, blending elements of folk, rock, bossa nova, and other samba-based Brazilian music with avant-gardist elements from his jazz heroes, Ornette Coleman and John Coltrane. Among his innovations, Metheny experimented extensively with alternate guitar tunings—and

sixteenth note   a note value representing one-sixteenth the duration of a whole note; notated as ♪.

TIME	SECTION	MELODY
0:00	FIRST CHORUS (HEAD MELODY): A	The sawtooth-shaped melody makes its first appearance. Bass and drums play sparingly, giving the guitar the first moment in the sun.
0:12	A	Second A of AABA form.
0:26	B (BRIDGE)	Drummer Moses turns to funky texture, which he will vary at each subsequent bridge.
0:36	A	The return of the sawtooth melody is the final A of the AABA form.
0:48	SECOND CHORUS	Guitar solo: Metheny starts his solo with a rising sequential figure. Once he arrives in a satisfying hand position, he will hover there.
1:10		Pastorius's figures become busier, and his tone becomes sharper.
1:17		Listen for Pastorius's bent dyad, one of his signature figures.
1:25		Moses's drumming gathers in density; Metheny's figures glide over the denser texture of bass and drums.
1:33	THIRD CHORUS	Metheny continues his solo.
1:35		Metheny's approach to the solo is to alternate double-time, sequential figures with sparser moments, as if to catch his breath.
1:56	BRIDGE	Metheny reinforces Moses's samba-based, funky drum pattern.
2:07		Metheny finishes the solo with sparse, high ringing notes.
2:18	FOURTH CHORUS	Pastorius solo: Pastorius's approach is almost entirely melodic. He plays a start-and-stop melody in a high register, allowing the tone to linger.
2:41	BRIDGE	Waiting for Moses's funk theme to get established, Pastorius then plays ascending double-time figures. His tone becomes more brittle.
2:55		Pastorius finishes the form with a cross-rhythm gesture, diving to the lowest reaches of the instrument. The solo's narrative arc is high-to-low and sparse-to-dense-to-moderately dense, letting both the high notes at the beginning and the low notes at the end resonate and recede.
3:04	FIFTH CHORUS	Pastorius continues his solo, reprising the cross-rhythms of before, abruptly shifting to an ascending figure of grouped **sixteenth notes**—a deceptively simple harmonic gesture difficult to execute.
3:15		Pastorius combines several techniques almost simultaneously: a spacious melodic line, interspersed with flashes of dense sixteenth notes, and a harmonic overtone for color.
3:26	BRIDGE	Pastorius uses the bent dyad repeatedly, working it as a solo idea, as opposed to a momentary accompaniment gesture.
3:40		Moses's playing is its most active, foregrounding cymbals and angular drum accents, helping build a sense of impending climax.
3:49	OUT CHORUS	The drums quiet down, as the sawtooth gesture, played in octaves by Metheny and Pastorius, signals that this will be the culminating chorus.
4:35	ENDING	As if reining in a galloping horse, the action suddenly slows and dies out in a satisfying major chord.

with alternate guitars. He commissioned, for example, a three-necked, 42-stringed guitar instrument from Canadian luthier Linda Mazur (*Quartet*, 1996). By 2010, he was exploring more new territory, as he toured and recorded playing an orchestrion—a giant set-up of mechanically triggered acoustic and acousto-electric instruments (*Orchestrion*, 2010).

Singer-songwriter Joni Mitchell, one of the leading voices in rock music's post-Beatles creative surge of the 1970s, brought many jazz fusion musicians into her stage and recording projects during the 1970s and 1980s. Her albums traced a trajectory of ever-deeper commitment to jazz exploration, yet she never abandoned the poetic voice that had made her a star in the folk-rock mold. Rather, the contemplative interiority in each of the two idioms clearly appealed to her. Her final album of the 1970s was a collaboration with jazz bassist Charles Mingus as he was fighting a losing battle against Lou Gehrig's disease (amyotrophic lateral sclerosis). The album, *Mingus* (1979), included Herbie Hancock and members of Weather Report, prominently featuring Jaco Pastorius on electric bass. Although Mingus supplied six new melodies for the album, and Mitchell re-worked his tribute to Lester Young, *Goodbye, Pork Pie Hat*, Mitchell and the other musicians resisted the temptation to produce a "Mingus" sound. Mitchell's lyrics achieve sophisticated word painting. Describing an encounter with a Las Vegas tourist who's impossibly lucky (*Dry Cleaner from Des Moines*), Mitchell (as Mingus) marvels, "He got three oranges/Three lemons/Three cherries/Three plums/I'm losing my taste for fruit/Watching the dry cleaner do it/Like Midas in a polyester suit." Elsewhere (*A Chair in the Sky*), she becomes Mingus floating into and out of consciousness, peering out from his Manhattan hospital room window "the rain slammed hard as bars" and trapped by dual ravages of disease and medication: "Daydreamin' drugs the pain of living/Processions of missing/Lovers and friends/Fade in and they fade out again/In these daydreams of rebirth." Throughout the album, Mitchell extends her penchant for inventive guitar tunings, resulting in fresh, quirky harmonies. Pastorius and Wayne Shorter (soprano saxophone) weave a *pas-de-deux*, with short bursts of melodic saxophone commentary amid Pastorius's characteristically angular, everywhere-at-once bass playing.

Pat Metheny in 1984. PHOTO COURTESY HULTON ARCHIVE/GETTY IMAGES.

TAKE NOTE

- How has fusion continued to develop and who are some current performers?

Conclusion

Fusion, as an approach to playing jazz, has continued. In 1985, Miles Davis, with bassist-producer Marcus Miller, created the R&B-laced *Tutu*. Likewise, Herbie Hancock has regularly confounded jazz purists (and purists of other varieties generally), breezily traversing from techno-funk (*Future Shock*, 1983) to the inclusion of hip hop (*Dis Is da Drum*, 1995) and to *Gershwin's World* (1998)—the latter ranging from post-bebop jazz juxtaposed with African and Afro-Caribbean drumming, to an orchestral arrangement of Gershwin's *Lullaby*, to a piano concerto movement by Maurice Ravel, to a stride piano cutting-contest piece performed as a duo with Chick Corea.

sampling (1) the use of a "sampled" section or piece of a preexisting recording in a new recording; (2) digitally recording a singer, instrument, or other sound to use as a "voice" in a synthesizer.

freestyle the improvisational style of hip hop.

MC; MCing rapper; rapping.

acid jazz a style of jazz fusion combining elements of jazz, funk, and hip hop, especially looped beat samples from earlier jazz.

Hip Hop and Jazz

The connections between hip hop and jazz are deeper and more integral than many are aware. The instrumentation and approaches of the two styles may seem totally different, yet hip hop can be seen as a generational extension of jazz, the two styles have idiomatic similarities, and both are part of the continuum of African American musical conception.

There are three key areas where jazz and hip hop overlap: sampling and quotation, rhythmic displacement; and improvisation.

Sampling: Just as jazz musicians borrow or **sample** melodies and quotations from other songs in their solos, hip hop artists also sample melodies and snippets from songs. The main difference is that hip hop artists sample the actual recording of the song, enabled by sampling technology. It is similar to the visual art technique of "pastiche."

Rhythmic displacement: This is used in hip hop as it is used in jazz. The swing feel of jazz musicians is a characteristic of playing "behind the beat." Musicians lay back while playing a musical line to create a bouncing pulse in the music. Hip hop artists use the same technique to create rhythmic interest in their music. They play "behind the beat" in their vocal delivery or in the track to give an underlying bounce to the rhythm. The main difference between hip hop and jazz in this area is that jazz emphasizes beats two and four where hip hop emphasizes "the one."

Improvisation: The improvisational form of hip hop is known as **freestyle**. The art of **MCing** actually began with freestyling but became a written form early in its development. Rhyming from the "top of the dome" (head) is the hallmark of freestyling and is very similar to improvising jazz in approach and method. Phrases and ideas are woven together spontaneously over a rhythm and MCs seek to create a meaningful statement.

Their histories are similar as well. Many critics of jazz over the decades wrote off the new movements in the music, as in the case of bebop and free jazz. Critics of hip hop have also been unfavorable to the art form and have underestimated the influence and importance of hip hop's artistic impact.

Fusions of hip hop with jazz have produced intriguing results, bringing jazz textures and recognizable "quotes" to hip hop's sonic collages. An **acid jazz** movement of the 1980s grew from nightclub deejays sampling hard bop grooves; by the 1990s some hip hop groups were sampling jazz snippets. In 1993 the jazz-rap group US3 found popular success with the track *Cantaloop (Trip Fantasia)*, which sampled Herbie Hancock music. The group A Tribe Called Quest sampled Cannonball Adderley, Roy Ayers, and Les McCann for their 1990 album *People's Instinctive Travels and the Paths of Rhythm*. Digable Planets' 1993 hit *Rebirth of Slick (Cool Like Dat)* sampled both Art Blakey and the Jazz Messengers and soul singer James Brown's backup band. Guru, of the hip hop duo Gang Starr, went further by employing a live jazz band rather than jazz samples, especially on his albums *Jazzmatazz Vol. 1–4* (1993–1997). Other notable hip hop integrators of jazz included the Roots and De La Soul.

Jazz musicians have turned to hip hop for ways to extend their creativity—and, in some cases, audiences. Miles Davis's final studio album, *Doo-Bop* (1991), was a jazz-rap project. Saxophonists Greg Osby and Branford Marsalis released albums that incorporated rap elements (Marsalis's 1994 disc *Buckshot LeFonque* featured producer DJ Premier on turntables, beats, and drum programming). M-Base founder Steve Coleman drew on hip hop (among other sounds) for a number of albums in the 1990s.

More recently, pianist Jason Moran achieved interesting results recording a piano version of *Planet Rock* (2002), achieving melodic atonality by copying the rap-vocal cadences on the original tune recorded by Afrika Bambaataa in 1982 (see Chapter 12).

Trumpeter Roy Hargrove sought to merge elements of hip hop (and soul and R&B) with bop in albums with his collective RH Factor (*Hard Groove*, 2003, and *Distractions*, 2006), while in *Def Jazz* (2005), he rendered smooth jazz versions of hit tracks from the hip hop record label Def Jam. Pianist Robert Glasper maintained parallel involvements in hip hop and jazz and showcased both in his 2009 album *Double Booked*.

His ability to achieve a ruminative jazz expressiveness against a tight funk drumbeat can be heard in the track *Downtime* (2009).

—*William E. Smith
and Tad Lathrop*

Hip hop/jazz fusion group the Roots in concert. PHOTO COURTESY MICHAEL JACKSON.

In the meantime, a younger generation of performers, eclectic in their musical backgrounds and catholic in their interests, have extended fusion's tendency toward hyphenation: acid jazz (Digable Planets, US3), jazz-house (Jamiroquoi, St. Germain), jazz-rap (the Roots, Black Science Orchestra), newgrass (Bèla Fleck and the Flecktones, Nickel Creek), free-funk (Ornette Coleman's Prime Time), M-Base (Steve Coleman, Greg Osby, Cassandra Wilson), and many more styles claim jazz parentage and listenership.

Fusion jazz experienced a heyday from the mid-1960s to the mid-1980s, but to bracket that time as "the fusion years" would be as much a disservice to a historical understanding as it would be to describe the 1940s as "the bebop years," as if that music hasn't continued to the present day. Fusing—hybridizing—has been a feature of jazz since day one; "the fusion years" merely refers to a time of increased attention to this hybridization. Fusion responds to musicians' exposure to, and investment in, a widening variety of musical influences. Beyond this, fusion, like jazz generally, responds to developments in audience demographics, music technology, the music industry, and political life. All of these factors continue to change and evolve, and fusion jazz continues to reflect these changes. From the moment it began to be called *fusion jazz*, critics disparaged the music as a kind of anti-jazz. Rather, fusion continues a line of engagement with popular and other music styles that has characterized jazz since the beginning.

 Explore Jazz Classics and Key Recordings on **mymusiclab.com**

TAKE NOTE

- **What is fusion jazz and how does it compare to other jazz styles?**

Fusion jazz attempts to extend jazz's traditional aesthetics of adventure and improvisation, using elements borrowed from a range of other music styles. One of the main sources of inspiration was the popularity of rock music, particularly rock rhythms and electronic instrumentation.

- **What were some of the early forms of fusion jazz?**

Precursors of fusion included western swing and jump blues from the 1940s and 1950s, and experimenting rock musicians from the Beatles, Jimi Hendrix, and Cream to Blood, Sweat and Tears. Miles Davis's experiments with electronic instrumentation, inspired by rock musicians such as guitarist Jimi Hendrix, yielded two important albums in 1969 and 1970: *In a Silent Way* and *Bitches Brew.*

- **What were some of the key fusion bands of the early 1970s, and how did their styles differ?**

Weather Report emphasized grooves, layers of timbre, and funk or Afro-Brazilian percussion; pianist Chick Corea's Return to Forever purveyed dense, aggressive rock; pianist Herbie Hancock's Headhunters favored funk; drummer Tony Williams's Lifetime pursued rock and avant-gardist experimentation; and guitarist John McLaughlin's Mahavishnu Orchestra combined rock energy with modalism, impossibly fast runs and challenging, odd meters.

- **How did fusion jazz become more commercial by fusing with R&B music?**

The Jazz Crusaders and a group of widely recorded session players developed a funkier, R&B-inflected approach to jazz that grew in popularity through the many hit records that these musicians played on. Players of R&B-jazz into the 1980s, 1990s, and 2000s included Pieces of a Dream, Spyro Gyra, Jeff Lorber Fusion, and, through the 1980s, the Brecker Brothers.

- **How has fusion continued to develop and who are some current performers?**

Smooth jazz—a brand of rhythm and blues fusion featuring a light funk rhythm combined with blues- and soul-styled soloing—achieved popularity during the late 1970s and early 1980s. Guitarist Pat Metheny is among the most successful of the more recent fusion artists. Other blends of jazz and popular music included hip hop/jazz fusions, notably acid jazz.

DISCUSSION QUESTIONS

1. Identify some of the forces and impulses—aesthetic, social, economic—that may have attracted jazz musicians to rock ideas in the 1960s and 1970s.

2. Do you think rock musicians were as attracted to jazz music? Why or why not?

3. Think back through the history of rock—jump blues, rockabilly, rock and roll, Beatles pop, British blues, Jimi Hendrix, guitar heroes, psychedelic rock, progressive rock in the 1970s, punk rock, heavy metal, jam bands, electronica, noise pop—and identify points of convergence with jazz. Which movements and musicians have had elements of jazz? And what were those elements?

4. How would you explain the differences between rock, jazz, and classical music to someone with very little knowledge about them?

5. Discuss the impact of Miles Davis on jazz-rock fusion. Then discuss Davis's impact throughout the history of jazz.

6. What were the key differences between the fusion bands Weather Report, Mahavishnu Orchestra, and Return to Forever?

7. Make an argument for the legitimacy of fusion music as a form of jazz. How would you answer critics' claims that fusion is simply an attempt to "cash in" on the pop charts?

KEY TERMS & KEY PEOPLE

acid jazz 248
bossa nova 229
Gary Burton 231
clavinet 242
Chick Corea 232
Larry Coryell 231
The Crusaders 244
Cubop 229
Miles Davis 229
Al Di Meola 228
flamenco 236
freestyle 248
funk 230
fusion jazz 228

groove 237
Herbie Hancock 228
Headhunters 235
Jimi Hendrix 230
hip hop 234
jump blues 229
Lifetime 235
Mahavishnu Orchestra 228
mambo 229
MC; MCing 248
John McLaughlin 228
Pat Metheny 228
Joni Mitchell 243
modal jazz 236

Jaco Pastorius 237
progressive rock (prog rock) 231
psychedelic rock 231
Return to Forever 228
sampling 248
session player 237
sideman 230
slap bass 244
synthesizer 237
vamp 233
Weather Report 228
Tony Williams 232
Josef (Joe) Zawinul 232

CHAPTER 10

Latin Jazz

by Isabelle Leymarie, Tad Lathrop, and John Edward Hasse

TAKE NOTE

- How did Afro-Cuban and Brazilian jazz draw on similar musical roots to create different musical styles?
- What native Cuban and Brazilian musical rhythms and musical instruments have influenced the development of Latin jazz?
- How did Latin music influence early jazz?
- Who were the key Cuban and Puerto Rican musicians in jazz history?
- What was the influence of Brazilian music on jazz?
- What other Caribbean music styles have had an influence on jazz?
- What are some more recent trends in Caribbean and Latin jazz?

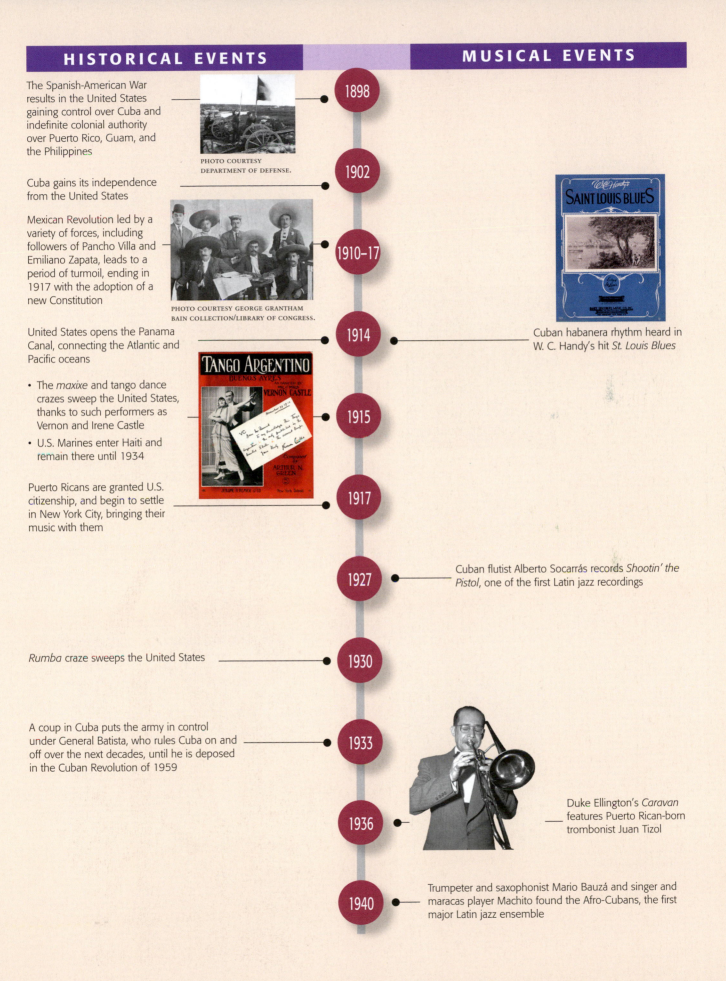

HISTORICAL EVENTS

1898

The Spanish-American War results in the United States gaining control over Cuba and indefinite colonial authority over Puerto Rico, Guam, and the Philippines

PHOTO COURTESY DEPARTMENT OF DEFENSE.

1902

Cuba gains its independence from the United States

Mexican Revolution led by a variety of forces, including followers of Pancho Villa and Emiliano Zapata, leads to a period of turmoil, ending in 1917 with the adoption of a new Constitution

1910–17

PHOTO COURTESY GEORGE GRANTHAM BAIN COLLECTION/LIBRARY OF CONGRESS.

1914

United States opens the Panama Canal, connecting the Atlantic and Pacific oceans

1915

- The *maxixe* and tango dance crazes sweep the United States, thanks to such performers as Vernon and Irene Castle
- U.S. Marines enter Haiti and remain there until 1934

1917

Puerto Ricans are granted U.S. citizenship, and begin to settle in New York City, bringing their music with them

1927

1930

Rumba craze sweeps the United States

1933

A coup in Cuba puts the army in control under General Batista, who rules Cuba on and off over the next decades, until he is deposed in the Cuban Revolution of 1959

1936

1940

MUSICAL EVENTS

Cuban habanera rhythm heard in W. C. Handy's hit *St. Louis Blues*

Cuban flutist Alberto Socarrás records *Shootin' the Pistol*, one of the first Latin jazz recordings

Duke Ellington's *Caravan* features Puerto Rican-born trombonist Juan Tizol

Trumpeter and saxophonist Mario Bauzá and singer and maracas player Machito found the Afro-Cubans, the first major Latin jazz ensemble

HISTORICAL EVENT	MUSICAL EVENTS

1947

Cuban percussionist Chano Pozo joins with Dizzy Gillespie's big band to record *Manteca* and *Cubana Be/Cubana Bop.*

1956

The U.S. State Department sponsors a jazz tour to South America, including Dizzy Gillespie

François Duvalier, known as "Papa Doc," takes control in Haiti; he and his family retain control of the government through 1986 — **1957**

Fidel Castro seizes power in Cuba, cutting off the Cuban music and dance scene from the United States — **1959**

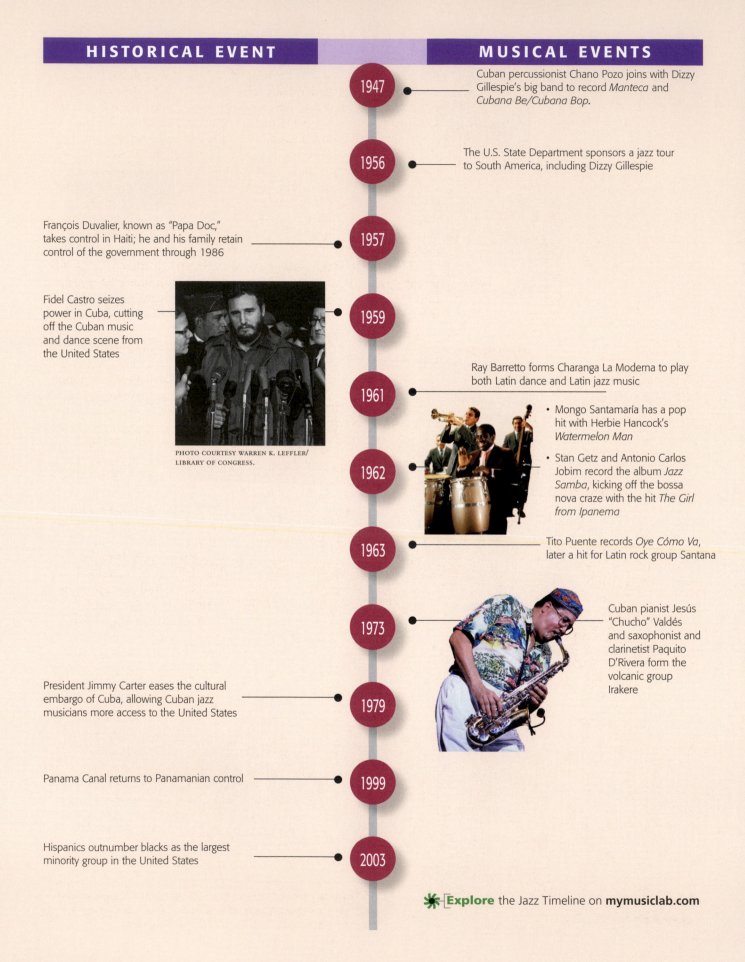

PHOTO COURTESY WARREN K. LEFFLER/ LIBRARY OF CONGRESS.

1961

Ray Barretto forms Charanga La Moderna to play both Latin dance and Latin jazz music

1962

• Mongo Santamaría has a pop hit with Herbie Hancock's *Watermelon Man*

• Stan Getz and Antonio Carlos Jobim record the album *Jazz Samba*, kicking off the bossa nova craze with the hit *The Girl from Ipanema*

1963

Tito Puente records *Oye Cómo Va*, later a hit for Latin rock group Santana

1973

Cuban pianist Jesús "Chucho" Valdés and saxophonist and clarinetist Paquito D'Rivera form the volcanic group Irakere

President Jimmy Carter eases the cultural embargo of Cuba, allowing Cuban jazz musicians more access to the United States — **1979**

Panama Canal returns to Panamanian control — **1999**

Hispanics outnumber blacks as the largest minority group in the United States — **2003**

✳ **Explore** the Jazz Timeline on **mymusiclab.com**

Jazz's richness can be attributed in part to its ability to assimilate and develop the most diverse musical influences. Eastern European folk melody, Indonesian gamelan, and Japanese scales are just a few of the sounds that over time have expanded the stylistic bounds of jazz. But no foreign influences on jazz have been more significant and pervasive than Latin American and Caribbean music. A key reason is that jazz and Latin and Caribbean music share African and European sources and are thus inherently compatible. The mixture of jazz and Latin music is, as Cuban singer and bandleader Machito aptly put it, "a marriage made in heaven." Latin jazz brings together the harmonic sophistication, instrumentation, and improvisational techniques of jazz with the complex polyrhythms and the percussion of Latin America and the Caribbean.

There is no single sound called Latin jazz. Rather, several different strains of Latin American and Caribbean music have seeped into the jazz playbook. These strains have brought jazz many intriguing "Latin" alternatives to jazz's standard instrumentation and swing rhythm.

Cuban jazz musician Paquito D'Rivera performing in 1991. PHOTO COURTESY DAVID REDFERN/REDFERNS/GETTY IMAGES.

One vital Latin-Caribbean strain (which has numerous variations) is Afro-Cuban. Characteristics such as syncopated bass lines and complex rhythms played on congas, bongos, *timbales*, *claves*, and maracas have marked Afro-Cuban styles as exciting settings for jazz improvisation, as evidenced in **Dizzy Gillespie**'s *Manteca* (CD II, Track 9/Download Track 33) and perhaps more familiarly in the recent popular music of guitarist Carlos Santana.

Another prominent Latin American influence is Brazilian. As rhythmically syncopated as Afro-Cuban, Brazilian jazz differs in some fundamental ways, especially in the **bossa nova** style, exemplified by **Antonio Carlos Jobim**'s *The Girl from Ipanema* (CD II, Track 10/Download Track 34). While Afro-Cuban is often extroverted, flashy, and "hot," Brazilian music can be soft, "cool," and bubbling with light syncopation, or it can be propulsive and densely textured as in the high-energy

---

bossa nova   Portuguese for "new tendency"; a syncopated, sensuous musical style refined from the samba and introduced in the late 1950s in Rio de Janeiro, Brazil.

samba *baterias* (percussion groups) led by giant pounding *surdo* drums overlaid with intricately interlocking *agogôs* (bells), shakers, and other percussion.

Common Sources, Different Sounds

Afro-Cuban and Brazilian jazz have both similarities and differences. The similarity accounts for the ease with which Latin music blended with jazz: essential

---

samba   (Portuguese, derived from the Bantu *"semba,"* meaning "navel") a Brazilian dance of Congo origin; percussive, propulsive music in $\frac{2}{4}$ time to accompany this dance; the symbol of the Rio carnival (called Carnaval).

bateria   percussion section of a Brazilian *escola de samba,* famed for performances during Carnaval.

surdo   (Portuguese) bass drum that keeps one of the fundamental rhythms in Brazilian samba; also the name of the rhythmic pattern played on the drum.

agogô   (Portuguese) a double clapper-less bell beaten with a stick, used in Brazilian music.

---

parts of both music styles are traceable to the same African sources. The slave trade of the seventeenth through the nineteenth centuries brought millions of West Africans across the Atlantic Ocean to ports all along the eastern seaboard of the Americas—in Brazil, Cuba, Haiti, and the southern United States. In each location, the displaced Africans—who included the Yoruba and Abakuá from Nigeria, the Arará from Benin (formerly Dahomey), and Bantu groups (including Congos) from what is now Angola and the Democratic Republic of Congo—sustained their cultural and religious identities through practice of their traditional music and dance. But their music also melded with that of the host cultures. In Latin music, an African-derived emphasis on rhythm was filtered through mostly European-derived cultures—Spanish in the case of Afro-Cuban, Portuguese in the case of Brazilian—yielding contrasting styles that eventually crossed paths and mingled through the movement of peoples.

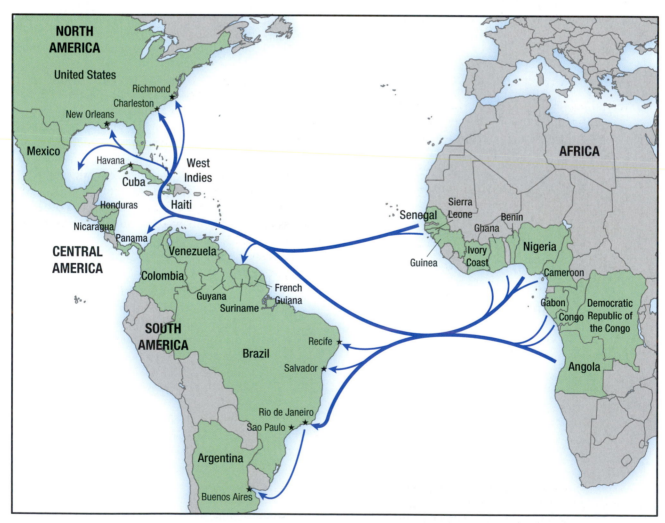

The slave trade of the seventeenth through nineteenth centuries brought millions of West Africans across the Atlantic Ocean to ports all along the eastern seaboard of the Americas—in Brazil, Cuba, Haiti, and the southern United States.

Music of Hope and Survival

How do Afro-Cuban and Brazilian musics reflect the troubled histories of the peoples who created them?

There's a key reason for Afro-Cuban music's fire and emotion and Afro-Brazilian music's passion and soulfulness. Both musics are descended from forms used to affirm identity in the face of violent uprooting and dislocation from native countries. Africans transplanted to points in Cuba and Brazil during the slave trade strove to preserve their social and religious traditions through music and dance. In Cuba, Yoruba slaves camouflaged their religious celebration to avoid persecution; behind a façade of Spanish Catholicism, slaves secretly invoked their own gods, called *orisha*, through the practices of song and dance and especially drumming. In Brazil, music helped slaves communicate their shared spirituality and native culture in an atmosphere of often violent subjugation. The same phenomenon took a slightly different form in the United States, where field workers ended their days with sung affirmations and prayers. Their songs evolved into the blues, an expression of vitality amid oppression that became a foundation of American popular music and jazz. Similarly, Cuban and Brazilian slave rhythm and song traditions integrated into Latin popular music over time, investing it with the depth of feeling and spirituality that slaves poured into the original music to affirm life in the face of impossible circumstances.

—Tad Lathrop

A Heritage of Rhythm and Percussion

Rhythm and percussion thrived in Latin American and Caribbean cultures, where drumming flourished and developed early on to a greater degree than in the United States. Stateside, during the pre–Civil War period, drums made by African Americans were systematically prohibited and destroyed. The white clergy viewed them as "devilish instruments" associated with "lewd" dancing, and slave owners feared that the slaves would use them to encode calls for rebellion. In the relatively more lenient and less puritanical Catholic countries of Latin America and the Caribbean, however, "black" drums and other percussion instruments were, although intermittently repressed, mostly tolerated.

Both social and religious activity and ritual played an important role in spreading African influences through Latin and Caribbean cultures. People of African descent often formed clubs and secret societies based on ethnic origin that helped preserve ancient traditions; and when organized under the aegis of Christian churches, these gave rise to syncretic religious cults (cults that combine native beliefs with elements of other religions, such as Christianity), such as *santería* in Cuba, *candomblé* in Brazil, and *vodun* in Haiti. Whether in secular or religious contexts, singing and dancing were (and remain today) accompanied by a vast array of drums and other percussion instruments.

Latin American percussion instruments. Top, from left to right: güiro, shekere. Middle, from left to right: caxixi, frying pan agogô bells, standard agogô bells, tamborim. Front, from left to right: maracas, double ganza. PHOTO COURTESY CHRIS STOCK/ LEBRECHT MUSIC & ARTS.

TAKE NOTE

- How did Afro-Cuban and Brazilian jazz draw on similar musical roots to create different musical styles?

Cuban Roots

Some of the most exciting sounds in jazz have come from Cuban-derived or influenced bands and musicians. Breakneck tempos and bravura instrumental solos over percolating multi-percussion blends—these and other characteristics have entertained audiences for decades in the bands of, among many others, Dizzy Gillespie, Machito, and Mongo Santamaría and, more recently, in the group **Irakere** and its alumnus **Paquito D'Rivera**. The widely known and enjoyed style *salsa* is derived in large measure from Cuban influences.

One source of the highly rhythmic and outgoing cast of Afro-Cuban music is the Spanish influence, invested with the passion of flamenco guitar and its dance propelled by the stomping of feet and the clicking of castanets. The other, perhaps key, reason for Cuban music's power is its rich African cultural heritage, well preserved throughout the island's history.

Prominent African influences in Cuba came from descendants of the Nigeria-originated Yoruba people, whose music and dance incorporated highly complex rhythms, call-and-response singing, and **batá** drums (three different-sized hand drums). The Yorubas' wide selection of intricate rhythm patterns (called **toques**) in combination with the low, middle, and high sounds produced by the different-sized drums, provided essential ingredients for Latin percussion of today. Additional influences came from the Nigeria-derived Abakuá sect and the Dahomey-descended Arará, who accompanied their dance music with batteries of drums, sticks, bells, and rattles. The Congo-originated Bantu people used large barrel drums from which evolved today's widely used congas.

These African influences mixed with Hispanic to yield core sounds and styles of popular Afro-Cuban music. In the 1800s there was the **canción** tradition—vocal music with guitar accompaniment—with its styles the romantic bolero and the earthier *guaracha*. A French influence entered from Haiti following the island's slave uprising of 1791: the **contradanza** (from French *contredanse*) became the favorite dance of Cubans, played on strings, woodwinds, brass, and percussion. It incorporated *clave* rhythms, and it generated the **danza** and the **danza habanera**—the latter being one of the first Cuban styles to travel to, and find popularity in, Europe

and the United States. A further permutation of danzas was the **danzón**—a light-classical dance music (generally using piano, flute, violin, and *timbales*) that for about a century prevailed as a favorite dance music in Cuba.

The rhythmic core of Afro-Cuban music is a pattern called the **clave**, typically (but not always) played on a pair of sticks called *claves*. The pattern commonly consists of two even beats followed by three beats the second of which is syncopated. This is called the 2-3 *clave*. Sometimes the reverse, 3-2, is used.

2-3 Clave

3-2 Clave

((•—**Listen** to these rhythms on **mymusiclab.com**

Linked in structure to patterns found in West African music, the *clave* carried over into Afro-Cuban dances including the rhythmically complex **rumba**, which developed in rural areas of Cuba in the mid-nineteenth century and later thrived in the cities of Havana and Matanza (before inciting a *rumba* craze in the United States in the 1930s). The *clave's* distinctive three-plus-two structure—simplified, over time—provided a compelling anchor for ensembles

---

contradanza   (Spanish) Cuban dance popular in the eighteenth century.

danza   (Spanish) a nineteenth-century musical genre, using the *habanera* rhythm, derived from the *contradanza*, popular in Cuba in the eighteenth and nineteenth centuries; a predecessor to the *danzón*.

danza habanera   a Cuban social dance in duple time and performed in a ballroom or on a stage; originating in the late nineteenth century, it became one of the first Cuban styles to become popular in the United States and Europe.

danzón   (Spanish) a light classical dance accompaniment derived from the *danza* and originating in Cuba in the late nineteenth century.

clave   (Spanish) a basic rhythmic pattern of Cuban and Puerto Rican music, played over two bars; the *clave* beat holds the band together. In Latin jazz, the *clave* is often implied, rather than stated by the *clave* sticks.

rumba   (Spanish, "rhumba" in English) a music genre derived from the Cuban *son* and popularized in the 1930s; also a ballroom dance performed by both Latino and non-Latino audiences in the United States and in Europe.

---

batá   (Yoruba) a set of three double-headed drums originally from the Yoruba people (present-day Nigeria and Benin) in West Africa typically used in *santería* ceremonies in Cuba.

toques   (Spanish) drum rhythms in ritual Afro-Cuban music.

canción   (Spanish) literally, "song": song style focusing mostly on lyrics/melody, with guitar accompaniment.

Drummers of Oyu, Yoruba tribe, Nigeria. PHOTO COURTESY M & E BERNHEIM/ WOODFIN CAMP AND ASSOCIATES.

of singers, **tumba** and **quinto** drums (later the names of, respectively, the lowest- and highest-pitched conga drums), and other miscellaneous percussion.

The *clave* was also a core element of **son**, a derivation of the *canción*. Considered one of the more complete syntheses of Cuba's African and Spanish cultures, *son* originated in the late 1800s as a combination of Bantu-derived rhythm and the poetry of Spanish-descended farmers. In the 1920s *son* replaced the more polite *danzón* as Havana's most popular dance music.

Son's instrumentation and rhythmic structure prototyped those of later Latin ensembles: acoustic bass and conga drum on a rhythm called the **tumbao** (from *tumba*, meaning drum); *clave* sticks on the rhythm of the same name; bongos, maracas, and shakers playing additional patterns; a scraper called a **güiro**; a guitarlike instrument called the **tres** plucking a repeating arpeggio cross-melody called a **montuno**; and a rhythmically active singer. Later *son* groups added trumpet. A two-drum instrument called the *timbales*—used in *danzón* groups—became central in later Afro-Cuban groups.

Danzón may have been driven out of style in Havana by *son*, but it reemerged in a new form when some musicians added to it elements of different styles including trumpets playing vocal lines from *rumbas*, and beefed-up rhythm including the *tumbao*. The

((• **Listen** to a demonstration of Afro-Cuban rhythms on mymusiclab.com

---

tumba (Spanish) the largest and lowest-pitched of the conga drums; national dance of Santo Domingo in the nineteenth century.

quinto (Spanish) the smallest and highest-pitched of the conga drums, which in Cuban music usually improvises.

son (Spanish) a genre that emerged in the late nineteenth century in the rural areas of eastern Cuba. It developed as an urban type of music in Havana in the 1920s and became commercialized in the United States under the name *rumba* or *rhumba*. The *son* forms the backbone of salsa.

tumbao (Spanish, of African derivation) a rhythm pattern played by the conga and the string bass.

güiro (Taino—the original Amerindian language spoken in Cuba) a serrated, rasped gourd used in Puerto Rican and Cuban music.

tres (Spanish) a stringed instrument used in traditional Cuban and Puerto Rican music.

montuno (Spanish) an improvised section, in Cuban popular music and salsa; kind of contrapuntal accompaniment used in salsa and in Cuban music in general.

Style & Technique

Cuban Rhythms

((•—Listen to these rhythms on **mymusiclab.com**

Following an African tradition, the various instruments of the rhythm section in Cuban folk and popular music create polyrhythms anchored by a basic pattern called *clave*. This *clave* can be implied or stated by a pair of *clave* sticks. There are different types of *claves* according to the type of music played. The most common one is the so-called "2-3" or "*son*" *clave*, characteristic of a genre called *son*, which began growing in popularity in Cuba in the late 1920s.

2-3 *clave*:

The **timbales**, consisting of two snare drums mounted on a stand, play a pattern called **cáscara**. (**Tito Puente** is one of Latin jazz's most celebrated *timbaleros*.) The left hand usually keeps the *clave* while the right hand can improvise around the *cáscara*. In Latin jazz, *timbales* may be replaced by a set of trap drums, or both instruments may be employed simultaneously.

Example of *cáscara*:

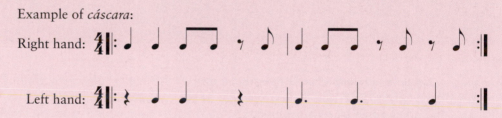

name eventually given to this highly popular blend was **mambo**. And from it, as mambo bands took their sounds to the United States and elsewhere, emerged big band mambo, *cha-cha-chá*, and salsa.

Brazilian Roots

With a land mass that covers nearly half of South America and a population ranked fifth largest in the world, Brazil dominates its continent. Brazilian

---

timbales   (Spanish) a drum set with two tuneable snare drums with different pitches, two cow bells, a cymbal or cymbals, and sometimes a woodblock; typically played with two sticks; developed in Cuba, inspired by the European tympani; used in Cuban music and in salsa music.

cáscara   (Spanish) a rhythmic pattern played on *timbales*.

mambo   (Bantu) a highly syncopated instrumental genre created by Cuban bandleader Pérez Prado and first performed by him in Mexico; a dance style highly popular in the 1950s that was a precursor to salsa.

culture—especially its musical culture—is richly developed and has global reach. As in Cuba, African-derived traditions thrive in Brazil, which has its own vast array of rhythms and percussion instruments. These are used to accompany a panoply of traditional events and local performances—including Carnaval sambas, cult ceremonies of African origin, and spontaneous street-corner jam sessions—that to this day feed into the broad spectrum of styles, from folk to rock to pop, that make up the Brazilian musical mix.

Accounting for why Africa-derived musical ideas developed differently in Brazil than in Cuba starts with the impact of Brazil's Portuguese culture. The colonization of Brazil by the Portuguese from about 1500 forward brought some distinctive characteristics and practices: a language considered to be one of the most lyrical and musical in the world; a sense of poignancy, soulfulness, and longing that would inform song lyrics; favored instruments including flute, guitar, clarinet, violin, accordion, piano, drums, triangle, tambourine; an appreciation for complex, syncopated rhythms; a celebration called the *entrudo*, which would be the

The conga and the bass both play patterns called *tumbaos*.

Example of *tumbao*:

On certain sections, especially during other instruments' solos, the piano (as well as the guitar, the vibes, the *tres*—a stringed instrument used in traditional Cuban and Puerto Rican music—and violins) may play patterns called *montunos*.

Example of *montuno*:

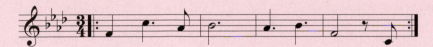

The bongos, the maracas, the *güiro*, the **shekere** (a big shaken gourd with a mesh of beads), the **campana** (cowbell) and other percussion instruments each play their own patterns.

Cuba has produced many musical genres. In the 1930s, jazz incorporated elements of the *rumba*; in the late 1940s and 1950s, Cubop mostly used mambo, *cha-cha-chá*, and bolero rhythms; and in the late 1970s, Cuban jazzmen experimented with a new genre called *songo*. Latin jazz has also delved into traditional secular and sacred Afro-Cuban rhythms, one well-known example of which is Mongo Santamaría's *Afro Blue* (1959), with its $\frac{6}{8}$ time feel (although for convenience's sake, it's written in $\frac{3}{4}$):

—*Isabelle Leymarie*

prototype of the later Carnaval tradition that would nurture so much Brazilian music; and, last but not least, a tolerance for African culture that permitted deep comingling of traditions.

Early on, the **lundu**, a kind of circle dance brought by Bantu slaves, entered Portuguese society as a song style with guitar accompaniment and gained wide popularity. Notably, the *lundu* and other Afro-Brazilian dances included a movement called the **umbigada** in which couples bump navels as an invitation to the dance—the pulse of which some contend is directly related to the samba.

It's the samba, perhaps more than any other musical style, that stands as the centerpiece of Afro-Brazilian music. Its distinctive $\frac{2}{4}$ rhythm, pounded out on giant *surdo* drums, anchors a dense, intricate, and thrilling matrix of interlocking rhythms played on numerous different African-derived percussion instruments: **repique** (**repinique**, medium-sized drum), **caixa** (smaller drum), *agogô* (double bell hit with a stick), **cuíca** (friction drum), **reco-reco** (scraper, derived from

shekere   (Yoruba) a rattle consisting of a large gourd with beads held, by a mesh net, on the outside, instead of on the inside as in *maracas*; shaken in rhythm and struck with the palm of the hand; of West African origin.

campana   (Spanish) a cowbell, played with a stick as a percussion instrument; used in Afro-Cuban and salsa music; also called *cencerro*.

lundu   (Bantu) song and dance with Angolan roots, brought to Brazil by slaves in the eighteenth century; an ancestor to various urban Brazilian song forms.

umbigada   (Portuguese) a movement in Afro-Brazilian dances during which the dancer touches navels with another dancer as an invitation to dance.

repique (repinique)   (Portuguese) a two-headed tenor drum; played in Brazilian samba.

caixa   (Portuguese) a Brazilian snare drum.

cuíca   (Portuguese) a Brazilian friction drum used often in samba music.

reco-reco   (Portuguese) a Brazilian scraper made of bamboo or metal.

Samba dancers dressed in colorful costumes are a mainstay of Carnaval celebrations in Rio de Janeiro, Brazil. PHOTO COURTESY ALEX ROBINSON/DK IMAGES.

roots as an expressive outlet for the underclass to a widely disseminated (via the newly invented radio) and highly popular national trend.

Starting in the late 1920s, Rio became the home of **escolas de samba**—samba schools that doubled as social clubs, in which their thousands of members would prepare samba performances for the annual competitive Carnaval samba parade. During the parades, watched by tens of thousands, the school's *baterias* (percussion ensembles of several hundred strong) would thrill audiences with highly synchronized rhythms supporting several thousand singers–vying against other *escolas* for highest ranking. The tradition continues to this day.

Early interaction with U.S. jazz helped Brazilian music evolve from samba to what would become Brazil's best-known musical export. As early as 1946 vocalist Dick Farney (with his hit *Copacabana*) and, a few years later, singer and pianist Johnny Alf—both Brazilians who were exposed to North American jazz—began signaling the coming of a new style of Brazilian music with jazz inflections. Further developments came in 1953, when the Brazilian guitarist Laurindo Almeida recorded in the United States the album *Laurindo Almeida Quartet Featuring Bud Shank* (reissued in 1961 as *Brazilliance*), an amalgam of Almeida's knowledge of the samba and saxophonist Shank's expertise in jazz. Almeida and Shank further pursued their experiments in "jazz samba," as they termed it, with *Holiday in Brazil* (1958) and *Latin Contrasts* (1959).

From 1955 to 1961, new artistic movements flourished in Brazil under the liberal government

original Brazilian Indians), *shekere*, **tamborim** (small tambourine without jingles), and **pandeiro** (similar to the tambourine).

Samba developed in Rio de Janeiro in the early 1900s with the influx of immigrants from the Afro-Brazilian population of Bahia to the coastal north. At informal social gatherings and jam sessions the samba was forged with influences from the *lundu* and several other precursors: the **maxixe**, a lively exuberant dancehall style born in Rio around 1880, mixing *lundu*, the Argentinian tango, Cuban *habanera*, and polka; and the **marcha**, an uptempo $\frac{2}{4}$ rhythm like the samba, derived about 1899 from the tango and *habanera*. Over time, different strains of samba emerged, and samba expanded from its

---

escola de samba   Brazilian organization or club where samba is practiced for performance in Carnaval and other events.

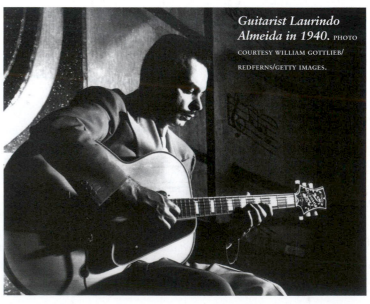

Guitarist Laurindo Almeida in 1940. PHOTO COURTESY WILLIAM GOTTLIEB/ REDFERNS/GETTY IMAGES.

---

tamborim   (Portuguese) a small, jingle-less tambourine played with a single or double stick, used in Brazilian music.

pandeiro   (Portuguese) a Brazilian percussion instrument similar to the tambourine.

maxixe   (Portuguese) a Brazilian couples dance, originating around 1870, with elements of the polka and the Brazilian tango. It became popular in the United States and in Europe at the turn of the twentieth century.

marcha   (Spanish) a march.

Brazilian Rhythms

((•◦—[Listen] to these rhythms on **mymusiclab.com**

Brazil boasts a wealth of rhythms and musical genres.

The samba, which began to develop in Rio de Janeiro at the beginning of the twentieth century, is an ebullient $\frac{2}{4}$ style. Good examples of jazz sambas are Luiz Bonfá's *Samba de Orfeu* (1959) and Dizzy Gillespie's *Winter Samba* (1966). In a jazz samba, the bass may play the following pattern:

while the piano and the guitar may "comp" (accompany with chords) in the following way:

The piano defers to guitar, which is the main chordal accompanying instrument in Brazilian rhythm section; typically, the guitarist picks with the fingers and plays the bass line independently with the thumb—and the thumb is often doubled by the *surdo.*

The bossa nova, created in Rio de Janeiro in the late 1950s and adopted by jazz musicians in the early 1960s, is a medium-tempo $\frac{4}{4}$ style characterized by an offbeat pulse. Some of the most famous bossa novas in jazz include Kenny Dorham's *Blue Bossa*, Lee Morgan's *Ceora*, and Antonio Carlos Jobim's *The Girl from Ipanema*, *Corcovado*, *Wave*, *How Insensitive*, *Triste*, *Meditation*, *Desafinado*, *No More Blues*, and *Once I Loved*. The piano and the guitar play variants of the following basic rhythm:

To add color, percussionists such as **Airto Moreira** have also used such small instruments as the *agogô* and the *cuíca.*

Agogô rhythm:

Cuíca rhythm:

—*Isabelle Leymarie*

of President Juscelino Kubitschek, and this burst of creativity extended to the local music. In Rio, a group of Brazilian musicians became increasingly drawn to jazz—and there were plenty of visiting U.S. musicians to fuel their interest, from Dizzy Gillespie (on a 1956 State Department-sponsored tour) to guitarists **Charlie Byrd** and Jim Hall to singer Ella Fitzgerald. The jazz-inclined Brazilian musicians, whose members notably included a composer named Antonio Carlos Jobim, began holding jam sessions in 1956 in a handful of clubs in the Copacabana neighborhood of Rio de Janeiro. From their creative interactions emerged a style that modernized and toned down the samba, adding sophisticated and intricate chord progressions and rhythmic accompaniment—often on guitar—that hovered always slightly ahead of the pulse, in syncopation to it. Compared to the more propulsive, extroverted samba (not to mention fiery Cuban rhythms), this Brazilian music was airier, more subdued, more intimate and cerebral. As it caught on, it acquired the label bossa nova—literally, the "new tendency."

The bossa nova was officially launched by guitarist and singer João Gilberto's recordings of Antonio Carlos Jobim's *Desafinado* (1958) and *Chega de Saudade* (1959), and then by Marcel Camus's 1959 film *Black Orpheus* (*Orfeu Negro* in Portuguese), which featured such classics-to-be as Luiz Bonfá's *Manha de Carnaval* and Jobim's *A Felicidade*.

In Brazil's two largest cities—Rio de Janeiro and São Paulo—a host of musicians and singers established their credentials performing the bossa nova. Many of these musicians would become well-known beyond Brazil's borders. They included pianists Sérgio Mendes, who offered his own brand of jazz samba; Eumir Deodato, who wrote arrangements for Frank Sinatra and Tony Bennett; and guitarist Baden Powell, with his exciting mixture of Afro-Brazilian, jazz, and classical strains.

After the decline of the bossa nova, a new generation of highly creative musicians emerged in Brazil. Starting in the mid 1960s a genre called **MPB**—for *música popular brasileira*—encompassed the work of diverse singer-songwriters who pulled freely from many sources, including bossa nova, jazz, rock, reggae, and music from all parts of Brazil, to frame their personal musical visions and lyrics. Especially notable were Milton Nascimento, whose high-pitched voice enhances the haunting quality of many of his compositions, including *Ponta de Areia* (from the Wayne Shorter album *Native Dancer*, 1974). That song was also recorded by the singer Elis Regina, whose vibrato-free, sometimes soaring vocal approach somehow embodied the Brazilian quality of *saudade*—longing, nostalgia, and yearning—for a brief period of acclaim until her death in 1982.

The creative environs of Brazil produced so many notable and distinctive musicians that a balanced and meaningful accounting is not possible in a short narrative. Still, there are standouts including the singer-songwriters Gilberto Gil and Caetano Veloso, who spearheaded the iconoclastic ***Tropicália*** movement with mixes of everything from traditional Bahian rhythm to rock and roll—spawning associated efforts in other art forms. Pianist-singer Ivan Lins, singer-songwriter Chico Buarque, and singer-guitarist-composer Jorge Ben have added their own distinct colors to Brazilian music.

A purely instrumental tradition existed in Brazil as well, including **choro**, which emerged in Rio de Janeiro in the late nineteenth century. An improvisational form predating jazz, *choro* involved soloing over European harmonies with Afro-Brazilian syncopation, typically on flute accompanied by guitar and the four-stringed *cavaquinho* in early *choro*. *Choro*, with an ever-expanding selection of instruments, remained an important part of the Brazilian music playbook over the years. Among those who employed it in the 1970s was the composer and multi-instrumentalist **Hermeto Pascoal**—while also exploring a virtually limitless array of other musical possibilities. Not widely known outside of Brazil, Pascoal acquired a reputation as a musician's musician in his country. Whether writing for standard instruments or nonstandard ones (toys, pots, pans), pursuing such experiments as writing a song a day for a year, or penning such notable compositions as the *choro/baião Bebe* (1973) and the *Missa Dos Escravos* (*Slaves Mass*, 1977), Pascoal proved a musical innovator unlike anyone else, although his

Herman Pascoal playing a button accordion, 2000. PHOTO COURTESY LEON MORRIS/REDFERNS/GETTY IMAGES.

MPB (música popular brasileira)   post–bossa nova Brazilian urban popular music, combining elements from different genres.

Tropicália   an experimental, style-mixing arts movement—with a strong musical component—of late 1960s Brazil.

choro   (Portuguese) a type of Brazilian popular music, improvised and usually instrumental, that originated prior to jazz.

Comparing Aspects of North American, Afro-Cuban, and Afro-Brazilian Jazz

Among the differences between Afro-Cuban and Afro-Brazilian jazz styles—as well as their antecedents—are their different approaches to the role of the bass and bass drum. Brazilian samba has the *surdo* (bass drum) and acoustic or electric bass *anchoring* the rhythm, emphasizing the main beats in $\frac{2}{4}$ time. Cuban music, on the other hand, has the conga and bass playing offbeats, *destabilizing* the core rhythm. The two feelings are substantially different. The following chart shows other differences—of the most general kind—between Afro-Cuban, Afro-Brazilian, and North American jazz. All three have complexities that extend far beyond these summaries.

—*Tad Lathrop*

	NORTH AMERICAN	AFRO-CUBAN	AFRO-BRAZILIAN
Heritages	African, French, English, Italian, German, Mexican, Cuban	African, Spanish, French	African, Portuguese
Root styles	blues, ragtime, marches	*son, danzón, contradanza, habanera, rumba*	*lundu, maxixe, marchá, choro,* samba
Developed styles	swing, bebop, cool jazz, mainstream, Latin jazz, Brazilian jazz	mambo, *cha-cha-chá*, bolero, salsa, *songo*	samba, bossa nova, MPB
Character	widely varied in expression, based on musicians' personal styles	"hot," brash, extroverted	*samba:* powerful, propulsive, infectious *bossa nova:* "cool," light, sensual, subtle, gentle
Rhythmic core (bass)	walking bass	*tumbao*	*surdo*
Main accompaniment instrument	primarily piano	primarily piano	primarily guitar
Rhythm matrix	even, four-to-the-bar pulse accented with syncopation	syncopated *tumbao* bass line, *clave* 3-2 or 2-3, *montuno*, cyclical maracas, cross-rhythms	*surdo* and bass anchoring the beat, cross-rhythms on accompanying percussion and guitar
Typical rhythm instruments	drum set	conga, bongo, *timbales, claves* (sticks), maracas, cowbell, *güiro* (scraper), *shekere* (shaker)	*surdo* (bass drum), *repique* (tom tom), *caixa* (snare drum), conga, *agogô* (bell hit with stick), *ganza* (shaker), *cuíca* (friction drum), *tamborim, reco-reco* (scraper), *berimbau* (stringed bow), whistle

propensity for experimentation brings to mind such stateside iconoclasts as Sun Ra and Frank Zappa.

Pascoal had many musical associates, among whom one standout is the multi-percussionist, singer, and occasional bandleader Airto Moreira. A master of playing arrays of popping, twinkling, chiming, fluttering, whistling, rasping, slapping, hiccupping, and pattering instruments—not to mention the standard drum set—as one ambience-creating percussion tool, Moreira was at the forefront of a trend started in the 1970s in which Brazilian multi-percussionists were employed by jazz bands in the United States to add dimension and color to the sound. This trend was just one of the several major intersection points of jazz and Brazilian music during the twentieth century and into the twenty-first.

> ### TAKE NOTE
>
> - What native Cuban and Brazilian musical rhythms and musical instruments have influenced the development of Latin Jazz?

Early Latin Influences on Jazz

The Cuban *habanera* song and dance form, an antecedent of the popular *danzón* style, found popularity in California by the late nineteenth century, brought there by Mexican composer Miguel Arévalo. The brass band of the Mexican Eighth Cavalry Regiment performed various Latin tunes, among them *danzas* of Cuban origin, in New Orleans in 1884. (One of

African Americans dancing and singing the bamboula, New Orleans LA (ca. 1790–1800).

THE BAMBOULA.

the band's members introduced the saxophone to the Crescent City.) In addition, Cuban rhythms may have been brought to Louisiana by members of New Orleans's Onward Brass Band, who were reportedly among U.S. troops who fought in Cuba for its independence from Spain in 1898.

Habanera rhythm.

((•—**Listen** to this rhythm on **mymusiclab.com**

When jazz erupted onto the New Orleans music scene, the city had a bustling Latin and Caribbean population comprising, in part, Mexicans, Cubans, freed slaves from Santo Domingo, and settlers from Martinique and Guadeloupe. The city's music reflected their varied traditions. Creole balls featured **quadrilles** (square dances of French origin), **mazookas** (a Creolized version of mazurkas, still danced today in some Caribbean islands), and Cuban *danzas* and *habaneras*, all of which enjoyed great popularity. Voodoo rhythms from Haiti pulsated through black neighborhoods, while drums accompanied the *bamboula* and the

kalinda dances—both of Congo origin—when they were performed in the city's famed Congo Square. The New Orleans composer Louis Moreau Gottschalk, whose work foretold ragtime and jazz, drew freely from these dance rhythms for such works as *Bamboula— Danse de Nègre* (ca. 1846). And some black Louisiana folk songs sung in *patois* (a dialectal mixture of French and African words and turns of phrases)—*Missié Banjo*, for example—were infused with such Caribbean strains as the calypso or the beguine.

The New Orleans–born pianist-composer "Jelly Roll" Morton, who claimed to be the creator of jazz, considered what he called "the Latin tinge" a foremost ingredient of this emerging musical gumbo. This Latin tinge can be heard in ragtime instrumentals such as Jess Pickett's *The Dream Rag* (evidently from the 1890s) and *Tiger Rag* (1917; see "Jazz Classics: *Tiger Rag*," page 52), in Morton's *New Orleans Joys* (1923) and *Mama Nita* (1924), and especially in W.C. Handy's famed *St. Louis Blues* (1914; see "Jazz Classics: *St. Louis Blues*," page 39), with its *habanera*-based second section. These all share a bass line, called **"Spanish" (or "tango" bass)**, which resembles that of the *danza* or of the Argentinian tango. (Similarities between the Cuban *danza* and the Argentinian tango were not coincidental. The *danza* and *danza habanera* had derived from the French *contredanse*, which in Haiti—before it was brought to Cuba around 1791 and changed to the

---

quadrille (French) a square dance of French origin for two couples; a piece of music to accompany quadrille dancing.

mazooka (Creole) a Creolized version of the mazurka (a Polish folk dance in triple meter), still danced today in the French Caribbean islands of Martinique and Guadeloupe.

"Spanish" (or "tango" bass) a bass line containing syncopated figures, typically in *habanera* rhythm. The term was used in the early twentieth century to describe syncopated bass lines of certain rags, blues, and jazz pieces.

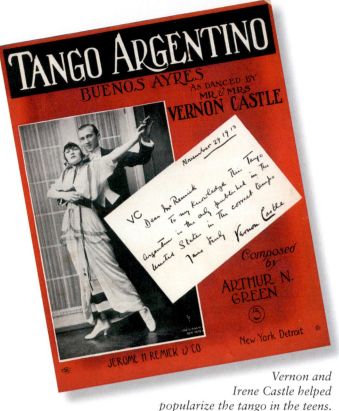

Vernon and
Irene Castle helped
popularize the tango in the teens.
COURTESY BENCAR ARCHIVES.

jazz. The band was nicknamed the "Hellfighters" because of their dedicated service in World War I as a colored U.S. regiment serving in France. They helped popularize proto-jazz in France during and after World War I.

Latin and Caribbean influences continued to be strongly felt in New Orleans. Tyers's *Panama* became a favorite of New Orleans brass bands, although they often dropped its *habanera* rhythm; and several Latin musicians performed in early New Orleans jazz bands.

Puerto Ricans, after being granted U.S. citizenship in 1917, migrated in increasing numbers to New York, where they first settled mostly in East Harlem. Their neighborhood, soon to be known as El Barrio, became a hub of musical activity and an incubator for many musical careers. The Puerto Rican trombonist **Juan Tizol** emigrated in 1920 to the United States. As a member of Duke Ellington's orchestra, Tizol began in the 1930s to introduce Latin-inflected compositions into Ellington's repertoire, among them *Conga Brava*, *Moon over Cuba*, and two of the most popular jazz standards, *Caravan* (1936) and *Perdido* (1942). (One day in 1936, Ellington remembered,

contradanza—had acquired an African tinge that came to be known as tango bass. In addition, Cuban sailors brought rhythms from their island to Argentina's Buenos Aires around 1850, and many Cuban musicians performed there in the late nineteenth and early twentieth centuries. Beyond this cross-fertilizing, Cuban popular music and Argentinian tango both have African roots in common.)

Latin and Caribbean elements also found their way into New York's pre-jazz music in such pieces as the *Cuban Cake Walk* (1901), performed by "Tim" Brymn, leader of the famed Clef Club Orchestra. Also in New York, the pianist and arranger William H. Tyers, who collaborated with the African American bandleaders James Reese Europe and Will Marion Cook, wrote several pieces influenced by Latin music: the tango-*maxixe Maori* (1908) and the tango *Panama* (1911)—both of which were recorded by Duke Ellington in 1928—and the Cuban dance *Trocha* (1913). Around 1915, the Brazilian *maxixe* (also known as "Brazilian tango" and the Argentinian tango became wildly popular in the United States.

In 1917, James Reese Europe recruited 15 Puerto Rican musicians—among them the famed composer Rafael Hernández—for his 369th U.S. Infantry Military Band, who performed highly syncopated material that forecast the coming of

Juan Tizol, *valve trombone player of Duke Ellington's orchestra at the Hurricane cabaret,* 1943. PHOTO COURTESY GORDON PARKS/LIBRARY OF CONRGESS.

Caravan

Ellington first recorded *Caravan* in 1936, with a septet, but the best-known version is the track he recorded a year later with his big band of 16 musicians. From drummer Sonny Greer's dramatic opening percussion effects to the final unresolved chord, this classic recording of *Caravan* paints an intriguing picture of some distant and exotic place. Its serpentine melody conjures an image of a Middle Eastern snake-charmer's trick, or a camel caravan undulating across the rolling sand dunes; yet at the same time, Tizol's inflections also bespeak his Latin American roots. *Caravan* is one of the Ellington orchestra's first efforts to incorporate influences from other cultures into its music.

Caravan is the single most-recorded Latin jazz composition. It is also the most-recorded composition with Duke Ellington's name on it. The Duke Ellington Orchestra made 191 recordings of *Caravan*, and other jazz musicians recorded it nearly 1,500 times. It has been recorded by a wide variety of musicians, ranging from Ella Fitzgerald, Chet Atkins, the Carpenters, and Phish, to the Latin artists Candido, Tito Puente, and Pérez Prado. It is included in the movies *Chocolat*, *Ocean's Eleven*, and *Ocean's Thirteen*; the Woody Allen films *Alice* and *Sweet and Lowdown*; and the television programs *The O.C.* and *The Simpsons*.

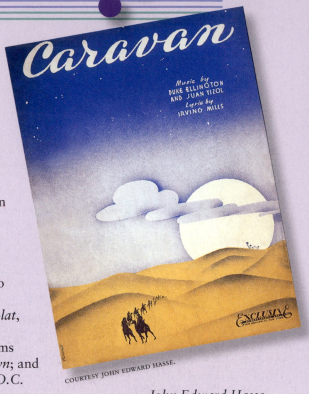

COURTESY JOHN EDWARD HASSE.

—*John Edward Hasse*

Tizol "came up with [part of *Caravan*]. See, it wasn't in tempo, he stood [and played it] sort of *ad lib*. He played it, [the] first ten bars, we took it and worked out the rest of it.")

 Watch the video of *Caravan* by Duke Ellington on **mymusiclab.com**

> **TAKE NOTE**
>
> • How did Latin music influence early jazz?

Cuban Music and Jazz

Cuba's proximity to the United States contributed to the mixing of their musical cultures. Only 90 miles separate the two countries, and for many years a steady stream of people traveled between the island and the United States. By the early 1920s American jazz had reached Cuba and was spreading throughout the island nation; several North American musicians formed jazz groups in Havana. Conversely, Cuban big bands such as the Lecuona Cuban Boys—most of them influenced by Fletcher Henderson's arrangements—gained first local then international exposure.

Musical exchanges between the United States and Cuba intensified over the years. During the 1920s, North American record companies took a growing interest in Latin music, especially Cuban music, and offered contracts to several bands. As a result, two Cuban rhythms—the *son* (commercialized under the name *rumba* or, in English, rhumba), and the **conga** (a Carnival rhythm of Congo origin, brought to the United States by the Cuban singer and actor Desi Arnaz)—became popular across the country. These rhythms aroused the interest of jazz musicians such as Sidney Bechet and Willie "The Lion" Smith (who together recorded *Rose Rhumba* and *Baba Rhumba*), and Cab Calloway (*Doin' the Rhumba* and *The Congo Conga*).

Then, in the 1930s, Cuban music took the United States by storm. The Cuban flutist Alberto Socarrás, who moved to Harlem in 1927, helped to establish it in the United States. From 1937 to 1940 Socarrás performed at the famous New York nightspot the Cotton Club, opposite Duke Ellington, Cab Calloway,

conga a dance of the Cuban carnival, which gained popularity in the United States in the 1930s and 1940s; a rhythm of Congo origin, it features a heavy fourth beat.

Cuban percussionist Machito and his orchestra, the Afro-Cubans, created some of the earliest Latin jazz. The band came into prominence in the 1940s as the Afro-Cuban style was gaining popularity through the bands of Xavier Cugat and Pérez Prado. Machito, with his brother-in-law **Mario Bauzá**, melded the *clave*-based rhythmic patterns of Cuban dance music with the dense instrumental textures of jazz big bands, with exciting bop solos thrown in

✳ **Explore** on **mymusiclab.com**

((• **Hear** a tribute to Machito and the Afro-Cubans by Bobby Sanabria on **mymusiclab.com**

for good measure. An irresistible combination, it propelled the Afro-Cubans to a career that lasted decades.

—*Jeff Rupert*

The Congas

The rhythm section in Afro-Cuban music, with its inclusion of several percussionists, reflects a West African heritage more than does the typical jazz band rhythm section. The conga player pictured is Carlos Vidal, who played with Machito and several important jazz bands including Stan Kenton's. Other important conga players associated with Machito were Cándido Camero and Patato Valdés. Just as in the West African tradition, Afro-Cuban drummers or percussionists take turns playing ostinato (repeated) figures and soloing.

The Bongos

Bongos, along with congas, *claves*, and cowbell, add to the variety of percussion sounds in Latin jazz. José Mangual, Sr., is seen here playing the bongos.

The Drum Set

Drums in Latin jazz are often supplemented with *timbales* (usually two free-standing drums with a cymbal or cowbell, played standing). Ubaldo "Uba" Nieto, Puerto Rican *timbale* player, is seen here playing the drumset.

The Bass

The bass part in Afro-Cuban music differs from the walking bass line known in jazz. It is more syncopated as it joins with percussion in a rhythm pattern referred to as the *tumbao*. The bass's rhythmic interaction with the percussion section is crucial to the feel of Afro-Cuban jazz.

PHOTO COURTESY FRANK DRIGGS COLLECTION.

Mario Bauzá • Trumpet

Cuban-born Mario Bauzá originally played clarinet, and switched to trumpet. As musical director for Machito's Afro-Cubans, he brought the influences of Dizzy Gillespie, Cab Calloway, Stan Kenton, and other jazz bandleaders to a cross-pollination of jazz and Afro-Cuban music. Bauzá came to the United States in 1930, and soon became a member of Chick Webb's band, one of the most prominent swing big bands in New York at the time. With the Afro-Cubans, he and his brother-in-law Machito introduced Latin music to the New York City jazz scene, influencing Dizzy Gillespie and Charlie Parker, among others. Bauzá was also responsible for bringing percussionist Tito Puente into prominence by hiring him as a member of Machito's Afro-Cubans.

Machito • Maracas and Bandleader

Machito (Frank Grillo) was a singer as well as a bandleader and percussionist. Raised in Cuba, he played music there professionally before moving to New York and establishing a presence in the Latin music scene. His founding of the Afro-Cubans cemented his place in jazz history, and he led the band through several eras and musical trends—such as salsa—that he helped create. Machito was also featured with non-Latin bands that capitalized on the mambo (a kind of Afro-Cuban beat, and a dance) craze of the 1950s and 1960s.

and Louis Armstrong, creating a stir. At different times in his career and according to the venues where he performed, Socarrás led several jazz-oriented Latin ensembles—among them the Afro-Cuban Rumbas, who appeared to acclaim at the Apollo Theater and at the Savoy Ballroom in Harlem—and helped break down racial barriers in previously segregated U.S. clubs. (Socarrás is also known for making what were probably the first jazz flute solos on record—on *Shootin' the Pistol* in 1927, and *Have You Ever Felt That Way*, 1929.)

Cuban music and jazz began to merge more completely in the early 1940s, with the creation in New York of the Afro-Cubans, the seminal big band founded by the Cuban-born trumpeter and saxophonist Mario Bauzá and his brother-in-law, singer and maracas player **Machito (Frank Grillo Gutiérrez)**. A well-schooled instrumentalist, Bauzá had played with some of the best ensembles in Havana and, after moving to New York in 1930, with popular U.S. bandleaders Chick Webb and Cab Calloway. Machito had sung with some of the top *son* groups in Havana. Comprising both Latin and jazz musicians, Bauzá's and Machito's ensemble—in which Bauzá served as musical director while Machito fronted the orchestra—combined the riffs and the brass and reed sections of jazz with authentic Afro-Cuban percussion and rhythms. At first, some black Americans—eager to dissociate themselves from the image of a "primitive and savage" Africa that the hand-held drums conjured in the minds of many whites—professed shock at the band's powerful percussion, completely new in jazz at the time. Nevertheless, many were soon won over by the Afro-Cubans' irresistible rhythms and eventually became ardent fans.

Bauzá's *Tanga* (1943; *JTSA* Disc 2/Track 22), a head arrangement influenced by Duke Ellington's "jungle" style of growling brass instruments, launched what came to be called **Cubop** (*Cuban* plus *bebop*). Cubop laid down a high-energy, multi-layered mix of sounds, with fluid, bebop-style melody lines played over *montunos*—brief yet intricate countermelodic vamps typically played on piano—unfolding against complex rhythmic textures. The Afro-Cubans brought

---

Cubop   from "Cuban" plus "bebop"; Afro-Latin-flavored bebop, pioneered in the 1940s by Cuban trumpeter-arranger Mario Bauzá.

Professional Cuban dance team known as Pete & Millie dancing the mambo at the Palladium Ballroom, 1954.

this recipe to their memorable rendition of *Tanga* at Carnegie Hall in 1949, a concert whose star power—with Charlie Parker, Duke Ellington, and Lester Young on hand—evidenced the growing popularity of the Latin strain in jazz.

The flowering of Cubop in the late 1940s and early 1950s coincided with crazes for the the big band mambo and the *cha-cha-chá*, two styles created by the Cuban musicians (Dámaso) Pérez Prado and Enrique Jorrín, respectively. Top Latin bands battled it out and the best dancers strutted their stuff at New York City's famed Palladium Ballroom, the "temple of the mambo." Located on Broadway, the Palladium was also a haunt for Dizzy Gillespie and other jazzmen, who performed just around the corner in the 52nd Street clubs (and was a hangout for such celebrities as actor Marlon Brando, who occasionally enjoyed trying his hand on the conga drums). The proximity of the Palladium Ballroom and 52nd Street nightclubs contributed to the cross-fertilization of Latin music and bebop.

Over the years, Gillespie, saxophonists Cannonball Adderley, Johnny Griffin, Dexter Gordon, and countless other jazzmen all performed and/or recorded with the Afro-Cubans. The longest-running Latin band in the United States, the Afro-Cubans lasted until Machito's death in 1984. They inspired many other orchestras in the United States, including those of Stan Kenton, Tito Puente, and Tito Rodríguez, as well as various aggregations in Cuba. Kenton recorded *Machito* (1947) as a tribute to the singer and bandleader, and borrowed part of the Afro-Cubans' rhythm section, including Machito himself on maracas, for his rendition of *The Peanut Vendor* (1947), which became his best-selling work.

The classically trained Cuban-born composer and arranger "Chico" (Arturo) O'Farrill imparted brilliance and sophistication to the Afro-Cubans, with arrangements that offered greater harmonic complexity than the more traditional approaches of the band's other arrangers. O'Farrill's *Afro-Cuban Jazz Suite* (1951), performed by the Afro-Cubans, guest-starred saxophonist Flip Phillips, powerhouse drummer Buddy Rich, and most notably Charlie Parker, who breezed with stunning ease through the complex Latin rhythms. O'Farrill led his own ensemble in the 1950s; worked with Dizzy Gillespie, Count Basie, and others post-1965; recorded with Gillespie and Machito in 1975 (*Afro-Cuban Jazz Moods*); and in the late 1990s recorded *Pure Emotion* (1995) and *Heart of a Legend* (1998–99). Over the course of his career, O'Farrill wrote and arranged for bandleaders as diverse as Benny Goodman, Lionel Hampton, and rocker David Bowie, among many others.

The appeal of Cuban music to jazz musicians was at least threefold: The energy and thrill of multiple percussion instruments playing complex rhythms induces a desire to move and dance. Cuban music also makes

Cuban percussionist Chano Pozo's work with Dizzy Gillespie in 1947–48 helped embed Afro-Cuban sounds in jazz, where they would remain often-used rhythmic and melodic ingredients. PHOTO COURTESY © HERMAN LEONARD PHOTOGRAPHY LLC.

frequent use of breaks, an effective device that helps spice up and propel songs. In addition, the simple harmonic structure of many Cuban tunes allows soloists to "stretch out" without overly worrying about chord changes, thus providing another source of excitement.

A large number of U.S. jazzmen took to Latin music: Duke Ellington recorded *The Peanut Vendor* (1931), Louis Armstrong *La Cucaracha* (1935) and *Mexican Swing* (1938), Artie Shaw *Frenesí* (1940), and Jimmy Dorsey *Aquellos Ojos Verdes* (under the name *Green Eyes*, 1941). But it was Dizzy Gillespie who was became the first North American bandleader to fuse bebop and Afro-Cuban rhythms. A close friend of Bauzá's since their joint tenure with Cab Calloway, Gillespie had become acquainted with the *clave* during his stint in Harlem with flutist Alberto Socarrás. In 1947, on Bauzá's recommendation, Gillespie hired into his big band the outstanding **conguero** (conga player) Luciano "Chano" Pozo, freshly arrived in New York from Havana. Pozo introduced hand-held drums into a U.S. jazz ensemble for the first time, as well as sacred Afro-Cuban chants and the rhythms of the **rumba brava** (a

---

conguero (Spanish) a player of the conga drum.
rumba brava (Spanish) refers to several Cuban traditional vocal and instrumental genres of Congo derivation, among them the *guaguancó*, the *columbia,* and the *yambú*. The *rumba brava*, also danced, is different from the ballroom *rumba*.

Tito Puente in performance, 1982.
PHOTO COURTESY MIKE ALBANS/AP PHOTO.

James Moody as well as with Latin musicians. But Pozo's career was cut short when, on December 2, 1948, he was shot down in a bar in Harlem. His impact on jazz, however, proved long-lasting. After Pozo's death, Gillespie later recruited a string of percussionists, and the conga drum and the bongo became mainstays of many jazz and dance ensembles, from singer-pianist Nat "King" Cole's 1950s trio to trumpeter Roy Hargrove's 1990s group Crisol.

By the 1960s, big bands that featured Latin jazz had given way to more intimate ensembles—called "combos" at the time in both jazz and Latin music—that usually consisted of piano, vibes or guitar, bass, bongos, and flute. Most representative of this era were the combos formed by Cuban percussionist **Mongo Santamaría**, American vibraphonist Cal Tjader, British pianist George Shearing, and percussionists Tito Puente and **Ray Barretto**, both Nuyoricans (Puerto Ricans from New York). Groups led by U.S. musicians generally accentuated the jazz side, while those led by Latinos leaned more toward a Latin feel. Santamaría's group served as an incubator for such talented newcomers (and future headliners) as pianists Herbie Hancock and **Chick Corea**. Hancock brought Santamaría his freshly penned *Watermelon Man*—a catchy, funky blues-like piece—which Santamaría recorded in 1962 to become the *conguero's* first hit.

A *timbalero*, vibraphonist, and highly prolific composer and arranger with hundreds of recordings under his name, Tito Puente—known as "El Rey" (The King)—popularized the *timbales* in the United States, as well as the flute in Latin jazz. Born in East Harlem in 1923, he grew up listening to both jazz and Latin music, and he studied piano, organ, trap drums, vibes, *timbales*, conga, and composition. He began to play professionally at the age of 14. At 18, in 1941, he worked six months with the Afro-Cubans, and later he led both dance-oriented Latin big bands and smaller, more experimental Latin jazz ensembles. Two of his most famous compositions are *Ran Kan Kan* (1949) and *Oye Cómo Va* (1963), the latter recorded

musical genre of Congo and Spanish origin). It took a while, however, to fine-tune things. Pozo didn't immediately fit the bebop mold, and, conversely, Gillespie and his bandmates needed a certain amount of coaching before they could adapt to the exacting idiosyncrasies of Afro-Cuban music. "Chano taught us all multirhythm; we learned from the master," reminisced Gillespie. "On the bus, he'd give me a drum, [bassist] Al McKibbon a drum, and he'd take a drum. Another guy would have a cowbell, and he'd give everybody a rhythm. We'd see how all the rhythms tied into one another, and everybody was playing something different."

Pozo's pyrotechnics tested the mettle of Gillespie and his men. The band soon made history though, with *Manteca* (1947), *Cubana Be/Cubana Bop* (also 1947), *Tin Tin Deo*, and other compositions. The fiery *Manteca*, with its introduction and A and A' sections based on authentic Cuban vamps (*tumbaos*, see "Cuban Rhythms," page 261)—peppered with Gillespie's shouts of "*Manteca!*"—and with its contrasting, jazzier bridge, was a novelty. Even more revolutionary was Gillespie's and upcoming composer George Russell's *Cubana Be/Cubana Bop*, with its advanced modal colors, and its middle section, on which Pozo let loose on conga and chanted ritual Yoruba chants.

The Gillespie band's February 1948 concerts at the Salle Pleyel in Paris turned the city on its ear. Audiences were stunned and Gillespie even witnessed a fistfight between the advocates of old-time jazz, whom modernists derisively nicknamed "moldy figs," and the fans of bebop, who were in turn dubbed "sour grapes."

Back in the United States, after his European tour with Gillespie, Pozo recorded with tenor saxophonist

Hear a tribute to Tito Puente on **mymusiclab.com**

by rock guitarist Carlos Santana in 1970. The tunes can notably be heard on an album representative of Puente's Latin jazz work, *El Rey* (1984), which also includes the jazz standard *Autumn Leaves*, as well as John Coltrane's *Equinox* and *Giant Steps*.

Like Puente, Ray Barretto, a powerful *conguero*, cultivated both jazz and Latin music. Born in Brooklyn in 1929, Barretto discovered the conga drum while stationed in Munich with the U.S. Army when he heard a record of Chano Pozo with Dizzy Gillespie. Back in New York, he participated in jazz jam sessions in Harlem. As a sideman, he performed and recorded with countless jazz musicians, ranging from pianist Red Garland and saxophonist Eddie "Lockjaw" Davis to Dizzy Gillespie and Herbie Hancock. In 1957, he replaced Mongo Santamaría in Tito Puente's orchestra, and then worked four years with Cal Tjader. In 1961 Barretto formed his own Latin group, called Charanga La Moderna, and he gradually shifted from Latin dance music, scoring a hit in 1963 with the catchy *El Watusi*, to Latin jazz. In the 1990s, his New World Spirit band included an eclectic mix of young musicians, from the Columbian pianist Héctor Martignon to the Japanese drummer Satoshi Takeishi (they can be heard on Barretto's album *Taboo*, 1994).

Another Nuyorican, pianist **Eddie Palmieri**, brought a somewhat different sound to Latin music in the early 1960s with his band La Perfecta. It was known as "the band with the crazy roaring elephants," due to its use of a trombone section instead of the more standard trumpets. Palmieri, who had studied *timbales* as a youth in addition to piano, went on to explore various fusions of Latin music with North American rhythm and blues, soul, funk, and jazz over a career that spanned more than 50 years. His 2007 *Sympatico* earned a Grammy Award for Best Latin Jazz Album, an accolade that was seconded by the Jazz Journalists Association.

The free exchange of musicians and musical ideas between Cuba and the United States—which had culturally enriched both countries—came to a halt in 1960, when Washington severed its ties with Havana after Fidel Castro nationalized all U.S. property. In the early 1960s, following the Cuban Revolution, Cuban government officials first looked upon jazz as "degenerate American music," but they eventually changed their views and new artists began to emerge. In 1973, pianist Jesús

Mongo Santamaría in performance (ca. 1960). PHOTO COURTESY BOB WILLOUGHBY/ REDFERNS/GETTY IMAGES.

"Chucho" Valdés and saxophonist and clarinetist Paquito D'Rivera formed the volcanic group Irakere (from a Yoruba word meaning "forest"). With its impressive array of percussion and bravura-style solos, Irakere gave a new impulse to Cuban jazz and rapidly became the most famous band in its country. Amid its battery of percussion the group made use of the *batá*—the set of three double-headed drums of Yoruba origin that had been such an early foundation in the development of Afro-Cuban music. The *batá*, then a novelty in jazz, gradually became more widespread in Cuban popular music.

In 1977, American jazz masters Dizzy Gillespie and **Stan Getz** performed in Havana, and "discovered" Irakere. When in 1979 President Jimmy Carter eased up on the cultural embargo on Cuba, Irakere was able to book a tour in the United States. The tour—the first performances of a Cuban jazz band in the United States in 20 years—earned huge acclaim, and their debut Columbia album earned them a Grammy Award in 1980.

In 1980, more than 100,000 Cubans defected from their country to the United States; their numbers included clarinetist D'Rivera and drummer Ignacio Berroa, who brought a new shot of Cuban energy to the States. Trumpeter **Arturo Sandoval**, also from Irakere, defected 10 years

Listening Guide

MANTECA • DIZZY GILLESPIE AND HIS ORCHESTRA

Music: Chano Pozo and Dizzy Gillespie, 1947. Personnel: Dizzy Gillespie, Dave Burns, Elmon Wright, Jr., Benny Bailey (trumpet); "Bill" (William) Shepherd, Ted Kelly (trombone); John Brown, Howard Johnson (alto saxophone); Joe Gayles, George "Big Nick" Nicholas (tenor saxophone); Cecil Payne (baritone saxophone); John Lewis (piano); Al McKibbon (bass); Kenny Clarke (drums); Luciano "Chano" Pozo (conga). Recorded December 22, 1947, in New York. Timing: 2:58.

Overview

Manteca (meaning "grease" but also "marijuana" in Cuban slang) is one of Cubop's most significant compositions. The tune, which had its public premiere December 27, 1947, at Town Hall in New York City, became a major hit for Gillespie and a staple of his repertoire until the end of his career. In 1948, *Manteca* also stunned listeners at the Salle Pleyel, in Paris, as well as at the Pasadena Civic Auditorium in California.

Key Features

- *Manteca* is fascinating for its jubilant mood, high energy, and contrast between the initial vamps and the "head"—based on traditional Cuban rhythm patterns called *tumbaos*—and the bridge, played with a straight-ahead $\frac{4}{4}$ jazz feel. The enjoyment shared between the musicians is palpable and infectious.
- Form: Initial vamps are followed by a melody in ABA' form: a 16-bar A section based on a B-flat *tumbao* (with saxophone chorus) and ending with a different rhythm pattern on the last two bars; a 16-bar swing bridge (with trumpet improvisation); and a 16-bar A' in B-flat, followed by a repetition of the initial vamps.
- Standard big-band instrumentation: Sections of trumpets, trombones, and saxophones, and a rhythm section of piano, bass, and drums, plus the addition—new in bebop at the time—of congas.
- Melody and harmony: The initial vamps and the A section stem from conga rhythms created by **Chano Pozo,** while the jazzy and very fluid bridge was composed by Gillespie with the help of saxophonist Bill Graham and arranger Walter "Gil" Fuller. The arrangement was ghostwritten by **Chico O'Farrill,** who used it again in his *Manteca Suite*, recorded by Dizzy Gillespie's Orchestra in 1954. O'Farrill again produced an excellent version of *Manteca* on *Heart of a Legend* (1999).
- Arrangement: The skillful arrangement creates a crescendo and decrescendo of intensity with several climaxes (at the end of the A and A' sections and during Gillespie's brief but highly charged solos). The Latin A and A' sections herald the rhythm of the mambo—a genre that would become highly popular in the United States in the early 1950s. The shifting textures of the riffs and the contrasts between the different sections sustain the sense of excitement throughout the piece.
- Rhythm: The introduction of the conga in jazz initially created a stir but the instrument soon became a fixture of many other jazz ensembles. Playing *tumbaos* also was a novelty for bass players. At first, bassist Al McKibbon had trouble mastering the new rhythm, but said that "*Manteca* really opened my eyes and mind and heart and everything." The conga, however, plods and feels somewhat unnecessary on the bridge. Gillespie often wished Pozo would refrain from playing on this section, but Pozo was a headstrong man who liked to have his way.

Paquito D'Rivera's role in the Cuban group Irakere brought him to the United States, where he remained to forge his own Latin-bop sound. PHOTO COURTESY ANDY FREEBERG.

- Stylistic variety: The orchestra led by Gillespie in the late 1940s was a revolutionary one and the first bebop big band in the history of jazz. Kenny Clarke, who played on this date, also pioneered bebop, creating a whole new way of distributing accents on his drums. There is nonetheless a marked difference between Gillespie's dazzling lines and Nicholas's tenor solo, which is still rooted in the swing style of the 1940s.

—Isabelle Leymarie

TIME	SECTION	MELODY/INSTRUMENTATION
0:00	INITIAL VAMP	Bass and conga enter with a B-flat *tumbao* while Gillespie shouts "Manteca!"
0:08	SECOND VAMP PLAYED OVER THE FIRST ONE	Baritone sax joins in with a different B-flat vamp which, superimposed on the first one, creates interesting polyrhythms.
0:18		Brass joins in with riffs while Gillespie improvises.
0:29–0:31		Short and powerful **tutti** riff.
0:32	INITIAL VAMP	Return to the bass-and-conga *tumbao*.
0:38	A (16 BARS)	Melody stated in call-and-response form by the reeds and the brass.
1:00	BRIDGE (16 BARS)	Bridge: First eight bars stated by the reeds against brass riffs while the conga adapts to the jazz feel.
1:12		Second eight bars of the bridge stated by Gillespie.
1:22	A'	Same as A section.
1:33	INITIAL VAMP	Initial bass-and-conga *tumbao*.
1:37		Baritone sax joins in.
1:39		Reeds join in.
1:42		Short and powerful *tutti* riff.
1:48	SOLO (VAR. OF A)	Tenor saxman "Big Nick" Nicholas plays a solo against riffs on the A section, briefly quoting *Blue Moon*.
2:10	BRIDGE	First eight bars stated by the brass with countermelodies by the reeds.
2:21		Second eight bars stated by Gillespie, who improvises around the melody.
2:32	A'	A' section stated by the reeds the brass and punctuated by a resounding "Manteca!"
2:43	SECOND VAMP	B-flat vamp by brass and reeds with shout of "Manteca!"
2:52	INITIAL VAMP	Initial *tumbao* by bass and conga.
3:03	END	Short final drums accent by Kenny Clarke.

later. D'Rivera and Sandoval both enjoyed fruitful and long-lasting careers in the United States, first joining Gillespie's United Nations Orchestra, established in 1990, and playing on countless record dates as both sidemen and leaders. (In 2000, Sandoval's life and defection were portrayed in the Home Box Office television docudrama *For Love or Country: The Arturo Sandoval Story*, and in 2005, D'Rivera became the first Latin jazz artist to earn a prestigious Jazz Masters Award from the National Endowment for the Arts.) These exiles were later joined by pianist Gonzalo Rubalcaba, whom Dizzy Gillespie had discovered while in Cuba in 1985, and who moved to Miami in 1997, proving himself one of the more interesting young pianists in jazz.

Beginning in the 1970s and 1980s, in New York, young Puerto Rican Nuyoricans such as Jerry and Andy Gonzalez and their Fort Apache Band, as well as pianist Hilton Ruiz and trumpeter Charlie Sepúlveda, created brawny, highly charged sounds that crackled with the city's electricity.

California also eagerly embraced Latin jazz, from the mambo orchestras of Pérez Prado and René Touzet in the 1950s to the boogaloo and funky Latin jazz of percussionist Willie Bobo in the 1960s, on to more recent sounds. In New Orleans, a Latin and Caribbean lilt continued to mark the styles of many mid-to-late-twentieth-century New Orleans musicians,

tutti (Italian) all; played by an entire ensemble.

Listening Guide

Listen to *Airegin* by Tito Puente on
mymusiclab.com
CD II, Track 8/Download Track 32

AIREGIN • TITO PUENTE

Music: Sonny Rollins, 1954. Arrangement: Brian Murphy and Tito Puente, 1989. Personnel: Robbie Kwock, David "Piro"Rodriguez (trumpet); Mary Fettig, Mitch Frohman (saxophone); Sam Burtis (trombone); Sonny Bravo (piano); Bobby Rodriguez (bass); Jose Madera (congas); Johnny Rodriguez (bongos); Rebeca Mauleón (synthesizer); Tito Puente (*timbales*); John Santos (*shekere*, bongos). Recorded July 31–August 1, 1989, in San Francisco. First issue: *Goza Mi Timbal* (Concord Picante CCD-4399), 1990. Timing: 4:11.

Overview

Tito Puente's version of Sonny Rollins's mainstream jazz standard *Airegin* (Nigeria spelled backwards) "cooks"as only Latin-energized jazz can. Here, the melody and improvised solos burn over a percolating, mambo-flavored brew of interlocking rhythms. Congas, bongos, *timbales* and the syncopated *tumbao* bass line—interlaced by the piano's catchy *montuno* (repeating countermelody)—complete the Afro-Cuban-derived recipe.

The A-B-A-C form of the melody departs from the standard 32-bar length (8+8+8+8) by adding an extra four bars to the B section. The resulting 36-bar form, 8+12+8+8, provides the structure for each solo chorus.

This track and others from Tito Puente's Grammy Award–winning 1990 album *Goza Mi Timbal* are considered some of the finest examples of mainstream jazz tunes fused with Latin rhythm.

—*Tad Lathrop*

TIME	SECTION	INSTRUMENTATION	MELODY
0:00	INTRO	Rhythm section	The rhythm section (percussion, bass, piano) introduces the tune with a syncopated *clave* pattern, climaxing to an abrupt stop.
0:09	CHORUS 1, A	Band	Trumpets and saxes lead into the melody (answered by trombone at 0:11 and 0:15). It is a ricocheting bop-style phrase (in minor key) played twice, low and high. 8 bars.
0:17	B		Long notes cycle smoothly through major keys descending in half steps. 12 bars.
0:31	A		As in the first A, the rhythm section drops out dramatically for the first and fifth measures. 8 bars.
0:39	C		Variation on B. 8 bars. Percussion marks the ending, and leads into Chorus 2.
0:48	CHORUS 2, AB	Trumpet solo, first half	As trumpet begins soloing, the rhythm section up-shifts to an exciting, propulsive groove—a traditional Afro-Cuban rhythm matrix of off-beat bass *tumbao*, *clave* variations by the *timbales*, and piano *montuno*.
1:10	A	Trumpet solo, second half	Sharp contrast as trumpet sustains a rapid **tremolo** (using a technique called triple tonguing). The *montuno* on piano becomes more audible.
1:18	C		Trumpet shifts the tremolo to ultra-fast riffs over the C section.
1:27	CHORUS 3, ABA	Trombone solo	As trombone enters, the rhythm continues to cook. The trombone solo moves rhythmically—playing off the underlying groove—as it outlines the chord changes of sections A, B, A.
1:58	C		Solo ends in continuous double-time phrases.
2:07	CHORUS 4, ABAC	Sax solo	Saxophone solos through sections A and B, with the same rhythmic feel as the trombone. The solo briefly doubles speed at 2:21. On the second A section and into C, the feel stays much the same as the sax hurtles forward over bubbling percussion.
2:46	CHORUS 5A	Horn unison	Horns all join in a new melody—three punchy unison riffs through section A, ending with two "hits."
2:55	B	Percussion solo	Percussion solos feverishly through the 12 bars of B.
3:08	A	Horns unison	Horns replay their melody over the second A section.
3:16	C	Percussion solo	More fiery solo percussion over section C (6 bars instead of the usual 8).
3:23	CHORUS 6, ABAC	Band	Head: The full band reprises the main melody, minus the last 2 bars.
4:00	CODA	Band	The tune's percussive 8-bar intro is repeated, this time with saxophone soloing freely until all end together in bar 9.

among them the rhythm and blues pianists "Professor Longhair" (Henry Roeland Byrd), Fats Domino, Allen Toussaint, James Booker, and Dr. John; drummers Vernell Fournier, Ed Blackwell, and Idris Muhammad; and the rollicking Dirty Dozen Brass Band. Finally, Latin jazz, which had largely disappeared from New Orleans since the days of Jelly Roll Morton, returned to the Crescent City in 1998, when the fiery Los Hombres Calientes was founded by percussionist Bill Summers, trumpeter Irvin Mayfield, and drummer Jason Marsalis. This band used Latin rhythms, but Summers, Mayfield, and Marsalis came from the jazz tradition and improvised more in a modern jazz style.

Many of Brazilian guitarist Antonio Carlos Jobim's compositions—including One-Note Samba, Triste, Corcovado, Desafinado, *and* Meditation—*have become cornerstones of the standard jazz repertory.* PHOTO COURTESY GENE LEES/DOWN BEAT ARCHIVES.

TAKE NOTE

- Who were the key Cuban and Puerto Rican musicians in jazz history?

Brazilian Music and Jazz

It didn't take long for Afro-Brazilian and jazz sensibilities, once exposed to each other, to bond into a sophisticated and sensuous musical hybrid quite distinct from Afro-Cuban and other flavors of Latin jazz. There were two moments in particular when Brazil and jazz reached their highest heights of interaction: the bossa nova infusion during the 1950s and the samba-fusion movement of the 1970s and 1980s.

Among the American musicians who tuned in to the bossa nova was Dizzy Gillespie. He received a recording of Antonio Carlos Jobim's *Desafinado* from Argentine pianist-arranger **Lalo Schifrin**, and he took in more bossa nova, enthusiastically, during a trip to Brazil in 1961. That same year, other U.S. jazz musicians including guitarist Charlie Byrd, trumpeter Kenny Dorham, flutist Herbie Mann, and saxophonist Zoot Sims made their own visits to Brazil and fell in love with this new genre. Byrd, back in the United States, introduced his friend saxophonist Stan Getz to the new sounds, and the two paired up to record an album. Their *Jazz Samba* (1962), which featured Jobim's *Desafinado* and *Samba de Uma Nota Só (One Note Samba)*, became a best-seller. In the same year, Herbie Mann issued *Do the Bossa with Herbie Mann*, and he and trumpeter Kenny Dorham flew to Brazil to record with pianist

Sérgio Mendes's Sexteto Bossa Rio. On November 21, 1962, a momentous bossa nova concert—featuring Jobim, **Luiz Bonfá**, and many others—was held at Carnegie Hall. The event attracted an overflow crowd, drew dozens of reporters, and brought into the audience such illustrious musicians as Gillespie, Miles Davis, pianist Erroll Garner, and singer Tony Bennett.

The popularity of bossa nova in the United States soon soared. In 1963, Stan Getz recorded Jobim's *The Girl from Ipanema* with Jobim on piano, João Gilberto on guitar and vocals, and Gilberto's wife Astrud on vocals. A year later its parent LP, *Getz/Gilberto*, became hugely successful (and it remains one of the most

Getz and Gilberto at the time of their major hits. PHOTO COURTESY FRANK DRIGGS COLLECTION.

---

tremolo dynamic effect achieved by rapid alternation of a note's loudness levels.

Listening Guide

THE GIRL FROM IPANEMA (ORIGINAL TITLE: GARÔTA DE IPANEMA) •
STAN GETZ AND JOAO GILBERTO

Music: Antonio Carlos Jobim, 1962. Portuguese lyrics: Vinícius de Moraes. English lyrics: Norman Gimbel. Personnel: Stan Getz (tenor saxophone); João Gilberto (vocals and guitar); Astrud Gilberto (vocals); Antonio Carlos Jobim (piano); Tommy Williams (bass); Milton Banana (drums). Recorded March 18, 1963, in New York. First issue: *Getz/Gilberto* (Verve V6-8545), 1964. Timing: 5:22.

Overview

For many all over the world, *The Girl from Ipanema* is the epitome of the bossa nova, if not of Brazilian music in general. The song was inspired by a beautiful, real-life woman who used to pass everyday by the Veloso—Jobim and lyricist Vinícius de Moraes's favorite bar in Rio de Janeiro—on her way to the beach. (De Moraes collaborated on many songs with Jobim, bringing a literacy and intelligence to the words that complement the subtlety of the music.) Jobim first recorded it in Brazil shortly before this 1963 New York session, supervised by producer Creed Taylor. Astrud Gilberto—João's wife—had only come to the studio to be with her husband, but Getz convinced her to sing the lyrics in English. While crooners and usually powerful vocalists were the norm in jazz, *The Girl from Ipanema* introduced a new nonchalant way of singing *sotto voce*, almost as if in a whisper. Verve, the record company, didn't believe in the commercial potential of the album and waited until 1964 before releasing it. When it finally was released, it earned three Grammy Awards and became a bestseller.

Key Features

- With its syncopated rhythm and relaxed atmosphere, *The Girl from Ipanema* perfectly exemplifies the charm of the bossa nova, a $\frac{4}{4}$ genre quite different from the more ebullient $\frac{2}{4}$ samba from which it claims to be derived.
- Form: ABA: 16-bar A section, 16-bar bridge, 8-bar A (with Getz improvising on the whole form). This could also be described as AABA: the 16-bar A section really consists of an 8-bar melody, repeated. The listening chart highlights that substructure. (The B section's length, 16 bars, is unusual. In standard AABA form the B section is 8 bars.)
- Mood: The general mood is graceful and subdued. Both João and Astrud Gilberto sing softly—Astrud with what has been described as a "little girl's voice." Jobim plays unobtrusive filigree lines under her and Getz, and when stating the theme, uses sparse but highly efficient chords. Getz blows with tender lyricism and, like Jobim, never intrudes on Astrud Gilberto's singing. The whole song gives a feeling of poise and utmost elegance, and the lyrics (both in Portuguese and in English) fit the melody perfectly.
- Rhythm: The syncopated interlocking of the bass, the guitar, the piano, and the drums is particular to the bossa nova. Its essence is in the steady beat of the bass overlaid with guitar chords played slightly ahead of or behind the beat.
- Harmony: Like many other compositions by Jobim, *The Girl from Ipanema* is harmonically very interesting. It modulates up a half step on the bridge, whose first 12 bars are characterized by an unusual chord progression and quarter-note triplets, which create a dreamy, languid atmosphere. Yet the tune is catchy and easy to remember, and has since given rise to countless cover versions.

—Isabelle Leymarie

popular jazz albums of all time). While some Brazilian musicians dismissed Getz's reading of the bossa nova as inauthentic, the album nonetheless contributed to the enduring popularity of Brazilian music in jazz circles. As for Jobim, a classically trained pianist and composer as well as a guitarist and vocalist, he made history as the figure most associated with jazz bossa nova, the composer of many exceptional pieces, a remarkable number of which have become jazz standards.

Bossa nova's rhythm, its chromatic melodies, and its intriguing harmonies provided jazz musicians a new direction—an alternative setting to the swing-based rhythms and blues-tinged melodies of mainstream jazz. The rhythm, in particular, provided

Astrud Gilberto sang on the memorable recording of The Girl from Ipanema, *accompanied by her husband, Brazilian singer-guitarist João Gilberto.* PHOTO COURTESY JAN PERSSON/REDFERNS/GETTY IMAGES.

TIME	FORM	MELODY	INSTRUMENTATION
0:00	INTRODUCTION (FOUR BAR)	João Gilberto, humming.	Guitar.
0:07	A, FIRST HALF	Gilberto sings the song in Portuguese.	
0:22	A, SECOND HALF		
0:24			Bass and the drums enter lightly—almo[st] inaudibly—under Gilberto.
0:36	B (BRIDGE)		
0:42			Jobim comes in on piano under Gilberto on the fourth bar.
1:06	A	Gilberto returns to the A section.	
1:21	SECOND VERSE, A FIRST HALF	Astrud Gilberto enters, singing in English.	Guitar, bass, and drums.
1:36	A, SECOND HALF		
1:50	B		
1:56			Jobim comes in on piano under Astrud Gilberto on the fourth bar.
2:20	A	Astrud Gilberto returns to the A section.	Guitar, bass, and drums.
2:35	A, FIRST HALF	Getz states the melody.	Saxophone, backed by the rhythm section minus the melody.
2:49	A, SECOND HALF	Getz improvises on the second eight bars of the A.	
3:03			Jobim (piano) comes in under Getz on the last bar before the bridge.
3:04	B	Getz solos on the bridge, embroidering the melody.	
3:33	A	Getz finishes his chorus.	
3:48	A, FIRST HALF	Jobim states the melody with very rhythmic chords.	Piano.
4:03	A, SECOND HALF		
4:17	B	Astrud Gilberto comes in on the bridge, singing it in English. The song fades out with a repeat of the words "but she doesn't see."	Guitar, bass, and drums, while Getz on saxophone plays countermelodies.

a fundamental shift in feel. In swing, the rhythmic undercurrent of soloing can be described as "swing" eighth notes, played with a dash of emphasis on the offbeats. But with bossa nova, the soloist's feel is of evenly spaced eighth notes, even though the band's rhythm may be highly syncopated. With the "swing" removed and with a stricter rhythm, the soloist's accents may stand out more, emphasizing rhythmic expressiveness.

As this rhythmic style took a permanent place in the jazz repertoire, a second wave of Brazilian influence brought a more overt rhythmic physicality and broader array of percussion color—more samba than bossa nova—into the mainstream jazz repertoire. Chief among the conduits were the Brazilians Airto

Moreira and his wife, singer Flora Purim, and U.S. musicians Chick Corea and Pat Metheny, who more than other jazzmen spread the samba sound through the jazz community and beyond.

Lured by jazz, many Brazilian musicians settled in the United States. Multi-percussionist Airto Moreira, among them, soon found work with no less than Miles Davis. Through his playing on the seminal fusion album *Bitches Brew* (1969) and five other Davis albums, Moreira's colorful arrays of percussion sounds caught the ears of associated musicians.

Two years earlier than *Bitches Brew*, an album titled *Duster* (1967) by Boston-based vibraphonist Gary Burton, offered some of the non-swing, straight-eighth-note rhythms of bossa nova but with

electronics and a bit more force. And in 1969, an album by a young pianist named Chick Corea became a must-listen-to "find" among musicians. That disc, *Now He Sings, Now He Sobs* (1969), explored innovative harmonies in an acoustic-piano trio format but was also notable for the samba and bossa nova rhythms that seemed to propel Corea to extraordinary heights of expression. (Corea also had Cuban sounds in his ear, having earlier played in the combo of conga player Mongo Santamaría.)

Corea (who had played on Miles Davis's *Bitches Brew*) connected with Moreira as well as Flora Purim, and with other musicians they made some of the earliest full integrations of samba and jazz on two 1972 albums by the group Return to Forever. The track *Spain*, with its pro-tracted and exciting samba-flavored solo section, became a touchstone for musicians who wanted to display their "chops" while enjoying the sojourn into impassioned, Spanish-tinged melody.

Moreira and Purim, meanwhile, applied themselves to their own group, Fingers, that displayed a fuller range of Brazilian rhythmic possibilities to U.S. audiences and musicians. Moving from banks of multi-percussion to a seat at the drum kit, Moreira powered sets of tunes that left little doubt about how exciting and eclectic an Afro-Brazilian and jazz mix could be. An album, *Fingers* (1972), captured some of that variety and excitement.

Airto Moreira rode into jazz on the 1970s Brazilian-percussion wave. PHOTO COURTESY INSTITUTE FOR JAZZ STUDIES, RUTGERS UNIVERSITY.

Not surprisingly, Moreira turned up on another seminal meeting of jazz and Afro-Brazilian music, Wayne Shorter's 1974 recording *Native Dancer*, featuring Brazilian singer-songwriter Milton Nascimento. An analysis of the opening track, Nascimento's haunting *Ponta de Areia*, could paint it as a musical portrayal of two cultures first encountering each other hesitatingly, then coming together joyously. At any rate, the album stands to this day as one of the main markers in the road to fully realized Brazilian jazz.

There was only one Airto, but there was increasing demand for what he did. Other multi-percussionists moved into the market, leaving colorful imprints of their own on a wide variety of jazz bands. Dom Um Romão—whose recording *Spirit of the Times* (1973, with U.S. guitarist Joe Beck) broke new ground in the building of tougher, grittier Afro-Brazilian jazz constructions—joined the fusion group Weather Report. Guilherme Franco, Naná Vasconcelos, and a host of others provided jazzmen such as Keith Jarrett, McCoy Tyner, and Pat Metheny their own beds of percolating percussion over which to express new ideas.

Guitarist Pat Metheny deeply absorbed the Afro-Brazilian feel and developed it into a distinctively airy, colorful, and obliquely accented mix that coalesced beautifully on the 1978 recording *The Pat Metheny Group*. Two tracks from that set, *Phase Dance* and *San Lorenzo*, pointed to a hybrid of subtly Brazil-tinted jazz with rock and even country music. Years later, on the 1994 recording *First Circle*, Metheny took the same blend to less surprising but at times equally soaring heights, with Afro-Brazilian percussion featured near front and center.

From that 1970s heyday, the wave of Afro-Brazilian percussion and rhythm swept further through jazz. It sometimes emerged as soft support for easy-listening "smooth jazz" and at others times

provided a robust, audience-pleasing break from otherwise straight-ahead jazz sets, but it always exemplified the successful blend of jazz with genres outside its immediate stylistic vicinity.

TAKE NOTE

- What was the influence of Brazilian music on jazz?

More Sounds from the Caribbean

Afro-Cuban and Afro-Brazilian sounds may dominate the Latin-Caribbean-jazz connection, but they are not the end of the story. The Caribbean islands host an intricate mosaic of cultures and languages, and their rich music reflects their diversity. Trinidad, for example, produced the **calypso** (first called *kaiso*), a carnival genre that spread to other islands as well as to the United States during the 1950s. Calypso, with its playful rhythms, offbeat phrasings, and cheerful melodies, was popularized stateside by a wide range of singers, including the Andrew Sisters, Ella Fitzgerald, and Harry Belafonte. Jazz musicians took to calypso as well. One of the most notable examples of calypso-infused jazz is Sonny Rollins's now-standard *St. Thomas* (1956; *JTSA* Disc 3/Track 12).

Latin artists who contributed to the spread of calypso include Tito Puente (*Calypso Mambo* and *Calypso Blues*, both from the early 1950s) and Mongo Santamaría (*Afro Lypso*, 1964). In 1976, Trinidadian steel-drummer Othello Molineaux introduced the **pans (steel drums)** into jazz, an instrument later taken up in the United States by Andy Narell.

Two foremost exponents of Caribbean jazz have been Jamaican: guitarist Ernest Ranglin (*Grooving*, 2001), and pianist Monty Alexander, whose repertoire often includes calypsos as well as reggae (the albums *Stir It Up: The Music of Bob Marley*, 1998, and *Jazz Calypso*, 2004).

The French-speaking Caribbean islands (Martinique, Guadeloupe, and Haiti) have created their own dance rhythms, among them the **biguine** (known as "beguine" in English), a medium-tempo genre somewhat akin to the calypso. In the late 1920s,

---

calypso (originally called *kaiso*) a music and dance tradition originally from Trinidad that, during the 1950s, spread to other Caribbean islands and the United States.

pan (steel drum) a musical instrument made from a large empty oil drum that has been tuned; originally from Trinidad.

biguine (French) a medium-tempo dance-based music originally from the French Caribbean; rhythmically similar to the calypso; "beguine" in English.

biguine orchestras, called "jazz" in Guadeloupe and Martinique, adopted the instrumentation of New Orleans jazz bands (clarinet, trombone, banjo, drums). Clarinetist Alexandre Stellio, from Martinique, adapted a rag as a *biguine* under the title *Serpent Maigre* ("lean snake," 1929) and popularized the *biguine* in France. In the early 1930s, Cole Porter heard the *biguine* and was inspired to write the song *Begin the Beguine* (1935), a major hit for bandleader Artie Shaw in 1938 and a jazz standard thereafter. More recently, pianists such as Mario Canonge (from Martinique) and Alain-Jean Marie (from Guadeloupe) recorded vibrant and compelling *biguine*-jazz albums such as, respectively, *Retour aux Sources* (1991) and *Biguine Reflections* (2000).

Saxophonist and flutist Jacques Schwarz-Bart and trumpeter Franck Nicolas, both from Guadeloupe, injected into their progressive jazz the stirring rhythms of *gwo ka*—a genre deriving from the drum music played by Guadeloupe maroons during colonial times to communicate with each other, and which, on the island, has since been revived as a symbol of cultural pride and resilience. Their work can be heard on *Soné Ka-La* (2006), and *Jazz Ka Philosophy* (2002), respectively.

TAKE NOTE

- What other Caribbean music styles have had an influence on jazz?

Later Trends in Latin and Caribbean Jazz

Over the years, many talented artists from all over the globe have been drawn to Latin and Caribbean jazz. Lalo Schifrin, an Argentinian pianist, composer, and arranger, became a leading film and television composer—he wrote the theme for the TV series *Mission Impossible* (in $\frac{5}{4}$ time, 1966)—while playing jazz alongside some of the music's top stars. They included Dizzy Gillespie, to whose band Schifrin contributed a percussion-laden composition, the *Gillespiana Suite* (1960). Tenor saxophonist Gato Barbieri, an alumnus of Schifrin's band and a fellow Argentinean, purveyed a distinctively aggressive jazz sax sound while capturing the nostalgia of the Argentine *pampa* on such recordings as *El Pampero* (1971) and *Caliente* (1977).

Puerto Rican saxophonist David Sánchez delved into the robust *bomba*, an African-derived genre from the northern coast of Puerto Rico, on his album *Sketches of Dreams* (1995). His fellow countryman trombonist William Cepeda explored the hybrid *plena* on *Afrorican Jazz* (1998). Panamanian pianist

Gato Barbieri playing at Chicago's Viva Latin Jazz festival in 2005. PHOTO COURTESY MICHAEL JACKSON.

Latin and Caribbean jazz seems to be evolving towards an increased eclecticism and syncretism. Like Lalo Schifrin, the American pianist Clare Fischer composed and arranged Cuban- and Brazilian-inflected material (*Morning*, *Pensativa*, *Poinciana*) as well as straight-ahead jazz. Clarinetist Paquito D'Rivera, pianist Danilo Pérez, and saxophonist David Sánchez, to name only a few, proved equally at ease with modern jazz and with *rumbas*, sambas, *guaguancós*, and other Latin rhythms. In the United States and the Caribbean, groups such as the Caribbean Jazz Ensemble and the West Indies Jazz Band offered compelling syntheses of various West Indian genres. British saxophonist Courtney Pine, of Jamaican descent, incorporated jazz, Indian, African, and Caribbean strains (*To the Eyes of Creation*, 1992). Some artists have injected individual tunes with more than one kind of Latin rhythm. Two examples of this, both moving from Brazilian samba to Cuban *montuno* patterns, are vibraphonist Jay Hoggard's *São Pablo* (on his album *Rain Forest*, 1980) and Clare Fischer's *João* (on Gary Burton's *For Hamp, Red, Bags, and Cal*, 2000).

From its origins in Cuba, Latin jazz remains a *lingua franca* for many musicians all over the globe. As is true of the United States, Latin America and the Caribbean have proven to be an inexhaustible wellspring of musical ideas and a fertile seedbed of talent. Fed by and successfully incorporating myriad musical influences from different corners of the Americas, while exerting its own pervasive influence, the music these countries produce is in a state of constant evolution and seems poised to remain among the most vital artistic languages in years to come.

Danilo Pérez skillfully reworked the music of his native land in such tunes as *Panama Libre* (1992), *Panama Blues* (1998), and *Cosa Linda* (also 1998), bringing to them an adventurous approach to harmony and dynamics.

U.S. jazzmen have also turned toward Latin horizons beyond Cuba, Brazil, and the Caribbean. Bassist-composer Charles Mingus looked toward Mexico with the album *New Tijuana Moods* (recorded in 1957), and Colombia with *Cumbia & Jazz Fusion* (1976–77). Duke Ellington revealed inspiration from points south with his compositions *The Virgin Islands Suite* (1965, with a calypso movement), *The Latin American Suite* (1968), and his 1956 album *A Drum Is a Woman*, a fantasy history of jazz that featured three percussionists.

TAKE NOTE

- What are some more recent trends in Caribbean and Latin Jazz?

Explore Jazz Classics and Key Recordings on **mymusiclab.com**

- How did Afro-Cuban and Brazilian jazz draw on similar musical roots to create different musical styles?

Essential elements of both Afro-Cuban and Brazilian jazz are traceable to the same African sources. In each area, the displaced Africans sustained their cultural and religious identities through practice of their traditional music and dance. But their music also melded with that of the host cultures. In Latin jazz, an African-derived emphasis on rhythm was filtered through mostly European-derived cultures—Spanish in the case of Afro-Cuban, Portuguese in the case of Brazilian—yielding contrasting styles that eventually crossed paths and mingled through the movement of peoples.

- What native Cuban and Brazilian musical rhythms and musical instruments have influenced the development of Latin Jazz?

Dance rhythms from both Cuba and Brazil were the major influences on Latin jazz, along with a wide variety of native percussion instruments that were incorporated into their bands. Important Afro-Cuban styles influencing jazz included *son*, *rumba*, *habanera*, and mambo. In the United States these yielded *rumba*, big band mambo, *cha-cha-chá,* and Cubop. Important Afro-Brazilian styles influencing jazz included *maxixe* (Brazilian tango), samba, and bossa nova.

- How did Latin music influence early jazz?

Several popular Latin dances came to the United States and were adapted by early jazz musicians. The Cuban *danza* and the Argentinian tango contributed to the "Latin tinge" that Jelly Roll Morton and others recognized as a vital part of New Orleans jazz. The Brazilian *maxixe* (also known as the "Brazilian tango") and the Argentinian tango became wildly popular in the United States around 1915, influencing early jazz performers in New York City.

- Who were the key Cuban and Puerto Rican musicians in jazz history?

The Cuban flutist Alberto Socarrás, who moved to Harlem in 1927, was among the first musicians to wed jazz with Latin rhythms. The Afro-Cubans, led by percussionist Machito and trumpeter and saxophonist Mario Bauzá, were the first successful Latin big band playing in New York, beginning in the 1940s. In the late 1940s, Dizzy Gillespie became the first North American bandleader to fuse bebop and Afro-Cuban rhythms when he hired the *conguero* (conga player) Chano Pozo. During the 1960s, the combos formed by Cuban percussionist Mongo Santamaría, and Nuyorican (Puerto Rican New Yorker) percussionists Tito Puente and Ray Barretto and pianist Eddie Palmieri helped further popularize the music. After the Cuban revolution of 1959, the interchange slowed somewhat, but picked up momentum in the 1970s–1980s, thanks to the work of artists like pianist "Chucho" Valdés and saxophonist and clarinetist Paquito D'Rivera.

- What was the influence of Brazilian music on jazz?

Bossa nova and samba were the two key Brazilian dance rhythms that were wed with jazz. The bossa nova craze was launched by the hit recording *The Girl from Ipanema* by saxophonist Stan Getz and Brazilian musicians pianist/composer Antonio Carlos Jobim, guitar player/vocalist João Gilberto, and vocalist Astrud Gilberto. In the 1970s and 1980s, jazz samba-fusion was very popular. Chief among the conduits were the Brazilians Airto Moreira and his wife, singer Flora Purim, and U.S. musicians Chick Corea and Pat Metheny, who more than other jazzmen spread the samba sound through the jazz community and beyond.

- What other Caribbean music styles have had an influence on jazz?

The calypso, a Trinidadian carnival genre, spread to the United States in the 1950s. A notable example of its use in jazz is the Sonny Rollins standard *St. Thomas*. The French-speaking Caribbean islands (Martinique, Guadeloupe, and Haiti) have created their own dance rhythms, among them the *biguine* (known as "beguine" in English), a medium-tempo genre somewhat akin to the calypso.

- What are some more recent trends in Caribbean and Latin Jazz?

Latin and Caribbean jazz seems to be evolving towards an increased eclecticism and syncretism. Some have explored more regional folk rhythms, such as the Puerto Rican *bomba* or the *gwoka* rhythm of the Guadeloupe maroons. Others have freely combined rhythms from different cultures to create something entirely new. Still others, like saxophonist Paquito D'Rivera, pianist Danilo Pérez, and saxophonist David Sánchez, to name only a few, proved equally at ease with modern jazz and purely Latin music.

1. Discuss some of the music you have heard that has elements of Latin traditions. Describe the feeling and the rhythm.

2. North American jazz, Afro-Cuban jazz, and Afro-Brazilian jazz are traceable to African origins. What developmental factors account for their differences?

3. Name some of the U.S. jazz musicians who helped popularize Latin elements at different points in the twentieth century. What do you think attracted them to the Latin elements?

4. Have you had any experience in dancing or watching Latin steps such as the *salsa*, *tango*, or *samba*? How do these steps differ from other steps you know?

5. Why do you think that despite Mexico's much larger population, Cuban and Puerto Rican jazz musicians have had much more overall exposure and influence in the United States?

6. The chapter mentions that such U.S. jazz musicians as Dizzy Gillespie were sent by the State Department to perform in Latin America as goodwill cultural ambassadors. Present arguments for why such tours are, or are not, a worthy use of taxpayer money.

7. After listening to *Manteca* and *The Girl from Ipanema*, compare them in terms of the moods and feelings they convey. Explore the cultural origins of any differences you perceive.

8. Discuss characteristics of Brazilian music that have been absorbed into jazz. Can you think of jazz standards (evergreens) that have a Brazilian flavor?

KEY TERMS & KEY PEOPLE

Ray Barretto 272	Dizzy Gillespie 255	Chano Pozo 274
Mario Bauzá 269	Irakere 258	Tito Puente 260
Luiz Bonfá 277	Antonio Carlos Jobim 255	*rumba* 258
bossa nova 255	Machito (Frank Grillo	samba 256
Charlie Byrd 263	Gutiérrez) 270	Arturo Sandoval 273
clave 258	mambo 260	Mongo Santamaria 272
conga 268	*montuno* 259	Lalo Schifrin 277
Chick Corea 272	Airto Moreira 263	*son* 259
Cubop 270	Chico O'Farrill 274	*surdo* 256
Paquito D'Rivera 258	Eddie Palmieri 273	Juan Tizol 267
Stan Getz 273	pan (steel drum) 281	*timbales* 260
	Hermeto Pascoal 264	*tumbao* 259

CHAPTER 11

Jazz Worldwide

by Kevin Whitehead

With contributions by E. Taylor Atkins ("Jazz in Asia and Oceania"); Mark Lomanno ("Jazz in the Middle East"); Cyril Moshkov ("Jazz in Eastern Europe"); and John Edward Hasse ("Jazz in Africa")

TAKE NOTE

- Who were the prominent musicians who brought jazz to Europe and how has a European jazz scene developed?
- What is the history of jazz in Asia and Oceania, and who are the vital figures creating original jazz music there?
- How did jazz develop in the Middle East, and who are some of the key players?
- Which musicians led the practice of jazz in Eastern Europe, and what were the characteristic styles?
- What styles of jazz are popular in Africa, and who are the dominant performers?
- How has global jazz continued to develop in the first decade of the twenty-first century?

Archduke Ferdinand of Austria is assassinated, launching World War I

1914

1917

James Reese Europe and his jazzy Hellfighters military band perform in Paris

Russian Revolution puts Vladimir Lenin and other Communists in power

1918

• Clarinetist/tenor sax player Sidney Bechet among first jazz musicians to perform in Europe

Treaty of Versailles ends World War I

1919

• Original Dixieland Jazz Band spends the year touring England

1921

Mitchell's Jazz Kings first black jazz band to record in Europe

Mussolini takes power in Italy

1922

La Revue Nègre opens in Paris, with clarinetist Sidney Bechet and singer Josephine Baker

1925

African American Ada Smith ("Bricktop") operates her famous Paris nightclub where many jazz musicians performed

1928–39

Adolph Hitler and Nazi party come to power in Germany

1933

• Duke Ellington performs in Paris

• Solomon "Zulu Boy" Cele's Jazz Maniacs, a 15-piece band, forms in South Africa

1934

Quintet of the Hot Club of France, with guitarist Django Reinhardt and violinist Stéphane Grappelli, debuts

1935

The Nazis block Coleman Hawkins from touring Germany because they view jazz as "degenerate" music

1938

English bandleader Ray Noble composes and records *Cherokee*, which becomes a jazz standard on both sides of the ocean

World War II begins with German invasion of Poland

1939

Gandhi launches civil disobedience movement demanding Britain return India to self-rule

1942

• Germany surrenders; Hitler commits suicide

• United Nations founded

1945

Paris holds the Festivale International du Jazz with an array of important musicians

Mao Zedung takes over as leader of China

1949

Oscar Peterson discovers Japanese pianist/composer Toshiko Akiyoshi while touring Japan, and arranges for her to record for Verve Records

Elizabeth II crowned Queen of England

1952

HISTORICAL EVENT	MUSICAL EVENT

1955 — The Voice of America begins long-running *Music USA* worldwide radio broadcasts of jazz, eventually reaching 100 million listeners

Soviet Union launches first successful satellite, Sputnik — **1957**

In Africa, 17 nations are granted independence, including Nigeria and the former Belgian Congo — **1960** — In England, alto saxophonist Joe Harriott releases Europe's first free-jazz record: *Free Form*

Berlin Wall divides East and West Berlin — **1961**

Nelson Mandela, South African black leader, sentenced to life in prison for opposing apartheid — **1964**

1967 — Dutch drummer Han Bennink and Russian pianist Misha Mengelberg found the Instant Composer's Pool Orchestra to perform their own contemporary jazz works

Arab-Israeli War — **1967**

1968 — Egyptian drummer Salah Ragab forms the Cairo Jazz Band, among Egypt's first big bands

1969 — German jazz fan Manfred Eicher establishes the ECM label to promote contemporary jazz players from around the world

1974

South African pianist Abdullah Ibrahim records *Manenberg*, which becomes a symbol of resistance against apartheid

Iran takes U.S. hostages — **1979**

Mikhail Gorbachev calls for "Glasnost" in Soviet Union — **1985**

Soviet Union collapses — **1991**

1994

950F 2009
NELSON MANDELA
RWANDA
COURTESY STAMPGIRL/SHUTTERSTOCK.

After fall of apartheid, Nelson Mandela elected president of South Africa — **1994**

1995 — French-Vietnamese guitarist Nguyên Lê, living in Paris, releases *Tales from Viêt-Nam*

Euro introduced as common currency of European nations — **1999**

2005 — Syrian Jazz Orchestra founded in Damascus, Syria

North Korea conducts first nuclear test — **2006**

✳ **Explore** the Jazz Timeline on **mymusiclab.com**

2008 — Guitarist and vocalist Lionel Loueke, from Benin, combines African pop and jazz on his album *Karibu*

I t's a rainy Sunday in December. The bassist Lelio Giannetto is at Palermo's airport on the Sicilian coast, where incoming flights are running late. He keeps looking at his watch.

Giannetto is an organizer of a three-day meeting—called "Dreamin' California"—of free improvisers from Sicily and the San Francisco Bay Area, that starts in a downtown theater tomorrow evening. Yesterday, he'd recorded with early arrival Tim Perkis, whose basic equipment is a laptop computer from which he coaxes abstract blurps and squeaks. Expected within the hour is Tom Nunn, who plays homemade instruments and has written a 300-page treatise on free improvisation, in which jazz is barely mentioned.

Think we're off the jazz map yet? Then ask Giannetto why he keeps checking the time. His answer is that he has a different kind of gig this afternoon, an hour or so away in the town of Salaparuta, with the Sicilian Jazz Dixielanders. In the nineteenth century, he explains, there was regular ship traffic between Salaparuta and New Orleans, a boat going out loaded with oranges and maybe a few hopeful immigrants and coming back full of cotton.

One couple who took the boat to New Orleans had a son who grew up to be Original Dixieland Jazz Band cornetist Nick LaRocca. All those Italians in old New Orleans were one reason opera was in the air, helping inspire Louis Armstrong's dramatic high-note endings.

The moral of the story is that you don't have to be American to see yourself in jazz. By the beginning of the twenty-first century, jazz was nearly everywhere, coming back around the bend just when you thought you'd left it. Colleges all over Europe were teaching it, wealthier European countries were subsidizing it. Even Beijing had launched an annual jazz festival, where musicians converged from the United States, Australia, Japan, Europe, and China itself—including the People's Liberation Army Big Band. But then, Shanghai had begun hosting itinerant jazz musicians as far back as 1926.

Tenor saxophonist Jan Garbarek brought distinctively Nordic elements to his jazz improvising. PHOTO COURTESY DAVID REDFERN/REDFERNS/GETTY IMAGES.

Jazz in Europe

The Early Years

Jazz went international early—no later than the fall of 1914, when the Original Creole Orchestra from New Orleans, including cornetist Freddie Keppard, toured western Canada for five weeks. They passed through again in 1916. The year after that, two homegrown Canadian jazz bands turned up, one in Vancouver and one in Hamilton, Ontario. Others quickly followed, in cities from Winnipeg to Montreal. (And Americans kept coming: pianist Jelly Roll Morton made Vancouver his base from mid-1919 through 1920.) In many ways, what happened in Canada set the pattern for jazz's reception in the rest of the world: the music was popular immediately, even if newspaper critics were hostile; musicians quickly attempted to do it themselves; a few African American musicians elected to stay around, because racial attitudes were less oppressive than in the United States; and many Canadian musicians got a good education listening to and playing with U.S. talent. As a practical matter, this meant working bands were racially integrated in Canada in the 1920s, much earlier than in the United States.

Jazz began crossing the oceans even before it turned up on records back home; for example, *Down Home Rag* was recorded in London in 1916 by the Versatile Four, an American vaudeville band then based in England. Their drummer, Charlie Johnson, was already swinging in a style based on military drumming.

In 1918, Australia's first jazz band was a smash hit in Sydney. In 1919, the Original Dixieland Jazz Band visited England and stayed a year. Around 1920, the Blue Band, from Holland, recorded in Berlin and London. Dutch colonials were playing jazz in Java by 1922; by 1926 they'd been joined by native Indonesians and itinerants from the Philippines.

The first great U.S. jazzman in Europe was clarinetist Sidney Bechet, who appeared in London in 1919 with Will Marion Cook's ragtimey Southern

The Original Dixieland Jazz Band, billed as "the creators of jazz" and the "sensation of America," played the Palladium and other London halls in 1919. They are shown here at London's Palais de Danse. PHOTO COURTESY FRANK DRIGGS COLLECTION.

Syncopated Orchestra. Swiss conductor Ernest Ansermet heard them often and wrote a now-famous review singling out Bechet as a harbinger of music that would sweep the world. Ansermet was astute enough to praise the quality of Bechet's blues at a time when Europeans may have had little knowledge of that style. When Cook's band broke up, its musicians scattered as far afield as Norway.

Back then, when the "jazz" label got pasted on nearly any music that moved, there was some confusion abroad about just what jazz was. Was its essence syncopation or improvisation? Was it futuristic noise music, or a novelty act with drummers doing tricks with sticks? Was it folk music or a more refined expression?

For that reason, American musicians on foreign soil were enormously important locally, even if little remembered back home. Take drummer Louis Mitchell, who in 1918 or 1919 took a jazz band to Paris and stayed over a decade. To quote John Szwed, jazz was "the shock to the system the French had been waiting for": modern, energetic, exotic. By 1922, composer Darius Milhaud was taking notes in Harlem nightspots, an influence you can hear on his *La Creation du Monde* (1923).

In Europe, black American musicians were suddenly in demand, and more than a few at home—encouraged by stories of racial tolerance told by black GIs returning from World War I—took the boat abroad. One pianist lured to Paris by an offer of $50 weekly was soon in London making $750 a week.

When U.S. musicians left a local band, or a group showed up a few players short, locals began filling in. One such precocious French player was trombonist Leo Vauchant, born in 1904. Hearing Mitchell's band, he quickly grasped that improvisation was the point and soon figured out how to do it himself. In 1924 Vauchant began exchanging music lessons with symphonic composer Maurice Ravel, who wanted to know about jazz. Relying on his practical experience, Vauchant formulated loose guidelines for what worked or didn't, what was hip and what wasn't—an early glimmering of "jazz education" (but not the only one: jazz instruction books were sold in England by 1926, and by 1927 the Frankfurt conservatory was offering a jazz performance class). Surreal postscript: In 1931 Vauchant traveled to the States as a dance-band arranger. On one band's bus tour in Louisiana, he and a guitarist went out in a field during a rest stop to play impromptu blues for African American cotton pickers. By age 30 he'd glimpsed both jazz's intellectual future and its formative past.

By the mid-1920s, jazz records were being distributed overseas, and before long England and France (like the United States) had jazz critics. Pianist Claude Hopkins, in Paris to accompany singer Josephine Baker in 1925, found that local musicians had been studying the latest Armstrong sides: "Some of the European bands were so like Louis's band, you could hardly tell the difference. . . . The tone and the range weren't as good but the overall picture was pretty similar."

Still, for many outside the United States, these records posed more questions than they answered. Labels on 78s typically gave no or misleading information about who the players were, and when and where they recorded the disc—information necessary to fit fragmentary pieces of the jazz puzzle together. Thus were born the jazz discographers, tracking down dates and personnel, often by peppering visiting Americans with vexing questions about sessions long past. Over the years, many of jazz's most diligent discographers have come from outside the United States: France's Charles Delaunay whose 1936 *Hot Discography* was a stylistic model for many later examples; England's Brian Rust; Denmark's Jørgen Grunnet Jepsen; Belgium's Walter Bruyninckx; and Canada's Tom Lord.

The line dividing discographers and critics from active jazz promoters and producers was thin enough for several Europeans to cross, just as John Hammond did in the United States. Delaunay and French writer Hugues Panassié both produced numerous recording sessions; together, they directed the A&R program of the French label Swing. Critic Andre Hodeir played, arranged, and produced jazz, in addition to writing several noteworthy books on the subject.

4ᵉ ANNÉE
NUMÉRO 22

PRIX : 4 FR.
(FOREIGN 5 FR.)

HOT

FRANK NEWTON
INTERNATIONAL REVIEW OF JAZZ MUSIC
REVUE INTERNATIONALE DE LA MUSIQUE DE JAZZ
DÉCEMBRE NOËL JANVIER

COURTESY FRANK DRIGGS COLLECTION.

Le Jazz Hot: Jazz in Paris between the World Wars

Jazz was born and raised in America, but in Paris between the wars it found its home away from home. Long a cosmopolitan city that encouraged personal and artistic freedom, the City of Light attracted hundreds of U.S. writers, painters, and classical and jazz musicians.

World War I jump-started Parisians' infatuation with syncopated music. In August of 1918, they discovered American Lt. James Reese Europe and his jazzy Hellfighters military band. Americans, thanks to their strong participation in the war, were loved by the French.

African Americans found a far more welcoming environment in Paris than in their native United States and drank in the greater freedom. When Mitchell's Jazz Kings recorded in Paris in December 1921, they made the first non-ragtime jazz disc by blacks in Europe. The St. Louis-born singer and dancer Josephine Baker achieved overwhelming success in *La Revue Nègre* (1925) and overnight became the darling of the French, while the African American singer Bricktop (Ada Smith) ran a highly successful nightclub in Paris (1928–39) where many top musicians performed. In 1920, Parisians had an opportunity to hear their first jazz artist of wide renown, Sidney Bechet, playing with Benny Peyton's Jazz Kings. In 1925, Bechet returned with *La Revue Nègre* and in 1928 played the nightclub Chez Florence, but then was expelled from the country for getting into a gunfight.

Bandleaders Paul Whiteman (1925) and Noble Sissle (1928) also played and made their marks in Paris, and at the end of the decade, many young, talented white Chicago musicians went to the city, among them Bud Freeman and drummer Dave Tough. France was also producing homegrown jazz musicians—the most important of the 1920s were trombonist Leon (Leo) Vauchant, trumpeter Philippe Brun, and pianist Stéphane Mougin, while the most outstanding orchestras were those of Ray Ventura and Grégor.

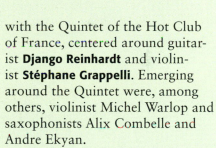

COURTESY FRANK DRIGGS COLLECTION.

In the 1920s, jazz was terrifically in vogue, but in the early 1930s, the mass audience seemed to turn its back. Still, *Jazz Tango* magazine emerged in June 1930. And in 1932, a handful of amateurs established the Hot Club of France to offer concerts under the direction of critic Hugues Panassié and jazz activist and discographer Charles Delaunay. American records were widely distributed, and radio followed timidly.

In the first half of the 1930s, most young Parisian jazzmen were still works-in-progress. But their music took a flying leap thanks to their microscopic analyses of the best jazz recordings; live concerts (Duke Ellington in 1933 and 1939, Louis Armstrong in 1934); and jam sessions with leading American jazzmen. Europe's *crème de la crème* burst forth in 1934 with the Quintet of the Hot Club of France, centered around guitarist **Django Reinhardt** and violinist **Stéphane Grappelli**. Emerging around the Quintet were, among others, violinist Michel Warlop and saxophonists Alix Combelle and Andre Ekyan.

Thanks to Delaunay, the second half of the decade saw the debut in 1935 of the bilingual (French and English) magazine *Jazz Hot* (continuous, except for a wartime hiatus, until century's end) and in 1937 of the label Swing, which captured marvelous encounters between French jazz artists and visiting U.S. jazzmen.

In 1939, as the German army advanced into France, American musicians fled Paris; jazz would take a lower profile until after World War II.

—*Philippe Baudoin*

If European musicians at first emulated the Americans stylistically, by 1934 the seeds were planted for an alternative approach. That's when guitarist Django Reinhardt and violinist Stéphane Grappelli put together their Quintet of the Hot Club of France. Grappelli's violin, notably on *After You've Gone* and *Limehouse Blues* (both 1936), was as sweet, urbane, and sophisticated as Parisian café music. Reinhardt, a Belgian gypsy who couldn't read music and who had limited use of his fire-damaged fretting hand, proved a phenomenal jazz-guitar innovator. He had a stinging attack and improvised complex single-note lines broken up by a short series of charging chords that goosed the music forward—all rendered with distinctive flair (*Swing Guitars*, 1936, and *Minor Swing*, 1937). Traveling Americans who heard and played with him related to it, even as they recognized that his harmonic and melodic vocabulary reflected his own roots at least as much as it echoed the blues.

Reinhardt was the model of the successful non-American jazz improviser. The Quintet inspired similar groups around the continent, and he belatedly spawned a raft of French or French-speaking pickers, including Raymond Boni, Philip Catherine, Boulou Ferre, Bireli Lagrene, and Belgium's electric-guitar wizard René Thomas. To date, no foreign-born jazz musician who didn't move to the United States has commanded nearly as much stateside attention or respect as Reinhardt.

((•●—[Hear a profile of Django Reinhardt on **mymusiclab.com**

Django Reinhardt, now considered a seminal jazz guitarist, first rose to fame as a member of the Quintet of the Hot Club of France. PHOTO COURTESY FRANK DRIGGS COLLECTION.

Listening Guide

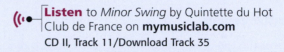

MINOR SWING • QUINTETTE DU HOT CLUB DE FRANCE

Music: Stéphane Grappelli and Django Reinhardt, 1937. Personnel: Stéphane Grappelli (violin); Django Reinhardt, Joseph Reinhardt, Eugene Vees (guitar); Louis Vola (bass). Recorded November 25, 1937, in Paris. First issue: Swing 23. Timing: 3:17.

Overview

This café-style music is a prime example of the premier European jazz group of the 1930s, a Parisian string quintet featuring suave violinist Stéphane Grappelli and guitarist Django Reinhardt, the most admired non-American jazz musician of his time. Reinhardt was an influence on early electric guitarists such as Charlie Christian. Here he and Grappelli romp over a simple minor-chord progression, infusing their jazz with a European sensibility.

Key Features

- Reinhardt's punchy flat-picking and heavy vibrato immediately distinguish his sound. His right hand had been damaged in a fire, and he did most of his fretting with index and middle fingers only.
- A chunky two-beat rhythm feel predominates. Two strummed rhythm guitars lay down a strong "one *and* two *and*" syncopated feel typical of early jazz, over which the soloists freely place their accents.
- Form: A 16-bar melody, with the two similar halves separated by a two-bar break. Reinhardt and Grappelli solo in turn over another 16-bar template built on the same simple three- and four-note chords (A and D minor, E7). The closing 16-bar melody recalls but differs from the opening theme.

—*Kevin Whitehead*

TIME	STRUCTURE	MELODY
0:00	THEME	Guitar and violin state the theme, which does little more than outline the underlying chords of A minor and D minor. At 0:08, one (upward sliding) bass note fills a two-bar break, when the rest of the band falls silent. The (slap) bass returns with a descending run on the second break at 0:17.
0:20	GUITAR SOLO—CHORUS 1	Reinhardt jumps in on the end of the bass break with a diminished chord, then switches to mostly single-note lines, played with a flat pick. Note the symmetry of his first three phrases (all of which end on the keynote of A).
0:39	GUITAR SOLO—CHORUS 2	Reinhardt begins the chorus emphasizing a high E note, and concludes it with a skittering downward run (0:53) that lands on the keynote.
0:58	GUITAR SOLO—CHORUS 3	Notice Reinhardt's use of bluesy bent notes, as at 1:01 and 1:10. The chorus ends with a variation on the shapely phrase that introduced it.
1:17	GUITAR SOLO—CHORUS 4	Reinhardt begins with one of his signature moves—a flurry of wildly flailed chords, and ends the chorus with chord forms that emphasize the octave. (To manage these, he employed his damaged fingers, over which he had some limited control.) This dramatic climax paves the way for Grappelli's entrance.
1:36	VIOLIN SOLO—CHORUS 1	Grappelli—bowing the strings—like Reinhardt, elegantly wends his way through the underlying chords. But his phrasing and feeling are a little more relaxed than the guitarist's, a contrast that made them excellent partners. Note his slightly scratchy tone, which gives his lines more bite.
1:55	VIOLIN SOLO—CHORUS 2	The rhythm guitars (three, now that Reinhardt's joined them) really shine with their loudly accented strummed chords, as at 2:05. Just as Grappelli is about to enter his last chorus, someone—Reinhardt maybe—offers murmurs of encouragement, in English—jazz's universal language, "Yeah, man. Come on."
2:14	VIOLIN SOLO—CHORUS 3	Grappelli's slurred, high-pitched phrases starting at 2:24 effectively build tension, and lead him into his last chorus.
2:33	VIOLIN SOLO—CHORUS 4	Note the punctuating upward "rip" at 2:34. Syncopated, matching phrases from 2:43 on bring the solo to a climax.
2:51	CLOSING MELODY	The melody here outlines the chords as in the opening, with minor variations. But this time, the whole band is playing, which gives it greater urgency, and the E7 chord is outlined as well. The bass break at 2:58 echoes the one at 0:17. To finish, Grappelli plays a fast chromatic run, E down to E-flat and then up to A. The band responds with murmurs of approval at their having nailed the tune—contrived, but well deserved nonetheless.

Controversies

Naturally the music encountered resistance. Italians circulated an anti-jazz petition in 1923. One French composer explained that collective improvising was mathematically impossible. Swedish critics denounced Louis Armstrong when he visited in 1933.

In post-revolutionary Russia, folks had fiercely debated jazz's merits—even before they'd heard any jazz. Abroad as at home, there was always someone ready to argue what the music should or shouldn't be.

In 1926, two contradictory visions of jazz came to Russia. Bandleader **Sam Wooding**, criss-crossing Eurasia with the theatrical revue *Chocolate Kiddies*, championed Paul Whiteman's symphonic jazz. Drummer Benny Peyton's Jazz Kings, with Bechet on board, backed the hot alternative. Predictably, the music establishment backed the dead-end former approach, while grass-roots musicians supported the latter.

Jazz, like any art form, must be free to develop as it will; it does not take orders from the top. But in the Soviet Union, where the official line on any matter could reverse itself in an instant, jazz was a small boat on a high sea. For example, in 1934, a pro-jazz movie swept Russia. In 1936, the newspaper *Pravda* denounced jazz, then reversed itself, but sister paper *Izvestiia* continued the attacks. In 1937, some jazz musicians were hauled off to labor camps, or simply disappeared. In 1938, a sanitized, 43-piece State Jazz Orchestra was organized, its musicians paid twice the compensation of their classical counterparts—a grand if grim exception to the rule that jazzers always make less money. Hip audiences booed anyway. In 1939, subsidized regional swing orchestras cropped up. During World War II, army and navy jazz bands entertained the Russian troops.

In Germany, the situation was similarly tragic and absurd. The Nazis portrayed jazz as Jewish-Negro degeneracy—and declared syncopated music incompatible with marching—but because of existing trade agreements were obliged to allow in Armstrong records.

The Germans unwittingly helped the cause of European jazz in 1935. Coleman Hawkins, on tour in Western Europe as a featured guest with English leader Jack Hylton's band, was forbidden to enter Germany because he was African American. (Hylton continued on without him.) Stranded in Holland, Hawkins

The reception accorded Sam Wooding (seated, center) and his band in travels through Eurasia and South America in the 1920s wasn't matched in the United States, where the returning Wooding found that other pre–swing era bands had staked claim on domestic listeners. PHOTO COURTESY FRANK DRIGGS COLLECTION.

Trumpeter Buck Clayton (center) took his 14 Gentlemen of Harlem to the Canidrome club in Shanghai, China, in 1934. The band split up there; Clayton stayed on until he'd earned enough money to return to the States, where he joined Count Basie's band. PHOTO COURTESY FRANK DRIGGS COLLECTION.

worked and recorded with the capable swing band the Ramblers and with expatriate pianist Freddy Johnson, in Europe since 1928.

Johnson was one of a few American musicians locked up by the Germans in the early 1940s. After World War II, Valaida Snow—the most widely traveled jazz woman of the prewar years—would claim to have been held in a concentration camp; in fact she'd been detained by Danish authorities, possibly for her own protection. Before that, she'd traveled from Sweden to Shanghai and hit a lot of stops between. When her fellow trumpeter Buck Clayton spent two years in Shanghai in the mid-1930s—at the instigation of pianist Teddy Weatherford, who'd been bouncing around Asia for years, and would spend his final years playing in India—he found that Snow had taught some Shanghai chefs how to cook soul food.

Hawkins was naturally much in demand, and he stayed in Europe until 1939, playing with locals in Holland, France, Switzerland, England, and Scandinavia. That the father of the tenor saxophone

found European musicians acceptable colleagues gave them a strong psychological boost. He was impressed by Reinhardt; by his own French admirer, tenor saxophonist Alix Combelle; and by at least one chart the Ramblers brought him. Having him around also helped the Europeans see how a musician's life and art intertwine— how the choices made on the bandstand relate to the kind of day a musician's having, for example.

The War Years and After

In Germany even before World War II, and in occupied countries during it, musicians were encouraged to play good European music rather than "degenerate" jazz— never mind how bad the proposed alternatives sounded. The occupation government in Holland and at least one German district issued regulations for improvisers—riffing was limited or forbidden, plunger mutes and scat singing were off-limits, and other restrictions applied.

American tunes were outlawed, too, but musicians found ways around that. If the French lament

La Tristesse de St. Louis (*The Sadness of St. Louis*) sounded oddly like the Czech patriots' anthem *The Song of Resetovd Lhota* or the German *Das Lied vom Heiligen Ludwig* (*The Song of Saint Louis*) it's because all of them were *St. Louis Blues*.

Jazz continued to be played in Berlin itself. Germans put jazz into propaganda broadcasts aimed at the British, and vice versa. There was even a jazz band, known as the Ghetto Swingers, at the Czech Terezin concentration camp, and it's said there was one at Buchenwald. For some in Germany and occupied countries (as in the Soviet Union), jazz became a symbol of freedom and resistance; then and there as now and elsewhere, however, to be a jazz fan was no sure sign of liberal politics. There were jazz fans in SS uniforms too. In the long run, the war had much to do with the dissemination of jazz around the world. The United States' Armed Forces Radio played a conspicuous role in spreading jazz in Europe and Asia, both during and after the war. U.S. soldiers also played an important part. During wartime, they shared their **fake books**—informal sheet music—with Russian allies, who picked up on harmonic refinements they'd been missing. (But as the Cold War dawned, the Soviets flip-flopped again, confiscating saxophones in 1949.)

Postwar U.S. service folk in Germany and Japan gave the defeated powers a taste for the music. (U.S.-based radio broadcasts helped too.) In 1948, Takatoshi Kyogoku reported from Japan to *Down Beat* magazine that jazz had "swept over this country like wildfire since the end of the war." In Europe, homegrown musicians got work entertaining off-duty U.S. troops. One, German trombonist Albert Mangelsdorff, later developed a method of coaxing harmonies from his horn by playing one note and humming another, a technique now widely used by other trombonists; he may have been the most influential European jazz musician to follow Reinhardt.

There was a major jazz festival in Paris in 1949, with bebop players Charlie Parker, Miles Davis, Tadd Dameron, and Kenny Clarke among featured performers. After Sidney Bechet played at the festival, music stores reported a run on soprano saxophones. Bechet moved to France in 1951; he'd record there often through the 1950s (*Olympia Concert*, 1955, and *La Legende de Sidney Bechet*, 1949–58), and would become a national hero. The French—like the Italians, mindful of old New Orleans's cultural makeup—considered jazz part of their own cultural legacy.

In France, Bechet usually performed in traditional settings, but also with the Algerian-born piano modernist Martial Solal, whose manic inventions, hopping all over the keyboard, suggested Earl Hines's influence. In his long and productive career Solal recorded with such thoughtful Americans as altoist Lee Konitz (*Satori*, 1974, and *Four Keys*, 1979) and Dave Douglas (*Rue de Seine*, 2005) as well as a host of Europeans. His recording of *Neutralisme* (1999) with saxophonist Johnny Griffin (*JTSA* Disc 6/Track 15) is one example of his excellent accompanying work.

Along with tenor saxophonist Don Byas, Bechet was in the first wave of postwar expatriates who gravitated to Paris, Rome, Copenhagen, Amsterdam, and other cities where they could find work, respect, and the good life. By 1965 there were so many American jazz musicians in Paris, the French musicians' union complained the Yanks were getting all the good gigs.

Not that Americans there neglected their French colleagues. Drummer Kenny Clarke often played with bassist Pierre Michelot, sometimes backing temporary Parisian Bud Powell, as on the pianist's albums *Cookin' at Saint Germain* (1957–59) and *The Complete Essen Jazz Festival Concert* (1960). (Powell's experiences in Paris were part of the inspiration for *'Round Midnight*, 1986, one of several feature films focusing on jazz abroad.) For 12 years, Clarke also co-led a successful pan-European big band with Belgian pianist Francy Boland, heard on the albums *Two Originals* (1967–68) and *Three Latin Adventures* (1968).

When Miles Davis visited in 1957 to tour with Clarke, Michelot, pianist Rene Urtreger, and tenor saxophonist Barney Wilen, director Louis Malle asked Davis to score his film noir *Ascenseur pour L'Échafaud* (*Lift to the Scaffold*). Jazz soundtracks were then a French fad: John Lewis, Art Blakey, and Duke Ellington also did one each, respectively, *Sait-on Jamais* (*No Sun in Venice*) (1957), *Des Femmes Disparaissent* (*The Disappearing Women*) (1958), and *Paris Blues* (1961).

Blakey, by the way, was later quoted as saying about jazz, "It's American music, and no one else can play it." But that didn't stop him from hiring, over the years, such musicians as Russian trumpeter Valery Ponomarev, Australian saxophonist Dale Barlow, Nigerian bassist Essiet Essiet, or Japanese bassists Isao Suzuki and Yoshio Suzuki—or from recording in the 1950s with drummers from Senegal, Nigeria, and Jamaica.

Regional Conceptions of Jazz

The indigenous sounds of cultures worldwide have played an important role as source material for new, regional conceptions of jazz as well as thematic material for jazz played by Americans.

---

fake book a collection of printed music in a kind of musical shorthand, specifying only melody line, chord symbols, and lyrics—musicians have to fake the rest; used by many jazz musicians.

The German jazz band Weintraub's Syncopators (shown here in 1931) appeared in the 1930 film The Blue Angel, *which rising Nazi official Josef Goebbels denounced as "offal."* PHOTO COURTESY ULLSTEIN BILD/THE GRANGER COLLECTION, NYC.

Jazz under the Nazis

Why did the Nazi government (and other totalitarian regimes) object to jazz music?

To many Germans of the 1930s who subscribed to the notion of a superior Aryan race, jazz—because of its black origins and its loose, danceable rhythm—was widely considered to be counter to German moral and cultural standards. Thus, immediately after the Nazi takeover in March 1933, Germany's new rulers banned jazz from all radio programs on the grounds that it was a form of musical decadence. Josef Goebbels, the Third Reich's minister for public enlightening and propaganda, referred to jazz as "talentless and unimaginative juggling with notes"(a position that didn't prevent him from employing a jazz band, Charlie and His Orchestra, in propaganda broadcasts to North America and Great Britain).

In many ways jazz was the antithesis of Nazi regimentation and a symbolic threat to the regime's control. The authorities disliked it not only because they associated it with despised racial minorities, including Jews, but also because it emphasized freedom, spontaneity, and individualism.

Under Nazi rule, Jewish dance and jazz musicians were unable to pursue their professions and were forced to leave the country. (One emigre, Francis Wolff, launched a record company in the United States that would one day become almost synonymous with jazz: Blue Note.)

The German government discouraged the public from playing, listening, or dancing to jazz, but the ban was difficult to enforce. American jazz recordings were readily available until the United States entered the war in 1941. Afterward, until 1944, the German companies Odeon, Brunswick, and Imperial pressed hot jazz records for sale in neutral and occupied countries, but the discs found their way back into Germany and were unofficially available "under the counter."

Not surprisingly, jazz became a symbol of resistance. In order to fool informers and the secret police, jazz fans and musicians organized clandestine sessions, cut off telltale composers' names and song titles from sheet music, and misled the censors by disguising jazz standards under new names.

Despite the repressive climate, jazz enjoyed unprecedented popularity during the Nazi years, not only in such occupied countries as Norway, France, the Netherlands, and Czechoslovakia but also in Germany. And jazz musicians somehow continued to play and evolve. Some of Germany's finest jazzmen—including Kurt Hohenberger, Heinz Wehner, Freddie Brocksieper, Max Rumpf, Ernst Hollerhagen, Helmut Zacharias, and Benny de Weille—emerged, played, and recorded under Nazi rule. And their ranks were supplemented by such visiting foreign players as Kai Ewans, Fud Candrix, Teddy Stauffer, Thore Ehrling, Jean Omer, Eddie Tower, Cesare Galli, and Tullio Mobiglia.

By the time the war ended with the Nazis' defeat, jazz was in Germany to stay.

—*Rainer E. Lotz*

Sidney Bechet (right), one of the earliest U.S. jazz players in Europe (1919), spent his last years in France. PHOTO COURTESY DOWN BEAT ARCHIVES.

Sidney Bechet's tours in the 1920s had also taken him to Sweden, Spain, France, Italy, Hungary, Czechoslovakia, Greece, and Egypt; his biographer John Chilton said that later in life Bechet surprised listeners by playing various folk themes he'd heard in such places long ago; he was in the vanguard yet again, as interest in world music was beginning to build. In post–World War II Japan, there was a fad for jazzing up traditional themes. In 1951, Stan Getz, in Sweden with a local rhythm section, recorded a Swedish folk tune that became a jazz standard as *Dear Old Stockholm.* Within a few years, Sweden's cele- brated baritone saxophonist **Lars Gullin** began record- ing original pieces with a folk flavor.

By now, foreign musicians had a good understand- ing of jazz as a reflection of the United States' cultural mix and of players' own experiences. It was inevitable that some would ask, "If U.S. jazz builds on indige- nous materials like the blues, shouldn't our jazz reflect our culture and upbringing?"

With that question, jazz abroad began to grow up and out, beyond imitating American models. Not that outlanders didn't still look to the United States for new directions. Australians after World War II, for example, shadowed successive American trends—New Orleans revival, bop, cool, modal, free, and jazz and poetry—and produced the brilliant neo-bebopper,

lightning-quick alto saxophonist Bernie McGann. But they, too, were mindful of what they brought to the table: in 1964 there was even an Australian TV series called *Jazz Meets Folk.*

A regional conception of jazz was developing in England too, where the growth of jazz had been complicated by a decades-long protectionist blockade of U.S. talent—which didn't stop Americans from making English bandleader Ray Noble's *Cherokee* (1938) and its chord changes into jazz evergreens. The long-running feud between stateside and English musicians' unions had made it impossible for jazz musicians from either country to play the other, from 1935 to 1956—a crucial period in the States, encom- passing the full flowering of the swing era and the birth and assimilation of bebop. The English scene lagged behind American developments, yet the ban also inspired a certain cocky, do-it-yourself attitude, heard in such period notables as trumpeter Nat Gonella. While the French continued to play with vis- iting Americans, the English made their own music.

That sense of independence bore fruit mostly in the years after the ban was lifted. In England, the folk-jazz connection was abetted by several factors: jazz musicians working in blues and folk-revival groups, several of which played Charles Mingus tunes; an influx of West Indians, including saxophonist

Joe Harriott and trumpeters Shake Keane and Harry Beckett, who brought island rhythms along; and the presence of black and white South Africans in exile, notably drummer Louis Moholo, pianist Chris McGregor, bassists Harry Miller and Johnny Dyani, trumpeter Mongezi Feza, and altoist Dudu Pukwana. The latter's "**township jazz**"—a blend of jazz sonorities, catchy tunes, and simple chord schemes (heard on *In the Townships*, 1973)—had a significant effect on the English jazz scene.

Curiously, polycultural South Africa remains the most jazz-oriented African country—a sign, perhaps, of the pronounced impact of European culture there. But that didn't stop such U.S. musicians as pianist Randy Weston, trumpeter Lester Bowie, multireedist Yusef Lateef, saxophonist Ornette Coleman, and drummers Max Roach and Ronald Shannon Jackson from going to various other African countries to play with local musicians or to investigate their music. And a number of U.S. musicians, including Weston, Lateef, Roach, and clarinetist John Carter, have deployed percussionists from North or West Africa on record as well.

The trend toward homegrown jazz styles really took off in the mid-1960s. Its Pied Piper and Johnny Appleseed was cornetist Don Cherry, one of several American modernists—among them, saxophonist Steve Lacy and pianist Mal Waldron—wandering Europe then, looking for work and partners. Cherry discovered Gato Barbieri, in Paris; sought out and studied with exiled South African pianist Dollar Brand, later called **Abdullah Ibrahim**, whose rolling polyrhythms—as on *African Piano* (1969) and *African River* (1989)—can suggest an African percussion choir; went to Milan to play with the remarkable pianist **Giorgio Gaslini** after reading about him in London; and spent many years off and on living and recording in Sweden, particularly inspiring musicians there. (Listen to Ibrahim's *Manenberg [Revisited],* CD II, Track 12/Download Track 36.)

Where most previous Americans in Europe sought out, not always successfully, musicians who could play on American terms, Cherry encouraged Europeans to be themselves: he was an avatar of world music, writing compositions flavored by various south-of-the-equator cultures. From 1978 to 1984, he was in a fine co-op trio, Codona, with Brazil's Vasconcelos

and American sitarist and tabla player Colin Walcott, of the groundbreaking world-jazz group **Oregon**, a spinoff of Paul Winter's band.

After 1970, the Scandinavians got another boost from the German record label ECM, which favored quiet, almost meditative music adorned with atmospheric studio echo. ECM's northern discoveries included pianist Bobo Stenson—whose out-of-tempo intros leading up to playing over a steady pulse reflected his interest in the music of India—and tenor saxophonist **Jan Garbarek**, who had played with Cherry and with U.S. composer George Russell. Garbarek worked with Norwegian folk materials in all manner of settings—one album featured a Nordic wind harp—and his pinched, restrained sound has been much imitated. In the 1970s he was in pianist Keith Jarrett's "European quartet"with Swedish bassist Palle Danielsson and the graceful Norwegian drummer Jon Christensen.

"What I'm playing today—whatever it is— I'm playing because I once learned the language of jazz,"Garbarek said, "but we also have our own blues equivalents, our own folk music."This Nordic consciousness was taken even further by Kristian Blak, a pianist

Drummer Kenny Clarke, 1946. PHOTO COURTESY FRANK DRIGGS COLLECTION.

---

township jazz jazz that originated in the black townships of South Africa, characterized by ostinatos.

from Denmark's remote Faroe Islands, who in 1984 recorded a jazz LP, *Concerto Grosso*, by his group Yggdrasil in a cave formed by the sea, to the accompaniment of crashing waves.

Other notable ethnic influences came from India, a country with no strong jazz tradition, but where improvisation is central to music making. Indian music was a full-blown fad in the 1960s: the Beatles and other rock bands adopted the **sitar** (a lute that features strings that are not directly played but vibrate "sympathetically" when other notes are plucked) and **tabla** (paired Indian drums); saxophonist John Coltrane recorded *India* (on *Live at the Village Vanguard*, 1961), albeit no more than a vague impression of droning Carnatic music; West Coast sax player Bud Shank recorded with sitar master **Ravi Shankar** on the album *Fire Night* (1962); British saxophonist Joe Harriott mixed jazz and Indian players in *Indo-Jazz Suite* (1966). In the 1970s, John Handy draped rhythmically supple alto saxophone improvisations over simplified Indian rhythmic cycles on the album *Karuna Supreme* (1975). Indian strings and percussion had been used for exotic color—as on some electric Miles Davis recordings from 1970—but India's contribution to the jazz vocabulary has been primarily rhythmic, its fiendishly complex additive rhythm patterns stimulating jazz much the way Latin rhythms have.

The most important figure in this connection was English guitarist John McLaughlin, with his strong feel for South Indian music and the blues, two traditions with the shared characteristics of string bending, floating pitches, and elaborations on basic compositional forms. His electric Mahavishnu Orchestras of the 1970s—which at various times included Czech keyboardist Jan Hammer and French violinist Jean-Luc Ponty—hinted at Indian influences on such albums as *The Inner Mounting Flame* (1971) and *Birds of Fire* (1972). (For an example of the Mahavishnu Orchestra's sound, listen to *Celestial Terrestrial Commuters* [*JTSA* Disc 5/Track 11].) The influences were more on the surface in McLaughlin's later acoustic group **Shakti**, which employed Indian violinist L. Shankar and percussionist Zakir Hussain and played fast and fiery jazz ragas. In the 1980s and 1990s, whippet-fast Indian hand-drummer Trilok Gurtu played with many Western musicians and groups, including Oregon and Jan Garbarek.

sitar Indian stringed instrument consisting of a resonating gourd and a long neck supporting seven principal strings, plus 12 to 20 sympathetic strings.

tabla a pair of drums of North India, played with the fingers, palms, and hands.

Experimental and Free Jazz in Europe and Beyond

Even nowadays, American soloists touring Europe sometimes encounter incompatible rhythm sections (although Stan Getz, who lived in Copenhagen from 1958 to 1961, found a compatible bassist in the U.S. expatriate Oscar Pettiford). In 1963 a strange album from Copenhagen rang in new changes from just such incompatibility: the rhythm section (which included bass prodigy **Niels-Henning Ørsted Pedersen**, who'd go on to work with pianist Oscar Peterson) played with a smooth sense of swing, but the visiting American seemed to be fighting the players all the way. That record, *My Name Is Albert Ayler*, announced the European debut of free jazz, which had even more profound consequences there than in the United States. If Americans could break free of their jazz past, so could Europeans. In England, alto saxophonist Joe Harriott had already made Europe's first free-jazz record—*Free Form* (1960)—on which he sometimes sounded strikingly (if coincidentally) like Ornette Coleman.

By the late 1960s numerous Western Europeans had declared that they no longer played jazz; rather, they were playing "European improvised music," employing scant if any predetermined material. It was a thoroughly transnational movement, with musicians crossing borders looking for like-minded souls. As English saxophonist Evan Parker put it, "It really was reassuring to know you weren't alone, you weren't crazy. Or if you were crazy there were other people who were just as crazy as you."

The major players came mostly from Germany (including saxophonist Peter Brötzmann, who personified his country's roaring high-energy take on the concept); England (where Parker and guitarist Derek Bailey helped define a quieter, more cooperative model); and Holland, where pianist Misha Mengelberg, drummer **Han Bennink**, and saxophonist Willem Breuker brought a sense of subversive fun to the music. A key contributor, Danish-Congolese saxophonist John Tchicai, had already made a dent in the United States, recording with Archie Shepp and with Coltrane on the latter's roiling album *Ascension* (1965).

That European movement eventually mushroomed into a worldwide circuit of free improvisers, many of whom recognized no kinship with jazz but (like Garbarek) wouldn't be doing what they did without its example. The Dutch model proved particularly attractive to some observers, because it embraced swing rhythm, while the German and English tended not to. The playing of Bennink—one of the heaviest swingers in or out of Europe, even while performing such visual stunts as bouncing his

Danish bassist Niels-Henning Ørsted Pedersen emerged as one of Europe's most in-demand players. He is shown here with pianist Oscar Peterson while the duo was touring in Denmark, 1998. PHOTO COURTESY JAZZSIGN/LEBRECHT MUSIC & ARTS.

sticks off the floor—even harkened back to vaudeville drummers. (A theatrical side also popped out in the Lithuanian trio that personified the new, liberal Soviet jazz of the 1980s: keyboardist Vyacheslav Ganelin, saxophonist Vladimir Chekasin, and drummer Vladimir Tarasov.)

Mengelberg—born in Russia, of temporarily transplanted Dutch and German parents—composed music that reflected his conservatory training, a finely honed sense of the absurd, and an admiration of Thelonious Monk and pianist Herbie Nichols. (Monk loomed large on the European scene when he was overlooked in the United States; some pianists who bore his stamp included Germany's Alexander von Schlippenbach, Switzerland's Irene Schweizer, England's Stan Tracey, and Russian-born nomad Simon Nabatov.) For this writer at least, Mengelberg's (and Bennink's) ICP—the **Instant Composers Pool Orchestra** of eight to ten pieces—offered one of the world's finest mixes of jazz chops and conceptual smarts; the group could twist Ellington, Nichols, and Monk tunes into elegant pretzels, as the album *Bospaadje Konijnehol* (*Forest Path Rabbit Hole*) (1986–91) attests.

Italy produced more than its share of good jazz musicians, ready to play with visiting American soloists—Chet Baker recorded with many of them. And Italy had no shortage of lyrical horn players, the best known of whom was trumpeter Enrico Rava.

Still, in terms of developing a national jazz identity, Italy lagged behind Western Europe; chalk it up to national disorganization rather than lack of ambition. Giorgio Gaslini, in particular, tried about all there was to try: bop just after World War II, cool and free jazz, jazzed-up folk songs, and reconciliations of jazz and 12-tone music.

For a period in the 1990s Gaslini played piano in the Italian Instabile Orchestra, the first successful attempt to bridge the musical gap between the industrial North and the rural South. It brought in musician-composers from all over the boot and provided a setting in which a pan-Italian sound could discover itself. The group offered a rich mix, including Rava; multireedist Gianluigi Trovesi, who combined jazz and folk elements in a natural way; the manically comic trumpeter (and IIO founder) Pino Minafra; and elder statesman and squirrelly altoist Mario Schiano. He began free-improvising in 1960 and said later he didn't consider himself a jazz musician anymore. Why, then, did he remain so fond of playing such chestnuts as *Moonlight in Vermont* and *Lover Man*? "Nostalgia," he said.

Of all the European scenes, Italy may be the richest in untapped potential, not least because it stands at the crossroads of so many cultures that have their own rhythmic and melodic traditions. It's one to watch in the future.

DISCOVER JAZZ

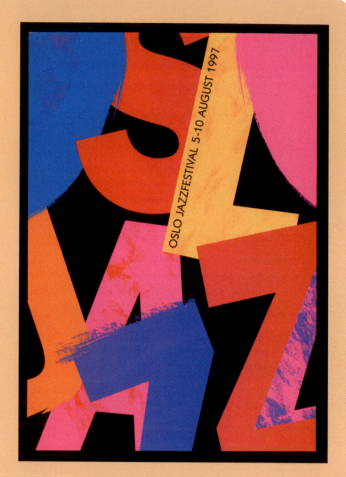

International jazz festivals offered audiences and musicians alike an idyllic alternative to cramped, smoky, noisy nightclubs. The hundreds of festivals presented every year—in such cities as Oslo, Paris, Berlin, and Edinburg—also added up to an important source of work for jazz bands.

COURTESY JOHN EDWARD HASSE.

As is Canada, the site of several pockets of independent jazz activity by late in the twentieth century. In Montreal—where Oscar Peterson came up before he arrived on the U.S. scene in 1949—an independent crop of French-speaking improvisers, such as saxophonist-flutist Jean Derome and electric guitarist René Lussier, were bringing Quebecois consciousness to improvised music's subversive/political aspect. In Toronto, the heart of the Canadian radio industry, and thus the center of big band activity, trombonist and arranger Rob McConnell led the best known. In Vancouver, such forward-looking improvisers as the percussive but lyrical pianist Paul Plimley and clarinetist François Houle helped keep things hopping. The influx of Asians into western Canada late in the century held the promise of spawning more

cross-cultural players, such as the Canadian-Chinese pianist from Toronto, Lee Pui Ming. Still, such cross-cultural contracts have been slow to develop in the new century, which is not to mention the many Canadian musicians—from high-note trumpeter Maynard Ferguson to neobop pianist Renee Rosnes, and the lyrical trumpet and flugelhorn player Ingrid Jensen—who made their mark in the States.

> **TAKE NOTE**
>
> • Who were the prominent musicians who brought jazz to Europe and how has a European jazz scene developed?

Jazz in Asia and Oceania

From its earliest days, jazz spread across the Atlantic, Pacific, and Indian Oceans with astonishing speed. Several factors helped speed its journey: new mass media (published sheet music and recordings); the European and American imperial presence in Asia and the Pacific islands; the growth of transoceanic tourism aboard passenger liners, with on-board orchestras; and the United States involvement in World War I. These conditions accelerated the movement of printed and recorded music and musicians, guaranteeing that jazz and its related dances would rapidly become worldwide forms of entertainment and expression.

Early Twentieth Century

The Philippines seems to have been the earliest site of jazz activity in Asia and Oceania; this may not be surprising, since it was a U.S. colony, yet the introduction and diffusion of jazz in the Philippine archipelago is not well documented. What we do know is that by the early 1920s, Filipino musicians were the most in-demand jazz musicians in Pacific Asia. Adept at "faking"(improvising mostly by ear), they earned a reputation second only to that of homegrown American talent, but Filipinos were in far greater supply. The dance halls, cabarets, movie theaters, and revues that began to appear in Shanghai, Osaka, Hong Kong, and Singapore in the years immediately after the Great War often featured Filipino jazz bands as headliners. The prominent Japanese saxophonist and composer Ryŏichi Hattori, who performed with a band called the Manila Red Hot Stompers in the mid-1920s, recalled that Filipino jazzmen were "weak readers" but blessed with intuitive musicality.

Post–World War I Years

In the interwar decades, several American musicians of African and European descent visited parts of Asia, although in smaller numbers than those who visited Europe. Pianist Teddy Weatherford performed extended engagements in China, the Dutch East Indies (now Indonesia), and India; he is remembered fondly for generously instructing Chinese, Indian, and Japanese musicians until his death in Kolkata in 1945. Prior to joining the Count Basie Orchestra in 1936, trumpeter Buck Clayton traveled the Pacific Asia circuit and lived it up in Shanghai, where he could afford to employ Chinese cooks and domestic servants. Singer Midge Williams and her three tap-dancing brothers went from a Shanghai engagement to Japan, where in 1934 she recorded with the Nippon Columbia Jazz Band and played a weeklong gig at Tokyo's famous Florida dance hall. The presence of these and other American-born musicians, coupled with the widespread availability of jazz recordings, meant that Asian jazz was often derivative of prevailing trends, techniques, and repertoire in the United States.

There were exceptions, however. Chinese musician Li Jinhui and Koichi Sugii of Japan composed, arranged, and recorded music that combined elements of jazz, show tunes, and East Asian folk melodies in the late 1920s and early 1930s. These strikingly successful experiments forecast more radical musical fusions later in the twentieth century. However, jazz was not always welcome in the region. Some Asian nationalists felt it was driving out native music. The Chinese communists took the party line that jazz was a bourgeois tactic to divert the oppressed masses from making revolution, dismissing Li's music as "pornographic." On the other hand, Sugii's recordings helped prolong jazz's presence in wartime Japan, despite ultranationalist, anti-American sentiments.

After World War II

Jazz swept through Asia with renewed vigor after the post–World War II dismantling of Europe's Asian empires. The expanded U.S. military commitment to the region during the Cold War brought thousands of soldier-musicians to the Pacific islands and East and Southeast Asia. More importantly, native talent was nurtured through expanded employment opportunities at and around U.S. military bases. Jazz also figured prominently in propaganda from both sides in the Cold War. The U.S. government sponsored radio broadcasts and tours by prominent American jazz artists from Pakistan to Japan, to demonstrate the virtues of American-style democracy and to deflect criticism of Jim Crow racism. By contrast, Asian communists condemned jazz as an example of cultural imperialism. However, the music's status on the political spectrum was unpredictable: Australian leftists embraced jazz as a signifier of radical populism, but in resolutely anti-communist countries like South Korea, jazz remained controversial and emblematic of generational tensions.

Asia's most developed scene emerged in Japan, where listeners were as enamored of jazz as they were of other forms of Western music. There, however, image at times won out over content. Fans and even jazz magazines occasionally invented fanciful jazz-player histories unencumbered by the facts. One gets the feeling that Japanese jazz's best days are ahead—which is not to slight such accomplished individualists as big band composer Toshiko Akiyoshi, a resident of the States, whose penchant for flutes suggested her roots; pianist Yosuke Yamashita, who combined Japanese-sounding materials with a hard-edged attack; and Toshinori Kondo, a free-jazzer capable of blasting earthy trumpet lines like an old New Orleans hero.

Toshiko Akiyoshi was raised in China and Japan before moving to the United States in 1956. Many of her compositions incorporate elements of Japanese music. PHOTO COURTESY MICHAEL JACKSON.

Late Twentieth Century

The last four decades of the twentieth century witnessed both the rise to international prominence of innovative Asian- and Oceanic-born jazz artists, and—despite the very different musical systems of Asia and the West—high-profile ventures to meld Asian classical and folk traditions with jazz. Since the 1950s, Japan has produced a slew of major artists, from bandleader-pianist Toshiko Akiyoshi and saxophonist Sadao Watanabe to guitarist Kazumi Watanabe and pianist Hiromi Uehara. Indian *tabla* drummers Trilok Gurtu and Zakir Hussain have earned esteem as jazz musicians through collaborations with Don Cherry, John McLaughlin, and Charles Lloyd. Filipina songstress Charmaine Clamor and Chinese singer Coco Zhao have tackled what is arguably the single greatest challenge for non-native English speakers—jazz singing—and have also composed and performed credibly in Tagalog and Bisaya (Clamor) and Mandarin (Zhao). Although better known for his political role at home, the Thai monarch Bhumibol Adulyadej is also a jazz saxophonist and composer, whom Lionel Hampton praised as "the coolest king in the land."

Since the 1960s an "Asian tinge" has colored many jazz performances, frequently (if not always) involving collaborations with Asian musicians. Because many Asian musical traditions embrace extemporaneous performance, spontaneous dialogues with jazz musicians can be artistically fruitful. Joe Harriott and John Mayer

Listening Guide

((•)) **Listen** to *Ting Ning* by Nguyên Lê on **mymusiclab.com** CD II, Track 13/Download Track 37

TING NING • NGUYÊN LÊ

Music: Nguyên Lê/traditional. Personnel: Nguyên Lê (electric, acoustic, and fretless guitars; guitar synthesizer; computer and synths); Hao Nhiên (zither, *dan bau, sao* flute, *sapek* clappers); Paolo Fresu (trumpet); Simon Spang-Hanssen (saxophones and flutes); Michel Benita (acoustic bass); François Verly (percussion and keyboards); Trilok Gurtu (drums, percussion). Recorded October and November 1995 in Paris. First issue: *Tales from Viêt-Nam*, ACT 9225-2. Timing: 3:44.

Overview

From the rustic percussion and folk melodies of rural Vietnam to electric, effects-saturated guitar and jazz-tinged saxophone, *Ting Ning* takes the listener on an exotic mini-journey. The track exemplifies the fusion of jazz, rock, and world music at its most organic sounding. The leader, French-Vietnamese guitarist and producer Nguyên Lê, made many recordings of similarly style-mixing music in the 1990s and 2000s. He counts among his influences rock guitarist Jimi Hendrix, the jazz-rock of Return to Forever and Mahavishnu Orchestra, and traditional jazz guitarists Wes Montgomery and Django Reinhardt. But where most others with similarly eclectic sources staked out comfortable positions in well-known musical zones, Lê built a multicultural soundscape of his own.

On *Ting Ning*, and its parent album *Tales from Viêt-Nam*, Lê mixed jazz players with Vietnamese traditional musicians to create "a journey back into my childhood, a return to lost roots."

Key Features

- Style: A mix of Vietnamese folk melodies, heavy-metal rock guitar, and jazz-tinged saxophone and drums.
- Colors: A blend and contrast of acoustic and electric—woody-sounding percussion mixed with acoustic flute, saxophone, and, later, electronically processed guitar. Textures evolve from the spare beginning to the densely textured climax.
- Rhythm and percussion: The band maintains a steady mid-tempo patter on rustic, acoustic instruments throughout, shifting up to double time (1:36) as the tune increases in excitement. The standard drum set, played by Trilok Gurtu, adds fullness and color to the rhythm sounds.
- Melodies shift among a Vietnamese-originated main melody with several variations (at 0:00, 0:15, and 0:36), a syncopated blues riff (2:01), and another syncopated riff that mixes blues with hint of the Vietnamese melody (2:32).
- Improvisation occurs most notably in the guitar toward the end of the piece (2:39). Lê uses the tune's melodic materials as the basis for screaming solo riffs.
- Form: The journey is from the spare, simple folk material to more contemporary jazz-rock fusion.

—*Tad Lathrop*

pioneered "Indo-jazz fusion," an effort later taken up by Nepalese-Bengali pianist Louis Banks and Goan saxophonist Braz Gonsalves, exploring the affinities between modal jazz and improvisatory practices of Hindustani *rāga*. Artists such as Alice Coltrane and Pharoah Sanders have composed and arranged with Asian instruments, modes, and motifs, creating music that has a deliberately mystical, meditative quality. On his 1961 album *In Fiesta*, Japanese drummer Hideo Shiraki seamlessly integrated Kinuko Shirane's fleet-fingered **koto** playing into his hard bop combo. Musicians of Chinese descent, such as Jon Jang, Fred Wei-han Ho, and Francis Wong, have created politicized "Afro-Asian" ensembles and compositions, sometimes integrating instruments such as the *erhu* (two-string fiddle) into their arrangements to a bluesy

effect. The American Voices Association sponsored the 2002 recording *Jazz Bridges Myanmar* incorporating the Burmese *pat waing* (tuned drum set) into jazz improvisations. Balinese composer I Nyoman Windha has written for **gamelan** ensembles with jazz quartet, while pianist Steve Suriajaya has done the same with Sundanese gamelan, creating richly layered pieces that illuminate the links between the *kotekan* (interlocking melody) and contrapuntal jazz aesthetics.

---

koto (Japanese) a Japanese zither (a stringed instrument) about six feet long typically with 13 silk strings.

gamelan Indonesian music, and set of instruments, notable for interlocking rhythms, microtones, repeating patterns, and metallophone-based sonorities.

TIME	FORM	MELODY/RHYTHM	INSTRUMENTATION
0:00	FOLK-LIKE MELODY	In a spare-sounding intro, a lively eight-bar melody is stated.	Flute duet with melodic percussion; cymbals provide accents.
0:14	FIRST VARIATION	Syncopated (uneven) rhythms in the melody interact with evenly spaced rhythms in the percussion.	Plus acoustic bass.
0:37	SECOND VARIATION	The texture thickens as saxophone enters, joining on a further variation of the melody, now shifted to a lower pitch area. Saxophone adds a "modern" tone to the previously rustic sound.	Plus saxophone.
0:50	THIRD VARIATION	The bass provides contrast with long, sustained notes. (Compare it with bassist Jaco Pastorius's work on *Birdland* (1:19; CD II, Track 5/Download Track 29).	The bass asserts itself, and drummer Trilok Gurtu fills in more.
1:05		Surprise! A tricky extra half-beat is inserted, shifting the melody slightly behind the established beat.	
1:18	FOURTH VARIATION	Texture thickens even more as a repetition of the melody is "doubled" in a higher register.	
1:35		A sustained stack of notes fades away as percussion continues. Rapid beats on hand drums and plucked eighth notes lead to drum-set improvisation.	
2:00	SYNCOPATED BLUES RIFF	A syncopated blues riff is played on saxophones.	Saxophones.
2:06		The riff ends on an offbeat and the notes sustain as drums maintain a propulsive, exciting groove for four bars.	
2:13	SYNCOPATED RIFF REPEATED	Saxophones repeat the syncopated blues riff.	Saxophones.
2:20		The riff ends again and notes sustain, as percussion continues grooving for eight bars.	
2:32	NEW MELODY	A new melody enters—a syncopated riff that mixes blues with elements of the main melody.	
2:39		Lê answers with a blistering set of bluesy guitar riffs spiced with extra "odd" notes.	Guitar.
2:45		The syncopated riff repeats, followed by more guitar improvisation.	
3:04	RETURN OF ORIGINAL FOLK MELODY	Echoes of the folk melody come in the form of full-band riffs. Guitar solos above the riffs and in response to them, with rapid phrases and howling high notes.	Full ensemble.
3:17		All join on final statement of melody ideas, leading to four closing accents.	

Nguyên Lê, born in France of Vietnamese parents, is one of the most innovative modern jazz guitarists. PHOTO COURTESY ACT/ ROLF KISSLING.

Twenty-First Century

In the early twenty-first century, most Asian and Oceanic metropolises boast respectable jazz scenes; even in communist China, there has been a revival of interest in Shanghai's former status as interwar Asia's jazz capital. And Asian musicians who are living far from their homelands have also made a large impact on the jazz world. These musicians don't always follow one musical path, but feel free to draw from various jazz styles. As just one example, French guitarist Nguyên Lê played in Orchestre National du Jazz, covered Jimi Hendrix tunes, and explored his cultural roots on *Tales from Viêt-Nam* (1996) with a cast including Italian trumpeter Paolo Fresu and drummers from India and England, Trilok Gurtu and Steve Argüelles.

 Watch a video of Nguyên Lê discussing how he composed *Ting Ning* on **mymusiclab.com**

TAKE NOTE

- What is the history of jazz in Asia and Oceania, and who are the vital figures creating original jazz music there?

Jazz in the Middle East

The term *Middle East* signifies not only a vast geographical region of the world stretching from Morocco to western India but also a diverse set of cultural constructs that derive from population migration, a variety of religious traditions (including Islam, Judaism, and Christianity), and shifting sociopolitical attitudes toward Western culture, including jazz music. Jazz in the Middle East has developed since at least the 1920s, incorporating and interpreting Western influences (through recordings and live performances) within local practices and styles of music, producing a rich and provocative milieu of sounds. Defining characteristics of jazz in the Middle East can be found most obviously in instrumentation, musical form/genre, and performance practices.

In the Middle East, some instruments are identified with particular cultures, while others retain a more pan-regional identity. Of the latter type, the **oud ('ūd)**, a **chordophone**, and **darbouka (dumbek)**, a goblet-shaped hand drum, are common in Middle Eastern jazz. Some instruments—the zither, for example—are shared among Middle Eastern cultures, although they vary locally in construction, performance practice, and repertoire.

Musical form and performance practice demonstrate the same dynamic range of pan-regional and culturally specific identities. Folk dances (such as the Bulgarian *horo*) composed in compound meters (groups of two and three beats, as in 3+2+2, or $\frac{7}{8}$) are common among Balkan cultures and have served as inspiration for many jazz compositions from this area. The **taksim (taqsīm)**, a solo instrumental improvisation found in Arab and Turkish music traditions, is another form that is frequently adapted to jazz contexts. Musicians also explore connections between musical systems, such as Middle Eastern melodic and rhythmic modes. The **maqam** is an Arabic or Turkish mode composed of tetrachords that forms the basis of melodic construction and improvisation. While these musical materials reference regional cultures, individual interpretations can vary greatly and transcend national and cultural borders.

---

oud ('ūd) (Arabic *al-'ūd*) a lute or chordophone common in Middle Eastern music.

chordophone a stringed instrument.

darbouka (dumbek) an Arabic goblet-shaped hand drum, common in Middle Eastern music.

taksim (taqsīm) a soloistic instrumental improvisation found in Arab and Turkish music traditions.

maqam (Arabic) an Arabic mode composed of tetrachords.

The Maghreb

The Maghreb, the region encompassing North Africa from Morocco to Libya, is said to include Andalucia, Spain, because of its history of multicultural influences, including the lasting influences of Sephardic Jewish and Muslim populations after their forced expulsion beginning in the fifteenth century. The legacy of Andalucia as a harmonious multicultural society continues to inspire musicians to explore the intersections of these cultures. Some of these influences (such as the highly punctuated and syncopated rhythmic patterns of *palmas* and *zapateo*, and melismatic vocal phrasing) can be heard in flamenco music, including the flamenco jazz of modern-day pianists Diego Amador (*Piano Jondo*, 2003) and Chano Dominguez (*New Flamenco Sound*, 2006). In the late twentieth and early twenty-first centuries Tunisian *oud* player Anouar Brahem (*Thimar*, 1998) and pianist Wajdi Cherif (*Jasmine*, 2006) both explored the intersections of Arab classical and Western European jazz traditions, shifting their emphasis among musical styles through collaboration with varied musicians.

The Mashriq

The Mashriq (the eastern coast of the Mediterranean, including Egypt) includes some well-established jazz cultures, especially in Israel and Egypt. Cairo, long regarded as a modern, cosmopolitan epicenter for music culture, hosts an annual jazz festival informed by a long history of local jazz performance. In the 1960s, Salah Ragab, a drummer, established several combos and a big band with which he recorded several albums, including collaborations with the American experimental bandleader Sun Ra (compiled in *The Sun Ra Arkestra Meets Salah Ragab in Egypt*, 1999).

Jewish cultures are active in countries around the world, and Israel serves as an epicenter of Jewish jazz music. Through institutionalized education and a vibrant festival scene, Israeli-born jazz musicians, such as bassists Avishai Cohen and Omer Avital, exhibit influences from the Middle Eastern, Western, and Eastern European branches of the Jewish diaspora. For example, Cohen's *Adama* (1998) includes *oud* and Middle Eastern melody and harmony. Oudist Marcel Khalife and vocalist Rima Khcheich, both of Lebanese descent, are internationally renowned musicians whose careers are bolstered by successful recordings and festival performances. Syrian Abdullah Chhadeh performs on **qānūn** (plucked zither) and fronts several projects that have garnered success among local jazz and international festival audiences.

Anatolia and Caucasus

Anatolia and the Caucasus region, which encompasses the nations surrounded by the Black and Caspian Seas, includes Turkey, home of the Middle East's most established jazz culture. Percussionist Okay Temiz, among others, has achieved much success, often collaborating with musicians outside of Turkey; one of his best recordings is *Magnetic Band*

Anouar Brahem, performing live onstage, playing the oud, 2007. PHOTO COURTESY PHILIP RYALLS/REDFERNS/GETTY IMAGES.

---

qānūn a Middle Eastern stringed instrument, like a plucked zither, with 72 to 75 strings.

Abdullah Chhadeh performs with his band, April 24, 2009, in Abu Dhabi. PHOTO COURTESY AFP/GETTY IMAGES.

Middle Eastern Influences on American Jazz

American jazz musicians have explored Middle Eastern music through jazz—both in collaboration with Middle Eastern musicians and in personal interpretations of the region. Randy Weston (*The Splendid Master Gnawa Musicians of Morocco*, 1995), Ornette Coleman (*Dancing in Your Head*, 2000), and Pharoah Sanders (*The Trance of Seven Colors*, 1994) all recorded with musicians from Morocco. In the 1960s, bassist Ahmed Abdul-Malik (*East Meets West*, 1960) and flautist Herbie Mann (*Impressions of the Middle East*, 1967) recorded jazz albums influenced by Middle Eastern music. The best known of these is Dave Brubeck's *Blue Rondo à la Turk* (1959; CD I, Track 21/Download Track 21) and Duke Ellington's *Far East Suite* (1966), inspired by his State Department tours of both the Middle East and Japan. (Listen to *Isfahan* from the *Far East Suite*, JTSA Disc 5/Track 7.) More recently, John Zorn and the musicians on his Tzadik record label have extended the sonic boundaries of Middle Eastern music and Euro-American jazz in recordings such as *Bar Kokhbar* (1996) and *Live at Tonic* (2001).

TAKE NOTE

- How did jazz develop in the Middle East, and who are some of the key players?

Jazz in Eastern Europe

In Eastern Europe, a region prone to political turmoil, bloody wars, and repression, jazz became an outlet for individual expression and a manifestation of artistic and personal freedom. Musically, jazz in Eastern Europe drew in varying measures from American jazz (filtered through the sensibilities of local players), a wide variety of native folk traditions (Jewish **klezmer**, Slavic folk songs, Gypsy dance music), and European classical music.

It was not until 1920–22 that the earliest accounts of jazz performances in Eastern Europe began to emerge. Some countries were visited by touring American musicians. In other countries, local enthusiasts listened to and tried to imitate early 78-rpm jazz records—most notably those of the Original Dixieland Jazz Band—imported (or smuggled) from the United States. In Russia, the first documented jazz performance took place in Moscow on October 1, 1922 (celebrated since 1982 as the

in Finland 1995 (released in 2004). Jazz in Armenia traces its history back 70 years, and several organizations in Azerbaijan have recently founded a Web site (www.jazz.az) that celebrates local jazz culture, including the publication of an anthology that features Azerbaijani musicians.

Arabian Peninsula and Central Asia

The Arabian Peninsula and Central Asia (encompassing Iran, Pakistan, Afghanistan, and neighboring former Soviet republics) reveal relatively little information on their jazz cultures, partly due to changes in political environments within the last several decades. In Iran, however, jazz thrived in the 1960s, through recordings, television programs, and music festivals. Iraqi-American Amir ElSaffar performs both as a classical Iraqi singer and a trumpeter in the tradition of American jazz (*Two Rivers*, 2007). In 2010 he collaborated with Hafez Modirzadeh, an Iranian-American saxophonist and scholar/educator. The collaborative work of these artists demonstrates the potential for jazz to serve prescriptive, socially conscious goals by emphasizing mutual respect and peaceful commonality that rise above political or cultural conflicts.

---

klezmer (Yiddish) traditional Eastern European Jewish music, which underwent a revival in the late-twentieth-century United States; such jazz musicians as John Zorn and Don Byron have sometimes blended klezmer with jazz.

birthday of Russian jazz). The band was local, led not by a musician but by a dancer. Valentin Parnakh, an innovator of European modern dance, and a poet and literature historian, had spent many years in Western Europe, where he fell in love with this exciting new music from beyond the ocean.

The first Russian jazz band to be recorded was pianist Alexander Tsfasman's, in 1928; within the next 10 years, the first Eastern European jazz recordings were made in Czechoslovakia, Poland, Romania, and other countries. Recordings contained either American standards, reproduced by local musicians with more or less accuracy, or dance tunes. Until the 1940s, the very word "jazz" for Eastern Europeans meant a certain type of band rather than a style of music (a band that, unlike a traditional brass band, included saxophones, a drum set, and, in many cases, violins and accordions along with the brass). Any modern danceable music, even with a strong influence from local folkloric traditions, was called "jazz" if it was played by a "jazz band." Soloists and vocalists could emulate the blues, or employ Eastern European sonorities (most notably derived from Jewish klezmer and local brands of Gypsy folk music), or simply stick to the melody without much improvisation; still, they were called "jazz musicians." Examples included the Czech dance bandleader Rudolf Antonín Dvorský, who would perform both jazz tunes and Czech folk songs, and the U.S.S.R. (Union of Soviet Socialist Republics)-based singer-actor Leonid Utyosov, whose State Jazz Orchestra of the Russian Soviet Federative Socialist Republic might play American jazz, klezmer, Gypsy romance songs, and Russian folk tunes during the same concert. German trumpet player Eddie Rosner, who emigrated to Poland after Hitler was elected Germany's chancellor in 1933, defected to the Soviet Union with his entire Polish band when Hitler's troops entered Poland in 1939; he gained wide popularity in the U.S.S.R. by adding local pop tunes and Polish songs translated into Russian to his repertoire of jazz standards.

Then, for more than a decade, World War II and subsequent political shifts across the subcontinent made it difficult for jazz to evolve there; its very survival was in question in the late 1940s. Jazz, although never officially banned, was depicted by the Communist authorities as "decadent bourgeois music" and went mostly underground. Even Utyosov's band, the most popular band in the Soviet Union, dropped the word "jazz" from its name and continued as the State Variety Orchestra. Eddie Rosner was arrested in 1946—officially for the "unauthorized attempt to cross the state border" (he tried to leave the U.S.S.R. for Poland without permission from the government)—and served a six-year term in Siberian labor camps (where he, not surprisingly, led a successful prison jazz band).

Change came in the mid- and late 1950s. Everywhere in Eastern Europe, new generations of musicians were turning toward jazz: they felt that the music, especially in its new styles of bebop, hard bop, and, later, free jazz, was the ultimate expression of personal creative freedom. Regional musicians tried to scale the new summits of jazz musicianship, mostly by picking up the music by ear from smuggled American vinyl records or from taped transmissions of the U.S. international short-wave radio service Voice of America. (Willis Conover, the VOA jazz host, became the general source of jazz information for thousands of musicians in Eastern Europe.) Slight liberalization of political regimes, first in the countries outside the Soviet Union and then within the U.S.S.R. itself, made it possible for musicians to emerge from the cultural underground to the mainstream of their countries' music scenes.

Poland

In Poland, the success of Krzysztof Komeda, a gifted jazz pianist and popular film score composer, opened the way for an entire generation of first-class jazz improvisors who were not only emulating the Americans but also trying to incorporate their own cultures' richest music traditions into their own, personal jazz voices. Two former members of the Komeda Quartet, saxophonist Zbigniew Namyslowski and trumpet player Tomasz Stanko, became the creative leaders of the Polish jazz scene (and the Eastern European scene in general) for the decades to follow. (Listen to Tomasz Stanko on *Suspended Night Variation VIII, JTSA*, Disc 6/ Track 16.) The present-day generation of musicians, including brilliant pianists Marcin Wasilewski and Leszek Mozdzer and saxophonist Adam Pieronczyk, keeps this legacy alive.

Czechoslovakia

In Czechoslovakia, similar processes were complicated by political upheaval in 1968; many jazz musicians emigrated to the West, which enriched American jazz with the likes of keyboardist Jan Hammer (who would join the fusion group Mahavishnu Orchestra), bassist George Mraz (born Jirí Mráz), and bassist Miroslav Vitous (an eventual member of Weather Report), but slowed down the evolution of local jazz scenes for almost two decades. Recently, musicians such as flautist Jirí Stivín and violinist/singer Iva Bittová have worked within a poly-stylistic idiom on the edges of jazz, avant-garde, and modern classical music.

Hungary

Hungarian jazz also suffered a substantial brain drain, as emigration from there was probably the easiest in the whole Eastern bloc; early émigrés such as guitarist Attila Zoller (who moved to Germany in 1948 and then made it big in New York in the 1960s) were followed by the likes of guitarist **Gábor Szabó** (who moved to the United States in the mid-1950s). More recently, however, a strong jazz scene enjoyed state support in Budapest, overseen by pianist and educator Károly Binder and influenced by Hungary's free-jazz patriarch, pianist György Szabados.

Romania

In Romania, although the local Communist regime was more hard-line than anywhere else in Eastern Europe, pianist Johnny Raducanu developed his local brand of jazz music, influenced by Romanian and Gypsy folk dance tunes, starting in the late 1950s, and his followers (pianist Ion Baciu, Jr., guitarist Ionut Dorobantu, and vocalist Teodora Enache, among others) kept the genre alive even in the worst years of the Ceausescu dictatorship in the 1980s.

Yugoslavia

Yugoslavia, although culturally part of Eastern Europe, never became part of the Warsaw Pact—the military alliance of Eastern European Communist countries. This enabled the 1971 launch (by an American company) of Eastern Europe's largest jazz festival, the Belgrade Newport Jazz Festival, in this federated country's capital in 1971. Twenty years later it was discontinued as the Balkan states entered a decade-long period of violence, civil wars, and the ultimate disintegration of Yugoslavia. In 2005, a group of enthusiasts in Belgrade revived the event under the name the Belgrade Jazz Festival.

Bulgaria

Bulgarian jazz, since its relatively late start in the 1960s, was always marked by incorporation of the complex, odd rhythmic patterns of local music into jazz improvisation; those rhythms became a trademark of pianist Milcho Leviev, who worked as a performer and arranger with the American trumpeter-bandleader Don Ellis and drummer Billy Cobham in the 1970s. (Leviev continued to influence the jazz scene in his native country by giving master classes in its capital, Sofia.) Most contemporary Bulgarian improvisers gravitate toward open concepts and cross-pollination of modern classical, Bulgarian folk, and avant-garde jazz music.

The Former Soviet Union (Union of Soviet Socialist Republics, or U.S.S.R.)

The jazz scene in the Soviet Union enjoyed a period of unexpectedly broad support from the state authorities following the 1960s and through the 1980s, as the Communist rulers felt that rock music was a more dangerous enemy of their ideology: jazz musicians, at least, did not sing protest songs, and they made the Soviet Union look good when they toured internationally. In Russia, the U.S.S.R.'s largest member republic, Moscow and Leningrad were the jazz centers, where several thousand professional musicians played in big bands, in combos, or solo, and practiced all existing jazz styles, from Dixieland and swing to free jazz, and from bebop to fusion.

Many Russians emigrated in the 1970s to 1990s. Some found success in the United States or in Europe. Some also returned to Russia: Leningrad-born saxophonist Igor Butman, active on the New York scene in the early 1990s, returned to run a successful jazz club, a superb big band, a record label, and a major jazz festival in Moscow. Several Russian musicians tried to be visible on the American scene without leaving their native land; they included Moscow-based saxophonist Oleg Kireyev, his fellow Muscovite pianist Ivan Farmakovsky, and St. Petersburg-based pianist Andrey Kondakov. As in other Eastern European countries, some Russian players opted to explore inter-genre possibilities; French horn virtuoso Arkady Shilkloper, active in both Europe and Russia, purveyed his own blend of jazz and modern classical music.

Other prominent jazz scenes in the former Soviet Union were Lithuanian, Estonian, Ukrainian, Armenian, and Azeri. While Azerbaijan is geographically in Asia, its jazz scene is well connected with Europe, where Azeri jazz superstar Aziza Mustafa Zadeh followed the steps of her father, the late pianist Vagif Mustafazadeh, who in the 1960s and 1970s pioneered the use of the native Azeri music style *mugam* in jazz improvisation. Jazz musicians in Armenia work in the same direction, incorporating the complex odd rhythms and ancient scales of Armenian music in jazz, most notably in the Armenian Navy Band (note the irony: Armenia is a landlocked country, and therefore has no navy!) led by American-born percussionist Arto Tunçboyaciyan, who in the 1990s moved to the land of his forefathers to explore his musical heritage.

The Ukraine

Many Ukrainian jazz performers during the period of 1990s economical instability moved to the United States, Europe, or Russia; still, the country offered a vibrant jazz scene, grouped around several strong jazz festivals in the capital of Kyiv and in Lviv, Odessa, Kharkiv, and Donetsk.

Estonia

Estonia, in its Soviet period, was the site of the Tallinn International Jazz Festival, which served as the meeting point for the entire Soviet jazz community in late 1960s. In independent Estonia, the festival flourished again, under the name Jazzkaar (Jazz Rainbow), now presenting musicians from all over the world, often in collaboration with strong local players (most notably, guitarist Jaak Sooäär).

Lithuania

Lithuania remains the country with one of the most original and well-evolved local brands of jazz in Eastern Europe, arguably ranking second after Poland. In the Lithuanian capital of Vilnius, in the early 1970s, three musicians from other Soviet locales began a collaboration that yielded a unique brand of free jazz—or "operative composition,"as they would call it. In 1986, as the Ganelin Trio, they became the first Soviet free-jazz band to tour the United States, garnering critical acclaim. Pianist Slava Ganelin left Vilnuis for Israel in 1987, but the other two, saxophonist Vladimir Chekasin and percussionist Vladimir Tarasov, still serve as Lithuanian jazz patriarchs, raising new generations of prolific improvisers with their unique individual voices.

> ### TAKE NOTE
>
> - Which musicians led the practice of jazz in Eastern Europe, and what were the characteristic styles?

Jazz in Africa

Jazz has deep roots in the music and culture of sub-Saharan Africa—most American slaves came from West Africa—and it was only a matter of time before the jazz impulse would reach and resonate in Africa. When it did, what happened varied widely in this large and diverse continent, which contains more countries—54—than any other.

Jazz spread primarily to urban areas in relatively better-developed countries. In the early years, jazz reached Africa through sheet music,

films, and especially phonograph recordings. For example, in the early 1930s, the Lagos (Nigeria) Police Band was listening to recordings of Louis Armstrong. In later years, radio, especially broadcasts on the Voice of America, helped spread the sound, as did occasional visits by American musicians. From 1956 to 1973, the U.S. State Department sponsored tours of such jazz musicians as Randy Weston, Woody Herman, Duke Ellington, and Dizzy Gillespie, which won many new fans for the music. Most of all, many Africans loved and still love Louis Armstrong, who toured about 30 cities across the continent, has been honored on the postage stamps of seven African nations, and remains the most popular American jazz musician in Africa.

South Africa

South Africa boasts the longest and by far strongest jazz tradition on the continent. Anthropologist David Coplan ascribes this to "similarities in the socio-historical experience of black Americans and South Africans, including rapid urbanization and industrialization and racial oppression . . . [and] the value of black American models for black South African urban cultural adaptation, identity, and resistance."

In the late 1910s and 1920s, slow boats from America brought not only cargo but also early jazz recordings. The music inspired black musicians in the segregated, impoverished townships and their speakeasies or *shebeens*, but the question of whether to absorb American musical elements sparked controversy in the local black press. Many performers imitated American styles, learning them from recordings, sheet music, or movies. In the 1930s, Solomon "Zulu Boy" Cele's Jazz Maniacs fused swing instrumentation, call and response between brass and reeds

Hugh Masekela performing in Chicago, 2005. PHOTO COURTESY MICHAEL JACKSON.

Listening Guide

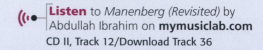
Listen to *Manenberg (Revisited)* by Abdullah Ibrahim on **mymusiclab.com**
CD II, Track 12/Download Track 36

MANENBERG (REVISITED) • ABDULLAH IBRAHIM

Music: Abdullah Ibrahim, 1974. Personnel: Carlos Ward (flute); Ricky Ford (tenor sax); Abdullah Ibrahim (piano); David Williams (bass); Ben Riley (drums). Recorded October 1985 in Englewood Cliffs, New Jersey. Original issue: *Water from an Ancient Well*, Black Hawk BKH50207. Timing: 6:12.

Overview

South African pianist Abdullah Ibrahim, known early in his career as Dollar Brand, grew up in the Manenberg section of segregated Cape Town surrounded by *kwela* music: peppy, melodically and harmonically simple major-key melodies originally played on pennywhistles (mass-produced metal flutes). His tune *Manenberg*, like other South African jazz, catches the flavor of *kwela*. This arrangement, for his New York band Ekaya, features an elaborate "solo" for melded flute and tenor sax, to offset the elementary tune.

Key Features

- The melody consists of two basic motifs over a recurring three-chord progression that anchors the entire piece. In Ibrahim's performances the number of repetitions has varied; the form as heard here is AAABBB.
- The scripted, unison "solo" for flute and tenor follows the same chords; there's no sense of a chorus structure or overall development. All the melodic and thematic material is derived from the F major scale, as if played on a pennywhistle.
- The long written episode is striking for what's absent. There are no blue notes, little fast virtuoso playing or variation in dynamics, no building to a climax or even a real ending. But it has the freshness and loose extemporized feel of real improvising. *Manenberg (Revisited)* has the timeless quality of folk art—as if its cycling motion could go on forever.
- Ekaya was an international band: three members were born outside the United States: Ibrahim, David Williams (from Trinidad), and Carlos Ward (Panama).

—Kevin Whitehead

TIME	SECTION	MELODY
0:00	INTRO/VAMP	A two-bar melodic figure (followed by two bars of gospel-like piano, rolling over the same chords) is played twice as an introductory vamp, at a stately pace. Note the **triplet**-like, skipping momentum of drummer Ben Riley, who uses brushes throughout. Bassist David Williams, the son of a calypso bass player, elaborates on and slides over the constant three-chord two-bar cycle. Note his inventive fills, at the ends of those cycles, in the entire performance. Throughout, Riley tends to go easy on the first beat of a $\frac{4}{4}$ measure, giving his drumming a Caribbean lilt. From 0:11, he sometimes plays his version of a reggae "one drop"—leaving out that first beat altogether.

(in the style of Fletcher Henderson; see Chapters 4 and 5), and *marabi*, a guitar or keyboard style of the slum yards, creating considerable excitement. By the 1940s, militant voices began advocating for the absorption of specifically *African* musical materials into jazz—a shift that would ultimately profoundly shape South African jazz. By the mid-1940s, bands such as the Harlem Swingsters began experimenting with fusing the cyclical harmonies of *marabi*, "a slow, heavy beat . . . and American swing," writes Chris Ballantine. "The result was nothing less than a new kind of jazz: its practitioners and supporters were eventually to call it African jazz, or *mbaqana*."

By the 1940s and 1950s, jazz groups large and small proliferated in cities and towns across the country. By the late 1950s, South African jazz was diverging in two directions: the *marabi*-oriented dance bands and a more overtly political, progressive style, inspired by the American avant-garde. The leading exponent of the progressive style was the Jazz Epistles—led by pianist Dollar Brand and featuring Hugh Masekela (trumpet), Jonas Gwangwa (trombone), and Kippie Moeketsi (reeds). They made one album (*Verse One*, 1959) before going into exile after the white racist government cracked down heavily in 1960. Other musicians joined the exodus including Brand's wife, singer Bea Benjamin, and white bandleader Chris McGregor, who organized a racially integrated band, the Blue Notes (*B My Dear*, 1964).

TIME	SECTION	MELODY
0:20	THEME A	Flute and tenor enter—voiced in unison throughout the performance (as if they're a single instrument). The A motif is the same as that introductory vamp, echoed here by piano, in classic call and response. Riley's "one drop" occurs at 0:21 and 0:25.
0:30	THEME A REPEATED	Flute and tenor sax continue to voice the melody.
0:40	THEME A REPEATED	Bass and drums subtly vary their accompaniment; otherwise, there is no development.
0:50	THEME B	The second figure is a slow, descending four-note run, with the first note repeated. It begins on the second beat of the bar. Piano then echoes the horns: more call and response.
1:00	THEME B REPEATED	As just heard, with response from imitative piano.
1:10	THEME B REPEATED	Note, again, the lack of development, of holding in place, reinforced by the verbatim call and response between winds and piano.
1:20	SCORED "SOLO" FOR HORNS	The horns begin by playing an answer to Theme B, as if moving into the next part of the melody—but the line proceeds without repetition. This "solo" continues for 100 bars (plus a two-bar **tag**). Its melody does not repeat itself, or make much overt reference to the opening themes, though it does rely on, and sometimes develops, small kernel phrases. The phrases are often linked by rhythmic imitation and variation, but the short sequences rarely run more than four bars. Minor subplots develop and disappear: a catchy, repeating figure will be introduced (as at 2:08 and 5:06) and dropped. At other times riffs will be spun out into longer, more complex variations (as from 3:22 to 3:47—with a false ending after the high note at 3:40 before the final phrase). Although there's no sense of overall development, Riley and Williams build tension by gradually accelerating the tempo very slightly, and with impromptu accents. Williams constantly varies his runs around the basic chords; Riley's brush slaps on snare drum get more emphatic. A two-bar tag (5:15) is squeezed in behind the (anticlimactic—almost cut off) end of the scored improvisation; note the loping, reggae-like feel of the rhythm trio.
5:20	PIANO VAMP (THEME A)	Piano vamps, as at the beginning of the performance (though with fewer repeats).
5:29	THEME A (HORNS)	In feel, the closing theme closely resembles the parallel sequence at 0:21.
5:38	THEME A REPEATED	As just heard.
5:48	THEME A REPEATED	Decelerating tempo signals an ending. Note how Riley's snare drum accents drill home the new tempo. We end with a rumble of cymbal rolls, piano tremolo chords, and bass thrumming the keynote.

During the decades of white oppression of black and colored (mixed-race) peoples, black and white musicians could not play on the same stage and a jam session might be broken up by the police. Jazz became a cry for freedom, which is why the authorities suppressed it and even forbade the public from listening to banned musicians. Converting to Islam in 1968, Dollar Brand became Abdullah Ibrahim and in 1974 penned *Manenberg*, named for one of the Cape Town townships where people settled after the government demolished the homes of 60,000 black people. *Manenberg* became an anthem for those resisting the government. In 1978, the exiled South African bassist Johnny Dyani recorded *Song for Biko*, for student leader Steven Biko, killed in 1977 while in police custody.

triplet   three beats fit evenly into the time span of two, as in

tag   a phrase tagged on or added to the end of a chorus or, more commonly, a piece; the latter is formally known as a *coda*.

((•—**Hear** a profile of Abdullah Ibrahim on **mymusiclab.com**

DISCOVER JAZZ

Against this backdrop, in 1983, at the University of KwaZulu-Natal in Durban, Darius Brubeck, son of the American pianist-composer, initiated the first degree-granting course in jazz studies offered by an African university. The fall of apartheid in the early 1990s brought new freedom for the music—lessening its political urgency, but also permitting the flowering of jazz radio programs, jazz recordings, jazz festivals (for example, the Cape Town International Jazz Festival, established in 1999), a training school for youth (Johnny Mekoa's Guateng Jazz Academy), and a South African Association for Jazz Education.

After fully free elections in 1994, some exiled musicians returned home, while longtime musicians made new recordings: "Big Voice" Jack Lerole improvised on the pennywhistle in *kwela*-style jazz on *Across Africa* (2003). New artists emerged, such as Moses Taiwa Molelekwa, who fused traditional and electronic instruments in *Genes and Spirits* and stacked alluring polyrhythms in *Ntatemoholo* (both from the album *Genes and Spirits*, 1998).

Ethiopia

If South African jazz sounds different than American jazz, Ethiopian jazz sounds even more exotic to American ears, because of its "oriental" or Arabic-sounding pentatonic scales. These Ethiopian scales figure prominently in the work of composer and multi-instrumentalist Mulatu Astatke, who worked with Duke Ellington and is "the father of Ethiojazz." His recording career runs from the 1960s (*Éthiopiques 4: Ethio Jazz & Musique Instrumentale, 1969–1974*) to 2010's *I Faram Gami I Faram*. Today, Ethiopia's capital, Addis Ababa, hosts a renewed jazz scene and even a nascent African School of Jazz.

Senegal

In Senegal, jazz became popular in the 1930s through recordings of U.S. and French musicians. During World War II, U.S. servicemen stationed there introduced American recordings, instruments, and dancing styles. After the War, the then-capital city Saint Louis became a center for jazz in West Africa, as bands playing New Orleans, swing, and bop styles became popular. In the 1950s and 1960s, Cuban and Latin styles took precedence. The Saint-Louis Jazz Festival, founded in 1990, pays homage to the city's one-time jazz prominence, and ranks as one of the most important in Africa. Intriguing new jazz, some incorporating indigenous sounds, is still heard in Senegal. The Senegalese saxophonist Abdoulaye N'Diaye has mixed *kora* and other African instruments with American ones, as on *Xarrit Sama* (2001).

South African pianist Abdullah Ibrahim (a.k.a. Dollar Brand) followed mid-1960s ventures into free jazz with a return to African musical ideas, yielding music of great harmonic and rhythmic variety and emotional depth. PHOTO COURTESY ANDY FREEBERG.

Other Locales

Elsewhere, jazz has made toeholds, and mixes with other kinds of music at venues such as Burkina Faso's Festival Jazz à Ouaga, established in 1992. By 2010, partly as a draw for tourists, jazz festivals were springing up in Angola, Mozambique, Cape Verde, and other countries.

In the United States, "jazz" has been a contested term; its meaning in Africa is often at least as variable as it is stateside, and can mean simply a band playing for social dancing. But however one defines it, American jazz has influenced a wide array of African musicians, from Ghanian Highlife and Congolese *rumba* bands, singers such as South Africa's Miriam

Ladysmith Black Mambazo performs Paul Simon's Under African Skies *at BAM on April 9, 2008, in New York City.* PHOTO COURTESY AMY SUSSMAN/GETTY IMAGES.

Makeba and Cape Verde's Cesaria Evora, to the South African choral group Ladysmith Black Mambazo, the Cameroon-born electric bassist Richard Bona, and the Afropop pioneer Fela Kuti.

TAKE NOTE

- What styles of jazz are popular in Africa, and who are the dominant performers?

Global Jazz in the Twenty-First Century

In the new century, jazz musicians and musicians inspired by it continued to come from all over the globe. Guitarist and vocalist Lionel Loueke, from Benin, played intricate rhythms that reflect African pop as well as jazz (the album *Karibu*, 2008). The Syrian Jazz Orchestra was founded in 2005—in the wake of a jazz festival in Damascus produced by the Swiss embassy—and involved Syrian, Dutch, German, and Greek musicians; the Brooklyn-based, Finland-born pianist Frank Carlberg has written music for them. The Israeli scene became productive enough to start exporting players to New York. In the late 1990s,

bassist Omer Avital led a sextet every week at the Greenwich Village club Smalls, and later employed his countryman Avishai Cohen on trumpet—not to be confused with the Israeli bassist Avishai Cohen. The trumpeter also worked with two of his émigré siblings in the band 3 Cohens, as on *Braid* (2007)— recorded as his clarinetist/saxophonist sister Anat was becoming a critical favorite.

By then jazz in Europe had become so vital the English critic Stuart Nicholson frequently made the case—as in his 2005 book *Is Jazz Dead? (Or Has It Moved to a New Address)*—that European jazz had taken the lead, the American variety, in his view, having fallen into a purely retrospective phase. But the musicians he touted as jazz's new European wave were steeped in American music: Norway's Nils Petter Molvaer's plaintive trumpet, electronics, and funk rhythms owe an obvious debt to 1970s and 1980s Miles Davis; the club/dance beats of Swedish pianist Esbjörn Svensson's trio E.S.T. (*Somewhere Else Before*, 2001) derived from techno and hip-hop—like the American group Medeski Martin & Wood that came before them. Indeed, it seemed Nicholson was unaware of progressive developments in New York, Chicago, and elsewhere, dismissing a scene across the Atlantic on the basis of incomplete information—the way some Americans, knowing no better, had written off jazz abroad.

European and American musicians maintained cordial relations however—particularly in Chicago, where Germans (Peter Brötzmann), Scandinavians (Swedish saxophonist Mats Gustafsson, Norwegian bassist Ingebrigt Haaker Flaten, and drummer Paal Nilssen-Love), Austrians (trumpeter Axel Dörner), and Dutch musicians (Misha Mengelberg and other members of his ICP) collaborated with local improvisers such as saxophonist Ken Vandermark. Gustafsson, Vandermark, and Nilssen-Love all play in Brötzmann's multinational band based in Chicago on *Chicago Tentet at Molde 2007*.

✳ Explore Key Recordings on **mymusiclab.com**

TAKE NOTE

- How has global jazz continued to develop in the first decade of the twenty-first century?

TAKE NOTE

- Who were the prominent musicians who brought jazz to Europe and how has a European jazz scene developed?

The first great U.S. jazzman in Europe was clarinetist Sidney Bechet, who first toured in 1919. By the mid-1920s, singer/dancer Josephine Baker achieved overwhelming success in Paris, where many top jazz musicians performed. In 1932, the Hot Club of France was established, which later in the decade became home to guitarist Django Reinhardt and violinist Stéphane Grappelli and their famed Quintet. In the 1930s, Louis Armstrong, Duke Ellington, and Coleman Hawkins performed extensively in Western Europe. However, under some of Europe's more repressive governments, such as the Nazis in Germany and the Communists in Russia, jazz was often viewed as "decadent" music and was seriously repressed. After World War II, regional styles developed by homegrown talent led to a blossoming of jazz across Europe.

- What is the history of jazz in Asia and Oceania, and who are the vital figures creating original jazz music there?

In the decades before World War II, a small number of jazz musicians toured in Asia and Oceania, and some homegrown music was also created. However, jazz swept through Asia with renewed vigor after World War II. While jazz remains controversial in some countries—such as China and Korea—in others it has become highly popular, notably Japan. Japan has produced many leading jazz performers, including big band composer Toshiko Akiyoshi; pianist Yosuke Yamashita; and trumpeter Toshinori Kondo. Since the 1960s, there have been various collaborations between Asian and American jazz players and new musical styles created by Americans of Asian descent. Asian musicians who are living far from their homelands have also made a large impact on the jazz world, notably French–Vietnamese guitarist Nguyên Lê.

- How did jazz develop in the Middle East, and who are some of the key players?

American jazz musicians such as Dave Brubeck and Duke Ellington have explored Middle Eastern music through jazz—both in collaboration with Middle Eastern musicians and in personal interpretations of the region. While jazz is not widely performed in certain Arabic/Islamic countries where Western music is resisted, there are many jazz cultures in the region, including in Egypt, Israel, Turkey, and the Balkans. The Israeli Avishai Cohen, Turkey's Okay Temiz, and Iraqi-American Amir ElSaffar are among prominent Middle Eastern jazz players.

- Which musicians led the practice of jazz in Eastern Europe, and what were the characteristic styles?

In Eastern Europe, a region prone to political turmoil, jazz became an outlet for individual expression and a manifestation of artistic and personal freedom. Polish trumpeter Tomasz Stanko, Czech bassists George Mraz and Miroslav Vitous, Hungarian guitarists Attila Zoller and Gábor Szabó, and Lithuania's Ganelin Trio are among the more prominent Eastern European jazz players. Musically, jazz in Eastern Europe drew from American jazz, native folk traditions, and European classical music.

- What styles of jazz are popular in Africa, and who are the dominant performers?

While jazz has its roots in African music, it has developed most strongly in certain areas, notably South Africa, which has a tradition of jazz music that goes back to the 1920s. Under apartheid, jazz played a key role in expressing resistance to the regime, particularly in the work of such musicians as pianist Abdullah Ibrahim. In Ethiopia, Arabic-influenced music has been predominant, particularly in the work of composer and pianist Mulatu Astatke. Jazz has long been popular in Senegal, where saxophonist Abdoulaye N'Diaye has mixed *kora* and other African instruments with American ones.

• How has global jazz continued to develop in the first decade of the twenty-first century?

In the new century, jazz musicians and musicians inspired by it continued to come from all over the globe. Some critics even feel that the most innovative jazz being made today is occurring outside of the United States. Jazz continues to flourish globally, with a free interchange of ideas and styles occurring.

DISCUSSION QUESTIONS

1. What were some of the ways American jazz spread around the world?

2. Why would jazz be viewed as subversive by the German government during World War II and by Iron Curtain countries during the Cold War?

3. What aspects of life in Paris and other cities around Europe made those places attractive to American jazz musicians?

4. In jazz music that you have heard and can recall, identify musical elements—instruments, songs, rhythms—derived from countries other than the United States.

5. Identify some of the technological advances of the twentieth century that contributed to the spread of jazz worldwide.

6. In light of jazz's spread to many parts of the globe, do you think it is still American music? Whose music is it?

KEY TERMS & KEY PEOPLE

Han Bennink 300
chordophone 306
darbouka (dumbek) 306
fake book 296
gamelan 305
Jan Garbarek 299
Giorgio Gaslini 299
Stéphane Grappelli 291
Lars Gullin 298
Joe Harriott 299
Abdullah Ibrahim 299

Instant Composers Pool
 Orchestra 301
klezmer 308
koto 305
Nguyên Lê 304
maqam 306
Niels-Henning Ørsted
 Pedersen 300
oud ('ūd) 306
Oregon 299
qānūn 307

Django Reinhardt 291
Ravi Shankar 300
Shakti 300
sitar 300
Gábor Szabó 310
tabla 300
taksim (taqsūm) 306
township jazz 299
Sam Wooding 294

CHAPTER 12

Jazz Forward

by José Antonio Bowen

TAKE NOTE

- How has mainstream acoustic jazz continued to flourish and develop?
- How has the avant-garde jazz movement of the 1960s and 1970s evolved and who are some of its key performers?
- How have some musicians begun to rethink the definition of jazz beyond the classic division between mainstream and avant-garde?
- Who are some of today's leading vocalists and vocal groups, and what roles do they play on the current jazz scene?

HISTORICAL EVENTS		MUSICAL EVENTS

1975 — Ornette Coleman's Prime Time band debuts its "free funk" musical style

1976 — Saxophonists David Murray, Hamiet Bluiett, Oliver Lake, and Julius Hemphill form the World Saxophone Quartet to explore free jazz music

1980 — President Reagan elected, moving the country to the right

1981 — Wynton Marsalis makes his first world tour at age 20 as trumpeter with the VSOP quartet

1984 — Alto sax player Steve Coleman forms the M-Base collective to explore wedding hip-hop and funk rhythms with jazz

1986 — Iran-Contra Affair shows United States secretly sold weapons to Iran to fund fighting rebels in Central America

1987 — Composer/saxophone player John Zorn forms the punk-jazz group Naked City with guitarist Bill Frisell and keyboardist Wayne Horvitz

1988 — Jazz at Lincoln Center Orchestra debuts

PHOTO COURTESY CARDAF/SHUTTERSTOCK.

1989 — Berlin Wall falls, leading to the reunification of East and West Germany, as the Iron Curtain crumbles

1990 — Smithsonian Jazz Masterworks Orchestra established

1992 — Bill Clinton elected President, bringing Democrats back to power

1997 — Wynton Marsalis's *Blood on the Fields* is awarded a Pulitzer Prize, the first for a jazz composition

1999 — Clinton impeached for having sex with a White House intern; he is eventually acquitted

2001 — • "9/11": United States attacked by Al Qaeda and the World Trade Center is destroyed
• Apple launches iPod player and digital music-listening revolution

2002 — The Smithsonian Institution launches the first national Jazz Appreciation Month (celebrated each April)

2003 — United States invades Iraq, toppling dictator Saddam Hussein

2004 — Jazz at Lincoln Center opens its own facility on New York's Columbus Circle, featuring three performance halls

2008 — U.S. economy crashes

2009 — Barack Obama becomes first African American president of the United States

PHOTO COURTESY ALAN FREED/SHUTTERSTOCK.

❋ Explore the Jazz Timeline on **mymusiclab.com**

Jazz has always been a music of fusion and change: many of its players welcome new influences and actively seek innovation. But at the same time, because musical sounds are evanescent and musical styles constantly evolve, cultures must work to preserve the music of the past. So in jazz, the creation of new work has been accompanied by preservation of the old.

In the 1930s, swing bands powered ahead as preservationists looked back to earlier styles from New Orleans. In the 1960s, as experimental sounds echoed through Greenwich Village, vintage Dixieland jazz could be heard as well. In the 1970s, just as jazz-rock fusion was gaining momentum, a flood of new acoustic jazz records appeared.

Change *and* preservation: that's the way it has been with jazz since the music's early years, and the combination continues into the present. Change has occurred along several interacting paths: fusing with surrounding styles, experimenting with the very foundations of jazz construction, and interacting with world cultures.

The tendency for jazz to fuse with other styles of music has been a theme from the beginning. Jazz was born a hybrid. In New Orleans, jazz was fashioned from European brass band music, African drumming, Delta blues, Missouri ragtime, old hymns, Spanish rhythms, and popular Tin Pan Alley songs.

Contemporary saxophone player Steve Coleman.

PHOTO COURTESY
MICHAEL JACKSON.

In each new style, jazz's emphasis on spontaneous improvisation led to a search for greater freedom. The beboppers wanted to play longer solos, free from having to follow the melody of popular songs, while players of cool jazz experimented with new textures and time signatures. Modal jazz freed players from having to follow chord changes, and players of free jazz sought sonic, harmonic, formal, and rhythmic freedom. The early jazz-rock fusion of Miles Davis, Weather Report, and Mahavishnu Orchestra was really a continuation of free jazz with an added emphasis on new electronic sounds, collective improvisation, and constant experimentation with rhythm, grooves, and meter.

The introduction of world music influences also brought forth new innovations in jazz. Latin jazz was inspired by the hope to reconnect more directly with African rhythm and be free of some of the European binary (march) rhythms of traditional swing. The new rhythms and scales of Indian music also offered freedom from Western conventions. Players from the United States and around the world fused jazz with native or ethnic musics in the continuing desire to find something new. These new fusions all involved improvisation over a rhythmic or harmonic repeating pattern, shareable across styles and cultures, so the basic language of jazz became a sort of new *lingua franca* for music making.

All of this occurred with remarkable speed, which brings up another constant theme in jazz: the unprecedented pace of change. Some eras of Western classical music lasted for longer than a century. But jazz generated its key historic styles—from New Orleans to big band swing, bebop, cool, hard bop, avant-garde, and fusion—in about 60 years. This pace continues as jazz evolves.

Balancing the "preservation" part of the jazz equation against the imperatives of change—maintaining the best of the old even as innovators invent the new—created debate and controversy about jazz and its definition. New Orleans revivalists argued against beboppers about the true nature of jazz. Mainstream purists denounced fusion as a sellout. Even when a revival movement appeared in jazz, it was usually accompanied by an alternative approach and a fresh battle over the definition of jazz.

Five broad phenomena that propelled jazz through its initial development continued to do so as jazz reached the end of its first century and entered its second:

1. Fusings: Jazz musicians sought to fuse jazz with an increasing diversity of other musical cultures and sounds, and players continued to interact with popular music grooves, techniques, and repertoire.

2. Neotraditional movement: In reaction to the experimentation of the avant-garde and jazz-rock fusion, a **neotraditional** movement arose—centering on trumpeter **Wynton Marsalis**—who sought to return jazz to its blues roots, while elevating the importance of key performer/composers such as Louis Armstrong and Duke Ellington.

3. Quest for the new: At the same time, an army of experimental and avant-garde players maintained their quest for change and new forms of freedom. The variety of these paths meant that the sound of jazz continued to diversify: any two jazz performances of the early twenty-first century were likely to be more different than ever before.

4. Accelerating change: The pace of change didn't let up: the tendency of jazz to fuse and morph accelerated in the jazz of the 1980s and beyond.

5. Redefining jazz: A group of jazz revivalists challenged the jazz practices of exploration with a new definition of jazz. This movement stoked controversy about the definition of jazz in the twenty-first century. The question became, "If all of these different sounds can be jazz, then what is jazz?"

The Continuing Life of Mainstream Acoustic Jazz

What jazz *was*, in its mainstream form, never disappeared. While jazz-rock fusion brought new attention to jazz in the

1970s, the core jazz approach—based on bop and swing—expanded during the same period. In 1970 and after, every jazz style ever created was still being played, and it was still possible to hear many of the legends who had created these styles: Louis Armstrong, Duke Ellington, Count Basie, Benny Goodman, Dizzy Gillespie, Ella Fitzgerald, Sarah Vaughan, Art Blakey, Charles Mingus, and Dave Brubeck were all still performing. Other players who had moved to Europe, such as Dexter Gordon and Stan Getz, returned to live in the United States and began recording again.

While the major record companies largely abandoned jazz for rock during the 1960s, several new companies appeared in the 1970s to keep the jazz tradition alive. In 1973, Norman Granz, who had earlier established Verve Records, founded Pablo Records and built an extraordinary roster of legendary jazz performers. Another label, Concord Records, was started in California by Carl Jefferson in the same year to record seasoned West Coast players.

Formal jazz education also focused primarily on core jazz principles associated with the mainstream. The initial rise of jazz education came in the 1970s. High school jazz bands and many university programs were founded, while a handful of educators—among them Jamey Aebersold, David Baker, and Jerry Coker—published educational materials that became standard. While every aspiring bass player knew the bass line from Herbie Hancock's *Chameleon* and every trumpet player wanted to be Maynard Ferguson playing *Gonna Fly Now* (the theme from the 1976 film

Dexter Gordon enjoyed renewed acclaim late in his career. PHOTO COURTESY ANDY FREEBERG.

---

neotraditional jazz   mainstream jazz as preserved and practiced by some jazz musicians in the 1990s, most notably Wynton Marsalis.

David Baker, musical and artistic director of the Smithsonian Jazz Masterworks Orchestra. PHOTO COURTESY THE SMITHSONIAN INSTITUTION.

Institutional Jazz Programs

It is perhaps ironic that jazz—noted for its outside-the-mainstream, anti-establishment ethos—has gained a great deal of support from public and private institutions over the last few decades.

Some wondered whether institutional involvement would change the music for the worse. But the arguments for such support were compelling: to preserve the growing history of jazz, to give jazz a stronger economic footing, to present it as a music equal in value to any other, and to help it reach new audiences.

Among the first institutions to embrace jazz were Tulane University in New Orleans and Hunter College in New York, each of which set up a jazz archive in the 1950s. (Hunter's Institute of Jazz Studies moved in 1966 to Rutgers University in Newark, New Jersey.) In 1971, the Smithsonian Institution in Washington, DC, established a presence in jazz that grew to be the world's most comprehensive set of jazz programs, including collections of memorabilia, artifacts, and oral histories, and the production of exhibitions, recordings, books, educational material, symposia, concerts, and radio and multimedia programs. The Smithsonian Jazz Masterworks Orchestra, founded in 1990 under the batons of David Baker and Gunther Schuller, plays the riches of the jazz repertory in the nation's capital and on national and international tours.

In the 1980s and 1990s, a number of other institutions got into the act.

Founded in 1986, the Washington-based Thelonious Monk Institute for Jazz has focused on nurturing young jazz performers, while the Kennedy Center, under advisor Billy Taylor, presented an ambitious series of concerts and school programs. The Library of Congress undertook a program of commissions to jazz composers. New York's Jazz at Lincoln Center, under the artistic direction of the charismatic Wynton Marsalis, developed its widely touring Jazz at Lincoln Center Orchestra in 1988, as well as the Essentially Ellington high school band contest (begun in 1995), a radio series, and lecture and film programs. In 2004, Jazz at Lincoln Center opened a new facility at Columbus Circle with three impressive performance halls, and as of 2011 offered 450 events per year in New York City and elsewhere. Carnegie Hall established its Carnegie Hall Jazz Band under trumpeter Jon Faddis in 1992 (although the band folded due to budget cuts in 2003), while the Brooklyn Academy of Music launched a cutting-edge performance series under clarinetist **Don Byron**.

Efforts began elsewhere in the United States to create jazz repertory orchestras and homes for jazz performance series and jazz archives. Among the latter were the Chicago Jazz Archive at the University of Chicago and the California Institute for the Preservation of Jazz at California State University, Long Beach.

The National Endowment for the Arts, founded in 1965, provided a modest stream of grants over the years for jazz and each year from 1982 to 2012, honored a series of distinguished musicians as NEA Jazz Masters. In the 1990s, three foundations stepped in to raise the ante: the Doris Duke Charitable Foundation; the Louis Armstrong Educational Foundation; and the largest jazz philanthropic donor of the twentieth century, the Lila Wallace-Reader's Digest Fund, whose grants included $7.5 million to the Smithsonian for a 10-year initiative of jazz programs and $6.9 million to National Public Radio.

European institutions include the National Jazz Archive in Amsterdam; the Norsk Jazzarkiv in Oslo; the Institute for Jazz Research in Graz, Austria; and the Jazz-Institut at Darmstadt, Germany.

—*John Edward Hasse*

Rocky), all of the new educational bands, programs, and materials were based on bebop as the essential style. Jazz-rock fusion might be on the radio, but acoustic jazz was in every classroom.

The presence of acoustic jazz hardly diminished in the 1980s. Trumpeter Clark Terry remained active as did saxophonists Phil Woods, Stan Getz, Dexter Gordon, and Sonny Rollins. There were also several important reunions of classic groups. Starting in 1981, the Modern Jazz Quartet reunited for regular concerts (with the same lineup they had maintained since 1955) and continued recording until 1993. Pianist Oscar Peterson also reunited with guitarist Herb Ellis and bassist Ray Brown, and the Heath Brothers (saxophonist Jimmy, bassist Percy, and drummer Albert "Tootie") went back on the road.

For an art form steeped in an aesthetic of change, it is hardly surprising that the history of jazz is dominated by young radicals reinventing the music of their elders. So jazz (like rock) has remained a challenge for older players. Do you play your old hits and abandon the fire of change that motivated you from the beginning, or do you continue to seek freedom and spontaneity even if it means reinventing your own style? For years Dave Brubeck avoided playing *Take Five*, but by the 1990s, he gave in and began including it at every concert. An exception, Miles Davis remarkably reinvented himself and jazz in surprising new ways throughout his career.

While producer Norman Granz introduced recordings of the "Great American Songbook" with Ella Fitzgerald and Oscar Peterson in the 1950s, jazz musicians in the 1960s and 1970s were keen on recording their own material. In the 1980s, however, collections of standards again became a mainstay for jazz players. This return to a format that once drew criticism for being populist and conservative occurred in the rock world, too: In 1983, rock singer Linda Ronstadt's album *What's New*, with arrangements by Frank Sinatra's arranger Nelson Riddle, proved the existence of a large audience for collections of standards; a host of aging rockers followed in her footsteps. Jazz singers, who had been interpreting standards all along, enjoyed growing audiences for their shows and recordings.

Through the 1980s and 1990s, the issues remained much the same for mainstream jazz musicians: the style and repertoire were established and were reinforced by both a graying audience and jazz schools. Most older musicians simply continued to play the same tunes in much the same style, and several found renewed success in the guise of "old masters."

Stan Getz, after popular success with the bossa nova in the 1960s and experiments with Chick Corea in the 1970s, returned in the late 1980s to his favorite ballads with a deepened sound and commitment to make some of his greatest recordings—with a quartet that included pianist Kenny Barron, bassist Rufus Reid, and drummer Victor Lewis. Saxophonist Joe Henderson, pianist Andrew Hill, and trombonist J. J. Johnson all returned to major labels and to critical success. Saxophonist Sonny Rollins continued to be as edgy and as popular as ever. On September 18, 2007, the 76-year-old Rollins returned to Carnegie Hall, 50 years after his debut there, to play with both his regular sextet and the 82-year-old (and equally young-sounding) drummer Roy Haynes.

Art Blakey was another powerful keeper of the flame. Like Miles Davis, Blakey also liked to hire young musicians, but Blakey continued to train them in his own thunderous style of hard bop. After the celebrated editions of his **Jazz Messengers** of the late 1950s (*Moanin'*; *JTSA* Disc 4/Track 1) and early 1960s (*One by One*; *JTSA* Disc 5/Track 1), the group made fewer recordings through the 1970s until Wynton and **Branford Marsalis** joined the band in 1980.

Watch the video *Build A New World* by Art Blakey and the Jazz Messengers on **mymusiclab.com**

Veteran bassist Ray Brown.
PHOTO COURTESY PAUL J. HOEFFLER/DOWN BEAT ARCHIVES.

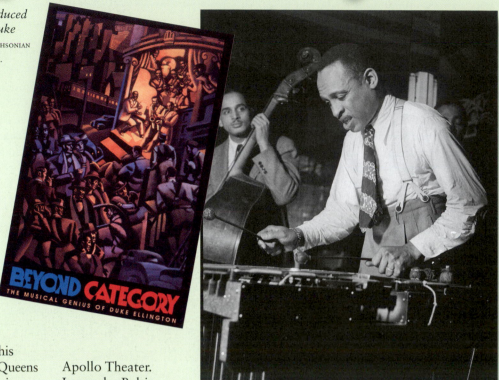

Jazz Museums

The need for the preservation of jazz history has propelled several major museums and institutions to collect jazz materials over the last half-century, and more new museums open from time to time.

In the East, Louis Armstrong's house (3456 107th Street in Queens, New York City) is open to visitors, and a selection of his memorabilia is on display at Queens College, which houses the Louis Armstrong Archives. In Manhattan, Jazz at Lincoln Center offers a small "Hall of Fame" display and periodic exhibits of photographs. Uptown, the National Jazz Museum in Harlem, until a regular museum is built, maintains a small visitors' center and organizes weekly public programs such as panel discussions and lectures.

Beginning in 1988, the Smithsonian Institution's National Museum of American History has displayed some of its national jazz treasures, which include the vast, 200,000-page Ellington archive as well as Dizzy Gillespie's angled-bell trumpet; the clarinets of Benny Goodman and Artie Shaw; the drum sets of Buddy Rich and Gene Krupa; the band "library" of Jimmie Lunceford; John Coltrane's manuscript for *A Love Supreme*; artifacts from Miles Davis, Thelonious Monk, Herbie Hancock, and Tito Puente; photographs by Herman Leonard and William Claxton; 350 films; and papers of Ella Fitzgerald and the

Apollo Theater. In nearby Baltimore, the Eubie Blake National Jazz Institute offers exhibits on this Baltimore-born ragtime and popular music composer/performer, along with Chick Webb, Cab Calloway, and Billie Holiday.

The South has a growing number of jazz sites. The Louisiana State Museum, in New Orleans, maintains a continuing exhibition on New Orleans jazz, while the city-owned Louis Armstrong Park features statues of hometown heroes Armstrong and Sidney Bechet. Also in the Crescent City, the New Orleans Jazz National Historical Park has rehabilitated Perseverance Hall near the old Congo Square and operates a visitors center in the French Quarter providing information, walking tours, demonstrations, and educational performances. In Florence, Alabama, the W. C. Handy birthplace (602 West College Street) is open to visitors, while

Hall of Famer Lionel Hampton performing in New York City (ca. 1946). PHOTO COURTESY WILLIAM P. GOTTLIEB/WILLIAM P. GOTTLIEB COLLECTION/LIBRARY OF CONGRESS PRINTS & PHOTOGRAPHS DIVISION.

the Alabama Jazz Hall of Fame, in Birmingham, honors 200 native sons and daughters, including Erskine Hawkins, Lionel Hampton, and Dinah Washington.

In the Midwest, the library at Indiana University in Bloomington features a Hoagy Carmichael room, displaying his jazz- and song-related memorabilia. In St. Louis, you can tour the restored Scott Joplin House State Historic Site (2658 Delmar). In Kansas City, Missouri, the handsome American Jazz Museum, in the historic 18th and Vine District, offers memorabilia of local musicians and has a performance space.

Out West, there is a Glenn Miller exhibit, chockablock with memorabilia, at his alma mater, the University of Colorado in Boulder.

—*John Edward Hasse*

Wynton Marsalis and the Hard Bop Revival

Despite all of the wonderful music being made by these old masters, it took an articulate young man from New Orleans to make mainstream acoustic jazz fashionable again. With a distinguished jazz pianist as a father, a childhood in the Baptist church, and a classical music education that included the Tanglewood Music Center and the Juilliard School of Music, Wynton Marsalis had the perfect pedigree to become the spokesman for a new jazz age.

Recognition came quickly. Marsalis had barely arrived at Juilliard in 1978 before he was playing with Blakey (in 1980), with whom he stayed for only a year before leaving at the age of 20 to tour the United States and Japan with the former Miles Davis rhythm section comprising pianist Herbie Hancock, bassist Ron Carter, and drummer Tony Williams. In 1982 he signed with Columbia Records and soon became the first musician to win Grammy Awards for both classical and jazz albums in the same year.

Marsalis's first quintet featured his brother Branford, drummer Jeff "Tain" Watts, and pianist Kenny Kirkland. His early groups were eclectic and carefully constructed, but they had mixed success. Indications of a personal style were evident on the album *Black Codes (from the Underground)* (1985), which featured changing time signatures and unusual phrase lengths. However, its absence of the names of the other musicians on the album cover—unusual in jazz—invited speculation about Marsalis's collegiality. When Branford and Kirkland left the band to tour with rock singer-composer Sting, Marsalis became publically angry. Controversy came slowly to Marsalis, but calling out his brother for playing "some [expletive] that's being called jazz" made it clear that Marsalis was already on a crusade to define jazz.

Three months later Marsalis formed a new group, retaining drummer Watts and bassist Robert Leslie Hurst III from the previous group and adding the remarkable blind pianist Marcus Roberts, who walked in with all of Marsalis's earlier material memorized. *J Mood* (1985) and *Marsalis Standard Time Vol. 1* (1986) followed quickly, and while the structures, texture, and meters were still complex, the finicky virtuosity of the earlier albums now seemed better reconciled with the imperfections of improvisation and the lyricism of his melodic style. Then in December 1989, Marsalis made his last recording in this style: "I knew

Drummer/bandleader Art Blakey in 1992.
PHOTO COURTESY MARC MARNIE/ REDFERNS/GETTY IMAGES.

that when I did that album *[Live] at Blues Alley*," he said, "that I wasn't going to make another record in that type of style—all those really complex rhythms, playing fast, wild."

Over the next two years, Marsalis's thinking, life, and music would undergo a remarkable transformation. First, he quit classical music: "I found there was not enough time for me to pay respects to the unarguable greatness of European music or jazz. . . . The time I spent bludgeoning Haydn could have been devoted to learning how to swing and reaching a functional appreciation of the blues." Second, he became deeply interested in early jazz, especially the music of Louis Armstrong and Duke Ellington. In 1988 he agreed to become the chair of a new task force to perpetuate New Orleans music. Third, he came to see the blues as fundamental not just as music, but as the social and ritualistic cornerstone of the black experience in America. In this he was influenced by his growing relationship with critic Stanley Crouch and by Albert Murray's book *Stomping the Blues*. The Marsalis-Crouch-Murray position became an increasingly

Watch the video of *Well, You Needn't* by VSOP on mymusiclab.com

The talented Marsalis clan has matched the prominence of such other jazz families as the Boswell Sisters (Connie, Martha, and Vet), the Jones brothers (Hank, Elvin, and Thad), the Montgomery brothers (Wes, Monk, and Buddy), and the Heath brothers (Jimmy, Percy, and Tootie). After Wynton Marsalis gained fame in the 1980s, national attention eventually turned to

✳ Explore on mymusiclab.com

the sources of his talent. A New Orleans upbringing proved to be part of it, but so did the influential presence of a musical father, Ellis. The father and four brothers, as a family, won a National Endowment for the Arts Jazz Masters Award in 2011.

Ellis Marsalis • Piano

The patriarch of the family, Ellis Marsalis is a well-known jazz pianist and educator. He nurtured the careers of many New Orleans jazz musicians, including his own children.

Branford Marsalis • Soprano Saxophone

Branford has had the most eclectic career of any of the Marsalis offspring. Besides performing in his brother's first quintet from 1981 to 1985, he gained recognition for his work with the pop singer Sting and as leader of the *Tonight Show* television band from 1992 to 1995. During the first decade of the twenty-first century, he performed primarily with classical ensembles and focused on composition.

Jason Marsalis • Drums

Jason is considerably younger than his other musician brothers. He has developed a distinct style as a drummer based on his training in classical and Brazilian percussion. In 2001, he made his first recordings on the vibraphone.

PHOTO COURTESY JACK VARTOOGIAN/FRONT ROW PICTURES.

Wynton Marsalis • Trumpet

Wynton, the best known of the Marsalis clan, burst onto the jazz scene in the early 1980s and drew accolades as the next great trumpet player. Winning Grammy Awards for both classical and jazz trumpet performance in 1983, Marsalis became a leader of the neotraditional jazz movement. He became known for his criticism of jazz-rock and fusion, and especially of Miles Davis, whom he felt had turned his back on jazz. Marsalis was named the founding Artistic Director of Jazz at Lincoln Center in 2004.

Delfeayo Marsalis • Trombone

Delfeayo is better known as a record producer than as an active trombonist, but he does perform and record both with his family and his own groups. He has also scored music for television, the off-Broadway stage, and ballet.

prescriptive lament that jazz needed to return to its (somewhat romanticized) roots in the blues.

All of these influences can immediately be heard in *The Majesty of the Blues* (1989) and in the three-volume *Soul Gestures in Southern Blue* (1991). The classical tone, intricate meter shifts, and complex modern harmonies of the previous albums are replaced with growling and muted trumpet, slow deep grooves, and a wide variety of blues, a form that hardly appears in his early work. The reorientation toward New Orleans is completed with some clarinet, "tailgate" style trombone, and even some banjo playing.

While it was significant that Marsalis had changed his style, a fourth change in his life was much more significant for the future of jazz. In the summer of 1987, already perhaps more famous and influential than any previous jazz player, the 26-year-old Marsalis became the co-founder of the first jazz series at Lincoln Center in New York: Classical Jazz. This acceptance of jazz into the institutions of high art was welcomed, but the idea of jazz as an institution seemed paradoxical. As artistic director of Jazz at Lincoln Center, Marsalis soon led an empire with competitions, commissions, a big band, a national education program, and, eventually, its own concert venues. Unlike previous jazz musicians whose influence was limited to the response to their music, Marsalis was now an institution himself, and his new vision of jazz became public policy. He gave frequent interviews, had his own national TV and radio programs, and wrote articles, letters, and books. His programming (initially only black artists, but excluding the then-living Miles Davis) became the subject of comment and controversy.

Marsalis's criticism of Miles Davis, if Marsalis were solely a musician, would have been controversial but ultimately just gossip. But as the head of the premier national jazz institution, Marsalis had an impact on who got heard. "Did some people lose some gigs because I don't like their style of music?" he asked. "Maybe that's true, maybe that's false, I don't know.

History & Culture

The Big Band Revival

After the swing era, the costs of maintaining big bands became prohibitive and the primary focus of jazz shifted to smaller units. Yet the big band sound continued to thrill, and over the years a variety of orchestras kept the unique big band experience alive.

The classic big band sound, with its accent on swing and its adherence to smooth ensemble lines, remained an important jazz niche and the focus of preservation-oriented jazz enterprises. Incarnations of the orchestras of Duke Ellington, Count Basie, Glenn Miller, and other swing bandleaders maintained demanding schedules performing in towns and cities across the United States and elsewhere. Repertory orchestras—purveying historic sounds and revitalizing traditions—emerged in the form of the Jazz at Lincoln Center Orchestra, the Smithsonian Jazz Masterworks Orchestra, and city-based units such as the Chicago Jazz Orchestra and outfits in New Orleans, Dallas, Columbus, Seattle, and elsewhere.

College and high school jazz education provided a platform for continuation of the big band tradition. University bands, such as the University of Wisconsin-Madison Big Band, remained standard formats for jazz study and performance.

More experimental big bands emerged alongside the classic ones. Through the second half of the twentieth century and into the twenty-first, some big bands absorbed elements from classical, rock, and other types of music to create a new kind of swing that was more suited for listening than dancing. Bandleaders such as pianists Carla Bley, Toshiko Akiyoshi, and McCoy Tyner; bassists Charlie Haden and William Parker; saxophonist **David Murray**; and composer Maria Schneider were among the better-known exponents of this newer approach. Influences on these innovators ranged from Basie and Ellington to Gil Evans and Charles Mingus. Indeed, the Mingus Big Band, a unit dedicated to its namesake's work, attracted a devoted following for its surprising and energetic sounds.

Other notable big bands included the Vanguard Jazz Orchestra, which began life as a band co-led by trumpeter Thad Jones and drummer Mel Lewis, and the Sun Ra Arkestra, which carried on the name of its visionary pianist-bandleader.

—*Calvin Wilson and Tad Lathrop*

Hear Maria Schneider discuss her piece *Concert in the Garden* on **mymusiclab.com**

But that's not controversial to me." But with this public persona and his ability to program his personal version of classic jazz, Marsalis set the terms for a new debate about the definition and future of jazz. This has made him perhaps the most important figure in jazz of the time, but also the most polarizing.

Still only in his thirties, but with a new septet and the new Jazz at Lincoln Center Orchestra at his disposal, in the early 1990s Marsalis turned his musical attention toward composition. Inspired by Ellington, Marsalis created postmodern epic journeys that mixed earlier jazz styles. *Citi Movement* (1993) is a 21-movement, two-hour suite written as

music for *Griot New York*, a modern ballet created by Garth Fagan (later a Tony Award winner for his choreography of Broadway's *The Lion King*). The movement *Down the Avenue* has a steady swing feel but is still a study in contrasts and references to the history of jazz. One minute the band plays almost a parody of 1930s dance-hall music, but then an edgy bop saxophone solo floats through, alternating with some New Orleans clarinet and growling trombone. The equally successful and lengthy *In This House, On This Morning* (1994) followed. While improvisation is still featured and the blues and the sounds of New Orleans made up the raw materials, Marsalis's music became increasingly intricate and composed. This period culminated in his three-hour oratorio *Blood on the Fields*, which, in 1997, became the first jazz composition to win the Pulitzer Prize in Music.

((•)) **Hear** a profile of Wynton Marsalis on **mymusiclab.com**

Listening Guide

((•)) **Listen** to *Down the Avenue* by Wynton Marsalis Septet on **mymusiclab.com**
CD II, Track 14/Download Track 38

DOWN THE AVENUE • WYNTON MARSALIS SEPTET

Music: Wynton Marsalis. Personnel: Wynton Marsalis (trumpet); Todd Williams (tenor saxophone); Wessell Anderson (alto saxophone); Wycliffe Gordon (trombone); Reginald Veal (bass); Herlin Riley (drums); Eric Reed (piano). Recorded July 27–28, 1992, in New York City. First issue: *Citi Movement (Griot New York)*, Columbia C2K 53324, 1993. Timing: 4:45.

Overview

Down the Avenue is the fourth of 21 movements from *Citi Movement*, one of the many extended works written by Wynton Marsalis in the 1990s after he turned his attention to the blues, his New Orleans roots, and the music of Duke Ellington (who also wrote suites). Marsalis would go on to compose even longer suites for even larger forces,

including the Pulitzer Prize–winning three-hour oratorio *Blood on the Fields* for his Jazz at Lincoln Center Orchestra, but *Citi Movement* is a more tightly constructed work for his working septet of the time. Its seamless mix of improvisation and composition across a variety of older styles simultaneously looks both forward and backward, while the relaxed but driving swing would be a model for any era.

Key Features

- The composition juxtaposes rhythmic feels and styles of different jazz eras. These self-conscious references to older styles were a hallmark of postmodernism in art but a new occurrence in jazz.
- Even the two parts of each chorus (A and B) seem from different

eras: A is twice as long and modal, while the B is a traditional harmonic sequence.
- While there is a basic A (16 bars) + B (8 bars) form to each chorus, the piece does not follow the typical head arrangement of bebop. Instead, the short solos and prearranged material are often mixed in the same chorus to blur the boundary between improvisation and composition.
- The "melody" first occurs as a "background" behind a tenor sax solo, thus also blurring the lines between background and foreground. In retrospect the first A is an introduction and the second A (0:20) is the opening statement of the theme.

—*José Antonio Bowen*

While Marsalis was looking toward the jazz past for inspiration, his brother Branford turned his attention to improvisation in a wide range of contexts, along the way becoming one of the most underrated big brothers in musical history. After playing with jazz veterans such as Dizzy Gillespie and Miles Davis, Branford explored collaborations with rock performers Sting, Tina Turner, and the Grateful Dead. He led the Tonight Show Band on NBC television, formed the hip-hop inspired band Buckshot LeFonque, and pursued greater freedom and flexibility in his solos in a piano-less trio with drummer Jeff "Tain" Watts and bassist Rob Hurst—the rhythm section he had left in his brother's band in 1985. Rarely has a single musician explored such diverse areas of music.

Branford and Wynton were among four brothers—the others being Jason and Delfeayo—who followed in the footsteps of musician father Ellis Marsalis, Jr. Pianist Ellis exerted a powerful influence as one of the relatively few New Orleans locals to specialize in mainstream styles instead of traditional New Orleans jazz. His own recordings feature elegant playing and a deep appreciation of swing. Jason, as a drummer, and Delfeayo, as a trombonist and producer, also established themselves as excellent professional musicians. In 2011, all five were given the prestigious NEA (National Endowment for the Arts) Jazz Masters Award—an unprecedented family honor.

TAKE NOTE

- How has mainstream acoustic jazz continued to flourish and develop?

TIME	SECTION	MELODY/INSTRUMENTATION
0:00	A (16 BARS)	The movement begins with a tenor sax solo over backgrounds from the other horns and a solid swing foundation with four beats to the bar.
0:20	A (16 BARS)	The solo continues, but the "background" horn line now starts to sound like a melody.
0:40	B (8 BARS)	The horns play quiet, long tones, acting like the piano, while the bass solos, changing the rhythmic feel.
0:51	A (16 BARS)	Both the tenor sax solo and the horn "background" return as in the previous A section.
1:12	B (8 BARS)	The quiet bridge returns, but this time with a piano solo over a two-beat feel from bass and a dainty riff from the band as "background." For a moment, we seem to be in an elegant 1930s ballroom with a swing band.
1:22	A+B (16 + 8 BARS)	A trumpet solos with only the rhythm section as background.
1:54	A (16 BARS)	An alto sax solo competes with the band "background" that is led this time by the soprano saxophone and seems to be an inverted (upside-down) and harmonized (multiple notes at once) version of the earlier "background."
2:15	B (8 BARS)	The trombone and soprano sax solo together in a reminiscence of old New Orleans.
2:25	A+ B (16+8 BARS)	The piano solos with only the rhythm section as background.
2:56	A (16 BARS)	The "upside-down" version of the "background" is heard alone, played by the entire band with no soloing.
3:16	B (8 BARS)	The alto sax gets to finish his solo chorus (started at 1:54, but interrupted at 2:15) while the band plays a background of quiet long tones.
3:27	C (20 BARS)	A new double-time section begins with call-and-response falls (that sound like simulated whistles or car horns) from the brass at twice the speed in the rhythm section.
3:40	C' (10 BARS/ 20 BARS IN DOUBLE-TIME)	Stop time: the drums and bass stop playing time and only play the "hits" with the horns. The C' section is the same length as C, but the feel of the speed is cut in half again.
3:54	A (16 BARS)	The piano solos over the "background" as it appeared in the beginning (0:20), and it is now clear this is the "melody" of the piece.
4:14	B (8 BARS)	The piano and bass solo over the quiet bridge with the "dainty riff" in the band from the second chorus, but the drums stay in the four-to-a-bar pulse.
4:25	½ A (8 BARS)	We hear the first half only of the inverted and harmonized "melody" from the band.
4:35	POSTSCRIPT	The band alone (without the rhythm section) adds a slower short postscript.

Avant-Garde Jazz Continues to Grow

Left out by Marsalis at Lincoln Center, avant-garde jazz and free improvisation continued to thrive further "downtown" in Manhattan lofts such as the Ladies' Fort and Studio Rivbea, and in clubs such as 8BC, the Knitting Factory, and Tonic. While Marsalis was busy raising money to build a new kind of exclusive jazz house, these clubs celebrated experimental music of all kinds, from the free improvisation of Terry Riley, Pauline Oliveros, and **John Zorn** and the performance art of Laurie Anderson to the minimalism of La Monte Young and Steve Reich. Experimental jazz, rock, punk, and no-wave bands shared the stage with classical and conceptual artists. The Kitchen, initially a venue for video art, was soon a place where the music from Philip Glass, Rocco Di Pietro, and Brian Eno could interact with other art forms. Instead of trying to limit what jazz could be, these "new music" artists were interested in expanding and fusing jazz with other experimental musics.

While hardly old, many of the pioneers of free jazz were now elder statesmen of this alternative jazz culture. After playing in lofts in the early 1970s, free-jazz

innovator **Ornette Coleman**'s response to rock and fusion was to add multiple electronic guitars to his new band, **Prime Time**, to create a music some called "free funk." Their first album, *Dancing in Your Head* (1975), was typically eclectic and included traditional musicians from Jajouka, Morocco. Once again, Coleman was prescient: this simultaneous fusion of jazz with both world and rock influences would become common in the twenty-first century.

Coleman's interest in the electric guitar led to performances with Jerry Garcia (of the jam-rock group the Grateful Dead) and a **Pat Metheny** collaboration (*Song X*, 1985) that became *Down Beat*'s Record of the Year. Classical commissions and further public recognition followed. Coleman brought his original quartet back together with—and in contrast with—Prime Time for the double album *In All Languages* (1987) and the Tufts University commission *DNA Meets E=MC²*, which Coleman described as a duel between the acoustic (natural) and the electric (atomic) forces of the universe. In the 1990s, Prime Time experimented with dancers, video, and even an appearance from French philosopher Jacques Derrida. With the first Guggenheim Fellowship awarded to any jazz musician and a Pulitzer Prize for *Sound Grammar* (2007), Coleman continues in his seventies to perform alternatives to the Marsalis jazz orthodoxy.

Cecil Taylor was also awarded a Guggenheim and continued to perform and record for solo piano (*For Olim*, 1986), with his Feel Trio of the 1990s with bassist William Parker and drummer Tony Oxley, and for some even larger big-band projects. Pianist and composer **Anthony Braxton**, who joined the Association for Advancement of Creative Musicians (AACM) in 1966 and later taught at Wesleyan University, also continued as one of the most prolific and rapacious musicians in history, recording more than 100 albums as he attempted to rework the entire musical tradition.

Coleman, Taylor, and Braxton all embraced both jazz improvisation and classical composition. While they shared rejection by the jazz establishment, their awards—all have won MacArthur Fellowships (informally referred to as "genius" awards)—testify to their welcome by the academy. It was an unexpected paradox of the 1980s that both the most traditional jazz (Marsalis) and most experimental (Coleman, Taylor, and Braxton) would find different sorts of institutional acceptance and in radically different venues.

Free jazz appeared to have a new proponent in the person of reedman David Murray, who had been influenced by saxophonists Archie

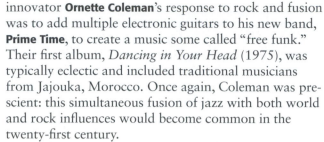

Ornette Coleman, 2000. PHOTO COURTESY ANDREW LEPLEY/REDFERNS/GETTY IMAGES.

Exploratory saxophonist and big band leader David Murray performing at the 2002 New Orleans Jazz and Heritage Festival. PHOTO COURTESY LEON MORRIS/REDFERNS/ GETTY IMAGES.

Shepp and Albert Ayler. Playing both tenor sax and bass clarinet, Murray expanded sonic possibilities by playing higher notes and with blistering speed and circular breathing. Murray continued playing in a wide variety of styles and influences, but by the 1980s Murray, guitarist Bill Frisell, and the George Adams-Don Pullen Quartet were all trying to make free jazz swing again.

Murray typified this new approach to connecting an improvisational world without musical borders back to the bop mainstream. Murray was voracious in his musical appetites, leading the David Murray Octet (whose Mingus-like recordings for the Black Saint label seemed both formal and reckless at the same time), an experimental big band conducted by cornetist-composer Lawrence D. "Butch" Morris, and his own driving quartet with pianist John Hicks. In 1977, he joined with saxophonists Hamiet Bluiett, Oliver Lake, and Julius Hemphill to form the **World Saxophone Quartet**. Working without a rhythm section, they combined this new interest in classical avant-garde composition with the solo saxophone recitals of the 1970s and the spirit of New Orleans's collective improvisation. On *Steppin'*, swing, free funk, and open meter all flow seamlessly together, integrating what is composed and what is improvised. (Listen to *Steppin'* by World Saxophone Quartet, *JTSA* Disc 6/Track 6.)

Other "new music" artists were equally interested in expanding jazz and experimental music. A haunting and unusual sound characterized the guitar playing of Bill Frisell, and he issued eclectic recordings on ECM Records with saxophonist Joe Lovano, trumpeter Kenny Wheeler, and drummer Paul Motian. A more volcanic approach to free jazz was kept alive by saxophonists Tim Berne and David Ware. For all of these avant-garde jazz musicians, categories of music disappeared. The trend away from strict compartmentalization of styles continues today. Electric or acoustic, classical or jazz, European or African—it is all ground for experimentation and improvisation.

New Collectives and Ethnic Jazz

The compactness of New York has always encouraged cross-pollination and collaboration, and during the 1980s two new downtown collectives emerged: **Steve Coleman's M-Base**—whose track *The Glide Was in the Ride* (*JTSA* Disc 6/Track 7) mixes the jazz tradition with experimentation—and the circle of musicians around John Zorn.

John Zorn

Like others in the new music movement, Zorn drew upon a tremendous array of non-jazz influences. As a record store clerk by day, he listened to all sorts of music and sounds: cartoon soundtracks, punk rock, klezmer music, duck calls, and the classical composers

((• **Hear** an interview with John Zorn about his group Masada on **mymusiclab.com**

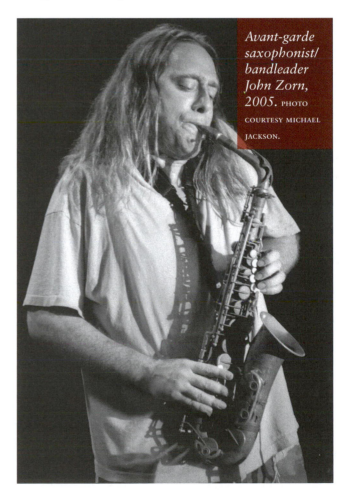

Avant-garde saxophonist/ bandleader John Zorn, 2005. PHOTO COURTESY MICHAEL JACKSON.

Webern, Cage, Stockhausen, and Philip Glass. After hearing an Anthony Braxton record, he switched from piano to alto saxophone and studied the music of avant-garde saxophonists Albert Ayler, John Coltrane, and Pharoah Sanders.

His hardcore punk rock group, Naked City (1987–93), with Bill Frisell and keyboardist Wayne Horvitz, thrived on short bursts of intense music with "jump cuts" to radically different sounds and back again. Like these musical "jump cuts," Zorn's career has moved rapidly from one style to another. His first experimental compositions were called "game pieces" (most important was *Cobra* from 1984) that used rules and cues to guide a group improvisation. After years of self-produced albums, *The Big Gundown* (1985) brought together much of the downtown scene in a series of radical reworkings of the "spaghetti Western" film scores of Ennio Morricone. Zorn would

go on to score for films and the concert hall, but he is best known for his klezmer jazz **Masada** groups (1994–2007).

Jump cuts, and the influence of Ornette Coleman, can also be heard in the acoustic version of Masada, with trumpeter **Dave Douglas**, bassist Greg Cohen, and drummer Joey Baron. *Kilayim* (*JTSA* Disc 6/ Track 13), for example, is based on one of Zorn's many new themes using Jewish modes, but what begins as a punk bar mitzvah band soon slams into a short blast of free jazz interspersed with screeching horns. Masada also appeared as a string trio and in an electric version.

While his music was hailed as a new form of jazz (called "thrash jazz" by some), Zorn himself questioned labels. "The term 'jazz,' per se," he asserted, "is meaningless to me in a certain way. Musicians don't think in terms of boxes." (His stance echoed an earlier one of

Style & Technique

Are Solos a Key Element in Jazz?

A debate arose in the 1990s over the role of improvisation and soloing versus composition in jazz. Is jazz primarily an art form based on the work of the composer, or are the individual performers' improvised solos the most important element in the music?

Wynton Marsalis took the position that jazz is fundamentally a *composed* art form and that the discipline of its tradition was essential. Marsalis's position was influenced by his belief that jazz had been unfairly lumped together with other forms of popular music. Jazz, he argued, is a highly structured musical form, and it requires years of training to achieve excellence in its performance. In the provocatively titled "What Jazz Is—and Isn't" (*New York Times*, July 31, 1988),

Keith Jarrett became noted for long solo piano improvisations—marked by his ecstatic utterances and expressive physicality—and for adventuresome but accessible small-band music. PHOTO COURTESY JAZZSIGN/LEBRECHT MUSIC & ARTS.

Marsalis proposed that pop musicians were simply riding on the coattails of jazz's reputation when they claimed to be performing a kind of jazz-rock fusion. Marsalis attacked rock and pop musics' lack of sophistication in their melodies and harmonies, contrasting them with the richness of the work of classic jazz composers such as Ellington.

In Marsalis's view, it is heroic to preserve what is truly great about jazz music. Marsalis saw Miles Davis's move to fusion not as a continuation of a tradition of jazz experimentation, but as a commercial sellout. He felt Davis— along with the record companies and promoters of jazz rock—were trying to cash in on jazz's artistic cachet. Marsalis's criticism of the avant-garde (from the late Coltrane and Ornette Coleman to the Art Ensemble of Chicago and

Duke Ellington, who resisted labels and categories.) This attitude was typical among the downtown musicians who were trying to forge something completely new. Speaking in general about the 1980s and 1990s new music scene in New York, Zorn wrote that "the music explicitly and violently resists the classifications that these so-called thinkers have so desperately tried to impose on it: from the ludicrous *comprovisation* to the ambiguous *postmodernism* to the meaningless *totalism*."

In 1995, Zorn founded the record label Tzadik to record "the best in avant garde and experimental music, presenting a worldwide community of musician-composers who find it difficult or impossible to release their music through conventional channels." While not all of the musicians on the label (or even in Masada) were Jewish, Zorn's recording series, Radical Jewish Culture, identifies the character of much of the music and a new emphasis on ethnic jazz.

In the same way that players from Norway or South Africa had tried to give the international language of jazz a local accent (a phenomenon sometimes called *glocalization*), downtown players such as trumpeter Steven Bernstein and cellist Erik Friedlander, and the band Hasidic New Wave, experimented with mixing free jazz with klezmer, a jazz-like folk music created by Eastern European Jews but now reborn in New York City. Other mixtures emerged, based on players' ethnicities: percussionist Roberto Juan Rodriguez and eclectic guitarist Marc Ribot mixed Cuban jazz with klezmer. This interest in making jazz reflect the player's culture can also be

---

collective improvisation   spontaneous composition performed simultaneously by members of an ensemble.

---

the World Saxophone Quartet) was to argue that it was not jazz.

While free jazz might appear to be uninterested in swing and the blues, it can also be seen as a pure form of **collective improvisation**, where, as in the original New Orleans jazz, multiple people improvised simultaneously. So the jazz world was stunned when Marsalis attacked the idea of solos and improvisation as central to jazz in a *Jazz Times* interview:

I think there is going to be an end to the old style of jamming on the bandstand that was really initiated during Charlie Parker's time. Historically, that was never a part of jazz music, not in the beginning . . . solos didn't come into fashion until Louis Armstrong and didn't become ingrained into jazz until the bebop thing came along. So I think there will be more emphasis put on presentation and composition as opposed to just soloing, which is a really boring and predictable way of presenting music.

A few months later, critic Ben Ratliff made use of this quote in an equally controversial article, "The Solo Retreats from the Spotlight in Jazz," that appeared in the May 28, 2000, *New York Times*. One of the many passionate letters printed by the *Times* in response included this one from pianist **Keith Jarrett**:

May I ask whose soloing Mr. Marsalis is referring to? And may I ask Mr. Ratliff what he thinks jazz actually is, if not those few precious exploding moments? And what does he think genius is? Those exploding moments can hold more sustenance than all the "jazz literature" (whatever that is) ever written. Look at Duke's band: how does his written music sound now, without those monster soloists-improvisers? Dry, lifeless, institutional. It is personal narrative we're losing, personal awareness: players with something to say. If that thread is broken (and it may well be), we're not going to write our way into the jazz future without important improvisatory voices, because

the narrative that is jazz will have died. The spirit of jazz is the spirit of personal freedom, only spontaneous individual acts. Jazz needs these acts of freedom to reconfirm itself in every era. It is in the player's art, not the writer's. There is no future if there is no present.

Duke Ellington is a key figure for both Jarrett and Marsalis. For Marsalis, Ellington's role as composer was the guiding force behind the band's unique sound, while the individual soloists were carrying out Ellington's vision in their performances. For Jarrett, however, it is the spontaneity and creativity of those solos that gives the music life and makes it jazz.

While new jazz has often raised questions about the old definitions of jazz, this more theoretical discourse about the nature of jazz indicates that indeed jazz has matured as an art; it has been around long enough to have a theory about itself. SOURCE: BILL MILKOWSKI, "WYNTON MARSALIS: ONE FUTURE, TWO VIEWS," *JAZZTIMES*, MARCH 2000; KEITH JARRETT, LETTER TO THE EDITOR, *NEW YORK TIMES*, JUNE 11, 2000.

—*José Antonio Bowen*

seen in the movement to create Asian American jazz ensembles, and even in Wynton Marsalis's emphasis on the importance of preserving the African American roots of jazz.

In addition to his work (as the non-Jewish member) with Masada, trumpeter Dave Douglas led both acoustic and electric bands and proved equally at ease with turntables, the progressive Dutch drummer Han Bennink, or celebrating the music of Mary Lou Williams (*Soul on Soul*, 2000). He considered John Coltrane, Igor Stravinsky, and Stevie Wonder to be his primary influences.

Issues

Jazz and Race Revisited

How have issues of race and class continued to play a role in jazz today?

Jazz lovers have always taken pride in the fact that jazz musicians have long been leaders in breaking down racial barriers. Long before the public would accept it, or the government would demand it, jazz musicians were integrating bands. By the 1960s and 1970s, jazz fans had come to expect racially integrated groups. At the same time, the idea that jazz was a black music became an important symbol for the Civil Rights and Black Power movements. (See "Jazz: The Sound of Freedom" in Chapter 8, page 200.) In his influential book *Blues People: Negro Music in White America* (1963), LeRoi Jones (later known as Amiri Baraka) argued that the history of African American music was the history of African Americans coming to recognize the vitality and emotional validity of their own culture. Jazz didn't just have soul, it *was* soul. His story of a unique and vital folk music constantly fending off dilution from American popular music became a cornerstone for a new argument about race in jazz.

By the early 1980s, the tide seemed to be turning when Billy Taylor in *Jazz Piano: A Jazz History* (1982) argued that jazz had moved beyond African American music to become *Jazz: America's Classical Music*, the title adopted by Grover Sales for his 1984 book. It was a surprise then, when race again emerged as a topic in jazz after Wynton Marsalis began presenting concerts honoring only black musicians with the almost exclusively black Jazz at Lincoln Center Orchestra. Marsalis wrote, "People who invent something are always best at doing it, at least until other folks figure out what it is." Jazz writers James Lincoln Collier, in *Jazz, The American Theme Song* (1993), and Gene Lees, in *Cats of Any Color* (1994), responded that there was now reverse racism in jazz. Collier and Marsalis exchanged heated words in the *New York Times Book Review* and even held a public debate at Lincoln Center.

When in 1999 Richard Sudhalter published an exhaustive, scholarly 890-page book, *Lost Chords: White Musicians and Their Contribution to Jazz, 1915–1945* that argued that white and black musicians had both contributed to jazz "often defying the racial and social norms of their time to create a music whose graces reflected the combined effort," he was loudly and publicly denounced by some.

Another flashpoint came in April 2003 with a column in *Jazz Times* magazine by Stanley Crouch called "Putting the White Man in Charge." Crouch criticized white jazz critics for praising white artists "as an antidote to too much authority from the dark side of the tracks" and for trying to destroy a "Negro aesthetic" based upon the blues and swing. He singled out white "downtown" trumpeter Dave Douglas (*Down Beat's* Trumpeter of the Year that year), writing that he "is far from being a bad musician, but he knows he should keep as much distance as possible between himself and [black] trumpet players like Wallace Roney, Terence Blanchard, and Nicholas Payton." Crouch was fired the next month.

For some, jazz has been a multicultural democratic space: a model environment where musicians of any race—"cats of any color," in Louis Armstrong's words—can play together. As jazz has become more global in the last 30 years, however, definitions rooted in the African American experience and the blues have become both more prominent and more controversial. World jazz musicians, like Jan Garbarek, readily admit that the blues isn't their tradition, and instead attempt to create a "native version" of jazz that is authentic to their own tradition. While the argument about the history and origins of jazz seems to have died down, future critics, players, and historians will need to determine how much of the past remains essential for future jazz cultures.

—*José Antonio Bowen*

Listening Guide

THE GLIDE WAS IN THE RIDE • STEVE COLEMAN GROUP

Music: Geri Allen. Personnel: Steve Coleman (alto saxophone); Geri Allen (piano); Lonnie Plaxico (bass); Marvin "Smitty" Smith (drums); collective vocal. Recorded March 1985, in New York City. First issue: *Motherland Pulse*, JMT 852 001. Timing: 4:03.

Overview

Both the rhythmic audacity and the collective voice of hip-hop were important influences for the musicians that Steve Coleman gathered in New York in the early 1980s under the banner of M-Base. Coleman insisted, however, that this was not a musical style, and indeed the pieces on this first album present a wide array of different approaches to improvisation. M-Base was also a community and Coleman emphasized the Chicago background of the musicians and the New Orleans rhythmic feel of the music. As with previous generations of jazz saxophonists, Coleman had an instantly recognizable sound and style, and his music relates clearly to the jazz tradition while also being both experimental and newly urban.

Key Features

- The familiar instrumentation is that of an acoustic jazz quartet, but the band strives to avoid familiar ways of playing and is comfortable with pop recording techniques of vocal overdubbing and an electronic fade of the band.
- Like much black popular music of the 1970s and 1980s, the bass line is a key element of both melody and rhythm—part of the composition's essence.
- The drummer establishes a relatively square rock pattern in four, but the bass line moves across the groove, creating an unconventional rhythm pattern where the bass is silent on the downbeat.
- The structure of the piece feels organic, with a saxophone melody followed by a unison bass, piano, and saxophone melody occurring only between the two solos.
- Improvisation is collective and structured; the improvisations and the melodies all relate to the opening bass line's juxtaposition of angularity and linear flow.
- The piece ends with a collective vocal chant (or "rap") satire of advertisement copy: "Before you take that final fall, if you do nothing else at all, tell the standbys on the side, the glide was in the ride."

—*José Antonio Bowen*

TIME	FORM	MELODY/INSTRUMENTATION
0:00	INTRODUCTION	The drums set up a quasi rock groove while the bass plays across the bar to set up an unusual rhythmic feel.
0:11		The piano joins and Steve Coleman begins his saxophone solo playing a series of related figures, also playing across the bar to further unsettle the rhythmic feel.
0:43	A	The saxophone introduces a new melody (A) and then continues to solo.
1:00		Five jabs from the piano across the time disturb the rhythmic pattern.
1:07	A	The saxophone again plays the A melody.
1:16	B	The bass, piano, and saxophone play a unison melody (B). It happens four times, with the saxophone making additions and further improvisations in each iteration.
1:45	PIANO SOLO	Geri Allen begins her piano solo with a series of one-handed, bop-ish runs, connecting the angularity of the melodies to bebop jazz.
2:05		The piano introduces some two-hand chords and unison figures.
2:22		The piano plays more vigorously and in the groove with two hands.
2:36		The piano and bass return to their opening figures.
2:46	A	The saxophone enters again with the A melody.
2:57		The piano returns to fast solo runs while the saxophone continues to experiment with the A rhythm.
3:08	B	The unison bass, piano, and saxophone B melody returns.
3:27		The band fades but continues with B, while an overdubbed group vocal chant/rap begins.
3:40		The band continues to play with B as the music fades out.

A musician of broad interests, clarinetist Don Byron ventured into klezmer, classical, salsa, rock, and jazz. PHOTO COURTESY DAVID REDFERN/REDFERNS/ GETTY IMAGES.

(1992), and *Def Trance Beat (Modalities of Rhythm)* (1995), Coleman updated the sound of Miles Davis's 1970s ensembles and Ornette Coleman's Prime Time band, making a persuasive case that the dance ethic that won jazz its following in the swing era still survived. All that was necessary was that it reflect contemporary styles.

Coleman had developed a strong straight-ahead bop technique before setting out on his own path, having performed in the Thad Jones-Mel Lewis big band and recorded with bassist Dave Holland. In turn, the M-Base movement exerted an influence on a generation of jazz performers who, while mindful of the music traditions, were also open to a multitude of ways to express themselves. Over the years, that spirit of exploration remained intact as Osby and Allen continued to push the limits of bop, Wilson helped to bring a broader audience to jazz singing, and Coleman remained open to a world of musical possibilities.

After graduating from the New England Conservatory, Don Byron helped revive the clarinet as an important jazz instrument, while also working as an important collaborator in many downtown projects and serving as artistic director of jazz for the Brooklyn Academy of Music (1996–99). He shared his interest in classical, klezmer, and hip-hop with the Philadelphia pianist Uri Caine. While both recorded albums of reworked classical music, Caine (often with Byron as a sideman) demonstrated notable fearlessness in reworking Bach, Beethoven, Mahler, and Wagner. He proved equally arresting playing a Fender Rhodes electric piano and a Hammond B-3 organ on *The Philadelphia Experiment* (2000) with Ahmir Thompson (drummer from the hip-hop band the Roots) and bassist Christian McBride. The album offers a world where jazz avant-gardist Sun Ra grooves next to Motown singer Marvin Gaye.

In the 1980s, the neobop movement garnered most of the media attention, but not all jazz artists were involved in that trend. Based in Brooklyn, M-Base was spearheaded by alto saxophonist Steve Coleman, a Chicago native whose eclectic musical tastes were readily apparent in his compositions and performances.

M-Base stands for Macro-Basic Array of Structured Extemporization. In Coleman's music, that meant funk that swung, hip-hop that drew on bop, and street rhythms that made room for improvisation. The company he kept in the late 1980s was, in retrospect, exemplary: M-Base adherents included such end-of-the-twentieth-century stars as singer Cassandra Wilson, pianist Geri Allen, and alto saxophonist Greg Osby.

Although M-Base had no formal organization, its flagship was Coleman's group, Five Elements. On albums such as *Black Science* (1991), *Drop Kick*

TAKE NOTE

- How has the avant-garde jazz movement of the 1960s and 1970s evolved and who are some of its key performers?

Reenvisioning Jazz

While some musicians preserved a conception of jazz that reached its zenith with bebop and its offshoots, and while others opened the doors of jazz to welcome far-flung styles, there were musicians (in addition to John Zorn) who set about completely rethinking jazz—in some cases to a point at which the term "jazz" perhaps became archaic. To some, "jazz" evoked a set of conditions, traditions, and practices that could impede artistic progress. Perhaps (for these musicians) the living legacy of jazz in the twenty-first century would be, simply, improvised music.

One of the thinkers whose work pointed toward a wide-ranging notion of improvised music, composer and pianist **Jason Moran**, emerged in the 1990s. Starting with the 1999 album *Soundtrack to Human Emotion*, Moran stood out as a voracious assimilator of whatever sounds he regarded as valuable, and a resourceful generator of ideas for producing new kinds of listening experiences. An alumnus of the Manhattan School of Music and a student of renowned veteran jazz pianist (and Charles Mingus band member) Jaki Byard, Moran embraced the avant-garde, classicism, and populism along with jazz roots. His 2002 reworking of the 1930 James P. Johnson classic *You've Got to Be Modernistic* transformed it into a showcase for an improvising style that easily commingled stride-piano pyrotechnics with Cecil Taylor–style atonality. In *Planet Rock* (2002), Moran translated the 1982 raps of Afrika Bambaataa into piano melodies, generating an atonality based on direct human expression (in contrast to the mathematical, at times soulless, atonal formulations of twentieth-century art music) that he pursued further in later years. His 2010 track *Feedback, Pt. 2* juxtaposed ruminative, abstract piano chording with samples of feedback from rock guitarist Jimi Hendrix, generating a contrast in texture suggesting soft textile alternating with sandpaper or gravel.

Steve Turre, for many years a trombone-playing member of the *Saturday Night Live* band on network television, found musical sound in unlikely places—the cavities of sea shells. Focusing primarily on the conch, Turre amassed a collection of shells that he tuned to specific pitches, and used to evocative ends with his shell choir, the Sanctified Shells, and in other settings. A means rather than an end, shells simply expanded the palette—in which trombone remained central—from which Turre rendered audioscapes of vastly varied hue. Turre's blue-chip background playing with salsa and jazz figureheads—Art Blakey, Dizzy Gillespie, Max Roach, and Tito Puente among them—informed his expansive conception of what might be called "open source" improvised music. Within it, he could conjure expression of limitless range: from the primitive-sounding, "talking" melodicism of *Morning*, 1995, to the full-bodied, brash declamation of *Midnight Montuno (Descarga)*, 1993.

One of the highest-profile of the jazz musicians to emerge in the 1990s, pianist **Brad Mehldau** worked largely in a trio setting (with bass and drums) as he applied jazz, pop, and associated ideas to structures suitable for his improvisational inclinations. These ranged widely, from free improvisation with no readily apparent stylistic source other than Mehldau's imagination (*Paranoid Android*, 2002) to reconstructing pop songs as platforms for inventive melodic departures (*Dear Prudence*, 2002).

Even the 1990s-spawned jazz star most likely to inherit the mainstream mantle of "jazz giant," burly tenor saxophonist **Joe Lovano**, made his own case for expanding the bounds of jazz simply by virtue of the musicians he chose to play with. A veteran of the Woody Herman big band and the Thad Jones-Mel

((•—[Hear] a profile of Jason Moran on **mymusiclab.com**

Jason Moran at the Newport Jazz Festival, 2010. PHOTO COURTESY DOUGLAS MASON/ GETTY IMAGES.

Listening Guide

**Listen** to *Planet Rock* by Jason Moran
on **mymusiclab.com**
CD II, Track 16/Download Track 40

PLANET ROCK • JASON MORAN

Music: Afrika Bambaataa and Soulsonic Force, Arthur Baker, John Robie, 1982. Personnel: Jason Moran (piano; piano prepared with erasers, paper, paper clips, and clothespins; sound loops). Recorded: April 12, 2002, in New York. First issue: *Modernistic*, Blue Note 39838. Timing: 5:41.

Overview

Planet Rock, from Jason Moran's solo piano album *Modernistic* (2002), showcases several of the inclinations Moran brings to music: openness to and incorporation of a broad range of music traditions (in this case hip-hop and, indirectly, 1970s techno-pop); use of spoken word as a source of melody; interest in experimental jazz of the 1980s and 1990s, and affinity for twentieth-century atonal music. In *Planet Rock* we hear a clear departure from traditional notions of jazz (to the point where some might question calling it jazz), and we get a clear window into the boundary-defying thrust of Moran's thinking—the kind of thinking that moves music forward to new forms.

The original *Planet Rock* was a 1982 hit by "godfather of hip-hop" Afrika Bambaataa and Soulsonic Force. At the time the track was a dance-floor revelation, and it prototyped the soon-to-be-popular genres hip-hop and electronica, blending rap (rhythmically spoken) lyrics with electronic beats inspired by the German electro-pop band Kraftwerk, and **sampling** an eerie modal melody from Kraftwerk's 1977 hit *Trans-Europe Express*.

For this version, Moran took on the task of translating most of those elements to piano—no small challenge. He achieved the goal by overdubbing several tracks, including "percussion" played on prepared piano and special effects produced by digitally manipulating recorded sound segments. "It was a matter of finding the connections between hip-hop and the piano-as-percussion-instrument, which I did via John Cage's prepared piano music," Moran recalled in 2007. "If I could put all that together, I thought, then *Planet Rock* could still work as a hip-hop piece, and not some jazzy version of it. It could still hold some of that drumbeat, it could still hold that bass line and I could play the lyrics."

Whether or not the track works as a hip-hop piece, the rap-derived melodies sound new, and conversely, they highlight the musicality of rapping.

Key Features

- Melody: Strikingly, Moran crafts "melodies" shaped by spoken word on the original hip-hop version of *Planet Rock*. It's an unorthodox technique for freeing melody from **tonality**, and Moran explores it further in a later tune, *Ringing My Phone* (2002), in which he "melodizes" recorded telephone conversations. In *Planet Rock* he also duplicates the repeated melody (0:54) that Afrika Bambaataa borrowed from Kraftwerk in the 1982 original.
- Rhythm: Generated via piano "prepared" by inserting erasers, paper, paper clips, and clothespins on the strings, the rock-style rhythm is a steady mid-tempo $\frac{4}{4}$, accenting the first and anticipating the third of every four beats. The intensity changes during the tune, receding in volume at 2:21, returning at 4:50, and slowing at 5:14 through the fade.
- Style: Defying stylistic labels, Moran draws from hip-hop and self-developed techniques ("playing the lyrics") to concoct a mixture of atonal and modal free jazz with a rock-derived beat.
- Texture: Moran varies the texture with acoustic piano, percussive "prepared" piano, and recordings played backwards, providing an electronic swelling sound that opens the tune and recurs throughout.
- Form and structure: Three primary kinds of sections form the structural material: "verses," in which Moran is "playing the lyrics"; melodic interludes, featuring a modal melody (borrowed by Afrika Bambaataa from the band Kraftwerk); and a slower-paced melody (based on half notes) that supports Moran's improvisation.

—*Tad Lathrop*

Lewis Orchestra—both hard-core jazz ensembles—Lovano branched out over the years. Free jazz pianist-composer Carla Bley, third stream conceptualist Gunther Schuller, fusion guitarist John Scofield, and a trio featuring guitarist Bill Frisell and drummer Paul Motian, all drew on Lovano's saxophone sound and, in turn, he assimilated theirs. The results are audible in such open-sounding tracks as *Us Five* and *Wild Beauty*

on the 2009 album *Folk Art*, credited to Lovano and his band Us Five.

One of Us Five's members, **Esperanza Spalding**, emerged to great acclaim as a soloist in 2008 with a concept—conveyed through her full-throttle singing, bass playing, and arranging—of improvisational music that could venture anywhere (while favoring a Brazilian bent). Proof could be found in both the title

TIME	SECTION	MELODY
0:00	INTRO	Following an electronic swell (a recording played backwards), piano enters with a four-note blues figure, played twice.
0:05		Moran plays a more complicated figure. It is stated three times, with the third ending (0:16) on an octave crescendo.
0:17		An electronic beat enters (played on prepared piano in a pre-recorded take). A series of chordal swells (backwards recordings) ensue.
0:38	VERSE (8 BARS)	Moran picks out a melody as he simulates the phrasings of Afrika Bambaataa's rap. The melody has an imperfect, atonal quality and rhythmic variety.
0:54	MELODIC INTERLUDE (8 BARS)	A fixed melody (Kraftwerk's synth melody "sampled" by Bambaataa) interrupts the piano "rapping." It repeats in two different registers.
1:10	VERSE (8 BARS)	Moran returns to "rapping," with ever-changing rhythmic figures and notes that fall "outside" expected musical patterns.
1:26	MELODIC INTERLUDE (8 BARS)	The fixed melody is played again, twice.
1:42	VERSE (6 BARS)	Moran emphasizes two notes repeatedly and at 1:49 raises them a half step.
1:54	(8 BARS)	Ominous-sounding chords in call and response, low to high.
2:10	IMPROVISED CHORUS 1 (16 BARS)	Moran introduces a new melody built on half notes moving evenly in upward and downward directions. A swelling effect emanates from the piano notes.
2:42	IMPROVISED CHORUS 2 (16 BARS)	The half-note melody continues, morphing (2:50) into half-note accompaniment to improvising, which evolves into fractured, high-pitched shards of melody.
3:14	IMPROVISED CHORUS 3 (16 BARS)	Texture changes as the swelling half-note melody (via backward recording) returns to the foreground and the percussion backbeat drops out. Improvisation continues.
3:46	IMPROVISED CHORUS 4 (16 BARS)	The half-note melody continues, now without the "swelling" effect, and it morphs into chordal accompaniment under soloing.
3:56		Moran plays jabbing octaves.
4:07		Moran returns to tumbling single-note lines ending on repeated single notes.
4:18	INTERLUDE (16 BARS)	An interlude ensues, with piano maintaining a low-key rhythm . . .
4:32		. . . until a melody emerges, echoing the half-note melody from earlier.
4:42		A series of electronic swells similar to the opening of the tune is heard.
4:48		The backbeat becomes more pronounced.
4:51	MELODIC INTERLUDE (4 BARS)	The fixed melody returns, one time.
4:58	CODA (4 BARS)	High notes echo the fixed melody. Electronic swells mix with high piano notes.
5:07		The beat becomes spare and ambiguous.
5:13		Steady beat returns, but slower, as the piano fades with high chords and electronic chordal swells.

sampling (1) the use of a "sampled" section or piece of a preexisting recording in a new recording; (2) digitally recording a singer, instrument, or other sound to use as a "voice" in a synthesizer.

tonality relationship to a tonal center or key.

of her 2010 album *Chamber Music Society* and the music contained within.

TAKE NOTE

- How have some musicians begun to rethink the definition of jazz beyond the classic division between mainstream and avant-garde?

Vocal Jazz

The variety of approaches in vocal jazz in the second half of the century mirrored the expansion of instrumental jazz. Veterans Tony Bennett and Mel Tormé, along with such younger singers as Diane Schuur, Dianne Reeves, Karrin Allyson, Kevin Mahogany, and Jane Monheit, continued to sing the great American songbook. A quartet of veteran women singers—Betty

The expressive singer/bassist Esperanza Spalding performing in 2010. PHOTO COURTESY DR. BILLY INGRAM/ WIREIMAGE/GETTY IMAGES.

In the 1950s, Eddie Jefferson and Jon Hendricks put lyrics to recorded jazz solos and created vocalese, a technique that continues to find favor with male vocalists. From his debut in 1956, Mark Murphy forged a long and distinguished career scatting and singing vocalese, while Dave Frishberg made his name as a wordsmith best known for singing his own clever compositions including *I'm Just a Bill* (written for ABC Television's *Schoolhouse Rock*), *My Attorney Bernie*, and the widely sung *Peel Me a Grape*? With a string of critics' and readers' poll awards and a huge baritone voice, Kurt Elling continued in this tradition, singing standards, new compositions, and vocalese.

The internationalization of jazz extended to jazz singing. After successful stints in the 1970s in front of the Thad Jones-Mel Lewis Jazz Orchestra and on Broadway, the American singer Dee Dee Bridgewater moved to Paris in 1986 and returned to singing jazz. Her 2007 album *Red Earth* features a Malian band led by Cheick Tidiane Seck. Londoner Norma Winstone began singing jazz standards, but her wordless improvisations became an important part of the progressive ECM sound, especially as a unique new texture in Kenny Wheeler's big band on *Music for Large and Small Ensembles* (1990).

While jazz instrumentalists were drawn to rock fusions, jazz singers saw R&B or pop as more of a crossover point. Al Jarreau, for example, won a jazz Grammy award for his scat singing on the track *Take Five* from his album *Look to the Rainbow* (1977), which also reached number 49 on the pop charts. Nnenna Freelon moved easily back and forth from the classic jazz singing of Billie Holiday to the pop-soul of Stevie Wonder.

Cassandra Wilson managed to integrate her country, R&B, pop, and blues interests into jazz. After time with Ellis Marsalis in New Orleans, in Steve Coleman's M-Base, and touring with experimental altoist Henry Threadgill, Wilson launched a solo career with *Point of View* (1986). Initially, her progressive funk repertoire seemed at odds with her ability

Carter, Abbey Lincoln, Nancy Wilson, and Shirley Horn—all learned the importance of a unique style and sound. All three recreated old melodies in their own image. Tierney Sutton continued this tradition of rethinking standards and **scat singing**. Following in the footsteps of Horn and Nat "King" Cole, Diana Krall emerged as an accomplished pianist who could swing and phrase as well as any jazz singer on the scene.

scat singing   vocal improvisation, typically wordless; notable practitioners have included Louis Armstrong; the Boswell Sisters; Cab Calloway; Ella Fitzgerald; Eddie Jefferson; Lambert, Hendricks and Ross; and Dizzy Gillespie.

Vocal Groups

Jazz has always meant something different for vocalists: jazz singers needed to swing and have a unique sound, but most sang only as soloists in front of a big band, coming out occasionally to sing a song. All of that changed with the Boswell Sisters—Connee, Martha, and Vet—a trio who sang together in the 1930s and whose vocal harmony was widely imitated, most famously by the Andrew Sisters. Their dramatic reworking of pop tunes with tempo changes, improvised solos, and group scat singing were radical and innovative (listen to *Everybody Loves My Baby*, *JTSA* Disc 1/Track 17). Ella Fitzgerald was a huge fan and was deeply influenced by Connee. Big bands responded by adding even larger vocal groups, rather than just soloists, to their ensembles. The Modernaires joined Glenn Miller, and the Pied Pipers joined the Tommy Dorsey band to back up Frank Sinatra.

Then along came Eddie Jefferson, who sang note-for-note recreations of famous jazz solos. This technique was called *vocalese* and required the singer not only to memorize an instrumental solo but also to create lyrics. The greatest lyricist of this genre is Jon Hendricks, who along with Dave Lambert and British vocalist Annie Ross formed a new sort of jazz vocal group. The first Lambert, Hendricks and Ross LP was *Sing a Song of Basie* (1957), in which the group recreated complete arrangements from the Count Basie Band by singing all of the parts and adding lyrics. They did this using the new technique of **overdubbing**, a way to layer new parts on top of previously recorded parts using multitrack magnetic tape. For *The Swingers!* (1959), they sang as a trio over a rhythm section, again singing versions of famous instrumental performances with lyrics by Hendricks, but now with increasingly modern arrangements by Lambert that featured tightly crafted individual vocal lines meshing together in dense clusters of sound.

This style of group vocal jazz became an important influence on 1950s and 1960s pop-oriented groups such as the Four Freshmen and doo-wop and R&B acts like the Drifters. The influences sometimes worked in both directions: One of the greatest arrangers of a cappella vocal jazz, Gene Puerling, came from a pop background, having founded the eclectic Hi-Lo's in 1953—they sang everything from barbershop quartet music to calypso. Puerling went on to lead the popular jazz vocal group Singers Unlimited.

Vocalese came to its peak with the Manhattan Transfer. After an aborted initial quintet (1969–71), bass Tim Hauser reformed a quartet with alto Janis Siegel, soprano Laurel Masse, and tenor Alan Paulin in 1972. They gained an early following in New York clubs and attracted the attention of Atlantic Records founder Ahmet Ertegun, who signed them to his label. The group's *Extensions* (1979) included a vocalese version of Weather Report's *Birdland* with lyrics by Jon Hendricks, which won a Grammy Award and remains a classic. The album is notable for its use of analog synthesizer backgrounds, but it also revived an interest (in both Europe and America) in close harmony singing and led to the creation of high school and college vocal jazz groups. This in turn led to a flourishing professional vocal jazz-group scene.

Darmon Meader, Peter Eldridge, Kim Nazarian, and Caprice Fox met at Ithaca College and formed the New York Voices with Sara Krieger in 1987. The New York Voices rejected vocalese for a new approach: they created their own arrangements of jazz standards and took improvised scat solos. (Meader is also an accomplished soloist on the saxophone.) Relentless rehearsal enabled them to swing as one voice.

Like instrumental jazz, group vocal jazz spread around the world and fused with other genres. Take 6 is a gospel-oriented a cappella sextet that formed at Oakwood College in Huntsville, Alabama, in 1980. Their brilliant 1988 debut album launched another revolution in college jazz singing that included a proliferation of "rockappella" groups. At the Royal Music Academy in Stockholm in 1984, the Real Group was inspired by **Bobby McFerrin** to create new versions of standards from *The Real Book* (the standard "fake book" collection of jazz lead sheets), while Vocal Sampling took male a cappella singing to Cuba. Zap Mama, a Belgium group of five mixed African European women, was led by Marie Daulne, who listened to blues and French music before returning to her native Congo to study traditional pygmy music and then sang in Brussels jazz cafés. The album *Zap Mama* (1991) may be an attempt to bridge Europe and Africa, but the improvisation over pygmy chants also feels like jazz coming home.

—*José Antonio Bowen*

overdubbing   the practice of recording in synchronization with previously recorded material; used primarily in popular music to build layers of sound.

to channel Billie Holiday in standards, but ultimately her ability to unite disparate elements, especially new takes on familiar tunes, became as much a stylistic trademark as her deep smoky voice.

No singer, however, brought more innovation to vocal jazz than Bobby McFerrin. Eclectic in taste and influence, *The Voice* (1984) was a unique solo outing, with nothing but the sound of his voice. Jumping from low bass to falsetto, making sounds as he inhaled, overdubbing his own voice to create multiple parts, and mimicking other instruments, McFerrin added an arsenal of techniques and fresh ideas to jazz and singing. Some of his genius can be heard on his hit recording *Don't Worry Be Happy*.

Conclusion

Even fully matured, jazz continues to wrestle with its own identity. Is jazz now a classical and conservative art? Is it still a radical and experimental music making up its own rules as it goes along? Can it be both? For world musicians or Americans influenced by John

History & Culture

Jazz in the Marketplace

In the United States, jazz continues to have approximately the same share of recorded music sales as classical music (about 2 percent). Jazz, however, has always been a "catalog" seller, meaning that older music in the back catalog continues to sell for years. So while Miles Davis's *Kind of Blue* sold extremely well in its first year, it did not go "gold" (signifying 500,000 units shipped to retailers in the United States as certified by the Recording Industry Association of America [RIAA]) until 1993, then it went platinum (one million units) in 1997 and continued to sell, eventually going triple platinum (three million units) in 2002. *Kind of Blue* and Dave Brubeck's *Time Out* remain in the top 20 jazz albums sold each year.

Like the rest of American popular music, jazz began its commercial life on 78 records, which featured two songs, one on each side of the disc. Since the rise of the LP in the 1950s, however, jazz sales have been almost entirely in LP records or CDs. As music sales shift back

to singles via download sites such as iTunes—nearly 30 percent of all music sales were digital in 2010, according to the International Federation of the Phonographic Industry (IFPI)—will jazz do better or worse? At least one new Web site (jazz.com) has responded to this trend by reviewing and rating individual jazz singles (generally single tracks from longer CDs) again.

Jazz has always had obsessive fans. In fact, "discography" (the study of sound recordings) was started by jazz fans in the 1930s who recognized that different takes of a jazz performance were substantially different and consequently began to identify and catalog recordings of different performances. The Internet has allowed thousands of fans to create Web sites devoted to their favorite players and genres. There is more information on jazz available than ever before, and many Web sites also allow users to hear sound clips.

There has also been a huge expansion of summer jazz festivals, although as Wynton Marsalis pointed out, there has also been an

expansion of the range of music presented at them, and different festivals have taken on different repertoires and missions. Jazz festivals routinely include R&B, rock, smooth jazz, and other broadly popular styles as a way to expand their potential market. The annual New Orleans Jazz & Heritage Festival, for example, has hosted pop singers Billy Joel and Stevie Wonder, country musician Tim McGraw, rock singer Sheryl Crow, and many other non-jazz performers.

While the internal jazz community has been arguing about traditional versus experimental types of jazz, a different argument about the classification of jazz has been continuing in the commercial world. Saxophonist Kenny G claimed to be the best-selling jazz instrumentalist of all time (with more than 50 million records sold). Yet many jazz fans would classify Kenny G in the "easy listening" category, and "smooth jazz" as an instrumental category of R&B. Both Kenny G and smooth jazz are listed on the jazz charts.

—*José Antonio Bowen*

Zorn, jazz seems less a style and more a set of interests: improvisation, rhythm, exploration, and new fusions. Creative musicians today are applying these interests across a range of musical cultures and ideas: jazz can now be Asian or Jewish and electric or acoustic. At the same time, others see the importance of returning jazz to its African American roots and traditions and re-establishing boundaries for jazz.

But with all of this controversy at home (outside of the United States, this local debate is largely ignored), the basic language of jazz has become established as the *lingua franca* of modern music making. Around the world, melodic improvisation and even the names and recordings of the greatest performers in American jazz are commonly known. Jazz and its techniques have become the world's music.

Explore Key Recordings on
mymusiclab.com

Bobby McFerrin's wide vocal range and ability to quickly shift between high and low registers enabled him to sing both melody and accompaniment.
PHOTO COURTESY MICHAEL WILDERMAN.

TAKE NOTE

- How has mainstream acoustic jazz continued to flourish and develop?

Mainstream jazz returned to fashion in the 1980s sparked by excitement surrounding trumpeter Wynton Marsalis. He would go on to mentor dozens of younger musicians, and shape the new Jazz at Lincoln Center as a highly visible home base for jazz. Jazz entered college curricula, music archives, and the repertoires of institutionally subsidized orchestras as an essential, still-evolving part of American cultural history.

- How has the avant-garde jazz movement of the 1960s and 1970s evolved and who are some of its key performers?

Downtown Manhattan lofts and clubs in the 1980s served as a home for a handful of experimenting musicians, including saxophonists David Murray and John Zorn, keyboardist Wayne Horvitz, and guitarist Bill Frisell.

- How have some musicians begun to rethink the definition of jazz beyond the classic division between mainstream and avant-garde?

Characteristic of jazz musicians later in the twentieth century was their ability and inclination to look back to bop for inspiration and to reach forward to new ideas. Notable in late-century jazz was a blurring, even a disintegration, of musical categories. Labels such as "jazz" and "rock" became decreasingly relevant.

- Who are some of today's leading vocalists and vocal groups, and what roles do they play on the current jazz scene?

Jazz singing has enjoyed a renaissance, with performers ranging from the inventive Bobby McFerrin, with his ability to sing percussion and bass accompaniment while also singing melody, to newcomers Kurt Elling, pianists/vocalists Diana Krall and Diane Schuur, Karrin Allyson, Jane Monheit, and Tierney Sutton.

DISCUSSION QUESTIONS

1. Before reading this chapter, which late-century jazz musicians were you most familiar with?

2. Discuss whether jazz of the 1990s and 2000s had any innovators with the originality and brilliance of Louis Armstrong, Charlie Parker, Duke Ellington, and John Coltrane.

3. Discuss what this chapter calls "an improvisational world without musical borders" and what it meant for jazz in the late twentieth century. Give examples.

4. Discuss institutional jazz programs. Do you feel that inserting jazz into institutions such as those discussed in this chapter has had any negative results for the music?

5. Identify some of the ways jazz singing in the late twentieth century differed from earlier kinds of jazz singing. Identify and compare leading singers of different jazz eras.

6. From what you've read and heard, do you feel jazz stopped evolving in the early twenty-first century? Or did it change so much that it was harder and harder to recognize?

7. Chapter 12 barely mentions what some radio stations call "light jazz" or "smooth jazz." Why do you think the book deemphasizes this kind of music?

8. Why do you think Wynton Marsalis has been a lightning rod for both praise and criticism?

9. There have been debates throughout the history of jazz about what constitutes "real" jazz—in the 1940s, swing versus bebop; in the 1960s, mainstream versus free jazz; in the 1970s, straight-ahead versus fusion; in the 1980s and beyond, acoustic/bop/straight-ahead versus everything else. Where do you stand in the latter debate?

KEY TERMS & KEY PEOPLE

Anthony Braxton 330
Don Byron 322
Ornette Coleman 330
Steve Coleman 331
collective improvisation 333
Dave Douglas 332
Keith Jarrett 333
Joe Lovano 337
Masada 332
M-Base 331

Branford Marsalis 323
Wynton Marsalis 321
Bobby McFerrin 341
Brad Mehldau 337
Pat Metheny 330
Jason Moran 337
David Murray 327
neotraditional jazz 321
overdubbing 341
Prime Time 330

sampling 338
scat singing 340
Esperanza Spalding 338
Cecil Taylor 330
tonality 338
Steve Turre 337
World Saxophone Quartet 331
John Zorn 330

Glossary

A&R artists and repertoire, a term used in the recording industry; an "A&R man" was a staff record producer, but now most recording sessions are supervised by independent producers.

accent expressive emphasis of a musical beat, note, or chord.

accent mark a symbol (>) over a beat, note, or chord, indicating emphasis.

acid jazz a style of jazz fusion combining elements of jazz, funk, and hip hop, especially looped beat samples from earlier jazz.

agogô (Portuguese) a double clapper-less bell beaten with a stick, used in Brazilian music.

aircheck a recording made from a radio broadcast by the station for its own purposes; sometimes, years later, they were issued.

altered chord a chord that includes a sharped or flatted alteration of a standard pitch for desired effect.

altered tone a sharped or flatted alteration of a standard pitch.

arpeggio the notes of a chord played sequentially rather then simultaneously.

arranger one who applies styling and instrumentation to a musical composition.

atonal composed without being based in traditional rules of harmonic relationships; for example, not in a key.

augmented raised a half step, typically applicable to the fifth degree of a scale, or the fifth in a dominant seventh chord.

aural tradition the practice of passing along a story, song, or tune by ear, rather than by written means.

avant-garde experimental, unconventional, cutting-edge.

backbeat emphasis on the 2 and 4 of a four-beat measure; a fundamental example of syncopation, characteristic of African American music, and in contrast to the European march rhythm emphasizing the 1 and 3.

balafon West African tuned percussion instrument, played by hitting tone bars with mallets.

band battle a performance of two or more bands billed as a competition; especially prevalent in the swing era, and generally used to boost the appeal to audiences; also known as a battle of the bands.

band book a band's repertoire of tunes.

bar also called a measure: a grouping of beats that determines the music's meter, as in "four beats to the bar"; indicated in music notation with bar lines.

bar lines on a staff, vertical lines that indicate beginnings and ends of measures.

bass clarinet the lowest-pitched instrument in the clarinet family.

bass clef a symbol in music notation indicating the assignment of pitches to the lines and spaces of a staff below middle C; also called the *F clef*: 𝄢.

batá (Yoruba) a set of three double-headed drums originally from the Yoruba people (present-day Nigeria and Benin) in West Africa typically used in *santería* ceremonies in Cuba.

bateria percussion section of a Brazilian escola de samba, famed for performances during Carnaval.

beam in musical notation, joined flags, as when an eighth note is connected to another eighth note.

beat a sonic event in time, the patterning of which is foundational to music; can also refer to a succession of beats, as in "the music has a slow beat."

bebop a style of jazz that emerged in the 1940s and established jazz as a music for listening rather than just dancing to; characterized by fast tempos, complex chord progressions, and virtuoso improvisation using multiple scales and altered tones; notable pioneers included Charlie Parker, Dizzy Gillespie, and Thelonious Monk.

biguine (French) a medium-tempo dance-based music originally from the French Caribbean; rhythmically similar to the calypso; "beguine" in English.

blue note a defining note in blues melodies and scales; a "bent" or slightly raised minor third or seventh.

blues a fundamental style of American music derived from the West African tradition of vocal call and response, reinvented as "field hollers" in America's rural south during the nineteenth century, combined with the European-style harmonies of hymns and simple folk songs; the three-chord, three-phrase structure of the blues has served as a central structure in jazz.

blues form typically, a twelve-bar musical structure comprising three lines of lyrics with the form AAB, consisting of a statement (A) sung over the home (tonic) chord, repetition of the statement (A) sung over the subdominant chord, and resolution of the statement (B) sung over the dominant chord resolving to the home chord.

blues scale a minor *pentatonic scale* supplemented with an augmented fourth (or flatted fifth if the melody is descending).

bolero (Spanish) originally, a Spanish dance in ¾. In Cuba, it became a slow, romantic 4/4 genre akin to jazz ballads.

bomb a pronounced or unexpected accent, most typically on a bass drum.

boogie-woogie a form of blues, often for the piano, with a repeating or ostinato left hand or bass pattern.

bossa nova Portuguese for "new tendency"; a syncopated, sensuous musical style refined from the samba and introduced in the late 1950s in Rio de Janeiro, Brazil.

break a brief pause in a band's playing to feature a soloist or soloists; the beat continues, but is implied.

bridge a segment of a tune, usually 8 or 16 bars, that departs from the main melody in order to provide contrast and development; the B in AABA form, for example.

caixa (Portuguese) a Brazilian snare drum.

call and response a pattern, common in jazz and African American music, in which a singer or instrumentalist (or group of them) answers a phrase or short passage from another; also found in some church services when the congregation answers the "call" from the preacher.

calypso (originally called *kaiso*) a music and dance tradition originally from Trinidad that, during the 1950s, spread to other Caribbean islands and the United States.

campana (Spanish) a cowbell, played with a stick as a percussion instrument; used in Afro-Cuban and salsa music; also called *cencerro*.

canción (Spanish) literally, "song": song style focusing mostly on lyrics/melody, with guitar accompaniment.

cáscara (Spanish) a rhythmic pattern played on *timbales*.

chamber jazz small-ensemble jazz intended for listening in concerts. The term is applied frequently to the music of the Modern Jazz Quartet, reflecting its intricacy, polish, precision, and formal presentation.

changes the arrangement of chords—the chord progression—that defines a tune; "*Rhythm* changes," for example, is jazz shorthand for "the chords of *I Got Rhythm*."

Charleston a fast, rhythmic African American dance step of the 1920s characterized by knocking the knees together and kicking out the lower legs. At the heart of the Charleston dance was the rhythm:

chart informal term for the notation of a tune; written music read by musicians.

chops informal jazz term meaning technical skills on an instrument, as in "Wynton Marsalis has great chops."

chord a stack of notes played simultaneously; the simplest chord typically contains a root, third, and fifth; more complex chords may include the seventh, further extensions, and altered tones.

chord changes a sequence of chords; also called a *chord progression*.

chord extensions additions to a basic chord using compound intervals such as the ninth, eleventh, and thirteenth.

chord progression a sequence of chords; also informally called *chord changes* or just *changes*; serves as the harmonic architecture of a tune.

[chord] substitution replacement of a chord that is standard or written with another to create musical interest; most often applied to transitory chords such as the dominant seventh.

chordophone a stringed instrument.

choro (Portuguese) a type of Brazilian popular music, improvised and usually instrumental, that originated prior to jazz.

chorus (1) in jazz, an iteration of a main theme; each time a jazz performer plays through, for example, a 12-bar blues or a 32-bar popular song, he or she is playing a chorus of that tune; (2) an improvised solo, as in "take a chorus"; (3) in a popular song, the main part of the song, which typically repeats, often preceded by its verse.

chorus form a formal structure, typical in jazz, consisting of one set of harmonic-melodic material—12 bars, 32 bars, or another length—that repeats over and over.

chromatic related to half steps, as opposed to diatonic and modal, which refer to arrangements of whole and half steps.

circular breathing technique used in playing wind instruments that permits continuous, unbroken phrasing.

clave (Spanish) a basic rhythmic pattern of Cuban and Puerto Rican music, played over two bars; the *clave* beat holds the band together. In Latin jazz, the *clave* is often implied, rather than stated by the *clave* sticks.

clavinet an electronic keyboard with a distinctive staccato, guitar-like sound; used notably for the main riff in Stevie Wonder's 1972 hit *Superstition*.

clef symbol in music notation indicating the assignment of pitches to the lines and spaces of a staff.

coda (Italian for "tail") the ending of a musical piece.

collective improvisation spontaneous composition performed simultaneously by members of an ensemble.

color in music, the timbre or tone of a sound.

comping playing chordal accompaniment for a soloist.

compound form a structure with multiple discrete sections; also called *multisectional form*; came to jazz from marches and rags; an example is AABBACCDD (*Maple Leaf Rag*).

compound interval a melodic interval of more than an octave.

conga a dance of the Cuban carnival, which gained popularity in the United States in the 1930s and 1940s; a rhythm of Congo origin, it features a heavy fourth beat.

conguero (Spanish) a player of the conga drum.

conjunct stepwise melodic motion.

consonant notes or harmonies sounding agreeably "in tune"; the opposite of dissonant.

contradanza (Spanish) Cuban dance popular in the eighteenth century.

contrafact a composition that superimposes a new melody on a preexisting chord progression; employed extensively in the bebop era, notably in the writing of new melodies to the chords of *I Got Rhythm* and *Indiana*.

cool jazz a style of jazz developed in the late 1940s and 1950s, in part a reaction to bebop; notable for its understatement, restraint, lighter vibrato-free lines, use of counterpoint, and use of atypical jazz instruments such as the French horn, tuba, and flute.

counterpoint interaction of two or more melodies. Music with counterpoint is characterized as having polyphony or being polyphonic.

Cubop from "Cuban" plus "bebop"; Afro-Latin-flavored bebop, pioneered in the 1940s by Cuban trumpeter-arranger Mario Bauzá.

cuíca (Portuguese) a Brazilian friction drum used often in samba music.

cut time a meter emphasizing two beats per measure.

cutting contest in jazz, the practice of two or more pianists or bands competing with each other, each taking turns, to determine the winner; common in early New Orleans jazz and among Harlem pianists of the 1920s and 1930s; also called a "carving contest."

cutting session a jam session featuring informal competition among soloists.

danza (Spanish) a nineteenth-century musical genre, using the *habanera* rhythm, derived from the *contradanza*, popular in Cuba in the eighteenth and nineteenth centuries; a predecessor to the *danzón*.

danza habanera a Cuban social dance in duple time and performed in a ballroom or on a stage; originating in the late nineteenth century, it became one of the first Cuban styles to become popular in the United States and Europe.

danzón (Spanish) a light classical dance accompaniment derived from the *danza* and originating in Cuba in the late nineteenth century.

darbouka (dumbek) an Arabic goblet-shaped hand drum, common in Middle Eastern music.

diminished lowered a half step, typically applicable to the fifth and seventh steps of a scale, and the fifth and seventh of a chord.

diminished scale a sequence of eight notes alternating whole steps and half steps.

disc jockey in radio, the on-air host who plays records; also called a "deejay."

disjunct melodic movement to a note several steps away.

dissonant sounding discordant; the opposite of consonant.

dominant the fifth degree of the scale.

dominant seventh chord built on the fifth degree of the scale, with an added seventh; resolves to the tonic.

doo-wop popular vocal music of the 1950s and 1960s, in which a lead singer was backed by harmony vocalists. A style of rhythm and blues, doo-wop was often sung a cappella (without instrumental accompaniment).

double time twice as fast as the established tempo; used in jazz to create excitement.

downbeat the first beat of a measure; can also refer to the first beat of a tune.

duration length in time.

dyad two notes.

eighth note a note value representing one-eighth the duration of a whole note; notated as ♪.

eights the jazz practice of showcasing a different soloist every eight measures, as in "trading eights."

enharmonic having the same pitch but a different name; for example, the note D-sharp sounds the same as E-flat.

escape tone a note that connects two stable tones, leaving the first by step and reaching the second by leap.

escola de samba Brazilian organization or club where samba is practiced for performance in Carnaval and other events.

F clef the bass clef; a symbol in music notation indicating the assignment of pitches to the lines and spaces of a staff below middle C: 𝄢.

fake book a collection of printed music in a kind of musical shorthand, specifying only melody line, chord symbols, and lyrics—musicians have to fake the rest; used by many jazz musicians.

feel the distinctive quality of a piece of music imparted primarily through its rhythm, felt by the listener in a combination of emotional and motor responses.

field holler an extemporaneous, solo cry made by African Americans in Southern cotton-picking and other work settings; it's likely a forerunner of the blues.

fill an improvised phrase inserted between phrases of a main melody.

flag an extender on a note beam, indicating an eighth note; multiple flags indicate halved note values.

flamenco (Spanish) a body of dance and music—guitar playing, singing, and percussion—from Andalusia in southern Spain.

flat (1) sounding off-pitch on the low side; (2) lowered in pitch by a half step; (3) symbol indicating lowering of the affected pitch by a half step: ♭.

flip side the reverse side of a 78-rpm or 45-rpm phonograph record; unlike CDs, these records were played on both sides.

form architecture or organization of a piece of music and its subdivisions.

formula a memorized or routinized musical pattern that becomes a building block for improvising solos, especially at fast tempos; popularly called a *lick*.

formulaic improvisation creating solos by manipulating, at the speed of thought, musical formulae or patterns that one has worked out and internalized.

fours trading fours: the jazz practice of showcasing a different soloist every four measures.

free jazz a style of jazz introduced in 1959 and developed in the 1960s and 1970s that relies on neither key nor chord progressions for improvisational structure.

freestyle the improvisational style of hip hop.

front line in New Orleans marching and jazz bands, the melody instruments of trumpet, trombone, and clarinet; by extension, *front line* in later jazz means the instruments played by musicians standing in front of the rhythm section—typically trumpet, trombone, and sax.

funk a style of late–twentieth century African American popular dance music, evolved from rhythm and blues and soul music, with a strongly accented first beat in each bar and highly refined syncopated rhythm—or groove—expressed throughout the ensemble.

fusion jazz a mixture of different musical styles; introduced in the 1960s as a term for the blend of jazz with rock and funk pioneered by Miles Davis, Weather Report, and others.

G clef the treble clef; a symbol in music notation indicating the assignment of pitches to the lines and spaces of a staff above middle C: 𝄞.

gamelan Indonesian music, and set of instruments, notable for interlocking rhythms, microtones, repeating patterns, and metallophone-based sonorities.

glissando a gliding slur or slide from one pitch to another.

gospel music demonstrative African American religious music originating in the early twentieth-century United States, associated with Protestant denominations.

groove the rhythmic architecture, or *feel*, of a tune, especially in late twentieth-century popular dance music and *funk*.

güiro (Taino—the original Amerindian language spoken in Cuba) a serrated, rasped gourd used in Puerto Rican and Cuban music.

habanera (Spanish) a long-short-medium-medium rhythm from Cuba; a dance and music genre in ²⁄₄ time popular in Cuba in the late nineteenth century; adopted in Bizet's 1875 opera Carmen and widely exported to the Americas; named for Habana (Havana).

half note a note value representing one-half the duration of a whole note; notated as 𝅗𝅥.

half step the smallest change in pitch up or down in traditional Western music; the interval of a half step is called a minor second.

half-diminished chord also called a minor 7♭5; a chord containing a minor third, a diminished fifth, and a minor seventh (contrasted with a fully diminished chord, in which the seventh is diminished); in jazz, commonly functioning as the ii in a ii–V7–i progression in a minor key.

hambone practice of using the human body as a rhythm instrument by using one's hands slapping against thighs, arms, chest, and other parts of the body.

hard bop a post-bebop style marked by simpler chord progressions and earthy soulfulness, in contrast to the cool restraint of another post–bop style, cool jazz.

harmonic minor scale a type of minor scale that features a major seventh degree.

harmonic overtones in acoustics, secondary tones that are subdivisions of a fundamental tone or frequency; generated in stringed instruments by touching, rather than plucking, the string at points marking shorter segments of the string length that generates the main tone.

harmonic progression a sequence of chords, also called a *chord progression*; also informally called *chord changes* or simply *changes*; serves as the harmonic architecture of a tune.

harmonic substitution replacement of an established chord in a progression with an alternative to counter expectation and add interest.

harmony the combination of two or more pitches, melodies, or melodies and chords; the aspect of music related to combinations of pitches changing in progression for expressive effect.

head in jazz, the main melody of a tune.

head arrangement an arrangement worked out, usually collectively, on an impromptu basis and typically played from memory.

heterophony the simultaneous playing or singing of two or more versions of a melody.

hi-hat cymbal a percussion instrument consisting of two facing cymbals on a stand operated with a foot pedal; pressing on the pedal brings the two cymbals together; functions as a time-keeping component of a drum set; can be played with a drumstick or brush in open and closed position.

hip hop a largely African American popular music characterized by talk-sung rhymes over funk-derived beats.

hot bands in the 1920s and 1930s, hot bands were ones that played considerable jazz, as opposed to the more commercial "sweet" dance bands, which seldom improvised.

hot rhythm mid twentieth-century term for rhythm that swings or has a strong, forward-propelling motion.

improvisation spontaneous composition; one of the central elements in jazz.

instrumentation the array of instruments called for in a piece of music or provided by a band.

interval the distance between two pitches, usually expressed as the number of steps—a second, third, fourth, and so on—and as minor, major, perfect, augmented, or diminished.

intonation tuning, that is, playing or singing in tune.

jam session informal playing session in which musicians play for each other.

Jitterbug another name for the *Lindy Hop*, a fast swing dance step that emerged in 1928.

jump blues a form of upbeat, jazz-tinged blues made popular in the 1940s and 1950s by bandleader Louis Jordan and others.

key signature the array of sharps or flats positioned on a musical staff at the beginning of a composition to indicate its tonal center, or key.

klezmer (Yiddish) traditional Eastern European Jewish music, which underwent a revival in the late-twentieth-century United States; such jazz musicians as John Zorn and Don Byron have sometimes blended klezmer with jazz.

koto (Japanese) a Japanese zither (a stringed instrument) about six feet long typically with 13 silk strings.

leading tone the seventh step of a major scale and some minor scales; important in harmonic movement due to its strong tendency to resolve to the tonic.

ledger line line added above or below a staff to allow notation of a pitch outside the range of the staff.

lick a brief melodic idea or phrase.

Lindy Hop a fast swing dance step that burst forth in 1928, and became widely popular in the 1930s; it featured improvised "breakaways" and athletic aerial movements; named for aviator Charles Lindberg.

long-playing (LP) record a disc recording that plays back on a turntable moving at 33⅓ revolutions per minute (rpm); the principal music delivery medium from about 1950 through the 1980s, until it was replaced by the digital compact disc (CD).

lundu (Bantu) song and dance with Angolan roots, brought to Brazil by slaves in the eighteenth century; an ancestor to various urban Brazilian song forms.

mainstream jazz acoustic jazz as practiced in the 1950s and 1960s and preserved in the present day; some define mainstream jazz as including earlier classic jazz.

major interval an interval between two pitches of a major second (one whole step), major third (two whole steps), major sixth (four steps and a half step), or major seventh (five steps and a half step).

major scale a sequence of consecutive notes arranged in the following order of whole steps and half steps: whole–whole–half–whole–whole–whole–half; the basis of much Western composition, including jazz.

mambo (Bantu) a highly syncopated instrumental genre created by Cuban bandleader Pérez Prado and first performed by him in Mexico; a dance style highly popular in the 1950s that was a precursor to salsa.

maqam (Arabic) an Arabic mode composed of tetrachords.

marcha (Spanish) a march.

maxixe (Portuguese) a Brazilian couples dance, originating around 1870, with elements of the polka and the Brazilian tango. It became popular in the United States and in Europe at the turn of the twentieth century.

mazooka (Creole) a Creolized version of the mazurka (a Polish folk dance in triple meter), still danced today in the French Caribbean islands of Martinique and Guadeloupe.

MC; MCing rapper; rapping.

measure also called a bar: a grouping of beats that determines the music's meter, as in "four beats to the bar"; indicated in notation with bar lines.

melisma in vocal music, a group of notes sung to one syllable.

melodic minor scale a type of minor scale that features major sixth and major seventh degrees on the ascent and minor sixth and seventh degrees on the descent.

melody an organized succession of notes.

meter the pattern of beats underlying a tune's rhythm; the number of beats occurring in a measure and the kind of note—quarter note, eighth note, or whatever—that is counted as a beat.

minor interval an interval between two pitches of a minor second (one half step), minor third (a whole step and a half step), minor sixth (four steps), or minor seventh (five steps). The minor interval is always a half step smaller than the major interval (see *major interval*).

minor scale a scale defined primary by the inclusion of a minor third; minor scales differ in their treatment of the sixth and seventh—in some those degrees are minor, in others major.

modal jazz a style of jazz developed in the late 1950s and 1960s in which modal scales serve as the basis of improvisation.

mode in jazz, a scale built on a distinctive order of whole steps and half steps creating a characteristic sound.

montuno (Spanish) an improvised section, in Cuban popular music and salsa; kind of contrapuntal accompaniment used in salsa and in Cuban music in general.

motif (or motive) a brief pattern of notes; typically the building blocks of longer phrases.

motivic improvisation improvisation that focuses on repeating a given motif by retaining its essential pattern but changing the pitches to match the changing chords of the compositional structure.

MPB (*música popular brasileira*) post–bossa nova Brazilian urban popular music, combining elements from different genres.

multiphonics two or more notes played at the same time by a single instrument.

musique concrète (French) musical composition created by recording and manipulating natural sounds; pioneered in 1948 by the French composer Pierre Schaeffer.

natural minor the scale whose tonic is the sixth degree of the major scale; also called *relative minor*.

neighbor tone a note one step up or down that connects two stable tones of the same pitch.

neotraditional jazz mainstream jazz as preserved and practiced by some jazz musicians in the 1990s, most notably Wynton Marsalis.

nonharmonic tone a note from outside the core harmony, used as embellishment or to connect harmonic tones.

note a single sound that has pitch and duration.

obbligato (Italian) a secondary melody that accompanies another, primary melody; also called a countermelody.

octave the interval of eight degrees, or twelve half steps, for example from the note C to the next higher note C.

octave tremolo a rapidly repeating oscillation between two notes that are one octave apart.

orchestration the assignment of instruments to the raw melodies and harmonies of a composition, affecting the color and texture of a performance.

organ trio a distinctive ensemble configuration consisting of electronic organ (usually a Hammond B-3), electric guitar or saxophone, and drums; introduced as part of the soul jazz and hard bop movements in the 1950s and 1960s primarily by organist Jimmy Smith.

ostinato maintaining a repeating figure in the bass; in jazz, sometimes serves as an anchor to the motion and development of other voices.

oud (*'ūd*) (Arabic *al-'ūd*) a lute or chordophone common in Middle Eastern music.

out chorus the final chorus of a performance (see *chorus*, definition 1); the out chorus ends the piece, unless there is a coda or tag.

overdubbing the practice of recording in synchronization with previously recorded material; used primarily in popular music to build layers of sound.

overtones harmonic overtones; in acoustics, secondary tones that are subdivisions of a fundamental tone or frequency; generated in stringed instruments by touching, rather than plucking, the string at points marking shorter segments of the string length that generates the main tone; also called harmonics.

pan (steel drum) a musical instrument made from a large empty oil drum that has been tuned; originally from Trinidad.

pandeiro (Portuguese) a Brazilian percussion instrument similar to the tambourine.

paraphrase improvisation paraphrasing, varying, and commenting upon—but not abandoning—the original melody.

passing chord transitional chord that connects stable chords; chord that conveys a sense of irresolution and tension, resolved by movement to another chord.

passing tone a note that connects two stable tones of different pitch by moving stepwise between them.

pedal point held or repeated note of one pitch, typically in the bass; sometimes used to create contrast with simultaneous melodic motion in other instruments.

pentatonic scale scale consisting of five notes.

perfect interval an interval of a fourth, fifth, or an octave.

phrase a short sequence of notes expressing an idea, analogous to a musical clause or sentence; sometimes constructed from shorter sequences called motifs; typically employed as units of longer melodies.

piano rag a syncopated, multisectional composition for piano, such as Scott Joplin's *Maple Leaf Rag*.

pitch the aspect of sound related to highness and lowness, determined by sound wave frequency; in music, pitches are given letter names from A to G; the pitch A above middle C has a frequency of 440 hertz (cycles per second).

plunger mute a type of brass mute, such as an ordinary sink plunger without the stick, that is cupped and manipulated against the bell of the instrument with the left hand. It produces human-voice-like tone colors. Trombonist "Tricky Sam" Nanton and trumpeters Bubber Miley and Cootie Williams—all in Ellington's band—were brilliant exponents of the plunger mute.

polymeter multiple meters played simultaneously.

polyphonic having a multi-melodic texture.

polyphony multiple melodies occurring simultaneously.

polyrhythm multiple rhythms played simultaneously.

polytonality multiple keys or tonalities occurring simultaneously.

popular-song form a standard architecture in American popular song and jazz: 32 bars, consisting of four 8-bar phrases, AABA, with a contrasting bridge or B section.

progressive rock (prog rock) rock music characterized by structural complexity and instrumental virtuosity.

psychedelic rock a style forged in the late 1960s with an aesthetic influenced by the hallucinogenic experience induced by mind-altering drugs such as LSD; notable practitioners included the Grateful Dead and Jefferson Airplane.

qānūn a Middle Eastern stringed instrument, like a plucked zither, with 72 to 75 strings.

quadrille (French) a square dance of French origin for two couples; a piece of music to accompany quadrille dancing.

quarter note a note value representing one-quarter the duration of a whole note; notated as ♩.

quinto (Spanish) the smallest and highest-pitched of the conga drums, which in Cuban music usually improvises.

race records a music industry term from the 1920s and 1930s to connote phonograph discs made expressly for blacks (whites could also purchase the discs); applied to blues, gospel, and some jazz recordings.

radio remote a radio broadcast not from the station's studio but rather from a remote location such as a nightclub, ballroom, or theater.

rag (verb) to syncopate a melody in the style of ragtime.

ragging the practice of creatively altering and syncopating an existing piece of music; a term from the early twentieth century, when *ragtime* music was popular.

ragtime a body of syncopated American popular music, especially popular from ca. 1897 to 1920; one of the roots of jazz. Ragtime included both instrumental or piano rags and ragtime songs.

reco-reco (Portuguese) a Brazilian scraper made of bamboo or metal.

regional band similar to a *territory band*.

register the range of the pitch spectrum, from low to high, available to an instrument or voice.

rehearsal band group of musicians who meet to rehearse and play for each other rather than for the public.

relative minor minor key that has the same pitches as a relative major—that is, its *tonic* is the sixth degree of a major scale.

repique (repinique) (Portuguese) a two-headed tenor drum; played in Brazilian samba.

resting tone a stable tone; a primary note, the expression of which imparts a feeling of stability, consonance, or resolution; a goal of musical motion.

rhythm the aspect of music related to the structuring of sound in patterns of unfolding time; the aspect of music that most people think of as "the beat."

rhythm and blues (R&B) style of popular music forged in the 1940s as an offshoot of urban blues; a precursor of rock and roll, soul music, funk, and hip-hop.

rhythm section the core instrumentation of the jazz ensemble: piano, bass, drums, and sometimes banjo or guitar.

ride cymbal one of several cymbals used in a drum set, providing a splashy metallic accompaniment that contrasts with the tight time-keeping of the hi-hat cymbal, the dramatic statements of the crash cymbal, and the more exotic effects of the sizzle cymbal.

ride-out chorus climactic final chorus, often with collective improvisation; term used especially in early jazz.

riff a short, repeated melodic phrase.

rip a loud tonal slide (glissando) up to a note, often ending with a sharp accent; can be heard in the playing of trumpeters Bix Beiderbecke and Louis Armstrong, among many others.

rock and roll genre of youth-oriented popular music that emerged in the 1950s as an amalgam of jump blues, rhythm and blues, and country music; early stars included Elvis Presley, Jerry Lee Lewis, Chuck Berry, Buddy Holly; as it matured, its name became abbreviated to rock.

rondo a multisectional musical form, dating from the Baroque period, in which the principal theme alternates with other themes; for example ABACADA.

root primary pitch of a key; also known as the *tonic* and "the one."

rubato freely; played expressively without adhering to a strict beat.

rumba (Spanish, "rhumba" in English) a music genre derived from the Cuban *son* and popularized in the 1930s; also a ballroom dance performed by both Latino and non-Latino audiences in the United States and in Europe.

rumba brava (Spanish) refers to several Cuban traditional vocal and instrumental genres of Congo derivation, among them the *guaguancó*, the *columbia*, and the *yambú*. The *rumba brava*, also danced, is different from the ballroom *rumba*.

run a rapid sequence of notes, ascending or descending.

samba (Portuguese, derived from the Bantu "semba," meaning "navel") a Brazilian dance of Congo origin; percussive, propulsive music in $\frac{2}{4}$ time to accompany this dance; the symbol of the Rio carnival (called Carnaval).

sampling (1) the use of a "sampled" section or piece of a preexisting recording in a new recording; (2) digitally recording a singer, instrument, or other sound to use as a "voice" in a synthesizer.

scalar related to a scale.

scale a sequence of consecutive notes arranged in a particular order; in jazz, may be used as raw material for melodic improvisation.

scat singing vocal improvisation, typically wordless; notable practitioners have included Louis Armstrong; the Boswell Sisters; Cab Calloway; Ella Fitzgerald; Eddie Jefferson; Lambert, Hendricks and Ross; and Dizzy Gillespie.

second line the procession of people marching and dancing behind a New Orleans jazz band parading down the street. A person who joins in is a "second liner."

secondary rag a melodic-rhythmic pattern that repeats three eighth or sixteenth notes, each repetition placing the accent on a different beat of the measure. Used to create a catchy effect in such piano rags as *Dill Pickles*, *Black and White Rag*, and *12th Street Rag*.

section subdivision of an ensemble defined by instrument group (as in reed section) or function (as in rhythm section).

semitone a half step.

sequence a short melodic phrase repeated at different pitch levels.

session player a musician who plays in recording studios.

sharp (1) sounding off-pitch on the high side; (2) raised in pitch by a half step; (3) a symbol indicating raising of the affected pitch by a half step: ♯.

shekere (Yoruba) a rattle consisting of a large gourd with beads held, by a mesh net, on the outside, instead of on the inside as in maracas; shaken in rhythm and struck with the palm of the hand; of West African origin.

sideman an accompanying or supporting musician, in contrast to the leader; a member of a backup band.

signify an African American rhetorical device featuring indirect communication or persuasion and the creating of new meanings for old words and signs; or in the words of Henry Louis Gates, "repetition with a signal difference."

sitar Indian stringed instrument consisting of a resonating gourd and a long neck supporting seven principal strings, plus 12 to 20 sympathetic strings.

sixteenth note a note value representing one-sixteenth the duration of a whole note; notated as ♪.

slap bass an acoustic bass technique made by pulling and releasing the strings sharply against the fingerboard, producing loud snapping, popping sounds; on the electric bass produced by slapping the thumb down on a lower string and plucking a higher string with the fore- and middle fingers.

snare drum narrow drum with a band of metal wires called "snares" stretched across the underside, which provide a distinctive rasp when the drum is struck on top with a drum stick; a central component of the rock, funk, and blues drum kit, where it typically supplies the backbeat; in bebop jazz it became used more for accenting.

son (Spanish) a genre that emerged in the late nineteenth century in the rural areas of eastern Cuba. It developed as an urban type of music in Havana in the 1920s and became commercialized in the United States under the name *rumba* or rhumba. The *son* forms the backbone of salsa.

soul jazz a funky, bluesy style of jazz made popular in the 1950s and 1960s by such musicians as organist Jimmy Smith; guitarists Wes Montgomery, Kenny Burrell, and Grant Green; and saxophonist Cannonball Adderley.

"Spanish" (or "tango" bass) a bass line containing syncopated figures, typically in *habanera* rhythm. The term was used in the early twentieth century to describe syncopated bass lines of certain rags, blues, and jazz pieces.

stable tone a resting tone; a primary note, the expression of which imparts a feeling of stability, consonance, or resolution; a goal of musical motion.

staccato played with shortened duration, detached from other notes in a phrase; not legato.

staff a five-line grid on which Western music is written.

stock arrangement standard, published orchestration of a tune, used by musicians in lieu of an original interpretation.

stop-time a technique to draw attention to a soloist; a stop-time passage typically suspends the beat except for one beat every one or two bars; for example, in King Oliver's *Dipper Mouth Blues* (CD I, Track 8/Download Track 8) and Jelly Roll Morton's *Black Bottom Stomp* (CD I, Track 9/Download Track 9).

stride a style of jazz piano developed in the 1910s and 1920s, derived from ragtime and featuring large, striding leaps in the left hand and syncopated figures in the right hand; pioneered by James P. Johnson; also called stride piano or Harlem stride piano.

subdominant the fourth degree of the scale.

suite a musical work with multiple movements or major sections; examples are Tchaikovsky's *Nutcracker Suite*, Ellington and Strayhorn's *Far East Suite*, and Mary Lou Williams's *Zodiac Suite*.

surdo (Portuguese) bass drum that keeps one of the fundamental rhythms in Brazilian samba; also the name of the rhythmic pattern played on the drum.

sweet bands a term, often used derogatorily in jazz, from the 1920s and 1930s to denote commercial dance bands that featured minimal improvisation—the opposite of hot bands.

swing a rhythmic characteristic of much jazz, swing is a forward momentum, an elasticity of the pulse, that defies precise definition.

syncopation accenting weak beats of a rhythm in a way that adds musical interest; a characteristic of jazz rhythm.

synthesizer a sound production device that blends waveforms to create new sounds; the device stores the sounds, which are playable via a keyboard or other controller.

tabla a pair of drums of North India, played with the fingers, palms, and hands.

tag a phrase tagged on or added to the end of a chorus or, more commonly, a piece; the latter is formally known as a *coda*.

tailgate trombone an uninhibited style of jazz trombone—with considerable slides, glides, and slurs—characteristic of early New Orleans players such as Kid Ory and New Orleans revival or Dixieland players.

take in a recording session, one run-through; several takes may be required in order to achieve an acceptable rendition.

taksim (taqsīm) a soloistic instrumental improvisation found in Arab and Turkish music traditions.

tamborim (Portuguese) a small, jingle-less tambourine played with a single or double stick, used in Brazilian music.

tango (Bantu) a ballroom dance born in Buenos Aires, Argentina, and stemming from Congo cult dances with slow movements and abrupt pauses; music, in $\frac{4}{4}$ time, to accompany this dancing. Danced in the mid-nineteenth century by blacks at the Buenos Aires carnivals, it later acquired European elements.

tempo the pace of rhythm—uptempo (fast), moderate, or slow.

ternary composed of three parts.

territory band in the 1920s and early 1930s, a jazz or dance band that played in a limited region or territory and found limited access to radio and recordings; some talented musicians, such as Harry James, rose from the ranks of territory bands to gain renown in national bands of the swing era.

texture the quality of sound determined by the density of instrumentation.

theme song the song or tune with which a musician or band is most associated; also called a signature tune.

third stream compositions blending jazz elements with classical forms and techniques; term coined in 1957 by composer Gunther Schuller.

tie a marking that connects two notes of the same pitch, indicating that the second is not to be played—rather, its durational value is to be added to that of the first note.

timbales (Spanish) a drum set with two tuneable snare drums with different pitches, two cow bells, a cymbal or cymbals, and sometimes a woodblock; typically played with two sticks; developed in Cuba, inspired by the European tympani; used in Cuban music and in salsa music.

timbre tone quality, or color, of musical sound.

time signature numbers on a staff that specify the meter of the music that follows: the upper number indicates the number of beats per measure, and the lower number indicates the kind of note that gets a beat.

tom-tom midrange drum used in the drum kit for sounds higher than a bass drum but lower than a snare drum; there are several sizes of tom-toms.

tonal center the key.

tonality relationship to a tonal center or key.

tone the quality of sound as determined by properties other than pitch, primarily sound shape, or waveform; also sometimes used to mean a note or pitch.

tone color same as *timbre*.

tonic the root of a key.

torch song in popular music, a sad or sentimental song describing an unrequited love; from the expression "to carry a torch" for someone. Examples are *My Man, Stormy Weather, Lover Man, Body and Soul,* and *One for My Baby (and One More for the Road).*

toques (Spanish) drum rhythms in ritual Afro-Cuban music.

(to) swing to play with a perceptible forward momentum, a propulsive rhythm, and a flowing beat; found in much African-rooted music

township jazz jazz that originated in the black townships of South Africa, characterized by ostinatos.

transcription recordings disc recordings made, especially in the 1930s and 1940s, exclusively for broadcast on radio stations; from the phrase "broadcast transcription."

treble clef a symbol in music notation indicating the assignment of pitches to the lines and spaces of a staff above middle C; also called the *G clef:* 𝄞.

tremolo dynamic effect achieved by rapid alternation of a note's loudness levels.

tres (Spanish) a stringed instrument used in traditional Cuban and Puerto Rican music.

triad a chord of three notes made up of scale tones separated by intervals of a third.

trill for ornamentation, a rapidly repeating alternation of a note with its adjoining note.

trio (1) a three-piece ensemble; (2) in a march or rag, a contrasting section that modulates to another key.

triplet three beats that fit evenly into the time span of two, as in 𝄴 ♩ ♩ ♩.

Tropicália an experimental, style-mixing arts movement—with a strong musical component—of late 1960s Brazil.

trumpet style a descriptor applied to Earl Hines's right-hand piano style, in which he played more like trumpeter Louis Armstrong—improvising single-note melody lines—than like other pianists.

tumba (Spanish) the largest and lowest-pitched of the conga drums; national dance of Santo Domingo in the nineteenth century.

tumbao (Spanish, of African derivation) a rhythm pattern played by the conga and the string bass.

tutti (Italian) all; played by an entire ensemble.

umbigada (Portuguese) a movement in Afro-Brazilian dances during which the dancer touches navels with another dancer as an invitation to dance.

unison simultaneous playing of the same pitch or melody by different voices.

uptempo played fast.

vamp a brief chord pattern, repeated an indeterminate number of times, used as filler and most commonly to introduce a piece.

vaudeville the popular theatrical entertainment style of the late nineteenth and early twentieth centuries in which different kinds of acts—singers, comedians, dancers, magicians, acrobats—would share billing; presaged later television variety shows and provided a career launching pad for many star musicians and performers.

veena (also *vina*) Indian stringed instrument with a resonating gourd and a long neck supporting four melody strings and three drone strings.

vibrato type of ornamentation or articulation in which a pitch is fluctuated slightly to enrich or intensify a tone.

vocalese the application of lyrics to an existing instrumental solo; notable practitioners have included Eddie Jefferson; Lambert, Hendricks, and Ross; and the Manhattan Transfer.

voice leading the interactional linear motion of voices within multi-voice music.

voodoo (or *vodun*) religious beliefs and practices that combine African and Roman Catholic elements; practiced in parts of the Caribbean, especially Haiti, and in some parts of the Southern United States.

wah-wah (1) a mute that, when manipulated over the bell of a trumpet or trombone, creates a vocal-like wah-wah sound. Popularized by King Oliver and a series of Ellington trumpeters. (2) The sound achieved by using such a mute. (3) From the 1960s on, an electronic pedal used by guitarists (popularized by Jimi Hendrix and Eric Clapton) and keyboard players.

walking bass the bass technique of producing a steady beat while playing and connecting notes of a chord progression.

West Coast jazz the collective name for jazz that emerged from Los Angeles and San Francisco in the 1950s and 1960s, generating much of what became known as cool jazz, but also offering experiments in instrumentation, composition, and counterpoint by such musicians as Dave Brubeck, Gerry Mulligan, and Jimmy Giuffre.

western swing a mixture of jazz and country music, popularized in the 1930s by Bob Wills and His Texas Playboys and, later, Asleep at the Wheel.

whole note the primary note value in traditional Western rhythm, the unit against which other note values (such as quarter notes and eighth notes) are measured: 𝅝.

whole step two half steps or semitones.

whole tone a whole step.

whole tone scale scale consisting only of whole steps; in jazz improvisation, especially applicable to the augmented chord.

woodshedding effort and time spent alone practicing.

Contributors

The Editors

John Edward Hasse is Curator of American Music at the Smithsonian Institution, founder and former executive director of the Smithsonian Jazz Masterworks Orchestra, and founder of Jazz Appreciation Month, celebrated in 50 states and 40 countries. He is author of *Beyond Category: The Life and Genius of Duke Ellington*; producer of a two-disc set of Ellington recordings, *Beyond Category*; editor of *Ragtime: Its History, Composers, and Music* and *Jazz: The First Century*; producer-author of *The Classic Hoagy Carmichael*; and co-producer/co-author of *Jazz: The Smithsonian Anthology*. Hasse is the recipient of two Grammy Award nominations and two ASCAP-Deems Taylor Awards for excellence in writing about music. He has lectured on American music in 20 countries on five continents.

Tad Lathrop has authored, produced, or edited more than 50 books on music, including *Jazz: The First Century* and two volumes on the business of music. He has been a music editor at Cherry Lane Music, Holt, Rinehart and Winston, and Billboard Books; has lectured on music and the recording industry at colleges and conferences; and has provided interviews and music consulting to such media outlets as Forbes.com and MTV Interactive. An accomplished guitarist, he has written about jazz guitar for *Guitar Player* magazine, taught privately and through the City University of New York, and performed at numerous venues, including New York's Blue Note.

Chapter Writers

Bob Blumenthal is the author of *Jazz: An Introduction to the History and Legends Behind America's Music*, a recipient of Grammy Awards for Best Album Notes (1999 and 2000) and the Jazz Journalists Association's Lifetime Achievement award, and the creative consultant to the Marsalis Music record label.

José Antonio Bowen is dean of the Meadows School at Southern Methodist University, has written over 100 scholarly articles, and has appeared as a musician on four continents with Stan Getz, Bobby McFerrin, and others. He has written a symphony (nominated for the Pulitzer Prize) and music for Hubert Laws and Jerry Garcia, is currently on the boards of the *Journal for the Society for American Music* and *Jazz Research Journal*, and is a Fellow of the Royal Society of Arts in England.

Michael Brooks is a six-time Grammy Award–winning record producer and writer with a track record of more than 2,000 reissue albums, including Time-Life's 84-disc *Giants of Jazz* series. He worked

as an assistant to Columbia's legendary talent scout John Hammond from 1971 to 1976 and is currently an archival consultant to Sony Music.

Isabelle Leymarie, a jazz pianist and musicologist, has taught at Yale and other American universities as well as at the Conservatoire Nadia et Lili Boulanger and the Bill Evans Piano Academy in Paris. She is the author of *Cuban Fire*, *Latin Jazz*, *Dizzy Gillespie*, *Du Tango au Reggae – Musiques Noires d'Amérique Latine et des Caraïbes*, *Les Griots Wolof du Sénégal*, and other books.

John Litweiler is the author of *The Freedom Principle: Jazz After 1958* and *Ornette Coleman: A Harmolodic Life*. His writings have appeared in *Jazz Monthly*, the *New York Times Book Review*, the *Chicago Sun-Times*, and *Down Beat*, for which he was also an editor.

Steven F. Pond is an ethnomusicologist and associate professor of musicology at Cornell University. He is the author of *Head Hunters: The Making of Jazz's First Platinum Album* and is currently writing about jazz historiography.

Neil Tesser is the author of *The Playboy Guide to Jazz* and has contributed to publications from *USA Today* to *Rolling Stone*. He has written liner notes for more than 225 albums, receiving a Grammy Award nomination in 1985 and a Deems Taylor Award from ASCAP in 2001. He lives in Chicago.

Kevin Whitehead is the author of *Why Jazz? A Concise Guide*, *New Dutch Swing*, and *Instant Composers Pool Orchestra: You Have to See It* (with photographer Ton Mijs). He is the longtime jazz critic for NPR's *Fresh Air* and jazz columnist for eMusic.com, and has written about jazz for many publications, including the *Chicago Sun-Times*, *Down Beat*, and the *Village Voice*.

Sidebar Writers

Larry Appelbaum is senior music reference librarian at the Library of Congress, a jazz radio host on WPFW Radio, and a contributor to *Jazz Times*.

E. Taylor Atkins is professor and director of undergraduate studies in the Department of History at Northern Illinois University. He is the author of *Primitive Selves: Koreana in the Japanese Colonial Gaze* and *Blue Nippon: Authenticating Jazz in Japan*, and is the editor of *Jazz Planet*.

David Baise, a guitarist and composer, is the recipient of a Monroe Berger–Benny Carter Jazz Research Grant.

David Baker, distinguished professor of music and chair of the Jazz Department, Indiana University School of Music, is musical and artistic director of the Smithsonian Jazz Masterworks Orchestra and the author of more than 70 books on jazz, including *Jazz Improvisation, Advanced Jazz Improvisation, Jazz Pedagogy,* and *How to Play Bebop.* He is an NEA Jazz Master and a Kennedy Center Living Legend of Jazz honoree.

Philippe Baudoin, a jazz pianist, taught the history and techniques of jazz at the Sorbonne in Paris. His books include *Jazz Mode d'Emploi, Vol. 1 et 2* and *Chronologie du Jazz* and he is writing a book on the history of jazz standards.

Richard Carlin is the author of several books on popular music, most recently *Worlds of Sound: The Story of Smithsonian Folkways.* He coedited the book *Ain't Nothing Like the Real Thing: How the Apollo Theater Shaped American Entertainment.* He has been an editor of music books at Schirmer, Routledge, and currently Pearson/Prentice Hall, where he is executive editor for college music texts.

Donna M. Cassidy is a professor at the University of Southern Maine and the author of *Painting the Musical City: Jazz and Cultural Identity in American Art, 1910–1940.*

James Dapogny is professor emeritus of music at the University of Michigan, a pianist and bandleader, and the compiler-editor of *Jelly Roll Morton: The Collected Piano Music.*

Gerald Early is director of the Center for the Humanities and the Merle Kling Professor of Modern Letters. His books include *Tuxedo Junction* and *One Nation Under a Groove: Motown and American Culture* and he has written extensively on jazz.

Sascha Feinstein received the 2008 Pennsylvania Governor's Award for Artist of the Year. His most recent books include *Black Pearls: Improvisations on a Lost Year* and *Ask Me Now: Conversations on Jazz & Literature.* He edits *Brilliant Corners: A Journal of Jazz & Literature.*

Rusty Frank, author of *Tap! The Greatest Tap Dance Stars and Their Stories 1900–1955* and producer of the documentary *Tap! Tempo of America,* is a professional tap dancer, Lindy Hopper, and dance preservationist.

Krin Gabbard is professor and chair of the Department of Comparative Literary and Cultural Studies at Stony Brook University. He has written on jazz, film, psychoanalysis, and African American studies. His most recent book is *Hotter Than That: The Trumpet, Jazz and American History.*

William Howland Kenney is the author of *Chicago Jazz: A Cultural History, 1903–1930* and *Recorded Music in American Life: The Phonograph and*

Popular Memory, 1890–1945. He is also a professor emeritus of history and American studies at Kent State University.

Ann K. Kuebler is an archivist at the Institute of Jazz Studies, Rutgers University. She has conducted research into the music manuscripts of Duke Ellington and Mary Lou Williams.

Mark Lomanno is a doctoral candidate in ethnomusicology at the University of Texas at Austin and a jazz pianist. In 2010 he recorded the album *Tales & Tongues* with Le Monde Caché, a San Antonio-based ensemble that performs African and Jewish diasporic repertoire.

Rainer E. Lotz is the author of record album notes, monographs, and scholarly articles and the publisher of the *German National Discography.*

Jeffrey Magee, associate professor of musicology at the University of Illinois, Urbana-Champaign, is the author of *The Uncrowned King of Swing: Fletcher Henderson and Big Band Jazz.*

Cyril Moshkow is the publisher of *Jazz.ru,* Russia's only jazz publication. He has published three Russian-language books: *The Jazz Industry in America, The Jazz Greats,* and *The Blues: Introduction to a History.*

Jeff Rupert heads jazz studies in the music department at the University of Central Florida. He earned his BM and MM degrees in Jazz Performance at the Mason Gross School of the Arts, Rutgers University. He also enjoys an active career as a freelance tenor saxophonist, composer, and arranger.

William E. Smith is the music industry coordinator at North Carolina Central University and the founder and president of the International Association for Hip Hop Education (IAHHE). He has recorded or performed with Kenny Burrell, Donald Byrd, and James Moody, among others, and has released three albums with his jazz ensemble the W.E.S. Group. He is the author of *Hip Hop as Performance and Ritual.*

Jack Stewart, a member of the New Orleans Jazz Commission and a frequent contributor to the *Tulane Jazz Archivist,* is writing a book on the history of New Orleans vernacular music and another on bandleader Jack Laine.

Michael White, a clarinetist and leader of the Original Liberty Jazz Band and a member of the New Orleans Jazz Commission, is heard on more than 20 recordings.

Calvin Wilson is an arts and entertainment writer at the *St. Louis Post-Dispatch* and coordinator of the newspaper's fine arts blog, *Culture Club.* Wilson has written about jazz for national magazines including *Emerge, Jazziz,* and *Schwann Spectrum.*

Index

Weintraub's Syncopators, *297*
Wells, Dicky, 98, 104
West Africa influence on jazz, 29–31
West Coast bop, 170, 172
West Coast jazz, 151–159, 170, 172.
    See also cool jazz
West End Blues (Armstrong), 57,
    62–63, 68
western swing, 4, 229
West Indies Jazz Band, 282
Weston, Randy, 119, 149, 299,
    308, 311
Wheeler, Kenny, 331, 340
Whetsol, Arthur, 78
White, Larry, 235
White, Maurice, 243
white big bands, 104–110
    commercial success, 105, 130
Whiteman, Paul, 72–73, *73*, 74, 91, 99,
    291, 294
    in film, 156
    use of vocalist, 83, 91
whole tone, 149
whole tone scale, 149
The Whoopee Makers, 76
Whyte, Virgil, 221
Wilber, Bob, 142, 150
Wildflowers Jazz Festival, 209
Wilen, Barney, 296
Wilkerson, Edward, 218, 219
Wilkins, Barron, 131
Williams, Clarence, 63, 72
Williams, Cootie, *75*, 76, 99, 150
Williams, John A., 189
Williams, Mary Lou, 69, 113, 133, 222
    Andy Kirk and, 57, 70

religious influence, 180
role of women in jazz, *220*, 221
Williams, Paul, 137
Williams, Martin, 186
Williams, Midge, 303
Williams, Sherley Anne, 159
Williams, Tony, 194, 211, 232, 233
    Lifetime (band), 235–236, *236*
Williamson, Claude, 172
Wills, Bob, 126, 229
Wilson, Cassandra, 250, 336, 340
Wilson, Joe Lee, 209
Wilson, Nancy, 340
Wilson, Ollie, *110*
Wilson, Teddy, 97, 107, 119, 121,
    123, 186
Windha, Nyoman, 305
Winding, Kai, *132*, 143, 171
    Birth of the Cool, 153
Winstone, Norma, 340
Winter, Paul, 299
Wolff, D. Leon, 137
Wolff, Francis, 297
The Wolverines, 66
women in jazz
    bands, 112–113
    growing role of, 220–221
    in New Orleans jazz, 45
    vocalists, 82–83
Wonder, Stevie, 244, 340, 342
Wong, Francis, 305
The Woodchoppers, 116
Wooding, Sam, 294, *294*
Woods, Phil, 172, 244, 323
woodshedding, 22
Woodstock, 198

Woody Herman's Herd, 109–110
world jazz, 285–316. *See also* Africa,
    Caribbean, Asia, Europe, Latin
    America, South America
The World Saxophone Quartet, 218,
    319, 331
World War I, 58, 81, 286
    African-American migration after,
        70, 125
    Europe and racial tolerance, 290
    jazz in Paris, 291
    jazz scene after, 303
World War II, 129, 142, 164, 286,
    298, 301
    African Americans and, 124
    boogie-woogie and, 125
    European jazz scene,
        295–296, 309
    jazz in Paris, 291
    jazz scene after, 303
    military jazz bands, 294
    post-war jazz scene, 130–131, 142
    women's role in jazz, 220–221

Y

Yamashita, Yosuke, 303
Yancey, Jimmy, 125
Yardbirds, 236
The Yerba Buena Jazz Band, 40, 123
Yggdrasil, 300
Youmans, Vincent, 15
Young, Al, 159
Young, La Monte, 330
Young, Larry, 194, 235

Young, Lester, 72, 73, 93, *101*, 121,
    123, 131, 133, 140, 141, 142, 143,
    144, 149, 151, 152, 153, 172, 178,
    186, 192, 199, 235, 248, 271
    Count Basie's Orchestra, *101*, 104,
        132, 137
    drug use, 146
    One O'Clock Jump (Basie),
        102–103
    'Round Midnight, 150
    as solo instrumentalist,
        116–117, *116*
YouTube, 187
Yugoslavia and jazz 310

Z

Zabor, Rafi, 189
Zacharias, Helmut, 297
Zadeh, Aziza Mstafa, 310
Zap Mama, 341
Zappa, Frank, 231
Zawinul, Joe (Josef), 166, 227,
    230, 232
    Birdland, 240
    Weather Report, 237, 238,
        238, 239
    Zawinal Syndicate, 235
Zawinul Syndicate, 235
Zhao, Coco, 304
Zinsser, William, 118
Zoller, Attila, 310
Zorn, John, 308, 330, 331–333, *331*,
    336, 342–343
    avante-garde jazz, 330
    Naked City, 319, 332